THE COMPLETE ILLUSTRATED GUIDE TO EVERYTHING SOLD IN HARDWARE STORES AND GARDEN CENTERS

(EXCEPT THE PLANTS)

THE COMPLETE ILLUSTRATED GUIDE TO EVERYTHING SOLD IN HARDWARE STORES AND GARDEN CENTERS (EXCEPT THE PLANTS)

BY STEVE ETTLINGER

COURAGE BOOKS

9 8 7 6 5 4 3 2
Digit on the right indicates the number of this printing

Library of Congress Cataloguing-in-Publication Number 2002112887
ISBN 0-7624-1493-6

The Complete Illustrated Guide to Everything Sold in Hardware Stores originally published by Macmillan in 1998.

The Complete Illustrated Guide to Everything Sold in Garden Centers originally published by Macmillan in 1990.

Cover design by Bill Jones
Edited by Michael Washburn

Published by Courage Books,
an imprint of
Running Press Book Publishers
125 South Twenty-second Street
Philadelphia, Pennsylvania 19103-4399

Visit us on the web!
www.runningpress.com

The first part of this book is dedicated to anyone
who has ever walked into a hardware store,
home center, or lumberyard and asked for
a whatchamacallit or thingamajig.

The second part is dedicated to all of us who
appreciate knowing the difference between
potting soil and top soil and between
a dibble and a widger.

THE COMPLETE ILLUSTRATED GUIDE TO EVERYTHING SOLD IN HARDWARE STORES

COMPLETELY UPDATED EDITION

ILLUSTRATIONS BY ROBERT STRIMBAN

Contents

PART III: General Hardware

PART IV: General Materials

PART V: Paints, Stains, Finishes, Wall Coverings, and Related Products and Tools

PART VI: Wood and Wood Products

PART VII: Wall, Floor, and Ceiling Materials and Tools; Doors and Windows

PART VIII: Plumbing Hardware, Materials, and Tools

PART IX: Electrical Products and Tools

PART X: Masonry Materials, Products, and Tools

PART XI: Safety Equipment

Preface

Why This Book

Whether you are a homeowner, an apartment dweller, or renovator, you no doubt have often entered a hardware store, lumberyard, or home center full of fear prior to making a small purchase. This uneasiness generally stems from two facts: first, people rarely know the actual, correct name of even the most everyday item and are reduced to visual descriptions that often leave a lot to be desired—and often leave the customer with an unusable and unreturnable purchase. Second, store clerks may often be unavailable, unknowledgeable, or downright rushed (or is it just that we feel guilty with all those folks in line behind us?).

Probably the most frustrating thing is that after you ask a clerk for an item, whether a succinct request for a paintbrush or pliers, or the more typical "whatchamacallit that fits over the thing that you turn to make the doohickey work" (accompanied, no doubt, by broad, dramatic, descriptive hand gestures), the clerk will come back at you, nine times out of ten, with a barrage of questions: "Well, what are you using it for?" "What size do you want?" "You want top-of-the-line or cheap?" "Silicone or acrylic?" "Galvanized or plain?" If you haven't thought these questions through, this can be pretty demoralizing, embarrassing, and intimidating. I know. That's just the kind of experience that gave birth to this book.

The Complete Illustrated Guide to Everything Sold in Hardware Stores should serve to end your intimidation, help you avoid wrong purchases, and enable even you, too, to walk fearlessly into a hardware store or lumberyard and get exactly what you need. I will expose the choices available to you so that you can be prepared for those rapid-fire questions.

How This Book Got Inspired

A cat's paw did it. No doubt about it—a cat's paw inspired this book. A few years ago, while I was helping a friend renovate her apartment, I asked a passing carpenter for advice about my next task—removing an old floor. The carpenter said casually, "Get yourself a cat's paw, and you'll have those floorboards ripped up in an hour!" So, armed for once with specific professional guidance, I strode boldly into the local hardware store and asked self-confidently for a cat's paw, even though I had never seen or heard of one before. "Cat's paw? Cat's paw?" The clerk reacted sarcastically. "Wha' d'ya think this is, a butcher shop?" Rolling his eyes, he completely demolished my assertive frame of mind. I mentioned almost apologetically that I wanted to rip up some old floorboards. After much gesticulating, the clerk said, "Ohhhh, what *you* want is a pry bar!" Relieved, he proceeded to sell me one. It turned out he was quite wrong.

About a week later I finally finished ripping up the floor, cursing the new tool all along and wondering why the carpenter had suggested it. Well, if you check Chapter 3, you'll understand what went wrong—the cat's paw and the pry bar are distinctly different tools, though they are members of the same family. I checked all the indexes of the heavy-duty complete how-to books and found them listed nowhere. And I thought, "someone ought to write a book that just lists all the items mentioned elsewhere—I don't want to keep looking past all those articles on how to install a garage door or a deck every time I want to check out some small item that is mentioned somewhere!"

And thus was this book born. I hope it answers your questions too.

Notes on the Revised Edition

What's changed in ten years? While the inventory of hardware stores and home centers has not changed dramatically, it certainly has increased. More importantly, the stores themselves have expanded. The prevalence and success of immense home centers is the norm, while they were more just a new trend back when I started research. With their extensive inventory (and increasing crowds of do-it-yourself folks), a revision and updating of this book was called for, and here it is.

A lot of the traditional tools are now made with better materials and ergonomic designs; there is also a general increase in the availability of top-quality, longer-lasting versions. Of course, the cheap stuff is still with us. Innovation is healthy: More gadgets are being introduced each month, it seems, most in the painting tools and fastener departments. Advances in electronics have led to a wide array of fully electronic measuring devices; advances in engineered wood have led to new products there, too. It seems that many improvements are found among paints, finishes, and materials like caulk and insulation, partly in response to environmental concerns.

One thing that hasn't changed is the need for a book that describes all the items and lists all the names people have for them—something no other book in this field does, despite the publication of several excellent, how-to books in the intervening years. Most of the how-to books' indexes don't even list the tools and gizmos that you need to buy. And contractors and sales clerks are still telling us to get some gizmo or some adapter by vague description, or use, or nickname, so the descriptions, including items merely referred to, have been made more detailed to help you make that purchase with a minimum of confusion.

A final note about the motivation for a revised edition: Over the years, I've heard again and again how much people really liked having this book. Some (even from outside my immediate family!) claim it's their favorite, though I doubt they mean to include all books in that praise. I've been told of at least one spouse who was kept up late at night while her husband read it voraciously in bed. With that kind of response, I felt that I owed my readers a thorough revision. Happy hardware hunting!

—Steve Ettlinger

New York City, 1998

Acknowledgments

Generous research assistance for the first edition of this book was provided by the editors of *The Old House Journal*, Brooklyn, New York, especially Patricia Poore and Gordon Bock.

This book began with a simple idea that I discussed over time with a variety of people ranging from friends and relatives to mere acquaintances. Their enthusiastic responses sustained my efforts and without them it is unlikely that this book would have happened. To those people who gave me such early encouragement I will be ever grateful. In particular, though, there are some people whose responses provided as much emotional as professional support at a time when the project was just a gleam in my eye. I will never forget Clem Labine's and Patricia Poore's quick response to my initial phone call. The original enthusiasm and help of designer Leslie Smolan of Carbone, Smolan Associates will be appreciated forevermore. My parents' continuous contributions of thoughts, critiques, and suggestions for both the manuscript and concept were truly wonderful and essential.

The following people and companies proved invaluable and patient in their generous assistance and technical expertise when reviewing sections of the manuscript, allowing me to explore their stores, and, in all cases, answering endless lists of questions: J. C. Valentine of J & G Plumbing and Heating Supplies, Brooklyn; Dan and the staff of Dan's Hardware, Brooklyn; Matthew Pintchik, Tom Mariano, John Heemer, Larry Reingold, Leon Cummings, Rudy Gentik, Floyd Stanislaw, and Allen Cohen of Nathan Pintchik, Inc., New York; James P. Balis and Dennis J. Vanette of APS Locksmith and Hardware, Brooklyn; Marvin Pereira and Lorenzo Otero of City Lighting, New York; Milton and Adam Greebler and the staff of Gurrell Hardware, New York; Byron Hathorn of SITA Construction Company, Ely, Vermont; Clem Labine (now of Historic Trends, Brooklyn); Jean McGrane, industrial hygienist, New York; Paul "Hocky" Hochberg, Chicago; Paul Murphy, Chicago; Gary Chinn of Garrett Wade Tools Catalog, New York; Chris Wadsworth of Peter Gisolfi Associates, Architects, Hastings; Gregory Warock, master mason, Asheville, North Carolina; and Martin Daly and Harlow Haagensen of the New York District Council of Carpenters Labor Technical College, New York.

I am also very grateful for the friendly expertise of the many manufacturers who responded to my numerous requests for technical information and catalogs.

I would especially like to extend my heartfelt thanks to: Al Barrett, The Stanley Works; Jack Murray; Stanley Zuba; Hugh and Mary Devaney of Centerport Hardware; and Henry Wetzel. John Trench, the incomparably articulate owner of A&B Hardware, Huntington, New York, contributed much important information and spent many long hours on the book for which I am extremely grateful.

Many friends and colleagues provided valuable editorial and administrative assistance, including Laura Anderson and Karen Richardson; Debnee Steele; Paul Wheeler of Wheeler Pictures (including a generous loan of a Macintosh); Sharon Rappaport; Johnny Truman; and Gusto Graphics, which provided graphic and editorial consulting services.

And special thanks to—

Robert Strimban, whose encouragement, generosity, enthusiasm, and upbeat attitude added to the pleasure of working with his beautiful illustrations.

The friendly, helpful staff editors of Macmillan who have been a delight to work with, and especially my first editor, David Wolff, who has always been a true, patient colleague, and who has always understood what I wanted.

Rick Smolan, whose early enthusiasm and suggestions were fundamental to the birth of this book, and who has shown that the book business can be a great entrepreneurial one.

The carpenter who suggested long ago that I buy a cat's paw, and especially to the obnoxious, anonymous hardware-store clerk who sold me a pry bar instead of the cat's paw I requested, neither of us aware of the difference. His attitude and error actually inspired this book—I understand he is no longer employed in this field.

The many hardware-store clerks around the country of whom I inquired about cat's paws, without ever buying one—I was just testing the need for the book. My apologies and sincere thanks.

And certainly I could never have done anything like this without the support of my wife, Gusty Lange. Projects like this take too many hours away from the pure pleasure of being together, and I will always be thankful for her sacrifices, understanding, suggestions, and shared pride. What more could you want?

For the Revised Edition

I am grateful for publisher Natalie Chapman's longtime enthusiasm and editor Betsy Thorpe's guidance on the revised edition. A note of thanks goes to Ed Lanctot, legendary co-founder of True Value Hardware, for his enthusiasm for my book.

A special acknowledgment goes to Dylan and Chelsea Ettlinger for their extraordinary patience during numerous mysterious trips to hardware stores and home centers. The most patient and helpful staff at those stores earned my respect and gratitude, especially at Home Depot, Norwalk, Connecticut; M. D. Joyce, Deer Isle, Maine; Lumberland, New York City; and (again!) Pintchik's Ace Hardware, also here in New York City. You're great. Thank you!

—Steve Ettlinger

Introduction

How This Book Is Organized

This book is organized in a way similar to a large hardware store or home center. However, it is not a perfectly clean breakdown. For example, though there is a section on hand tools, specialized tools for particular products or projects, such as masonry tools, are found in their own section.

I have put what I think are the more common items in the front of each section, and groups of items follow this in a logical sequence wherever possible. Also, do make use of the index, as it includes every item alphabetically.

The item names are the result of months of research with manufacturers and catalogs, and though these names reflect the most accurate and common terms you'll find on a store's label, in many cases it may not be the name with which you are most familiar, the name you hear on the job site, for example. That's where the "Also Known As" element comes into play. This section comes from the original inspiration for this book, when someone told me to get a cat's paw, which is not the most common name for the tool I needed, a nail claw.

We all call these tools by the names we've learned informally—from where we grew up, in the Navy, on the farm, from some old boss who picked up hardware nomenclature from who knows where. It has been fun collecting all the various aliases that might be out there (tongue-and-groove pliers are the tool with the most aliases: 19) and I continue to try to collect them (please send me any you come across). Some are dead wrong and may come from authoritative sources (even a popular TV show host), others are rare and folkloric, but someone somewhere calls the thing by that name, and so it finds its way into print.

"Use" and "Use Tips" are meant to be succinct, with just enough information to help you identify the item and avoid common problems.

There is also a conscious avoidance of extensive "how-to" advice. The tips we give are meant to echo the friendly advice a good clerk would give you as you leave a store; they are definitely not the comprehensive and detailed instructions required for many projects. I would never have been able to do justice to them in a book of this size.

This is, after all, a buying guide, so the individual "Buying Tips" with each item are essential, as are the more general ones in the various "About" sections. And please also keep in mind the following generalities:

■ So many items are available in different sizes, models, and materials that you should always try to take in an old item in order to purchase proper replacement parts or materials.

■ Most small hardware items sold "carded" in see-through plastic packages are much more expensive than the same item sold in bulk. Always ask if something is available in boxes of 100, or by the pound, or merely loose.

■ While the technical terms concerning metals and finishes of tools and devices may be complicated, you can often determine quality merely by hefting the item and comparing weight and finish quality to other brands. (See Appendix A for information on metal finishes.)

■ Most stores group their merchandise in a manner similar to our book. However, there are many overlapping uses as well as interior-design considerations that may make it difficult for you to find something. Be sure to ask—even small stores may have over 15,000 items in stock!

What This Book Does Not Include

Though a good hardware store, lumberyard, or home center carries tens and even hundreds of thousands of items in stock, I have included only those that the average homeowner/handyperson will find necessary for typical repairs, do-it-yourself projects, renovation, and restoration.

You will not find heavy construction materials, or professional tools, or esoteric cabinetmaking tools, or hobby materials. I drew the line at including automotive, boating, electronics, gardening items, home security items, and housewares.

Yet these items may all be sold in many hardware stores. Nonetheless, for practical reasons, which I trust you understand, I had to stick to my decision: this is about traditional do-it-yourself hardware, products, and materials, and not meant to include anything more.

How to Use This Book

It's very simple. When you are preparing for your next foray into the hardware world, check out the relevant sections in this book. Wherever it is noted that a particular item "comes in various sizes" (or types, or styles, or colors, or grades) you should be alerted that you have some thinking and shopping to do. These are questions that must be answered prior to a purchase.

In other words, there is no such thing as "just a door lock" or "just a paintbrush" and so on. When you ask for these items the clerk will ask you questions back, and invariably they are questions you can anticipate. This book tells you in advance what you have to figure out before you leave home. The key word is "usage." You have to think about what you are going to use your purchase for before you go to the store.

I

Common Hand Tools

About Common Hand Tools

This section includes the more common tools used in do-it-yourself projects, particularly those used with wood, plastic, and metal. Although many of these tools have more specialized applications, those tools that are more often used with specific types of work are not listed here but are found at the ends of their respective sections, such as tools for **painting and finishing** (Part V), **hanging drywall** (Part VII), **plumbing** (Part VIII), **electrical work** (Part IX), and **masonry work** (Part X). Many innovative, ergonomic designs have been introduced recently, making shopping for even the simplest tool exciting.

Hammers

About Hammers

A hammer is usually the first tool for most of us and indeed was one of mankind's first tools.

Safety glasses or goggles are recommended, as a hammer can send a chip flying like a shot into your eye. Never strike another hammer or other striking tool—both could chip or be damaged so that they chip later. Never use a hammer with a loose head. Never use the side, or "cheek," of the head to strike anything—it is likely to crack.

Search for the most comfortable handle you can find—many new materials and ergonomic designs are now available.

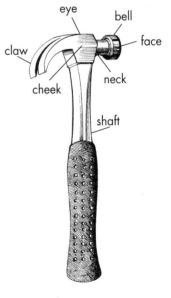

Claw Hammer

Claw Hammer

Also Known As: Curved claw hammer, nail hammer, carpenter's hammer

Description: The most common, standard hammer. Metal head, with a striking surface (the face) and opposite it a notched, curved claw for pulling nails out of wood. Usual head weight is 16 ounces; sometimes lighter or heavier. *Rip hammers*, also called *straight claw*, *ripping claw* or *flooring hammers*, have a straighter claw. *Casing hammers* (8 ounces) are for cabinetwork. Hammer handles can be of wood, steel, or fiberglass.

Use: Driving and pulling nails. Rip hammers are useful for demolition. Also, their straight claw can be jammed into a roof deck if you start to slide off.

> **Use Tips:** The 16-ounce size is best for most carpentry, but the 20-ounce size is highly recommended for construction work when driving long nails into soft wood—the weight of the head gives the hammer greater momentum. Some models have magnets or slots that hold nails for starting.

> **Buying Tips:** Quality hammers have heads with slightly beveled, or "chamfered," edges to avoid chipping, and slightly curved, or "crowned," faces, which are well polished. Research with friends and experts the choice of handle material.

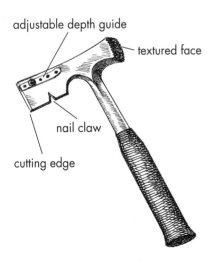

adjustable depth guide

textured face

nail claw

cutting edge

Shingler's Hatchet

Shingler's Hatchet

Also Known As: Roofing hatchet, shingling hatchet

Description: Hammer-sized hatchet with notch in lower edge and thumbscrew and small, sliding, replaceable metal blade along top edge; "heel" of blade has a milled pattern and is square. A *shingler's hammer* is a similar tool but without the sharp hatchet edge, while the small *roofing knife* has only the edge.

Use: Ripping up and replacing old shingles in a small repair or re-roofing job. The sliding metal blade with holes in it can be set to keep the blade from going too far under old shingles; it is used for cutting asphalt or fiberglass shingles, while the hatchet blade is for splitting shakes. The hammerhead is for driving roofing nails. The notch is for prying out nails from the roof decking.

> **Buying Tips:** A specialized tool that helps a big job go faster. For a larger job, get the larger **roofing shovel (Part IV, Chapter 33).**

Drywall Hammer

Also Known As: Drywall hatchet

Description: Smallish hammer with a notched blade instead of a claw. Hammerhead is scored.

Use: Driving drywall nails when hanging drywall and removing old drywall and nails. The notch in the blade is for removing exposed nailheads.

> **Buying Tip:** Screws are the preferred method for hanging drywall.

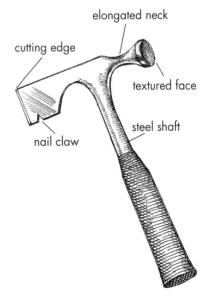

Drywall Hammer

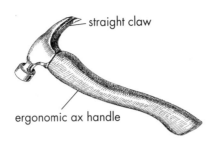

straight claw

ergonomic ax handle

Framing Hammer

Framing Hammer

Also Known As: California Special, California Framer's hammer, Framer's hammer

Description: Extra-long (up to 17") and heavy (21 to 30 ounces) hammer with straight claw, available with either a smooth or patterned (milled, checkerboard) face. Handle is usually straight but some models are available with an "ax-handle" curve to them. Developed by framers in California during the post-war housing boom. Quite similar to the lighter, smaller **rip hammer (above)** but sturdier.

Use: Rough carpentry, such as framing in a house with 2 × 4's, where accuracy is less important than power and speed. The extra length and weight give the carpenter more leverage, reducing the number of blows needed to drive a nail home. Straight claw is more useful for prying than for nail removal.

> **$ Buying Tips:** Checkerboard-patterned faces reduce the chance of glancing blows and flying nails. Top-quality models reduce vibration and arm fatigue. Look for unique features such as square heads and side-pull claws.

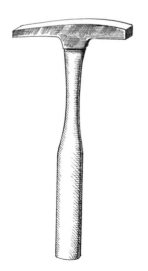

Tack Hammer

Description: Light, narrow, square head, with one face split and magnetized. Similar, but lighter and with a rounded head, is an *upholsterer's hammer*.

Use: For driving tacks or small nails. The magnetized face holds tacks that are too small to be held by hand.

Tack Hammer

Use Tip: Likely to be damaged if used on heavy nails.

Brad Driver

Also Known As: Brad pusher

Description: Round handle on short, spring-loaded, two-piece metal shaft. Brads are loaded into the open end of the shaft.

Use: Drives brads (small finishing nails) without a hammer.

spring-loaded barrel

Brad Driver

Ball Peen Hammer

Also Known As: Ball pein hammer, machinist's hammer

Description: A flat striking surface on one face, like a standard hammer, and a rounded striking surface on the other. A similar model, a *Warrington pattern* or *cross-pein hammer*, has a horizontal wedge-shaped face instead of the rounded face. A *straight-pein hammer* has a vertical wedge.

Use: Driving metal punches, working on sheet metal or rivets. Warrington model has a wedge face that can be used for starting small brads without hitting your fingers. The ball-shaped end is used for forming metal.

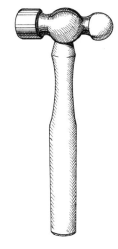

Ball Peen Hammer

Mallet

Mallet

Also Known As: Soft-face hammer

Description: Large cylindrical or square wooden, rubber, plastic, or rawhide head with a wooden handle. A *carver's mallet* has a vertical cylindrical wooden head; a *carpentry mallet* has a big, squarish wooden head; a *deadblow hammer* is rubber filled with shot to eliminate rebound.

Use: For striking wood-handled wood-carving chisels; for bending metal; for tapping wood into place in cabinetmaking (a metal hammer face would mark the wood).

Sledgehammer

Description: Oblong, faceted, extra-heavy head secured to a wooden handle. Available in a range of weights and lengths, the longest ones being two-handed tools. Common small one has a 3-pound head. *Double-face* means both faces are the same; a *single-face sledgehammer*, or *maul*, has one flat striking face and one wedge-shaped face for splitting wood. It is also called a *log splitter*.

double-face head

Sledgehammer

Types:

Drilling, hand drilling, or *stone cutter's, hammer:* For striking masonry chisels, such as a **star drill (Part X, Chapter 75)**.

Engineer's hammer: Very small sledge (or metal mallet).

Blacksmith's hammer: One face wedge-shaped ("New England pattern").

Note: Some manufacturers consider same as engineer's.

Use: Heavy work, such as driving chisels into brick or stone, driving heavy spikes or stakes, or breaking up concrete.

Wedge

Description: Heavy forged steel wedge about 7 to 9 inches long weighing 3 to 5 pounds, with a straight V-shape that has a cutting edge on one end and a wide striking surface on the other.

Use: Splitting logs for firewood. Must be struck with a sledgehammer. Can only work *with* the grain—not a cutting tool.

$ Buying Tips: Quality steel is worth the expense. The striking end on cheaper wedges will "mushroom" out with use and the blade dulls quickly.

Hammer Wedge

Description: Tiny steel wedge with slight steps. Sold in various widths and thicknesses.

Use: Driven into the head ends of wooden hammer, ax, hatchet, and mallet handles to expand the wood and better hold the head in place.

Hammer Wedge

Struck Tools: Nailsets, Punches, and Chisels

Nailset

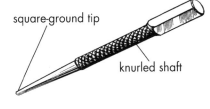

square-ground tip

knurled shaft

Nailset

Also Known As: Countersink

Description: Small shaft of metal, a few inches long, with one end round or square and one tapered to a point. Tapered point is usually blunt, but on some models is concave, or cupped, to hold nailheads. Nailsets come with various-sized tips—$^1/_{32}$" to $^5/_{32}$" at $^1/_{32}$" increments. This tool is often confused with a **center punch (below)**.

Use: Countersinking nails, i.e., driving nailheads beneath the surface of wood.

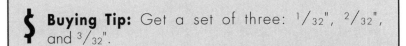

Use Tip: Use the nailset sized to the nailhead being driven to avoid enlarging the hole.

Buying Tip: Get a set of three: $^1/_{32}$", $^2/_{32}$", and $^3/_{32}$".

Punches

Description: Short, cylindrical steel shape like a **nailset (above)** with square head and knurled (or hexagonal) area for gripping. Tapers to a point. *Self-centering* models have telescoping sleeve.

Types:

> *Center punch* (point has short bevel, also known as a *nail punch*)
>
> *Drift punch* (long taper to a flat tip)
>
> *Pin punch* (straight shaft to a flat tip)
>
> *Prick punch* (point has long bevel)

Use: For marking and starting holes in metal or wood (*prick* and *center punches*), for aligning bolt or rivet holes (*drift* or *center punches*), or for driving out bushings (*pin punch*) or rivets after their heads have been removed (*center punch*). A *prick punch* makes a first, light mark that can be enlarged by a center punch.

Use Tips: Punches should always be hit with a ball peen or light sledgehammer with a head slightly larger than the end of the punch. Safety glasses are recommended. Self-centering models are helpful when making holes in hinges and the like.

Buying Tip: The center punch can take care of most punch jobs.

About Chisels

Chisels are classified according to the kind of material they cut—wood, metal, and brick or **stone (masonry tools, Part X, Chapter 75).** Very few are interchangeable. Wear safety goggles when striking these tools.

Cold Chisel

Also Known As: Flat chisel, rivet buster

Description: Thick, short, hexagonal steel bar about 6 to 10 inches long, with a flat, tapered point.

Other Types:

> *Diamond point chisel* (sharp square end, for sharp corners and V-shaped grooves)
>
> *Round nose chisel* (for curved grooves)
>
> *Cape chisel* (arrowhead-shape tip, for shearing off rivet heads and mashing bolt threads to keep nuts in place)

Use: Strike with a ball peen hammer or small sledge to cut and chip such "cold" metals as brass, copper, aluminum, and unhardened steel. Also good for removing bolts and rivets.

Use Tips: Do not use for cutting masonry, which is a common mistake with cold chisels. There are specialized chisels for **masonry (Part X, Chapter 75).** Always wear safety glasses to protect your eyes from flying chips. Deformed tips can be reground.

---

hammer anvil

cutting edge

Cold Chisel

plastic hand guard

Cold Chisel with Hand Guard

Wood Chisels

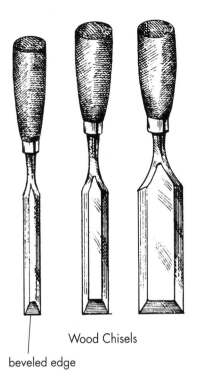

Wood Chisels

beveled edge

Description: Long, narrow steel blades in a variety of shapes, ranging from 2¹/₂" to almost a foot long and ¹/₈" to 2" wide, with a wooden or plastic handle. Only the beveled, front cutting edge is sharp. If the sides are beveled, then it is a *bench*, or *bevel-edged*, chisel, which is the most common style.

Types:

Butt chisel (short blade)

Firmer chisel (medium duty, square-sided)

Framing chisel (long and up to 2" wide, for deep furrows)

Flooring chisel, or *Electrician's chisel* (3" wide, 10" long, all steel)

Mortise chisel, or *mortising chisel* (narrow, thick, and strong)

Paring chisel, or *cabinet chisel* (light duty, for trimming)

Use: Making cuts in wood by chipping small pieces away at each hit.

Use Tips: Protect and keep sharp. Hit with a mallet rather than a hammer, except for the all-steel models. Wood-handled chisels should be hit only with a wooden mallet.

Buying Tips: Some top-quality chisels are works of art, and there is great competition among woodworking tool suppliers in this area. Bevel-edged chisels are common for the home workshop. Get a set.

Bars and Claws

About Pry and Wrecking Bars

While the following lineup of demolishers will help you take a house to the ground, they also do other jobs. Some tools allow you to remove nails and boards with minimal damage to treasured wood or plaster. Since some old trim may be irreplaceable, it is desirable to have, as usual, the right tool for the job. Happily, most bars are not expensive. The choice is easy. And lots of specialized bars are available (but not included here).

Safety note: When standing on anything other than flat, firm floors, don't put all your weight into pulling on a wrecking bar. When the piece you are wrecking pulls free, all your pulling energy is released, and you can go right down unless you are braced and ready.

Wrecking Bar

Also Known As: Crowbar, ripping bar, pig's foot, gooseneck bar, pinch bar

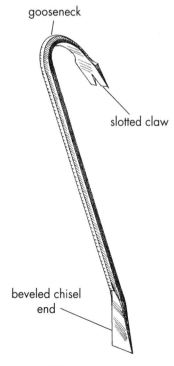

gooseneck

slotted claw

beveled chisel end

Wrecking Bar

Description: High-carbon steel bar, from 1' to several feet in length, with ends designed for prying and nail-pulling. Typically, one end is bent back in a hook and has a forked, nail-grabbing tip. The opposite end has a solid chisel shape and is slightly angled. Cloven appearance of nail puller is the source of the nickname *"pig's foot."* T-headed *wrecking bars* (or *rocker bars*) are common alternatives, too.

> **Note:** To some the *crowbar* or *iron bar* refers to a wrecking bar without a curved end. A bar with a curved end is known as a *gooseneck bar*. However, common usage is as presented above.

Use: Heavy prying and wrecking, particularly where some damage is acceptable. Also popular for lifting heavy objects, such as flagstones or crates, the distance necessary to place wedges and other items under them.

> **Use Tip:** The longer the model, the more leverage you'll have (and the more weight to maneuver).

> **Buying Tip:** A 24" or 30" model is handy for most jobs.

Pry Bar

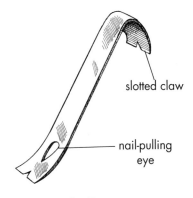

Pry Bar

Also Known As: Wonder Bar™, Super Bar (brand name), Utility Bar (brand name), Action Bar (brand name), pinch bar, molding chisel, shipscraper (small models), flat bar

Description: Flat, thin steel bar, a foot or so long, with beveled notches in both chisel-type ends, one slightly curved and one bent at 90 degrees. Some smaller, lighter models, less than 10" long, are called *pry bar scrapers.*

Use: For prying paneling, molding, crates, and the like where a thin, flat tool is needed and you are trying to avoid damage. Also for removing nails and spikes whose heads are exposed, either by using the notches in the ends or the teardrop-shaped hole (the "eye") in the middle.

> **Use Tips:** Not for extremely heavy prying. The flat shape is less strong than the hexagonal shape of **wrecking bars (above)**.

> **Buying Tips:** Useful to have around, in both light and heavy weights (short and long, 6" and 14").

Ripping Chisel

Offset Ripping Chisel

Also Known As: Ripping bar, rip chisel, angle bar, flat bar, double-end ripping bar

Description: Hexagonal or I-beam steel rod, usually 18" long, with a wide chisel end, a beveled notch, and a teardrop-shaped nail slot for removing nails. Also made in an *offset* version, with a short, beveled, and notched end bent at a 90-degree angle opposite the wider chisel end.

Use: Basically a heavy-duty model of the **pry bar (above)**, for removal of items with small gaps between them. Made to be driven with a large hammer and used like any chisel.

> **Use Tips:** Particularly useful when removing floorboards. Don't overload.

> **Buying Tip:** Many variations exist. Get the one you need.

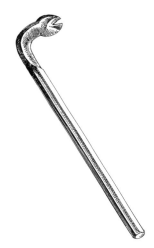

Cat's Paw Nail Claw

Nail Claw

Also Known As: Cat's paw, nail puller, nail puller bar, cat's paw puller, tack claw (smaller models)

Description: Hand-sized, hexagonal or round steel bar with a small, nail-grabbing slotted tip at one or both ends. Typically each tip is cup- or spoon-shaped, and at 90 degrees to the shaft. Some models are L-shaped. Usually around 1' long.

Use: Pulling out sunken nails. Driven below nailheads with a hammer so that nails can be pulled all the way out with the claw of a **hammer (Chapter 1), pry bar, ripping bar,** or **wrecking bar (above)**.

> **Use Tip:** Try to avoid driving the claw too deeply into the wood.

Double-End Cat's Paw

Tack Puller

Description: Short metal shaft with flared, slightly curved, notched end and cylindrical handle, no more than 6" long.

Use: Prying out tacks.

Tack Puller

Lumber Wrench

Also Known As: Tweaker® (brand name), board bender (brand name), warped lumber straightening tool

Description: Foot-long, heavy, octagonal steel bar with uneven U-shaped end, the points of which are tapered to resemble hammer claws. The inside of the U is squared off. Some models have an angled handle with a hinge.

Tweaker®

Use: Multiple uses, but its distinctive shape is primarily for tweaking 2 × 4 studs and deck joists or any other 2"-**dimensional lumber (see Chapter 48)** into place with a gentle twist. The hinged model also squeezes deck floorboards tight. Also suited for wedging a door or other panel to move it slightly, and for removing nails, as well as miscellaneous demolition jobs.

Screwdrivers

About Screwdrivers

There are a number of screwdrivers of potential use to the handyperson, but two kinds predominate: the *slotted* and the *Phillips*. Both types are available with square or round shanks. A *square shank screwdriver* can be gripped with a wrench for added turning power; some brands have a round shank with a hex bolster (a small section just under the handle) for the same purpose. The slot must conform to the type of **screw (Part III, Chapter 21)**.

Slotted Screwdriver

Also Known As: Standard screwdriver, straight-slot screwdriver, machinist's screwdriver, mechanic's screwdriver

Description: Narrow steel shank with flat tip, or blade, and a plastic or wooden handle. *Machinist's screwdrivers* have blades with a slight shoulder and taper. *Cabinet, electrician's,* or *thin-blade* screwdrivers are similar, but the blade tip is narrower and there is no shoulder (straight sides); for finish or electrical work. Cabinet models have a wide blade under the handle.

Use: Driving and removing standard, slotted screws.

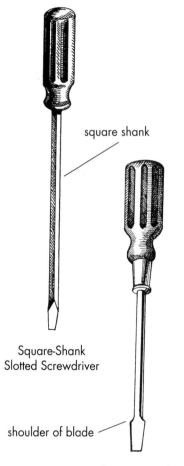

square shank

Square-Shank
Slotted Screwdriver

shoulder of blade

Machinist's (Standard)
Slotted Screwdriver

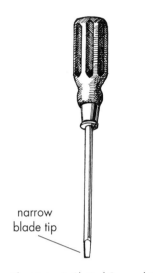

narrow
blade tip

Electrician's Slotted Screwdriver

> **Use Tips:** Always use a screwdriver with a tip that fits the screwhead snugly; otherwise the slot can be damaged, making it difficult to turn the screw.

> **Buying Tips:** Cheap, low-quality screwdrivers are worthless. Get screwdrivers with the bigger, softer handles.

Phillips Head Screwdriver

Also Known As: Cross head screwdriver, star screwdriver, Phillips-type screwdriver

Description: Long, narrow steel shank with pointed, crisscross end and a plastic or wooden handle. Comes in a range of five sizes: 0 (smallest) to 4 (largest). Industrial variations are the *Reed & Prince,* and *Pozidriv* screwdrivers.

Use: Driving and removing Phillips head screws.

> **Use Tip:** Always use a properly sized screwdriver. Using the wrong size can ruin the screw slot.

> **Buying Tips:** Buy at least a #1 and a #2 so you can use the right size each time. The smallest sizes are good for electronic devices. Get good quality only.

Phillips Head Screwdriver

Torx® Screwdriver

Description: One of several new styles of screw slots found in manufactured items, Torx® screwheads are designed with an internal, faceted hole. Sizes are denoted by numbers, such as T8, T15, T40, etc. Somewhat similar to Phillips or Hex Head, Torx® screws are most often used on automobiles (in headlights and the dashboard) and computer cases.

Use: Driving Torx® screws only.

Torx® Screwdriver

> **$ Buying Tip:** You must match the Torx® screw size to the driver.

Stubby Screwdriver

Description: Standard or Phillips blade but only about 1¹/₄" long.

Use: Good in tight spots where a regular-size screwdriver won't fit.

> **$ Buying Tip:** Handle should be large enough to grip comfortably.

Stubby Screwdriver

High-Torque Spiral Ratchet
Screwdriver

High-Torque Spiral Ratchet Screwdriver

Also Known As: Ratchet screwdriver, wrist ratchet screwdriver, mechanical screwdriver

Description: Has a ball or a T-handle instead of a regular handle and a ratchet mechanism enabling you to turn the tool without regripping the handle. Has more turning power, or torque, than an ordinary screwdriver. Most models have interchangeable blades, for both slotted and Phillips screws.

Use: For easier driving and removing of screws.

> **Use Tip:** Good in tight spots where gripping and regripping the handle is difficult.

Return Spiral Ratchet Screwdriver

drive/remove switch

lock ring

spiral grooves

chuck

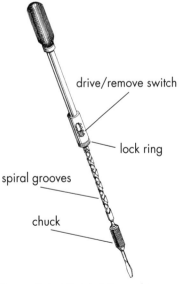

Return Spiral Ratchet Screwdriver

Also Known As: Ratchet screwdriver, auto-return screwdriver, Yankee® screwdriver, in-and-out screwdriver, mechanical screwdriver

Description: Crosshatched shank, with short, interchangeable, ratchet-operated blade and large handle. Turned by pushing down on the handle. Some models can store different type blades in the handle.

Use: Driving and removing screws quickly. Can also drill small holes in soft materials.

Offset Screwdriver

Also Known As: Cranked screwdriver

Description: 4" or 5" long, S-shaped shank with either standard slot head blades or Phillips head blades on each end, perpendicular to the shank; some combination models have both. Also sold in pairs with one of each kind. Available in an *offset ratchet* version made plain **(see ill.)** and with a large handle. For the hardest to reach spots, there is a *flexible screwdriver*, a rare accessory that has a spring-like shank.

Use: Primarily for turning screws in tight places, its added leverage is also helpful in turning difficult screws.

Offset Screwdriver

Offset Ratchet
Screwdriver

Screw-Holding Screwdriver

Screw-Holding Screwdriver

Also Known As: Screw-gripper screwdriver

Description: Similar to a standard screwdriver, but with a split blade that holds screws on the tip of the blade. A variation is a *spring-clip*, which has two springs, or arms, and fits on the end of the blade.

Use: Starting screws in places where they are difficult to hold.

 Use Tip: Screwdriver size must match size of screw being driven.

Saws and Accessories

About Saws

Saws come with various-sized teeth and specific numbers of teeth per inch (tpi) simultaneously designated by "points," such as an "8-point" or "8-tpi" blade. The higher the number, the finer and slower the cutting. All saws should be kept sharp through careful use and, if possible, professional sharpening. They should be of fine-tempered steel. A little lubricating spray helps keep things moving more easily, too.

Crosscut and Rip Saws

Description: Wood or plastic handle secured to a wide, slightly tapered, steel blade with jagged teeth along one edge. Lengths run from 20" to 28"; 26" is most popular.

Use: *Crosscut saws* are used to saw boards across the grain. *Rip saws* have teeth designed to saw along, or with, the grain going the length of the board.

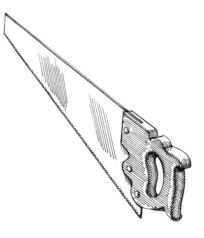

Crosscut Saw

> **Use Tips:** The crosscut saw is *the* basic handsaw for most projects. Use a rip saw at a slightly steeper angle than a crosscut saw—60 degrees as opposed to 45 degrees.

Buying Tips: Taper-ground blades (thinner along the top), which reduce binding, are recommended, as is purchasing brand names. *Skewback saws*, which have slightly curved topsides, are lighter and better balanced. The 8-point size is best for general crosscut work on most home projects; 10-point is for finer work and for plywood and paneling. Rip saws are in the 5- to 6-point range, and are not needed if you have power saws Also, a crosscut handsaw can suffice for the occasional rip job.

About Specialized Handsaws

Saws come in a wide variety of specialized models, but the most useful ones are listed here. Only serious cabinetmakers will need more models. There are also a number of particularly useful Japanese saws; typically, such saws are made of harder steel and cut very well but, unlike American-made saws, cut on the "pull" rather than the "push" stroke, giving you more control for a smoother, more accurate cut.

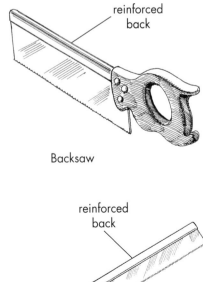

reinforced
back

Backsaw

reinforced
back

Dovetail Saw

Backsaw

Also Known As: Miter-box saw, miter saw

Description: Rectangular, fine-toothed saw with a stiff reinforcement piece along the top or back. Smaller versions of the backsaw, the smallest having handles in line with the blade, are for very fine joint work and include *the dovetail saw, cabinet saw, blitz saw, gent's* or *gentleman's saw, slotting saw, razorback saw,* and *tenon saw.* The reinforced back gives greater control for fine cutting. Generally smaller than a regular saw—12" to 16"; 18" to 30" models are for use in **miter boxes (below)**.

Use: For making very accurate cuts, such as for molding. Also for use in a **miter box (below)**.

Miter Box

Also Known As: mitre box

Description: Wood or plastic box with matching slots on both sides cut at 45-degree and 90-degree angles. Also available in metal with guides for the saw rather than slots.

Use: To cut wood at precise angles.

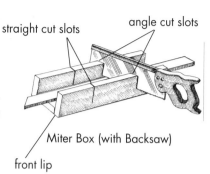

straight cut slots — angle cut slots

Miter Box (with Backsaw)

front lip

> **$ Buying Tips:** Indicators of a quality metal miter box are roller bearings in the saw guide and grips, which allow the stock to be held so both hands can be used. Some miter boxes have magnetic mounts, which make it easier to cut more accurately.

Compass Saw

Also Known As: Keyhole saw, nesting saw

Description: 12" to 14" long, thin, tapered blade. Similar to a **drywall or wallboard saw (Part VII, Chapter 50)** but finer-toothed. Smaller versions are called *keyhole saws* and have fine teeth, which can often cut metal as well as wood. Also very useful are still smaller models with metal, open construction, *pistol grip* or *turret-head* handles, which can hold the smaller blades at various angles. All of these saws are often sold with several different-sized blades, and are therefore sometimes called *nesting saws* or *nest of saws*. When the handle is in line with the small blade, it may be called a *jab saw*, or *pad saw*, as well as a *keyhole saw*.

Use: Cutting holes and curves.

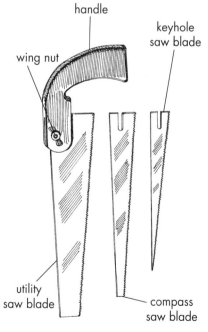

handle

wing nut

keyhole saw blade

utility saw blade

compass saw blade

Compass Saw and Interchangeable Blades

> **Use Tips:** You must drill a hole to start a cut. Some of the smaller blades may cut on the "pull" stroke.

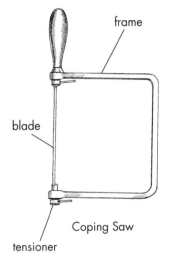

frame

blade

Coping Saw

tensioner

Coping Saw

Description: Extremely thin blade, usually around 6½" long, held by a C-shaped metal frame. Deeper-throated models are known as *fret saws, scroll saws,* and *deep-throat coping saws.*

Use: Extremely fine cutting of all decorative patterns and curves.

> **Use Tips:** Keep blade highly tensioned. Adjust angles and direction of teeth for the work at hand.

> **Buying Tip:** Many specialized blades exist for cutting plastic, metal, and wood.

Japanese Saws

Also Known As: Pullsaw

Types:

Ryoba saw

Dozuki saw

Azebiki saw

Keyhole saw

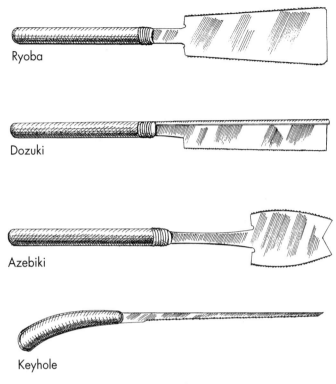

Ryoba

Dozuki

Azebiki

Keyhole

Japanese Saws

Description:

Ryoba: Thin-bladed *combination saw* with fine teeth on both sides—crosscut teeth on one and ripsaw teeth on the other.

Dozuki: Thin, fine-toothed saw with very sharp teeth and stiffening weight rib (usually of brass) along backside. Cuts very fast.

Azebiki: Short, thin, slightly curved blade with fine teeth on both sides. Similar to small **flooring saw (below)**.

Keyhole: Very narrow, pointed blade with large teeth.

Use:

Ryoba: Traditional carpenter's general-use saw; also flush cuts.

Dozuki: For fine cabinetry work and joint cutting, such as for dovetails.

Azebiki: Starts cuts in middle of panels; also for flush cutting in awkward places.

Keyhole: Like its American counterpart, for cutting holes with very small radii; "pull" stroke method allows for a finer blade.

Use Tips: As mentioned, Japanese saws cut on the "pull" stroke rather than the "push" stroke. This certainly aids accurate cutting, makes it easier and faster, and prevents blade buckling. It also allows the use of thin blades. Warning: They are easily damaged.

Buying Tips: An absolutely superior design. The *ryoba* as a combination model is an excellent gift item for anyone of any skill level. A definite purchase for all tool boxes.

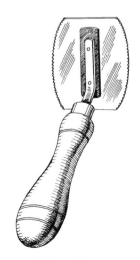

Veneer Saw

Veneer Saw

Description: Small handle secured to small, slightly rounded blade with large-toothed edges.

Use: Cutting veneer (extremely thin pieces of wood) and any small cuts flush with a surface.

Flooring Saw

Description: Short, 8-point crosscut saw with a curved bottom cutting edge and a short cutting edge on the topside of the front end.

Use: Cutting floorboards and baseboards where you need to keep the blade away from neighboring surfaces.

Buck Saw

Also Known As: Bow saw

Description: Extremely large-toothed blade secured between two ends of a metal bow, or handle. Not to be confused with a *frame saw*, popular with cabinetmakers, which is a rarefied traditional saw made of two parallel wooden pieces joined at one end by a blade and at the other by a tension cord or wire, with a bar of wood in the middle.

Use: Rough cutting of logs for firewood or pruning.

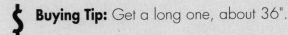

$ Buying Tip: Get a long one, about 36".

Flexible Saw

Also Known As: Pocket saw

Description: Flexible wire coated with sharp tungsten-carbide particles. Has a ring on each end instead of a solid handle.

Use: Limited rough cutting. Made to be portable, used by hikers.

Hacksaw

Description: An adjustable or fixed-frame saw that holds a narrow, fine-toothed blade 8" to 16" long. Number of teeth per inch varies from 14 to 32 tpi, and they may be of various designs such as *wavy* or *raker*. The frame is bought separately from the blades, which are easily (and often) replaced. Some models are extra-strong and have many convenient features such as blade storage and special shapes, called *high-tension* hacksaw frames. Others have just a small handle in line with the blade for use in close quarters, called *mini, jab, handy, close-cutting,* or *utility hacksaw,* depending on the manufacturer. Blade may be mounted at a 90-degree angle for flush cutting.

Use: Cutting metal or plastic.

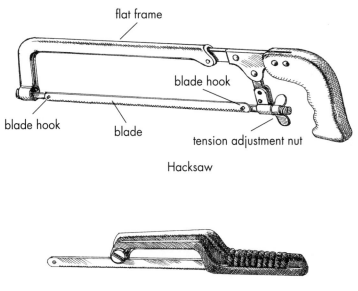

flat frame

blade hook

blade hook   blade

tension adjustment nut

Hacksaw

Mini-Hacksaw

Use Tips: The thinner the material to be cut, the finer the blade should be. Use an 18-tpi (teeth per inch) blade on soft metals; a 24-tpi blade on medium metals; and a 32-tpi blade on hard metals. Always use higher-tpi blades on thinner material. Blade should have three teeth on the work piece.

Buying Tips: Keep a supply of different-toothed blades on hand. Specialized blades are available for cutting glass or tile. Both the *rod saw,* a wire or rod covered with bits of tungsten carbide, and the *grit saw,* with a normal-shaped blade also covered with abrasive material, can cut almost anything. A 10" simple model is sufficient for most DIY jobs. Standard, high-carbon steel blades are usually fine, but a few more expensive, tougher bi-metal blades are good to have on hand.

Saw Set

Description: Pliers-like tool with thumbscrew and small vise for holding a saw blade. Some models have a small magnifying glass built in.

Use: Setting (bending back) teeth on all kinds of hand saws, from 4 to 12 tpi, and on some fine-toothed circular saw blades. The goal is to prevent the saw from binding in the kerf (cut) after getting banged up or worn out.

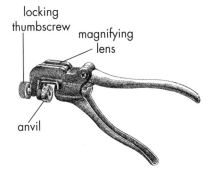

locking thumbscrew

magnifying lens

anvil

Saw Set

Buying Tip: Not your usual weekend handyman necessity, but a good way to save money and extend the life of a tool.

Knives and Cutting Tools

Utility Knife

Also Known As: Trimming knife, carpet knife, Sheetrock knife, drywall knife, mat knife

Description: Two common models: either a hollow metal handle with a large angular blade that is held in place by screwing the two sides of the handle together or else a push-pull type. Some *breakaway utility knives* have sectioned narrow "breakaway" blades; each section can be broken off with pliers when it dulls. Then the new blade section is slid forward. One model even stores blades in a rotating barrel inside the handle.

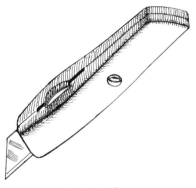

Utility Knife

Use: Cutting wallcovering, drywall, tape, string, roofing, and most any soft material. *Hook blades* allow cutting without damaging material underneath.

Use Tips: Be sure to use sharp blades only; dull blades are inefficient and unsafe. You can reverse the large angular blades and use the opposite end before replacing them. Store with blade retracted for safety's sake. Keep away from children. Hide it in your tool box.

> **$ Buying Tips:** One of the handiest tools to have around. Look for the newer ergonomic models (some even have holsters—wow!).

Razor Knife

Razor Knife

Description: Wooden- or plastic-handled grip that holds single-edged razor blades.

Use: Cutting wallcoverings, paper, etc. Slices and trims with precision.

> **Use Tip:** Change blades as often as every cut, depending on material.

Precision Knife

Also Known As: X-ACTO®, hobby knife

Description: Pencil-sized metal knife that holds a variety of triangular and curved blades in a chuck. The blades are made from surgical steel and are especially sharp. Some models can store blades in their hollow handle. Larger, heavy-duty models are available.

Use: Precision cutting of paper and other lightweight materials, usually on a flat surface. A regular staple of the graphic design business.

Precision Knife

Use Tips: Use a metal rather than a plastic straight-edge to guide your cutting, as the knife will cut into plastic. Wrap worn blades in tape before discarding to protect anyone who might handle the waste basket.

Linoleum Knife

Also Known As: Vinyl knife, flooring knife, hook-bill knife

Description: Short, hooked, wide blade with short, thick handle.

Use: Cutting resilient flooring, such as linoleum or vinyl sheets.

Use Tips: Keep blade sharp. A small file works as well as an **oilstone (below)**.

Linoleum Knife

Oilstone

Also Known As: Whetstone, benchstone, sharpening stone, Arkansas stone, waterstone, carborundum, craftsman's stone, hone stone

Description: Polished stone, either silicon carbide or aluminum oxide. Comes in various sizes. The standard oilstone is $1/2$" to 2" wide by $6^1/2$" to 8" long and 1" thick. It is kept in a holder and the blade is ground on it. If the stone is shaped, small, and can be ground against the blade, it is known as a *slipstone*. A *combination stone* has a different roughness on each side. *Japanese waterstones* are now becoming popular with craftspeople.

Oilstone

Use: Sharpening ("honing") tool and knife edges.

Use Tips: Clean the stone with a stiff brush and kerosene if it becomes clogged with metal shavings. Treat with honing oil.

Buying Tips: Oilstones come in a range of coarseness, or grit: fine, medium, and coarse. Medium is best for most uses.

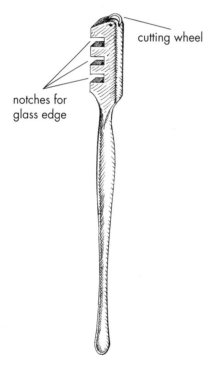

cutting wheel

notches for
glass edge

Glass Cutter

Glass Cutter

Description: Pencil-like metal tool with one notched end with a small cutting wheel on the tip. Roller may or may not be carbide.

Use: To cut glass by scoring and then breaking glass along the line. Models are made for cutting plastic, too.

Use Tips: Warmed glass cuts more easily than cold glass. Never go over the same score twice.

Buying Tip: Table model also available for cutting circles.

Plastic Cutter

Description: Short metal blade and flat handle

Use: For cutting and scoring acrylic plastic sheets.

Tin Snips

Types:

> *Aviation snips*
>
> *Duckbill snips*
>
> *Hawk's bill snips*
>
> *Offset snips*
>
> *Straight snips*
>
> *Universal snips*

Also Known As: Metal shears, tinner's snips.

> *Straight*: Standard, flat blade (duckbill pattern, with pointed tips)
>
> *Aviation*: Compound action, compound leverage

Description: Large, heavy, scissor-like tool with different-shaped noses. *Aviation snips* are smaller, with spring hinges and smaller noses. *Offset snips* have jaws that are at a slight angle to the handle.

Use: Cutting thin metal, as follows:

> *Aviation*: For cutting both straight and curved lines, but spring action gives you better leverage. Available in left- and right-cutting models.

Aviation Tin Snips

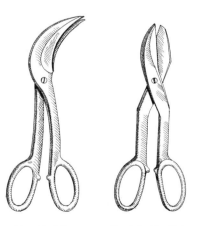

Hawk's Bill Snips

Straight Tin Snips

Hawk's bill: For cutting tight circles without distortion.

Straight and duckbill: For cutting straight lines.

Universal: For cutting both straight and curved lines.

Use Tips: Wear gloves when cutting metal. Cut edges are very sharp.

Buying Tips: For really thin materials, smaller, lighter models called *shears* are available. Offset and aviation snips are slightly easier to use than the large, heavy, *straight* snips.

Bolt Cutter

Bolt Cutter

Also Known As: Rod and bolt cutter, cutter

Description 14" or 24" long blade-and-anvil type shears. Handles work with two sets of hinges and a compound cutting action for extra leverage. Even larger models are made, some over 3' long.

Use: Cutting chain, bolts, rods, small padlocks, or other thick wire.

Use Tips: The 24" model cuts up to $3/8$" diameter bolts; the 14" model only up to $1/4$" diameter. Keep lightly oiled to prevent rust, as this is not a tool one uses often.

Ax (or Axe)

Description Heavy steel, slightly curved wedge with a cutting edge, about 4" to 8" long, attached to a handle, usually of hickory, which ranges in length from 20" to 36"; 36" is most common. Some handles are now made of fiberglass. Handle is curved to increase leverage.

Types:

> *Single-bit ax* has only one sharp edge, for cutting; the other is slender but blunt, for driving large stakes and the like. (A *maul* has a wedge-shaped head with a large, blunt heel.)
>
> *Double-bit ax* has two sharp cutting edges and a straight handle.

Shapes of the ax head vary slightly and carry many different names, some of which are regional, such as *Western* and *Michigan* single edge. Names also vary with the specialized use, such as *fireman's* and *forester's*. Smaller versions of axes are known as **hatchets (below)**.

Use: Chopping trees and branches, splitting logs for firewood.

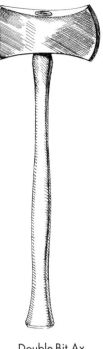

Double-Bit Ax

> **Use Tips:** Double-bit axes are very dangerous for beginners. Safety glasses to protect eyes from flying chips are recommended when using any ax. Don't use the blunt end of a single-bit ax for striking anything hard, like stone or a steel post—use a *sledgehammer* instead. An ax no heavier than 2¹/₄ pounds is recommended for the average user; heavier heads are harder to control and therefore slightly risky to use. A *maul* and *wedge* are best for splitting logs.

> **$ Buying Tips:** A good-quality ax head should ring when you snap your fingernail against it; lesser-quality heads will sound dull. Also look for a thin profile.

Hatchet

Half-Hatchet

Also Known As: Hunter's belt ax

Description: Hammer-sized single-bit ax. Half-hatchet model has a hammerhead where the heel normally is.

Use: Demolition, splitting of small logs into kindling, making stakes.

> **Use Tip:** Be especially careful when swinging this tool.

> **$ Buying Tips:** Many handy, specialized versions exist, including one suited for drywall (called a *wallboard* or **drywall hammer, Chapter 1**) and one for roofing (called a **shingler's hatchet, Chapter 1**).

Adze

Also Known As: Adz

Description: A heavy steel head with a cutting edge perpendicular to the handle, resembling an ax head turned sideways. Often sold as a head only, and you must supply the handle. A general-purpose adze has a 3-pound head, while a finishing adze is a little slimmer and lighter. Finishing adzes may come with slightly curved or straight blades, depending on their intended use.

Use: Shaping and smoothing logs and timbers into beams, notching logs for log cabins, or for wood sculpture. Cuts can be made only with the grain, not across it.

> **$ Buying Tip:** Rarely found in stock, but easily ordered from major manufacturers.

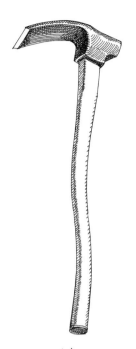

Adze

Pliers

About Pliers

Pliers are some of the most common and useful tools around the house. Some can be up to 20" long, with the jaw opening getting progressively wider as the handles get longer. The variety is necessary—a good toolbox should have a number of types. Many pliers have the capacity to cut wire, with, in most cases, just a small notch on the outside edge or a cutting edge inside, near the hinge. Special-task models abound.

All pliers are scissor-like, usually made of drop-forged steel, with handles on one side of a joint and jaws on the other. Some pliers handles are plastic-covered for improved grip and identification, but this plastic is not protection from electrical shock. Insulated pliers are marked as such, but are very rare.

Slip-Joint Pliers

Also Known As: Pliers

Description: Slightly curved, toothed jaws, and a hinge that can be "slipped" to make the jaw opening wide or narrow. The classic, standard pliers. Some models with a large, round

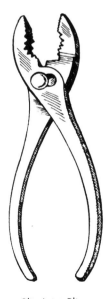

Slip-Joint Pliers

opening in the jaws are called *gas pliers*. Sometimes a type of **tongue-and-groove pliers (below)**, which have a similar slip-joint, are called by the same name.

Use: Gripping small objects.

> **Use Tips:** Not always the best tool for gripping—the specialized pliers described below are better for many jobs. It may slip.

> **Buying Tips:** One of the most common tools to have around, but one that is easily out-performed by more up-to-date models.

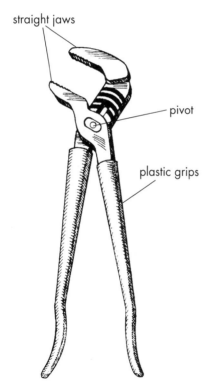

straight jaws

pivot

plastic grips

Tongue-and-Groove Pliers

Tongue-and-Groove Pliers

Also Known As: Channellocks® (brand name and most commonly used name), Channel-type pliers (referring to brand name), arced pliers, curved jaw pliers, jointed pliers, mechanic's pliers, pump pliers, water-pump pliers, pumphouse pliers, pipe-wrench pliers, slip-groove pliers, groove-joint pliers, rib-joint pliers, multiple-joint pliers, channel-joint pliers, C-joint pliers, utility pliers, adjustable pliers—and, incorrectly but often, just plain "pliers."

Description: Pliers-like tool with long jaws and a movable pivot that allows jaws to be set at a variety of widths. Choice of models is large; jaw widths range in size from about 1" to over 5". 1^1/$_2$" is average. Jaws may be either flat or curved. Some manufacturers make two models: *tongue-and-groove,* which has a number of slots or channels for positioning the jaws, and *water pump, box joint* or *slip-joint,* which has a long slot with scalloped edges for different jaw positions.

Use: For gripping items too large for standard pliers; their jaws remain parallel, making them more secure than slip-joint pliers. Plumbers use them for small repairs all the time. Curved jaw models are frequently used to hold pipes. Thinness allows access to tight spots.

> **Use Tips:** Long handles allow for great leverage and gripping power, which can cause you to dent or mar soft metals like brass and copper. Those with solid rivets at the pivot hold better than those with nuts and bolts.

> **Buying Tips:** Larger sizes are harder to handle; 7" and 10" are best to have around. Very versatile—useful also in cars and on boats.

Robo Grip® Pliers

Also Known As: Self-adjusting pliers

Description: Pliers-like tool with an adjustable pivot and handles connected by a moving bar for compound action. Jaws are curved, with deep teeth. Handles and jaws stay roughly parallel as they are moved.

Robo Grip® Pliers

Use: Where extra-strong gripping is required, this design provides needed leverage.

Buying Tip: Like a better mousetrap, building better pliers remains a valuable goal for manufacturers. This is a good attempt. Brand name is used here; imitators may be available under different names.

wire-cutting jaws

box joint

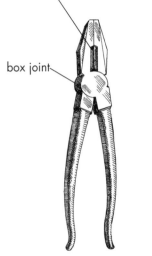

Lineman's Side-Cutting Pliers

Lineman's Side-Cutting Pliers

Also Known As: Lineman's pliers, linesman pliers, electrician's pliers, engineer's pliers (uninsulated handles), telecommunications pliers, wiring pliers, side-cutting pliers

Description: Similar to **diagonal side-cutting pliers (below)**, but of heavier construction and insulated handles with square jaws for gripping and cutting. Those with rounded jaws are known as *New England style*. Combination or universal models have a middle section in the jaws that has a more concave set of gripping teeth, and these may be called *gas* pliers. The pivot is a "solid joint" or "box joint."

Use: For heavy-duty cutting and handling wire with more control than **slip-joint pliers (above)**.

Use Tips: As mentioned before, plastic handles are for comfort only—not for protection against shock.

Buying Tips: Heavy-duty models are very good to have. The combination model, which is quite versatile, is the standard design of pliers in Europe. *Solid-joint* or *box-joint* design is superior.

Locking Pliers

Also Known As: Vise-Grips®, combination plier-wrench, plier wrench.

> **Note:** These are more often called by the brand name Vise-Grips®.

Description: Curved or straight, short jaws and what appears to be one double handle. Jaws may be opened and set as needed by turning a knurled screw in the back of one handle. The jaws are then clamped together by squeezing the handles. Available in a smaller, long-nose version, too, as well as **clamp versions (Chapter 9)**, and flat, smooth jaws for holding sheet metal, etc.

Use: Works like a clamp—they can provide up to a ton of pressure—and can be turned with two hands to free frozen nuts—or used with no hands, just to hold something in place.

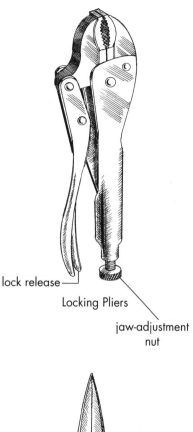

lock release—

Locking Pliers

jaw-adjustment nut

Long-Nose Pliers

Also Known As: Needle-nose pliers, thin-nose pliers

Description: Short, curved handles with long, thin, tapered jaws. Most have a wire-cutting area by the hinge. Those with the longer, more slender noses are more often called *needle-nose pliers*. Many specialized, hooked designs are available.

Use: For reaching into tight spots and/or to hold and bend wire, such as for the small radii necessary in electrical connections or for delicate work.

Long-Nose Pliers

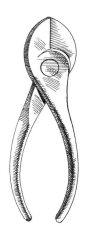

Diagonal Side-Cutting Pliers

Diagonal Side-Cutting Pliers

Also Known As: Wire cutters, diagonal cutting pliers

Description: Small pliers with curved handles and short, pointed nose with cutting jaws (no teeth) at a diagonal to the handles.

Use: General cutting of wire and thin metal items like cotter pins.

> **Use Tips:** Cutting a "live" wire can cause a dangerous short. Don't do it. And again, plastic-coated handles are not necessarily insulated. If you need to cut something thicker than wire, such as a bolt, a lock hasp, chain or cable, use a **bolt cutter (Chapter 6)**, which are huge versions of wire cutters.

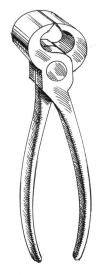

End-Cutting Nippers

End-Cutting Nippers Pliers

Also Known As: Nippers, end nippers, end cutters, carpenter's pincers, nail outener, end nipper plier, nail puller/cutter

Description: Beveled, wide jaws that meet at a right angle to the handles.

Use: For cutting off or pulling nails whose heads are close to the surface.

> **Use Tips:** If you are pulling a nail, don't grip so tight as to cut its head off. These pliers have great leverage.

Fence Pliers

Also Known As: Prong and hammerhead pliers, fenceman's pliers or tool, fencing pliers, fence tool

Description: Pliers-like tool around 10" long with a head that consists of jaws, a hooked part, and a flat, hammer-like end. Combination wrench, pliers, hammer, and stapler puller/driver.

Use: Made for the erection of wire fencing, but good for all wire work. The flat section is used to hammer staples into fence posts, the hook part to pull staples out, and the jaws to pull wire. Generally handy around the house too.

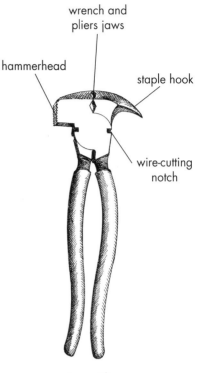

wrench and
pliers jaws

hammerhead

staple hook

wire-cutting
notch

Fence Pliers

Wrenches

About Wrenches

Within the variety of wrenches available there are generally two kinds: those for general use and those for plumbing. The **plumbing**, or **pipe wrenches**, as they are known, are detailed in **Part VIII, Chapter 63**. Basically, the wrenches described below are for turning any type of hex or square nut or bolt or object with flat surfaces, while most pipe wrenches can grip round surfaces with their teeth. All wrenches are available in either fractional (inches) or metric (millimeters) sizes, and only their openings are noted.

The quality you pay for at purchase time will be evident over the years: heavy, good-quality wrenches do not wear out. Cheap ones do, and can slip when in use, damaging the nut you are trying to loosen.

The rare term *spanner* is sometimes used for wrench terminology. It is in general use in England to denote a variety of wrenches, and it may have been used almost as often here prior to World War II. However, our research shows that usage here limits it to plumbing wrenches for large, special nuts.

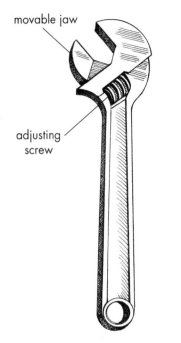

movable jaw

adjusting screw

Adjustable Wrench

Adjustable Wrench

Also Known As: Crescent® wrench, adjustable open-end wrench, knuckle-buster

Description: Long, narrow, polished steel handle with parallel jaws that open or close by adjusting a screw gear. Typically 4" to 16" in length; the size of the jaw opening is proportionate to the length of the tool.

Use: For tightening or loosening nuts and bolts, spark plugs, and small pipe fittings, and larger, chrome-plated pipe fittings that would be marred by the teeth of a pipe wrench. Considered by some to be the modern replacement of the **monkey wrench (Part I, Chapter 8)**.

Use Tips: Not intended for really heavy turning pressure—it may slip. Turn toward the movable jaw. Jiggle as you tighten it for best fit.

Buying Tips: Of all the wrenches you buy, this one should be of the highest quality as it tends to be used quite often around the home and lower-quality wrenches do not grip as well. Helpful to have both a small (6") and a large (10" or 12") model. Check out new versions that may replace this standard such as a *self-adjusting wrench*, which may even have a ratcheting feature.

About Open-End, Box, and Combination Wrenches

These three similar wrench types are available in sets of various sizes. Their openings are fixed, as opposed to the adjustable opening of the wrench described above. All are sold in sets. Ingenious new universal, adjustable, designs may render the fixed style obsolete.

Open-End Wrench

Also Known As: Double-end open-end wrench

Description: Narrow steel handle with ends that have open, fixed jaws. 4- to 16" length; the openings getting larger as the tool gets longer. Like **box wrenches (below)** wrench sizes are described by the size of the nut that each end can fit, such as $3/8" \times 7/16"$. Usually ends are of different sizes.

Use: For tightening or loosening nuts and bolts, especially those accessible only from the side.

Open-End Wrench

> ⚡ **Use Tip:** Generally can be used in tighter quarters than an adjustable wrench.

> 💲 **Buying Tips:** A completely flat version with several different-sized jaws on each end is made for bicycles, but is not very usable around the house.

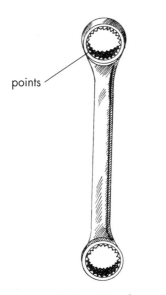

points

Box Wrench

Box Wrench

Also Known As: Ring wrench, double-end box wrench, offset box wrench, box-end wrench

Description: Long, narrow, polished, plated steel handle with two ring-shaped ends with six or twelve interior facets called *points* or *teeth*. Typically 4" to 16" long; the size of the rings is proportionate to the length of the tool. The rings are usually different sizes (³⁄₈" and ⁷⁄₁₆", for example) and may be slightly offset from the handle, so this is sometimes called an *offset wrench*. Also available in a ratchet form, called a *ratcheting box wrench*. Sizes are denoted by the size of the nut that each end can fit, not the wrench length.

Use: For tightening or loosening nuts and bolts when the wrench can be slipped over the end of the work.

> **Use Tip:** Generally can be used in tighter quarters than an adjustable wrench and with more leverage.

> **Buying Tip:** 12-point rings are faster and more versatile.

Combination Wrench

Also Known As: Combination open-end box wrench

Description: Literally a combination of the open-end and box wrenches described above. A narrow steel handle with one ring end with six or twelve points (as described above) and one open end with fixed jaws. Typically 4" to 16" long; the openings are larger if the tool is longer. The two ends are usually for the same size nuts, and that is the size denomination for the wrench, i.e., a $5/16$" wrench is for removing or installing $5/16$" nuts. Also available as a *ratcheting combination wrench*.

Use: For tightening or loosening nuts and bolts.

 Use Tip: Generally can be used in tighter quarters than an adjustable wrench.

Buying Tips: Most common type of fixed-end wrench. The ratcheting version is very handy.

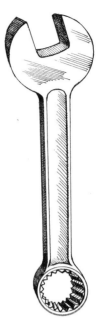

Combination Wrench

Adjustable Box End Wrench

Also Known As: Pocket socket wrench

Description: 8", 10", or 12" long steel bar with slightly angled head containing small sliding, notched jaws. Jaws are tightened in place with a thumbscrew or lever, depending on the make. Other designs use an eccentric oval head.

Use: Gripping and turning nuts and bolts of all sizes, metric or standard. Eliminates need for a set of different-sized wrenches or sockets.

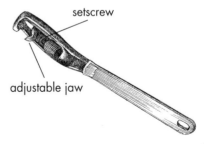

setscrew

adjustable jaw

Adjustable Box End Wrench

Use Tip: Angled handle allows you to work without endangering your knuckles.

> $ **Buying Tips:** Much cheaper than buying set after set of
> sockets (below) or standard **open-end** or **box wrenches**
> **(above)** and less likely to slip than an **adjustable wrench**
> **(above)**. Despite the appeal of its efficiency, some people
> prefer the solidity of size-by-size wrenches.

Bone Wrench

Description: Shaped like a small toy dog bone, usually made of cast aluminum. The two spherical ends have various-sized hex openings. Sort of a spherical version of the **box wrench (above)**.

Use: Light-duty nut tightening and loosening around the house, boat, or on a bicycle.

Nut Driver

Also Known As: Hex nut driver

Description: Round steel shaft and handle, like a screwdriver, but with a small hex opening in the end (which fits over nuts) instead of a screwdriver tip. Available in a variety of fractional and metric sizes from $3/_{16}$" to $1/_2$", denoting size of nut to be driven, but $5/_{16}$" is most common. An *adjustable nut driver* uses a **socket (below)** that tightens down to size.

Use: Driving and removing hex nuts or bolts. Works like a screwdriver.

Nut Driver

> **Use Tips:** Commonly used in plumbing for turning gears on *hose clamps* ($^5/_{16}$"). Very helpful in confined spaces, such as in automotive work, where a wrench would be difficult to "swing."

Socket Wrench

Also Known As: Ratchet wrench

Description: Long steel handle (the "drive") with a round head containing a reversable ratchet mechanism with a square point sticking out. The point snaps into short, cylindrical sockets. The size of this drive point is the size of the wrench, i.e., $^3/_8$" or $^1/_2$". Each socket has an interior opening with either six or twelve points, or in the case of the single-socket, *universal socket,* a spring-loaded pin system that fits a wide range of nuts and bolts. Sold in sets of drives and sockets. A socket wrench set may also include an *extension,* which fits between the socket and the handle to allow better access to certain jobs; and an *adapter,* which allows a combination of socket sizes.

Also made with a hinged handle *(universal joint, flex joint, or flexible head ratchet socket wrench)* for tight spaces. Ratchet mechanisms with more, smaller teeth *(fine tooth ratchet socket wrench)* allow for working in tight spaces with a smaller ratcheting arc. At least one model ratchets with a squeeze-action handle. Available in a cordless electric version.

Use: Driving and removing nuts and bolts that are accessible from their ends and in work where a lot of turning power is needed. The ratchet mechanism allows it to work well in limited space.

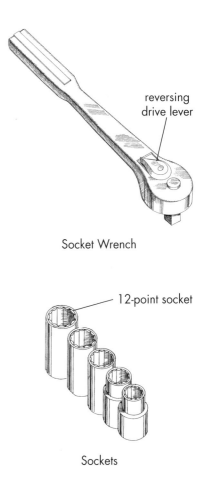

reversing drive lever

Socket Wrench

12-point socket

Sockets

> **$ Buying Tips:** Sockets are available in a wide range of sizes, in the metric, fractional, or Torx® systems, and specialty designs, such as for fitting spark plugs or for use with screwdriver blades. Because this can get expensive, check out the universal sockets.

Crow's-Foot Wrench

Crow's-Foot Wrench

Also Known As: Gimmick wrench, crowfoot wrench

Description: An abbreviated (just the head), open-end wrench with a square hole into which a socket wrench or extension can be inserted for driving.

Use: Tightening and loosening nuts accessible only from the side and in places difficult to reach.

Open-Back Socket Wrench

Open-Back Socket Wrench

Description: Steel rod with open ends that fit over long bolts. Ends contain hex-shaped openings that fit over nuts and bolts of various sizes. Sold in standard and metric sets. Also available in ratchet version, with a hole in the center of the head for bolts to pass through.

Use: Installing nuts on long, threaded rod or bolts. Eliminates the need for deep sockets designed for special uses, such as spark plug removal.

> $ **Buying Tip:** Considered a specialty item, but extremely helpful if needed. Similar effect can be had just by using the old-fashioned **open-end** or **box wrench (above)**.

Finger Wrench

Description: Probably the world's smallest wrench, this small stainless-steel sleeve just barely fits over any size fingertip (it is adjustable). A small notch in the end holds nuts or bolts.

Use: Holding a small nut (up to $7/16$") or bolt in an awkward spot so that the matching nut or bolt can be tightened.

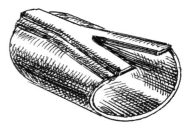

Finger Wrench

> $ **Buying Tip:** An inexpensive (and lightweight) gadget worth its weight in gold.

Allen Wrench

Also Known As: Hex-key wrench, setscrew wrench, hexagon key, L-wrench, hex-L

Description: L-shaped, short hexagonal metal bar, ranging in diameter from $1/20$" to $3/8$". Also available in a set (see illustration) in a screwdriver form and in a T-handle (or T-head) form as well. Some have a rounded "ball" tip for ease of use.

Use: For turning screws or bolts with a hexagonal opening. Typically found in setscrews on machinery.

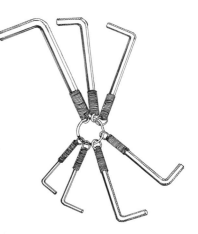

Hex-Key Set

Nut Splitter

Description: Small, hardened steel, P-shaped device with hex-head knob on the tail and small jaws in the P part that have a sharp cutting blade.

Use: Splits open nuts that are "frozen" onto a bolt or whose hex edges have become rounded, rendering a wrench useless.

Clamps and Vises

About Clamps

Clamps (and their mirror image, *spreaders*) are used for holding items in place on a workbench while they are being glued or otherwise assembled. They come in a variety of types. Clamps should not be tightened so much that they damage the surface of the clamped item; often it is wise to insert a piece of scrap wood or cloth in between the clamp and the item. It is always good to have a number of types and sizes in your workshop.

C-Clamp

Description: A piece of cast iron in the shape of the letter C with an adjustable screw on one leg, which actually makes it look more like the letter G. Comes in a variety of sizes ranging from 1" to 12" deep, measured by the gap, known as the throat, between back, or vertical, part of the C and the clamping part, at the opening. The opening between clamping faces can be as large as 8".

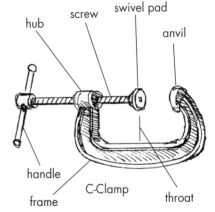

Types:

Deep-throat c-clamp (deepest gap)

Square-throat c-clamp

Heavy-duty c-clamp (rounder shape)

Use: For a wide variety of clamping jobs. Most common kind of clamp.

3-Way Edging Clamp

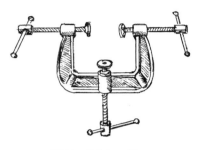

3-Way Edging Clamp

Description: C-clamp with an additional screw in the center of the throat. A plain-edge clamp is a **bar clamp (below)** with two spindles on the side for pieces too big for a C-clamp.

Use: Applies right-angle pressure to the edge or side of work. Ideal for holding trim in place while glue sets.

Hand Screw Clamp

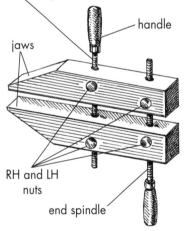

middle spindle

handle

jaws

RH and LH
nuts

end spindle

Hand Screw Clamp

Also Known As: Jorgenson®, screw clamp

Description: A pair of hardwood (usually maple) jaws connected by two large screw spindles.

Use: General clamping of woodwork, especially where protection of the work is important. Can be adjusted to clamp at various angles.

Hold-Down Clamp

Description: Clamp that attaches to workbench surface and has a vertical screw.

Use: Holding work against the workbench.

Pipe Clamp

Also Known As: Furniture clamp, cabinet clamp, Pony® clamp

Description: Clamping devices that slide on pipe and are locked into place where desired. Can be as long as any length of pipe. Generally made for $1/2$" and $3/4$" pipe.

Use: For clamping very large, flat objects.

> **Use Tip:** For smooth operation, use black iron pipe, not galvanized.

> **Buying Tips:** Tend to be cheaper than **bar clamps (below)**. Look for reversible models that can be converted into spreaders.

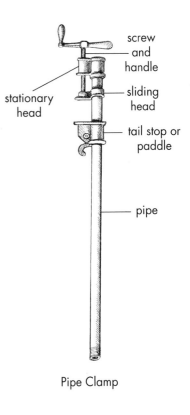

Pipe Clamp

Bar Clamp

Also Known As: Furniture clamp, cabinet clamp, joiner's clamp

Description: Similar to the **pipe clamp (above)** but has flat bars 6" to 4' long instead of pipes. Some models, called *quick-action one-handed clamps,* have a wedge-type trigger mechanism for locking one head in place.

Use: For clamping large objects.

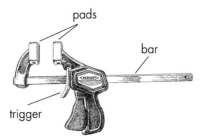

One-Handed Bar Clamp

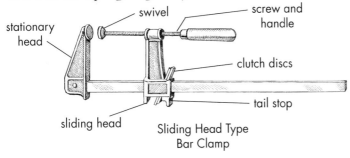

Sliding Head Type
Bar Clamp

$ Buying Tips: Trigger-grip models are great for one-handed use. Always buy in pairs.

Pinch Dog

Pinch Dog

Also Known As: Joint clamp, joiner's dog

Description: Small, U-shaped metal piece with two sharp, pointed legs.

Use: Holds boards together edge-to-edge while glue sets. The pinch dog is driven into the ends of abutting boards and naturally pinches them together.

Use Tip: Edges of boards must be truly flat.

Vise-Grip® Clamp

Also Known As: Locking pliers clamp

Description: Oversized jaws that function and look like a C-clamp with a handle—actually a pair of Vise-Grip® pliers. Various sizes and shapes available.

Use: Clamping irregularly shaped items. Squeezing the Vise-Grip quickly locks the clamp onto the item.

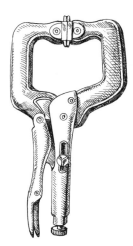

Vise-Grip® Clamp

Spring Clamp

Also Known As: Jiffy clamp

Description: Two flat metal pieces linked by a hinge and a spring, much like a large clothespin. Comes in a variety of sizes.

Use: For quick use with thin materials when not much force is required.

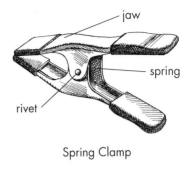

Spring Clamp

Web Clamp

Also Known As: Band clamp, tourniquet clamp, strap clamp

Description: Belt a few feet long made of hard nylon or cloth material that is locked into place with a buckle-like device. Some consider a 1" wide, light-duty clamp a *band clamp* and a 2" wide, heavy duty model a *web clamp*.

Use: For applying even pressure to an irregular shape, such as a chair, or around a large object, such as a box.

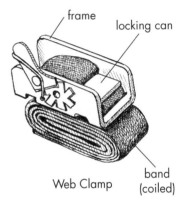

Web Clamp

Corner Clamp

Also Known As: Splicing clamp (same, but with ability to move small vises alongside one another to hold two pieces in a line), miter clamp, or miter box vise (same, but with adapter that holds a guide for sawing)

Description: Flat base with small vises that are at a 90-degree angle.

Use: For gluing picture frames, screen frames, and trim.

Vise

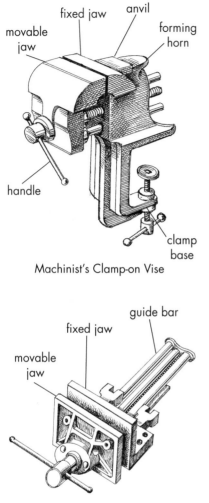

movable jaw — fixed jaw — anvil — forming horn

handle

clamp base

Machinist's Clamp-on Vise

Description: Two flat jaws drawn together and opened by a gear device. If the jaws are made of steel, known as a *machinist's vise;* if made of or faced with wood, known as a *woodworker's vise,* which is generally screwed to and flush with the edge of the bench. If bolted to the top of a workbench, known as a *bench vise.* May have a swivel base or just clamp to the bench.

Use: Holding pieces steady during a job.

Use Tips: Vises designed to hold pipe are also available. Lining the jaws of a machinist's vise with wood allows it to hold wood workpieces without damaging them.

Buying Tips: Models with a half-thread screw handle are easier to work. Most machinist's vises have a swivel base, allowing rotation of the jaws.

guide bar

fixed jaw

movable jaw

Woodworker's Vise

Measuring and Layout Tools

About Measuring and Layout Tools

Electronics have changed this category more than any other in recent years, now that there are electronic measuring devices of all kinds. Some are merely enhanced versions of the classics, such as a tape measure with digital readout. Others are really quite evolved, such as laser levels. Most are big improvements, but at a cost. In fact, the bulk of the state-of-the-art, high-tech measuring devices are designed, both price-wise and function-wise, for the professional. However, that still leaves a few models of interest to the DIY worker, and they are certainly a big help.

Tape Rule

Also Known As: Measuring tape, tape measure, rule, tape, push-pull tape, flex or flexible tape or rule, power return rule, pocket tape (if very small), steel tape, blade tape

Description: Slightly concave steel tape coiled inside a case, from 3' to 33' long and from ¼" to 1" wide. Retracts automatically after use. Another type has flat tape that can be up to 100' long and may be known as a *reel tape* or *engineer's tape*. A small hook is riveted loosely on the end for hooking over the edge of the object being measured (the looseness

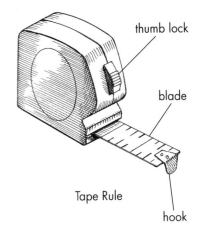

thumb lock

blade

Tape Rule

hook

Reel Tape

compensates for the thickness of the hook). Some tapes have clips on the back for hanging onto a belt or holster. Available with electronic, digital readout, as well as with a small recording/playback device for dictating measurements.

Use: Measuring objects.

Use Tips: If you are working with someone else, make sure you both use the same brand rule, as the actual dimensions may vary somewhat from brand to brand. Note that the case can be part of the measurement if you want; it is marked and is usually 2". Be careful not to touch the edge of the tape as it is returning to the case—you could get a nasty cut.

Buying Tips: Signs of quality are epoxy or Mylar coating on the tape, solid cases, and reliable return mechanisms. Domestic brands are generally better than imported. A wider, $3/4$" tape is easier to handle at long distances and may more easily be extended beyond your reach, say to a ceiling, which is a convenience that makes up for the bulkier size. Buy a small one to carry in your pocket if need be.

Electronic Distance Measuring Tool

Electronic Distance Measuring Tool

Also Known As: Electronic measuring tool, rangefinder

Description: Palm-sized, calculator-like tool with an ultrasonic transmitter/receiver on one end and an LCD display, plus an acoustical signal on some models. Contains a microprocessor and several command buttons. Available in a variety of models, which vary in range capacity (such as 1'6" to 60') as well as computing ability and accuracy. A separate target extends the range exponentially.

Use: Measuring linear dimensions and computing them into volume measurements for estimating wallpaper, flooring, or paint work. Works from one spot; no need to move furniture or walk to different spots in the room being measured.

> **$ Buying Tips:** An excellent time-saver that can convert a two-person job into a solo job. Some of the extra functions in the better models are well worth the price, such as automatic shutoff, ability to display distances in a variety of units, and memory.

Bench Rule

Also Known As: Ruler, steel ruler

Description: Plain, flat steel bar from 6" to 36" long with various measuring markings, usually down to $1/16$" or $1/32$" and metric increments down to millimeter increments.

Use: Measuring pieces around the workshop.

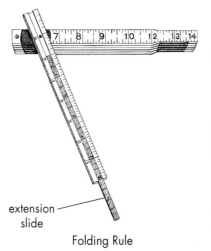

extension —
slide

Folding Rule

Folding Rule

Also Known As: Zigzag rule, carpenter's rule, folding wood rule

Description: A number of 6" to 8" segments hinged together. Made of hardwood, steel, or aluminum. Segments lock to form a long rule when folded out. A model with a small extension in the end segment for small measurements, called an *extension rule,* is also available.

Use: Measuring distances when it would be difficult to extend a tape rule.

> **Use Tip:** Take care of rule so that the markings remain clear and the hinges tight.

> **Buying Tip:** Quality rules have easily read markings, highlighted common measurements, and protective coatings.

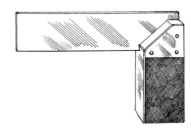

Tri/Miter Square

Try Square

Also Known As: Tri-square, rosewood square, engineer's square

Description: L-shaped tool with a thick wooden section that has a flat metal blade projecting at a right angle from it. Sizes range from 6" to 12". A similar tool, called a *miter square,* has its handle at 45 degrees and is used only for measuring and marking 45-degree miter cuts. A try/miter square has a 45-degree edge at its corner.

Other Types: *Engineer's,* or *machinist's,* try squares, which are made completely of steel.

Use: Checking, or "trying," workpieces to see if they are square. Good also for making 90- and 45-degree marks.

Combination Square

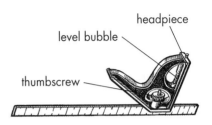

Combination Square

Also Known As: Machinist's square, 45-degree miter square

Description: Straight steel rule, usually 12" long, to which is attached a head section containing a small level (short tube with a bubble inside). The head can be slipped along the rule and then locked in place at any point. A center head is available.

Use: As its name denotes, it can be used for a variety of functions: a level, a steel rule, a try square, and for measuring or marking miter cuts.

> **$ Buying Tip:** A versatile but sometimes expensive combination tool good to have in your workshop.

Framing Square

Also Known As: Square, rafter square, steel square, carpenter's square, flat square, carpenter's framing square, roofing square, builder's square

Description: L-shaped piece of flat steel or aluminum with one long section, the *blade,* and one shorter section, the *tongue.* Typically 24" by 16". Both sections have measure-

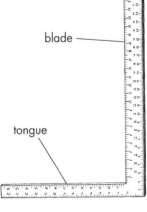

Framing Square

ment marks, including common carpentry measures such as the standard distance between studs (sargent tables); hence the names above.

Use: Mostly for laying out, for squaring up large patterns, and for testing the squareness and flatness of large surfaces. Use **stair guides (below)** for marking repetitive measurements.

> **$ Buying Tip:** The best-quality square has engraved, not stamped, markings.

thumbscrews

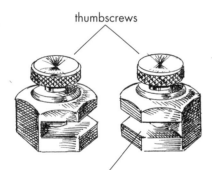

gap for square blade

Rafter and Stair Gauges

Rafter and Stair Gauges

Also Known As: Stair gauges, stair gage fixture attachments, stair gage fixtures, square gauge, square gauge set, angle gauge

Description: Small (³/₄"–2" wide) hexagonal or sometimes tear-drop-shaped cast iron, zinc, or steel clamp with a thumbscrew and a large slot that fits over a **framing square (above)**. Brass clamp screw available on better models. Always sold in pairs.

Use: When attached to a framing square forms a handy gauge for laying out stair stringers, hip, valley, and other rafter cuts, or any other repetitive measurement.

> **$ Buying Tip:** Worth its reasonable price for even a small job.

Speed Square

Speed Square

Also Known As: Pocket square, quick square, deck and rafter square, rafter square, rafter triangle square, rafter angle square, rafter layout square, angle square

Description: Small (6" × 10") plastic or light metal triangle with one wide, thick edge and various angle measurements marked on its surface and edges.

Use: Laying out a variety of cuts in ways similar to other, more specialized squares such as the **try square** and the **framing square (above)**. Its wide edge can be used as a *power saw guide,* and it also functions as a *protractor.*

Bevel Gauge

tongue or blade

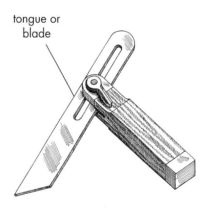

Bevel Gauge

Also Known As: Bevel, T-bevel, combination bevel, sliding T-bevel, sliding bevel, adjustable T-angle, angle bevel, bevel square, adjustable try square

Description: Flat metal blade about half a foot long with a wooden or plastic handle. The handle slides along the blade and can be locked into position at any angle.

Use: Marking a wide range of angles—more than other measuring tools—by copying them for transfer to another piece.

> **Use Tips:** A bevel gauge can be set to the desired angle with a protractor if it isn't copying an existing angle.

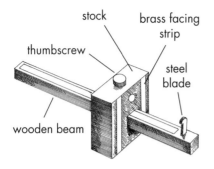

stock   brass facing strip

thumbscrew

steel blade

wooden beam

Marking/Cutting Gauge

Marking Gauge

Also Known As: Cutting gauge

Description: A long wooden, metal, or plastic bar, up to 9" long, with a marking pin on one end and a round section that slides along it and is locked where wanted with a thumbscrew. A *mortise gauge* has two marking pins; a *cutting gauge* has a small blade in place of the pin.

Use: Scoring lines parallel to the edge of a board. The round section is pulled along the board edge and the pin in the end of the long piece marks the face of the board.

> **Use Tip:** Before scribing, double-check desired dimensions with a ruler.

window vials

Carpenter's Level

Carpenter's Level

Also Known As: Level, spirit level, bubble level, magnesium level, aluminum level

Description: Wood or wood and metal (magnesium or aluminum) piece usually around 3" by 24" to 48" long containing from three to six small glass tubes ("vials") with bubbles in them. A *mason's level* is similar, but 48" or longer. Some levels have adjustable and replaceable bubble tubes. Some have magnets. A *bubble stick* or *bubble level* is a lightweight plastic ruler with one or two bubble tubes.

Use: Checking the level, or *true* (flatness), of surfaces or pipes. The glass vials are positioned for measuring the level of surfaces at horizontal, vertical, and 45-degree angles. A bubble stick is for installing wallpaper.

Torpedo Level

Also Known As: Canoe level, marine level

Description: Typically 1" × 9" lightweight bar containing three glass vials with bubbles in them. Some have magnets to hold them against pipes.

Use: Handy where a longer **carpenter's level (above)** won't fit, as in many electrical and plumbing jobs. Small enough, and shaped to fit in your pants pocket.

Torpedo Level

Electronic Level

Description: Plastic, electronic version of a **carpenter's level (above)** or **torpedo level (above)** with either a video or digital LED display as well as an audio signal to indicate level or off-level instead of the traditional bubble (some models include a traditional bubble as well). May have a pipe groove

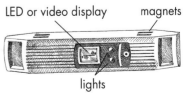

LED or video display   magnets

lights

Electronic Level

for stability on uneven surfaces, magnets for attaching to pipes and studs, or other accessories. Better models have memory and instant recalibration. Models intended for professionals (in other words, very expensive models) incorporate a laser beam as well, or angle measures (protractor arms) with digital readouts.

Use: Finding level or plumb (vertical) as well as (depending on the model's abilities) slope, pitch, or grade stored in memory. Visual and audio displays allow for ease of use in dark areas

$ **Buying Tip:** Easier to use and more precise than traditional levels.

Sight Level

Description: Small viewing tube with bubble level and crosswire.

Use: Simple leveling work, such as lining up the tops of fence or deck posts, or for grading jobs.

Sight Level

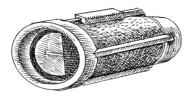

rubber band

vertical level

Post Level

Description: Small, plastic L-shaped item with a large rubber band on one side and three bubble vials (two horizontal and one vertical).

horizontal levels

Post Level

Use: Hands-free, one-person installation of posts that are plumb.

> **$ Buying Tip:** A gadget that saves time and possibly the need for a partner.

Line Level

Description: Short length of tubing containing a glass vial with a bubble, with hooks on each end for hanging from a line.

Line Level

Use: Hung from a taut *mason's line* prior to laying bricks; also used when installing a ceiling or constructing a floor.

> **Use Tips:** Make sure line is really taut before using level.

Water Level

Also Known As: Flexible Tube Level

Description: Clear tubing containing colored liquid and bubble, 25' to 200' long. Also available in an electronic version that beeps when one end is level with the other.

Use: Establishing level over long distances, such as when making suspended-ceiling lines, in landscaping, or around corners.

> **$ Buying Tips:** Some hardware stores will make up flexible tube levels to any length you wish. Or you can try making your own with a ¹/₄" plastic tube filled with water. Hold up the two ends in a U shape and the water will be at the same level at both ends. Add some food coloring for easier viewing.

Surface Level

Also Known As: Bull's-eye level, circular level

Description: Small liquid-filled circular plastic piece with a bubble in the middle.

Use: Determining the levelness of a surface over a range of 360 degrees, such as for record turntables or washing machines.

Contour Gauge

> **Use Tips:** May give misleading reading if surface is uneven; because of its small size, it can "read" only the levelness of the actual point it is touching, not the entire surface.

Plumb Bob

Plumb Bob

Also Known As: Plumb line

Description: A pointed, tapered weight a few inches long that is suspended from a cord. The bob commonly weighs from 6 to 24 ounces.

Use: Determines true verticality, or *trueness,* when hung by a cord.

🔧 **Use Tips:** Because a plumb bob is a precision instrument, it should be handled carefully. Dangle into a bucket of water for use on windy days.

💲 **Buying Tip:** Some plumb bobs' tips are replaceable.

Contour Gauge

Description: Hand-sized bunch of parallel, thin metal or plastic rods held together by a metal bar. See illustration on previous page.

Use: Making a template for transferring shapes to various materials, such as when cutting floor tiles or carpeting to fit snug against an odd-shaped piece of molding in a doorway. The rods are adjustable and are moved by pushing them all against a contoured piece. The result is an exact, traceable contour of that piece.

Calipers

Description: Precision metal instrument about 10" long consisting of two legs and a spring-type hinge with a small handle on the end about half a foot long. *Inside calipers* have straight legs slightly turned out at the ends; *outside calipers* have tips pointing in. Another version, *vernier calipers,* consists of a steel bar with a measuring scale on it and a sliding head.

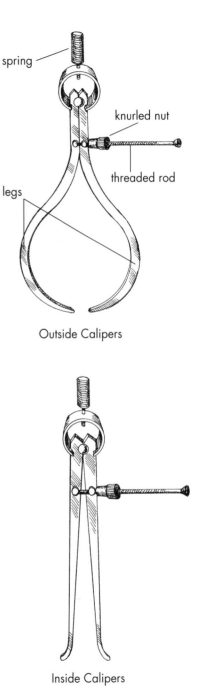

Outside Calipers

Inside Calipers

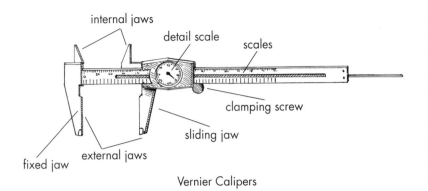

internal jaws
detail scale
scales
clamping screw
sliding jaw
external jaws
fixed jaw

Vernier Calipers

Dial calipers are like vernier calipers, but the measurement is read on a dial rather than on the bar itself. Extremely precise.

Use: For measuring the inside or outside of round objects, for transferring dimensions, or for precision measuring.

wing

Compass

Compass

Also Known As: Wing dividers

Description: Two pointed metal legs, hinged at the top, with a metal band that locks the legs in a desired position. One leg may or may not have a small pencil attached to it for marking; if not, this is more often known as a *pair of dividers*.

Use: Scribing circles or transferring measurements from one item to another.

Trammel Points

Trammel Points

Also Known As: Trammel heads, trammels

Description: Pencil-like metal points with adjustable clamps (or setscrews) for securing on a suitable beam or bar.

Use: Duplicates measurements or marks large arcs when a compass or divider is too small for the job.

> **Use Tip:** A pencil can often be substituted for one of the points.

Carpenter's Pencil

Description: Wide, flat pencil containing soft lead. A similar item, *lumber crayon,* is a 6" long hexagonal crayon.

Use: Like any pencil, for marking measurements and cut lines, etc. Its advantage is that, being flat, it won't roll away. Its design makes it easily sharpened with a penknife.

Chalk Line Reel

Also Known As: Chalk line, chalk box, snapline

Description: Coiled string in a metal or plastic housing containing powdered chalk. Line may be 50' or 100' long. Chalk is available in various colors.

Use: Marking long, straight lines on large, flat surfaces, such as floors, ceilings, and walls.

Chalk Line Reel

> **Use Tips:** Can be used as a **plumb bob (above)** by simply hanging it by its own string. Chalk for refilling is sold in plastic bottles; replacement string is also available. Rewind after each use to re-chalk string.

> **Buying Tip:** Much easier to use than the old-fashioned system of a half sphere of chalk, which was rubbed onto the string each time it was used.

lights

Electronic Stud Sensor

Stud Finder

Also Known As: Stud and joist locator, stud sensor

Description: A small magnetic or electronic device that comes in many types of designs. Small magnets, or metal detectors, indicate nails in studs; some use sonar to sense density, shown in LED's or audio tones.

Use: Indicating locations of studs behind finished walls or under floors for hanging cabinets, shelves, or light fixtures (studs are the vertical pieces of wood holding your wall up).

> **Buying Tips:** The more expensive electronic models can search through thicker walls, flooring material, and even concrete. They are also more accurate.

Drills and Braces

Hand Drill

Also Known As: Eggbeater drill

Description: Straight tool with a crank handle and gear on the side very similar to an eggbeater. Drives bits up to $1/4$" in diameter. The handle is usually hollow and used to store assorted bits.

Use: Basic, simple drill for making holes up to $1/4$" in diameter.

> **Use Tip:** Can use most standard drill bits and accessories intended for power drills.

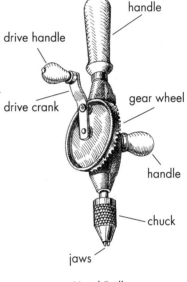

Hand Drill

About Drill Bits for Hand Drills and Braces

Most drill bits and accessories can be used both in hand and power drills. Because of the popularity of power drills today, we have placed all information about interchangeable drill bits in the **power tools section (Part II, Chapter 16)**. Those bits that can be used only by a hand drill or brace are described below in this chapter.

Push Drill

Also Known As: Yankee push drill

Description: Ratchet screwdriver-like tool whose end rotates a bit when the handle is pushed down. Uses special drill bit, sort of a small gouge, called a *drill point*.

Use: Drilling small holes in soft material.

Gimlet

Also Known As: Screw starter

Description: Short steel shank with a sharp, fluted tip and a wooden T handle.

Use: For starting screw holes in wood up to around ³/₈".

shell

lead screw

Gimlet

> **Use Tips:** Be sure gimlet is pushed in straight because the screw will follow the hole. Don't use a hammer—the gimlet would then be hard to remove.

Awl

Also Known As: Scratch awl

Description: Ice pick–like tool with wooden handle and pointed rod about 3" long.

Use: For starting holes for drill bits, screws, and nails, and for making "score" marks.

Awl

Brace

Also Known As: Hand brace, carpenter's brace, bit brace, brace and bit

Description: A type of large hand drill made of a crank handle with a knob on one end and a knurled nose that holds large drill bits with specially designed square or hex ends, called **auger bits (below).**

Use: To bore large holes in wood.

> ⚔ **Use Tips:** Traditional way to use brace is to press against the knob with your body. Some braces have ratchet mechanisms that allow the brace to be turned in very tight quarters.

> $ **Buying Tips:** Not available much anymore, having been replaced by power drills.

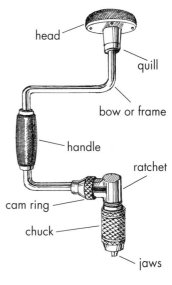

head

quill

bow or frame

handle

ratchet

cam ring

chuck

jaws

Brace

Auger Bit

Description: General name for bits used in a **hand brace (above).** Large spiral bit that averages 10" long but available as long as 30". Tail end of shank is a tapered square or hex. Common designs include the *Jennings,* or *Russell Jennings* (high-quality, double twist), and solid center (most common design—single twist). Special versions are made for end grain, creosoted timbers, wood containing nails, and so on.

Some Special Types:

Ship auger: Deep boring, often used with power drills.

Ship head car: Deep boring in soft wood.

Dowel bit: Short, 5" long, for precision work.

Door lock bit: Wide, for installing cylinder locks or piping.

Use: For drilling large holes in wood with a **brace (Part I, Chapter 11)** and with a $^3/_8$" or larger power drill if shaft end is round or otherwise adapted for power drills. *Power* auger bits are designed specifically for use with power drills and will have the properly designed shaft (round end) as well as other features that make them more suitable for high-speed use.

Use Tips: To avoid splintering where the bit leaves the piece, drill just until the small screw point emerges, then turn the piece over and drill back in the opposite direction. Solid center bits are less susceptible to bending.

Files, Rasps, and Abrasives

About Files and Rasps

Many people confuse rasps and files. The distinction is essentially one of use: rasps (technically a "cut" of file) are used on wood, whereas files are used on both wood and metal. They also differ in that rasp teeth, which are rougher, are individually shaped teeth, while file teeth, which are finer, are actually a series of lines or grooves cut into a metal bar.

When you buy or use a file, there are four basic distinctions that need to be made, depending on the work you want it to do:

1. **Length.** Length is measured from the tip, or *point,* to the *heel,* the shoulder where the file narrows to the *tang,* the narrow part that fits into and is secured to a handle **(see ill.)**. The coarseness of a file or rasp is also affected by its length: longer files and rasps have bigger teeth than shorter ones, and are therefore coarser.

2. **Shape.** The biggest distinction among the various types of rasps and files is their shape, as detailed below. However, some basic shapes are **(see ill.)**:

   Flat (*mill, flat,* and *hand,* in order of thickness)

   Pillar (thick and flat)

   Half-round

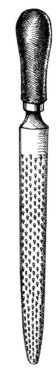

Wood Rasp with Handle

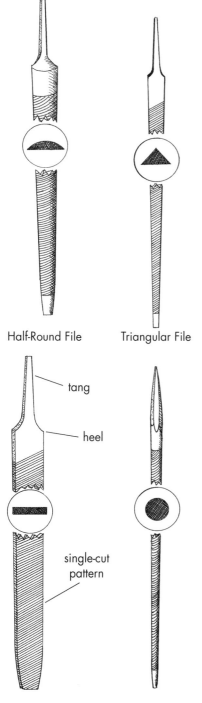

Half-Round File

Triangular File

tang

heel

single-cut
pattern

Flat File

Rattail File

Round (also known as *rattail*)

Square

Taper (also known as *three-square* or *triangular*)

3. **Cut, or coarseness.** There are three common grades:

Bastard-cut (coarsest; for rough work)

Second-cut, or *double-cut* (medium rough; for quick work)

Smooth-cut, or *single-cut* (smoothest; for finish work)

Two more extreme cuts are sometimes found—coarse and dead smooth. It is good to have a range of coarseness in the files of your workshop.

Rasps themselves are often rated with a slightly different set of names: *wood* (coarsest, for quick removal work), *cabinet* (finer), *bastard* and *cabinet rasp second cut* (finest).

Swiss pattern or *European patternmaker's* files range in seven cuts from 00 to 6.

4. **Kind or pattern of teeth.**

In one of the more confusing traditions in the world of tools, the terms for tooth pattern and coarseness are identical: cut. Good luck!

Single-cut (parallel rows of teeth)

Double-cut (two sets of parallel rows of teeth in a crisscross pattern)

Curved-cut (slightly curved rows, used primarily in autobody work)

Rasp-cut (short, triangular, separate teeth—just called a rasp)

> **General Use Tips:** Files should be cleaned with either a wire brush, or a specialized **file brush** or **card (below)**. They should be stored carefully—not piled in a box with other tools—so as not to chip teeth. Clamp whatever you are working on in a vise or clamp for better control.

Files

Description: Long, narrow metal bar of various shapes with shallow grooves or teeth. **(See About Files and Rasps section, above.)** Most are slightly tapered; they are known as *blunt* if they are not.

> **Note:** Usually the teeth are not cut on the edges of files, and the edges are then known as *safe* or *uncut*. When they are cut they may have a different coarseness than the face, and also may differ from side to side, being safe on one side only. Some "handy" or "utility" models have different cuts on each working side of the file, which is very convenient.

Common Types, Description and Uses:

Cabinet file (half-round, blunt tip)

Cantsaw, also known as *cant file, lightening file* (diamond shape, for certain saw-blade sharpening or other small work)

Equaling file (blunt, rectangular, for rapid stock removal)

Flat file (rectangular, for general work on metal)

Half-round file (one side flat, one side curved, pointed tip, for general use on curved surfaces)

Hand file (thick, flat)

Knife file (wedge shape, for sharpening crosscut saws, etc.)

Mill file (thin, flat, single cut, good general-purpose metal or tool sharpening)

Needle file (very small and slender, for finishing work; also known as *die sinkers*)

Pillar file (rectangular, thick)

Rattail file, or *tapered round* (slender, round, for enlarging holes and various detail work)

Round file (slender, round, usually tapered, also known as *rattail,* for enlarging holes and various detail work)

Square file (slender, square shape for corners and slots)

Taper saw file (triangularly tapered, very fine and slender, for sharpening saw teeth and other fine work)

Warding file (smaller, for fine metal work, such as keys)

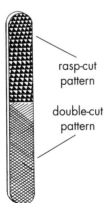

rasp-cut pattern

double-cut pattern

Four-in-Hand Rasp

Four-in-Hand Rasp/File

Also Known As: Shoe rasp, combination shoe rasp, horse rasp

Description: Steel bar with one flat face and one convex face, with vertical sides. Half of each face is file cut and half rasp cut.

Use: Variety of typical shop filing tasks.

Surface-Forming Tool

Surface-Forming Tool

Also Known As: Surform® tool, surface-forming rasp, surfoam

Description: Basically an open-weave zinc alloy metal that looks like a cheese grater. Shapes include plane-like, rasp-like, and hand scraper–like forms.

Use: Very fast removal of wood, plastic, rough drywall edges, hardboard, soft metals, plastic fillers and patchers, etc. Popular in auto-body repair work.

Use Tips: Comes with replaceable blades.

Buying Tips: Versatile and easy to use, especially in smaller, curved version. Good to have around.

Riffler Rasps and Files

Also Known As: Rifflers, bent rifflers

Description: Small, fast-cutting rasps or fine-cutting files. Only the tips have teeth; the center portions are very thin. Most tips are curved. Available in various shapes such as flat, triangular, round, and half-round. Sometimes rifflers are referred to by their country of origin, as in *German* or *Italian* rifflers.

Use: For finishing details in wood or metal.

Rifflers

File Card

Also Known As: File brush, file cleaner

Description: Small, wide brush with fine wire teeth.

Use: Clearing metal scrapings from file teeth.

> **Use Tips:** Use a file card frequently to keep files working efficiently. When filing nonferrous metals, use chalk on teeth to help prevent clogging teeth.

Wire Brush

Block Handle Wire Brush

Also Known As: Painter's wire brush

Types:

> *Block wire brush* (rectangle filled with bristles, like a scrub brush)
>
> *Curved handle wire brush* (curves slightly up)
>
> *Shoe handle wire brush* (finished, arc-shaped handle)
>
> *Straight handle wire brush*

Shoe Handle Wire Brush

Description: A wooden handle with several rows of stiff wire bristles embedded in it. Some models have a scraping blade at the tip for scraping before brushing.

Use: Cleaning material from rough surfaces, such as files, or old, flaking paint from metal or concrete.

> **Use Tips:** Keep dry—bristles will rust easily, making a mess of the next job.

> **Buying Tips:** A concave handle that curves away from the bristles may be more comfortable to hold than a straight one, and will protect your knuckles.

Sandpaper

Also Known As: Abrasive paper, coated abrasive, garnet paper, production paper

Description: Sandpaper is made in various degrees of coarseness, with different abrasive materials adhered to various backings. Some (the very finest grades) can be used dry or wet—that is, moistened with water or oil. This keeps the dust down—very important indoors.

Sandpaper comes described both by number—either of two kinds—and verbally. The higher the number, with either system, the finer the paper. The range commonly available includes:

Very fine (8/0 to 6/0, or 280 to 220 grit)

Fine (5/0 to 4/0, or 180 to 150 grit)

Medium (3/0 to 1/0, or 120 to 80 grit)

Coarse (1/2 to 1 1/2 or 60 to 40 grit)

Extreme ranges include 12/0 or 600 on the fine end to $4^1/_2$ or 12 on the coarse end. Grit numbers refer to the size of the abrasive grains themselves; the numbers are higher for finer grades because there are more pieces of grit per square inch.

This classification is only relative and varies somewhat from manufacturer to manufacturer and material to material. Remember that the grit, or mesh, is your most accurate guide from brand to brand.

Sandpaper also comes with *closed* and *open* coat, meaning the grit is farther apart or closer together. If closed coat, the grit covers 100 percent of the surface, while it covers only 60 to 70 percent of open coat. Open coat tends to clog up less with sawdust, which is a big advantage on *belt sanders,* and lasts longer, but closed coat will cut faster.

Three common kinds of paper are *flint* (least durable and least expensive), *emery* (called *emery cloth* or *paper*), and *aluminum oxide* (most common). Flint is cream or tan, emery black, and aluminum oxide a reddish color. It is the most commonly used abrasive. The backing weight is designated by letters A–E, thin to thick. C or D is best. X-rated sand paper is a medium-weight cloth used for heavy-duty and power sanding.

The material is normally available in small sheets, but can also be purchased with peel-and-stick or Velcro backing for easy adhering to power sanders. Abrasive cord or tape *rubber contoured sanding grips,* and *flexible sanding sponges* are also available, though not widely, for detail sanding work of contoured surfaces.

Sanding Block

Use Tips: For even hand sanding, secure the sandpaper to a *sanding block* or a long, narrow *sanding stick*. You can make this with a block of wood or buy a rubber one of various shapes. Many common materials, some types of paint, plaster, and treated wood, yield a toxic sawdust. Use wet sandpaper and/or a respirator in such situations.

> **Buying Tips:** Sandpaper is available in sheets or in packaged assortments. Buying by the sheet is more economical. *Sleeves* are packages of 50 or 100 sheets, depending on the grit, and are a good deal. Overall, aluminum oxide is the best buy in sandpaper for general sanding tasks because it lasts longer than other types.

Steel Wool

Description: Steel thread of various finenesses loosely woven into hand-sized pads; also sold in bulk packages. *Bronze wool* is also available and is simply steel wool made of bronze. Now *synthetic steel wool* (also known as *abrasive nylon pads* or *sanding pads*) is widely available. Pads are made from synthetic fibers and abrasive particles in various thicknesses that resemble dishwashing scouring pads.

Use: Steel wool is used for a variety of purposes, including a final wiping of wood and other surfaces prior to finishing, taking the gloss off a surface prior to painting or finishing, removing hardened substances such as dried paint, and applying final finishing materials such as wax.

Steel wool comes in six or seven grades ranging from 0000, which is super-fine, through 000 (extra-fine), 00 (very fine), 0 (medium fine), No. 1 (medium), No. 2 (medium coarse) and No. 3 (coarse).

> **Use Tips:** Bronze, stainless steel, and synthetic pads are better for use with water-based finishes as loose strands will not rust.

Buying Tips: For removal jobs, synthetic steel wool is the way to go. It won't shed, splinter, or rust. It can be rinsed and reused a few times, and it is generally longer-lasting, safer, and cleaner to use.

Planes and Scrapers

About Planes

Planes are one of the oldest designs of hand tools still in use. They are all used to shave wood from boards, and to do this their blades should be kept very sharp. There is quite a variety of planes, and we have omitted some that are really just for advanced cabinetry. The art of plane-making is a fine one, and they can be very expensive. And no matter how well they are made, you must fine-tune them—adjust the blade angle and so on—for best results.

> **Note:** See also **paint- and finish-removal tools, Part V, Chapter 45,** for more specialized scrapers.

Bench Planes

Also Known As: *Jointer,* foreplane, gage plane

Types:

Jack plane

Jointer (or *joiner*) *plane*

Smooth, or *smoothing plane* (most common)

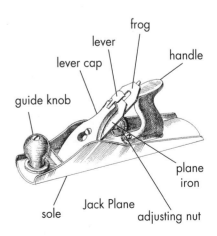

frog
lever
lever cap
handle
guide knob
plane iron
sole
Jack Plane
adjusting nut

Description: Metal or wooden device generally 9" to 22" long and several inches wide, with two handles—a knob in front and a grip in the back for pushing. Planes contain blades that protrude at an angle from the smooth wooden or steel bottom by a small, usually adjustable, amount. The *smooth plane* is smallest (9"–10"); *jack planes* are medium-sized (around 14"); and the *jointer* is the longest model (around 22" long).

Use: Smoothing, trimming, shaping, beveling wood along the grain.

Jack: Heavier, high capacity for rough work, medium size, popular model.

Jointer: Heaviest, for trimming long board edges prior to joining, or door edges.

Smooth: Lightweight, wide, good for most home workshop tasks.

> **Use Tips:** Cut with the grain, using both hands, and at a slight angle across the board.

> **Buying Tip:** The better-quality planes are more adjustable.

depth adjustment wheel

cam or locking wheel

guide knob

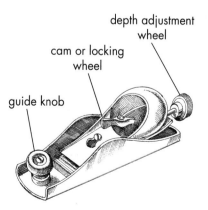

Block Plane

Block Plane

Description: Small plane, adjustable in many ways, with blade at 12–20 degrees, not 45–50 degrees as with most other planes.

Use: Shaping end grain and finishing cuts.

> **Use Tips:** For fine finishing, a plane with a very narrow mouth is desirable; a wider mouth removes wood faster. Keep a scrap piece of wood against the end of a board when planing end grain to keep from splintering off the edge. Plane in from the edges toward the middle. Common, handy model.

Rabbet Plane

Description: Similar to others, but blade projects from side as well as bottom.

Use: Cuts a rabbet, a recess, or step, in the edge of a board.

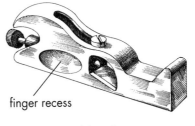

finger recess

Rabbet Plane

Bullnose Plane

Description: Extremely small, compact, usually metal block with small handle and blade right near the front of the plane.

Use: Very detailed work inside corners.

Router Plane

Description: Unlike other planes, a flat metal plate with a small blade in the center.

Use: Makes recesses, called *dadoes,* and grooves in a board.

Use Tip: More commonly done with power router.

adjusting screws

handle   cutter

cap iron

Spokeshave

Spokeshave

Description: Winged, two-handed handle with a small blade in the middle. There are many specialized variations for different types of work and wood.

Use: Fine scraping and planing of curved wood such as spokes.

Cabinet Scraper

Also Known As: Scraper plate

Description: Either a small **spokeshave (above)**, or sometimes just a flat piece of metal, rectangular or curved, with a cutting burr on one edge.

Use: Very fine shaving, as in removing glue.

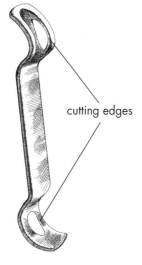

cutting edges

Cornering Tool

Cornering Tool

Also Known As: Chamfering tool, edge-rounding tool

Description: Looks something like a beer-can opener with holes that have cutting edges in each curved end. There are different sizes on each end, two tools to a set.

Use: Beveling corners of boards. Cuts a specific radius and no more.

Fastening Tools

Glue Gun

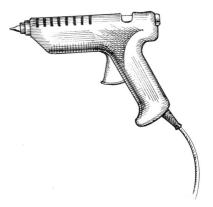

Description: Smaller models look like a regular gun, with a long handle and a triangular trigger. Cigarette-like *glue sticks* (*hot melt* glue) are melted inside the gun and the glue extruded either by pushing the stick in with your thumb or, on some models, merely by squeezing the trigger; it generally dries within a minute.

Use: For any large wood or household gluing jobs using hot melt glue. It can also be used with caulk sticks, and various specialized glue sticks for different materials.

Glue Gun

Glue Injector

Description: Syringe-like tool with a long probe-like applicator that can be filled with a variety of glues. Epoxy glue injectors have two cylinders.

Use: Applying glue in furniture joints and other narrow places.

Glue Injector

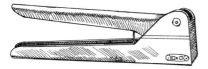

Rivet Tool

Rivet Tool

Also Known As: Rivet gun, Pop® Rivetool, riveter

Description: Consists of two pliers-like handles with a nose that accepts special nail-like **rivets (Part III, Chapter 23)** that form a sandwich bond when squeezed.

Use: Good for repairing anything made of thin metal, canvas, or leather, items ranging from toys to briefcases to gutters, especially when only one side of the material can be reached.

> **Use Tips:** Rivets come in various diameters (typically from $1/8$" to $3/16$") and "grip ranges"—determined by the thickness of the two pieces to be fastened together (typically from $1/16$" to $5/8$"). Selection of the proper rivet is easily made by following directions on the rivet-gun package. Rivets may be aluminum or steel; steel rivets are stronger.

> **Buying Tip:** Some rivet guns have interchangeable noses and can set rivets of three different diameters.

Staple Gun

Also Known As: Staple gun tacker, hand stapler

Description: Essentially a stapler with a grip and lever handle for shooting staples that are rectangular in shape. Comes in a variety of sizes and with varying degrees of power. Also made in an electric, power model. The *hammer tacker* is a heavier-duty model that is swung to hit against the surface, not squeezed.

Use: Securing a wide variety of thin materials to wood by shooting staples with great force: insulation, stair treads, carpet, ceiling tile, plastic sheet, poultry netting, etc. Much faster than nails and more secure.

> **Use Tips:** Standard staple guns can accept staples from $1/4"$ to $9/16"$ long. Choice of staple length is based on the material being secured, but the width and type of staple that you can use are limited to your particular brand and model, and these must be specified when purchasing staples.

> **Buying Tip:** The *hammer tacker* is a real time-saver for large projects.

Soldering Gun

Description: Similar to a **soldering iron (below)**, but shaped like a gun. Has a finer tip.

Use: Melts solder for making electrical connections.

Soldering Gun

Soldering Iron

Also Known As: Soldering tip

Description: Resembles a fat pencil with a copper rod or broad blade at the tip and an insulated handle that has a wire cord and plug attached to the tail end. Tip heats to 15 to 240 watts.

Use: Melts solder for making electrical connections.

> **Use Tip:** As soldering irons are available in a variety of sizes and types, be sure to use the proper one for your job.

Power Hammer (gun type)

Power Hammer

Also Known As: Low-velocity powder-actuated fastening tool

Description: Gun-barrel device in either a trigger or hammer-activated version, operated with bullet-like *power loads* (that look like .22 cal. bullets) and fasteners (hardened steel nails) sold separately, often called *powder-driven* or *power fasteners*. A back-up disc helps control the depth of the fastener.

Use: Fastening items such as door frames or studs to concrete or other masonry.

> **Use Tips:** These fasteners are actually shot out of the hammer, so make sure that the receiving wall is thick enough to "take" the hit; should the fastener continue through and exit a wall, it could injure someone. Make sure that fasteners are solid in the masonry, and that they have not shattered the wall instead.

Miscellaneous Tools and Equipment

Drop Light

Also Known As: Trouble light, safety light, work light

Description: Incandescent bulb housed in protective cage, secured to a long electrical cord and plug.

Use: Provide light for working wherever needed.

Use Tips: Hang carefully where it won't be snagged or bumped as you move around the worksite. Keep a few spare bulbs on hand, though. You might want to try using **construction grade bulbs (Part IX, Chapter 67)**.

Buying Tip: Could be replaced in some situations by a battery operated, portable mini-fluorescent lamp that is commonly sold for auto or camping use.

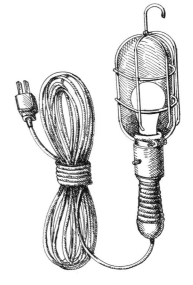

Drop Light

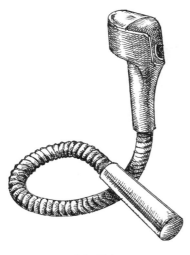

Grip Light

Grip Light

Description: Cordless flashlight with long, flexible snake-like neck that twists and holds position on horizontal surface or snakes around pipes. Light bulb is generally more intense than regular flashlight bulb. Some models have heads that pivot for more control.

Use: Providing hands-free light at worksite.

> **Use Tip:** Try wrapping it gently around your neck and shoulders for light that moves with you.

> **Buying Tip:** A terrific improvement over older models of portable lighting equipment.

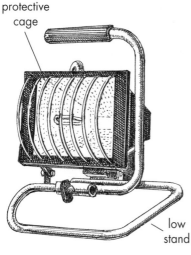

protective cage

low stand

250-Watt Halogen Light

Halogen Work Light

Description: Aluminum housing and caged reflector holding a halogen bulb. Available in a variety of forms, including clamp, low stand, and tripod for heights up to 8'. Bulbs offered in 250 and 500 watt versions.

Use: Lighting up an entire jobsite such as a room under construction with no other light source.

> **Use Tips:** These lights get dangerously HOT! They can easily cause a fire if they come into contact with combustible material. Exercise extreme caution around them! Stay clear of them, and make sure that nothing flammable is directly above them.

> **$ Buying Tips:** Extra-bright, pure white light is a pleasure to have, especially if you are used to making do with **clamp-on lamps (Part IX, Chapter 67)** with their small incandescent bulbs and small reflectors. Especially good for large painting jobs where reflections help you keep track of wet edges and drips.

House Jacks

Also Known As: Jack post, single post shore

Description: Two heavy steel pipes, one inside the other, in various lengths up to about 8', with flat metal plates on either end. A large screw extends the post a short distance for raising. A similar-looking item is the *lally column,* which has no jacking ability and may be filled with concrete once in place.

Use: For temporarily raising a sagging floor joist. Can be boxed off and left permanently in place, though this is not recommended (a lally column is used for a permanent installation). Shorter, heavier versions are used to jack up an entire house for moving or major repairs.

> **Use Tips:** Jack up floor joists, or any house framing member, very, very slowly—like less than an inch a day. Make sure the bottom part of the jack is well supported on thick concrete or wood. A hydraulic house jack, a large-scale version of a standard jack, may be useful for heavier loads.

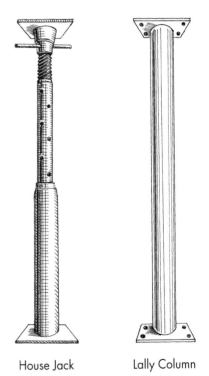

House Jack   Lally Column

Jay Roller

Description: Small wooden roller and handle

Use: Pressing down freshly glued veneers and laminates to help bond them.

Siding Removal Trool

Siding Removal Tool

Description: Hand-sized metal tool with slightly angled, 1" wide blade that has a hooked tip.

Use: Grabbing underside lip of vinyl siding to unlock it for easy removal and replacement. Eliminates cutting and scoring.

Ladder

Also Known As: Rung ladder

Description: Made of aluminum, fiberglass, or wood. Consists of two parallel rails flanking round or rectangular steps. *Extension ladders* are made of two similar sections that fit together and are linked by a line or mechanical device and locked into place with hinged hooks called *dogs*. Extension section can be pulled out to almost double the height of the ladder. *Folding* or *articulating* combination ladders are more expensive but can act as scaffolds and stepladders as well.

Use: For climbing heights.

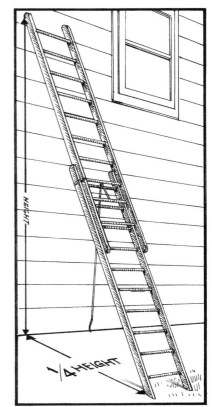

Extension Ladder

> ⚑ **Use Tips:** For safety, (1) extreme care should be exercised in securing the base so it doesn't slip, such as by using a ladder with rubber grips, by tying the bottom rung to a stake between it and the wall, or by having an assistant hold it; (2) the ladder base should be one-fourth of the height of the ladder away from the wall (an arm's length at shoulder height is usually correct); (3) move the ladder often rather than lean too far to one side when working; (4) look up before raising an aluminum ladder to avoid hitting electrical wires; (5) and never place a ladder in front of an unlocked door or on muddy ground. (6) Try using *ladder stabilizers*, or *guards*, C-shaped aluminum arms about twice as wide as the ladder, for better stability when leaning a ladder against a wall. Triangular metal brackets called *ladder jacks* can be attached to a heavy-duty **(Type 1A—see below)** ladder to make scaffolding. Tie off rope, check your dogs to see that they are locked.

Buying Tips: Aluminum ladders are lightweight and easier for one person to handle than wood, but they can be hazardous if there are electrical wires nearby. Flat "D"-shaped aluminum rungs are more comfortable and safer to stand on than the round ones found on wooden ladders. Look also for resilient rubber *ladder mitts end caps,* and rubber or metal swiveling *ladder shoes.* Ladders are rated for safety and construction four ways: *type 3:* household; *type 2:* commercial; *type 1:* industrial; and *type 1A:* extra-heavy-duty industrial. The commercial type, type 2, is highly recommended. The ratings indicate load limits ranging from 200 pounds (type 3) to 300 pounds (type 1A).

Stepladder

Description: Consists of what appears to be two separate ladders connected by a hinge at the top. Actually only one side has rungs. Available in wood, aluminum, and fiberglass and in various heights.

Use: Self-supporting ladder that can be used without leaning against a wall. Ideal for interior painting and repairs up to heights of 10 feet.

Use Tips: Never stand on the top two rungs—it is unsafe, due to the increased leverage of your weight. Never leave a hammer or other tool on the top when you come down, as it is very likely that you will forget it's there when you move the ladder and then it will fall and cause real damage.

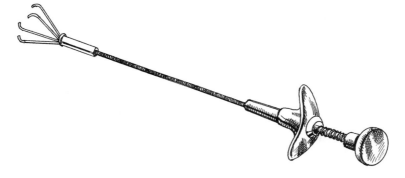

Mechanical Fingers

Magnetizer/Demagnetizer

Use: Magnetizing and demagnetizing screwdrivers, drill bits, wrenches, and other tools. Passing tools through the hole magnetizes items; passing tools repeatedly over the outside edge demagnetizes tools.

> § **Buying Tip:** Magnetized screwdrivers and wrenches are much easier to use because they hold screws and bolts automatically.

Nail Apron

Also Known As: Nail bag, carpenter's apron

Description: Canvas or leather pouch or pouches that attach around your waist.

Use: Holds large amounts of nails and screws handy.

Propane Torch

Description: Self-contained gas torch. Canister of pressurized propane gas with a screw-on burner and valve assembly. Uses propane but also higher-temperature fuels such as Mapp® and butane gas.

Use: Supplies clean flame that can be used for a variety of purposes, including removing resilient tile (heating the tile softens and loosens the adhesive), softening putty, removing paint, soldering pipe.

Use Tips: Both wide and narrow burner tips are available, and one may be more suitable for a particular job than another. Take precautions when working with flame; this is very intense heat and always risky.

Buying Tips: In addition to the standard propane torch, there are mini-propane torches, self-igniting ones, and those that can be linked by hose to a large canister of gas.

Spark Lighter

Description: Looking somewhat like a 6" long safety pin, this spring-wire tool has a replaceable flint on the end of one arm and a bowl-shaped striking surface on the other. When the spring arms are squeezed together, the flint sparks as it is dragged across the striking surface.

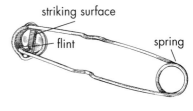

Spark Lighter

Use: Lighting propane and other pressurized gas torches. The tip of the torch is placed in the striking bowl and then turned on while the spark is created.

Buying Tips: This is the best way to light torches. Get one when you get a torch. Inexpensive.

Rubber Knee Pads

Rubber Knee Pads

Description: Flat rubber cups with straps

Use: Protects knees when installing floors or roofs.

Sawhorses

Also Known As: Horses

Description: Crosspiece supported by two pairs of legs set at angles. Typically made of two-by-fours.

Use: Temporary support for a worktable or shop work.

> **$ Buying Tips:** Sawhorses are typically homemade. Also, specially made hinged metal joints are available for making collapsible sawhorses from two-by-fours. Nonhinged metal or plastic *sawhorse brackets* are available as well. Both are big conveniences.

Toolbox

Description: Metal or plastic box with compartments for tools and hardware. Most have a piano-hinged top and a removable tray. Some small, open plastic models are designed only for use on a per-job basis—you load it only with the tools needed for a particular job.

Use: Carrying tools and miscellaneous hardware and materials to a work site (a *tool chest* is usually larger, with drawers, and designed for stationary use on a workbench or has built-in casters).

> **Use Tip:** Though they may seem convenient, larger toolboxes present a formidable problem when fully loaded with a complete set of tools—they are dangerously heavy and may be impossible to lift. Better to have a few smaller, specialized ones. The plastic boxes will not scratch floors or counters at the worksite.

5-Gal Bucket Pocket Tool Carrier

Description: Polyester sheet loaded with pockets that sit inside and out of an empty 5-gallon plastic bucket, such as that used for joint compound or paint.

Use: Definitely the modern, portable tool chest. Much better than dumping all your tools into an empty bucket. Plastic bottom is easy on floors, too.

> **Buying Tips:** Good gift item. Look for other bucket-related accessories, such as plastic compartment trays and seats that fit over the top, or removable screwtop lids that create an airtight, waterproof container.

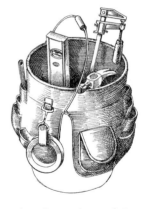

5-Gal Bucket Pocket Tool Carrier

Shop Vacuum

Also Known As: Shop vac, wet/dry vac

Description: Large canister or drum, some as large as several feet high, with a vacuum motor on top and $2\frac{1}{2}$" diameter vacuum hose. Most are wet/dry models. Six to 16 gallon capacity, with 2 to 6 hp motors. Smaller versions are designed to attach directly to portable electric tools with 1" or $1\frac{1}{4}$" adapters.

Use: Sucking up all kinds of workshop and worksite debris, such as sawdust, wood, glass, nails, gravel, water, paint chips, and the like. Also excellent for cleaning cars and gutters. Convertible to blower.

> **$ Buying Tips:** Invaluable time saver for any major interior project. Great gift item.

Portable Workbench

Also Known As: Workmate® (often used generically)

Description: Small, collapsible metal framework workbench with many convenient attachments and design elements, such as built-in clamp mechanisms (the two halves of the work surface slide open and shut).

Use: Home workshop and renovation projects—holding boards for sawing, clamping, and much more.

vise peg holes
adjustable vise jaws
adjusting crank
foot rest

Workmate® Portable Workbench

Power Tools

About Portable Power Tools

The real news in portable power tools is that not only are almost all of them now available in cordless form—you charge a battery for a few hours and off you go—but that many are now available in more powerful versions than ever before. This is a terrific convenience both for repairs at home and for major construction sites (just eliminating the mess of power cords is a major change). But in no way do cordless tools replace plug-in tools for steady use or for tasks where size and strength really matter. The smaller models, especially, are substantially weaker than their corded siblings.

When buying either kind of power tool, buy good quality and characteristics. With cordless tools, look for a short recharge time ("charge rate") and substantial voltage (upwards of 12 volts where power is important). Also compare cycle life, the number of charge/discharge cycles a battery can be expected to handle before failure—500 to as many as 3,000. With corded tools, check the amperages, not the horsepower, for determining the relative power—the more power, the better. The trade-off in both cases, besides price, is usually weight and size. Ball or roller bearings are better than sleeve bearings. Double-insulated tools are safer. Cheaper tools often are difficult to open for repair, if they can be opened at all.

In general, a good rule of thumb is to purchase a model somewhere in the middle range between heavy-duty professional and the lightweight, least expensive. "Light-duty industrial" is often best. You won't get every feature possible, but you'll get what is most often needed in a model that will last.

And remember, most power tools are available for rent.

Portable Power Drills, Tools, and Accessories

Power Drill

Also Known As: Portable electric drill, hole-shooter, drill-driver

Description: Gun-shaped tool with a chuck (nosepiece) that comes in one of the three common sizes: $1/4$", $3/8$", or $1/2$"; the size of the drill is denoted by the largest-size drill-bit shaft that can fit into the chuck. The better ones come with variable speed triggers and reversing switches (may be indicated by "VS" or "VSR"). Rpm's run 130 to 400 at low speed, and for corded models up to 2000 or so at high. A *close-quarters* drill has a head at 55 degrees to the handle.

Use: Drilling holes of various sizes. Also, with proper **accessories (below)**, a drill can be used to grind, sand, polish, and do other jobs. And with a **screwdriver bit (below)**, a VSR drill can be used as a very convenient power screwdriver. Can be mounted on a workbench on a special stand to work, use the half-inch drill, as the larger chuck means a more powerful motor; for major masonry drilling jobs, use a special model drill, the *hammer-drill*. This vibrates as it drills, and requires special *percussion* bits, also called *impact bits* (use the even larger *rotary hammer* for pure concrete and cement).

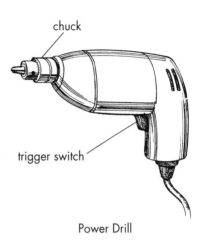

Power Drill

> **Use Tips:** Get a proper, heavy-duty extension cord with two or three female receptacles. This will allow you to use two or three power tools on the same job without having to unplug and plug as you switch tools.

> **Buying Tips:** Get a good one. The $^3/_8$" size is best for the do-it-yourselfer. Variable speed and reversibility are good features. If the plug is the two-prong type, the drill should be marked as "double-insulated" for protection from shocks. Cordless models of more than 12 volts are too heavy for most of us. Get the most amp-hours you can afford. A 9.6 volt cordless model is o.k. only for the casual DIY user.

Cordless Screwdriver

In-Line Cordless screwdriver

Also Known As: Compact cordless screwdriver

Description: Lightweight, straight cylinder of lower power and speed (under 200 rpm max) than the **power drill (above)**.

Use: Driving screws in light-duty household or repetitive small woodworking projects.

> **Buying Tips:** Though less expensive than the *drill-driver*, for only a little more money you can purchase a much more versatile and useful tool—the **power drill (above)**. On the other hand, the screwdriver is a lot lighter and smaller, and may be easier to handle for the DIY'er.

Chuck Key

Also Known As: Key

Description: Small, L- or T-shaped steel piece with one conical, fluted end. Literally a small gear. Comes in various sizes and types that vary by manufacturer as well as universal models. Also made in a ratchet version.

Use: Opens and closes the chuck on *electric drills* and *drill presses*. (The chuck—technically a *Jacob's chuck*—is the part of the drill that holds the bits.)

Chuck Key

 Use Tips: Always good to have a spare. Check for the proper fit if replacing your key. Always tighten the bit securely, using all three holes.

Keyless Chuck

Description: Knurled knob about 2" in diameter and length.

Use: Allows hand-tightening of chuck to hold bits in cordless and corded drills and drivers, depending on model.

Keyless Chuck

Buying Tip: Much easier to use than a *key*; a real advantage if the bulkiness doesn't bother you.

Drill Guide

Description: Consists of a bracket to hold a portable drill, two steel rods, and a round plate. Might be confused with a *hinge bit,* another type of drill guide. (A hinge bit—a hollow, beveled jacket housing a drill bit—merely centers a drill bit in the hole of a hinge plate.) A larger version is a *drill press stand,* which converts a portable drill into a **stationary drill press (Chapter 19)** for use on a workbench.

Use: Enables you to drill perfectly perpendicular or angled holes with a portable drill. Particularly helpful for mounting items on door edges.

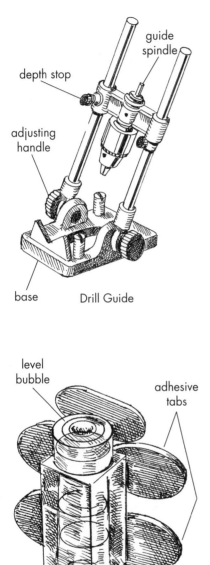

depth stop

guide spindle

adjusting handle

base   Drill Guide

Drill Level

Description: Small *bubble level* (either horizontal, vertical, or surface **(bull's eye—see Chapter 10)** that attaches to a drill with self-adhesive rubber mounts. Different models are designed for different types of drills, and may fit either the front, top, or rear of a drill.

Use: Judging when a drill is exactly vertical or level; also useful for portable machinery that must be leveled.

level bubble

adhesive tabs

Drill Level

> **Use Tip:** Useless if the piece being drilled is not also level or plumb.

> **Buying Tip:** Some newer models of portable drills have built-in levels.

Dowel Jig

Also Known As: Dowel jointing jig, doweling jig

Description: Rectangular metal block with various-sized holes and brackets for holding it in place.

Use: Allows accurate placement of holes for dowels in furniture and cabinetry.

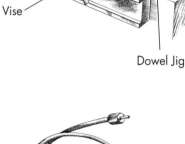

Vise

Dowel Jig

Flexible Shaft

Also Known As: Flexible drive

Description: A cable housed in a flexible cover material with a shank that fits into a drill on one end and a chuck that holds bits on the other. Various lengths up to 4'.

Use: Allows drilling in hard-to-reach places. Shaft can be snaked around various obstructions.

Flexible Shaft

Offset Screwdriver Head

Also Known As: Bevel gear offset screwdriver

Description: Though there are many different versions of this useful item available, the one shown here is smallest. $5^1/_2$" long, lightweight cylinder with a small chuck for screwdriver tips at 90 degrees to its axis. A small flange protrudes from one side and a hex shank extends out the back end. Magnetized. Also sold with a large, solid, standard screwdriver handle for hand use as a plain **offset screwdriver (Part I, Chapter 4)**. Sold with a set of various screwdriver tips.

hex shaft goes into drill chuck

Offset Screwdriver Head

Use: Converting a cordless or hand screwdriver to an *angle drive screwdriver* or just for more control, when you need to support the drill bit with your hand.

Right Angle Drive

Also Known As: Angle Drive

Description: Small gearbox that fits into the chuck of a power drill and has its own chuck at a 90-degree angle.

Use: Enables you to drill holes at right angles.

> **$ Buying Tip:** Less expensive than buying a whole *right-angle drill.*

Power Drill Accessories

Description: Small devices with shanks that fit like bits into power drill chuck just like regular hole-drilling bits, but for wood or metal shaping or finishing instead of drilling. Some are best used when the drill is mounted on a workbench in a horizontal or vertical drill stand, which turns a portable drill into a stationary tool.

Types:

Drill saw, or *router drill, saw bit:* A drill bit with cutting edges on its sides, made for either metal or wood.

Drum sander: Short, small cylinder wrapped in sandpaper.

Drill stand: Base and clamp for benchtop use.

Flap wheel, or *contour, sander:* Wheel with flaps of abrasive cloth, for rough contour sanding.

Grinder: Abrasive wheel.

Paint sprayer: Powers a small compressor.

Rotary file: Very small bit with file teeth in various shapes, such as cylindrical, cylindrical with round end, tapered round, conical, and ball.

Rotary rasp: Same as above, but with rasp teeth; some models have a knob on one end which you hold in your hand for control.

Note: Rotary files and rasps are also known as *burrs.*

Sanding disk, or *wheel:* Rubber backing disk about 5" in diameter that supports all kinds of sandpaper.

Screwdriver and nut-driver (or *nut-setter*) *bits:* Short blades (1" to $3^1/_2$") that turn a drill into a power screwdriver or nut driver. Magnetized tips are easiest to use. Available in straight-slot or Phillips head. Excellent for installing drywall or decks.

Socket wrench set: A power version of the standard socket wrench.

Water pump: Connects to garden hose; self-priming, up to 250 gallons per hour.

Wire brush, or *wheel:* Flat wire brush of various sizes. A wire cup brush has wires going parallel to the drill shaft.

Flap Wheel
Drill Accessory

Grinder Drill
Accessory

Rotary Rasp Drill Accessory

Screwdriver Bit

hose connections

goes into
drill chuck

Drill-Powered Pump

> **$ Buying Tip:** If you do a lot of very small-sized jobs requiring these attachments, you may want to purchase a precision, high-speed tool instead, called a **rotary tool (below)**. Get top-quality, hardened steel screwdriver bits with ribbed tips.

Screw Starter

Screw Starter

Also Known As: Bit finder and driver, screw starter/driver, bit holder, bit extender, drill bit holder

Description: Any one of a number of designs that consist of a short steel cylinder with a hex shank on one end (to fit into a power drill) and an open end that holds driver bits for screws up to a certain size (labeled by model). A *sliding sleeve* (plus, usually, magnetism) holds the screws in place; this is clear on some models so you can see the screw as it is driven in. A *manual screw starter* looks more like a hefty ballpoint pen (it even has a clip for pocket storage) and holds screws with springs and/or magnetism.

Use: Driving long screws or driving screws in hard-to-reach places, with more accuracy and less wobble. The nonpowered version is used only for starting or retrieving loose screws, not for driving.

> **$ Buying Tips:** Very handy item. Get the magnetized version, or magnetize yours. Look for one which can double as a quick-change bit for converting your drill into a driver and back again rapidly.

Quick Change Adapter

Quick Change Adaptor

Also Known As: Quick change chuck

Description: Spring-loaded collar a little over 1" in diameter that slides back over a bit-holding hole; a hex shank sticks out one end and fits into the chuck of a $3/8$" or $1/2$" drill.

Use: Converts a power drill into a quick-change power screwdriver. Makes changing bits almost instant, as there is no need to tighten the chuck.

> **$ Buying Tip:** Ideal if you have to change bits often.

> **Note:** Works only with $1/4$" hex shank bits with a power groove, but hex adapters for round bits are available.

Screw Gun

Screw Gun

Also Known As: Drywall screwdriver, drywall driver, drywall screw gun, power screwdriver

Description: Similar to power drill, above, but lighter, and with a clutch mechanism that disengages when the screw has reached its proper depth. Tips used should be magnetized for holding screws. Runs at a much higher rpm than a drill—around 4,000 rpm.

Use: Driving screws and removing screws, especially drywall and other self-tapping screws.

Buying Tip: Worth its price if you are hanging drywall in any quantity. Lighter than a drill with a screwdriver tip, and the clutch mechanism prevents driving screws beyond the paper surface of drywall or stripping the hole when driving into wood.

Drywall Adapter Bit

Drywall Adaptor Bit

Also Known As: Drywall screw adapter bit, depth driver, drywall bit

Description: Small, conical **Phillips #2 drill bit (above)** inside a larger cone, with a shaft that fits into $\frac{1}{4}$" and $\frac{3}{8}$" power drill chucks.

Use: Converting a power drill into a power screwdriver, expressly for driving drywall screws into **drywall (Chapter 50)** without piercing the surface paper, but with just enough of a dimple to make hiding the screwhead with **joint compound (Chapter 50)** more easy.

Use Tip: Practice setting the depth and getting used to the speed on pieces of scrap.

Buying Tip: Much cheaper but less effective than a **screwgun (above)**.

About Drill Bits for Both Power and Hand Drills

Many different bits and accessories may be used in drills. All drill bits are made of steel, have a pointed cutting edge or end, and are for drilling holes in wood and metal, unless otherwise noted. Many specialized types are made but not listed here. Oddly, the terms *drill* and *bit* are both commonly used to describe what we call *drill bits* (the actual hole-making instrument); we reserve the term *drill* for the tool that holds the bit. Buy many to save time on the job.

Twist Drill Bit

Also Known As: Drill bit (most common), twist drill, drill, drill point, screwdriver bit, bit

Description: Short steel rod ranging in diameter from $1/16''$ to $1/2''$ in increments of $1/64''$, about half of its length spiral and half smooth. Typical bits range from about $1^1/2''$ to 4" long. Drill bit sets are available in $1/4''$, $3/8''$, and $1/2''$ diameters; a $1/4''$ drill takes bits up to $1/4''$ in diameter; a $3/8''$ drill takes them up to $3/8''$, and so on. *Oversize,* also called *step-down* or *reduced-shank* twist drill bits, have narrower shanks at the chuck end than at the bit end, and therefore allow a $1/4''$ bit to drill a $1/2''$ hole, for example. Be careful to avoid overloading (drawing too many amps).

Specialized Types:

Brad point bits: Tip has a tiny screw-type lead point in front of the normal cutting teeth. For making $1/8''$ to 1" holes in hardwoods with great precision and for preventing splintering (you can tell when the bit has reached the far side by the lead point protruding). For use in wood only.

Twist Drill Bit

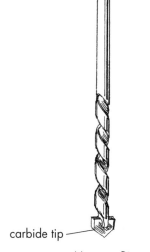

carbide tip ——

Masonry Bit

Taper point bits (also known as *tapered shank drill bits*): Tapered to match profile of wood screws.

Masonry bits: Recognizable by the flat wedge in the drill-bit tip. Carbide-tipped for drilling into masonry, tile, and marble.

Cobalt bits: For drilling stainless steel and other hard metals.

Installer bits: (also known as *Bell Hanger bits*): Long (up to 18"), hardened steel, large bore for creating holes for wire and small pipe installation. May be able to drill through nails.

Use: The most frequently used small hole–boring instrument. Suitable for either power- or hand-operated drills. Though most work in wood or metal, some are for wood only. Check the label.

Use Tips: Be sure to replace dull bits. Smaller ones break easily, too, so it is not a bad idea to have extras on hand. To choose the right-sized bit, hold it in your line of sight next to the screw being used. Bit should be the diameter of the center shaft of the screw. Charts matching the exact bit size for screws can be found in hardware stores.

Buying Tip: High-speed steel (HSS) bits are recommended over carbon steel bits—they tend to last longer and are more efficient and versatile. Chrome vanadium steel bits can be used only in wood and plastic.

Countersink Bit

Description: Short, pointed, mushroom-shaped bit. Also made with a knob handle in a hand-operated version.

Countersink attachments are available that work simultaneously with the bit making the original hole. Bits with this feature are known as *pilot bits*. Another version is the *counterbore,* which makes a straight-walled hole, leaving room for a wooden plug. Combination drill bit/countersink/counterbore units do it all at once.

Use: To make beveled, recessed holes for screwheads, enabling them to be driven until the top of the screwhead is flush with or slightly below the surface of the piece into which they are screwed. Actually drills an angle around the hole itself.

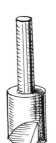

Countersink Bit

Pilot Bit

 Buying Tip: Adjustable combination models offer many advantages.

Spade Bit

Also Known As: Power wood-boring bit, flat boring bit

Description: Usually a 6" long bit consisting of a rod with a flat, paddle-like end with a triangular point. Width of paddle is diameter of hole, ranging up to about 2". A similar item, a *corner drill* or *3D-Bit,* has cutting edges on the sides too.

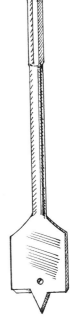

Spade Bit

Use: For drilling large holes with power drills. May have a small hole in the blade for pulling wire through holes. Typical uses include holes for installing door locks and electrical wiring. A *corner drill* can cut curved holes and half-holes (grooves) and due to having cutting edges on its sides and rear, can be used for milling in all directions.

Extension Bit

Description: Similar to a regular drill bit, but extra-long, usually 6" to 12".

Use: Reaching places a regular bit would not fit, such as between studs.

> **$ Buying Tip:** Not to be confused with a *drill bit extension*, or *extension shaft*, a plain shaft with a collar and two setscrews, which can extend the length of any drill bit.

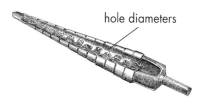

Extension Bit

Step Drill Bit

Description: Conical metal drill bit with 6 to 13 steps and a gouge out of about a third of the whole bit. Dimensions are marked inside the gouge. Made of high-grade, high-speed, heat-treated molybdenum steel. Available in both $1/4$" and $3/8$" shank sizes and several different shapes, ranging from more squat to more elongated. Each shape cuts different sizes and quantities of holes, in different increments.

Use: Making perfectly round holes of various sizes in thin materials such as most metals.

hole diameters

Step Drill Bit

Glass And Tile Drill Bit

Glass and Tile Drill Bit

Description: Plain steel diameter shaft with spear-like carbide tip. Shaft sizes available from $1/8$" to $1/2$". Different bits are suitable for different recommended drilling speeds, measured in rpm's, from 250 (the largest bit) to 1000 rpm's (the smallest bit).

Use: Smooth, accurate drilling in ceramic tile, mirrors, marble, and so on, usually for installation of fasteners or accessories.

Hole Saw

arbor (mandrel)

Hole Saw

Also Known As: Saw-blade cutter

Description: Cup-shaped metal blade with a bit, called a *mandrel*, in the center and saw teeth on the bottom. Attaches to chuck on electric drill or drill press. Comes in small-range diameters up to 2 $1/2$", all of which fit onto the same mandrel. Sold in kits for installing door locks.

Use: Cuts large holes in wood, drywall, and metal.

> $ **Buying Tip:** Best quality are *bimetal blades*, that is, teeth are made of high-speed steel and welded onto a regular steel body.

Circle and Wheel Cutter

set screws

cutting
blade

Circle and Wheel Cutter

Also Known As: Fly cutter

Description: Large drill bit with attached horizontal arm that has a cutting blade at the end.

Use: Cutting circles up to 7" in diameter, and, if adjusted to cut twice, wheel shapes.

> **Use Tip:** Primarily for use on a **drill press (Chapter 19)**.

Drill Stop Collar

set screw

Drill Stop Collar

Also Known As: Nail setters, stop collars, drill stop

Description: Circular steel piece that attaches to drill bits at any point and is held in place by a set screw.

Use: Limits the depth a bit can go so that you don't drill farther through the work than you want.

> **Use Tip:** The stop itself will mar a surface if you continue bearing down once it touches, so be careful on delicate surfaces.

Plug Cutter

Description: Hollow bit with saw teeth. Various sizes up to ³/₄".

Use: Cuts plugs of wood for insertion into the tops of screw holes (to conceal the screws) or for dowel joints.

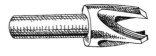

Plug Cutter

Forstner Bit

Description: Rimmed bit with small, pointed center guide. Available from ³/₈" to over 2".

Use: Drilling large-diameter, clean, shallow, flat-bottomed holes without great danger of the bit wandering, i.e., following the wood-grain pattern. Can replace any large bit where accuracy and cleanliness are desired. Best used in **drill presses (Chapter 19).**

> **Use Tips:** The precision of Forstner bits makes them particularly useful for drilling into veneer. To start the bit, tap it into the material first.

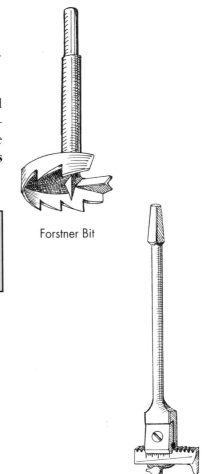

Forstner Bit

Expansive Bit

Also Known As: Expanding bit, adjustable bit

Description: Long bit with adjustable cutting bit on the end.

Expansive Bit

Use: Cutting large holes in wood. Diameter may be adjusted to avoid having to purchase different bits for different-sized holes. Different shaft designed for use in a **brace (Part I, Chapter 11)** or **power drill (above)**. Normally for use in a **drill press too (Chapter 19)** as opposed to a *portable drill*.

Rotary Tool

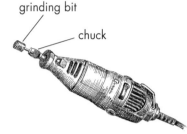

grinding bit

chuck

Rotary Tool

Also Known As: Dremel (brand name), hobby/craft tool

Description: Hand-sized, cylindrical, high-speed (up to 30,000 rpm) motor with many drill-bit like attachments available. Commonly has a $1/8$" collet for bits. Usually sold in kits, some with as many as 72 accessories or bits for grinding, drilling, sanding, and so on.

Use: Grinding, sharpening, drilling, polishing, sanding, and generally shaping small areas of all kinds of materials.

> **Use Tips:** Handy for furniture making and sculpture as the odd repair. Due to its high speed, the rotary tool can be used to drill small holes in hard materials.

> **Buying Tip:** More useful to hobbyists than home repair nuts, but a great gift item for either.

Portable Power Saws

Circular Saw

Also Known As: Power saw, cuttoff saw, Skilsaw® electric hand-saw, contractor's saw; sometimes confused with **table saw (below)**.

Description: Handle on a housing in which a high-speed circular blade is mounted. Blades vary in diameter, but $6^{1}/_{2}$", $7^{1}/_{4}$", and $8^{1}/_{4}$" are most popular. Cordless models are smaller, starting at $3^{3}/_{8}$" **(see below for more details on blades).** Size of saw indicates the largest size of blade it can use. Can be adjusted to cut on an angle. Side-drive is most common, and worm (rear)-drive more common for heavy-duty models; this denotes the position of the motor relative to the blade. Various motor sizes and rpm capacities are available.

Use: To make straight cuts (either crosscut or rip) in a wide variety of materials such as plywood, lumber, particleboard, plastic, and so on. Probably the one power tool most often used by carpenters. Good for materials that are difficult to cut by hand. Cordless version can cut wood only up to about 1" thick.

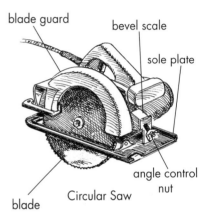

blade guard · bevel scale · sole plate · angle control nut · blade

Circular Saw

> **Use Tips:** Most circular saws have a rip guide attached so the saw won't waver during a long cut, such as across a plywood panel. You can buy one as an accessory.

Note: The circular saw is proven the most dangerous portable power tool. Always use it with two hands on the saw, and make sure the guard snaps back into place before putting it down. Some models have a brake that stops the blade from spinning as soon as the trigger is released.

$ **Buying Tips:** A quality circular saw has a chute that directs sanding dust away from the cutting line. It also has higher amperage and rpm ratings. Look for one with at least 10 amps of power and ball or roller bearings. Cordless models are good for trim or clapboards.

Circular Saw Blade with Large Carbide-Tipped Teeth

Circular (and Radial and Table) Saw Blades

Description: Blades for circular saws, **radial arm saws, compound miter saws,** and **table saws (Chapter 19)** are available in types and styles that can make jobs easier. The diameter and the arbor, or center hole, of the blade must be the right size for your model. Most blades have a "knockout" center piece that enables the blade to fit saws that take either round or diamond arbors. Some now have open slots for heat and noise reduction as well as to minimize resin build-up. Only some types are listed here.

Types:

Abrasive blade, masonry blade, or *abrasive cutoff wheel:* Different materials, such as metal, masonry, ceramic tile, concrete block, and the like can be cut by a circular saw as long as you match the blade to the material (carbide-tipped blades should not be used on such materials). Abrasive cutoff wheels should be used only if the saw has an aluminum or magnesium guard.

Carbide, or *carbide-tipped blade:* Expensive but last as much as ten times longer than ordinary blades. Use them if you do a great deal of cutting. Available in many styles.

Chisel-tooth combination blade: Excellent for exterior plywood, massive softwood-cutting projects where speed is most important, tempered plastic or hardboard laminates, and for other materials or contruction jobs that normally cause blades to dull rapidly and where a rough-edged cut is not a great concern. Common general-purpose blade.

Combination, combo, general-purpose, or *all-purpose blade:* The most commonly used blade, adapted for ripping, crosscutting, mitering hard- or softwood, plywood, composition board, and veneer. Generally has groups of medium-sized teeth separated by spaces every four teeth or so. Makes for a slightly rougher cut than you would get with specialized blades but smoother than a chisel-tooth blade. Usually included with saw when purchased.

Crosscut flooring, nail-cutting, or *remodeling blade:* Smooth cutting blade particularly good for hardwoods; stays sharp even when cutting old, nail-embedded lumber.

Crosscut and rip blades: Just like their handsaw counterparts, except that the crosscut has smaller teeth. Crosscut blades are sometimes called *cutoff blades,* as they cut boards off across the grain. Rip blades are sometimes called *framing blades,* designed for fast, rough cutting.

Flat ground blade: These have teeth angled a bit to each side, or "set" in such a way that the blade makes a wide cut and does not bind. Especially useful for plywood, fiberboard, and other hard materials.

Hollow ground blade: Also called *planer* or *taper ground,* this style of blade is sort of the opposite of flat ground. They are manufactured to be slightly concave so that when the cut is made the blade can go through the material smoothly, without binding. There is no "set" to their teeth, which means they are aligned. Look for this style in combination blades, as it makes for more precise, clean cutting, although it is more expensive. Little sanding is needed afterward.

Metal cutting blade: Available for cutting either ferrous or nonferrous metals.

Plywood and veneer blade: These have extremely small teeth and resist the abrasion of plywood glue and prevent splintering. The finest version of this blade is called a *thin-rim blade,* which cuts splinter-free.

Circular Saw Blade for Plywood

Use Tips: Many types can be resharpened. The center hole (the arbor) varies in size from brand to brand (usually $5/8$" but also $1/2$"), so it must be specified or the blade must come with an insert that fits. Wear safety goggles, especially when cutting wood that chips or has nails. Store blades carefully, and clean them after use if they have gum and pitch on the teeth.

> $ **Buying Tips:** Combination blades suffice for general use. In general, the more teeth per inch, the smoother the cut will be—and the slower. Make sure you get the proper-sized center hole to fit your machine. Carbide-tipped blades are worth the extra expense.

Ripping Guide

Description: Circular saw accessory. An adjustable metal rail that attaches to the saw.

Use: Helps guide the saw during very long cuts, such as of 8' long plywood sheets.

Saber Saw

Also Known As: Portable jigsaw, jigsaw, sabre saw, bayonet saw

Description: Has a short, thin blade that moves up and down, cutting on the upstroke. Barrel grip or overhand grip.

Use: For making intricate cuts in a variety of thin materials, but may be used for crosscutting and ripping. Heavy-duty saws can cut through hardwood up to 1" thick and softwood up to $1^1/_2$" thick. It can also be equipped with a wide variety of specialized blades to cut through a variety of other materials, including metal and glass. Starting from a drilled hole, it can cut from inside a larger piece. Accessories include a rasp blade.

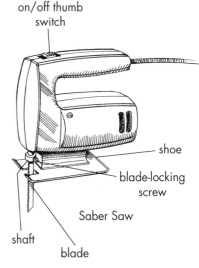

on/off thumb switch

shoe

blade-locking screw

Saber Saw

shaft

blade

Use Tips: If you are making straight cuts, you are better off with a circular saw as the saber saw does not have the high-speed stroking necessary to keep the blade straight. Toss blades the minute you suspect they are dull.

Buying Tips: Check for the following features:

- *Stroke.* Good machines have long ones, up to 1". May be adjustable. Some are orbital and some vertical—orbital is best for wood.

- *Adjustable cutting angle.* Blade can be oriented to cut at a 90-degree angle, for corners, or at angles for bevels.

- *Strokes per minute.* Quality machines have a stroke speed of around 3,000 strokes a minute. Look for variable speed settings.

- *Blade attachment.* Quick-blade change features make things go a lot easier.

Reciprocating Saw

Also Known As: Bayonet saw, Sawzall®, Cut Saw®, Supersaw

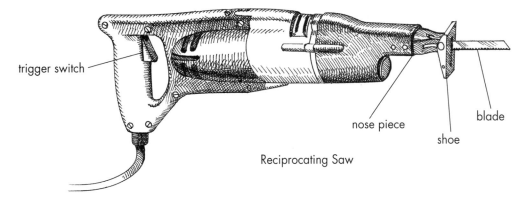

trigger switch

nose piece

shoe

blade

Reciprocating Saw

Description: Tubular housing with straight blade projecting from end. A cordless version is similar but smaller, and may be called a *multipurpose saw* or *utility saw.*

Cordless Multipurpose Saw

Use: A good saw to use in tight quarters and the only one for rough cutting in major renovation work, such as when cutting into existing framing members and through pipes and walls. Variety of blades available that simultaneously cut through nails and wood and the like.

> **Use Tips:** A large variety of specialized blades are available, developed for different materials (drywall, wood, metal) and types of cuts. The cordless model is handy for pruning.

Chain Saw

Description: Gasoline- or electric-powered motor with a long, wide blade around which a toothed chain revolves.

Use: Rough timber cutting, primarily for firewood or pruning.

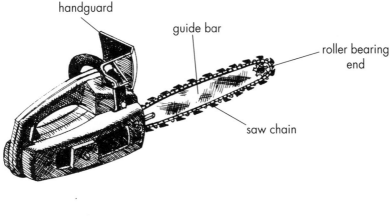

handguard

guide bar

roller bearing end

saw chain

Chain Saw

Portable Power Sanders, Scrapers, Routers, Joiners, and Planes

Finishing Sander

Also Known As: Pad sander

Types:

Orbital or *random orbit sander*

Oscillating sander

Also Known As:

Orbital: Speed finish sander (if high-speed type)

Oscillating: Straight-line sander

Description: The finishing sander has a handle and a base pad of felt or other soft material to which pieces of sandpaper are secured. *Oscillating/orbital sanders* combined two models in one tool. The dimension of the pad is the *size* of the sander; sometimes the model name notes the size of a standard sheet of paper that it takes, such as $1/3$ sheet. The finest finishing is done with small *palm grip–type* orbital sanders called *palm sanders.*

The oscillating sander moves the pad in a straight line, back and forth, while the orbital moves the pad in a circular motion. The motion, in either case, is usually not more than $\frac{1}{4}$" and is extremely rapid. The more rapidly it oscillates, the finer the sanding action.

Use: For fine finishing—not for quick, heavy removal of wood.

> **Use Tips:** Use only aluminum oxide or silicon carbide paper; inexpensive flint paper will tear apart quickly. Paper cut to the correct size is sold in packages. Remember that an orbital sander will inevitably go across the grain and thus is not good for some sanding operations.

> **Buying Tip:** Look for flush sanding in quality models, which allows you to sand right up to corners.

Detail Sander

sanding pad

Detail Sander

Also Known As: Corner sander, triangle sander

Description: Long, narrow, cylindrical tool (some would say "svelte") with small, offset, triangular flat head to which sanding pads are attached by hook and loop system or adhesive. Models available that vibrate (oscillate) up to 12,000 SPM (strokes per minute); 7,600 is average (orbital models may be rated in orbits per minute, or OPM). Accessories available include scraping blades and polishing or buffing pads; a *profile sander* includes small profile pads with rounded or cupped shapes; one brand even adds a saw blade. Some models are designed to vibrate only in a back-and-forth motion (*in-line sanders*).

Use: Sanding in small areas, such as corners and edges, where attention to detail is paramount and where discs and square pads of larger sanders can't reach. The sanding head on this tool is out in front of the handle, so you can get into spaces that other sanders can't. In-line sanders can be used specifically for sanding curves of millwork, with the help of narrow rubber profiles.

> **Use Tips:** Holding one of these for a long time may set your bones to vibrating. Don't overdo it.

> **Buying Tips:** Extremely welcome development in the world of sanders. Great gift item.

Belt Sander

Description: This sander has fore and aft grips to guide it, with a rapidly revolving (usually 1,300 feet per second) abrasive belt that rides on rollers beneath the housing and ranges, depending on the model, from $2^1/_2$" to 4" wide and 16" to 21" long. Some models have bags for collecting sanding dust. Many come with a special stand for benchtop work, upside down. At least one company has introduced a compact belt sander to bridge the gap between the **detail sander (above)** and the belt sander. Made with a sharp point in place of the front roller, it takes $1^1/_2$" wide belts and can sand close in to corners.

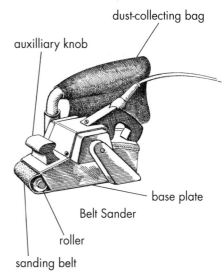

dust-collecting bag

auxilliary knob

base plate

Belt Sander

roller

sanding belt

Use: For the fast removal of finish or wood. You might think of a belt sander, with a coarse belt, as the first sander you'd use to remove a layer of wood or paint; with a fine belt it can also do the finish sanding (the belt going with the grain) better than **orbital sanders (above)**.

Use Tips: Take care when using a belt sander. It removes material so rapidly that it's easy to gouge a surface without realizing it.

Buying Tips: The heavier the model, the better. An occasional problem is the belt tracking off the pulleys. Most models have an adjustment feature that prevents this. *Open-coat sandpaper* is best, as it is less likely to clog. Get the biggest and heaviest model you can heft; sturdiness counts here. 3" × 21" models are good bets.

Disk (or Disc) Sander/Polisher/Grinder

Also Known As: Rotary sander

Description: Comes in two configurations. In the *vertical* type the disk, which revolves rapidly, operates in a plane perpendicular to the motor; in the more common *angle grinder,* or *angle-head grinder,* type the disk is parallel to the motor.

Use: Sanding, polishing, or grinding metal or wood, depending on the disk used. Disks for use on wood, plastic, and concrete are also available. Really for heavy-duty use; a disk sanding attachment on a power hand drill will take care of most homeowners' tasks.

Use Tip: The extreme speed and heavy weight of this tool make it easy to gouge something by mistake.

Buying Tips: Especially suited for long-use periods and high pressure. Otherwise a **portable hand drill with a sanding disk accesory (Chapter 16)** will do. A good tool to rent.

Router

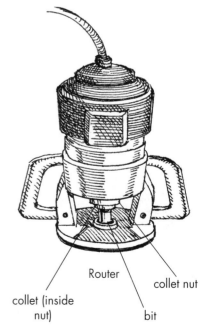

Router

collet nut

collet (inside nut)

bit

Description: Canister-shaped tool with two handles and a bit that revolves at high speed underneath the center of the tool. (A shaper performs similar functions but is a stationary tool.) Sold in two versions: *fixed-base router (see illus.)* and *plunge-type router.* A smaller, handle-less model is called a *cut-out tool* or *rotary cutter.*

Use: There are a few dozen bits available for use with a router that allow fast and accurate cutting of wood and plastic edges into molding shapes, making grooves (dadoes and rabbets) and mortising for door hinges. A special, smaller model, a *laminate trimmer,* is made for trimming plastic laminate, such as for countertops. A *plunge router* can start a cut in the middle of a solid surface. Cut-out tools are used for cutting electrical and plumbing openings.

> **Use Tips:** Think of the router wherever you want to achieve a very smooth-cut surface along an edge; its high-speed operation ensures this. Because the router bit is exposed, make sure to exercise extreme caution. New bits may chip at first. Don't put bits snug against bottom of collet.

> **Buying Tips:** Ask for a tool that has both accurate depth adjustment of the bit and ball-bearing construction. Routers come with motors of various horsepower and higher rpm's are better. For the do-it-yourselfer a $^7/_8$- to $^1/_2$-horsepower motor is adequate, but home renovators need at least a $1^1/_4$ horsepower model; also look for $^1/_4$" to $^1/_2$" collet capacity (or better, one with both). Check to see whether replacing bits is convenient or awkward. Bits come three ways: carbide-tipped, pure carbide, and heat-treated. Carbide is more costly than heat-treated but lasts longer. Plunge routers are more handy. *Cut-out tools* are a big help in new construction jobs. *Door hinge* and *strike and latch templates* are worthwhile accessories for big jobs.

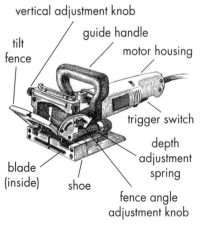

vertical adjustment knob
guide handle
tilt fence
motor housing
trigger switch
depth adjustment spring
blade (inside)
shoe
fence angle adjustment knob

Biscuit Joiner

Biscuit Joiner

Also Known As: Plate Joiner

Description: Cylindrical motor about a foot long, housed above a square base, with a handle on top and a vertical front (the "fence") with one sliding piece and thumbscrews for guidance for depth and angle of cuts. Contains a small cutting blade, usually about 3" to 4" in diameter, in the square base.

Use: Cutting half-circle slots in sides of pieces to be joined with glue and wooden or plastic inserts, called **biscuits (below)**.

> § **Buying Tip:** Excellent and simple way to assure strong joints between pieces of wood, though not as strong as tenons or dowels—just much easier to make.

Joiner Biscuits

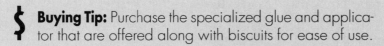

Also Known As: Plate joiner biscuits, splines, wood biscuits, plate, biscuit

Description: Thin oval ($^3/_4$" to 1" × $1^7/_8$" to $2^3/_8$") of wood (often compressed beechwood) or plastic. Sold in bags of 50 to 1000, by dimensions and thickness (#00 to #20 gauge).

Joiner Biscuits

Use: Joining two pieces of wood by placing wooden biscuits into slots cut by a **biscuit joiner (above)** with glue (some plastic biscuits are self-locking and eliminate the need for clamping).

> § **Buying Tip:** Purchase the specialized glue and applicator that are offered along with biscuits for ease of use.

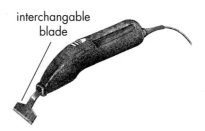

interchangable blade

Power Scraper/Carver

Description: Hand-sized, cylindrical, vibrating motor with off-set head that holds a variety of blade-like tools (scrapers, gouges, chisels, and knives) for scraping and carving.

Power Scraper/Carver

Use: Quick, uniform scraping or carving for quick removal of (depending on the choice of interchangeable metal blades) adhesive, caulk, glazing compound (from windows), foam carpet backing, wood filler, paint splatters, putty, stucco, mortar overflow or splatters, and of course, wood stock.

> **$ Buying Tip:** Good gift item.

Portable Plane

Types:

> *Block plane*
>
> *Jack plane*

Description: Just like hand planes, portable planes come in small and large versions. Rotating cutter blades protrude slightly from a smooth bottom; a high-speed motor and handle grip are on top.

Use: For smoothing surfaces and edges of wood and for some rabbeting (grooves on edges).

> **Use Tip:** Block planes, being smaller, are handier.

Engraver

Description: Hand-sized plastic tool with pencil grip and a small metal point that vibrates at high speed.

Use: Engraving identification on tool housings or other equipment.

Stationary Power Tools

About Stationary Power Tools

The ultimate power tool for the do-it-yourselfer is the stationary or benchtop one: Unlike portable tools, which you take to the work, you take the work to the stationary power tool.

Radial Arm Saw

Also known As: Cutoff saw

Description: A cutting table with an arm over it that houses a circular saw. The saw can be set to various angles, and turned 90 degrees for ripping. To operate, grasp the handle and pull the blade forward for cutoff operations. Move the work through the blade for ripping cuts.

Uses: Can be set to crosscut, rip, and do a variety of other jobs—shaping, dadoing, sanding, jigsawing—with the proper accessories, such as *molding heads,* **dado heads (below),** and *panel cutters.* Can also be set for compound and bevel cuts.

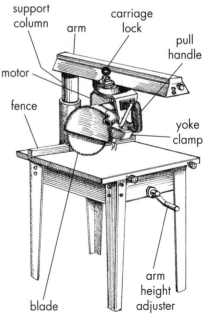

Radial Arm Saw

> ✂ **Use Tips:** Does many different things than a **table saw (below)**. Ripping especially can be very dangerous—be sure to feed the work to the blade from the correct side.

> 💲 **Buying Tips:** Many people consider the radial arm saw the most useful stationary power tool of all, and it should be the first major purchase for your shop. The models that take smaller-sized blades are better for a first purchase. **Compound miter saws (below)** are a close competitor for that No. 1 purchase.

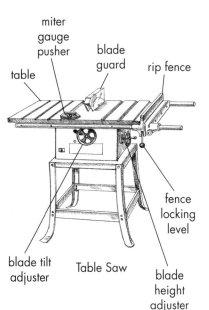

miter
gauge
pusher   blade
             guard   rip fence
table

fence
locking
level

blade tilt   Table Saw
adjuster   blade
                      height
                      adjuster

Table Saw

Also known As: Bench saw, contractor's saw, arbor saw, circular saw (not to be confused with the **portable circular saw, Chapter 17**), variety saw

Description: Consists of a table with a slot from which the circular saw blade protrudes. The blade can be raised or lowered as needed for depth of cut, and either the blade or the table, depending on the model, can be tilted for angled cuts (tilting blades are much more common). To operate the saw, wood is fed into the revolving saw blade (unlike the **radial arm saw, (above)** where the saw is run across the stock). The motor and works of the machine are located under the table.

Use: Very good for ripping large pieces of wood, but how large depends on table size. Special blades such as *molding heads* or *panel cutters* can be used to cut special grooves and contours, like a router or a more advanced tool, a **shaper (Chapter 18).** Grooves are also cut by **dado heads (below).**

> **Use Tips:** If you have to cut very narrow lengths of stock, protect your fingers by using a push stick to feed the stock into the blade. Floor stands with rollers are available for supporting extremely long workpieces.

Compound Miter Saw

Also Known As: Chopsaw, chop saw, chop box

Description: Benchtop-mounted, circular saw with blade and motor mounted on a hinged yoke-style arm that raises up and lowers for cutting at various angles. Not necessarily attached to the workbench, this saw can be used at the worksite. Small models start at about 1$^1/_2$ hp, take eight $^1/_4$" blades, and can cut up to a limited degree of angle. Larger models are offered at 2 to 3$^1/_2$ hp with greater amperage and can cut at a wider range of angles with 10" and even 12" saw blades. All saws are sold labeled by their various stock capacities, such as crosscutting up to 5$^1/_2$" × 2$^1/_{16}$" thick, and the like.

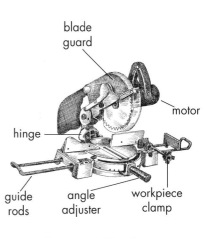

Compound Miter Saw

Use: Accurate and fast miscellaneous angled (miter and bevel) or cutoff (straight crosscut) cuts in trim stock.

> **Use Tip:** Use as often as possible for accurate cutting.

> **Buying Tips:** One of the most successful developments in power tools in recent years. Extremely helpful tool for finish carpentry of all kinds.

> **Note:** Not all miter saws are *compound miter saws* (angles off vertical *and* horizontal).

About Power Saw Blades

Radial arm, miter, and table saws use the same types of blades as circular saws, as mentioned above in **Chapter 17**, except that these stationary tools, due to their higher speeds, tend to use blades with larger diameters and greater thicknesses (and generally cost more). Be sure to check your old blade and tool model before purchasing replacement blades.

Dado Head Blades

Dado Head Blades

Also known As: Dado set, dado assembly

Description: Composed of two kinds of blades: small, thicker-than-usual *circular saw blades,* and *chippers,* which are cutters mounted, or flanked, by the blades when in use. Generally 6" to 8" in diameter. An alternative is a single-blade type, called an *adjustable dado.*

Use: To cut grooves or slots, called *dadoes,* across boards.

> **Use Tips:** For most purposes the 6" size will be fine. To vary the dado size, use fewer and/or wider chipper blades or make multiple cuts. If you have it resharpened, be sure to sharpen the entire set so the sizes remain constant.

Band Saw

Description: Large tool with a saw blade in the shape of a loop or circle that rotates continually in one direction through a table guide that holds the workpiece. The table on many models can be tilted 45 degrees.

Use: For cutting intricate curves in wood, particularly in thick wood (6" or more). With the proper blades, a band saw can cut a variety of other materials, including steel, plastic, and aluminum.

> **Use Tip:** Sanding attachments can be substituted for blades for sanding intricate shapes.

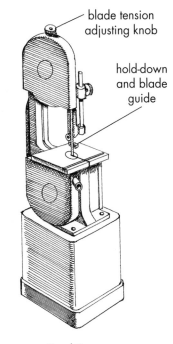

Band Saw

Scrollsaw

Also known As: Jigsaw, bench jigsaw

Description: Small blade in the middle of a steel worktable, supported by a long arm anchored in the rear. Blades are extremely narrow and of two types: the *jeweler's blade,* which is held at both ends, and the *saber blade,* which is a bit heavier and held only from below. Blade moves vertically in a reciprocating motion.

Use: For cutting curves and sharp corners in patterns and for cutting from within a starter hole inside a workpiece. Table tilts for miter and bevel cuts.

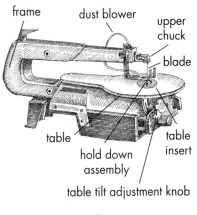

Scrollsaw

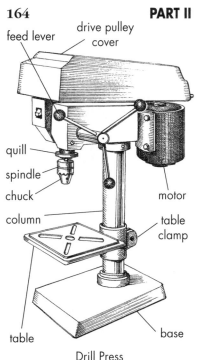

feed lever
drive pulley cover
quill
spindle
chuck
column
motor
table clamp
table
base

Drill Press

Drill Press

Description: Has a heavy base and a vertical arm that holds drill bits and can be raised or lowered with a crank or lever. The table or base can be adjusted to various angles. A variation on the regular drill press is the *radial* type, which can be rotated completely around the arm.

Use: A handy machine, though mainly for precision or production drilling. With accessories a drill press can shape, mill, groove, or rout. For metal as well as wood.

$ **Buying Tip:** Recommended as the second stationary power tool in your shop, after the **radial arm saw (above)**.

Bench Grinder

Also known As: Grinder

Description: Usually has a motor flanked by two grinding wheels. The tool itself is mounted on a workbench. Various wheels include *abrasive grinders, lamb's-wool buffers,* and *wire brushes.*

Use: A variety of polishing, grinding, and sharpening jobs.

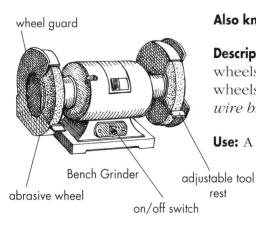

wheel guard
abrasive wheel
Bench Grinder
on/off switch
adjustable tool rest

Jointer

Also known As: Jointer-planer

Description: Table with a housing from which cutterheads protrude. Stock is pushed against housing into cutters that revolve at up to 4,500 rpm.

Use: A variety of jobs similar to a hand plane: to smooth, groove, taper, or bevel wood edges and surfaces. Particularly helpful prior to gluing precision joints. One of the basic cabinetmaking tools.

> **Use Tip:** For safety, use a stick to push stock into cutters.

> **Buying Tip:** One sign of a quality jointer is three or four cutters; lower-quality machines have only two.

Lathe

Description: Two heads ("stocks")—one movable, the other stationary—mounted on a metal bed, with wood inserted between them or attached to one. As the head spins so does the wood. A chisel, supported by a tool rest, is held against the wood.

Use: All kinds of wood shaping, from making bowls to adding a filigree to a piece of molding.

Lathe Gouges

Also known As: Gouges, turning tools

Description: Long, narrow, variously shaped high-speed steel blade set into a wooden handle, similar to a chisel. May be *flat* or *fluted*.

Basic Types:

Plain gouge: For roughing shapes, cove cutting.

Roughing out gouge: Trims square to round.

Spindle gouge: For hollows and beads.

Skew and square end gouge: General planing action.

Parting gouge: Sizing and beading.

Scraping gouge: Flat, for bowls and faceplates.

Use: Shaping wood on a **lathe (above)**.

Buying Tip: Use only the highest-quality turning tools.

General Hardware

Nails

About Nails

There are two categories of nails: those ordinarily used for assembling wood members, be it fine work or rough construction, and specialized nails—those having a variety of single purposes. Actually, there are hundreds of different types when you include various esoteric coatings, ends, materials, and heads. We deal only with the more commonly found ones here. Most of the regular wood nails may be referred to as wire nails.

For wood, though you can get nails smaller and larger, nails are generally available in 1" to 6" sizes; as the nail gets longer it gets larger and thicker in diameter. After 6" in length, nails are often called spikes, and can range up to 18" long.

Basic wood nails are sized according to length, expressed by the letter d (verbalized as "penny"). Originally this was an early English symbol for a pound of weight—from the ancient Roman coin, the denarius—and related to the weight of 1000 nails in pounds. Sizes run from 2d (2-penny or 1") to 60d (6-penny or 6")—6d nails are 2" long, 10d nails are 3" long, etc. This is shown on the following table.

About Determining Nail Length and Quantity With the D System

As mentioned in the above About section, nails are commonly sold by length, which is denoted by the symbol d and a number. Here is how it works:

2d—1"	8d—2$\frac{1}{2}$"	30d—4$\frac{1}{2}$"
3d—1$\frac{1}{4}$"	9d—2$\frac{3}{4}$"	40d—5"
4d—1$\frac{1}{2}$"	10d—3"	50d—5$\frac{1}{2}$"
5d—1$\frac{3}{4}$"	12d—3$\frac{1}{2}$"	60d—6"
6d—2"	16d—3$\frac{1}{2}$"	70d—7"
7d—2$\frac{1}{4}$"	20d—4"	80d—8"

Approximate quantities of common nails per pound by size are, for example: 845 2d nails, 165 6d nails, 65 10d nails, or 30 20d nails. Check with your dealer for specifics regarding whatever nail you are purchasing.

Another antique term is still used too—*penny,* again probably referring to the number of nails you could get for this amount in England. Thus a 10d nail is sometimes called a *10-penny nail,* and a box of 3" long, common-type nails would be labeled *10 common.* Don't worry—these days you can order nails just by their length in inches if you want.

Finishing nails are sized by length in inches and diameters in gauge, with higher numbers denoting thinner nails.

Nails are generally not as strong as screws; however, the holding power (and driving ease) of nails is increased by coating them with resin. These are called *cement-coated ("c.c.") nails, resin-coated nails, coated sinkers* or *sinkers,* or *coolers.* Other coatings, such as zinc, are for rust resistance. Holding power is even more greatly increased by various deformations, or threading, of the shaft, such as *barbs, chemical etching, annular rings, spiral threads* or *flutes,* and by *clinching,* or *bending,* the tips. These nails, though, are very difficult if not impossible to remove without damaging the wood, while screws are easily removed. In general, if strength is your requirement, use screws.

Plain common nails with no coating are called *bright.*

> **Note:** Because of the increased holding power of coated or deformed nails, they are a little bit shorter than the same d-size common nail.

Nails come in boxes, brown paper bags, and carded; the latter is the most expensive way to buy them. If you are going to use a lot of nails, buy 25- or 30-pound kegs at a reduced price. Your dealer can show you a chart to help you figure out the quantity of a particular nail per pound.

Common Nail

Description: Fairly thick with a large, round, flat head

Use: General construction work such as framing and a wide variety of other purposes. Comes in many different sizes. Its large, flat head acts like a washer.

> **Use Tips:** When driving common nails with a hammer try to snap your wrist rather than hitting the nail with arm power. If you are using cement-coated nails, do not stop hammering until the nail is driven all the way in. If you stop, the cement, which is actually a friction-sensitive glue, will set, and when you start again the nail might bend.

Common Nail

Box Nail

Box Nail

Description: Looks like the common nail but is thinner and a little shorter than the common nail d-length indicates. Smooth sides. Made of specially hardened wire.

Use: A variation on the common nail. It is used for the same purposes but its thinner diameter (lighter gauge) and slightly blunted tip make it good where there is a danger of the nail splitting thin wood. Does not hold as well as common nails.

Finishing Nail

Also Known As: Brad

Description: Thin, with a very small, cupped head. Comes in both very small and fairly long sizes and may be sized according to wire gauge (diameter) with a number from 12 down to 20 as well as by the d system.

Use: For wherever you don't want nailheads to show, such as when making cabinets, fine paneling, and the like. A very commonly used nail, it is also thinner than the common nail, but the real difference is the head: because it's small and cupped, it can be easily countersunk, that is, driven beneath the wood surface with a **hammer** and **nailset (Part I, Chapters 1 and 2)** and then the depression above the head filled with wood putty and sanded for a near-invisible finish.

Finishing Nail

Casing Nail

Description: Looks like a **finishing nail (above)**, but is thicker and has a flat rather than a cupped head.

Use: This is a close cousin of the finishing nail and gets its name from its main use: securing **case molding (Part VI, Chapter 49)** and other rough trim. It is thicker and harder than a finishing nail, so you can use fewer of them.

Ringed, Threaded, or Barbed Nails

Types:

Annular ring (or ring shank, or ring drive, or underlayment) *nail*

Drywall nail

Roofing nail

Spiral (or spiral flooring, or spiral shank, or spiral screw, or spiral drive, drive screw, or underlayment) *nail*

Description: Nails with shanks that have been shaped to have the greatest holding power possible, such as

Annular ring: Shank has many sharp ridges. Various uses include underlayment, shingles, siding, paneling.

Drywall: Has a partially barbed or ringed shank and may be resin-coated; has a large head. A *plasterboard* or *lath nail* is another version of this, with a larger head and smaller barbs.

Roofing: Large head and a barbed shank, usually galvanized. Metal roofing model available with a lead or plastic washer under head. *Cap nail* has extremely large head—up to 1" (metal or plastic).

Spiral: Small head with a spiral shank.

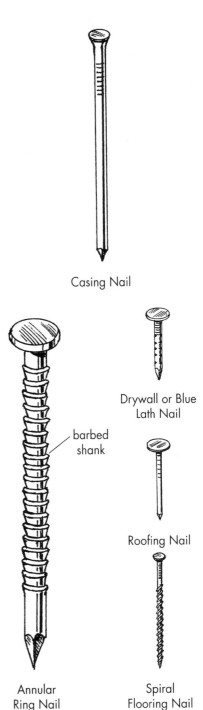

Casing Nail

Drywall or Blue
Lath Nail

barbed
shank

Roofing Nail

Annular
Ring Nail

Spiral
Flooring Nail

barbed shank

Cap Nail

Use:

Annular ring: For generally increased holding power, such as in paneling or delicate floor repair work.

Drywall: Securing **drywall (Part VII, Chapter 50)** to framing.

Roofing: Securing asphalt shingles and roofing paper.

Spiral: Usually used to install or repair wood flooring but can also be used in rough carpentry.

> **Use Tips:** *Drywall:* Hit it just hard enough so that the nailhead dimples the surface paper but goes no deeper. Screws should generally be used with drywall.
>
> *Roofing:* Comes in various sizes up to $1^{1}/_{4}$". Carefully size the nail to the thickness of the roofing being fastened. Available in rust-resistant materials, such as aluminum or stainless steel. Strike as few times as possible to avoid scratching off the rust-resistant coating.

> **Buying Tips:** Galvanized roofing nails are the least expensive. Get double-hot-dipped galvanized nails.

Cut Flooring Nail

Description: Flat, tapered shank and head. Looks like old-fashioned, hand-forged nails.

Use: For nailing into sides of floorboards without splintering and for decorative purposes in restoration.

Use Tips: As it is very difficult to nail sideways at a precise angle, we recommend the use of a *nailing machine*. This can usually be rented from your hardware store or flooring supplier.

Duplex Head Nail

Also Known As: Duplex nail, sprig nail, double-head scaffold nail, staging nail

Description: Regular common nail with a flat ring about $\frac{1}{4}$" below the head.

Use: For temporary work, such as scaffolding. You drive it in up to the first head like a normal nail but can easily remove it by pulling on the second head.

Panel Nail

Description: Decorative brads available in a variety of colors. The best come with **annular rings** for better holding power **(see above)**.

Use: Securing wood paneling to wall when nails are to be inconspicuous.

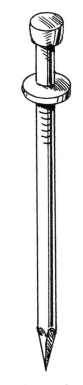

Duplex Head Nail

Common
Tack

Ornamental
Tacks

Tack

Types:

Common tack

Ornamental or ornamental tack

Description:

Common tack: Short, flat- or round-sided nail, some with extra-sharp "cut" end.

Ornamental: Has a tack-like shaft, or shank, and a large, fancy head, often mushroom-shaped.

Use:

Common tack: Mainly used for securing carpeting.

Ornamental: For securing upholstery.

Use Tips: Available with a blued finish or in copper and aluminum. The latter are impervious to weather and are good for boating applications but also for securing webbing on outdoor furniture. Starting tacks without a small-headed hammer, such as a **tack hammer (Part I, Chapter 1)**, is difficult but can be done by holding the tack with a hairpin instead of your fingers.

Nail-like Fasteners

Chevron

Also Known As: Corrugated fastener, corrugated nail

Types:

Chevron

Corrugated fastener

Staple

Description:

Chevron: Small, thin metal piece bent at 90 degrees with several sharpened points on one side.

Corrugated fastener: Short, wide, wavy piece of thin metal with one sharpened side.

Staple: Small U- or J-shaped wire with sharpened ends.

Use:

Chevron: Nailed into corners of boxes and the like.

Corrugated fastener: Nailed across miter joints, such as in picture frames and boxes.

Staple: Usually driven into wood to hold wire or screening.

Masonry Nail

round shank

Masonry Nail

Also Known As: Concrete nail

Description: Looks like a thick common nail but is made of case-hardened and tempered steel. Its shank comes four ways: *round, fluted* (or knurled), *flat* (cut), or *square.* The cut-type masonry nail looks just like the old-fashioned normal cut nail. Another version is the *hammer drive pin,* a ¹/₄" diameter pin inside a flanged sleeve.

Use: Securing items such as electrical conduit furring strips to masonry (brick, concrete, block, etc.), where great holding power is not needed. Hammered in.

> **Use Tips:** You should use a two-pound or bricklayer's hammer to drive these nails. Definitely wear safety glasses to protect against flying masonry chips, and use as few blows as possible.

Screws, Screw Eyes, and Screw Hooks

About Wood Screws

Screws should be the choice when a woodworking job calls for strength. They can be removed—unscrewed—without damaging the item. All screws are driven with screwdrivers except a **lag screw,** or **lag bolt (below)**, which is driven with a wrench, and all are pointed and tapered (unlike *bolts,* which have blunt ends and are straight) except for the machine screw, which is actually a **bolt (Chapter 22)**. Still with us? *Lag* means threaded only on about a third of a long screw or screw eye.

When selecting a screw for a job, a number of factors come into play: finish, length, gauge (diameter), head style, and slot type, as follows:

Finish may be plain steel, blued, or dipped—partially immune to weather—galvanized, brass, brass-plated, chrome-plated, or stainless steel **(Appendix A, Metals and Metal Finishes)**. Remember that brass is softer than brass-plated steel, and thus brass screws' slots are more easily damaged than those of brass-plated screws.

Screws range in size from $1/4$" up to around 6" long; the longer the screw the more difficult it is to turn with a screwdriver. Indeed, if you need a screw more than 4" long use a *lag bolt* or *screw,* which is turned with a wrench. Length is measured in inches.

Screw "gauge," or diameter, of the unthreaded shank under the screwhead is described according to numbers commonly ranging from No. (or #) 5 to No. 14, with the higher number being the larger. The total range is No. 2 to No. 24. A No. 5 screw is about $1/8$" in diameter. Screws of the same gauge are available in different lengths. Always order a screw by length and number: $1/2$" No. 8, for example. Screwheads may be flat, round or oval. See illustration.

Slot types differ. Most common are *slotted* (one straight slot) and *Phillips* (crisscross slots). Other slot types exist, but are not widely available. However, one specialized kind is often found on computers, car headlights, and dashboards—the **Torx head**, which resembles a small star-shaped Phillips head style **(Chapter 4)**. Another type, used often in furniture assembly, is the *square drive,* or *Robertson,* and features a small square hole in the head. All are vast improvements over the slotted type. All require their own screwdriver **(Part I, Chapter 4)**.

Standard Wood Screw

Description: Threads along three-fourths of a tapered shaft, with a variety of heads. **See About section, above.** Most common material is zinc chromate-treated steel. Commonly sold 100 to a box as well as in smaller and larger containers.

Use: Securing wood items to one another. Generally, *oval-* and *flat-head* screws are used when countersinking for decorative purposes or with hardware such as hinges, but oval head is generally easier to remove and slightly better-looking. *Round-head screws* are used with thin woods and with washers.

Slotted
Screwhead

Phillips-Type
Screwhead

Flat Head
Wood Screw

Torx® Screwhead

Oval Head
Wood Screw

Round Head
Wood Screw

Dowel Screw

Description: Slightly heavier than a regular screw, and with threads from both ends. (A similar item is the **hanger bolt,** or **hanger screw, listed in Chapter 22.**)

Use: Furniture assembly of pieces end-to-end.

Dowel Screw

Lag Bolt (or Screw)

Lag Bolt (or Screw)

Description: Looks like a fat, oversize screw that is partly threaded (hence the name *lag*). However, it has a square or hex head for turning with a wrench (hence the name *bolt*). Always on the large side, though not in many sizes.

Use: Heavy-duty fastening when a standard wood screw is not strong enough, such as for securing framing members on a deck, for outdoor furniture, or for hanging kitchen cabinets. Think of it as the largest screw available.

> **Use Tip:** Drill pilot and shank holes so that the screw will be easier to drive. It must be turned with a wrench. Use a washer when tightening against soft wood.

> **Buying Tip:** Lag bolts are cheaper than **carriage bolts (Chapter 22)**, so if you have a choice, use a lag bolt.

Drywall Screw

Drywall Screw

Description: Thin, straight, blued (looks black) screw with deep threads, especially sharp point, and a flat Phillips head (actually a special design called a *Bugle head,* which prevents tearing the surface paper of drywall). Self-tapping—needs no predrilled hole in soft materials. Although there are two kinds—fine thread for metal studs and coarse thread for wooden studs—they are basically interchangeable. In any case the kind intended for metal works fine in wood. *Deck screws* have a coarse thread and are rust-proof galvanzied or stainless steel.

Use: Securing drywall or wood to wood or metal (stud fram-ing, beams, furring, or joists).

> **Use Tips:** Where you are using screws just for basic construction, use drywall screws. They work quite well, due to their self-tapping design: they pull themselves right in, hold securely, and do not need a predrilled hole in soft wood. However, they are not very strong, and the heads may shear off under stress. Particularly convenient when used with a **screw gun** or an **electric drill** with a **screw-driver bit (Part VII, Chapter 50)**.

> **Buying Tip:** Drywall screws are much cheaper than other types when bought in packages of a pound or more. Avoid buying small bags or bubble packs.

Sheet Metal Screw

Description: May be flat-head, oval, or *pan* head, a button-like top (as shown). Unlike wood screws, they are threaded their entire length. Self-tapping (creates its own threaded hole). Heads and gauges are similar to wood screws.

Use: Fastening thin metal to thin metal. Holds extremely well in wood, too, due to its deep threads and self-tapping de-sign.

Sheet Metal Screw

Concrete Screw

Description: Wide-threaded, incredibly hard steel screw, with either tapered flat head or hex washer head; coated against corrosion. Sold with special carbide-tipped masonry drill. Available in $\frac{1}{4}$" and $\frac{3}{8}$" diameters and a variety of lengths.

Use: Screws directly into cement and cement board **(Part VII, Chapter 50)** of all kinds. No anchor needed. Useful when attaching wood to concrete foundation, as well as for electrical installation.

> **Use Tip:** Carefully drill appropriately-sized hole first.

Countersunk Washer

Flush Washer

Screw Washers

Description: Small metal circles that come in three shapes: *flat, countersunk* (slightly cone-shaped), and *flush* (slightly funnel-shaped). The latter two are known as *finishing washers*. Size matches screw being used.

Use: Washers provide a hard surface for a screw to be tightened against, thereby preventing damage to the surface and allowing a tighter fit. Countersunk (for oval-head screws) and flush (for flat-head screws) are more attractive as well. Flat washers are for use with round-head screws.

About Screw Eyes and Screw Hooks

There is an entire family of devices called *screw eyes* and *screw hooks.* They are classic hardware-store items and have been around for many years. Some of these screws can be installed with hand power alone. Many are finished for outdoor use.

Both screw eyes and screw hooks are available in various wire gauges or diameters and lengths and are classified by number: As the eye gets smaller the number gets larger. For instance, a No. 000 screw eye has an inside diameter of 1" while a No. 9 would have an inside diameter only $1/2$". As the eye gets larger the screw eye or screw hook gets longer. Lengths generally range from $1/2$" to 3".

Screw Eyes

Screw Eye

Description: Metal shaft with one end formed into a ring, the other threaded and pointed like a screw. Models are available with a loose ring looped through the eye, called an *eye and ring*. Another, heavy-duty model has a round plate underneath the eye for added stability.

Use: Various uses but basically for hanging objects and hooking them together. The screw eye with a plate is used for anchoring cables, such as for TV antennae.

Screw Eye with Plate

Screw Hooks

Types:

    Ceiling hook

    Cup hook

    L-hook

    Utility hook

Screw Hook

Cup Hook

Shoulder Hook

L-Hook

Also Known As:

L-hook: Square bend screwhook, support hook, curtain rod hook

Utility hook: Bicycle hook, storage hook

Description: Same basic design as a *screw eye* but the ring part is open, forming a hook.

Ceiling hook: Very large hook for screwing directly into ceiling joists.

Cup hook: A rounded screw hook with a shoulder, or plate. Cup hooks vary from $1^1/_4$" long and, because they are decorative, are usually brass- or plastic-coated. "Safety" models have a snap across the opening.

L-hook: A screw hook in the shape of the letter L. L-hooks come up to 2" long. A *shoulder hook* is an L hook with a small shield like a cup hook.

Utility hook: Extremely large, squared-off, plastic-coated screw hook with large threads.

Use: Hanging things from wood shelves, walls, and ceilings.

Cup hook: Hanging cups in a cabinet.

L-hook: Hanging utensils, securing picture frames directly to walls (without hanging from a wire), holding curtain rods.

Utility hook: Great for hanging bicycles from a ceiling in an apartment or a garage. Screw directly into a joist. Also for rakes, shovels, lawn mowers.

> **Use Tips:** A small screw hook can be installed in soft wood by simply pushing it in place and turning it by hand.

Swag Hook

Also Known As: Ceiling hook

Description: Decorative cup hook with enlarged base and exaggerated relief. Comes in various decorator colors and with either large screw threads or a **toggle bolt (Chapter 23)**.

Use: Anchoring swag lamps and hanging plants from ceilings.

Clothesline and Hammock Hooks

Description:

Clothesline hook: Like an enlarged cup hook with a plate with holes to accept screws.

Hammock hook: Like the clothesline hook but three kinds are available. One is simply a large screw eye or hook; another has a plate with screw holes in it and a hook that hangs from it, and a third is a hook hanging from a screw eye.

Use:

Clothesline hook: For mounting clothesline, particularly where mounting material is thin.

Hammock hook: Heavy-duty anchor for hammocks.

toggle bolt

Swag Hook with Toggle Bolt

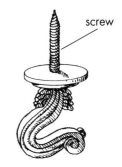

screw

Swag Hook with Screw

> **⚒ Use Tips:** *Clothesline hook:* When mounting to thin material, such as siding, use the type with the plate on it. The plate type allows you to use small screws, which will not bite deeply into the mounting material, possibly cracking it.

Gate Hook

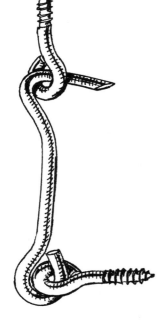

Gate Hook and Eye

Description: Consists of a screw eye that screws into a gate post and a corresponding screw eye and hook that is secured to the gate. Gate hooks commonly come 1" to 5" long but can be obtained up to 18" long. A "safety" version is available with a spring-loaded bolt that snaps across the hook opening to keep small children from unhooking the gate.

Use: Keeps gates and doors closed in a lightweight manner.

> **⚒ Use Tips:** Gate-hook parts must be sized to work together. This shouldn't be a problem because they come as kits.

Nuts and Bolts

About Nuts and Bolts

Bolts are generally for fastening metal to metal, not wood to wood (except for the **carriage bolt, below)**. They can be turned only with wrenches (except for **machine screws** and **stove bolts, below)**. Their threads, known as *machine threads,* cannot, unlike *wood-screw threads,* hold in anything except a nut. And they have blunt ends, not pointed ends like wood screws.

Bolt diameters are noted in inches, not in gauge numbers as with screws. Thread size is noted in a number following the diameter in terms of threads per inch, i.e., $^{1}/_{4}" \times 20$. Common machine bolt has 20 threads per inch. This nomenclature is often confused by various manufacturers, who may use two different systems on similar packages. Caveat emptor and good luck.

> **Note:** A **lag bolt**, also called a *lag screw*, is discussed in **Chapter 20**.

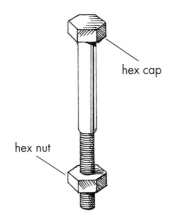

hex cap

hex nut

Machine Bolt

Machine Bolt

Description: Partially threaded with a flat end and either a square or hex head. The standard, classic bolt. Called a *tap bolt* or *hex head* capscrew when threaded its entire length; a hex head (or cap) bolt when threaded only part way up the shaft. In addition, a *capscrew* or *socketscrew* is threaded its entire length but has a round head (cap) for use with an **Allen wrench (Part I, Chapter 8)**.

Use: Assembling metal items.

Use Tips: There are several ways to keep nuts from coming off of bolts because of vibration, such as on machinery: the "double-nut" technique (two nuts per bolt); using a **locknut (below)**; using a **lock washer**, either the **split-ring** type or the **internal-tooth** type **(below)**; or using **anaerobic adhesive (Part IV, Chapter 32)**, a type of adhesive that comes in small plastic tubes, one drop of which hardens inside the threads.

Carriage (below) and machine bolts come with *rolled* or *cut* threads, but the cut thread is better. Here the thread is cut directly into the steel shaft used for the bolt, while the rolled thread is added separately after the shaft is machined. The rolled-thread type uses less metal. In smaller sizes this may not matter, but in larger sizes the shank part of the bolt may match the drilled hole perfectly but the rolled or threaded part may not. The result is a sloppy fit.

Machine Screw

Machine Screw

Description: Threaded along its entire length, it has a flat tip, a round or flat head, and is designed primarily to be screwed into prethreaded holes in metal, though of course it works with nuts too. Actually a type of bolt, but a bolt that is driven with a screwdriver instead of a wrench.

Machine screw threads are of two sizes: coarse (24 per inch) and fine (32 per inch). When a screw is specified (such as in electrical work) as a 6-32 screw, what is meant is a 6 gauge diameter, or No. 6 size, with fine threads. The length should be given in inches after the size, as in 6-32 × $3/4$". **See the About section, above**, for more information.

> $ **Buying Tip:** Most **electrical boxes (Part IX, Chapter 71)** need 8-32 machine screws.

Stove Bolt

Round Head Stove Bolt

Description: Usually threaded its entire length, with a round or flat head that has a straight screw slot; driven with a screwdriver. The most often used sizes (diameters) are $1/8$", $5/32$", and $3/16$". Exactly the same item as a **machine screw (above)**, the difference being that stove bolts are supplied to the customer with nuts and intended for use with nuts, while the machine screw is intended for use in prethreaded holes in metal (shown with a square nut).

Use: Light assembly (such as basic kitchen appliances), because a screwdriver has less tightening power than a wrench.

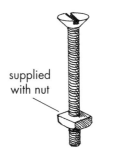

supplied with nut

Flat Head Stove Bolt

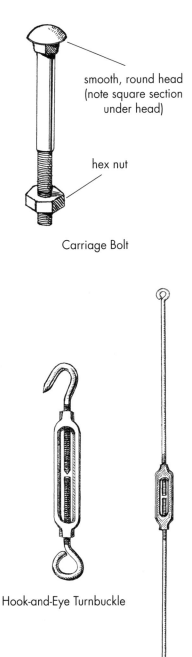

smooth, round head
(note square section
under head)

hex nut

Carriage Bolt

Hook-and-Eye Turnbuckle

Screen Door and
Gate Turnbuckle

Carriage Bolt

Also Known As: Carriage screw

Description: A large bolt, partially threaded, with a smooth, rounded head that has a square-sided portion just beneath it. That square part cuts into wood as the nut is tightened and resists the turning motion. A similar but smaller version is the *ribbed bolt*.

Use: Used in wood where particular strength is required, where you will not be able to reach the head with a wrench, or where you do not want a turnable head exposed (there is no slot in the oval head).

> **Use Tip:** Use washers under the nut on carriage bolts where the wood is very soft and you don't want the nut to dig in and cause damage, such as in outdoor redwood furniture.

Turnbuckle

Description: An open barrel-like metal device, internally threaded on both ends, with two threaded rods screwed in, one a left-handed thread, the other right-handed. The rods may have an eye at both ends, a hook on one end and an eye on the other, or hooks on each end, and are usually less than a foot long.

Use: Acts as an adjustable segment of a cable or wire. The various forms this comes in give one flexibility of use: for instance on one end a cable could be attached to a hook while on the other a snap fastener and rope. A common use for a turnbuckle is to brace a door. Another use is bracing a gate to remove a sag.

 Use Tips: The smaller sizes are zinc-plated, but the larger ones (all the way up to 2', in case you have any mountains to brace) are galvanized.

Buying Tips: Turnbuckles can be obtained in kits, such as for straightening out a screen door.

U-bolts and J-bolts

Description: Threaded steel rod bent into either a U or J shape (rounded or squared off). Most useful U-bolt has a slotted bar across both ends that clamps down as the nuts are tightened. A very small version with a large cast-metal piece across the opening is used for clamping cable ends.

Use: Clamping odd shapes or hanging items. Often used in conjunction with *S-hooks* and *8-hooks* (figure 8-shaped steel pieces).

Buying Tip: Can be made from **threaded rod (below)** that you bend yourself.

Threaded Rod (Shown in Use)

Threaded Rod

Also Known As: All thread

Description: Metal rod threaded along its entire length. Commonly available in 2' and 3' lengths and in the following diameters: $3/16$", $1/4$", $5/16$", $3/8$", and $1/2$". Much larger sizes can also be obtained on special order. Think of it as an infinitely long bolt.

Rod may also be made of stainless steel, plain steel, electroplated, or zinc-coated; the latter is suitable for outdoor use.

Use: Used with nuts and washers for many different jobs: hanging, bracing, fastening, supporting, and mounting. Also useful where a bolt doesn't have sufficient threads to work. For example, a 6" bolt may have only $1^1/2$" of thread; a threaded rod will have sufficient threads.

> **Use Tips:** To avoid burrs when cutting rod (it may be cut with a hacksaw or bolt cutters), make the cut between two nuts, then turn the nuts off the cut ends to remove the burrs.

Eye Bolt   Hook Bolt

Square-Bend (L)   Hanger Bolt
Bolt

Miscellaneous Bolts

Types:

Eye bolt

Hook bolt

Hanger bolt

Square-bend (L) bolt

Also Known As: *Hanger Bolt:* stud bolt hanger screw, handrail bolt, bolt hanger, table screw

Description:

Eye, hook, and *square-bend bolts:* These usually come galvanized or zinc-plated and resemble screw eyes or hooks, except the end is flat and it has bolt threads.

Hanger bolt: Has large screw threads on one end and bolt threads on the other, with a smooth portion between.

Use:

Eye, hook, and *square-bend bolts:* For hanging hooked items.

Hanger bolt: Commonly used to assemble commercial furniture. For do-it-yourselfers the hanger bolt is excellent for mounting in a joist or ceiling beam in order to hang fixtures.

> **$ Buying Tips:** The above bolts are available loose and are cheaper than packaged bolts.

Miscellaneous Nuts

Types:

Axle (or *axle cap) nut*

Cap nut

Fiber insert nut

Flat square nut

Cap Nut

Wing Nut

Hex nut

Locknut

Square nut

Wing nut

Also Known As: *Cap:* Acorn

Description:

Axle: Stamped, unthreaded cap.

Cap: Closed-end nut that resembles an acorn.

Fiber insert: Consists of a nut with a fiber insert.

Flat square: Thin, four-sided nut.

Hex: Standard five-sided nut.

Locknut: Thick hex nut with a plastic insert.

Square: Same thickness as a hex nut but with only four sides.

Wing: Two upward projecting wings flanking a threaded middle.

Use: All nuts screw onto bolts to tighten them against whatever is being fastened. Some have special applications though:

Axle: Caps the end of an axle to keep a wagon, baby carriage, or cart wheel on.

Cap: Decorative uses.

Fiber insert: This is self-locking and is used where much holding power is desired.

Locknut: Maintains tension even when vibrated repeatedly, such as on machinery.

Wing: Good for light use when something needs to be regularly disassembled by hand. Not intended for use with wrenches.

Nut and Bolt Washers

Types:

Flat washer

Split-ring lock washer

Internal tooth lock washer

External tooth lock washer

Split-Ring
Lock Washer

Internal Tooth
Lock Washer

Also Known As: *Split ring:* Lock washer, spring lock washer

Description: Small steel or aluminum donut-shaped pieces with holes that match the diameter of the bolt being fastened through them.

Flat: Flat circular shape. Smaller sizes provide a smooth surface for a nut or bolt head to be tightened against, while the larger ones are used with carriage bolts to prevent the nut from piercing the wood piece being attached.

Split ring: Spring action of slight spiral creates pressure that keeps a nut from loosening.

Internal tooth lock washer: Many small teeth pointing in toward hole that serve to keep nut from loosening.

External tooth lock washer: Many small teeth pointing outward that serve to keep nut from loosening. Can be used with wood screws.

Use: Provides a surface for a nut or bolt head to be tightened against, and in the case of lock washers, helps prevent the nut from loosening.

Bolt Extractor

Bolt Extractor

Also Known As: Easy Outs (brand name), screw and bolt extractor

Description: Fluted, tapered steel bar that resembles a nailset. Variety of diameters.

Use: Removing bolts or screws that cannot be turned out by normal means, such as when the threads have been completely stripped. It is driven into a hole made in the screw and then turned out; the threads, which are the reverse of the screw threads, bite into the screw and pull it out.

> **Use Tip:** As mentioned in the plumbing section **(Part VIII, Chapter 63)**, good for removing faucet seats when other means fail.

Taper Tap

Tap

Also Known As: Cut thread tap

Description: Short shaft of hardened steel with sharp, fluted threads and one squared-off end.

Types:

Taper tap

Plug tap

Bottoming tap

Tap Wrench (Stock Style)

Use: Cuts screw threads inside holes drilled in steel. The three types are sometimes numbered 1–3 and used in that order to create a properly shaped hole. Most common use would be repairing or making a new air-valve hole in a radiator.

> **Use Tips:** Use a T-handle tap wrench or a long tap stock handle rather than a regular wrench. Make sure everything is perfectly aligned. Back off $1/4$" turn for each full turn to break off cut material.

T-Handle Tap Wrench

Die

Also Known As: Threading die

Description: Small round piece of hardened steel, resembling a cookie cutter, containing several half-holes and extremely sharp internal teeth. Held in a two-handed handle, called a *die stock,* with a circle in the center for holding dies.

Use: Cutting threads on the outside of a metal rod.

Types:

Adjustable die

Solid die (most common)

Hexagonal die (can be used with a wrench instead of a handle)

> **Use Tip:** Make sure everything is perfectly aligned.

Die

Die Stock

Miscellaneous Fasteners, Braces, and Anchors

Cotter Pin

Description: Metal bent back upon itself, with slight open loop at the bend. Generally only about 2" long, but available in smaller and larger sizes.

Use: Generally used for holding metal rods or shafts. The cotter pin is put through a tight hole and has its tips bent to prevent it from sliding back out. The pin is removed by bending the tips straight again and pulling the ring on the other end with pliers or a hook.

Cotter Pin

> **Use Tip:** If you have to remove cotter pins repeatedly, get a small tool that looks like a hooked screwdriver, called a *cotter pin puller.*

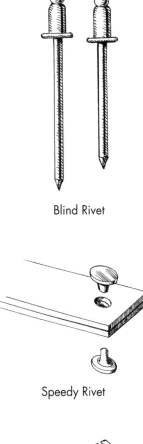

Blind Rivet

Rivets and Other Small Fasteners

Types:

> *Blind rivets*
>
> *Speedy rivets*
>
> *Teenuts* (or *T-nuts*)
>
> *Threaded inserts*

Also Known As: *Blind rivets:* Pop® rivets, aluminum rivets

Description:

> *Blind rivet:* A nail-like, two-piece item, usually made of aluminum, with a nose cap that is inserted in a drilled hole in the object to be riveted. A special **rivet gun (Part I, Chapter 14)** is then used to compress the rivet, fastening the parts together. Available in *grip range* sizes corresponding to the thickness of whatever is to be riveted.

> *Speedy rivet:* Consists of a barbed section and threaded part. The two parts are hammered or clamped together with a special plier-like tool. Similar are *grommets,* which form a ringed hole.

> *Teenut fastener:* Two-part fastener consisting of a threaded core and top with prongs (the "tee"). The core is inserted into a hole drilled into a piece of wood and then the top hammered in on top. A bolt screws into the core.

> *Threaded insert:* Steel or brass cylinder with large threads on its outside and bolt threads on the inside.

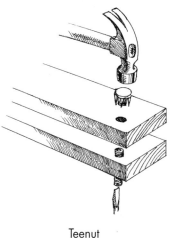

Speedy Rivet

Teenut

Use:

Blind rivets: Fastening pieces of light metal, leather, or canvas on objects such as toys, bikes, and appliances as well as briefcases and suitcases when accessing from one side only.

Threaded Insert

Speedy rivets: Fastening soft materials such as canvas to canvas or canvas to leather.

Teenut fasteners: For joining wood members, such as two-by-fours.

Threaded inserts: When steel (machine) threads are required in wood, such as for furniture assembly.

Floor Squeak Eliminator

Description: Actually a system of a small metal jigs, often with three feet and a platform with a hole to guide screws in the center, and special screws. May be supplied with a special, long screwdriver bit for use with a power screwdriver. The screws are scored to break off at the surface of the floor.

Use: Eliminating floor squeaks by attaching the floor surface more securely to the subfloor, without leaving a screwhead showing.

Floor Squeak Eliminator

Nylon Cable Tie

Also Known As: Nylon Tie

Description: Small piece of plastic strap 4" to 8" long, one end of which has a small fitting that the other end is pulled through. Available in self-locking and releasable versions. Disposable item. Sold by the bagful.

Nylon Tie

Use: Originally developed for binding cables together in electrical systems, can be applied to household tying tasks such as securing large plastic bags, coils of rope or hose, and so on.

Use Tips: CAUTION: Because these ties are easy to use and usually impossible to loosen, do not let unsupervised children play with them.

Inside Corner Brace

Braces and Plates

Also Known As: Door and window braces

Types:

> *Inside corner brace*
>
> *Flat corner brace* (or *iron*)
>
> *Mending plate*
>
> *T-plate*

Description: All are flat metal, available in zinc- and brass-plated finishes.

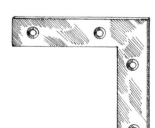

Flat Corner Brace

Inside corner brace: L-shaped piece with screw holes for mounting inside a corner. Comes in sizes 1" long and 1/2" wide to 8" long and 1" wide. Screw holes are staggered rather than being in a straight line. Specialty sources sell a thicker version excellent for chairs.

Flat corner brace: L-shaped piece with screw holes for mounting on surface, at right angles to the **corner brace version (above)**. A thicker, embossed version is specially made for screens.

Mending Plate

Mending plate: Flat length of metal with screw holes.

T-plate: Flat metal piece made in the shape of the letter T; both horizontal and vertical legs of the T are the same length.

Use:

Corner brace: Strengthening and supporting box and chair corners.

Flat corner brace: Bracing corners on window frames and doors.

Mending plate: Joining two pieces of wood end-to-end. Many different applications, from reinforcing screen doors to furniture.

T-plate: Common use is for joining horizontal and vertical screen-door members.

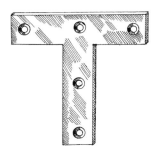

T-Plate

Chair Brace

Drop Leaf Brace

Description: Collapsible metal rod, attached to furniture parts at both ends, which snaps into place when extended.

Use: Supports table leaves or extra shelves.

Corner Brace for Screens

> **Use Tip:** The shorter part is installed to go on top, or on the "leaf" side.

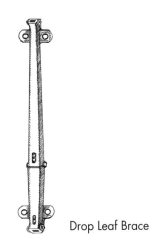

Drop Leaf Brace

Framing Fasteners

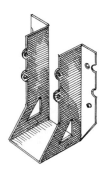

Joist Hanger

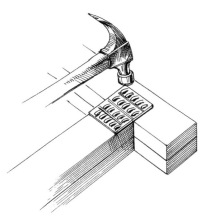

Nailing Plate

Angle Bracket

Examples:

Joist hangers

Nailable truss plate

Prong plate

Reinforcing angles

Also Known As: Framing, carpentry, or metal connectors, framing anchors, Tecos®, clips, structural wood fasteners, beam hangers, joist supports

Description: 16- or 18-gauge zinc-coated sheet metal in various forms with predrilled nail holes and, in some cases, metal prongs. Generally made to fit 2-by lumber, that is, 2×4's, 2×6's, etc.

Use: Conveniently connecting various framing members and assemblies, mostly at right angles. For example, there are framing fasteners to connect joists to beams, to secure roof beams, to mount posts, and much, much more. Also used as framing reinforcement in areas subject to hurricanes, tornadoes, and earthquakes. The nailable truss plate is used with special $1^1/_2$" truss nails supplied by the manufacturer.

> **$ Buying Tips:** *Hurricane anchors* are expensive and basically designed for framing that will withstand a lot of stress, such as in hurricane country. If severe weather isn't a problem in your area, then they likely aren't a good buy. However, they also enable framing to be assembled more quickly. You may count this as a plus and be willing to pay the extra money.
>
> Framing fasteners can be bought singly, in small packages containing a few fasteners, and in bulk—25 to 50 pieces per carton. Buying in bulk can save you up to 50 percent over buying singly or in small packages.

About Wall Anchors

Wall anchors, or fasteners, are particularly useful on two kinds of wall construction—hollow wall (usually drywall), if there is no stud or solid material to simply drive a screw or nail into, and hardwall, where the wall material is too hard for screws to take hold in, such as plaster or masonry. Wall anchors come in a variety of sizes and types, and new designs and brand names appear often. Be sure to check all your sources for the best ones available in your area. Below are some of the most popular types, which fall into three categories: *light duty,* for any kind of wall; *masonry;* and *hollow-wall fasteners.*

Light-Duty Anchor

Light-Duty Anchor

Also Known As: Tubular anchor, plastic anchor, hollow anchor, plastic shield, plastic expansion anchor

Description: Plastic or jute fiber cone-shaped or cylindrical sheaths of various sizes corresponding to various-sized screws. They expand against the sides of the hole when the screw is driven into them. One version of this is made especially for use in particle board.

Use: Anchoring wood screws in plaster, drywall, or masonry. They are inserted into a predrilled hole. Not for extremely heavy objects.

> **Use Tips:** The hole must be just the right size—too big and the anchor won't hold, too small and it won't go in far enough to work.

Flat Wall Anchor

Flat Wall Anchor

Also Known As: Expanding anchor

Description: Flat, wide, nail-like item with a chisel point and a large, flat head with a hole in the middle. Made of hardened steel. Sold in various lengths (for different wall thicknesses) and styles for either hollow walls or concrete.

Use: Depending on the model, either anchoring light to medium-weight items in drywall, pegboard, wood paneling, and hollow-core doors, or concrete.

> **Use Tips:** The hollow-wall (drywall) model does not require any drilling and when removed, leaves only a small slit.

Universal Expansion Anchor

Universal Expansion Anchor

Description: Similar looking to the slightly conical plastic expansion anchor, this is made of a softer material and has two halves that mesh together with alligator-like teeth (most common brand name is Alligator® Anchor, by Toggler®). Sold in both a flange and no-flange version, in various dimensions and lengths ranging from $3/16$" to $5/16$" in diameter and about 1" to 2" in length.

Use: Heavy-duty mounting in any kind of material and with a wide range of screw sizes in the same anchor. Designed for use with a screw gun.

> **Use Tips:** Special, soft plastic conforms to the outside shape of the hole, and allows the screw to cut threads inside. Pre-installs without screw.

> **$ Buying Tip:** Because of its universal applicability, a very cost-effective anchor.

Expansion Shield

Also Known As: Lead shield, shield

Description: The most common type consists of a thick, slotted metal sleeve usually made of lead. There is a one-piece design for use with wood screws and a two-piece design for use with lag bolts (most popular) and machine bolts. Another version, a *hammer drive pin,* is a nail-like device that is hammered in place. The shield expands slightly against the hole as the screw is driven into it.

Use: For anchoring items in masonry (brick, block, concrete).

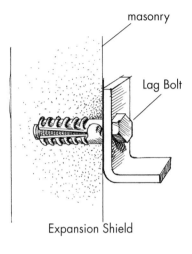

masonry

Lag Bolt

Expansion Shield

> **Use Tips:** Bear in mind that these shields require very large holes to be drilled in masonry. You need a power drill and a **masonry (carbide-tipped) bit (Part II, Chapter 16)** to make such holes, and alignment is not always easy. An alternative may be to use simple **masonry nails (Chapter 20)** and furring strips (thin boards). If you are putting up a large job with furring strips, you may want to rent a **power hammer (Chapter 14)** powered by .22-caliber blanks for *powder-driven* or *power fasteners.*

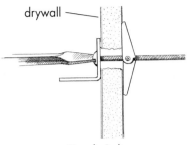

drywall

Toggle Bolt

Toggle Bolt with Decorative Head

Toggle Bolt

Also Known As: Toggles, spring-wing toggle, umbrella bolt

Description: A machine screw with collapsible "wings." One type has spring-loaded wings that squeeze together and open when released; the other type uses gravity. The wings push up against the back side of the drywall when the fastener is tightened. Available with decorative head, suitable for hanging mirrors.

Use: Hanging heavy items to hollow-wall construction (drywall), especially overhead.

> **Use Tips:** Note that the toggle will drop if the bolt is removed, and large holes are required.

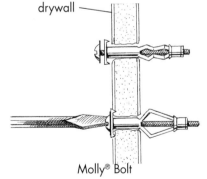

drywall

Molly® Bolt

Molly® Bolt

Also Known As: Mollies, collapsible anchors, expansion bolts, screw anchor, expansion anchor, hollow wall anchor

Description: Consists of a machine screw built into a sleeve with wings that expand out as they are tightened. A similar but smaller model is made for hollow-door anchoring, called *jack nuts*. Some brands have a plastic-tipped model that is hammered into drywall like a nail and then screwed tight.

Use: Fastening medium to heavy items to hollow-wall construction (drywall).

Use Tips: Drill a clean, solid hole so the anchor can be anchored tightly in it and not turn around as you turn the screw. The anchor will remain in place even if the screw is removed, making it slightly more convenient than a **toggle (above)**. A small wrench, a V-shaped wire device, is sometimes supplied to keep the sleeve from turning as you tighten the bolt.

Hinges, Hasps, and Latches

About Hinges

Hinges come in a tremendous array of styles and types, but there are some basics you can learn to help you make the best selection from the various models available.

Technically, hinges are "handed"—specified for use on left- or right-hand doors. But this can get complicated, and unless you're doing a special job you can forget it. Just flip the hinge over and it becomes left- or right-handed as needed.

Hinges come in different sizes to support different weights. But this, too, can get complicated. To select the proper size just determine if the hinge is in proportion, size-wise, to the door being hung and you'll be fine, even if you're undersized a bit—hinges are up to eight times stronger than they need to be.

Hinges also come in a variety of finishes, from plated brass to pure brass to paint. The variety available is virtually sure to give you the selection you require. They also are either surface-mounted or recessed ("mortised") on one or both sides. *Self-closing hinges* include spring-loaded hinges and *rising hinges* that are designed with an angular joint that uses gravity.

Because of the extreme range of models available, with minute variations in and combinations of style, prepare to ask for by

Butt Hinge

description, using a catalog or old hinge as a guide. Below is a small selection of common hinges.

Hinges

Types:

Butt hinge

Loose pin hinge

T-hinge

Strap hinge

Gate hinge

Invisible hinge

Piano hinge

Double-acting hinge

Also Known As:

Butt: Utility hinge

Invisible: Barrel hinge, Soss hinge (brand name), concealed hinge

Piano: Continuous hinge

Double-acting: Swing-clear hinge

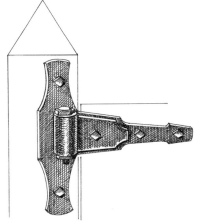

T-Hinge (Ornamental Style)

Description:

Butt: Two rectangular leaves of metal with screw holes and a pin joining the leaves; to remove door, hinge must be unscrewed. Each pin hole is called a "knuckle."

Loose pin: Similar to butt, but pin is removable for easy removal of door. Most common type.

Gate Hinge (Ornamental Style)

Note: Sometimes this removal distinction is not made obvious.

T: Shaped like the letter T, with a vertical strap going on the doorframe and a horizontal strap in the door.

Strap: Center pin from which extend two narrow leaves.

Gate: L-shaped part that screws into a fence post and a leaf part with a knurled nut that fits over the L-shaped part and is screwed to the gate.

Invisible: Two barrel-shaped parts joined by a pin segment with both barrel-like parts recessed into the edges of the door and frame.

Piano: Two long leaves, each with many screw holes, joined by a pin.

Double-acting: Two sets of leaves and knuckles, somewhat loose-jointed, so that both leaves can be opened simultaneously.

Use:

Butt: Hanging regular exterior house doors. The nonremovability of the pin is a security feature.

Loose pin: The most common hinge for hanging interior doors.

T: Mostly used on gates and cabinet lids.

Strap: Gates and cabinet lids.

Gate: As the name suggests, on gates.

Invisible: Cabinet doors where you don't want the hinge to show.

Piano: Cabinet lids.

Double-acting: Folding doors that open two ways or fold flat.

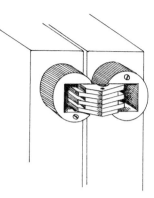

Invisible Hinge

Strap Hinge (Plain)

Strap Hinge (Ornamental Style)

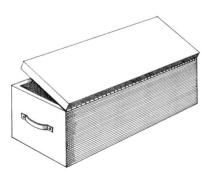

Piano Hinge

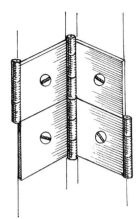

Double-Acting Hinge

Use Tips: *Butt:* These are mortised in door with a chisel; one leaf is recessed into door, one into the frame. Installation is easier using a flat template device called a *butt gauge, butt marking gage,* or *butt marker.* Also, should you want to take a door down, just remove the hinge pin, separating the leaves.

Invisible: These are very difficult to install since they must line up exactly opposite each other. There is no room for error.

Buying Tips: *T:* In addition to plain T-hinges, ornamental-looking T-hinges are available. Regular T-hinges come in plain and galvanized finishes.

Strap: Available in plain and galvanized as well as bronze finishes; the latter is ordinarily used on boats. They are available in large and small sizes. The length of the leaves makes them an unlikely selection for use on ordinary doors. They are also available in ornamental styles.

Gate: 5" and 6" sizes are commonly available, though other sizes can be obtained.

Invisible: These are very expensive.

Piano: Usually available in brass finish.

Hasps

Description: Hasps may be plain or decorative, with the length of the slotted part ranging from 2¼" to 6¼" with staples (the part with the ring for the lock) of proportionate sizes and hasp widths 1" to 2". Some models may have a key lock instead of a ring.

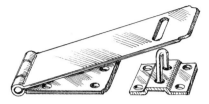

Hasp (Safety Style)

A *safety hasp* has a slotted part that conceals the screws securing the hasp when it is closed. Other safety hasps are heavy duty and have a square hole for insertion of a ⁵/₁₆" carriage bolt.

Another type of hasp is designed for use on chests and sliding doors. Here the end is upturned and also hides the mounting screws.

Decorative hasps are available with bright brass finishes.

Use: Securing doors, usually outdoor types, with a padlock that goes through the ring.

Latches

Description: Generally consists of a horizontal piece attached to the door that either slides, falls, or snaps into a catch on the door or gate post. Many different types and styles.

Barrel Bolt Latch

Basic Types:

Gate latch: Rod projects from gate and fits into catch on gate post.

Sliding, or *barrel, bolt:* Long bolt with handle projecting from middle slides in and out of curved piece on doorframe. Available in light weight for decorative purposes and in extreme heavy weight, also called a square

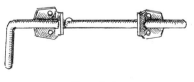

Cane Bolt

spring bolt, for security purposes, such as on the insides of exterior doors. Larger bolts come with a hole in the bolt so that it can be padlocked.

Cane bolt: L-shaped bolt that slides into two-holed mounting brackets. Installed vertically to use gravity action.

Use: Devices that keep gates and doors closed but not locked. They can also block gates open.

Cabinet and Furniture Hardware

About Cabinet Hardware

Hardware for cabinets consists of hinges, door catches, and knobs/pulls. Because so many of these items are made in decorative styles, the array of models and quality are vast.

> **Note:** See **Chapter 24** for larger items in this category.

Catches

Types:

> *Friction*
>
> *Magnetic*
>
> *Roller*

Description:

> *Friction:* Consists of a male and female part that work by spring tension similar to roller type. Another version, used to prevent little children from opening cabinets, has a long plastic lever called a *safety catch*.

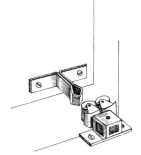

Roller Catch

Magnetic Catch

Magnetic: Part on frame is magnetic; plain metal part of this catch mounts on door.

Roller: One or two rollers set close together, mounted on the cabinet frame, that interlock with projecting part on door, similar to friction type.

Use: Keep cabinet doors shut.

> **Use Tips:** Catches are for lightweight doors only. The magnetic catch is best because it will work in situations where others won't, such as when the door warps and only part of the magnet section is contacted.

The friction catch is good when you don't want any hardware to show. This will be invisible on a **lipped door (see below)**.

About Cabinet Hinges

Cabinet hinges are made for three kinds of doors: lipped, overlay, and flush. The lipped door has a recess cut around the edge. The overlay overlaps the frame opening. The flush door's face fits flush with the face of the framework.

Hinges come in many different styles, sizes, thicknesses, and finishes. Chrome is popular, but there is also plated brass and pure brass as well as antiqued copper and black. Most hinges come carded; the card is used as a template for drilling screw holes.

On a replacement it is best to take the old hinge into the store to ensure getting the correct size. Knobs and pulls are also available in matching styles.

Cabinet Hinges

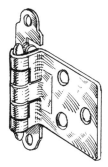

Pivot Hinge

Types:

Pivot hinge

Self-closing hinge

Butterfly hinge

Also Known As: *Self-closing:* S/C hinge

Description:

Pivot: One hinge is mounted on top of the door and one on the bottom, with portions of each hinge bent over and screw-mounted to frame and door. The hinge is concealed.

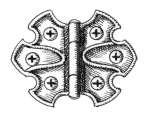

Self-Closing Hinge

Self-closing: Has a spring inside and operates with just a nudge.

Butterfly: When open resembles a butterfly.

Use:

Pivot hinges: Designed for use on the overlay door.

Self-closing: May be used on any door.

Butterfly Hinge

Butterfly: For use on flush doors only. Many people also like to use them on chest lids, where they add a decorative touch.

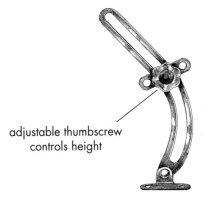

adjustable thumbscrew
controls height

Lid Support

Lid Support

Description: Long, narrow, slotted arm with small hinge on base plate and a sliding screw or thumbscrew on a flange that forms the opposing base plate. Available in a range of sizes around 5" to $6^1/_2$" long and $^1/_2$" to $^3/_4$" wide, sold in left-handed or right-handed versions. Brass or brass-plated steel.

Use: Locking cabinet or chest lids open at infinite positions. Used in conjunction with a regular hinge.

Knobs and Pulls

Description: Knobs and pulls come in a wide variety of styles and finishes. Pulls are handles mounted to doors or drawers with screws or bolts. Knobs may be mounted this way or have a screw built in, sort of like a screw with a knob for a head.

Use: Grasped to open and close cabinet doors.

> **Use Tips:** Small knobs that have screws built in are easier to install than larger ones that require separate screws.

Chest Handles

Description: A metal plate for mounting and a handle, or "bail," for pulling. One type has no screw holes but is designed to be welded or riveted to a chest. Another type is a *trapdoor (hatch cover) ring,* in which the bail, or ring, is smaller and lies in a recess flush with the surface.

Chest Handle

For a narrow box, chest handles may be obtained with narrow plates and larger bails. One manufacturer shows a chest handle with a plate $3^7/_{16}$" long but less than $1^1/_2$" wide.

Use: Handles for opening chests, cabinets, and trapdoors. Used for hatch covers on boats.

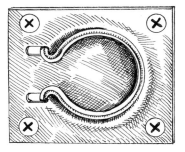

Trapdoor Ring

> **Use Tips:** If you are installing a trapdoor type in a floor, make sure the whole thing is well recessed so no one trips over it.

Flat Hook-and-Eye

Description: Similar to the hardware item of the same name mentioned above **(Chapter 21)**; a two-piece item that is flat, instead of round, and made of decorative material such as brass. The eye is the part that the hook goes into.

Flat Hook-and-Eye

Use: Often used to secure cabinet and chest lids, shutters, and the like, wherever light fastening is all that's required.

> **Use Tip:** The hook can be hooked over a plain screw or nail instead of going into an eye if precision fitting is difficult.

About Casters

Casters come in a variety of styles and for a variety of purposes. They are available to support heavy or lightweight items and the wheels may be hard plastic, rubber, or metal for particular kinds of flooring. For example, hard rubber works best on concrete floors, soft rubber on resilient flooring, and plastic best on carpet. They are available for mounting on hollow as well as solid legs and may turn 360 degrees or lock in place.

Casters come in a variety of finishes from plain to polished metal. They are characterized by wheel size: a 2" caster has wheels 2" in diameter. Other parts of the caster will be sized proportionately, and the larger the wheel, the easier it is to roll.

Stem Caster

Stem Caster

Description: Has a stem mounted above the wheel for insertion in a hollow leg.

Use: For use on any hollow-legged item.

Use Tips: To remove old sockets you can drive a 10-penny nail into the socket until it catches under the top, then pull out with pliers.

Plate Caster

Plate Caster

Description: Flat plate on top with screw holes for mounting.

Use: Use on any items that have solid wood legs that can accept screws.

> **Use Tips:** First drill pilot holes for screws. Before buying a caster make sure the leg is big enough to accept it. If wood is thin, bolts work better.

Ball-Bearing Caster

Description: Plate-type caster with ball bearing instead of a wheel.

Use: Good where headroom is scarce. A ball-bearing caster only adds $1/2$" in height to the piece it's on rather than the 2" on a standard caster.

Ball-Bearing Caster

Ball-type Caster

Also Known As: Shepard (most common brand name)

Description: Ball-like metal wheels come in both plate and stem types. Usually shiny, decorative metal (chrome, brass).

Use: Usually used on furniture where there is carpeting or resilient-type flooring.

Ball-type Caster

Furniture Glides

Description: Wide range of smooth-surfaced metal and plastic designs that attach to the ends of furniture legs either by a built-in nail or screw.

Use: Allows furniture to be pushed over a floor easily.

Furniture Glide

Leg Tips and Carpet Savers

Description: Little cup-shaped plastic or rubber devices that either slide over the ends of furniture legs (leg tips) or sit on the carpet or floor underneath a caster or leg (carpet savers).

Use: Protecting wooden floors or carpets from damage by furniture legs.

Appliance Rollers

Description: Two long, flat devices with about a dozen small plastic wheels linked by an adjustable metal bar. Sold in pairs.

Use: Goes underneath a refrigerator or washing machine to make for easy removal from a recessed space and to prevent scratching floor.

> **$ Buying Tip:** Difficult to find. Used-appliance stores may help if your hardware store does not stock this item.

Drawer Hardware

Types:

> *Drawer track*
>
> *Drawer slides*
>
> *Drawer rollers*

Description: Various types of guides mount either in the center or on the sides of drawers; those on the sides may be either on the bottom, middle, or top edge.

Track: Metal sections mounted on the sides of drawers that interlock with sections mounted inside the drawer cabinet.

Slides: Plastic sections or rollers mounted on drawers or inside cabinets.

Rollers: Small rollers mounted on drawers or inside cabinets.

Use: Allows drawers to slide freely in and out.

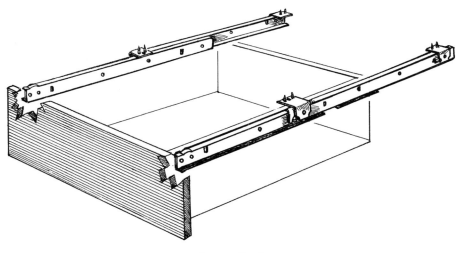

Drawer Track

Door and Window Hardware

About Door Locksets

Doorknobs and locksets, called *locks* here, are either interior or exterior. The exterior type is usually built more ruggedly for security purposes and more care is devoted to their style and finish. Following are some helpful pointers:

There is a tremendous variety of locks, which actually consist of doorknob, lock mechanism which fits into the door, escutcheon or rose (the decorative plate that fits against door), strike plate (plate that goes over the latch hole in the door jamb), and knob.

Locks are sized to fit into holes of a certain size and "backset" — a certain distance from the edge of the door, i.e., measuring from the door edge to midpoint of the knob or handle. Most locks have a $2^3/_8$" backset and are installed in a $2^1/_8$" hole; some are installed in a $1^3/_4$" hole. If the hole is backset $2^3/_8$" but is only $1^3/_4$", it can be enlarged by filling the hole and redrilling. Some locks come with a drill bit for the exact size hole needed.

Some locksets have a backset of 5". Here the bolt on the lockset wouldn't be long enough normally. A link mechanism that goes between the bolt and lock may be used to compensate.

Pin tumbler locks offer the greatest security; five tumblers are better than three.

Locksmiths can rekey your locks so one key will open all locks in a house.

Lock styles and finishes vary greatly and buying a stylish lock does not necessarily mean you'll get quality. You're more likely to get quality by buying a more costly, basic, brass-plated lock.

Heft and examine a number of different locks. Quality will soon become evident. Avoid locks made of lightweight pot metal. Following is a lineup of common interior and exterior locks.

Passage Lock
No locks on either side

Privacy Lock
Push button lock, one side only

Interior Doorknobs and Locksets

Also Known As: Tubular locks, tubular spring-latch locks, non-keyed locks

Types:

Passage lock

Privacy lock

Bathroom lock

Description: Two doorknobs that may have lock buttons in one or both knobs, but no keys, as follows:

Passage: No locking mechanism of any kind, just a latch.

Closet locks: like passage locks but may have smaller knobs or only a turnbutton on the inside.

Privacy: Has lock button on the inside knob only, which unlocks automatically when the knob is turned from the inside.

Bathroom: Like a privacy lock but chrome-plated to blend with bath fittings and fixtures.

Knobs are available that are only for decoration and have no latch mechanism, called *dumb trim.* Many special use–type knobs are available, such as for hospital rooms and patios.

Use: Passage locks are used on bedroom and hall doors where privacy is not absolutely required. Privacy and bathroom locks are used on rooms where locking is required or desired.

> ⚒ **Use Tips:** Privacy locks have a small slot or hole in the center of the outside doorknob that allows the door to be unlocked with a narrow screwdriver in case of an emergency.

Entry Locksets

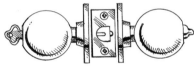

Entry Lockset
key on outside
turn button on inside

Also Known As: Entrance-door locks, exterior cylinder locks, entry locks, tubular spring-latch locks, keyed locks

Description: Two doorknobs that can be locked and unlocked from both sides. Models vary with a keyway or turn button in one or both knobs. Below are four basic types, though there are many specialized types.

1. Lock can be opened and closed from inside while outside stays locked ("all-purpose" or "communication").

2. Lock opened on the inside also unlocks the outside.

3. Unlocked on both sides by twisting a turn button inside ("dormitory" or "motel").

4. Locked with a key on both the inside and outside ("institutional").

Less common variations include models like the *vestibule lock,* which is always open from the inside and locked from the outside, and the *classroom lock,* which is always open on the inside but lockable with a key on the outside. Others include the *service station* and *storeroom* models, each with different locking combinations.

Use: As medium-security entrance-door locks.

> **Use Tips:** Type (1) lock is usually the culprit when people lock themselves out of their homes. On the type (2) lock a drawback is that you can't try the door to see if it is unlocked without unlocking it. The type (4) lock is often used on doors with glass sections because even if a thief breaks the glass he won't be able to open the interior knob without a key. But caution: this type of lock can be hazardous in case you have to get out fast, such as in a fire, and can't find the key. It is recommended to not lock this kind when you are inside the house; the door should have a second, more easily released lock, or else the key should be kept in the lock when you are inside.

All types of locks come with different striking, or latch, mechanisms. Some allow the latch to be depressed when the door is locked, a poor security factor (a credit card can easily be used to open this lock). Better are locks that have a small rod, sometimes called a dead latch (actually a mini-deadbolt), adjacent to the latch that will prevent this.

> **Buying Tip:** Models with just the cylinder lock itself, and no doorknobs, are also available. Keyways and cylinders are all replaceable if you have to change keys for any reason.

Deadbolt Lock

Also Known As: Deadlock

Description: A squarish lock that is mounted on the surface of the door if the lock is the older type (rim lock), or a recessed round one if of modern construction. The essence of a deadbolt lock is that the bolt, once in the strike (the part on the jamb), cannot be released without turning it with a key or turn knob—there is no spring action allowing it to be pushed or pried out of the strike. It is one solid piece of steel.

Deadbolts of both types have horizontal bolts, and the surface type can have a vertical "throw." They also come either as a single or double cylinder, meaning that they either require a key only from the outside (using a turn knob inside) or else require a key from both sides. These cylinders are easily replaceable if you need to change keys.

Use: Security locks on entrance doors. Generally backs up the cylinder lockset as an auxiliary lock. The door or the jamb would have to be pried way out in order to break through.

Use Tips: Never put a lock that can only be opened from the inside by key on a sole interior exit—or else keep a key in the lock.

Buying Tips: Deadbolts that are constructed of cast steel are easiest for a thief to drill through, a favorite method of entry. Deadlocks with an interior core of hardened steel are better.

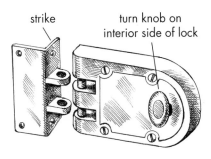

Angle Strike Surface-Mounted Vertical Deadbolt Lock

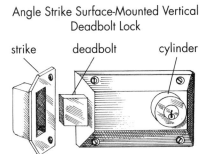

Horizontal Strike Surface-Mounted Deadbolt Lock

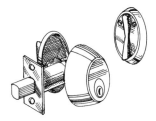

Recessed Deadbolt Lock with turnknob on inside

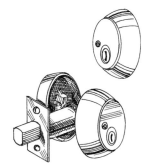

Recessed Deadbolt Lock with two keyways

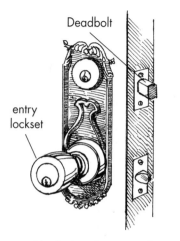

Deadbolt

entry lockset

Deadbolt with Entry Lockset

A thief could conceivably drill out the cylinder on any deadbolt, then use a screwdriver to turn the bolt out. For this there is the *jimmy-proof deadbolt*. The cylinder may be drilled but then a spring-actuated plate will stop further penetration.

Horizontal deadlock bolts come with various "throws," the distance the bolt protrudes from the lock. Sizes are commonly $1/4$", $1/2$", and 1". Theoretically, the more the bolt protrudes, the greater the security, but this is questionable on a wooden door where a well-placed kick could bring the door itself down. On a steel door it would be an entirely different story. In other words, the lock is only as good as the doorframe is solid. Look for heavy steel and brass, and sturdy screws.

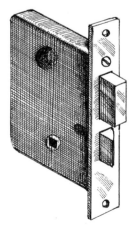

Mortise Lock

Mortise Lock

Description: Combines features of various other locks—the spring latch and the deadbolt. Consists of a flat, rectangular box, which fits into a recess in the door from the edge, and two faceplates (one for each side) containing the knobs, turn knob, and keyholes. Usually contains a deadbolt and a regular strike latch as well as two locking buttons on the side that control the locking settings. Comes left- or right-handed.

Use: Standard house entrance-door lock.

Night Latch

Also Known As: Night lock, slam lock

Description: Mounts on inside surface of door. Large, spring-loaded latch locks automatically when the door is closed.

Use: Light security, typically in addition to another lock such as a mortise or cylinder entrance lock.

Night Latch

Storm- and Screen-Door Hardware

Main Parts:

> Lock mechanism
>
> Door closer
>
> Retainer

Also Known As:

> *Door closer:* Pneumatic cylinder

Description:

> *Lock mechanism:* Consists of small regular knob outside, mounting plates and turn handle inside. May have locking feature from outside.

> *Closer:* Usually a bicycle-pump type consisting of a pneumatic cylinder and plates with screw holes for mounting to door and doorframe. There is usually also an extension spring, sometimes called a *snubber,* which attaches between doorframe and door.

> *Retainer:* Wire chain and spring with mounting brackets.

Pneumatic Door Closer

Use:

> *Lock mechanism:* Open, close, and lock storm door.
>
> *Door closer:* Regulates speed at which door closes. The door should close quickly enough but not slam and be unable to latch. The spring keeps the door from being pulled open too far.
>
> *Retainer:* Prevents damage of door closer, or, in the absence of a door closer, keeps the door from being ripped off its hinges.

Use Tips: Some lock mechanisms come with a flip lever that allows you to lock the door from inside. Locks that operate with keys are also available.

Buying Tips: Storm-door hardware is like window hardware—there are many variations and screw holes on replacement parts must align with the old screw holes. If you have a problem with your storm door, such as the wind always catching it, make sure that the closer used is the right size—they vary according to size and weight of door.

Sliding-Door Hardware

Description: Consists of a top metal track, wheels that attach to the door, and bottom guides (sometimes a track) that attach to the floor. Exterior, or patio, doors are similar but heavier duty. Two doors that slide past each other are *by-pass doors;* doors that slide into the wall are *pocket doors.*

Use: To enable a pair of sliding doors to work.

> **Use Tips:** When part of a sliding door doesn't work properly often all that is needed is a slight hardware adjustment. Some tracks are delicate and may be bent out of shape easily.

> **Buying Tips:** Hardware for sliding doors normally comes in kits containing all parts so that when one part goes bad—say a wheel becomes misshapen—you will probably have to buy all parts. Size is by track thickness. Exterior (patio) types tend to require the original-brand replacement parts.

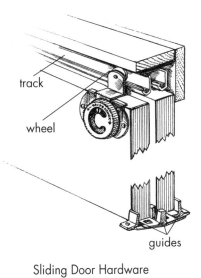

Sliding Door Hardware

Bifold-Door Hardware

Description: Six or seven different pieces of hardware, including hinges, track, top and bottom pivot, snubber, knob, and bottom jamb bracket.

Use: For mounting and using either two- or four-set bifold doors. There is a pivot on the floor that mates with a corresponding socket on the door, or the reverse—socket on the floor, pivot on the door. Four-door set also includes a bracket to align the doors at the bottom when closed.

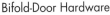

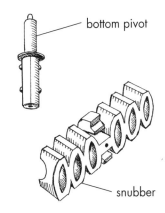

Bifold-Door Hardware

Miscellaneous Door Hardware

Types:

> *Doorstop*
>
> *Peephole*

Also Known As: *Peephole:* Door viewer, viewing eye, safety door viewer

Description:

> *Doorstop:* Metal rod or spring with rubber point that mounts on the wall or floor.

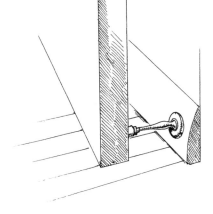

Doorstop

Peephole: Cylinder with internal viewing lens that goes in the center of the door.

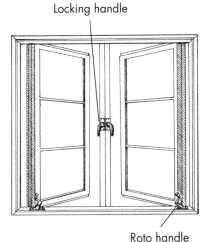

Peephole

Uses:

Doorstop: Keeps doors from banging into wall when opened.

Peephole: Lets home occupants view visitors without opening the door.

Window-Opening Hardware

Typical Parts:

Casement operator for roto handle (opens window)

Casement locking handle (locks window shut)

Casement keeper (handle, above, latches onto keeper)

Double-hung tape balance (rides in track to keep window open at desired position)

Double-hung sash lock (locking mechanism)

Locking handle

Roto handle

Casement Window

Description: There are thousands of different window parts but they can be grouped into hardware for either wood or metal casement windows and hardware for double-hung windows.

 Buying Tips: Since parts vary so much, it is essential to take the old part to the store when getting a replacement.

Glazier's Point

Turn Button

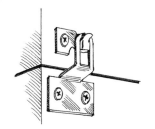

Screen- and Storm-Sash Hanger

Miscellaneous Window Hardware

Types:

Glazier's points, or *push points*

Turn button

Sash lift

Sash (window) handle

Screen- and storm-sash hangers

Storm-sash adjuster

Shutter dog

Also Known As:

Hanger: Hinge hook

Shutter dog: Shutter turnbuckle

Description:

Glazier's points: Tiny flat metal triangles or odd-shaped, pointed pieces with small flaps.

Turn button: Small galvanized or zinc-plated bow-shaped device with a raised turning edge.

Sash lift: Small metal plate with protruding lip.

Sash handle: Small pull handle.

Screen- and storm-sash hangers: Small two-part hanger consists of a hook that goes on the frame and a mating part on the storm window or screen.

Screen- and storm-sash adjuster: A folding leg, one end of which is attached to the window frame, the other to the storm sash.

Shutter dog: Bow-shaped flat metal piece on a center pivot.

Use:

Glazier's points: Pushed into wood window frame to hold glass plate in place prior to applying glazing putty.

Turn button: Retains screen or storm window.

Sash lift: Provides a small fingergrip for raising a window.

Sash handle: Provides handgrip for raising a window.

Storm-sash adjuster: For opening a storm sash to a certain point.

Screen- and storm-sash hangers: For hanging screens or storm windows.

Shutter dog: Holds exterior shutters open.

Drapery Hardware

Types:

Fixed drapery rod

Traverse drapery rod

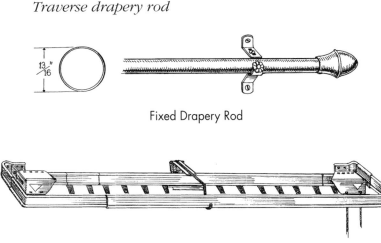

Fixed Drapery Rod

Traverse Drapery Rod

Description:

Fixed rods are hollow metal tubes that are either exposed (in full view) or concealed and come 48" and 60" long. They are also available spring-actuated to fit virtually any dimension.

Traverse rods are similar but come with an opening and closing mechanism controlled by hanging cords.

Use: Hanging drapery and enabling it to be opened and closed.

Use Tips: Accessories for either fixed rods or traverse rods must be matched but are readily available. Fixed rods require hanging rings as they have no mechanism for moving drapes. These must be slightly bigger in diameter than the rod. For traverse rods hooks are used and the hooks must be sized to hook onto eyelets, or hangers, that move along the traverse rod. Hooks come in three basic patterns: *slip-on* (hook goes into an eyelet on the traverse rod or over a plain rod, and a double-ended long piece slides under the heading of the drape); *pin-on* (large hook goes over a rod, and a sharp pin pierces the drapery heading); and *pleater hook* (large hook goes over a rod or into an eyelet, and three or four round-tipped prongs or shanks form pleats when inserted into the drapery heading).

Buying Tip: Fixed rods and traverse rods come in kits complete with fasteners and instructions for installing them.

Curtain Hardware

Description: Commonly lightweight, C-shaped metal channels that may expand, or *telescope,* to fit a window. Not decorative per se. Another version is the *spring-tension rod,* which expands to fit within a window casing and requires no mounting—it is held in place by its own tension. And of course there are just plain metal rods, such as *cafe rods,* which are held by supports designed to go with each type of rod and are generally more decorative than the above two types. Similar to **fixed rod (above)**.

Use: Supports curtains or draperies in a fixed position or allows only limited movement.

> **Buying Tip:** Additional supports are needed for large expanses, such as over 48".

Spring-Tension Curtain Rod

Springs

About Springs

There are literally hundreds of kinds of springs available, but for around-home use three kinds are common: extension, compression, and torsion. Most springs are zinc-plated so they can be used outdoors. Some are painted black enamel, and these are for indoor use only. Chrome-plated springs are also available but are not common.

Springs differ in terms of gauge of wire used and number of coils. On extension springs the heavier the gauge and the more coils, the greater the springs will expand. The quickest way to get the same size replacement spring is to take the one you are replacing to the store for a match. Dealers have boards on which are mounted many different springs and you can match up what you have to what's on the board.

Springs come loose and carded; carded is more costly. Spring assortments can also be bought, but before buying determine that you'll use them—many could go unused in the average household.

Extension Spring

Extension Spring

Description: Wire in a coil shape with ends that have closed loops, hooks, or a variation.

Use: Those with long hooks are useful for getting into tight places, such as attaching a spring to an oven door—the long hook enables you to attach it more easily. Another extension spring useful on a screen door is one with a threaded eyebolt, which you can turn to make the door open and close with more or less tension. Since extension springs come with hooked and closed ends, flexibility of use is ensured—you can either hook the spring onto the item or vice versa.

Compression Spring

Description: Wire in a coil but, unlike the extension spring, it does not have hooks or loops at the ends; ends are either plain or cut off.

Use: Used where you want to push parts together such as on wheels, shafts, and toys. Mostly a replacement spring. Compression springs with squared-off ends are useful where you need a spring that lies flat between two parts of a machine or toy.

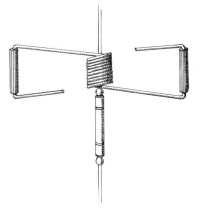

Torsion Spring

Torsion Spring

Description: Two-armed spring with the arms extended out, wing-like, several inches.

Use: Used only occasionally. It is slipped over the top of a hinge pin to give a door a spring-closing action. A similar type is a *door-closer, coil door spring,* or *gate spring,* which goes diagonally over the gap between the hinged side of a door and the wall and is attached with clamps or plates at both ends.

Chain and Cable

About Chain

Chain comes in around forty different varieties, but most of your needs will be filled by the small selection commonly available in stores, as described here. Sections are usually cut from reels to your order, though some decorative chain comes packaged. Size denominations vary from type to type, so study the label on the reel or package for important technical information.

Chain may be put into two groups: chain whose primary purpose is strength and chain whose main purpose is decoration. Whatever type you buy, however, check to make sure it's strong enough for the job at hand. All chain is classified and marked according to its *working load limit,* meaning what kind of stress may be applied before the chain snaps. Most are specifically marked "not for overhead lifting."

Load limits vary according to the thickness of the chain and the metal it's made of. So, for example, #10 (1" long links) brass jack chain, which is decorative, has a working load limit of 34 pounds. Grade 30-proof coil chain, however, in about the same size but made of steel, has a load limit of 800 pounds. And a cam-alloy version has a limit of 5,100 pounds in the same size. Check the label of the chain container or the manufacturer's catalog for the chain's working load limit.

> **General Use Tips:** Links of most lighter chain can be pried apart with fingers or pliers. Use pliers to crimp the links shut.

In addition to the specific chains detailed below, which are mainly available from reels, there are packaged chains designed for specific purposes such as dog runners, hanging porch swings, and various vehicular jobs. Chain also comes in pails, boxes, drums, and bags.

For safety, you should observe the following:

- Follow load limits on a chain—don't overload it. Dealers can supply load limits from charts they have. However, it is okay to load it right up to its limit.

- Don't use a chain for overhead lifting unless it is specified for that use.

- Don't apply tension if a chain is twisted.

- Pull a chain gradually from an at-rest position—don't jerk it.

- Don't use a chain that looks damaged.

Bead Chain

Description: Hollow, round metal beads joined by dumbbell-shaped connectors. Beads may also be elliptically shaped. Comes in chrome-, brass-, and nickel-plated finishes.

Use: Used for decorative purposes around the home and as lamp pulls.

Bead Chain

> $ **Buying Tips:** The main advantage of bead chain is that it will not kink or tangle. You can twist it every which way and it will fall out straight.

> $ **Buying Tips:** At local stores you are likely to get only a couple of sizes of bead chain, plus packaged chain for lamp pulls. Hardware stores carry catalogs that list manufacturers from whom you can get a much wider selection. You can buy connectors separately, such as when you want to lengthen a bead chain.

Decorative Chain

Decorative Chain

Also Known As: Decor chain

Description: Lightweight chain available in a variety of handsome finishes, including brass and colors—antique white, antique copper, and black. Loops are generally large ovals of wire.

Use: Hanging lamps, plants, and for hanging on draperies and other decorative effects.

Double-Loop Chain

Also Known As: Weldless, Inco (brand name), Tenso (brand name), Bowtie

Description: Lightweight steel links that are knotted into long double loops for linkage instead of being welded. Sizes run from No. 5 (smallest) though 0 to 8/0 (largest). A *single-loop,* or *lock link* version is available, primarily for use in machinery.

Use: Household jobs from decoration to shelf supports. Among the strongest of the decorative chains. Heavier sizes—over 1/0—can be used to hang hammocks and playground equipment.

Proof Coil Chain

Description: Strongest steel chain of welded, slightly oblong links. Comes in galvanized, plain steel, and zinc finishes. Comes in four grades: Grade 30 (most common), 40, 70 ("high test"), and 80 (made of alloy steel, with the highest load limits—up to 80,000 pounds). The $5/16$" size Grade 30 has a working load limit of 1,900 pounds. The fractional sizes refer to the diameter of the steel.

Use: Very heavy pulling jobs where motorized equipment is involved, such as in agriculture or for towing cars.

Jack Chain

Jack Chain

Description: A strong decorative chain of varying load limits made of twisted figure-eight links. Comes in hot-galvanized, brass-plated, bright zinc, and solid brass, and in single and double versions.

Uses: Often used for functions where decoration and light support are needed, such as for hanging large plants, signs, and children's toys.

Welded General Use Chain

Straight-Link Machine Chain

Types:

Coil chain

Machine chain

Passing link chain

Description: Similar to but not as strong as **proof coil chain** (above). Material is less than $1/4$" thick. Sizes are measured in gauges, from No. 4 (smallest—inside of links about half an inch long) through 3, 2, 1, and on to 1/0 to 5/0 (largest—inside of links about an inch long).

Coil: Longest link of these three. Available in straight-link and twist-link styles.

Machine: Slightly shorter links. Also available in straight-link and twist-link styles.

Passing link: Slightly rounded links which prevent binding and kinking.

Use: Wherever a strong chain is needed. Commonly used on agricultural implements, tailgates, overhead doors, security purposes, general utility.

Safety Chain

Safety Chain

Also Known As: Plumber's chain

Description: Flat, stamped brass chain of oval links that resist entanglement.

Use: Used by plumbers in toilet tanks (as link between flush rod and ball valve) and as a general utility chain. It is available in bright zinc and solid brass and may also be used for decorative purposes.

Sash Chain

Sash Chain

Also Known As: Weldless flat chain

Description: Flat, teardrop-shaped stamped links that appear folded over one another.

Use: Good replacement material for sash cords on double-hung windows as it rides over window pulleys easily, and for tub and basin stoppers. Often used to hold small animals.

> **Buying Tips:** Sash chain comes in plain metal and bronze, but if you live in an area where sea air is present, sash chain is inadvisable—it can rust out.

Plastic Chain

Description: Available in colors, usually red and yellow, and in light as well as heavy chain shapes.

Use: Decorative jobs such as hanging light fixtures, and drape accessories.

About Chain Accessories

Generally, accessories for chain are either designed to connect chain sections permanently or temporarily. There are a couple of other useful attachment/accessory pieces that stand alone.

Temporary Chain Connectors

Types:

> S-hook
>
> Clevis slip hook
>
> Clevis grab hook
>
> Lap link
>
> Quick link

S-Hook

Also Known As: *Lap Link:* Repair link

Description:

> *S-hook:* Open-ended metal link shaped like the letter S.
>
> *Clevis slip hook:* Looks like a hefty fishhook.
>
> *Clevis grab hook:* Shaped like a clevis slip hook but is narrower.
>
> *Lap link:* Partially open link that looks like it has almost been cut in half sidewise.
>
> *Quick link:* Link with a gap on one side that has a nut on one end and threads on the other.

Clevis Slip Hook

Clevis Grab Hook

Lap Link

Use:

S-hook: Connecting chain sections; they are crimped shut with pliers after being hooked onto the sections, but they are not designed for anything that requires a high degree of safety, such as swings and other play equipment.

Clevis slip hook: Looping chain around different-sized items, such as tree stumps, and pulling them out; in effect it allows you to make a chain lasso. The clevis (pin) end of the slip hook is secured to the end of the chain while the chain is slipped through the hook to form the lasso loop.

Clevis grab hook: Works like a clevis slip hook but its narrowness allows it to lock onto one link.

Lap link: Can be used wherever life or limb does not depend on link's integrity to link two sections of any chain together.

Quick link: Similar to lap, a fast but not the strongest solution to linking.

> **Use Tips:** S-hooks come in various strengths, and for safety the hook should be the same strength as the chain links it's being used on.

Permanent Chain Connectors

Types:

Connecting link

Cold shut

Description:

Connecting link: These look like individual links cut in half sidewise, with one half of the link containing rivet projections and the other holes to accept rivets.

Cold shut: Open-ended link device designed to be hammered shut.

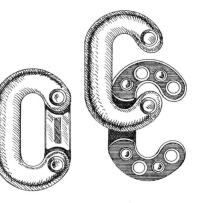

Connecting Link

Miscellaneous Chain Accessories

Types:

Ring

Snap

Description:

Ring: Heavy welded rings of steel.

Snap: Small metal device with spring-loaded locking device available in a variety of models, combining four features:

    Swivelling or fixed *(solid)*

    Eyes: round or rectangular *(strap)*

Cold Shut

Double-Ended Bolt Snap

Snap Types: large latch *(cap);* sliding bolt; flat strap *(spring);* lever on outside of a ring *(trigger);* or solid half-circle catch *(animal tie);* and other special ones for boats, horse harnesses, and dog leashes.

Snaps on one or both ends *(double-ended)*

Uses:

Ring: A variety of chain linking jobs with other connectors or snaps.

Snap: A variety of temporary connecting jobs, such as a gate closer.

> **Use Tip:** Most of these accessories can be used with rope as well.

Cable

Description: Multiple small strands of wire woven together to form a strong rope. Many different types and strengths. *Aviation cable* is the smoothest and strongest.

Use: Dog runs, anchoring trees, fences, and satellite dishes, and so on. Cable does not stretch and is generally stronger than rope and easier to use than chain.

> **Use Tip:** Cable clamps, a type of small U-bolt with a horizontal bar, are necessary for securing cable.

Wire and Wire Products

Wire

Description: May be *single-strand drawn wire* or *twisted strand;* the first is a single piece of wire, the latter three or four strands twisted together. Both types come galvanized for outdoor use (short lengths are available in copper and aluminum too) and both may be had in various gauges, specifically 10, 12, 14, 16, and 20. Wire also comes plastic-coated. *Aviation wire* is the strongest—cut it with a **cold chisel (Part I, Chapter 2)**. Very thin wire may be called *hobby* or *flower wire*. *Picture wire* is woven cable of medium strength.

Use:

> *Twisted:* Most often used, and commonly used as guy-wire support and for dog runs. In the very light gauges—18 and 20—it can be used for hanging pictures or tying Christmas wreaths.
>
> *Plastic-coated wire* is used for clothesline.
>
> *Aviation wire* or *cable* is for supporting the heaviest objects, such as trees or satellite dishes.

Screening

Also Known As: Bug screening, insect screening

Description: Screening is made in four different materials: aluminum, galvanized steel, bronze, and fiberglass. It is sold by the foot in a variety of widths, 24", 28", 32", and 36"—up to 4' wide—as well as in precut lengths and widths by the package. Screening is normally bright or galvanized metal, but green, gray, and gold are also available. Fiberglass may be gray, green, or charcoal. Solar screening is also available. This is made of a material and mesh that limit the amount of sun that can get through. Finally, you can buy small, prepackaged sections of screen for patching purposes.

Use: Permits open windows while providing a barrier to insects, leaves, and pets.

> **Use Tips:** It is a simple matter to install your own screening with a pair of **C-clamps (Part I, Chapter 9)** to hold screening to the frame while you use a special **screening tool (below)** to roll it into the grooved edges of the frame.

> **Buying Tips:** Screening bought by the foot costs a lot less than precut material.

Screening Tool

Screening Tool

Description: Cylindrical handle with blade-type wheels on each end; one wheel is convex, the other concave.

Use: Installing screening in frames with channels for this purpose.

Hardware Cloth

Also Known As: Wire mesh

Description: A kind of rugged galvanized, welded, and woven screening that is relatively flexible and comes in rolls of widths ranging from 2' to 4'. It also comes in various meshes, stated 2×2, 4×4 mesh, etc., which refers to the number of squares per inch, usually ranging from 2 to 8 mesh. As the number of squares per inch increases, the gauge of the metal gets thinner.

Use: Various: as a sifter of sand, cement, topsoil; a pet cage material; as a fence wherever you want extra security. It is frequently used to keep birds, bats, and squirrels out of houses and rabbits and deer out of gardens.

> **Use Tip:** You can cut hardware cloth quite easily with tin snips (Part I, Chapter 6).

> **Buying Tip:** Hardware cloth is sold by the foot.

Hardware Cloth

Wire Netting

Also Known As: (if openings are hexagonal) Chicken wire, poultry netting, hexagonal netting

Description: Galvanized wire woven—not welded—into a netting that has large squares or hexagons—1" or 2" wide—and comes in various heights up to 6' and lengths of 50' to

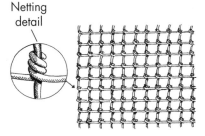

Netting detail

Wire Netting

150'. The wire is of a lighter gauge than **hardware cloth (above)**. Some brands have horizontal lines of wire through the lower hexagons to make a tighter mesh.

Use: Protection against encroachment of small animals on property; for example, installation on a split-rail fence as a way to keep a dog confined.

> **$ Buying Tips:** Though not as strong as hardware cloth, netting is very inexpensive and can serve well for many jobs.

Miscellaneous Hanging Hardware

Hinged Tool Holder

Also Known As: Broom hook

Description: "S"-shaped hook mounted as a hinge on a small plate. Plastic coated.

Use: Hanging light or average weight brooms, light shovels, hand tools, and the like. Items can be hung by the straight handle, as the holder design uses gravity to hold items in place.

> **$ Buying Tip:** Handy in confined areas such as closets or hallways where it is good to avoid installing hooks that stick out from the wall.

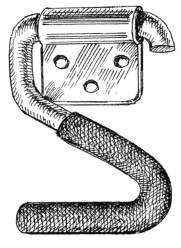

Hinged Tool Holder

Coat and Hat Hook

Description: Cast or solid metal (steel, aluminum, brass, or bronze) or wire double hook, with a short one on the bottom and a long one on top, and an integral wall plate with screw holes.

Use: Hanging coats (small hook) and hats (big hook).

> ✂ **Use Tip:** If you are prone to hanging many heavy pieces of clothing on a hook, be sure to get a solid and not cast metal hook. Otherwise it will bend.

Peg-Board® Fixtures

Description: Various shapes but designed to mount in holes in **Peg-Board (Part VI, Chapter 47).**

Use: Hanging a wide variety of items from tools to condiment containers.

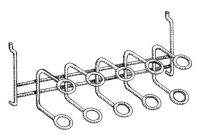

Peg-Board® Holder

> ✂ **Use Tips:** Hooks must be sized according to the thickness of the Peg-Board—$1/4$" Peg-Board takes $1/4$" fixtures, $1/8$" Peg-Board takes $1/8$" fixtures.

Peg-Board® Bracket

Peg-Board® Clip

Picture-Hanging Hardware

Types:

Picture hooks

Adjustable sawtooth hanger

Adhesive hanger

Hardwall hanger

Mirror hanger

Also Known As: *Picture hook:* Nail hanger

Description:

Picture hooks: Metal fasteners with holes for driving nails through. Come in various sizes and in plain and ornamental styles.

Adjustable sawtooth hanger: Piece of metal with serrations on one edge, nailed onto frame.

Adhesive anchor: Hook secured to adhesive strip that, in turn, is secured to wall.

Hardwall hanger: Consists of a hook with pins capable of being driven into hard material such as masonry and plaster, with the four-pin model capable of holding up to 100 pounds.

Mirror hanger: Small offset clip with screw hole in one end.

Use: Hanging pictures, mirrors, etc. of various weights.

Plain Picture Hook

Ornamental Picture Hook

Mirror Hanger

> **Use Tips:** Picture hooks needn't be driven into studs. They may be secured to plaster, plasterboard, and wood materials directly. To keep plaster from flaking, a small piece of transparent tape can be applied to the area where the nail is to be driven.

Hanging Plant Track

Plant-Hanging Hardware

Types:

Brackets

Chain

Macramé

Shelves

Track

Description:

Brackets: Decorative scroll hook that mounts on wall and has a small swiveling hook on the end. This allows plant to be rotated toward the sunlight.

Chain: This is decorative chain, either metal or plastic. It is secured with other hardware to the plant and ceiling. See **chain (Chapter 28)**.

Macramé: Fancy woven rope to which plant is secured at one end; the other end of the macramé is secured to a screw eye, toggle bolt, or other hanger.

Shelves: These may be as various as shelves are, but the brackets used to support them are fancier than most.

Decorative Scroll-Type Bracket

Swivel Hanger

Track: Formed metal pieces into which sliding sections are inserted and to which, in turn, hooks or swivel hangers are secured.

Use: To hang potted as well as other kinds of plants.

Shelf Supports

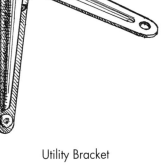

Utility Bracket

Types:

> *Utility brackets*
>
> *Standards and brackets*
>
> *Pilasters and clips*
>
> *Pin and hole*

Also Known As:

> *Utility:* Steel angle bracket.
>
> *Pilasters:* Pillars, standards.
>
> *Pin:* Plug-in clips, shelf supports, pin clips, plug-in shelf supports, clips, shelf rests, plugs.

Description:

> *Utility brackets:* L-shaped metal forms with a center ridge and screw holes for securing to walls. One leg is longer than the other. Usually gray, but also gold and black. Flat versions, called *braces,* are available. A newer version is larger and has a hooked part in front and below the shelf for a closet pole *(shelf and closet pole combination);* it has a diagonal brace that goes from the front down to the bottom of the vertical part in the rear. Fancy versions are available with some scrollwork or in solid wood.

Fancy Shelf Bracket

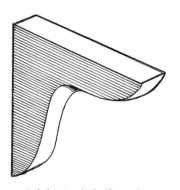

Solid Wood Shelf Bracket

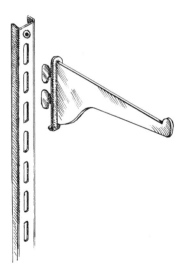

Standard and Bracket Shelf Support

Standards and brackets: C-shaped, long pieces of strong metal, with many small vertical slots, that are mounted on a wall. Brackets, which come in various lengths from 4" to 18" for corresponding shelf widths, have hook-shaped sections that slip into the slots and enable the brackets to support the shelves that are laid across them.

Pilasters: Shallow C-shaped light metal standards with horizontal slots that are placed in the sides of the cabinet or bookcase with small, V-shaped metal clips that snap into the vertical standard. Made in two versions: for surface mounting and for recessed mounting.

Pins: May be metal or plastic. Very small piece with plug on one side and flat support on the other, of various designs, including a rounded one called *spoon type.* Pins fit into predrilled $\frac{1}{4}$" holes in the sides of the cabinet or bookcase to support shelf ends.

Use: As the name suggests, shelf supports do just that—support shelving. All are adjustable except the utility brackets. The first two are mounted on the wall behind the shelves; the second two are mounted on the walls or sides at the ends of the shelves.

Utility: Mounted on wall studs with shelves laid across them and screwed down. They are considered strictly for utility in basements and garages. Not adjustable.

Standards and brackets: Mounted directly on walls and usually considered more decorative.

Pilasters: Mounted inside cabinets and bookcases at the ends of the shelves. Clips then fit into slots at any convenient position. When recessed can be used in the finest cabinets.

Pins: Fit into holes drilled inside bookcase or cabinet sides, with shelves resting directly on them. Adjustment limited to the positions of predrilled holes, so you want a lot of holes.

Use Tips: *Standards and brackets:* For better holding mount these on studs. You can use any kind of shelving that fits across the brackets. Shelf height can be varied simply by moving brackets on the standards, enabling you to accommodate shorter or taller items. Standards may be mounted with **hollow wall fasteners (Chapter 23)** if only light items are going to be supported, but anchor in studs with screws if heavy items are going to be supported; heavy items could pull light anchors from walls.

Pilasters: These are made of both aluminum and steel; when maximum strength is needed, use steel. Shelf length should be on the short side.

Pins: Drilling a series of $1/4$" holes in a straight line is not easy. For best results, make a template for hole drilling.

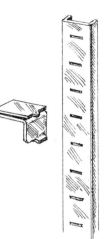

Pilaster and Clip Shelf Support

Buying Tips: *Utility:* For inexpensive shelf supports choose these.

Standards and brackets: These are more costly than utility brackets. They come in a variety of finishes. The standards and brackets of different companies are sometimes interchangeable but usually they're not.

Pins: Perhaps the simplest and least expensive adjustable shelf system.

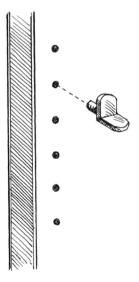

Pin-Type Shelf Support

CHAPTER

31

Miscellaneous Hardware

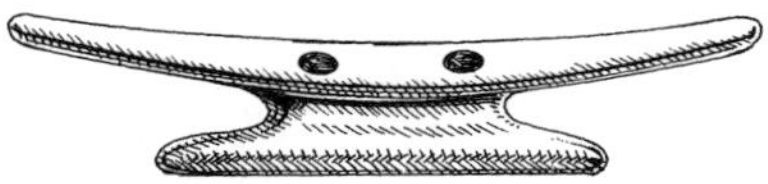

Cleat

Description: Long, narrow metal piece with screw holes on flat part in center for anchoring on wall and with ends raised slightly. Various lengths. A rope hook, which has a flat part with screw holes, is used to hold the coiled rope.

Use: Quick tying of rope to cleat from flagpoles or window blinds and the like.

Cleat

> **Use Tip:** The larger models are easier to use.

Engine Hoist

Description: Two sets of pulleys, usually three in one and four in the other, connected by a long rope that is threaded through the pulleys; each set of pulleys has a hook or hooking device.

Use: Obviously, as its name implies, for hoisting heavy objects. However, this is not limited to engines. Smaller models are useful for raising bicycles for storage to the ceiling of a garage or hallway, for example, or when installing heavy items in holes that are filled with cement and must be supported until it sets.

Siding Wedges

Siding Wedges

Description: Small aluminum wedges.

Use: Inserted under clapboards or shingles to allow air to circulate, thereby eliminating moisture and eventually preventing peeling paint.

Line Tightener

Line Tightener

Description: Small bullet-like cylinder with small funnel inserted in one end, ball bearings inside, and a large loop handle extending from its middle. Made of cast aluminum.

Use: Adjusting laundry lines. The line is threaded through the cylinder, which grabs onto it when the line is pulled tight and releases it when it is loose. The other end of the line is tied to the loop handle.

Padlock

Description: Small metal lock that is not mounted but attaches temporarily to hasps, lockers, or between links of chain. May be made of brass, plates of steel, or hardened or stainless steel. Opens either with a key or combination of numbers; some of the better models that require keys are called *tubular cylinder locks*.

Use: Temporary locking, both interior and exterior.

Use Tips: Lubricate often if used outside. Tubular cylinder locks offer the ability to have key changes without buying a new lock, a useful characteristic if many people have keys to the same lock.

Buying Tips: Domestic makes tend to be stronger, and hardened or stainless-steel locks are the strongest. The five-pin lock mechanism is the best.

General Materials

Adhesives, Sealers, and Caulk

About Adhesives

Adhesives and glues (the former generally refers to man-made products, the latter to natural ones) can be confusing because of their overlapping uses. They can generally be divided into products primarily used for wood and products used for other materials. Another source of confusion is that the term *glue* is used generically.

Adhesives for Wood

Types:

Casein glue

Clear cement

Hide glue

Hot melt glue

Plastic resin adhesive

Waterproof adhesive

White glue

Woodworker's glue

Also Known As:

Hot melt: Glue stick

Plastic resin: Urea resin, urea-formaldehyde adhesive, PRG

Waterproof: Resorcinol

White: PVA (polyvinyl acetate, polyvinyl resin)

Woodworker's: Yellow glue, carpenter's glue, aliphatic glue, aliphatic resin glue

Description:

Casein: Comes as a powder that you mix with water. Has a heavy consistency, clearish or brown.

Clear cement: Clear liquid adhesive. Sold in small tubes.

Hide: One part liquid or flake.

Hot melt: 2" to 4" long sticks sold by the box or package.

Plastic resin: Powdered material mixed with water.

Waterproof: Brown powdered material mixed with water.

White: One part white liquid glue that dries clear. Usually sold in soft plastic squeeze bottles. Very common, such as Elmer's Glue-All, a popular brand.

Woodworker's: One part yellowish liquid glue. Sold in soft plastic squeeze bottles. Relatively thick.

Use:

Casein: Good gap-filling characteristic for furniture with loose joints that must be filled. Stains wood and may attract mold. Good on high-moisture and oily woods such as teak.

Clear cement: For lighter wood and paper-porous materials. Somewhat water resistant.

Hot melt: Extruded by an **electric glue gun (Part I, Chapter 14)**. Excellent general-purpose, fast-setting adhesive particularly suited for complicated fits without clamping, such as household repairs and crafts using a variety of materials.

Hide: Traditional furniture glue, for both construction and repair, though not waterproof and with a longer "set up" time than white or yellow glue.

Plastic resin: Any kind of interior wood. Water resistant.

Waterproof: Designed for gluing wood indoors, resists chemicals and temperature changes. Good for wooden bowls and trays.

White: Excellent general-use glue, including wood, but not moisture or heat resistant and too thin for some jobs. Thinned with water can be used as an edge-sealer. Tends to run—not gap-filling. Medium strength.

Woodworker's: Strong glue, good and easy to use for general indoor woodworking jobs. Medium heat and moisture resistance. Excellent gap-filling characteristics.

Use Tips: Read adhesive labels very carefully. Be sure to use as much adhesive as needed to ensure total coverage (it should squeeze out of the joints), and try to match the adhesive closely to the usage. Clamping is necessary with most adhesives. Mix two-part glues very carefully.

Buying Tips: Glue is cheaper when bought in the larger-sized containers. For all-around use every household should have a bottle of either white or yellow glue around.

Adhesives for Other Uses

Types:

Acrylic resin adhesive

Anaerobic adhesive

Contact cement

Cyanoacrylate adhesive

Epoxy adhesive

Mastic adhesive

Urethane adhesive

Also Known As:

Anaerobic: Liquid lock washer, thread-locking compound

Cyanoacrylate: Instant glue, super glue

Mastic: Construction adhesive, construction mastic, Liquid Nails®, panel adhesive

Description:

Acrylic resin: Two-part adhesive that sets in less than a minute without clamping. Will adhere even if surface is oily.

Anaerobic: One-part adhesive that cures without air. Common brand is Loc-Tite®, which has almost become a generic term.

Contact cement: Heavy, sticky adhesive that is allowed to become tacky before surfaces are bonded.

Cyanoacrylate: One-part clear glue that bonds items instantly with just a drop or two. Made for either porous or nonporous surfaces.

Epoxy: Two-part material consisting of a catalyst and hardener. Available in clear, metallic, and white. Often sold in two-tube syringe. Not to be confused with **epoxy putty (Part VIII, Chapter 60)**, which is for filling holes and patching pipes.

Mastic: A general term applied to any thick adhesive, especially asphalt, rubber, or resin-based, thick, doughy material. Usually sold in cartridges used in **caulking guns (below)** as well as in cans or tubes for application by **notched trowel (Part VII, Chapter 51).** Includes rubbery, all-purpose adhesive.

Urethane: One-part, multipurpose, expensive adhesive that requires at least 24 hours to set.

Use:

Acrylic resin: Waterproof; good for repairs to two dissimilar materials, exterior or interior. Excellent for filling gaps and extremely strong. Mix to preference for job. Cleans up with acetone. Sold with syringe.

Anaerobic: Good for sealing nuts and bolts that are subject to vibration and otherwise tend to loosen, such as on machinery, doorknobs, or eyeglasses.

Contact cement: Bonds on contact (after it becomes tacky) and is a favorite material for bonding plastic laminate countertops and veneers. Also used to secure hardboard to metal. Applied with a paint brush or roller.

Cyanoacrylate: One version of this glue instantly bonds all kinds of nonporous materials like metal and glass instantly and another bonds porous materials—cardboard, leather, etc. Dangerous to use due to instant bonding quality. Not gap-filling.

Epoxy: For bonding just about anything to anything—masonry, metal, plastic—inside or outside the house. Waterproof, oil-resistant, strong. Excellent for china repairs. Difficult cleanup with acetone.

Mastic: Heavy-duty. Bonding paneling, flooring, drywall, or ceiling tiles to wood, metal, or masonry. Different formulations are made for different types of materials.

Urethane: Can be used anywhere you would use an epoxy, including wood. Can be applied with electric glue gun, brush, or as a stick. Waterproof, very stainable, slightly elastic, and almost invisible.

Use Tips: Make sure surfaces to be bonded are clean and dry. Most contact cements are dangerously volatile and should be used with caution. On top of that, once the two pieces being glued are put together, they cannot be repositioned.

Buying Tips: When you have a job that you can't imagine a glue doing, think epoxy. Some rubbery mastics labeled for special uses are actually all-purpose adhesives handy for most household and plumbing repair or sealing jobs. Keep some on hand.

Blacktop Sealer

Also Known As: Driveway sealer

Description: Heavy black liquid with coal tar or neoprene base. Ordinarily comes in 5-gallon cans but also available in smaller containers as a *crack patcher*.

Use: To renew the appearance of asphalt driveways and to provide a waterproof coating that also protects against oil and other staining materials. Also for sealing small cracks.

> **Use Tips:** Blacktop sealer can be applied with brush, roller, or push broom. Using a roller on a stick or a push broom makes the job easier.

> **Buying Tips:** Blacktop sealer can vary in quality greatly; poor-quality material can be as thin as water. The thicker the material, the better.

Blacktop Patcher

Also Known As: Cold patcher, cold-mix asphalt

Description: Chunky black material with the consistency of very soft tar. Comes ready to use in various-sized bags; also available in standard 10.5-ounce caulk cartridges.

Use: Repair cracks and holes in asphalt driveways; used to pave small walks.

> **Use Tips:** Cold-mix patcher is poured in place and then tamped to a solid density. Driving a car back and forth over a small patch is one good way to compress it, or use a heavy lawn roller.

Caulk

Also Known As: Sealant, sealer

Caulking Cartridge

Description: Elastomeric (flexible) and adhesive goo of various materials and colors most often sold in 6-ounce squeeze tubes or 10–11 ounce, 8" long cartridges made to be used with a **caulking gun (below)**. May or may not be paintable; may or may not be mildew-resistant; more or less flexible or adhesive depending on formulation and quality. Sold either by binder material or by specialized use. The terms "caulk" and "sealant" are interchangeable and are used differently by each manufacturer. Some of the common binders and combinations are:

Silicone caulk

Siliconized acrylic latex caulk

Silicone latex caulk

Acrylic or vinyl latex caulk

Latex caulk

Butyl rubber caulk

Polyurethane (also known as *urethane*) *caulk*

Rope caulk (also known as *caulking cord*)

Neoprene (also known as *rubber adhesive*) *caulk*

Use: Filling gaps or sealing between a wide variety of materials. Each kind has a different degree of flexibility, resistance, and adhesion. General use caulk is used to seal out water and/or air or just to fill in gaps around the house. Specialized uses run from driveway repair to roof repair to duct and gutter work. *Liquid caulk* is for sealing small cracks. General purpose caulks are listed under **Buying Tips.**

All replace the old-fashioned limestone-and -linseed oil product called putty. Following are some special use caulks listed by main ingredient:

Butyl rubber caulk: For metal-to-metal or metal-to-masonry joints (gutters, window and door frames, etc.).

Neoprene caulk: For metal-to-metal, metal-to-masonry, and masonry-to-masonry joints (driveway/foundation joints, window and door frames, foundations, etc.), plumbing and miscellaneous household repairs.

Polyurethane caulk: For masonry-to-masonry joints, highly stressed joints (driveway joints, marine construction).

Rope caulk: For temporary use and for large gaps. Applied by hand. Often called by the brand name Mortite®.

Use Tips: Experiment with the kind of caulk you find easiest to use. Have plenty of water and rags or paper towels around for quick cleanup. Fill extra-large gaps part way with foam rubber, fiberglass insulation, or **oakum (Part VIII, Chapter 60)** first to keep the caulked part relatively thin. Remember to have a long, thin nail on hand to puncture a new tube top, and a thick nail or plastic cap to seal it when you are done.

Buying Tips: In general, get the good stuff and avoid the cheap stuff. There are plenty of specialized caulks that are worthwhile for their particular purposes. Read the labels carefully. Always note whether a caulk is labeled paintable.

Among the general purpose caulks, there are some basic price and quality differences as ingredients (silicone, acrylic or vinyl compounds, and latex binders) are mixed in various recipes by different manufacturers under confusing names. Ultimately, price may be the best indication of quality as it relates to flexibility, durability, and adhesion (you need to decide which qualities are most important).

As with paints, the less expensive stuff has more water and filler in it. The cheap stuff is going to peel away or crack in a couple of years while the better stuff is going to last for decades, though some "lesser" quality caulks might be more suitable for a particular job than those of "greater" quality, such as filling small holes, depending on the manufacturer.

Listed here are the most basic formulas, with the most generally durable at the top:

100% silicone caulk: The most durable, flexible, water-repellent, and adhesive of all caulk products, but it cannot be painted (it is offered clear and in a range of colors), is a little harder to work with (because it is so sticky, though it doesn't stick to some materials), is slightly toxic in its uncured state (and cleans up with mineral spirits), and is often more than twice the cost of all other caulks. It is typically guaranteed for 50 years or even life. Best all-purpose caulk, especially for bathtubs. Worth the price.

Siliconized acrylic latex caulk: A hybrid of the lesser and greater types of caulk listed here, with some of the benefits and drawbacks of both. Most likely a general-purpose caulk. 15–35 year life.

Silicone latex caulk: Good adhesion and flexibility (depending on the brand) make this a common exterior general purpose caulk. 15-year life.

Acrylic or vinyl latex caulk: Suitable as a spackling compound for small holes and cracks prior to painting. Often marketed for its adhesive qualities or as a general purpose caulk. May be marketed as *painter's caulk.* Good for 10 to 15 years exterior use, longer indoors.

Latex caulk: Easily applied, easily cleaned up, inexpensive. May not be very flexible after a short time. May be marketed as *painter's caulk.* Best for stress-free interior use. Five- to 10-year life.

Accessories include different-sized *caulk tips, cartridge nozzles,* and the money- and caulk-saving *cartridge caps,* all worthwhile. Always avoid "bargain" caulks. They aren't!

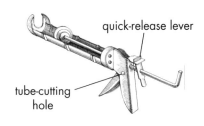

Caulking Gun

Caulking Gun

Description: Metal device about a foot long with a trigger handle and an L-shaped rod coming out the back. When the trigger is squeezed the rod is forced forward and squeezes caulk out of the cartridge in a ratchet or spring-pressure action. A cordless electric model is also available.

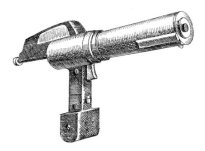

Cordless Caulking Gun

Use: Applying caulk and sealant from standard 10.1-ounce cartridges. This is the only way such cartridges can be used.

Use Tips: Keep the caulking gun moving evenly as caulk is forced out the tip of the cartridge to get an even "bead." Remove caulk tubes after use and clean gun.

> **$ Buying Tips:** Get a model with a little lever that releases easily, with one hand. The choice between a ratchet action and spring-pressure action is one of personal preference. Both have points that tend to wear out and are a little hard to use because of the constant squeezing. Definitely get a model with a metal spike attached for piercing the liner seals on new caulk cartridges—a tremendous help. Also look for models with new tube cutting holes. For smoothest and steadiest flow, use the cordless electric caulking gun.

Caulk Smoothing Tool

Also Known As: Caulk finishing tool

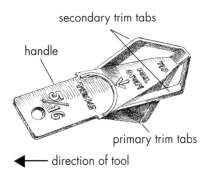

Caulk Smoothing Tool

Description: Small, open-winged, plastic trowel-like item with a slight scoop shape. Sold in a kit with two sizes ($1/4$" or $5/16$") and a specially shaped flat piece for cleaning it out. An alternative, a *caulk and putty square,* is a flat piece of plastic with different-sized rounded corners.

Use: Perfect smoothing of freshly caulked or glazed joints without using your finger or a plastic spoon. Works by trimming excess.

> **$ Buying Tip:** For the perfectionist, mostly. For everyday small jobs, fingers or plastic spoons aren't that bad, but for larger jobs or more toxic caulks, fingers and spoons do have their disadvantages.

Caulk Remover

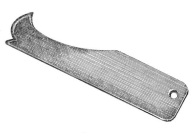

Caulk Remover

Description: 6" long, flat, plastic tool with a slightly hooked tip.

Use: Removing old caulk/sealant from around bathtubs or other areas. The small point is pushed under the caulk to loosen it and the hooked tip is pulled under the loosened caulk to remove it.

$ Buying Tip: Excellent for hard-to-remove caulk, but not necessary for most caulk, which can be pulled away by hand.

Roofing Materials

About Roofing

Roofing materials come in many more varieties and styles than can be described here. The intention is simply to give you a general orientation concerning the stuff that you may need in order to make minor repairs.

All roofing is available in a variety of colors. If you live in a very hot climate, consider the use of a light-colored roof; it absorbs less heat than a dark-colored one.

Roofing is sold by the square, meaning a 10' × 10' area or 100 square feet.

Working on a roof can be a hazardous activity, so it would be well to observe safety considerations. Professionals use safety hooks called *roof jacks* on which boards can be mounted. These are a good idea and can be rented.

Roofing Material

Types:

> *Asphalt roofing*
>
> *Built-up roofing*

Glass fiber shingles

Modified bitumen roofing

Roll roofing

Slate shingles

Tile roofing

Wood shingles

Also Known As: *Glass fiber:* Fiberglas (brand name), fiberglass

Description:

Asphalt: Usually comes in strip form with two, three, or four tabs per shingle and heavily coated with mineral granules on the weather side. Shingles range from around 11" to 22" wide and 36" to 40" long.

Built-up: Made of layers of tar-impregnated **roofing felt (below)** and base sheet with hot moppings of tar between the layers and a layer of asphalt on the very top. May also be all asphalt.

Glass fiber: These are partly asphalt and partly glass fiber, i.e., fiberglass is used as a base for asphalt and mineral granules instead of felt. (All asphalt shingles may be called *organic.)*

Modified bitumen: 36" wide, 10 square foot roll of rubbery material, similar to **roll roofing (below)**. Applied with a torch so that it melts into the surface adjoining rolls. Often called *rubber roofing;* it isn't.

Roll: 36" wide asphalt-impregnated material made in rolls containing 108 square feet. The weather side of this material is plain or covered in part with mineral granules (the uncovered part is the *selvage*). Sold in *weights;* typical is 90-pound type, and it may be sold in two *exposures*—half exposure being for use in double layers.

Slate: Available in various colors—green, gray, black, purple—depending on the quarry it's from. Slate has a nominal size $3/_{16}$" and an overall size 10" × 6" and 24" × 16".

Tile: A burned clay or shale or concrete product. Shapes vary greatly.

Wood: Made of cypress, cedar, or redwood. Comes in lengths of 16" to 18" and in bundles containing random widths 3" to 12". Available in either *shingle form,* which is machine-made, or *shakes,* which are hand-split. Some communities require expensive fireproofing treatment.

Use: To protect a home from weather and, in some cases, provide a degree of insulation. *Modified bitumen* and *roll roofing* are for flat roofs.

Use Tips: All roof installation is really a professional task. Installing or repairing slate and tile especially are better left to professional roofers; special tools and much experience is required to do the job right. In fact, you should limit your roofing work to repairs.

Buying Tips: The cheapest roofing materials are asphalt and fiberglass shingles. They are relatively easy to install. The heavier the shingle the better. Manufacturers guarantee their products, some types for 15 years and some for 25.

> **Use Tips:** Even though it is flat, a built-up roof is harder to install than it might seem. It is not that simple to make it leak-free. Keep some **asphalt plastic cement (below)** on hand for patching. You may want to coat it occasionally with asphalt or aluminum roof coating to extend the life of the roof.

Roofing Felts

Also Known As: Saturated felts, perforated felts, base sheet, tar paper

Description: Dry felt impregnated with an asphalt saturant and perforated to avoid trapping air. Different weights are available, the most common being No. 30, which weighs about 30 pounds per square. Comes in squares about 30" wide and in rolls.

Use: General patching of flat roofs, but mainly constructing bottom layers of a built-up roof. It is placed over the sheathing paper, which simply protects the basic roof from the asphalt in the felts.

> **Use Tips:** Felt can be installed with a staple gun or, for patches, plenty of roofing nails.

Roofing Cements

Types:

Asphalt plastic roof cement

Damp patch roof cement

Lap/double-coverage roof cement

Quick-setting asphalt roof cement

Also Known As: Mastic

Description: All these roofing cements contain petroleum solvents. Use outdoors only.

Asphalt plastic cement: Fairly viscous black goo of asphalt and mineral fibers. Comes in two grades, regular and flashing, which is thicker. Adheres to any dry surface. Like most cements, comes in 1- and 5-gallon cans. However, some similar products are available in standard 10.5-ounce caulking cartridges for application with a **caulking gun (Part IV, Chapter 32)**.

Damp patch cement (also known as *wet or dry roof cement*): Similar to the above, but specially formulated to adhere to wet surfaces.

Lap cement: Thick black adhesive, similar to the above cement but thinner.

Quick-setting asphalt cement: As the name implies, this sets very quickly. Basically an asphalt plastic cement with more solvent in it. Comes in various consistencies from fluid to thick.

Use:

Asphalt plastic cement: The standard material for sealing edges of flashing and patches in flat roofs, as well as installation of the bottom layers of roll roofing. Also for repairing leaks in gutters. Applied with a trowel over *reinforcement fabric* or *roofing tape*, a 4" to 6" wide loosely-woven glass fiber or cotton mesh membrane, sold in long rolls.

Damp patch cement: Emergency repairs under extreme dampness, such as leaks under snow buildup or during a major rainstorm. Applied with a trowel.

Lap cement: Used to seal overlapping strips of roll roofing or shingle tabs. Applied with a brush or roller.

Quick-setting asphalt cement: Adhering strip shingles in windy areas.

Use Tips: Patching over and over again may indicate a more serious problem that needs to be solved by a new roof or an overall coating with a material called *roof coating,* or *asphalt roof paint,* which is applied with a big brush. This will fill small gaps. Roof coating, also called *foundation coating,* is a masonry waterproofer. Both can extend the life of a flat roof.

Buying Tips: Always keep repair material on hand. Consult with manufacturers for best product in your situation (there are many variations on the themes noted here). Try the convenient 10.1 oz cartridges, used with a **caulking gun (Part IV, Chapter 32)**.

Reflective Roof Coating

Also Known As: Roof paint

Description: Either of two kinds, aluminum flakes suspended in an asphalt and solvent mixture, or white acrylic elastomeric suspension.

Use: Coating asphalt, modified bitumen, rubber, or metal roofs to protect them from damaging sunlight (U.V. rays) as well as to reduce thermal transmission.

> **Use Tips:** Worthwhile to apply every few years or so to extend the life of your roof. Easily applied with large brush or roller.

Flashing

Types:

Metal flashing

Metalized flashing

Mineralized roll roofing

Description:

Metal: This may be copper .01" thick or more, but aluminum is much more common. It is available in 6" and 8" squares and in rolls in 6" to 20" widths in 50' rolls. Other materials available are galvanized steel, lead, plastic, felt, and rubber.

Metalized: Very flexible paper-backed aluminum, almost like heavy aluminum foil.

Mineralized roll roofing: This is standard 36"-wide roll roofing cut to sizes desired.

> **Note:** *Flashing* is also a verb and may refer to the use of roof cement products around chimneys, skylights, and edges of roofs.

Use: Flashing is used to fill the gaps in a roofing job, such as at peaks, in valleys (where sloping roof sections abut), around chimneys and vent pipes, at roof edges, or against walls to carry off water. It is also used for repairs.

> **Use Tips:** Make sure that the flashing used is compatible with the roofing. For example, don't use copper with red cedar shakes because copper will darken the cedar. Be sure to seal it at the edges.

> **Buying Tips:** Metalized flashing is poor-quality material. The most commonly used flashing is aluminum. Roofing manufacturers also offer specialized products not listed here. Be sure to ask for them.

Soffit Vent

Soffit Vent

Also Known As: Vent louver, vent plug

Description: Small, round, metal, or plastic louvered vents ranging in size from 1" to 4" in diameter. Screen inside. Also available in rectangular lengths to run all the width of a house.

Use: Ventilation of the *soffit,* the part of the roof that overhangs the outside wall of a house. Helps prevent paint peeling and blistering.

> **Use Tips:** Be sure to keep paint off these small vents or it may close them up.

Shanty Cap

Also Known As: Coolie hat, rain cap

Description: Cone-shaped galvanized sheet-metal construction of large pipe section with roof suspended like a gazebo on top. Comes in diameters from 3" to 12" to fit pipe as needed (adjustable models are available). Other types are *turbine* and ones with *multiple cones.*

Use: Covers top of roof vent (drain stack or other vent) or chimney to keep rain out.

Shanty Cap

Ridge Vent

Description: Two Types: The stand-alone type is 5' or 10' lengths of either plastic, aluminum, or galvanized steel formed to fit over the open ridge of a roof; internal baffles on the underside allow for air circulation. The other type is a dense, synthetic mesh material about 1" high which is secured over the ridge gap, to which shingles are nailed. Each model has a specific ventilation capacity measured in square feet.

Use: Ventilating attics and barns efficiently of both moisture and heat.

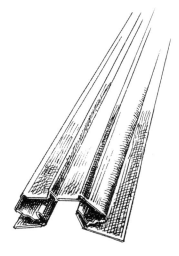

Ridge Vent

> **Use Tip:** More suitable to new construction than to retrofitting.

> **Buying Tip:** Be sure the unit is designed to block out insects.

Shingle Puller

Shingle Puller

Also Known As: Slate ripper, slater's ripper, shingle remover, shingle ripper, shingle nail remover

Description: 24" long, 2" wide flat steel bar with two fishhook notches on one end and an offset, thick, in-line handle.

Use: Driven up under and down to either shear off or pull out shingle nails or hooks when removing shingles carefully for a repair or remodeling job.

> **Buying Tips:** This is not the tool for removing an entire roof; for that use a *roofing shovel*, which generally looks like a flat garden spade with a notched edge for cutting nails and wedges for prying up shingles, or a garden hoe–like *shingle removal tool* that has a flat, angled blade instead of a shovel blade. Both can be used from a standing position. Handle asbestos shingles only after checking with authorities about their proper removal and safe disposal.

Gutter and Fittings

Types:

Aluminum, standard cut gutter

Aluminum, custom cut gutter

Copper gutter

Galvanized gutter

Vinyl gutter

Wood gutter

Gutter accessories and fittings

Also Known As:

Aluminum, standard and *custom cut:* Reynolds wrap
(if thin gauge)

Aluminum, custom cut: Seamless

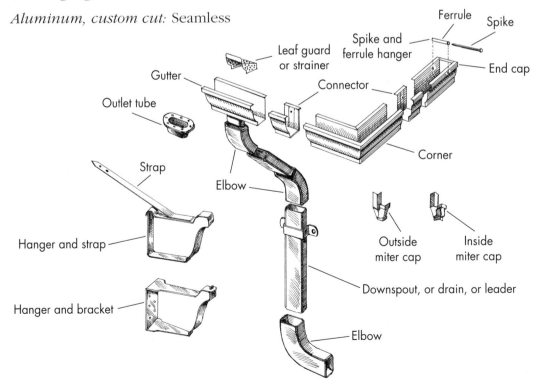

Description: Gutter is made of five different materials: copper, wood, vinyl, galvanized metal, and aluminum.

Aluminum, standard cut: Normal thickness, or gauge, is .027", but it also comes in 32' lengths of .032" at building supply houses that specialize in gutter. Standard-cut gutter is ordinarily available only in white.

Aluminum custom cut: Cut on the site by a jobber to the exact length desired; it is seamless. It is commonly available in white, brown, black, gold, and green.

Copper: This comes in standard 10' lengths; joints are soldered.

Galvanized: Comes in various baked enamel finishes and in lengths of 10' and 20'. It also comes 4" or 5" wide, rectangular or round and fluted.

Vinyl: This is PVC (polyvinyl chloride). It is available in one width, 5", and in lengths of 10', 16', 21', and 32' and in white and brown. Components snap together easily.

Wood: Usually made of fir, redwood, or red cedar, available at lumberyards in lengths up to 50'. It weighs five or six times as much as a metal gutter.

Accessories and fittings: These include *downspouts* (also known as *drains,* or *leaders*), *end tubes, leader hangers, spikes and ferrules* (tubes through which gutter spikes fit) for hanging, and *leaf guards,* which are grids that prevent leaves from entering the gutter.

Gutters are hung by one of three ways, and fittings will attach accordingly: with hangers attached to straps, with hangers attached to brackets, and with spikes that are driven through the ferrules and the gutter into the house.

Use: To carry water off the roof and away from the house.

Use Tips: The most common mistake in installing gutter is to assume that the house is level and pitch the gutter off that. Houses are rarely level. A level line must be established and the gutter pitched according to that for water to run down it properly. Clean gutters often.

Buying Tips: The best gutter buy is probably custom-cut aluminum. Besides being available in different colors, it is seamless—fewer places for leaks to occur—and .032 gauge; when you lean a ladder against it, it won't buckle, like the thinner (.027) aluminum will. But vinyl systems are easier to install and maintain by the homeowner.

Plastic, Metal, and Fiberglass

About Do-It-Yourself Materials

Plain, small sheets and lengths of aluminum and plastic can easily be used in a variety of innovative projects around the house. Many shapes are available; below are the basic ones. The first three items below are actually sold as "do-it-yourself materials" and are often found in specially designed display units.

Metal Sheets

Types:

Aluminum sheet, plain

Aluminum sheet, perforated

Galvanized steel sheet

Also Known As:

Aluminum sheet, perforated: Radiator grill, decorative aluminum panel

Galvanized steel: Sheet metal

Description: Thin metal (less than $3/16$" thick) that is easily bent and cut without special equipment other than tin snips.

Aluminum sheet, plain: Most often sold in 2' × 3' and 3' × 3' squares.

Aluminum sheet, perforated: Sold in 3' × 3' squares and 3' × 8' sheets in various perforations. Available also in anodized finishes, such as gold, and many different patterns.

Galvanized steel: Sold in rolls 2' wide, commonly 8' long.

Use:

Aluminum sheet, plain: Lining walls next to stoves, hobby projects, etc.

Aluminum sheet, perforated: Forms a grill in front of a radiator for decorative purposes.

Galvanized steel: Variety of repair and hole-patching jobs.

Angle Iron and Bar Stock

Description: L-shaped or flat aluminum or steel pieces in a variety of sizes up to about $1\frac{1}{2}$" wide, up to around $1/4$" thick, and sold by the foot. Generally available up to 8'. Some kinds of heavier steel angle iron or barstock come with slots and holes for bolts, allowing for easy construction of shelving or support brackets.

Use: Protecting corners, supporting shelves, and so on.

Rigid Plastic Sheet

Also Known As: Plexiglas®, Lucite®

Description: The most common rigid plastic is acrylic, and comes clear or in textures and colors. Generally cut to order from a 4' × 8' sheet, it comes covered with a protective paper coating that must be removed by the user. Most dealers stock a variety of sizes—2' × 3' is common. Lumberyards have larger pieces. Available in various thicknesses, of which ⅛" and ¼" are typical.

Use: Extremely versatile product used in an infinite array of decorative and functional projects, including art, hobbies, small shelves, and repairs. Can be bent by heating slightly, drilled at slow speed, cut with fine-toothed saw blades, glued, sanded, and polished.

> **Use Tips:** Easily cut with a special knife called a **plastic cutter (Part I, Chapter 6)**. Just score it several times along a line and then break it off. When drilling holes support it directly underneath the hole with a block of wood.

Plastic Film

Also Known As: Clear poly sheeting, plastic sheeting, plastic sheet

Description: Available in roll form and in various gauges— 2 mil, 4 mil, etc.—and widths.

Use: Many different uses, but chiefly as covers and drop cloths or for insulating windows.

> **Use Tip:** Do not use thin plastic film on floors—it is extrememly slippery.

> **Buying Tips:** Plastic film is just as effective an insulation material as glass, which is to say it stops drafts but transmits temperature. If you are using plastic as a drop cloth, make sure you get the thicker kind—the thinnest ones available tear very easily, making them worthless for that purpose (and are generally hard to use).

Fiberglass Panels

Description: Most commonly these are available in sheets 8', 10', and 12' long and 26" wide, with corrugations $2^{1}/_{2}$" apart. Fiberglass comes in a variety of colors and in various light weights—4, 5, 6, and 8 ounces per square foot. Installation is with aluminum nails. Fiberglass is also available in flat sheets and rolls up to 4' wide.

Use: As awnings over patios, carport roofs, porches, and the like. They let light in but keep out some of the sun's rays and heat.

> **Use Tip:** Fiberglass panels can be cut with a fine-toothed hand- or power saw.

Plastic Tubing

Description: Clear and frosted flexible vinyl in a wide variety of diameters and in lengths cut to suit. Often a large variety is for sale on a stand of reels.

Uses: Any number of uses, including making very long **liquid levels (Part I, Chapter 10)** for measuring levelness over long distances, such as in construction of a room's ceiling.

Plastic Laminate

Also Known As: Laminate, 'mica, Formica®, Micarta®

Description: Hard and brittle $\frac{1}{16}$" thick, sheet material sold by length and from 24" to 60" wide. One type has a hard plastic color surface and a base or core that's brown; newer material has the top color all the way through (color core). Plastic laminate has great stain resistance and easy-clean qualities and, once installed, can take a lot of punishment.

Use: Plastic laminate is considered the standard material installed on kitchen and bathroom countertops because of its easy clean feature and its imperviousness to water.

> **Use Tips:** Handle plastic laminate with care before installation. It's very brittle. *Contact cement* is used to install it. An easier way to apply this is with a paint roller. Laminate with color clear through makes trimming edges easier.

> **Buying Tip:** Color core is triple the cost of regular laminate.

Roll Laminate

Description: Plastic laminate in roll form, which is thinner than the better-quality laminate.

Use: Same as **sheet laminate (above)**.

$ **Buying Tip:** Roll laminate is not as good as sheet laminate but it does work.

Vinyl Patching Kit

Description: Kit containing patching material, graining "papers," and backing material.

Use: For repairing holes in vinyl upholstery.

Use Tip: Don't expect color-match perfection when using one of these kits.

Synthetic Marble

Also Known As: Corian®, 2000X®

Description: This is acrylic plastic combined with minerals to form an extremely hard material. It comes 30" wide and up to 10' long and in thicknesses of $1/4$", $1/2$", and $3/4$". It is a very heavy material and comes in a limited number of colors simulating marble.

Use: To cover countertops in kitchen or bath. Can be used as a cutting surface and repaired with minor sanding, but it dulls knives quickly.

Use Tips: Cut Corian® with carbide-tipped tools. Very easy to work with, perhaps even more so than plastic laminate.

Buying Tip: Synthetic marble is very expensive.

Insulation and Weatherizers

About Insulation

This is a highly technical field in which many specialized products are found. Below is only a basic overview of the main types commonly available. Thorough research for your specific application is necessary; many helpful publications are available at your local library, bookstore, or utility company. And of course from the manufacturer.

House Insulation

Types:

Batt and blanket (or *quilt) insulation*

Fill (or *loose fill) insulation*

Foam (or *foamed-in-place) insulation*

Rigid board insulation

Siding with insulation

Description: All insulation comes in a variety of thicknesses for different degrees of performance. All work on the same principle of tiny pockets of air trapped in something fluffy or foamy. The most common types of material are such fibers as rock or mineral wool, fiberglass, and cellulose.

Batts and blankets: Batts are precut flexible sections of insulation 4' or 8' long and 16" or 24" wide and are designed to fit between framing members. Blankets are as wide but come in lengths up to 100'. Both batts and blankets consist of mineral wool or fiberglass and have a vapor barrier, either kraft paper or aluminum. Both types also have edging strips or flanges, which are nailed or stapled to framing members (studs or joists).

Fill: A granular material, such as vermiculite, or chopped-up and chemically treated paper, which is poured or blown into place.

Foam: Applied as a liquid, it foams up instantly and becomes rigid.

Rigid: This comes in board form anywhere from 8" squares to 4' × 12' sheets (2'   8" sheets are the most popular, it seems) and may be urethane, expanded polystyrene or beadboard, fiberglass, Styrofoam®, or composition. Runs from $1/2$" to 2" thick.

Siding with insulation: Siding, wood sheating or aluminum, with insulation sheets adhered to the back side or in a sandwich form.

Use:

Batts and blankets: Normally installed between open ceiling and wall framing members (studs and joists).

Fill: May be poured in place between attic joists or blown into walls inaccessible to other kinds of insulation. Good for retrofitting.

Foam: Like fill-type installation, foam is for pumping into walls otherwise inaccessible to boards or batts and blankets. Professional installation is definitely required. Good for retrofitting. Aerosol cans of foam are excellent for filling small gaps, such as around windows, behind electrical boxes, and so on.

Rigid: Basement walls or areas with difficult access.

Siding with insulation: Exterior walls.

Use Tips: Do-it-yourselfers favor batts or blankets because they are very simple to install. Be sure to use *attic rafter vents* or *vent baffles* in attic installation to allow some movement of attic air from the *soffit,* under the sheathing. The most important area of the house to insulate is the top floor, simply because heat rises. For safety you should wear a suitable mask and gloves when handling insulation. Rigid insulation can be attached directly to walls of all kinds with **mastic adhesive (Chapter 32).**

Buying Tips: The key consideration when buying insulation is its R, or heat resistance, factor. The higher the R factor, the greater the ability of the insulation to limit heat passing through, and thus the more effective the material. Different climates require different R factors. To avoid installing too little—as well as too much—insulation, find out from your local utility what's sufficient.

Note: Foam has the highest R value per inch but gives off noxious gases in a fire.

Pipe Insulation

Blanket Insulation

Also Known As: Insulating pipe wrap, insulating pipe cover

Types:

> *Fiberglass insulation*
>
> *Foam rubber insulation*
>
> *Foam polyethylene insulation*

Description:

> *Fiberglass:* Comes in 4' and 6' lengths and in various diameters to fit all sizes of pipe, some with self-sealing tape. Paper or vinyl facing. Also in 3" wide rolls.
>
> *Foam rubber:* Sold in common pipe diameters and in 6' lengths with lengthwise seams which must be sealed with adhesive at joints, or wrapped with **cable ties (Part III, Chapter 23).** Foam rubber pipe wrap also comes in $1/4$" thick, 2" or 3" wide, 15' long rolls, with a self-adhesive foil cover. Duct wrap is similar, but 12" wide.
>
> *Foam polyethylene:* Also sold in common pipe diameters and in 6' lengths. Must be sealed lengthwise at joints with adhesive.

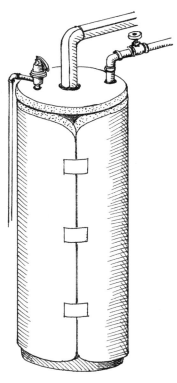

Insulation Jacket

Note: A similar but extra-large version, called an *insulation jacket* or *water heater blanket,* is available for use on hot-water heaters.

Use: Insulating hot-water pipes to conserve heat and to prevent cold water pipes from sweating.

Use Tip: Self-sealing fiberglass is easiest to use.

Outlet Seal

Description: Small pad of insulating material in the shape of a wall plate for either an outlet or a switch.

Use: Installed between the wall plate and the wall to seal out cold air.

Weatherstripping

Also Known As: Energy-saving products, weatherizers, sweeps (when installed on the bottom of a door; the vinyl or brush sweeps onto the threshold, or saddle, to make the seal).

Description: Many designs are available. Here are some basic ones:

Adhesive-backed foam: Foam rubber strip about 1" wide with peel-away paper, usually sold in rolls of 17'.

Aluminum saddle with vinyl gasket (threshold weatherstrip): Threshold with vinyl gasket in its middle.

Aluminum saddle with interlocking door bottom: See illustration.

Aluminum and vinyl strip sweep: Strips of aluminum with screw holes and a vinyl flap.

Caulking cord (Mortite®): Soft, putty-like cord supplied on a multiple-roll coil.

Felt strips: Strips of hair or cotton felt $3/4$" to 2" wide and about $1/4$" thick. Sold in 17' rolls, enough to surround an average window or door.

Foam-edged wood molding: Rigid molding with foam edging.

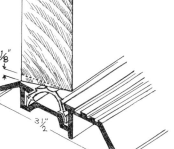

Aluminum Saddle with Vinyl Gasket
Weatherstripping

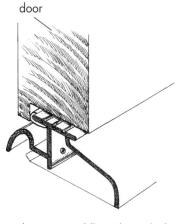

Aluminum Saddle with Interlocking
Door Bottom Weatherstripping

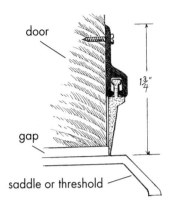

door

gap

1¾"

saddle or threshold

Aluminum and Vinyl Stripsweep
Weatherstrip

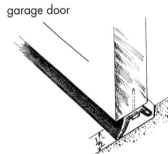

garage door

½"

Garage-Door-Bottom
Weatherstripping

Nylon pile: Soft, carpet-like strip with solid edge for nailing.

Polyethylene tape: Clear, wide tape.

Rubber garage-door stripping: Wide flaps of vinyl or dense foam rubber secured to bottom of garage door.

Serrated metal/felt: Felt encased in metal with holes for nailing.

Spring metal: V-shaped bronze strip with holes for nailing.

Interlocking metal: Two parts, one (male) installed on door, the other (female) on frame (see illustration).

Tubular vinyl gasket: Tube with a nailing lip; best have foam-filled tubes.

Vinyl channel: U-shaped strips.

Use: All weatherstripping prevents cold air from entering a house through gaps around doors and windows. Each of these items is more specialized, as follows:

Adhesive-backed foam: Sits on doorframe and door is closed against it.

Aluminum saddle with vinyl gasket: Sealing beneath door. Here, saddle is installed on floor, vinyl on door.

Aluminum saddle with interlocking door bottom: Interlock is installed on bottom of door.

Aluminum and vinyl strip sweep: Installed on door bottoms.

Caulking cord (Mortite®): Excellent temporary filling of large gaps. Easily applied.

Felt strips: Used to seal around windows and doors, especially over large gaps.

Foam-edged wood molding: Used around doors and windows.

Interlocking metal: Seals doors well, while also protecting against forced entry.

Nylon pile: For sealing around storm doors and windows. Nailed to bottom of door, sweeps up against the threshold.

Polyethylene tape: Seals around windows, sometimes with plastic film over the window too.

Rubber garage-door stripping: Nailed to garage door bottom, seals bottom and helps reduce shock when door hits floor.

Serrated metal/felt: Seals around windows and doors.

Spring metal: Nailed around a wooden doorframe to seal tightly when door is closed.

Tubular vinyl gasket: Nailed to door or window frame; can be used to replace factory weatherstripping on windows.

Vinyl channel: For sealing around metal casement windows.

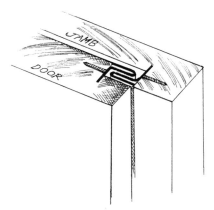

Interlocking Metal Weatherstripping

Tubular Vinyl Gasket
Weatherstripping

> **Use Tips:** Spring metal and interlocking metal are the best permanent types; polyethylene and dense, foam rubber (EPDM) are the best nonmetal materials; nylon pile can flatten out over time; tubular vinyl is more likely to seal better. You still can't beat new, double- or triple-glazed windows (windows with several layers of glass and air spaces) for energy conservation.

Rope and Cord and Accessories

About Rope and Cord

Rope is defined as any material $1/8$" (some say $3/16$") or more in diameter while cord is anything less than $1/8$". Both rope and cord have what is known as *safe working loads*—how much pressure they can take before breaking. If you use rope or cord in any situation where safety is important, check out the safe working loads. Your choices are of material, weave, and diameter.

Rope

Types:

> *Manila rope*
>
> *Nylon rope*
>
> *Polypropylene rope*
>
> *Sisal rope*

Description:

> *Manila:* Made from hemp. Resists sunlight, doesn't melt or stretch, and ties easily. Like most rope, it is available in diameters ranging from $1/4$" to $3/4$" and is normally sold by the foot from reels.

Polypropylene Rope   Sisal Rope

Nylon: Two types: One twisted, the other solid braid. Very strong. The twist type can unravel when cut. *Polyester rope* is similar.

Polypropylene: This is rope that floats. It comes in bright yellow and sometimes red. Least expensive material.

Sisal: Another natural-fiber rope; has less strength than Manila.

Use:

Manila: Where strength is important.

Nylon: Its big advantage is that it stretches, so if you have a job where the rope may need to take a shock and stretch, by all means use nylon—but beware of jobs where stretching would be a problem.

Polypropylene: Since it floats, it is used as a marker in pools and as a tow rope for boats. Hard to tie.

Sisal: Because of its relative low strength, use it only for temporary jobs.

> **Use Tip:** The ends of both nylon and polypropylene ropes can be melted with a match flame to prevent unraveling.

> **Buying Tips:** You can buy rope prepackaged in various lengths, but it's cheaper by the foot, taken off a reel. Match load limits to your jobs.

Cord

Types:

Clothesline

Twine

Masons' line

Description: Any rope product less than $1/8$" in diameter.

Clothesline: There are various types. One is braided cotton and has a filler inside to add body and bulk. Usually sold by the hank (a convenient length, coiled and packaged). Another clothesline is plastic—a film of vinyl over a wire. Another clothesline is *poly,* which is braided.

Twine: This could be described as a lightweight version of rope and cord made of plies twisted just once. There are different kinds: *Polypropylene* is strongest and sometimes the least expensive. *Jute* and *sisal* twine have fuzzy surfaces that stick well when tied.

Masons' line: Strong thin cord that comes in balls.

Twine

Use: All twine is good for lightweight tying jobs. Masons' twine is very strong and is used to mark off masonry projects, such as rows of bricks being laid. Jute and sisal are popular in rural and gardening applications because they will rot quickly.

Swiveling Round Eye Cap Snip

Swiveling Strap Eye Bolt Snap

Miscellaneous Rope Accessories

Types:

Pulley

Snaps

Description:

Pulley: 5" to 7" diameter grooved wheels in housings with eyes or hooks.

Snaps: Small metal device with spring-loaded locking device available in a variety of models, combining four features:

Swivelling or fixed *(solid)*

Eyes: round or rectangular *(strap)*

Snap Types: large latch *(cap);* sliding bolt; flat strap *(spring);* lever on outside of a ring *(trigger);* or solid half-circle catch *(animal tie);* and other special ones for boats, horse harnesses, and dog leashes.

Snaps on one or both ends *(double-ended)*

Uses:

Pulley: For clothesline but can also form the core of a rig winch for hauling up do-it-yourself materials.

Snaps: Where temporary hooking up of things is required. Swivel snaps are good for dog runs and other places where there is a lot of motion.

> **Use Tip:** Most of these accessories can be used with chain as well.

Lubricants

Household Oil

Also Known As: All-purpose oil, 3-in-1®

Description: Light oil in cans or sprays.

Use: Lubricating small machinery, doors, and tools around the house. Particularly good for breaking up rust. Cleans and polishes, removes tarnish.

> **Use Tip:** Although suitable for most lubrication needs, keep in mind that there are many specialized oils for sewing machines, cycles and mowers, and so on.

Dripless Oil

Also Known As: White lubricant

Description: White, high-viscosity oil—virtually a grease—that will not dry up and become ineffective (as **silicone, below,** does).

Use: For hinges and typewriters.

Graphite

Description: Comes as a powder and is applied with puffer tube.

Use: Usually used on locks but also good for squeaking floors and stairways.

Lock Fluid

Description: Graphite in fluid or spray form.

Use: Freeing up lock mechanisms.

> **Use Tip:** Take care when applying graphite. It can create a mess.

Penetrating Oil

Also Known As: Bolt loosener, easing oil

Description: Extremely thin petroleum/graphite mixture in liquid or aerosol spray. Liquid Wrench® is a common brand, as is WD-40®, which comes only as an aerosol spray. Both contain solvents.

Use: Loosens "frozen" nuts and bolts, "seized" machinery, or corroded galvanized-steel piping when allowed to penetrate for several minutes. WD-40® can be used as a plain solvent as well as a rust preventer on large metal items such as shovels and lawnmowers. Liquid Wrench® can also be used to remove rust.

Use Tip: After applying penetrating oil, make sure you give it enough time to work. The spray type is good for spots with limited access.

Buying Tip: Liquid Wrench® makes all-purpose and other specialized lubricants as well, so be sure you have the right item if you ask for it by brand.

Dry Spray Lubricant

Description: Teflon or silicone available in aerosol cans.

Use: Often used to slicken surfaces of drawers, doors, and windows for smoother operation. Works on paint, plastic, wood, glass, leather, and many other surfaces not suitable for liquids. Best lubricant for lock mechanisms.

Stick Lubricant

Also Known As: Stainless stick, stainless lubricant

Description: Comes as a grease stick and is applied like a crayon. May be made of silicone.

Use: Can be used on metal, plastic, glass, wood. Good for keeping drawers moving freely as well as enhancing the use of drills, saw blades, and other cutting tools.

Tape

About Tape

There are new kinds of tape appearing every day that combine various attributes of the ones below. This list is merely a grouping of some of the most common. All tape is known as *pressure-sensitive tape* and typically has adhesive on a backing of some sort.

Anti-Slip Tape

Description: Heavy tape with gritty surface, available in light and medium duty, and in various widths.

Use: Provides traction for bare feet around pools, on stairways, and in bathrooms.

Double-Faced Tape

Also Known As: Two-sided, cloth carpet tape

Description: Reinforced cloth with adhesive on both sides (one side protected with a removable wax-type paper).

Use: Securing carpeting and other flooring.

Duct Tape

Also Known As: Duck tape

Description: Reinforced cloth tape with a gray vinyl facing, commonly sold 2" wide (available in other widths too) and in up to 60-yard-long rolls. Most common is a rubber, waterproof adhesive, but other formulations are available that are flame-retardant or metalized.

Use: Wide variety of repairs and worksite holding jobs inside and outside the house such as gutter, leaking pipe and hose. Also seals heating and cooling ducts.

> **$ Buying Tips:** Inexpensive duct tape is not a good buy— the adhesive will be gummy and the tape may slip. Probably one of mankind's most useful inventions. Keep at least two rolls on hand.

Electrical Tape

Description: Black tape usually no more than 1" wide. Two kinds: One is a fabric that is sticky on both sides, known as *friction tape,* and adheres only to itself; the other is plastic with adhesive on one side only. The plastic tape stretches quite a bit and thus creates a tightening tension when wrapping wires.

Use: For wrapping electrical wires.

Foil Tape

Description: Thin, adhesive-backed insulation with foil face.

Use: For wrapping and insulating pipes against condensation.

> **Use Tip:** Does not prevent a significant energy loss as real pipe insulation would.

Masking Tape

Description: Paper-backed adhesive tape that comes in various widths up to about 3". Some have adhesive only along one half.

Use: Masking off areas to be painted, for packaging, general light use.

> **Use Tips:** Remove masking tape immediately after use, as otherwise it tends to leave a gummy residue that can be removed only with a strong solvent like lacquer thinner. Everyday translucent tape leaves no residue on windows. Don't use very old tape.

> **Buying Tip:** A serious paint store is likely to have a variety of specialized tapes available.

Paints, Stains, Finishes, Wall Coverings, and Related Products and Tools

About Paints

There is no question that painting jobs are made easier and better when you use top-quality paint, brushes, and rollers. Scrimping here is not a good idea. Getting the cheapest paint will almost always yield an inferior job that takes longer, requires more paint, and needs repainting sooner. You can expect to pay more for the best-quality paint, but in the end it will cover better, be easier to apply, and last longer than lower-quality paint. Stick with the top grades of nationally advertised brands, such as Benjamin Moore, although professionals may recommend some regional brands.

To save money, comparison shop by telephone—paint prices can differ dramatically from store to store. Also, buying paint by the quart is very, very expensive—it can be over double the price per gallon, although generally it should be about a third of the gallon price. Paint does keep a long time, so buy by the gallon (or the 5-gallon container) if possible.

Check paint-can labels to get an indication of quality. Paint is made of three components: a *vehicle* (solvent or water); a *pigment* (color); and a *binder,* usually a resin, to hold it all together. Resin can be natural (old-fashioned linseed oil) or synthetic (alkyd, or acrylic polyvinyl acetate). The more pigment and resin the better; likewise, the more vehicle the cheaper it is and the less covering power it has (and what good is paint that won't cover well?). For common household paints, pigment content of about one-third and a vehicle and binder content of about two-thirds is considered good. Ask for the technical specifications sheet.

Regular decorative paints are generally divided into two types: *interior* and *exterior.* Those types are generally available in either alkyd/oil-based or latex/water-based, as explained below. Where you will be using paint defines what kind of paint you should buy. Your choice will be determined by which rooms or walls it is going on (bathroom, ceiling, shingles, etc.) and what kind of surface it is going to be used on (old glossy paint, brick, drywall, etc.).

A final note: The paint job can be torpedoed by bad surface preparation. This cannot be overemphasized. Good wall preparation will make any job that much better—and poor preparation will ruin it. When in doubt about any aspect of a job, first try a test patch of paint in an inconspicuous spot. Follow directions.

About Alkyd and Latex Paints

Almost all decorative paints are available today in either of two types—alkyd or latex, which means either oil- or water-based.

Alkyds, the modern replacement of old-fashioned linseed oil-based paint, are actually a blend of cooked vegetable oils and resins that dry faster and have less odor than the old petroleum oil paints. Alkyds are often called *oil-base* or *oil-alkyd* paints just like their old counterparts. You can use either alkyd or latex paint for most painting jobs, but not always. These differences are detailed in the items below and on the paint-can labels.

Adding to the confusion is an inconsistency on the part of manufacturers in names. Some latex paints are labeled "acrylic" or "vinyl"; these are the synthetic resins that act as binders of the paint to the water and do not define any inherent difference for the end user because each manufacturer's process and formulations are different, prohibiting direct comparison. Latex paints are also referred to as "waterborne" products.

The basic difference is that alkyd (or oil) paints are thinned and cleaned up with paint thinner, or turpentine, while latex paints are thinned and cleaned up with warm water, making them mighty popular with the average user. Latex paints dry much faster than alkyd paints, have less odor, no noxious fumes, and are slightly porous to moisture. However, alkyd paints tend to cover a bit better, are slightly more durable, and are less prone to showing brush marks. Quality and manufacturing differences make a blanket comparison impossible, though, and in the long run personal preference dictates most decisions as to which paint to use. Furthermore, paint manufacturers are putting more and more research into latex paints so that the differences are becoming less significant. One day soon latex will be the norm and alkyds the exception, especially if environmental protection laws make the manufacture of alkyd paint or high V.O.C. (volatile organic compounds) finishes impossible.

Note: Most spray paints are oil-based.

Interior Paints

Standard Interior Paint

Also Known As: Finish paint

> **Note:** This term applies to any top coat, exterior or interior.

Description: Either latex, alkyd oil, or old-fashioned linseed oil paint labeled for interior use. Interior paints are generally available in flat, semigloss, high-gloss and enamel formulations, though some manufacturers have intermediate designations of eggshell and satin between flat and semigloss, and some manufacturers consider semigloss to be satin. Actual finish depends on the manufacturer.

The term *latex enamel* is actually a misnomer, as enamels technically are oil-based varnish with pigments, but in this case latex enamel describes a hard, glossy-finish paint. In the extreme, latex paints are not as glossy as alkyd paints, and alkyd paints are not as flat as latex paints.

Most deck, floor, and other enamels are oil-base types— mostly polyurethane or varnish (oil)-based, though some are lacquer-based. (Varnish and lacquer are discussed in **Chapter 42**.) Plastic paints are good for metal and wherever extreme gloss is desired.

Use: Flat latex or alkyd is ordinarily used for walls, while semigloss, high-gloss, and enamel are for woodwork trim, bathrooms, kitchens, and furniture. (Paints for metal are covered in **Chapter 41**.)

Use Tips: Flat paints dry lighter than the color on the label, while glosses tend to dry darker. Latex can be applied over old oil-base only if the surface is sanded and primed. A gallon will generally cover 400 square feet.

Interior and Exterior Primer

Types:

> *Alkali-resistant primer*
>
> *Alkyd primer*
>
> *Enamel undercoat*
>
> *Latex primer*
>
> *Stain-blocking primer*

Also Known As: Sealer, conditioner, undercoater, base coat, primer-sealer. *Stain-blocking primer:* stain killer

Description: Primers are almost always a white paint with a thin consistency. Alkyd is thinned with solvent, latex with water, and shellac-based stain-blocking primer with denatured alcohol.

Use: Providing a good, solid, even base for finish paint, because pigmented finish paints cannot sink in and bond as well as primer. Primer generally is used on previously unpainted (especially porous) surfaces, surfaces that have been heavily patched, when using high-gloss paint, and when changing from a dark to a light color. Finish print label will indicate the primer recommended. Stain-blocking primer (B-I-N, Kilz, and Enamelac are some brand names) is used when hiding stains, graffiti, soot, crayon, tape, grease, or knotholes, although some new latex and oil paints have *stain killer* in them. *Block filler* is used on masonry surfaces. *Alkali-resistant primer* is for damp masonry. (**Metal primers** are covered in **Chapter 41**.)

> **Use Tips:** Any primer helps seal and bond. However, when a surface is water- or otherwise stained, use a shellac-based, stain-killing primer (this stuff solves more problems than any other paint).

> **Note:** Nailheads will rust through latex primer unless they are sealed off. Alkyd is best for new drywall that is going to be wallpapered; latex primer should be used if the drywall is going to be painted. Figure coverage of about 250 square feet to the gallon. It is o.k. to paint over alkyd primer with latex.

Primers can be tinted with **colorants (below)** to give them a little more hiding power and to make the finish paint "holidays" (missed spots) less evident.

> **Buying Tips:** Stain-blocking primer is good to have on hand for all types of problems. Always use a primer when painting or the binder in the finish coat will soak in. Spray cans designed for use on ceilings area are a big help. Shop thoroughly—many product variations now exist.

Ceiling Paint

Description: White, glare-resistant paint in both latex and alkyd formulations with more and coarser pigment than wall paint.

Use: For ceilings. Some people use ceiling paint on walls, but it is very dull and not as washable as wall paint; it gives a dead flat effect. However, wall paint is perfectly all right for use on ceilings.

> **Use Tips:** Painting ceilings is usually easier if you paint against the light from a window to detect wet, freshly painted areas. If white ceiling paint doesn't cover well, add a teaspoon or two of either lamp black or burnt umber **colorant (below)**.

> **Buying Tip:** Ceiling paint costs less than wall paint.

Texture Paint

Description: Thick-bodied paint in various consistencies ranging from relatively thin liquid to material that can be worked almost like cement. Comes as a powder that is mixed with water or other base; can also be an additive, such as sand or perlite, bought separately or premixed. In any case it is tinted with colorant. Even "popcorn" texture is available, in aerosol form to boot.

Use: Excellent for covering a badly scarred and cracked ceiling or wall. Good for filling cracks in stucco. Also just for decorative purposes, such as a stipple finish.

> **Use Tips:** Many different items from crumpled paper to a trowel including **special rollers and sponges (Chapter 44)** may be used in working texture paint while wet. If you don't like one effect, you can always rework it. Cannot help badly peeling or flaking paint, as its weight will pull the rest of the old paint off; also, the cause of the damage must be cured first.

> **Buying Tip:** Because of its thick consistency, coverage per gallon of texture paint is limited, and therefore it is expensive, but it does solve minor problems.

Acoustical-Ceiling-Tile Paint

Description: Looks just like regular paint, but when it dries it is particularly porous.

Use: Painting acoustical tile. It does not interfere with the noise-absorbing qualities of the tiles.

Epoxy Paint

Description: Paint that comes in two containers, the contents of which are mixed together before use; dries to a hard, glass-like finish.

Use: Painting porcelain fixtures such as sinks and tubs, metal, concrete—just about anything.

> **Use Tips:** Epoxy is volatile and can be dangerous to use. Read cautionary material on the label and make sure area where you're working is well-ventilated. It is not cost-effective to use epoxy where other, less-expensive paints can be used.

> **Buying Tips:** A true epoxy is a two-container material. There are one-container so-called epoxy enamels but these are not true epoxies and will not perform like the two-container material.

Paint Colorant

Also Known As: Tinting colors

Description: A wide variety of colors in paste form, either oil-based or universal (oil and latex). Comes in tubes or cans.

Use: Tints primers or finish paints various colors.

> **Buying Tip:** Paint colorant is cheaper by the can than the tube.

Use Tips: Oil-based colorants can be used only with oil-based (alkyd) paint while universal colorants can be used with both latex or alkyd. Colorant cannot be used to darken a paint deeply—only to tint it. If you use too much colorant (see label for amounts suggested), the paint will become streaked with the colorant. One good use for lamp black or burnt umber colorant is to slightly darken ceiling paint so it covers better; the tinted paint may appear a bit gray in the can but will dry white.

Exterior Paints

Standard Exterior Paint

Description: Generally available in all formulations of flat and glossy. Some specialized paints are available, such as for aluminum siding or with "chalking" characteristics (a sort of weatherizing/fading process) that may or may not be desired. The final coat is called the *top* or *finish* coat.

Use: Painting siding and trim.

> **Use Tips:** To save your energy, try to paint only in the shade. Also, many manufacturers recommend you paint only in the shade to avoid problems with the paint. In any case, do not paint late in the day, as the dew and reduced daylight will prevent the paint from drying properly.

> **Buying Tips:** The same as for **interior paint (Chapter 39)**: buy the absolute best quality you can—and shop around for the best price. Each surface and location has particular needs, so choose paint with care.

Exterior Stains

Types:

> *Solid* (or *opaque*) *stain* (also known as *shingle paint*)
>
> *Semitransparent stain*
>
> *Preservative stain* (also known as *waterproofers*)
>
> *Specialized stains*

Description: Oil- or latex-based, with pigments and additives to resist mildew and moisture. Somewhat like a diluted paint with preservatives.

> *Solid stain:* Like flat paint, imparts an opaque finish.
>
> *Semitransparent stain:* Contains less pigment and allows the wood grain to show through.
>
> *Preservative:* Clear; merely darkens the wood slightly.
>
> *Specialized stains:* Include deck stains, weathering stains, and others.

Use: Penetrates and preserves exterior wood. Solid and semitransparent stains are designed for use on all kinds of wood siding. They color the wood to varying degrees and enable it to repel water. Preservatives enable wood to repel water and kill wood-rotting organisms, especially for wood in contact with soil or water. Among the specialized stains, deck stains are for application on decks only, while weathering stains give cedar and redwood an aged look upon application.

Use Tips: Solid and semitransparent stain is not as forgiving of incorrect techniques as paint. The chief problem is *lap marks*—stain dries so quickly that before you can apply a fresh brushful the previously applied stain is dry, causing lap marks. The key is to work in small areas quickly, always keeping a wet edge. Also, stir stain frequently to ensure that pigment is properly mixed with the vehicle. Depending on label instructions, may be applied with brushes, high-nap rollers, or spray. Wet the wood before staining on hot days or in direct sun.

Note: Observe safety precautions on can when using stains. Some are toxic, especially preservatives.

Buying Tips: Some cheaper, lower-quality stains do not contain preservatives, so all such stain does is color the wood—it offers no protection. Check label to ensure preservative is there.

Cement Paint

Also Known As: Portland cement paint, concrete paint

Description: Cement paint is available both as a powder that is mixed with water before use and premixed. Comes in various colors.

Use: Cement paints are good where a masonry surface is porous or badly damaged—the thick paint fills the cracks. Some brands are also intended to prevent damp basement walls and floors as well as for exterior use. For more serious waterproofing, see masonry sealers.

Use Tips: Read the cement paint label carefully—a special etcher, cleaner, or primer may be required and it may not work on floors or roofs. Some are made just for floors, ideal for garage floors. A specially made, pliable fiber brush is the best tool for application. The paint should be scrubbed into the surface.

Buying Tips: In many cases exterior latex paint works very well on masonry, but if the surface needs filling, use cement. Cement paint is specially formulated to not react to the powerful chemicals in cement.

Metal Paints

Metal Primers

Types:

Zinc chromate

Zinc oxide

Description: Zinc chromate is a white or yellow paint primer thinned with a chemical solvent, such as turpentine. Zinc oxide is a red primer also thinned with a chemical solvent.

Use:

Zinc chromate: For metal that is inside and not expected to be subject to moisture.

Zinc oxide: For metal that will be exposed to moisture.

> **Use Tips:** Follow primer labels for how to use the material. Once primed, you can use any finish paint—latex or alkyd—on the metal as long as it's compatible with the primer. Read the label on the paint. Alkyd primer will generally stand up better.

Rust-Inhibiting Paint

Description: Paint with a rust-inhibiting agent, or primer, that is part of the formula of the paint. In other words, the paint is primer and finish paint in one.

Use: Painting metal.

Use Tips: Read the label carefully to ensure that the paint is a primer/finish in one. Some companies make alkyd enamels that are purportedly single-coat metal paints, but they require that a primer be used.

Aluminum Paint

Description: Aluminum-colored paint consisting of aluminum with a resin base.

Use: Painting any kind of exterior or interior metal—fences, radiators, sheds, mailboxes, flashing, etc.

Use Tip: Aluminum paint should be allowed to dry overnight before recoating.

Buying Tips: Cheaper than other metal paints. Great results are easy in spray form.

Interior Stains and Clear Wood Finishes

About Interior Stains

Stains are an alternative to paint when you want the grain of the wood to show. As for which is best to use in which cases, it is often a matter of personal preference. Surface preparation and application are extremely important to a good job, if not more so than with paint. Some manufacturers mix stains with other products like tung oil, varnish, or polyurethane so that not only do they stain wood, but they also seal or coat it to provide protection. In most cases, however, another product is applied over the stain to protect it against moisture and wear—even when the stain totally hides the wood.

Using this kind of product correctly is almost an art. Test for results in an inconspicuous area first.

Interior Stains

Types:

Pigmented stain

Dye stain

Also Known As:

Pigmented stain: pigmented wiping stain, pigmented oil stain, wiping stain.

Dye: Aniline, spirit stain (if mixed with lacquer or other solvent), water stain, alcohol stain, NGR stain (if mixed with certain solvents), penetrating, dye-type.

Description:

Pigmented: Tiny particles of pigment suspended in either oil or latex (latex is water-based but not a water stain). Most common kind; almost like very thin paint. Designed to be brushed or wiped on with a cloth.

Dye: Aniline dye in powder form, mixed by user with water, oil or alcohol. When mixed with certain solvents becomes an NGR (non-grain-raising) stain, which dries very fast.

Use: All stains color wood and enhance its grain to varying degrees but provide no protection.

> **Use Tip:** Read product label closely for recommended method of application.

Pigmented: Stir constantly, as the pigment never dissolves—it is merely suspended. Wiping-type is easiest to use because you have more control over the rather slow process. Even though the colors are not as pure or transparent as dye stains, the results are quite good and colorfast.

Dye: Clearest, deepest penetrating colors—but the hardest to obtain and hardest to apply. Tends to raise grain. Surface and NGR types, or any mixed with lacquer, alcohol, or varnish, are hardest to handle and should be left to professionals. Used on the finest hardwoods; not sun-resistant.

Buying Tip: Pigmented, or wiping, stain is the best for the typical do-it-yourselfer.

Stain Remover

Also Known As: Aniline stain remover

Use: Removes deeply imbedded stains and water marks.

Use Tips: If stains cannot be completely removed, sanding the wood will make it lighter. If it is an alcohol-based or lacquer-based stain, the wood can be lightened slightly by rubbing with denatured alcohol, lacquer thinner, or a mixture of both.

Bleach

Also Known As: Bleaching solution, wood bleach

Description: Liquid product, generally sold in two parts. Similar product but less strong (although poisonous) is *oxalic acid,* which is sold as crystals or powder.

Use: Applied to bare wood prior to final finishing to produce lighter tones, remove water marks, or to make an uneven surface color even.

> **Use Tip:** Use caution when working with these caustic products.

About Clear Wood Finishes

Technically, paint is just another finish for wood. But when one thinks of wood finishes one ordinarily thinks of products that allow the wood to show through to varying degrees. Here two such kinds of finishes are considered: *surface* and *penetrating*.

Clear finishes do one of two things: They protect the wood or, if they have some stain mixed in them, both color and protect it at the same time. However, even the clearest finish will darken wood somewhat. Think of varnish as oil paint without the pigment. Whatever you use, it is always a good idea to test the product on a separate piece of wood in an out-of-the-way spot to ensure that you will be getting the finish you really want.

Choosing the best finish for woodwork and furniture can be very confusing, as there are not only a number of very different products with similar end results but manufacturers blend all of them and call them by names that can be misleading. For example, someone might put a tiny amount of tung oil in a can of polyurethane and call it "tung oil varnish" or mix polyurethane with old-fashioned varnish. The end result is a blurring of some already fine distinctions. Caveat emptor: experiment.

About Surface Finishes

This group of finishes stays right on top of the wood, sometimes giving a plastic-coated look, and can chip. They can be applied in successive layers to achieve a buildup.

Polyurethane

Also Known As: Urethane, poly, plastic varnish

Description: Available as both a petroleum derivative with a resin base and in a water-based formula. Very similar to traditional oil-based varnish, of which it is the modern version. Dries quickly, and when thinned can act as its own primer/sealer. Comes in satin or high-gloss, often called *gymnasium finish*.

Use: All-around protective coating for wood furniture, trim, and floors. Resists alcohol, household chemicals, abrasion, and chipping. Most durable finish. Usually applied with a brush or lamb's-wool applicator, but also can be wiped on.

Use Tips: Can outlast traditional varnish two to one. As rugged as it is after curing, polyurethane must be carefully applied and directions for temperature, thinning, and surface preparation followed rigorously. Also, oil-based polyurethane vapors and sanding dust are potentially harmful, so use maximum ventilation and an appropriate respirator. Allow planty of time for each coat to cure—days in some cases.

> **$ Buying Tips:** Only the more expensive polyurethane is reliable. Get the very best—it is too hard to redo a floor if the finish doesn't bond correctly. Water-based finishes are generally less durable than oil-based, though some can be mixed with hardeners.

Varnish

Types:

Alkyd varnish

Spar varnish

Tung oil varnish

Also Known As:

Spar: Marine spar, outdoor, phenolic

Tung oil: Penetrating oil varnish

> **Note:** The term *varnish* is sometimes used generically for all clear surface finishes and usually includes polyurethane, which is listed separately here because it is used so widely.

Description: Various durable formulations that dry with anywhere from a flat to a high gloss. Regular varnishes take a day or more to dry, but quick-drying, rubbing varnishes take only five hours or so to dry.

Thins with turpentine or mineral spirits (see label). New technology is being used to produce water-based varnishes.

Use: Finishing wood trim inside and outside the house.

> ⚒ **Use Tips:** Most varnishes take a long time to dry, so dust can be a problem. Varnish generally needs renewing from time to time. Spar varnish resists sunlight, water (and salt water), and alcohol more than others, but is not recommended for indoor use. Alkyd is less durable.

> 💲 **Buying Tips:** The alkyd formulation is least expensive; tung oil the most expensive.

Shellac

Description: A mixture of a liquid traditionally made from an Indian insect, the lac bug, and alcohol. Currently artificial substitutes are used as well. Comes as a cream-colored liquid known as *white* shellac as well as an amber-colored one known as *orange*. It is available in a number of different "cuts," referring to the number of pounds of lac flakes, the basic shellac component, per gallon of denatured alcohol. For example, a 3-pound "cut" means 3 pounds of flakes mixed with one gallon of alcohol. Also available in flake form for mixing on location.

Use: Furniture finish that dries very quickly. Also used as a paint primer/sealer over hard-to-hide colors, patterns, or knotholes.

> ⚒ **Use Tips:** Shellac is not waterproof and responds badly to alcohol; it is also brittle. But as easy as it is to damage, it is easy to repair. It may be waxed for protection too.

> **Buying Tips:** Shellac has a short shelf life—do not buy anything over six months old. If a can is not dated, test it for clarity and drying time.

Lacquer

Description: High-gloss finish that dries almost instantly. Thins with lacquer thinner.

Use: Favored by professional furniture finishers because it dries so quickly. Somewhat similar to varnish. Goes on in thin coats.

> **Use Tips:** Apply with spray. It dries too quickly to be applied by brush unless specifically formulated. Somewhat delicate to use for amateurs, except as a touch-up using aerosol spray cans.

About Penetrating Oil Finishes

These finishes are absorbed into the fibers of the wood and actually become part of the wood. They are known for giving the more natural appearance of being "hand-rubbed" and are thus quite different from the surface finishes described above. However, the principle is similar—protecting wood.

Penetrating Oil Finishes

Types:

Linseed oil

Tung oil

Also Known As:

Blends: Danish oil, antique oil, Danish penetrating oil, drying oil finish

Tung: China wood oil, China nut oil

Description: Oil that penetrates into wood fibers and hardens (polymerizes). Typically leaves a satin finish with a hand-rubbed look. Many different types of blends are available, but most are formulations that include either tung oil and/or linseed oil and solvents and dryers. They often have stains incorporated as well. Some of the most popular brands are mostly linseed oil, which costs much less than tung oil. Some purists still use pure linseed or tung oil, but the blends solve a multitude of problems of the pure oils.

Tung oil is made from the nut of the tung tree, originally found only in China, and is a major ingredient in enamels and varnishes. Many finishes with varying amounts of tung oil in them use "tung oil" in their name, but some might only have a little in them. Check the label. Somehow it seems logical to put an oil made from a tree onto wood in your home.

Use: Protects wood trim and furniture inside the home. Easy to apply—brushes or wipes on with rag or hand. Very durable—needs little maintenance. Successive layers make for a greater sheen.

Use Tips: Some types are safe for surfaces that come into contact with food. Tung oil is highly resistant to water and mildew and dries fast. However, it is harder to get good results with pure tung oil than with the many modern penetrating oils that mix tung with various additives to give a much more predictable product. Similarly, linseed oil, squeezed from flax seeds, is the prime ingredient in some of the more popular blends but can be found pure. It should be "boiled" rather than "raw." Raw takes months to dry or may not completely dry at all.

Linseed oil tends to darken with age and need renewal. It is difficult to apply by itself. Like tung oil, it is a common ingredient in other products. Pure linseed oil is not recommended to the average do-it-yourselfer.

Sealer

Description: Clear oil that penetrates deep into wood fibers and seals surface.

Use: Protects against grain raising, moisture, and general weathering; as a conditioner and as a primer for varnish, penetrating stain, polyurethane, or high-gloss paints, preventing blotches. Can also be used as a rust inhibitor on metal.

Wood Filler

Description: Finely ground silex (rock) paste.

Use: Fills pores of open-grain wood and acts as a primer for varnish, polyurethane, and some lacquer. Can be tinted to match wood.

> **$ Buying Tips:** Some brands are available in a combination with stain and sealer for one-step usage. Others are formulated for filling small gaps.

Thinners, Cleaners, Removers, and Preparers

About Thinners

Thinners are known generally as solvents, or reducers. Most are petroleum distillates and therefore volatile and flammable. Handle with care.

Paint Thinner

Also Known As: Mineral spirits

Description: Petroleum distillate product. Lowest of a number of grades of chemicals distilled from coal, such as benzene, acetone, or naphtha. Extremely volatile and flammable. Generally has only a mild odor.

Use: Thinning and cleaning up oil-based paints; cleaning up various adhesives and other materials.

> **Use Tips:** Avoid splashing in eyes or prolonged contact with skin by wearing goggles and gloves. Avoid diluting final coats of paint; use primarily on prime coats.

$ Buying Tips: Least expensive of this family of products. Can be made even cheaper by buying in bulk, using your own metal container; used thinner can also be recycled, as paint sinks to the bottom of the container. Don't buy premium-priced "odorless" thinners. It's the paint that smells, and you can't do much about that.

Turpentine

Also Known As: Pure gum spirits, turps

Description: Distilled from pine sap. Slightly lower-quality turpentine, called *steamed distilled* turpentine, is distilled from steamed pine tree bark. Has pronounced odor.

Use: Thins fine paints; particularly good for thinning exterior oil-based paints, making them easier to apply; general cleanup of all paints. Excellent for cleaning smooth surfaces.

⚒ Use Tip: Better, quicker, stronger solvent than paint thinner, but has odor.

$ Buying Tip: Much more expensive than paint thinner, which does most of the jobs that turpentine does.

Lacquer Thinner

Description: Extremely volatile petroleum-based solvent.

Use: Cleaning, removing, and thinning lacquer or other oil-based paint products. Cleaning any durable surface, especially tape or adhesive residue.

Use Tip: Extremely flammable; use with maximum ventilation.

Denatured Alcohol

Description: Volatile solvent.

Use: Thinning and removing paints and varnishes, removing grease and other smudges, fuel for chafing dishes. Main solvent for shellac.

Use Tip: Safer than wood or methanol alcohols, which are strong poisons.

Buying Tip: You can buy in bulk at a very low price from a gas station that mixes its own gasohol.

Paint and Varnish Remover

Types:

Water wash off remover

Solvent wash off remover

No-wash remover

Latex paint remover

Also Known As: Stripper, chemical stripper, paint remover

Description: All are dangerous, strong chemicals with varying degrees of volatility.

Water wash off: Liquid or paste containing detergents that allow it to be washed off with water. Very volatile, but nonflammable, unlike other removers.

Solvent wash off: Liquid or paste that is washed away with solvent, either a petroleum distillate or denatured alcohol.

No-wash: Remover that can be merely wiped off surface with an absorbent cloth.

Latex paint remover: Solvent or water-based chemical that acts only on latex, not oil-based paints.

Use: Removes paint, varnishes, and other finishes from wood. Typically the remover is applied, allowed to remain a specified time, and then it—and the old finish—are scraped off. Latex paint removers also remove crayon, tape residue, gum, and grease.

Use Tips: Removers work, but most are dangerous, very strong chemicals, and are messy. You must read labels carefully for cautions. Use proper safety equipment: goggles and heavy rubber gloves, long sleeves and long pants, adequate ventilation, and keep a water source ready in case you get some caustic chemical on your skin. Do not use in direct sunlight. Note that a remover may not be necessary in the first place. Other chemicals can remove finishes. For example, denatured alcohol will remove shellac as well as some varnishes. Lacquer thinner takes off lacquer. Heat takes paint (but not varnish) off very well, through the use of **heat guns** or **plates (Part V, Chapter 45)**, and it is not toxic—though the old paint may be. Use a liquid remover only on horizontal surfaces or it will run off. A paste remover can be used on vertical and horizontal surfaces. Water-based strippers raise the wood grain. Plastic abrasive pads are excellent substitutes for steel wool when removing gooey paint residue.

Buying Tips: There are many different removers available, but only some are nontoxic. Among the toxic ones, those containing methylene chloride work best. Check labels; the more of this ingredient the better.

Roll and Brush Cleaner

Description: Caustic liquid, paint stripper with additives.

Use: Alternative to paint thinner for cleaning extremely paint-encrusted brushes and rollers.

> **Use Tips:** May harm some synthetic-bristle brushes; definitely harmful to foam applicators. Can be saved and recycled.

Sanding Liquid

Also Known As: Liquid sandpaper

Description: Liquid abrasive.

Use: Scoring glossy surfaces prior to repainting with another high-gloss or latex paint; gives the new paint a "tooth" to hold on to.

> **Use Tip:** Dangerous, strong chemical. Use goggles and gloves.

Rubbing Agents

Types:

> *Rottenstone*
>
> *Pumice stone*
>
> *Tripoli*
>
> *Rouge*

Also Known As: Flour pumice, rubbing powder

Description: Finely ground stone powder.

Use: To rub with water or special oil (usually paraffin) to give final, delicate polish to surfaces.

Rottenstone: For high-gloss finish on varnished or lacquered wood surfaces, sometimes used after pumice.

Pumice: For soft, satin luster on varnished or lacquered surfaces.

Tripoli: Finer in texture than both the above. For polishing fine metal and jewelry.

Rouge: Finest rubbing/polishing agent for metal.

Painting Tools and Accessories

About Painting Tools

There are many kinds of painting tools, but a number of them are more gimmicky than useful. The tools presented below are all of good practical value, though in a number of cases one can be used for a variety of jobs.

Brushes

Description: Brushes come in a great variety of sizes and styles, but for the do-it-yourselfer brushes ranging from 1" to 4" wide and made of either a synthetic material or animal hair—normally Chinese hog bristle—will serve well. *Flat ends* have evenly trimmed bristles; *chisel ends* are V-shaped.

chisel end cut

chisel end cut

Sash Brush

Wall Brush

Radiator Brush

Types:

Angular or *angle sash brush* (1" to 3" wide, end cut on angle, long handle)

Calcimine brush, or *block brush* (heavy and thick, 7" wide)

Oval sash and trim, varnish and enamel brush (round, sized by number, 2-20)

Radiator brush (sash brush at 45-degree angle to long handle)

Sash and trim brush (flat end, 1" to 4" wide)

Varnish or *enamel brush* (chisel end, 2" to 3" wide)

Wall brush (chisel or flat end, 3" to 5" wide)

Use: Apply paint to any surface inside or outside the house and on a great variety of other items. Also used to apply many other finishes, such as varnish.

Use Tips: When applying paint try not to wipe the paint brush on the edge of the can. Instead, dip the brush in about one-third of the way, tap it back and forth inside the can, then apply the paint. A $2^1/_2$" brush is perfect for use with quart cans.

Brushes made of synthetic bristles serve well for both oil and latex paints, especially polyester, but do not use natural-bristle brushes with latex—they are not compatible and will soak up the water in the paint. Nylon bristles may dissolve in some solvents.

For trim a 2" brush is good. If you have large areas to paint, such as cabinets, a 3" or at most a 4" brush should be used. Brushes wider than this would be too heavy. Note special types listed above. Chisel ends and angular cuts make it possible to "cut in," or start painting from a corner, such as a window, and are generally better. Longer handles help when doing detailed trim work. *Angled radiator brushes* are helpful for painting trim in corners or at ceilings, as well as for reaching behind radiators. Large, thick block brushes are excellent for priming (indeed, sometimes they are called *priming brushes*). *Stain brushes* are thicker and bulkier than paint brushes.

$ Buying Tips: As quality varies, compare brushes against one another. Quality brushes have a lot of bristles. The bristles are of varying lengths and the tips are *flagged*—they have split ends, just like hair—so the paint can be applied more smoothly. And they taper to a point. Good brushes cost more but stand up to repeated cleanings and do a much better job. Get good ones.

Cheap brushes lose bristles in the paint and are generally much less efficient in carrying paint, making the job take longer and you work harder. Bristles should also be relatively long. Beware of China or ox hair "blends" of bristles—they may be cheap brushes with only 1 percent of those bristles. The good ones say "100% China Bristle" or the like. The most inexpensive brushes (made for one-time use) may be called *chip brushes.*

About Paint Rollers

A paint roller actually consists of two parts, the handle and a fabric-covered cylindrical cover that slips onto it. Both parts are often called rollers whether assembled or not.

Paint Roller

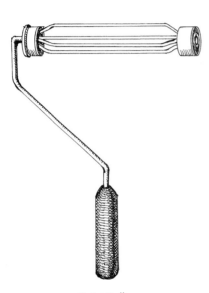

Paint Roller

Also Known As: Roller frame, roller

Description: Handle attached to metal rod that holds roller covers. Should have threads in end of handle for attachment to an extension pole for painting walls and ceilings. Handles come with either a wire cage–like section for mounting a sleeve or a wing-nut arrangement. Sold in 7" or 9" as well as 1" to 3" sizes.

Use: Painting walls and ceilings and other large, flat areas. Small rollers are for trim or radiators. Longer rollers are made for painting vast areas of flat wall.

Use Tips: Heights can be reached by screwing a broom-stick or *special handle extension pole* into the threads in the end of the handle for that purpose. Lengths of over 10' are unwieldy and messy and should be avoided, but they do limit time spent on a ladder. Some models come with **shields (below)** for catching the spatter. At least one manufacturer makes a hollow tube handle with a pump mechanism for continuous feed of paint to the roller.

Buying Tips: The cage-type handle works better than the kind with wing nuts. Choose a heavy-duty model where possible. More expensive but worth it.

Roller Cover

Roller Cover

Also Known As: Sleeve

Description: 9" long by about 2" thick tube made of cardboard or plastic, covered with naps or fabric coverings made of synthetic material (such as nylon or rayon) or natural lamb's wool in different thicknesses. Also available in narrower, "mini-roller" 1" to 3" long sizes. *Texture rollers*, for use with texture paint or for special effects, are also available. *End caps* fit in the end of the cover to convert roller to a full-sized corner painter.

Use: Applying paint to wide areas with a **paint roller, (above).** Roller covers are removed after use either for cleaning or to be discarded.

End Cap for Roller Cover

> **Use Tips:** The rule is, the rougher the surface being painted, the longer the nap should be. A $3/8$" nap works well for smooth walls and ceilings, while $3/4$" is good for semirough surfaces, such as stucco. You need a short nap for satin, eggshell, and other high-gloss paints. *Texture,* or *specialty rollers,* made of plastic loops, foam, carpet, rag, leather, and other materials, are used for special effects. The whole range of naps is from $1/4$" to $1 1/4$".
>
> Nylon and some other synthetics work well, but rayon is a poor choice. Lamb's wool is fine for long-nap rollers, but never with latex paint (it will absorb all the water). Small rollers, intended for trim, work well for touch ups or when you wish to use paint directly from a can with a **bucket grid (below).**

Leather Mottling Texture Roller

> **$ Buying Tips:** Good-quality roller covers have tubes made of plastic or some other hard material such as metal covered with plastic. Poor-quality rollers have cardboard or paper tubes that may come apart when wet. Mini-rollers don't hold that much paint.

Paint Roller Spatter Shield

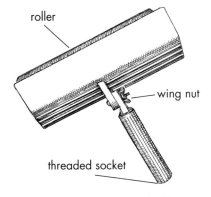

roller

wing nut

threaded socket

Paint Roller Spatter Shield

Also Known As: Spatter guard, spatter shield

Description: Plastic cover for paint rollers shaped to hide all but the part in contact with the surface being painted. Attaches to extension poles with an adjustable wing nut and clamp that permits use at any angle.

Use: Preventing droplets of paint from being sprayed onto the floor and you.

> **Use Tips:** Don't use too much paint on the roller, and move slowly to prevent excess splatter. Empty out the shield from time to time.

> **$ Buying Tip:** Good insurance.

Roller Washer

Description: Plastic tube about a foot long and 2" wide with two removable cap ends, one with a drain hole and one with a garden hose attached. It is forced over a paint-laden roller.

Use: Removing leftover latex (water-based) paint from a roller by forcing it off with pressure and back into the paint can, then by washing the roller in water by attaching it directly to a faucet.

Foam Rollers

Also Known As: Trim rollers, specialty rollers

Types:

> *Foam corner roller*
>
> *Foam paint tongs*
>
> *Foam pipe roller*
>
> *Foam edge roller*
>
> *Foam trim roller*

Description: Small foam rubber rollers of various shapes suited to specific tasks, mounted on short, special handles.

> *Foam corner roller:* Doughnut shaped roller with pointed edge.
>
> *Foam paint tongs:* Small rollers on ends of wire tongs.
>
> *Foam pipe roller:* Concave roller.
>
> *Foam edge roller:* 1" wide roller.

Foam trim roller: 3" wide roller, about 1" in diameter. A 3 or 4" long *tight spot roller*, *mini roller*, or *radiator roller* may use short foam or fabric roller covers with various naps, but on a 12" to 21" long handle.

Use:

Foam Paint Tongs

Foam corner roller: Painting corners.

Foam paint tongs: Painting fences or other thin items such as radiators two sides at a pass.

Foam pipe roller: Painting pipes, half the surface at a pass.

Foam edge roller: "Cutting in" along corners instead of using a brush.

Foam trim roller: Painting wider trim and radiators, as well as touchups. 3" and 4" rollers, with their narrow diameters, allow you to paint directly from a 1-gallon can instead of having to use a tray.

Foam Pipe Roller

> **Use Tip:** As with full-sized rollers, don't put too much paint on at any one time or it will drip.

> **Buying Tips:** Specialty rollers are a great time-saver and quite inexpensive to boot. Some trim rollers are sold with a small tray, excellent for small projects. Those with *covered ends* (the nap extends over one end of the roller) allow you to paint corners and walls at the same time.

spring

Roller Tray

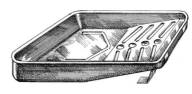

Roller Tray

Description: Shallow metal or plastic pan about 10" square, with one deep end and short legs at the upper end. May come with a grid insert. Inexpensive disposable plastic liners may be used to eliminate the need for cleaning the tray after use.

Use: Holds paint for use with rollers. Grid aids spreading paint evenly onto roller and thereby helps prevent splatter and drips.

> **Buying Tip:** Quality trays have deeper paint wells and hold more paint than cheaper models.

Paint Pourer

Paint Pourer

Description: Large plastic ring with spout that fits into a standard 1-gallon paint can. Some models have flip-top lid that re-seals between uses.

Use: Makes it possible to pour paint without dripping or messing up the ridge of the can. Protects label from drips, preserving it for future reference.

> **Buying Tips:** Handy if you are pouring paint into trays. If you are anti-gadget, punch holes in the ridge to drain paint, and pour quickly, and wipe up drips immediately.

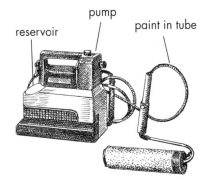

Bucket Grid

Bucket Grid

Also Known As: Paint grid, roller grid

Description: 7" square expanded steel grid with short legs, one set of which is curled (5-gallon model), or 4" × 8" plastic grid with loop handle (1-gallon model).

Use: Removing excess paint and spreading paint evenly on a roller within a can of paint, without having to use a **roller tray (above)**. The 1-gallon model can only be used with 3" or 4" long rollers.

> **Use Tip:** Remember to keep stirring the paint that remains in the can, and not to leave it open too long.

> **Buying Tip:** Great way to speed up a big job and reduce material to clean up.

Cordless Electric Paint Roller

reservoir — pump — paint in tube

Cordless Electric Paint Roller

Description: Not just a power version of the *manual roller*, but a painting system made up of a large container for paint, an electric pump, a hose that takes paint from the pump to the roller (through the handle), and a roller with a splatter guard.

Use: Continuous painting of large surfaces, such as walls. Pump keeps roller continuously wet with new paint. Eliminates the need for a **roller tray (above)** and the related repeated pauses to use it.

$ Buying Tip: For big projects only.

Paint Pad

Also Known As: Painting pad, brush pad

Description: Pads of varying widths, around 1" to 8", with a rigid back with a synthetic or natural nap, like rollers, and of varying lengths. Pads slip in and are held by a handle.

Use: Painting all the surfaces that rollers can paint, but with the versatility of a brush.

Paint Pad

Å Use Tips: Pads are faster than a brush but not as fast as a roller. They generally do a smoother job applying paint than a roller.

Foam Brush

Also Known As: Foam paint applicator

Description: Tapered slabs of foam mounted on handles, usually wood.

Use: For testing, touch-ups, or painting trim.

Foam Brush

Å Use Tips: Since their cost is so low, discard foam applicators after use. People are divided as to their effectiveness, so experiment.

Lamb's-Wool Paint Applicators

Description: A short nap of natural lamb's wool mounted on wood. The two most common designs are flat sticks (often paint-mixing sticks) and a more serious model that resembles a floor sponge, about 4" by 10", attached to a broom handle.

Use: The sticks are used for painting radiators or wrought-iron fences, where you need to get into narrow spaces, and the flat floor applicator applies polyurethane to floors.

>  **Use Tip:** Clean thoroughly and carefully.

Stippling Sponge

Description: Foam rubber cylinder, 3" thick × 5" wide, with a textured pattern on one side and threaded extension pole socket on the back.

Use: Creating a textured effect in painted surfaces. The sponge is dabbed, swept, or rotated to create different patterns.

Stippling Sponge

> 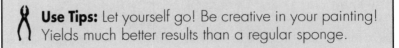 **Use Tips:** Let yourself go! Be creative in your painting! Yields much better results than a regular sponge.

Graining Tool

Graining Tool

Also Known As: Heart grainer

Description: Quarter or half cylinder of rubber with curved, raised ribs and a handle out one side. Also available in a *graining roller* version. A similar item, a *check roller*, is made of a series of metal plates. See illustration on the facing page.

Use: Creating a heartwood grain effect with paint or stain.

> **Use Tips:** Experiment to see what grain effects you can create and how much pressure to use. Wipe off tool after each pass.

Magnetic Brush Holder

Description: Steel clip about 3" to 6" high that slides onto side of paint or joint compound can. Large magnet at top.

Use: Holding paint brushes or **taping knives (Chapter 50)** by their metal ferrules or blades.

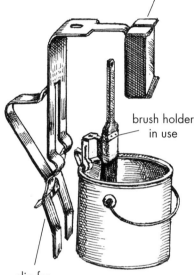

Magnetic Brush Holder

Extension Brush Holder

Description: Small, hinged two-part device, one side of which clamps onto paintbrush handles, the other side of which is threaded to fit onto the end of a broomstick or *roller handle extension pole.*

Use: Painting with a paintbrush instead of a roller on the end of a long pole.

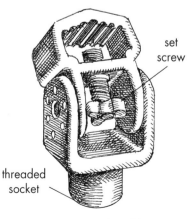

Extension Brush Holder

> **$ Buying Tips:** Handy for the odd touch-up or trim problem where using a ladder is too time-consuming or cumbersome, such as in a room full of furniture (or when the painter is not willing or capable of handling a large ladder).

Painter's Mitt

Description: Fabric or lamb's wool-covered mitten.

Use: The mitt is worn like a regular mitten and dipped into the paint, and then touched to whatever is being painted—your hand becomes the tool. Ideal for speedier painting of items such as pipes and wrought-iron fences, where the surface is relieved, shaped oddly, or otherwise difficult for a roller or even a brush to get into.

> **Use Tip:** Dip the mitt only about one-third of the way into the paint.

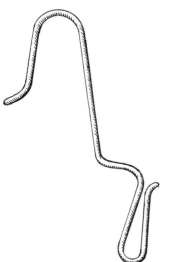

Pail Hook

Pail Hook

Also Known As: Paint-can hook, pot hook

Description: Large, heavy wire S-hook. Also made with a swivel and snap hook.

Use: Hangs from ladder rung to hold a 1-gallon can of paint by its handle.

Pail Opener

Pail Opener

Also Known As: Lid opener

Description: Plastic handle with C-shaped opening that has hooked ends.

Use: Opening plastic 5-gallon buckets of anything, such as paint or joint compound, without breaking the rim (or your tools or fingernails).

> **Use Tip:** Doubles as a pail hook.

> **Buying Tip:** A handy, inexpensive item.

bottle top opener

Paint Can and Bottle Opener

Paint Can Openers

Description: Various types are available. The multipurpose tool model is a flat, solid bar of steel with a chisel on one end and a fishtail on the other, with a teardrop hole and a small tongue on either end. A curved and a square notch are on either side. Another version, the *paint can and bottle opener,* is made of steel wire, with a loop handle and flat, slightly bent end.

Use: Opening paint cans gently, so as to preserve the sealing ability of the lid. Also, depending on the model, for opening bottles, pulling nails, and cleaning rollers and putty knives.

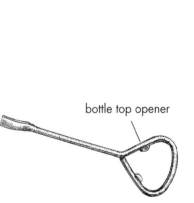

sharp edge for prying lids

bottle top opener

nail remover

curved edge for prying lids

Paint Can Opener

> **Buying Tips:** Very handy and much better than screwdrivers or quarters. Some of the more successful paint stores actually give them away at times. Keep your eyes peeled for such a wondrous deal.

Power Paint Mixer

Power Paint Mixer

Also Known As: Power mixing paint mixer, mixing paddle, paint blender, power mixer, paint mixer, drill mixer

Description: Propeller, spiral, or small paddle on end of metal rod that fits into power drill. Made for 1-gallon and 5-gallon cans.

Use: Inserted into paint cans for vigorous stirring without splashing, like a kitchen blender.

> **Buying Tip:** A must for 5-gallon cans.

Paint Shield

Paint Shield

Also Known As: Trim guard

Description: Long, slightly curved, or flat metal or plastic with a handle.

Use: Allows the painter to "cut in" narrow areas such as trim without getting paint on adjacent surfaces. Also used as a straight edge for trimming wallpaper.

Glass Masking Solution

Description: Fast-drying liquid solution applied with a wide applicator.

Use: Masking off glass without using tape, prior to painting windows. The material is scraped off with a razor knife after the paint is dry. Also used as a straight edge for trimming wallpaper.

Glass Masking Solution

Buying Tip: Faster and easier to use than masking tape.

Drop Cloths

Also Known As: Drops

Description: Large plastic, paper and plastic, or canvas sheet, commonly 9' × 12'. Plastic comes in a variety of thicknesses as well as from 1 mil (service weight) to 4 mil (extra-heavy).

Use: Protects floors, furniture, and landscaping from paint splatter and other mess.

> **Use Tips:** Fold up carefully after use and keep one side clean. Plastic is very slippery, so avoid using it on floors. Anything less than a 4 mil thickness is likely to tear too easily.

> **Buying Tips:** Get a good, big canvas one—it makes work go faster. Cut into small pieces for more convenient handling on small jobs.

Brush Comb

Brush Comb/Roller cleaner

Also Known As: Comb

Description: Plastic- or wood-handled comb with long steel teeth. Also made as a *brush comb/roller cleaner,* which has jagged teeth as part of a blade and a round notch on the opposite side for cleaning rollers.

Use: For straightening and cleaning bristles of a brush or cleaning a roller at the end of a paint job.

Brush and Roller Spinner

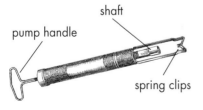

shaft

pump handle

spring clips

Brush and Roller Spinner

Also Known As: Brush cleaner, paint brush/roller cleaning tool, brush spinner, brush and roller cleaner

Description: Somewhat like a bicycle pump, with a loop handle and a metal cylinder, but with a spring-tension gripping device on one end to hold paint brushes or roller covers. Pump action spins the head very rapidly, creating strong centrifugal force on brushes and roller covers.

Use: Spinning paint brushes or roller covers at high speed to remove paint quickly and thoroughly without the use of excessive amounts of water or chemicals.

> **Use Tip:** Don't be like an unwanted wet dog. Spin inside a bag or a large bucket, as this thing makes the paint really fly. Very handy when working with a variety of colors.

> **Buying Tips:** An amazingly effective tool. Helps preserve expensive, high-quality brushes. Worth its relatively high price.

Cheesecloth

Description: Loosely woven, light cotton cloth.

Use: Originally used to strain old-fashioned paints; it's now used mainly in the kitchen (excellent for straining chicken stock). Also useful for applying stains and as a lintless cloth for wiping down surfaces with denatured alcohol before a final finish.

Tack Cloth

Description: Waxy **cheesecloth (above).**

Use: Final wiping of sawdust prior to painting or finishing. Its waxiness picks up dust.

Spray Can Handle

Spray Can Handle

Description: Pistol grip and trigger device with large ring instead of a barrel.

Use: Snaps on to almost any aerosol can to make pressing the paint can button easier, cleaner, and more controllable.

> **$ Buying Tip:** Makes any spray paint job easier and better.

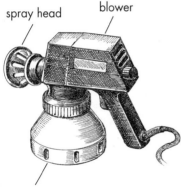

spray head   blower

paint reservoir

Airless Paint Sprayer

Airless Paint Sprayer

Description: Electronic pressurizer with trigger handle that sits atop a small paint container. Paint is atomized without mixing with additional air.

Use: Painting or staining large, irregular surfaces or items such as fences, decks, house siding, lattice, and concrete block. Also good for items such as wicker furniture, where using a brush would take too long.

Paint and Finish Removal Tools

Heat Gun

Description: Looks like a heavy-duty hair dryer—gun-shaped, electric, hot-air source (500 to 750 degrees).

Use: Softens multiple layers of paint for removal from molding or other detail.

Use Tips: Don't linger too long in one spot or a fire could start. Be especially cautious when removing lead paint.

Buying Tips: Avoid inexpensive plastic guns—they tend to drop their heat level as you work and do not have replaceable elements. The best are industrial-duty, with a cast-aluminum body and a ceramic heating element.

Heat Plate

Description: Electrified metal hot plate with handle that works up to about 1,100 degrees.

Use: Softens multiple layers of old paint for removal from large flat surfaces such as doors and clapboards.

About Scrapers

Even the semiactive handyperson frequently uses various kinds of scrapers, so it is a good idea to buy quality tools—they will last longer and be easier to use. The inexpensive ones tend to rust very easily, get dull quickly, and lose their handles.

Wall Scraper

Wall Scraper

Also Known As: Scraper, push scraper

Description: A stiff or slightly flexible, flat, triangularly shaped metal blade, commonly $3^1/_2$" wide at the front, with a wooden or plastic handle. A particularly long, narrow, and stiff scraper is called a *burn-off knife*.

Use: For scraping off peeling paint (whether old or while being softened with heat or chemicals), old plaster, or wallpaper. Can also be used as a trowel for *small* patching jobs, though that is easier with **flexible knives** made for the job **(Part VII, Chapter 50)**.

> **Buying Tips:** Look for such signs of quality as a one-piece blade that extends through the handle, is individually ground (or shaped), mirror-finished, and is of slightly flexible high-carbon steel. Good handles have large rivets and often a reinforced end for tapping nails into place, called a *nail-setting end*.

Shave Hook

Also Known As: Molding scraper, window scraper

Description: Long handle with small triangular or variously shaped blades perpendicular to handle. Generally sold in sets of three shapes (square, circular, and triangular), although models with interchangeable heads are available and convenient when scraping different shapes of molding. A large, heavy-duty version is called a *strip,* or *glue scraper.*

Use: Scraping softened paint or other finishes from window frames, moldings, doors, and other flat and curved surfaces.

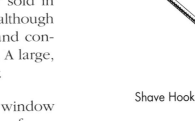

Shave Hook

> **$ Buying Tip:** Get a set of blades so that you can select a blade to match the contour of whatever you are scraping.

5-in-1 Tool

Also Known As: 6-in-1 putty knife, combination glazier's knife

Description: Stiff metal blade and handle similar to the **wall scraper (above)** that has a notched chisel end with a point on one side.

5-in-1 Tool

Use: Scrapes paint (with chisel end), opens cracks, cleans rollers (with large notch), removes putty (with point), and spreads adhesives.

> **$ Buying Tips:** Very handy to have. If it has a *nail-setting (hammer) end* (metal cap on end of handle) it can drive home small nails.

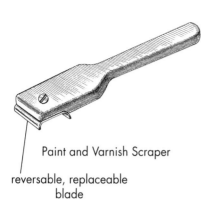

Paint and Varnish Scraper

reversable, replaceable
blade

Paint and Varnish Scraper

Also Known As: Wood scraper, hook scraper

Description: Consists of a short, hooked metal blade, 1" to 5" wide, with a long wooden, plastic, or metal handle. Blades are replaceable. Some models have four-sided blades that can be rotated around a central screw as they become dull.

Use: Removing old paint and varnish and smoothing wood.

> **Use Tips:** Take care not to gouge soft wood. Sharpen or replace blades often to make work easier.

> **Buying Tips:** Blades should be of high-carbon steel; long-lasting tungsten-carbide scrapers are also available.

Razor Blade Scraper

Razor Blade Scraper

Also Known As: Retractable blade scraper, glass scraper, window scraper

Description: Small, flat metal handle that holds a retractable single-edged razor blade.

Use: Mainly used to scrape paint off windows but can be used for other scraping jobs where you are dealing with a hard, nonporous surface.

> **Use Tip:** Blades dull quickly, so keep replacement blades handy.

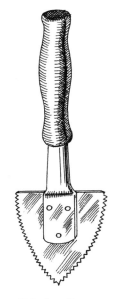

Window Opener

Window Opener

Also Known As: Window zipper, Windo-Zipper™

Description: Short spatula-like metal blade with toothed edges and a short handle.

Use: Cutting paint around windows that is blocking them shut.

> **Note:** See **Part VII, Chapter 50** for taping and putty knives.

Wall Coverings, Materials, and Tools

About Wallcoverings

Once there was only wallpaper—a wallcovering literally made of paper—to decorate walls and ceilings. Today, wallpaper is still plentiful but a variety of other materials are used, and thus the term *wallcoverings* is more apt.

Wallcoverings

Types:

> *Wallpaper*
>
> *Vinyl wall coverings* (popular brands include Wall-Tex® and Sanitas®)
>
> *Special materials wall coverings*

Also Known As: Wallpaper (only sometimes literally accurate, but often used generically to describe material that is not paper)

Description: Wallcoverings generally come 20½", 27", 36", and 54" wide, but almost always contain a total of 36 square feet of wallcovering per roll; more and more coverings are coming from abroad, though, and are measured in the metric system, yielding about 28 square feet per roll. Smaller widths, known as borders, are sold by the linear yard. Wallcoverings come prepasted or unpasted. Some are *dry strippable,* meaning that once installed they can be easily removed from the wall in one strip without using messy chemicals. Sold in "bolts"—one to three rolls, depending on the thickness of the material, but usually priced by the single roll. They are sold this way to cut down on waste when covering a standard 8' high wall.

> *Wallpaper:* Simply paper on which a design has been imprinted.
>
> *Vinyl:* This comes in various forms. One has a very thin clear vinyl coating over wallpaper; another has a strong fabric backing. While the vinyl may be solid, smooth, and shiny, it is also made "expanded" or textured to simulate many other materials from wood to suede. The patterns, colors, and textures are virtually endless. Vinyl may be either "washable," which can be washed mildly, or "scrubbable," which may be vigorously scrubbed.
>
> *Special materials:* These are woven textile, grass cloth, and materials other than vinyl or paper, such as metal foil.

Use: Chief use is decoration of walls as an alternative to painting or paneling, but in the case of vinyl, protects from moisture as well. Borders are used along the tops of walls. Most coverings can be used on ceilings too.

Use Tips: Vinyl is highly recommended for its cleanability and variety of surface appearances. Some fabrics, and especially grass cloth, are very hard to keep clean. 54" wide rolls are extremely difficult to handle but leave fewer seams. Recommended only for nonpattern types of covering, such as canvas. Use as thick a wall covering as possible to cover walls in poor condition; a product called *lining paper*, a plain wallcovering available in many weights, is good. A new polyester fiber-fill material is heavier and more versatile. Be sure to follow the manufacturer's directions closely, especially when selecting paste and when matching covering to the surface. Avoid applying paper over latex paint less than 6 months old.

Buying Tips: The more expensive types are fabrics, grass cloth, flocked paper, embossed paper (anaglyphic), and the like. Patterns and colors that are out of style are always cheaper. How-to books have many formulas for determining how much paper to buy for a particular room. Try for a 10-percent discount when you buy wallcovering; many retailers will give it to you just for the asking. Avoid untrimmed paper that comes with *selvage*, the unprinted edge that must be trimmed off.

Wallpaper Paste

Description: Specially formulated glue for hanging wallpaper; heavy vinyl wall coverings need a specified type. Usually water soluble.

Use: Holds wall coverings to wall.

> **Use Tips:** Follow directions carefully for wall prepara-
> tion. Using **wall size (below)** is usually a good idea.

Wall Size

Also Known As: Wallpaper primer

Description: Powder sold in bags or boxes. Mixed with water
for use. Some specialized mixtures contain different types of
primer as well.

Use: Applied as a primer to porous, especially plaster, walls
before using **wallpaper paste (above)**. Prevents the paste from
soaking into a porous wall and thus not adhering to the
paper, and provides a smoother surface for the paste that
allows more "open time" for positioning the paper (also called
slide time) as well as, eventually, better bonding. Generally
makes for a better wallpapering job. Some primers are designated for use with "strippable" wallcoverings.

> **Buying Tips:** *Primer/wall size* with additives to fit a
> variety of wall surfaces and paper is available and
> worthwhile. Note the details of your walls and paper and
> check the labels for the right one for you.

Wallpaper Remover

Description: Liquid or gel that is sprayed, rolled, sponged, or
brushed onto old wallpaper. May contain wetting agents and/
or enzymes.

Use: Softens old adhesive so that wallpaper may be scraped away.

> **Use Tips:** Gently slit or score (perforate) the paper first to foster better absorption. Wipe down the wall with remover solution after the paper is removed to eliminate any adhesive residue.

About Wallcovering Tools

One of the more common household decorating activities calls for a few specialized tools. Some typical items also often used but listed elsewhere are a **plumb bob (Part I, Chapter 10)** and a **razor knife (Part I, Chapter 6)**. Rent a *steamer* for removing stubborn old wallpaper.

Seam Roller

Also Known As: Oval seam roller, hardwood roller

Description: Small wooden roller with a wooden handle.

Use: Flattens wet wallcovering seams.

Seam Roller

> **Use Tip:** Wipe clean after each use.

Paste Brush

Paste Brush

Description: Typically a 6" wide, thick, long-bristle brush with a large wooden or plastic handle.

Use: Applying wallcovering paste.

Smoothing Brush

Smoothing Brush

Also Known As: Smoother, wallcovering smoother

Description: Very wide (up to 12"), very thin, flat, short-bristle brush.

Use: Smoothing wallcovering just after it is applied to the wall.

> **$ Buying Tip:** A flexible *plastic smoother*, a large flat rectangular plastic sheet with a handle, might be a good alternative.

Casing Knife

Casing Knife

Also Known As: Roller knife, smooth-blade casing knife

Description: Small wheel blade with a wooden handle; resembles a pizza cutter.

Use: For safely trimming excess wallcovering from windows, doors, baseboards, and so on.

> **Use Tips:** Even though this is the one tool specifically designed to trim wallcoverings, the **razor knife (Part I, Chapter 6)** actually works better (use a fresh blade after every cut or two; it is worth the slight expense in blades to avoid ruining a piece of wall covering with a dull blade alongside a straight edge (wallcovering tool) such as a **trim guard** or a **wide taping knife (Part VII, Chapter 50)**.

Magnetic Wrist Band

Description: Plastic wrist band, available in neon colors, with a rectangular, magnetic square instead of a watch.

Use: Holding single-edge razor blades, screws, or nails conveniently.

> **Use Tip:** Aim carefully when putting blades back on your wrist after use.

Magnetic Wrist Band

Wallpaper Scraper

Also Known As: Wallpaper stripper, slitter

Description: Extremely sharp, flat metal blade, usually about 3" wide, housed in a long metal handle. Often has a slightly angeled head.

Use: Scraping old wall coverings from wall after they have been steamed or chemically treated to release glue.

Wallpaper Scraper

> **Use Tips:** Try to avoid gouging soft plaster wall surface. A plain **wall scraper** may be easier to use.

> **Buying Tips:** Keep plenty of replacement blades on hand. Angled head makes it easier to use.

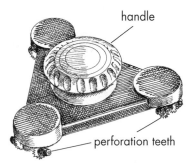

handle

perforation teeth

Wallpaper Scoring Tool

Wallpaper Scoring Tool

Description: Unique device made of a small, triangular, wheeled platform with a knob handle on top. The wheels are sharp-toothed blades, and there are six of them.

Use: Perforating old wallpaper so that removal chemicals or steam can penetrate more easily.

Wood and Wood Products

Manufactured Wood Products

About Manufactured Wood Products

All *manufactured wood products* are made from wood that has been cut, shaved, chipped, or ground into particles of various shapes and sizes, and then compressed under heat with synthetic resins and binders. The result is a product that is dimensionally stable and that can be designed for specific uses that go way beyond what mere boards and lumber can do.

For most people, the term *manufactured wood products* (also called *engineered wood*) does not include plywood, which is manufactured nonetheless from layers (not little pieces) of wood; indeed, some manufacturers call everything other than plywood *engineered board products*. Some of those products are smoother and flatter than plywood, or have less voids inside, or are stronger and lighter, though most are heavier because they are more dense. In most cases they are less expensive but in any case they are different from plywood.

Manufactured wood products are made with various kinds of adhesives and additives, some of which may emit slightly toxic gasses (especially when they are cut), presumably within stringent government standards. If you are particularly sensitive to formaldehyde or other gases, check with the manufacturer and note the technical specifications on the product for appropriate precautions. Often nothing more than covering the product or ventilating the room is called for.

About Plywood

Plywood is a manufactured item consisting of various thin layers of wood glued together. There are a number of characteristics to know about any plywood in order to make the proper selection. In other words, there is no such thing as "just plain plywood"—there is a specific plywood for each use.

Plywood is graded for either interior (INT) or exterior (EXT) use because of the different glues used (exterior grade is made with waterproof glue). It is also graded by the quality of its two faces, or sides, and each side may be graded differently. For grading, each plywood side, or face, has a letter designation that indicates quality. Plywood stamped Grade A should have no blemishes. Grade B will have a few blemishes and repair plugs of knotholes. Grade C will have checks (splits) as well as small knots and knotholes. In Grade D large knotholes are permitted. So, for example, if you buy Grade AC plywood, one side will be perfect while the C side will have some knotholes. This is often called *good one side* plywood. Plywood is also graded for the maximum span it can tolerate between roof rafters or floor joists.

Theoretically, you can buy any combination of sides, but in practice you will most often find: AC Exterior, AD Interior, AC Interior, and CD, or CDX (exterior), which is used for house sheathing.

Plywood

Plywood

Description: Plywood is either composed of various plies—thin panels of wood—bonded together at right angles to one another (veneer core plywood) or a single thickness of lumber sandwiched between a veneer of woods (lumber core). Some plywood is made with fine oak, birch, or lauan (Philippine mahogany) surfaces for shelving or cabinetry. Most is just plain pine, though.

Plywood is normally available in various thicknesses from $1/8$" to $3/4$" and in 4' 8' sheets and in exterior (EXT, or X) and interior (INT) use formulations. You may special-order other sizes, such as 4' × 10'. The only difference between interior and exterior plywood is that exterior plies are bonded with adhesive that can withstand harsh weather that glue for interior use cannot. *Marine plywood* is also available and has yet another specialized glue; even more specialized versions can be found, too, such as *fire-treated* or with *tongue-and-groove edges* for flooring.

A distinction between lumber and plywood is that nominal size is actual size—$3/4$" thick plywood is $3/4$" thick. In **lumber (Part VI, Chapter 48)** this is not so.

Use: A tremendous variety of building projects ranging from rough carpentry to building fine cabinets.

The following should give you an idea of how face grades are used:

A-A EXT: Outdoors, but very costly, used only when both sides show.

A-B EXT: Outside when both sides show.

A-C EXT: When only one side will show.

C-C EXT: Good for framing construction.

B-B EXT: Utility plywood for concrete forms, walks, and the like.

A-A INT: Best for cabinets and other fine furniture when both sides will show.

A-B INT: Similar to A-A, but a little less smooth-looking.

A-C INT: Paneling where one side will show.

B-D INT: Underlayment (subflooring) for flooring.

C-D: Used for sheathing, but cannot stand exposure to weather—must be kept covered.

CDX: Sheathing grade, exterior quality, for when you expect panels to be exposed awhile.

Sometimes carpenters refer to the lower grades as *construction grade* or *shop grade.*

$ Buying Tips: here are a number of ways to save money when buying plywood. One is to buy panels that are just good enough for the job at hand. If, for example, the plywood will be painted, you don't need an expensive plywood with a beautiful grain pattern. Check the so-called cut-up bin at the lumberyard where cutoffs or other scrap pieces are put. The pieces there may be big enough for the project—and the cost will be greatly reduced. Remember: If doing exterior work, make sure the pieces you buy are stamped EXT. Also, ask the dealer if he has any shop plywood available. This is material that has been chipped or otherwise damaged, but it is often possible to cut away the damaged area and use the rest of the panel. And shop plywood costs half of what nonshop plywood costs. Finally, *veneer-core* plywood is generally less expensive than *lumber-core.*

> ✂ **Use Tips:** Plywood is a wonderful material, but the edges are unsightly. To hide them you can (1) plan the project so the plywood edges don't show in the finished item, (2) cover them with thin wood strips, or (3) cover them with **veneer tape (below)**—thin strips of wood in flexible rolls.

OSB (Oriented-Strand Board)

Also Known As: Flakeboard, waferboard, waferwood, wiggle board

Description: Usually 4' by 8' panels made by bonding layers of wood strands and flakes oriented at right angles to one another with phenolic resin. Panels range from $3/8$" to $3/4$" thick; lengths longer than 8' are also available. Panel edges are both tongue-and-groove and square. Panels are available in three different degrees of stiffness for use as roof and/or wall sheathing, subfloors and underlayment, and single-layer floors.

(OSB is actually second-generation *waferboard*, an older product that has randomly-oriented flakes and is now almost only used in industrial applications where it is prized for its uniform strength in any direction. OSB is stronger in the long dimension of a panel.)

Uses: Light framing jobs, underlayment and roof sheathing (the material that goes under roofing). Some say OSB will be the plywood of the future.

> ✂ **Use Tip:** Dulls saw blades quickly. Keep dry.

OSB

> **$ Buying Tip:** More environmentally friendly in fabrication and slightly more uniform than plywood. Also less expensive.

Particleboard

Also Known As: Chipboard, fiberboard (incorrect), flakeboard (incorrect)

Description: Very hard, heavy material made of small reconstituted wood particles. Available in various thicknesses—$3/8$", $1/2$", $5/8$", and $3/4$"—and 4' wide by 8', 10', and 12' long. Particleboard is also available at some lumberyards precut as shelving 8", 10", and 12" wide, sometimes with plastic laminate already on it.

Use: For a variety of interior building jobs—closets, base for kitchen countertop plastic laminate, and underlayment. It does not warp.

> **Use Tips:** Particleboard is very heavy, so its use should be carefully calculated before obtaining it. The edges do not hold screws or nails well. Particleboard is also tough on saw blades. Cutting with a carbide blade is suggested. And don't let moisture get into it—it'll swell.

This material is often made with urea formaldehyde, which emits harmful vapors (outgassing) for some time after it is cut. Let new boards sit for a few days in a well-ventilated area.

> $ **Buying Tips:** Particleboard costs less than half of what plywood costs and can be very good material if used for the right project. It is particularly good for kitchen countertops and underlayment. You can also build with it, but be aware of its limitations.

Hardboard

Also Known As: Masonite®

Description: Made of densely compressed, very fine wood fibers and pulp. Standard hardboard comes 4' wide and in lengths of 8', 10', and 12' and in thicknesses of $1/8$" and $1/4$". Usually comes with one side tempered, which makes a harder, more moisture-resistant surface. The tempered side is normally smooth, the untempered side crosshatched and rough (available with both sides smooth). Another, substandard version is *service grade.*

Use: Various building purposes, but particularly useful as underlayment (subflooring) prior to installing resilient flooring, although some people think it is inferior to lauan or other plywood. For this you can get 4' × 4' squares or 3' × 4' hardboard rectangles, which are easier to manage than larger sizes. Also a common material for decorative wall paneling.

> **Use Tips:** Although screws do not hold well in hardboard, you can use sheet-metal screws if there is no alternative. The $1/8$" thickness takes glue poorly; *flooring nails* are best for underlayment.

> **Buying Tip:** Since hardboard is cheap, use it instead of plywood whenever possible.

Perforated Hardboard

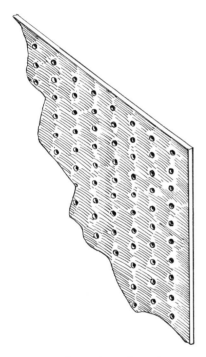

Perforated Hardboard

Also Known As: Peg-Board®

Description: Hardboard (above) with holes that can accept various hooks and hangers. Peg-Board comes either plain or prepainted and $1/8$" and $1/4$" thick.

Use: For hanging a wide variety of items, from tools in the shop to kitchen utensils. Special **Peg-Board fixtures** are used **(Part III, Chapter 30)**.

> **Use Tips:** When mounting Peg-Board make sure there's enough clearance behind the board for the hooks. Use special rubber spacers that go over the wall mounting screws.

MDF

Also Known As: Medium density fiberboard

Description: Heavy, flat, smooth panels of various sizes, most often $1/2$" or $3/4$" thick but in fact made from $1/4$" to $1^1/2$" or more thick. All edges are smooth; may come with shaped edges intended for use as bookshelves, stair treads, or flooring. Also sold as *molding*. Made from extra-fine wood fibers and resins or other bonding agents (glue) compressed under heat. Studier than particle board.

Use: Shelving (needs much support), cabinets, paneling, millwork, and furniture. Extra-smooth surfaces take paint and veneers extremely well.

> **Use Tips:** Stable, but not structural. Smooth edges are ready to paint (doesn't take stains). Routs easily.

> **Buying Tip:** Often half the price of birch veneer plywood, and two-thirds the cost of pine molding.

Fiberboard

Description: Very soft, low-density, light brown material made from wood fibers, available $1/2$" thick in panels of various sizes. A thicker, softer version of **hardboard (above)**. May be treated with chemicals for fire resistance. *Homosote® panels* are a similar, lighter item.

Use: As a light building material—closets and the like—and for sound deadening. Also as a "backer board" for nailing shingles.

> **Use Tips:** Fiberboard has significant limitations. It is not very strong and is subject to swelling from moisture; it should not be used in the bath or kitchen. Also, it should not be nailed to studs more than 16" apart.

Wood Scratch and Hole Fillers

Types:

> *Color stick*
>
> *Lacquer stick*
>
> *Liquid colorant*
>
> *Shellac stick*
>
> *Wood putty*

Also Known As: *Wood putty:* wood dough, Plastic Wood® (premixed type), Water Putty® (powder type), wood filler

Description:

> *Color stick:* Relatively soft, crayon-like stick in various wood colors.
>
> *Lacquer and shellac sticks:* Lacquer and shellac in hard stick form. They come in a variety of wood colors and are melted for use.
>
> *Liquid colorant:* Aniline dyes in small bottles in various colors.
>
> *Water putty:* Available two ways: cellulose fiber with a putty-like consistency, in small cans and ready to apply, and in powder form, which is mixed with water to obtain the proper consistency. Comes plain and in various wood colors.

> **Note:** These items are all made from wood fibers or wood-like products; **spackling compound (Part VII, Chapter 50)**, a plaster-like substance, is one of the most common and best wood gap fillers you can use prior to painting.

Use: *Shellac, lacquer stick*, and *water putty* are for holes, though they can also be used on deep scratches. *Color sticks* and *dyes* are for scratches; the former is rubbed over the scratch while the latter is applied with a tiny brush.

Use Tips: Wood putty may be colored to suit. Professionals favor lacquer and shellac sticks, but they are more difficult for the beginner to use than putty. Color sticks and dyes are simple to use.

Buying Tips: Powdered water putty is amazingly useful. Unused portions can be stored indefinitely (the premixed kind tends to dry out), and it can be used for large holes and even as a floor leveler. No worker should be without a large can.

Wood Restoration Material

Description: A variety of either polyester, polymer, or epoxy materials. Usually a two-part mix. Liquid form is considered a consolident for soft wood; putty form is a structural adhesive that fills and replaces whole sections of wood. Can be sawed, nailed, planed, and sanded like wood. Moldable.

Use: Restoring damaged architectural wood parts where replacement with new wood is not possible or desirable, and where plaster-like patchers would fail. Common items for which this is ideal include most exterior repairs, rotted or damaged windowsills, columns, frames, structural or decorative wood components in trim, and broken furniture. Liquid form is poured onto damaged wood so it penetrates and is absorbed and impregnates the wood fibers so that it hardens into a high-strength mass within minutes. It also acts as a primer for putty or paint. The putty is applied with a knife and does not shrink or crumble when dry. Both merge totally with sound wood.

> **Use Tips:** Follow directions for safety and use scrupulously. Some of the chemicals involved are toxic. Don't expect rotted wood to support a strong piece of this material—remove all rotted wood down to a sound base for repair. No material bonds well with wet wood. Make sure it is dry, dry, dry.

> **Buying Tips:** Especially formulated for use with wood. Do not confuse with the **epoxy repair putty** intended for **plumbing repairs (Part VIII, Chapter 60)**. Some people like to use polyester-based auto-body repair material, which is an acceptable substitute.

Wood Veneer

Description: Extremely thin strips of various types of fine woods, sold in narrow ribbons on rolls or in wider, packaged units. $1/28''$ or $1/40''$ thick. Available in many different beautiful wood grains.

Use: Furniture repair, hobbies. The ribbon type is used to cover edges of plywood; the sheets for furniture.

Lumber

About Lumber

There are a number of basic systems by which lumber is classified. These may seem confusing at first but are in fact very helpful.

1. **Type of Wood.** Trees can be broken down into two basic kinds: softwood and hardwood. The names are botanical distinctions and have nothing to do with the hardness of the wood: Softwoods come from trees that have cones, while hardwoods come from leaf-bearing trees.

   Theoretically, lumber is available in a vast variety of wood types. But in reality what you'll usually find in the average lumber outlet is pine, fir, and spruce. Pine alone comes in some 25 different varieties. But names don't matter. What matters is that you get the right material for the job at hand.

2. **Length.** Lumber is sold by the *board foot,* a volume measurement meaning a 1" thick, 1' square of wood. This is a common denominator used by dealers in pricing lumber. Sometimes it is sold by the *linear* (or, incorrectly, lineal) *foot,* too, but usually only with preformed, or milled, pieces such as molding.

3. **Major Groups: Lumber and Boards.** Lumber includes all sawed wood more than 2" thick, but is divided into

two broad subgroups: lumber (or *dimension lumber* or *framing lumber*), which is used for structural purposes— to make *studs* (basic vertical framing of walls) and *joists* (horizontal framing of floors and ceilings) and the like. Boards are thinner (no more than 2" thick) and are used for siding, decking, making furniture, or for decorative purposes. And there's yet another category for lumber larger than 5" × 5"—timber **(see dimension lumber and boards, below)**.

4. **Size.** Most important, boards and lumber, like many other wood products, have nominal, or named, sizes and actual sizes. This is because when it is dressed (cut, smoothed, and dried) lumber loses some wood from its original named size. Thus, when you buy a normal 2 × 4 you will actually get a piece of wood that is $1\frac{1}{2}$" × $3\frac{1}{2}$". If you buy a 1 × 4, the board will be $\frac{3}{4}$" × $3\frac{1}{2}$". Check with your dealer on the actual sizes of material before buying.

Boards and lumber come in a tremendous array of sizes, of course, but lumberyards don't carry everything, and in reality you will likely find boards ranging in size from 1" × 2" to 1" × 18" wide, with sizes increasing by 2" increments after 3". Lumber sizes start at 2" × 2" and go up in 2" increments after 3". Carpenters often call lumber by its dimensions only, such as a "2 × 4" or a "2 × 6." The "2×" dimension is so common that it is sometimes just called a "2-by," as in the most common lumber cuts, 2 × 2, 2 × 3, 2 × 4.

5. **Grading.** The most common boards are classified according to the amount of defects, such as knotholes, that they contain and are roughly divided into boards that have none or few defects, called *clear* or *select*, and boards that have varying degrees of defects are called *common*. Each of those has subcategories, too, and there are so many grades and systems (some regional, and some just

for one species!) that we've outlined them in a separate section **(below)**. However, many outlets just group their boards into these broad categories, or perhaps clear or select and two or three categories of common (No. 1 common, No. 2 common, on down in quality). For average projects that is all you need to know.

About Lumber and Boards Grading

Like plywood, lumber is graded according to quality, and prices reflect this quite strongly. *White pine,* one of the most common pines carried by lumberyards, is graded in nine categories for boards, though only about half of these grades are normally carried in your average, small lumberyard.

There are two basic divisions: *clear,* or *appearance* (almost perfect, clear of imperfections), and *common* (which has varying numbers of knotholes); these are in turn divided into four and five subdivisions. Again, most lumberyards do not carry all grades.

Here is how white pine is graded, from the top, or best, grades to the bottom:

Clear Grades:

A Select: Also known as: Clear

B Select: Also known as: A and B are sometimes lumped together and called *B or Better* or *1 and 2 Clear*—no knots or blemishes.

C Select: Perhaps only a few blemishes on one side.

D Select: Slight blemishes on both sides. Most widely obtainable of this group.

Common Grades:

> *No. 1 Common:* Also known as: 1C, Select Merchantable; overlaps with D Select.
>
> *No. 2 Common:* Also known as: 2C. Some knots and blemishes. Good for most projects.
>
> *No. 3 Common:* Also known as: 3C, Standard; knots and holes, okay for shelving; generally needs painting or staining.
>
> *No. 4 Common:* Also known as: Utility; much cheaper; okay for construction.
>
> *No. 5 Common:* Also known as: Economy; extremely unsightly; suitable for crating.

Dimension lumber (see below) is similarly graded, and ranges from select structural, the best, down to No. 1, No. 2, and No. 3, with No. 3 the lowest. However, these are commonly reduced to three names for lumber for light framing uses, or studs: *construction, standard,* and *utility.* To add to the confusion, wood intended for studs (basic vertical 2 × 3 or 2 × 4 framing) may be classified as just that: stud grade. Keep in mind that the lowest-quality grade is not as strong as the higher grades. Some low grades may be referred to by a rather descriptive term, *sound wormy.*

Here again, grade names really don't matter so much—just examine the wood and match it to the job at hand. If you want wood grain and pattern to show, buy lumber that has such qualities.

A final note: This grading system holds for white pine. Some of the more special woods have their own grading systems, so when you buy Idaho pine, redwood, and most hardwoods, ask to have that particular grading system explained to you. For example, hardwoods have a top category called *firsts and seconds,* abbreviated FaS.

CHAPTER 48

Dimension Lumber and Boards

Also Known As: Lumber, construction lumber, framing lumber

Description: In brief, dimension lumber is anywhere from 2" to 5" thick, while boards are less than 2" nominal size. Remember, nominal means that a 1" board is actually $3/4$" thick. If dimension lumber has smoothed surfaces on four sides, it may be noted as "S4S," which is a type of **molding (below)**.

Some boards come precut or trimmed for particular purposes, especially stair building. There is *stringer* (or *carriage*—zigzag cut or grooved to hold treads), *stepping* (treads), and so on. Others may be trimmed for decorative use, such as *nosing,* boards with one rounded edge. 1" boards 6" to 10" wide are often referred to as *shelving board*. Because of these time-saving cuts, your local dealer will often ask what you intend to use the board for.

Use:

> *Dimension lumber:* Framing rooms, porches, and a wide variety of other basic construction (structural) tasks. These are your studs (vertical framing), joists, and beams (horizontal framing), etc.

> *Boards:* Siding building boxes, cabinets, shelves, and many other, more finished items.

$ Buying Tips: You'll likely get a better buy at lumber-yards than at other outlets simply because you'll have a larger choice of material. Also, some home centers sometimes pick out the best pieces in a lot of common and sell them as select, so even if you can pick wood there you are not picking among the best material. Some lower-priced outlets sell lumber that lumberyards won't take. In fact, in smaller stores the only distinction made may be between clear and common—probably the No. 2 grades of each. And remember, grades are reflected in the prices. But don't fret—you can just ask for boards "with or without knots" if you have trouble with these terms.

When buying always check for the following, rather than just relying on complicated grading terms:

1. *Is it straight?* Tip the board up and sight down it. Is it flat or warped?

2. *Does it have knots?* If so, are they tight? If they are, they may not interfere with your project.

3. *Does the board have pitch pockets*—broken lines running down the board? Sap pockets? If so, don't buy the board. It will eventually warp.

4. *Does the board have splits?* Edges of bark that are rounded? No good.

5. *Is it kiln-dried, or air- (surface, or seasoned) dried?* Or green (wet)? Dried lumber does not warp, which matters a great deal if the wood is not nailed in place right away. Kiln-dried is the best, but air-dried is fine for most projects. The drying grade is often abbreviated, as in S-Dry for surface-dried and S-Green for high moisture content.

One Other Buying Tip: With boards, "common" is usually the cheapest material available. If your project requires clear wood, you may be able to buy common, cut away the knots, and still have enough usable material for your project. You can buy three times as much common as needed for the job, and if you can get the boards you need out of it, you'll still likely save money over buying clear—it's not that much more expensive. This is especially true for wood that you intend to paint, in the No. 2 and 3 categories, but you must paint the knots with **shellac (Part V, Chapter 42)** or other stain killer first, or else the knots will show through.

Furring

Description: Narrow strips of wood. Usually 1" × 2" boards, but sometimes 1" × 3" or 1" × 4" boards.

Use: Applied to walls and ceilings, provides a level nailing or adhesive surface for materials such as paneling, drywall, and ceiling tiles, a process known as *furring out.*

Use Tips: When using furring on walls, space the pieces horizontally. Proper spacing is more critical on ceilings than walls—especially when used as a base for tile.

Buying Tips: Select pieces of furring that are straight. Placing them length-to-length against one another and then turning them over will reveal any gaps between them and, therefore, any curves.

Pressure-Treated Lumber

Also Known As: Treated lumber, PTL, CCA (more common)

Description: Standard lumber that has had chemicals injected into it under pressure and is to varying degrees—depending on the treatment—decay- and rot-proof. CCA refers to one very common chemical used, copper chromate arsenate, but there are different ones and some manufacturers use their own formulations: Wolmanized® lumber is one very common example of this. These are strong and, in some cases, toxic chemicals.

Use: Used in place of naturally decay-resistant woods, such as redwood or cedar, in outdoor building projects such as decks, furniture, exterior trim, landscaping, and the like, where constant moisture is a problem.

Use Tips: Pressure-treated lumber was not intended to be painted for protection, at least when fresh (it "outgasses" chemicals for 4–6 months), but you may want to paint it to reduce the possibility of toxic splinters in bare feet. These days painting is being considered more often. Cut ends should be treated—ask at your lumberyard for assistance. Observe safety precautions when sawing, sanding, and handling treated lumber—the preservative chemicals used are toxic, and therefore so is its sawdust. Never burn pressure-treated lumber as it may give off toxic smoke. Make sure scrap is disposed of in a way that prevents it being used as fuel, especially for barbecue fires.

Buying Tips: Treatment is often done locally, and some communities are banning this work for environmental reasons. New, nontoxic treatments are being developed and some are already in use.

Milled and Preformed Wood Products

About Milled Wood Products

A stroll through the average lumberyard or home center can turn up a number of useful items, all assembled, milled into special shapes, or otherwise ready for use. Also known as *millwork.*

About Molding

Molding, or interior trim, is the material used to trim a job, and it often spells the difference between a job well or poorly done. There is a wide array of molding available, and lumberyards usually have a board on which are displayed their variety of moldings. The descriptions and illustrations here describe only a fraction of what's available.

Molding may be made of hardwood or softwood, depending on wood availability in the area you live in. Cedar, pine, fir, larch, poplar, and hemlock are common.

Molding comes unfinished in 2' increments up to 16' long, and the increments can be odd or even. 8' and 10' lengths are the most common and useful. Widths vary from a fraction of an inch up to 6", but molding, like lumber, is described in nominal and actual sizes—a 3" nominal size, for example, will only be 2⅝" wide.

Although this is a section on wood products, note that a common substitute for base molding around a floor-wall joint is

Base Molding

Shoe Molding

Casing Molding

vinyl strip, cove, or *straight base molding,* a 2" to 6" wide strip sold in various lengths and easily installed with its own adhesive. It is available in a range of colors.

Molding

Types:

Base molding

Base cap molding

Base shoe molding

Casing molding

Chair rail molding

Corner guard molding

Cove molding

Crown molding

Half round molding

Mullion

Quarter round molding

Stool

Stop

Threshold

Also Known As:

> *Base shoe:* Shoe, toe
>
> *Base:* Baseboard, clam, clamshell
>
> *Casing:* Case
>
> *Corner guard:* Corner bead (same term as metal base for joint compound)
>
> *Threshold:* Saddle

Description: Sold in lengths of 3' to 20' (usually stocked in the longer lengths only) and generally not cut to order. Dozens of shapes available, with many similarities. Here are a few of the most common.

> *Base:* Flatish with square bottom and tapered top, various surface patterns. Plain surface called *clam base.*
>
> *Base cap:* Square bottom and convex or concave top, generally small.
>
> *Base shoe:* In profile looks like a slightly offset quarter of a circle. Another type is concave with a square bottom. Always small.
>
> *Casing:* Flatish to slightly convex with almost square bottom and top with slight taper; fancier ones with more curves in the surface may be called *Colonial casing.*
>
> *Chair rail:* Flat, grooved, or fluted; generally fairly wide.
>
> Corner guard: V-shaped channel.
>
> *Cove:* Slightly curved, a little like the letter C. Also similar to a concave base shoe.
>
> *Crown:* Curved face on flat back with 45-degree beveled edges.
>
> *Half round:* Half-circle profile.
>
> *Mullion:* Fluted molding.

Half Round Molding

Quarter Round Molding

Quarter round: A quarter of a circle.

Stool: One square and one molded edge.

Stop: Thin molding with one square and one tapered edge.

Threshold: Usually oak, flat, beveled piece.

Use:

Base: Goes along bottom of walls.

Base cap: Goes over top of base for added trim.

Base shoe: Covers the gap between baseboard molding and floor.

Casing: Trim around outside of doors and windows.

Chair rail: Placed a few feet up a wall to divide the space and protect from chairs rubbing against the wall.

Corner guard: Covers corners to protect from damage.

Cove: Standard moldings usually forming an inside corner if small, such as on stairs, or if larger, trim at the wall-ceiling juncture, like crown molding.

Crown: Decorative cover of the wall-ceiling juncture; greatly enhances any room.

Half round: Variety of uses, including enhancing other moldings.

Mullion: Vertical trim between windows.

Quarter round: Fills the cap between wall and floor. Often used in small sizes on stairways.

Stool: Inside horizontal section of window molding (sill is outside section).

Stop: As trim that abuts windows and doors; actually "stops" the door at its closing point.

Threshold: Doorways, over joint between floors of two rooms.

Use Tips: When cutting molding at an angle, use a **miter box (Part I, Chapter 5)**—don't try to do it freehand. Keep in mind when determining how much molding to get that these cuts create waste by themselves as well as in the unfortunate case of errors. You can create very distinctive and fancy-looking trim by combining some of the simplest molding shapes. Old-fashioned trim often consists of three or four moldings—some just plain, flat boards—placed together with some simple shapes. Molding may be nailed or glued, and often both are used in difficult spots.

Buying Tips: Molding described as the same size can differ fractionally if produced by different mills. This can affect the looks of a job so hold pieces against one another to make sure they match. Buy more than you think you'll need to cover cutting errors. Also, beware of buying *paint grade molding* that's not one continuous piece but, rather, joined by so-called finger joints. Molding of this quality is suitable for only one finish—paint. For staining, get *clear-grade molding* (or *select-grade* or *stain grade*). If you want molding that has fancy designs milled in it, this is also available. Every metropolitan area has at least one major lumberyard that is a major supplier of finish wood trim. They would have, or sometimes even produce, a catalog or a sheet showing all kinds of shapes. Finally, shop around for molding prices—they vary greatly. One trick of lumberyards is to offer paneling at a great discount and companion molding at a great markup.

Wood Shims

Description: 6" to 8" long wooden wedges, no more than about $1/2$" thick at the "heel" end, and about 2" wide. Generally sold in bundles of a dozen or so.

Use: Stabilizing and leveling counters, appliances, and walls under construction.

> **§ Buying Tips:** Although your own scrap pile can help, having many of these on hand is a good way to speed up a major job. Alternatives are wooden shingles, or *shakes*.

Dowels

Also Known As: Dowel rods

Description: Wood rods, sold usually in 3' or 4' lengths and ranging in diameter from $1/8$" to $1\,1/4$" in $1/16$" and $1/8$" increments. Larger sizes—$1\,3/8$" and $1\,5/16$" diameter—are sold as *closet rods* or *poles*; *socket sets* are sold for installation, and come with cup-like parts that attach to the closet walls.

Use: Various woodworking projects, including making glued joints with perfectly matched holes and short lengths of dowel rod.

> **§ Buying Tip:** These are often sold in a DIY materials floor display.

Dowel Pins

Description: Short, specially milled dowels with spiral grooves or channels (fluted).

Use: Gluing two pieces of wood together, especially furniture parts. They are inserted in holes drilled in the edges with glue; the spirals or flutes are paths for excess glue and air to escape. Makes a very strong joint.

Dowel Pins

> **Use Tip:** Drill accurately matched holes in the two pieces with the aid of a **dowel jig (Part II, Chapter 16)**.

> **Buying Tip:** Although they are available commercially, you can easily make your own pins from dowel rods.

Furniture Legs

Description: Legs are available in unfinished wood as well as other materials—wrought iron, tube steel, and in a variety of styles from modern to Mediterranean. Lengths range up to around 30". Sold alone or with metal mounting plates.

Use: Used in the making of new furniture as well as repairing and resuscitating older pieces. They screw right into existing mounts.

Furniture Leg

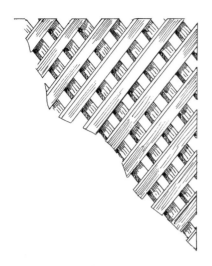

Lattice

Lattice

Description: Thin boards assembled in crisscross fashion into panels of various sizes—2' × 4', 2' × 8', and 4' × 8'—and made of interior or exterior wood. Also now available in plastic, which resists termites. Unassembled boards are sold as molding.

Use: Decorative material for inside and outside the house, such as for dividers, trellises, flanking entryways, to wall off the space between deck and ground to keep rubbish from blowing in.

Spindles

Description: Turned-wood posts of various lengths of around 6" to 72" and diameters of 1" to 4". In some cases the spindles screw together. Posts may be unfinished, raw wood, or finished. Related parts include finials, spacers, bases, and connectors.

Use: Spindles can be assembled to serve a variety of decorative and functional purposes, including dividers, shelf supports, candle and lamp holders, and stair or porch railings.

Use Tips: Prefinished spindles are available in a wide variety of finishes, so if you want to avoid having to finish the wood yourself, it's likely you can find what you need in prefinished form.

Shutters

Types:

Exterior shutters

Interior shutters

Description:

Exterior shutters: Made of plastic or wood that is primed.

Interior: Almost always made of pine, these come in widths from 6" to 12" and heights from 16" to 48". They may be unfinished and without hardware or finished with hanging hardware attached. Shutters are available with *louvers* (slats) and panels into which fabric or other decorative material may be inserted.

Use: Interior shutters can be used over interior windows or as cafe doors. Exterior shutters usually aren't operative and are intended for decoration only.

 Use Tip: If shutters require painting, aerosol spray paint is usually the easiest way to a smooth finish.

VII

Wall, Floor, and Ceiling Materials and Tools; Doors and Windows

Drywall, Plaster, Materials, and Tools

Drywall

Also Known As: Sheetrock®, wallboard, gypsum wallboard, gypsum board, gypsum drywall, gypsum panel, gypboard, plasterboard, GyProc®.

> **Note:** Sheetrock®, U.S. Gypsum's trade name, is used generically.

Description: Sheet material composed of a core of gypsum or other plaster-like material, covered on both sides with heavy paper. The paper on the backing and face is different according to use: drywall is available with both sides of backing paper, for use when another piece of drywall is going to be glued right to it (*backer board*); with green paper (*greenboard*) that is moisture-resistant, and with blue paper (*blueboard*) for skim-coating. Other specialized types are available.

Drywall panels come 4' wide and in 6', 7', 8', 10', 12', and 16' lengths with 8' the most common and $1/4$", $3/8$", $1/2$", and $5/8$" thick. Edges may be tapered, straight, beveled, tongue-and-groove, rounded, or square; tapered is most often sold and allows for three layers of **joint compound (below)** to be applied to the gap between panels without bulging out. Although all gypsum is somewhat fire-resistant, *Type X fire-rated* ("Firestop") or *boiler-room*, drywall types are also available.

Use: New walls and ceilings, resurfacing damaged walls. Moisture-resistant drywall is excellent for baths. It is secured with special **drywall nails** or **screws (Part III, Chapters 20 and 21)** to wooden or metal studs (the vertical framing members of the wall) or glued to existing walls and to ceilings with special **panel adhesive (Part VII, Chapter 51)**.

> **Use Tips:** Install panels so that the number of seams is minimized. This reduces the amount of joint taping you must do. $1/2$" thick drywall is generally used for light residential purposes and $5/8$" for everything else; $1/4$" can be used to cover an existing but damaged surface. Don't use moisture-resistant drywall on ceilings. Drywall is one of the heaviest materials around, so plan carefully how to transport it from the store to your home and within the construction site. Not a job for one person in any way. Even with two, look into renting a special hoist (called a *panel lift* or *drywall jack*) for holding panels in place on ceilings prior to screwing, or construct a "dead man," a cross of 1" × 2" or similar lumber that is jammed up against the panel while you screw it in. For best painting results, especially with glossy paint, put a "skim coat" of joint compound over all. Prime properly. Rent or buy a **screw gun (Part II, Chapter 16)**, if you are installing any large quantity.

> **$ Buying Tips:** As building materials go, drywall is the same: one manufacturer's product will be the same as another; there are no hidden defects. This material is either smooth and solid or it isn't. If you see it on sale, buy it. Drywall is cheap, but the price can vary somewhat from lumberyard to lumberyard, so check it out.

Cement Board

Also Known As: Backer board, tile backer board, underlayment board

Description: Cement version of gypsum **drywall (above)**, consisting of an aggregated portland cement core sandwiched between two layers of glass fiber mesh. One side is smooth and one textured; the side edges are smooth and rounded to allow for joint mortar, but the ends are square cut. Resistant to water damage. Standard board is $1/2$" or $5/8$" thick and 32", 3', or 4' wide in 4', 5', 6', or 8' lengths. Underlayment board made specifically for floors and countertops is $5/16$" thick and 4' × 4'. Should be sold with joint tape and polymer-coated screws made specifically for use with cement board.

Use: Substrate or underlayment for ceramic tile in wet areas such as bathrooms or kitchens, or for floors.

> **Use Tips:** Smooth side is for adhesives, rough side for thin-set mortar. Use only alkali-resistant glass fiber tape on joints, and only latex-fortified, thin-set mortar or Type 1 organic adhesive, as well as either $1^1/_2$" hot-dipped galvanized roofing nails or polymer-coated screws made specifically for use with cement board. Otherwise the strong chemicals (alkalis) in the cement or the moisture in the environment will corrode the screws and tape. Floor underlayment must be totally secured according to directions, using $^5/_8$" plywood.

Corner Bead

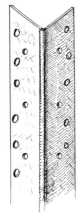

Corner Bead

Description: Long galvanized steel strip with an L-shaped profile. Sold in 8' lengths. Available also in a flexible version, *metal corner tape*, made of a steel strip sealed into paper tape. Many specialized designs available, such as J-profile, Bullnose, or offset.

Use: Finishes off corners where drywall panels abut. Provides base for **joint compound (below)**. Corner tape is for arches, cathedral ceilings, or any odd angle.

Joint Compound

Also Known As: Drywall compound, mud

Description: Comes both as a ready-mixed paste and in powder form that is mixed with water. Dries fast and is very easily sanded wet or dry, or smoothed with a wet sponge. Specially formulated for easy workability over large surfaces, made with the finest granules of the **wall patching/preparing products (below)**, including gypsum, vinyl, and other additives. Setting (*taping*) and *topping compound* are for professionals using a two-product system; *all-purpose joint compound* is the most common for the DIY market. Available also in a "light" formulation.

Use: Sealing drywall joints with joint tape as well as extremely shallow patching, such as in areas where paint has peeled. Intended for use over wide areas in thin, successive coats. A number of applications will likely be required because joint compound shrinks as it dries. Must be primed prior to painting; diluted flat latex wall paint is recommended. Only setting-type joint compound should be used with **fiberglass tape (below)**.

Use Tips: Joint compound is always applied in thin, multiple, smooth layers, each layer feathered out beyond the previous one. Use lots of joint compound and a proper **taping knife (below)**—it is an easy material to work with. Don't let any dried chips fall into your fresh supply (working out of a 14" long mud pan or mud tray instead of the compound container may help). If used in a high-traffic area, remember that joint compound is much softer than its cousin, plaster, and easily damaged. Nor is it as smooth. Sanding (done with fine-grade sandpaper) produces lots of bad dust, so use a proper respirator or use wet sanding or a damp sponge to limit your dust. Try using a damp sponge or a stiff felt pad *blister brush* instead of sandpaper but avoid wetting the surface paper. If you have much sanding along the ceiling or high walls, use a **drywall sander (below)** with a broom handle–type attachment. Sanding can be limited by proper application in the first place. "Light" compound generally needs less sanding (it is also easier to sand) and doesn't shrink or crack. Supposedly only two coats are needed. Some brands may be used as texture paint when diluted with water. Can replace **spackling compound (below)**. Powdered *setting-type joint compound* is a good plaster-like patcher.

> **$ Buying Tips:** Premixed "all-purpose" joint compound is recommended. It is always at the proper consistency and stores well. "Light" compound is usually more expensive, but you might use less, and it is easier to sand. Fiberglass tape requires setting-type compound that you must mix, but needs only two quick-setting coats and can be finished in one day.

Joint Tape

Types:

> *Paper joint tape*
>
> *Fiberglass mesh joint tape*

Also Known As: Wallboard tape, perforated tape, drywall tape

Description: 2" wide, strong, perforated (and nonperforated) paper or fiberglass mesh in various lengths, usually 75 and 250 feet. Paper tape comes in rolls as long as 500' and with a convenient crease down the middle (*corner tape* has steel strips in the middle). The perforations are necessary for the tape to imbed itself in the joint compound. Fiberglass mesh is also available in 36" by 75' or 150' rolls.

Use: Component in sealing and reinforcing the seams between drywall panels; always used in conjunction with **joint compound (above)**. Large rolls of fiberglass mesh are used to repair entire walls or ceilings of old, cracked plaster.

> **Use Tips:** Fiberglass mesh is applied with staples or is self-adhesive and may be easier to use, especially when patching holes (the adhesive eliminates the need for a first coat of joint compound). It also makes for a stronger joint. Fiberglass tape requires the use of the stronger *setting-type joint compound* and may be covered with two coats in only one day.

Self-Adhesive Wall Patch

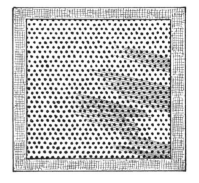

Self-Adhesive Wall Patch

Also Known As: Metal drywall repair patch

Description: 4" to 8" square piece of fiberglass mesh with adhesive backing, containing a perforated aluminum plate in its center. Peel-and-stick *patching tape* has no metal and is slightly flexible.

Use: Patching large holes in drywall, plaster, or hollow-core doors with a minimum of patching material. The aluminum eliminates the need to fill the hole and the adhesive mesh eliminates the need for preplastering. Also eliminates the need to cut drywall patches and holes to size. Smaller versions, made only of very stiff mesh, are specifically designed to bridge the gap between drywall and electrical boxes, a gap that is particularly hard to fill without cracking. They are placed over the whole hole and then the inside is cut out to leave the electrical box open while providing surface around it for patching compound. *Patching tape* is for small holes and cracks in plaster.

> **Buying Tip:** Another good effort in the search to simplify hole patching.

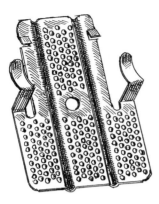

Drywall Repair Clip

Drywall Repair Clip

Description: Small, perforated, flat metal clip with openings on opposite sides.

Use: Provides instant bracing for repair of large holes in drywall. The "filler" piece of drywall is simply clipped in place and then covered with patching compound. Eliminates the need to cut back the good wall to studs or to create a home-made brace.

Wall Patchers

Types:

> *Plaster*
>
> *Patching plaster*
>
> *Spackling compound*

Also Known As:

> *Plaster:* Plaster of Paris, painter's plaster, wet-wall plaster
>
> *Patching plaster:* Wall patch
>
> *Spackling compound:* Spackle®, spackling putty, spackling paste

Description: Plaster, or plaster of Paris, is the generic name for a very common product made of ground-up and treated gypsum rock (originally mined near Paris) that comes as a white powder that is mixed with water for use. Different manufacturers use different additives and manufacturing processes, much as with paints, to produce similar products that they market under various names. The three basic groups of products noted here differ in their drying, or *set*, times, their ease of application, their plasticity or "workability," and their strength. These differences are due to chemical additives and the different grades of ground gypsum rock used.

Plaster: Mixed with lime to form the basic material in wet-wall construction, i.e., commonly known as *plaster walls*. Sets in about ten minutes and forms an extremely hard surface. May be mixed with aggregates such as sand for base coats and varying amounts of lime for different finishes and hardnesses. Must be applied over a proper surface, such as wooden or metal lath, a net-like metal sheet.

Patching plaster: Plaster that contains additives that make it dry much more slowly and has a slightly more plastic "feel" to it when being applied, making it slightly easier to work. **Setting-type joint compound (above)** is almost the same.

Spackling compound: Finest ground gypsum, with many additives. Extremely fast-setting and nonshrinking. Also available in paste form ready to apply (in tubs, tubes, and even pencil-like dispensers), as well as in versions with additives such as vinyl that make it more flexible or adhesive. The verb "to spackle" comes from the German verb *spachteln,* meaning to fill or smooth a surface; Spackle® is a popular brand name that is used—incorrectly—in a generic way for this family of products.

Use:

Plaster of Paris: Constructing walls, filling very large patches, anchoring ceramic bathroom fixtures, hobby projects. Making plaster walls is an art done only by seasoned professionals.

Patching plaster: Filling large cracks and breaks in plaster surfaces, but not holes.

Spackling compound: For small holes and cracks in drywall, plaster, or wood. If in powder form, use only inside the house; for outside use a *spackling paste,* made for both interior and exterior work. Lately manufacturers have been coming out with so-called *light* spackling mixtures that permit coverage of larger patches than before, though **joint compound (above)** suits this purpose, too. They cover well but are not as hard. Light spackling dries instantly and can be painted right after application.

Use Tips: Plaster sets so quickly that it can create problems. But you can triple the setting time by adding a dash of vinegar to every batch you mix. Use a **bonding agent (below)** to assure adhesion. Regular plaster is extremely hard to apply just right, and also hard to sand, so use spackling compound as a final leveler of uneven surfaces—spackling compound, like joint compound, is extremely easy to sand down.

Buying Tips: Plaster is available in 4- and 8-pound plastic tubs and 5-pound bags, but it is suggested you buy only what you need; it doesn't stand up to moisture well in storage. Take care when buying spackling paste—some brands are relatively gritty, while the better ones are very smooth. Stick with major brands. Specialized mixtures abound—even *popcorn ceiling patch* is available.

Bonding Agent

Description: Resinous emulsion that is brushed or rolled onto wall surface and allowed to dry until it becomes tacky.

Use: Dramatically increases bonding of new plaster or cement to any structurally sound surface. Virtually welds the patch to the old material. Useful for applying skim coats of plaster.

> **Use Tip:** While it is necessary to wait until this becomes tacky, it is o.k. to wait as much as two weeks after application to apply the plaster to it.

> **Buying Tips:** Yields excellent results. Some types are made specifically for plaster or concrete, while others work with both or are marked for interior or exterior use. Check the label carefully.

About Drywall Finishing Tools

A number of tools have been specifically developed to help in this common job of installing drywall, and you should not hesitate to buy them if you are doing a job even as small as one room.

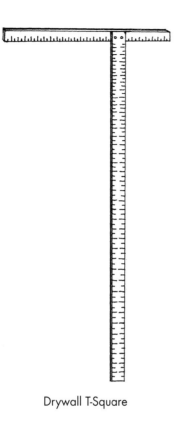

Drywall T-Square

Drywall T-Square

Also Known As: Wallboard T-square, drywall paneling T-square

Description: Flat aluminum T usually 22" wide and just over 4' long with measuring markings. The crosspiece is either off-set or has a lip to catch the edge of the drywall sheet, and may be adjustable.

Use: Acts as a guide for cutting drywall with a **utility knife (Part I, Chapter 6)**; extremely useful for marking any large sheet material (plywood, sheet metal, etc.). This is for cutting square shapes; for holes use a **drywall saw (below)**.

Drywall Saw

Also Known As: Wallboard saw, jab saw, Sheetrock® saw, utility saw

Description: Big-toothed saw with narrow, pointed, stiff blade and in-line handle, like a knife with a jagged edge. Teeth are specially hardened. Same name is given to a saw with similar large teeth, which has a blade that resembles a regular crosscut saw, but this is a rarely used version. Quite similar to a **keyhole saw (Part I, Chapter 5)**.

Use: Cutting openings in drywall for pipes and electrical outlets. (Larger sections should be cut side to side with a **utility knife, Part I, Chapter 6**, not a saw.)

Use Tips: You can start a cut by jabbing the point of the saw into the drywall or else punching it with a screwdriver and a hammer.

> **Buying Tips:** Stick with a knife for small jobs. Use a compass-like *drywall circle cutter* or **cutout tool (Part II, Chapter 18)** for big jobs.

Taping Knife

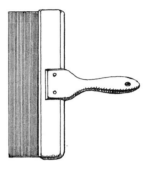

Taping Knife

Also Known As: Joint knife, tape knife, drywall knife, drywall tool, filling knife, broad knife, finishing knife, spackling knife, wallboard knife

Description: Wide, flexible metal blade with a riveted handle. Two types are made: a triangular shape about 4" to 8" wide at the tip *(broad knife)* and a rectangular shape, commonly 10" to 12" long *(finishing knife)*. The triangular type is sometimes called an *elastic knife,* referring to its flexibility; and the rectangular one, which is usually blued steel, may be called a *blue steel knife.* Some pros use a rectangular trowel with a slight curve to it, called a *drywall trowel.*

> **Note:** The triangular knife is often erroneously confused with a **wall scraper (Part V, Chapter 45),** which is narrower and stiffer but looks very similar.

Broad Taping Knife

Use: Spreading **joint compound (above)** smoothly over the **joint tape (above)** covering seams between **drywall panels (above)** or surface patches.

> **Use Tips:** Using the widest knife possible for the finish application makes the job easier, as there are fewer edge beads of compound created. Narrower knives are acceptable for the first application. Use a long, narrow *mud pan* to hold the compound for wide knives.

> **$ Buying Tips:** The key consideration in getting a quality joint knife that makes the job easier is flexibility in the middle of the blade itself—a *hollow ground blade*. Good knives have "give" while poor ones are stiff.

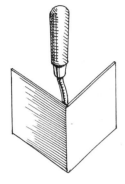

Corner Taping Tool

Corner Taping Tool

Also Known As: Corner tool, corner trowel, angle plow, inside corner wipedown tool, butterfly trowel

Description: A large, slightly flexible metal blade bent at just over 90 degrees; has a wooden handle. Outside corner versions, bent the opposite ways, are available as well.

Use: Applying joint compound or plaster to inside or outside corners.

> **Use Tip:** With this tool you can apply compound to both sides of a corner simultaneously—without it you have to wait for each side to dry before touching the other.

> **$ Buying Tip:** Hard to use well—not for everyone.

Spackling and Putty Knife

Putty Knife

Also Known As: Spackling knife

Description: Narrow blade, usually about 1" wide, with squared-off end and a simple handle.

Use: Applying *glazing compound* (putty) to windows, small scraping jobs, very small spackling jobs, such as nail holes and hairline cracks.

> ⚒ **Use Tip:** The more flexible knives are for patching and the stiffer ones for scraping.

> $ **Buying Tip:** Like many tools, putty knives come in varying degrees of quality. Cheap ones don't work very well.

Drywall Sander

Description: Open-mesh abrasive sanding screen made of steel, about 3" × 7", with a handle with a threaded hole so it can be attached to a broomstick or roller extension pole. The *vacuum drywall sander* attaches to the hose of shop vacuum. *Drywall sanding screens*, open metal mesh pieces that fit directly onto the sander, are sold separately, and in several levels of abrasiveness, or grit (80-120-150 grit, or coarse-medium-fine).

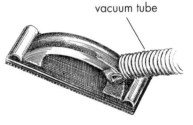

vacuum tube

Drywall Sander

Use: Sanding joint compound smooth in preparation for painting. The vacuum drywall sander sucks up all the fine dust produced by sanding.

> ⚒ **Use Tips:** Joint compound sands so easily that it is likely you will remove too much or gouge it. Go lightly.

> **$ Buying Tips:** Try to avoid sanding joint compound. The dust is fine, voluminous, and potentially unhealthy. Apply the compound carefully, use wet sandpaper or a damp sponge, or use the *vacuum drywall sander.*

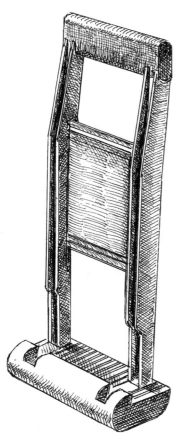

Panel Carrier

Panel Carrier

Description: 15" long plastic, L-shaped handle with slight bend in it.

Use: Carrying large, heavy panels of gypsum drywall.

> **$ Buying Tip:** Drywall is heavy and delicate. This helps overcome both attributes.

Drywall Lifter

Also Known As: Foot fulcrum, dry wall foot lift

Description: A number of small accessories are available that are generally a foot or so long, with a fulcrum. Some have small rollers for short movements.

Use: Placing and moving panels of drywall.

Crack Opener

Description: 6" long tool consisting of a hooked, stiff steel rod with a point, and a simple in-line hardwood handle.

Use: Cleaning and opening small cracks in plaster sufficiently for the most efficient filling and anchoring of patching material.

Crack Opener

Use Tip: Try to create a wider base to better anchor the patch.

Crack Patcher

Also Known As: Utility patcher and trowel

Description: Small, lightweight plated steel trowel with one pointed end and one rectangular end. Slightly flexible.

Use: Patching small holes and cracks in drywall, masonry, and plaster with various patching materials.

Crack Patcher

Cement Board Knife

Description: Carbide-tipped hand knife. Tip is semicircular with sharp points on either end of oval.

Use: Cutting **cement board (above)**. Carbide tip in handle is for chiseling and shaping. Score the fiberglass mesh on BOTH sides and then snap the board.

carbide cutting blade

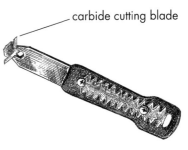
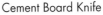

Cement Board Knife

Use Tips: Score deeply and hope for the best (it is rough material). For more, longer cuts, try a **carbide-tipped saw blade in a circular saw (Part II, Chapter 17)**.

Buying Tip: Cutting cement is not for your usual razor knife.

Paneling and Tile

Wall Paneling

Types:

Manufactured wood product paneling with paper, vinyl, or wood veneer face

Plastic laminate wall paneling

Wood planks (solid board panels)

Description:

Manufactured wood product: **Hardboard, plywood, particleboard**, or similar product **(Part VI, Chapter 47)** with a thin layer of decorative paper or vinyl attached that is generally a simulated wood-grain pattern; grooves are usually incorporated to give the impression of narrow wood panels. A fancier type is a fine hardwood veneer such as birch on plywood and may be used to cover cabinets as well as walls. Typically available in 4' × 8' panels ¹/₈" to ¹/₄" thick.

Plastic laminate: ¹/₁₆" thick plastic sheet with a decorative style laminated to a backing panel generally of particle board but may be applied directly to **drywall (Part VII, Chapter 50)**. In any case a strong adhesive is required. Comes in 4' × 8' sheets.

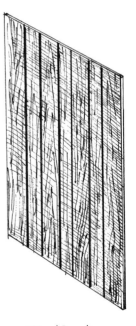

Wood Paneling

Wood planks: Solid hardwood or softwood boards 3" to 12" wide and $1/2$" to $7/8$" thick with smooth and rough as well as knotty and clear wood grades. Edges are *tongue-and-groove.* Length varies, and patterns can be custom-ordered (indeed, may have to be ordered, as this classic product is less and less commonly found).

Uses: Paneling walls in new construction and to cover badly damaged walls—or just to change the look of the room. May go directly over layer of **drywall (Part VII, Chapter 50)**.

Use Tips: Use a **router (Part II, Chapter 18)** for cutting and trimming paneling and laminate. It's faster and allows intricate cuts. If paneling is going to be applied directly to furring strips or studs, it should be at least $1/4$" thick; use **panel nails (Part III, Chapter 20)**. Thinner panels can be secured to plaster with special adhesive. Panels that are $1/4$" thick are best for installation directly on drywall.

Buying Tips: The plywood types are considered best; vinyl or paper wood-grain patterns never look as good as veneer does. There is a vast range of quality, and you should insist on fire-rated panels, because some are highly flammable and give off much smoke when burning.

Ceramic Wall Tile

Description: Extremely hard product that comes in various shapes from square to octagonal and various thicknesses and textures. Standard tile is $4^{1}/_{4}$" by $4^{1}/_{4}$" with projections, or nibs, on the edges for proper spacing.

Use: Wherever an easy-to-clean, waterproof surface is desired. Mainly in the bath, but also on kitchen countertops.

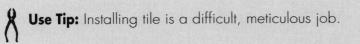

Use Tip: Installing tile is a difficult, meticulous job.

Tile Spacers

Description: Little white plastic crosses, ranging in size from $^{1}/_{16}$" to $^{3}/_{8}$" thick; all are less than an inch across. Sold in bags of 50 to 300, and boxes of up to 1500 pieces. Different types for wall tile or floor tile. Best quality models are molded, not extruded, for consistency.

Use: Maintaining even spacing between tiles prior to applying grout. Also to speed up the layout process.

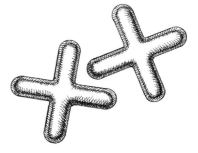

Tile Spacers

Buying Tip: Necessary for a professional, even installation when the grout space between tiles is bigger than the space made by the bumps on the tile sides.

Grout

Description: A cement-based material. Comes as a powder in various sizes and colors that is mixed with water for use; also in tubes.

Use: Filling gaps between ceramic tiles up to $\frac{1}{8}$". Sand is added when grout is intended for joints wider than $\frac{1}{8}$". Think of it as a thin mortar.

> **Use Tips:** Mix grout with *acrylic latex additive* for surfaces that will have water on them. Seal it later with *silicone grout sealer*. On large jobs, or when using sanded grout, use a **rubber float** or **grout float (Part X, Chapter 75)** instead of a sponge.

Grout Saw

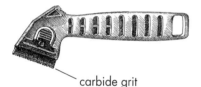

carbide grit

Grout Saw

Also Known As: Grout rake, grout scraper

Description: Plastic palm-sized handle with a short, round blade of tungston-carbide grit or hardened steel teeth.

Use: Removing old grout prior to regrouting.

> **Use Tip:** Take it easy—you need to remove the loose grout only to a depth of an eighth of an inch for the new grout to hold. No need to remove everything.

$ Buying Tips: Get replacement blades if available for your model. Some people get the same result with an old beer-can opener.

Notched Trowel

Also Known As: Trowel spreader, serrated trowel

Description: Rectangular metal or plastic blade with a handle and with notches of varying shapes and dimensions along the edges.

Use: Spreading adhesive (mastic) for tiles and panels of all kinds.

Notched Trowel

Use Tip: Use tooth size specified by adhesive manufacturer.

$ Buying Tip: Dealers will often give you a free notched trowel when you buy adhesive and tiles.

Tile Pliers

Also Known As: Tile-cutting pliers, tile cutter

Description: Pliers-like device with one flat jaw and one vertical blade, and a sharp, carbide wheel cutter.

Use: Splitting ceramic tiles along straight, scored lines.

carbide wheel cutter

Tile Pliers

Use Tips: For small quantities only. For large jobs rent specialized tile-cutting tools—they are great time-savers. The most common is the *tile cutter,* or *snap cutter,* with a blade that slides on two guide rods. Dealers will often lend you these tools.

Tile Nippers

Tile Nippers

Description: Blunt-headed pliers with wide pincer-like blades.

Use: Nibbling away at ceramic tiles to remove curved sections for fitting around plumbing, etc.

Doors and Windows

Doors

Types:

Interior doors

Exterior doors

Insulated doors

Folding doors

Bifold doors

Sliding doors

Swinging doors

Garage doors

Storm doors

Also Known As:

Swinging: Cafe

Exterior: "Entrance" doors

Description: Most doors are 6' 8" high and come in various widths. They also may come prehung, complete with frames and hinges.

Interior: Either hollow-core construction—sheets of wood veneer over a ribbed core of cardboard or wood strips—or solid-core. Usually 1 $^3/_8$" or 1 $^3/_4$" thick.

Exterior: Made of solid wood or wood material, such as particleboard. Usually 1 $^3/_4$" thick and assembled with exterior glue (interior doors use interior glue). Available insulated. Both interior and exterior doors come in two types: *panel* or *sash* doors, meaning they are composed of separate wood sections with visible joints (stiles, rails, and as many as 15 panels), and *flush* types, meaning the exterior is one homogenous, solid piece of wood veneer. Both types come with "lights," or windows. Doors come in a variety of widths and heights.

Insulated: Core of wood or particleboard encased in galvanized steel sheets. Such doors have R values up to R-15.

Folding: May be woven or laminated. Woven have louvers and may be made of wood or PVC. Laminated doors are commonly laminated to steel.

Bifold: Two folding doors with each of the two sections hinged together. They come solid and louvered.

Sliding: Made of wood, glass, and metal as well as vinyl-covered wood and metal. Exterior, or patio, doors of glass panels are normally insulated; there is a dead air space between the sheets of glass used in their construction. *Bypass doors* slide past each other; *pocket doors* go into the wall.

Swinging: Mounted on the sides of a doorway and swing open and shut when pushed.

Garage: Consists of panels hinged together. Panels may be wood or have air spaces or polystyrene inside for insulation. Doors ride on track and may be automatic or operated by hand.

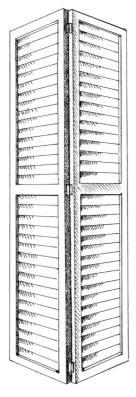

Louvered Bifold Door

Storm: Metal- or wood-framed doors with glass or plexiglas windows. Available ready-made or as a do-it-yourself package. *Cross Buck doors,* with an X-pattern on the bottom and a window on top, are a common model.

Use Tips: Because of the close tolerances, hanging most doors is a very difficult job, and prehung doors, where possible, are a great advantage. Hollow-core doors make excellent office tables when placed across low file cabinets. Prehung steel doors are the best for security.

Buying Tips: Doors are available in much greater variety in "panel" types. Doors covered with veneer are usually suitable only for painting rather than clear finishing. Wooden doors usually come unfinished.

About Windows

There are far too many types and details concerning windows to do justice in this book, so only a general classification will be given to guide you at the very start of your purchase. One term is helpful: *sash* refers to the wooden or metal framework that the glass panes are attached to.

Windows

Types:

Double-hung windows

Sliding windows

Casement windows

Fixed, or *picture windows*

Description:

Double-hung: Most common, with two units, or sashes, that slide up and down on separate tracks.

Sliding: Similar to double-hung, but horizontal.

Casement: Window swings outward from a side hinge. May be operated by a small crank. If they are out-swinging, hinged at the top, they are called *awning windows;* bottom-hinged, in-swinging models are called *hopper windows.*

Fixed: Generally large window, mounted permanently in a non-opening frame.

Use: Installed in walls to allow entry of light and air.

Glass

Types:

Safety glass

Standard glass

Composition glass

Description:

Safety: There are a number of types: wire-reinforced, laminated, tempered. Wire-reinforced: $1/4$" thick, has wire embedded in it that keeps the glass from shattering on impact. Laminated: $1/4$" thick and consists of two pieces of glass adhered to a middle layer of plastic to make it shatterproof. Tempered: if this breaks, it crumbles into zillions of harmless pieces rather than sharp shards.

Standard: Standard door and window glass, nonsafety, comes in three grades: B for general work, A for superior, and AA, the highest grade.

Composition: This glass has metal particles embedded in it with the result, manufacturers say, of retaining heat from the sun's rays longer, thereby keeping a house warmer in the winter and cooler in the summer.

Use: Use safety glass in storm doors, shower and bath doors, patio doors, interior and exterior doors—wherever there is a possibility the glass may accidentally be broken by a person's body.

Glazing Compound

Also Known As: glazing putty, window putty

Description: Soft, pliable material worked with fingers and/or **putty knife (Chapter 50)**. Sold in cans, tubs and cartridges. Also available in roll form, called *glazing tape*. Oil or latex (water) based.

Use: Glazing (attaching glass to window frame) and patching small exterior holes. Not a substitute for caulk.

> **Use Tips:** When dealing with bare wood, apply a coat of paint before applying the glazing compound. This keeps the wood from absorbing oils from the compound. Check the label for both suitability to either wooden or metal frames and for painting directions—it should be sealed with either latex or oil paint. Apply with a **putty knife** designed for this purpose **(below)**. Glazing tape needs no knifing, nor does compound sold in cartridges used with **caulking guns (Part IV, Chapter 32)**.

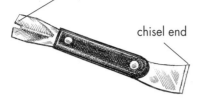

notched "V" end

chisel end

2-in-1 Putty Knife

2-in-1 Putty Knife

Also Known As: Double-ended window tool, glazing tool, glazier putty knife

Description: Small, hand-sized tool with hardened steel blades on each end, one of which is wide, and has a sharp, chisel end, and one of which is angled and folded into a V shape, with a small notch in the middle.

Use: Chisel end removes old putty from around windows, and notched V end smoothes new window putty or glazing compound.

> **$ Buying Tips:** A combination of two other tools, the bent putty knife and the putty chisel. A good buy.

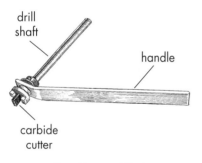

drill
shaft

handle

carbide
cutter

Putty Removal Tool

Putty Removal Tool

Also Known As: Putty Chaser™

Description: 6" long steel shaft with small carbide blade on one end, as well as a 6" long flat handle extending from the blade end. Fits into a power drill like a drill bit. The distance that the blade protrudes from the guide to cut over the sash is adjustable by a small collar on the shaft.

Use: Quickly removing old, hardened window putty without cracking the glass.

Use Tip: Works only with corded drills, as a minimum of 2,000 rpm is required. Wear safety glasses and a respirator. Hand removal of putty is onerous and usually involves removal of the window frame as well as breaking of the glass.

Buying Tip: Highly efficient solution to a big problem.

Floor and Ceiling Materials

About Flooring Materials

If there ever was a mantra to keep in mind while preparing a job, it is "make the floor level and solid" prior to laying floor covering. Anything else and things pop, crack, loosen, trip, wear out, and so on. Do it right the first time. Rent a variety of professional installation tools.

Resilient Flooring

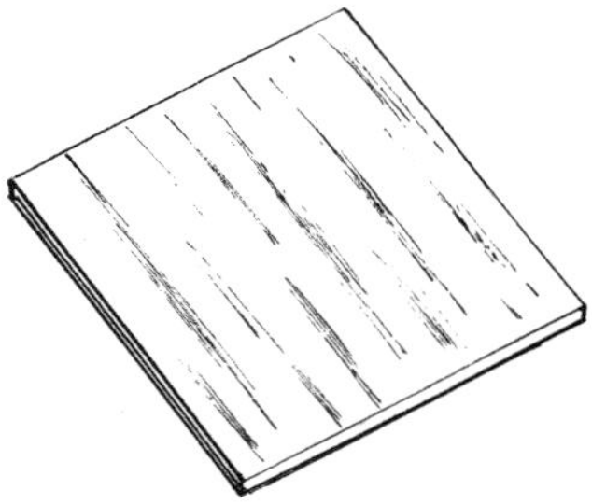

Groups:

Tile

Sheet goods; sheet goods types:

   Inlaid structure

   Rotovinyl

Vinyl Floor Tile

Also Known As:

Sheet goods: Sheet flooring; vinyl sheet flooring; roll flooring; linoleum (no longer manufactured in the U.S.)

Rotovinyl: Roto flooring, flexible

Description:

Tile: Vinyl and vinyl composition tile dominate tile flooring today. It commonly comes in 12" squares. It is approximately $3/32$" to $1/8$" thick and is available in a tremendous number of colors and styles. It is also available 3" wide by random lengths up to 36" to simulate wood planks. *Vinyl composition tile* has for the most part replaced asphalt tile, a 9" × 9" brittle material. Tile is available in self-stick form; the "dry-back" kinds must be laid in a bed of special adhesive, or **mastic**, made for this purpose **(Part IV, Chapter 32)**. Tile manufacturer should specify type of mastic required as well as other installation requirements.

Sheet goods: All sheet goods are available in a wide variety of colors and patterns and are generally cut to order off a large roll or else sold in rolls of convenient dimensions. *Inlaid structure vinyl* is a thick, durable material with color and pattern manufactured as one piece through to the backing material and a glossy, "no-wax" finish. It usually comes 6' and 12' wide and is relatively stiff; top-quality flooring. Rotovinyl consists of a core of vinyl with pattern and color printed on top and covered with a clear vinyl wear layer of varying thicknesses and perhaps a urethane coating. Rotovinyl is usually "waxless" —no waxing is required for maintenance. Rotovinyl is available 9', 12', and 15' wide. May be very thin and not long-lasting, and may have a cushion layer. Some come with kits of specialized installation tools.

Use: Tile and sheet goods can be used as flooring in any room in the house and on virtually all smooth and secure surfaces, but asphalt tile is still used for commercial installations and in below-grade basements, where it can "take" moisture.

Use Tips: Tile is easier to install than sheet goods; self-adhesive tiles are easier to put down than dry-back—those that require a separate adhesive. Among the sheet goods, inlaid is difficult to install and best left to professionals, while rotovinyl and cushioned flooring are easier because of their lighter weight and flexibility. Some manufacturers make a cushioned flooring that has to be held down only by molding or cemented at the edges rather than over the entire floor, the normal procedure. This makes for easy removal later on, which is convenient with the cheaper, thinner types that are bound to wear out quickly. Vinyl composition tile is more durable than plain vinyl.

Buying Tips: Better-quality tile is also thicker. Asphalt tile is much cheaper than vinyl composition tile, and plain vinyl is the most expensive. Inlaid, generally the best kind of sheet vinyl, comes with $1/16$" and $1/8$" wear layers; the $1/8$" thickness is best. The wear layer on rotovinyl is measured in thousandths of an inch; experts figure five thousandths of an inch equals about five years' wear. Hence, the thicker the wear layer the better the quality. In general, quality sheet goods are more expensive than tile. Get the kits with specialized installation tools.

About Carpeting

Carpeting is available in either roll form with padding—widths are usually 36", 54", 72", 108", and 144" —and tiles that are 12" × 12". Carpet materials vary, but the test of quality is the density of the pile. Bend the carpet. The less backing you can see, the better the carpet. The underlayment should be strong rubber padding for carpet used in high-traffic areas. Indoor/outdoor carpet can be used in high-moisture areas as well as outside the house. Rent a variety of specialized tools for installation.

Carpet Tiles

Description: As mentioned above, made of various materials. Some are self-adhesive, some installed with mastic, others installed with double-faced tape.

Use: Carpeting most rooms of the house and patio area, if outdoor type. Such tiles can also be used in the bath.

> **Use Tips:** Carpet tiles are easier to install than roll goods.

Roll Carpeting

Also Known As: Roll goods

Description: As mentioned in the **About section**, roll carpeting is made of various materials, such as nylon, acrylic, polyester, wool, and others. It comes in a variety of piles from velvet to plush. Paddings are made of felt, horsehair, rubber, or foam plastic. It may have to be glued down or held with a *pad and tackless strip,* which is a wooden strip with the points of tacks protruding from underneath; the carpet is laid upon it. In either case the carpet backing determines the method.

Use: Carpeting any room in the house.

> **Use Tips:** Roll carpeting is normally glued to the floor, but it can also be tacked in place, a professional job. Put metal strips called **carpet binder bars (below)** at doorway edges in high-traffic areas.

Ceramic Floor Tile

Description: Extremely hard ceramic pieces usually $4^1/_4" \times 4^1/_4"$ (often stated "4 × 4") but also 1", 2", 6", 8", and 12" in square as well as hexagonal and octagonal shapes. Texture may be smooth or rough, shiny or dull, and colors and patterns vary greatly. Tiles are also available in a variety of other shapes. Additionally, ceramic tile is also available in *mosaic* form— a number of small tiles on a mesh backing. **Grout (Part VII, Chapter 51)** is used to fill gaps between tiles.

Use: Normally used as bath or kitchen flooring but also used outside on patios, walks, etc.

Use Tips: Ceramic floor tiles can be installed on either a thin set sand/cement mortar mixture or adhesive; each will vary according to the tile being installed. Installation on adhesive is easiest for the do-it-yourselfer. Different tiles require different adhesives, so check. Keep in mind that the additional thickness of tile may cause problems for various built-in appliances. Use a slightly rough finish for traction in bathrooms and other areas likely to be wet. Dealers will normally furnish the tools, either free or for rent, for installing tiles. Tools would include a *trowel* for the adhesive, a *cutter* for square cuts, and *nippers* for odd-shaped cuts. Remember that a good, solid underlayment is particularly important. No "give" can be allowed.

Note: Floor tile is laid on a bed of mastic and filled with grout the same as wall tile, and the tools used are the same except that a *rubber float* is used to push the grout into the tile spaces. **See Chapter 51**, for the **notched trowel** and **tile cutters** and **nippers**.

Wood Flooring

Types:

Parquet (wood block) flooring

Plank flooring

Strip (prepackaged) flooring

Description: Usually hardwood—oak, maple, pecan, birch—but also softwoods such as redwood and southern pine—in flooring form. Flooring is available either finished or unfinished and most of it is $3/4$" thick.

Parquet flooring: Comes in 9" to 36" squares but sometimes in rectangular shapes or in individual strips that are assembled to form parquet blocks. It is $13/16$" thick and usually prefinished.

Plank flooring: Also tongue-and-groove and comes in standard widths $6^1/2$" to $7^3/4$" and random widths from 3" to 7" wide. Attachment is by installing screws in predrilled holes in the ends, which are covered with plugs; the result is a "pegged" effect.

Strip flooring: Narrow boards $1^1/2$" to 3" wide that come in random lengths and go together tongue-and-groove fashion. Usually $3/8$" thick, though pros use $3/4$" thick wood. May be prefinished.

Use: As flooring in all rooms of the house.

> **Use Tips:** Strip and plank flooring is normally nailed in place but there are planks with square edges that can be installed on a mastic base. Parquet is normally installed with **mastic (Part IV, Chapter 32)**. Do not install if there is excessive humidity present. If you are nailing tongue-and-groove flooring, rent a *nailing machine* especially designed for the purpose of shooting nails into wood flooring at a precise and low angle.

Floor Leveler

Also Known As: Floor and wall patch

Description: Cementitious plaster-like product that usually comes as powder that is mixed with water for use. A very common brand is Dash Patch®. Latex liquid binder may be added for more strength and adhesiveness.

Use: Leveling floors to provide a smooth base for floor coverings such as resilient tile or carpeting. Also general large area patching.

Ceiling Tiles and Panels

Also Known As: Panels, suspended ceiling, lay-in panels, pads

Description: Tiles are normally 12" square and made of either fiber or fiberglass. They are usually white but come in other colors as well. Tile faces have a striated or fissured surface for sound absorbency. Some also have a vinyl surface so they can be cleaned easily. Tiles are tongue-and-grooved, made to fit together when installed, either by bonding them directly to the ceiling or *furring* strips with adhesive or by stapling them. Ceiling panels normally are 2' × 4' and are designed to be installed in a grid system. They are made of fiber, fiberglass, or plastic.

Use: Ceiling installations for nonformal rooms. Panels installed in a grid system form a suspended, or dropped, ceiling, useful if you want to hide a ceiling with pipes running on it, such as in the basement. Translucent plastic panels are used to form a luminous ceiling in which lights are installed above the panels.

Use Tips: Take care when installing mineral fiber panels on a suspended ceiling: The wires to support the grid can cut through a panel easily. Also, panels are fairly delicate and can chip. Check your building code before installing. Getting a ceiling perfectly level is very difficult. Make extensive use of a **flexible tube level (Part I, Chapter 10)**. A good time to call in the professionals.

Binder Bar

Description: Long, thin, narrow metal strip, either gold or silver colored, with a slight bend down its length and several screw holes.

Use: Protecting the edge of floor covering when it is a little higher than the floor, especially in doorways.

Buying Tips: Cheap insurance for an extended life of floor covering. Don't hesitate to use it.

Floor Scraper

Also Known As: Floor stripping tool

Description: Long-handled, broom-sized steel tool with hardened steel business end and a sliding weight inside the tubular handle. The weight is slammed down to create 150 pounds per square inch of impact. Other versions, with no sliding weight, merely have a slightly angled steel head.

Use: Removing tile, linoleum, carpet, roofing, ceramic tile, and other adhesive floor coverings. Also helpful in removing old shingles from rooftops.

> **Buying Tips:** Certain jobs are incredibly tough without specialized tools. Removing old flooring is one of them, and this tool helps make it easier.

Plumbing Hardware, Materials, and Tools

$ General Buying Tips: Before shopping for any plumbing products, bear in mind the following, which could save you a lot of money.

- High-quality plumbing tools are worth the price difference in efficiency and safety. Cheap tools can truly interfere with a job.

- Many plumbing parts come both packaged and loose. The loose items can be as much as 30 percent less expensive than the items in "view," or plastic bubble packages.

- Some packaged products contain a number of the same item, meaning that they include many unneeded parts. For example, you'll most often need only one "O" ring to repair a faucet but a package contains at least four or five.

- In the same vein, washerless faucet-repair kits contain multiple parts but only one or two are usually needed for repair. A well-stocked hardware store or plumbing supply shop carries all kinds of individual parts for washerless faucets at much less than the kit price. To ensure getting the correct parts we heartily recommend that you make a habit of taking in the old part to identify the brand and the model of the faucet. You will always be better and more quickly served. Such a tremendous array of plumbing parts is sold that virtually any part of any plumbing device can be replaced. For example, an old toilet can be kept going virtually forever—there would likely be no need to replace it. A good hardware store stocks an amazingly wide variety of parts or will order what you need, as will a plumbing supply store.

- At this writing American-made plumbing products are generally better than ones imported from the Far East, as are most products imported from Germany. The country of origin must, by law, be on the package or product. The price difference is worth it.

- Check closely when buying a brand name to make sure that it is indeed the real brand. Some companies in the Far East make inferior products (especially tools) and package them to look just like well-known American brands.

- Look for "loss leaders" when buying at home centers. They often offer big discounts on common items such as faucets and tools. On the other hand, their prices on smaller, more unusual items tend to be higher than at hardware stores.

- You needn't buy an expensive, specialized tool that you may need only once or very rarely. You can rent virtually anything from a rental store, hardware or plumbing supply store, and such tools are generally of a heavier duty and higher quality than the average person would be inclined to buy. On the other hand, if you cannot find one to rent, and you are confident that you know what to do, then the purchase of a specialized tool to avoid the expense of a plumber's house call may be worthwhile.

- A plumbing supply store or good hardware store might be open to giving a 10 percent discount if you are planning to buy a large quantity of pipe and fittings, such as when you are renovating a house or apartment.

A Note About Plumbing Code

Any consideration of what plumbing products to purchase should take into account local building and plumbing codes, which are sets of rules and regulations set up by local governmental authorities on what products may be used and how the installations must be done. Similar codes exist for electrical and general construction work.

Plumbing codes have a simple purpose—to ensure that the installed plumbing is done safely and does not jeopardize the health of a building's occupants. However, despite this seemingly straightforward goal, plumbing codes vary greatly from community to community, sometimes in a contradictory manner. But they must be followed. If they are not, a plumbing inspector can order the removal of any installation that violates the code, even though the installation may be perfectly safe. This can also be a problem when selling a house and the prospective buyers have it inspected professionally. For example, plastic pipe may have been used where the code allows only metal.

Before embarking on a home improvement project by all means check the plans out with the local building code authority to ensure that they conform with the law. Your local plumbing supply or hardware store can usually advise.

Pipe and Accessories

About Pipe and Fittings

Three kinds of pipe are used for home plumbing, *water supply, water distribution,* and *waste.* Water supply pipe supplies clean cold water, water distribution pipe carries hot and cold water inside the house, and waste pipe transports waste, "used," or soiled water to a sewer, cesspool, or other disposal facility. Water piping in the home is rarely over 1" in diameter; waste piping is always of a larger diameter, like 2" to 4".

Water supply pipe is also known as *supply pipe* or simply *water pipe.* Waste pipe is also known as *drainage pipe, soil pipe, sewer pipe, drain pipe, DWV pipe* (for *drain-waste-vent*), and *discharge pipe,* although technically waste pipes do not carry toilet discharge, only soil pipes do, as they carry all waste. A *stack* is the general term for any vertical line of this kind of drain piping; *riser* is the general term for any vertical water supply piping. It's simple—the former goes down, the latter goes up.

Pipe sections are connected with **fittings (Chapters 55 and 56)** that allow piping to be routed around turns throughout a building and connect them to fixtures such as sinks, tubs, and toilets. Every type of pipe has its own type and kind of fittings, i.e., copper pipe/copper fittings.

Pipe size is almost always described and ordered in terms of its inside diameter—a 1" pipe has a 1" inside diameter. This is the "nominal" size; it is not meant to be exact. The outside diameter varies with the wall thickness of whatever the pipe is made of. For example, cast-iron pipe is thicker than copper pipe of the same nominal size. You do not have to specify it for retail purchases, but if the outside dimension is critical to the job, such as when fitting it through a hole in a wall, be sure to ask for specifications as sizes do vary.

Pipe is considered *male* and the fittings into which it fits *female*. Male pipe has threads on the outside; female fittings have threads on the inside. This male-female designation is used to describe all fittings.

On a large project it is advisable to buy all the fittings from the same manufacturer to ensure a better fit, as the manufacturing tolerances can vary from one brand to another.

Also, you should avoid mixing types of pipe, such as galvanized, brass, plastic, copper, and so on, as well as different thicknesses of the same type. Where different types must be connected you can use specialized fittings to avoid creating *electrolytic action,* a corroding condition that occurs when dissimilar metals are in contact with one another.

Galvanized Steel Pipe

Also Known As: Iron pipe, malleable pipe, steel pipe

Description: Gray, zinc-treated steel. The zinc, or galvanized, treatment, makes the steel rust-resistant if not scratched. Commonly comes in 21' lengths, which plumbing stores and larger hardware stores will cut to order, as well as in shorter precut lengths, usually in sections of 6" up to 6', threaded on both ends. Pipe diameters range from $1/8$" to 6". Common water sizes are $3/8$" to 1". Common waste sizes are $1\frac{1}{2}$", 2", and 3". Both ends should be threaded to be screwed into correspondingly threaded fittings; lengths can be threaded on one end only (T.O.E.) if you want.

Use: Carries water or waste as needed in a building.

Use Tips: Most hardware or plumbing supply stores will custom cut and thread lengths for you. Galvanized pipe cannot be used for gas or steam.

Buying Tips: Check to see that the threads are not damaged before leaving the store. Because galvanized pipes can eventually rust out, copper, brass, or PVC is usually used.

Black Iron Pipe

Also Known As: B.I. pipe, black pipe

Description: Similar to galvanized steel pipe, but not treated for rust resistance. Darker and often seamless. Slightly greasy to the touch.

Use: For steam or gas.

Use Tips: Only black fittings can be used with black iron pipe. Best left to a professional plumber.

Cast-Iron Pipe

Also Known As: Soil pipe, soil stack

Description: Very heavy pipe that comes in two weights—*service* and *extra-heavy*. It is commonly sold in lengths of 5' and 10' and in diameters of 2", 3", and 4". Two kinds exist. The old, classic kind has a bell hub on one end and a spigot hub (raised end) on the other, but the new kind is plain and known as No-Hub® or *hubless*. Sections of the old kind are joined with a packing of oakum and lead, while the hubless kind is joined with a special **hubless fitting (Chapter 55)** that is simply tightened down over the joint.

Use: As a waste pipe.

Use Tips: Only a professional should tackle oakum and lead joints. The new, hubless pipe can be done by the do-it-yourselfer, if allowed by local code, but the pipe is so heavy and hard to handle that is not recommended. Your supplier may cut pieces to length for you or you can rent a device called a *snap-cutter* for the purpose. It can also be cut with a cold chisel and a hammer. You can remove unneeded cast-iron pipe, such as during renovations, by shattering it with a sledgehammer.

Plastic Pipe

Types:

ABS (acrylonitrile-butadiene-styrene) pipe

CPVC (chlorinated polyvinyl chloride) pipe

PB (polybutylene) pipe

PE (polyethylene) pipe

PEX (crosslink polyethylene)

PP (polypropylene) pipe

PVC (polyvinyl chloride or vinyl) pipe

SR (styrene rubber) pipe

Description: Two basic kinds, *flexible* (PE, PEX, PB, PP) or *rigid* (PVC, CPVC, ABS, SR) some with ends prepared for joining in various ways, such as flared or threaded. Wall thickness for home use is generally referred to as "Schedule 40." Comes in same nominal diameters as all other water or waste pipe and in lengths of 10' and 20', as well as in 25' and 100' coils of flexible tubing. PVC, CPVC, and ABS are the most common kinds in general use.

Use: Different materials are made for use as either water supply (cold potable water), water distribution (hot and cold), or DWV (waste). PVC and ABS are commonly used for DWV. CPVC, ABS, PEX, and PB are used for water distribution; PB, PEX, and PE pipes can withstand freezing with water inside them without bursting and are often used outdoors. PB and PP are most popular for traps due to their excellent chemical resistance.

Use Tips: Plastic pipe can be cut with a special, large-bladed *plastic pipe saw*, **hacksaw (Part I, Chapter 5)**, or a special pruning shear–like *PVC cutter* or *plastic tubing cutter*, a great work-saver with pipes up to 1" diameter. PE and PEX not only can withstand freezing water but remain flexible in extreme cold. You can use **transition fittings**, or **adapters (Part VIII, Chapter 55)**, to join plastic to copper or steel plumbing systems. Be sure to get the kind of fittings specified for your pipe.

Buying Tips: Plastic is less expensive than steel or copper (by half), easier to use (it is one-twentieth the weight of steel and has a simpler method of joining), and works just fine. Use various plastic pipe accessories, such as a *deburring cone* or *edge bevel*, to speed your work and ensure tight joints. But make sure it is acceptable by your local plumbing code.

Copper Pipe and Tubing

Description: Rigid copper pipe for water comes in diameters from 1/8" to 12" (measured on the outside diameter, or "O.D."), and of various wall thicknesses known as types K (thick), L (medium), and M (thin), as well as DWV type (thin). Available in rigid 20' or 21' lengths with unthreaded ends, 10' lengths with threaded ends capped for protection, and coils of 45', 60', 100', and 200' (types K and L). *Drawn* is hard; *annealed* is soft.

Use: Water or waste pipe.

Use Tips: Type L is most common for residential use. It can be cut with a hacksaw but a specialized tool called a **tubing cutter (Part VIII, Chapter 65)** makes it easier. Connections are usually made with **sweat-soldered fittings (Chapter 55)**, but **compression and flare fittings (Chapter 55)** can also be used to avoid using the propane torch necessary for soldered fittings. Use only the same thickness (types K, L, or M) in one line of plumbing.

Buying Tips: If copper tube is on sale for a very low cost, make sure that it is indeed type L and not the thinner-walled type M. Although type M is suitable for some uses, it has been called *see-through pipe* by some plumbers who think it is too lightweight. Copper is the highest quality pipe, but it is relatively expensive and connections must be made with care and specialized tools. This said, it can be worked by the average handyperson.

Brass Pipe

Description: Solid brass, usually sold in unthreaded 12' lengths and in all standard sizes. Comes in various weights.

Use: Water supply and distribution, where resistance to corrosion is the main concern.

> **Use Tips:** All threaded connections. Not commonly used in homes.

> **Buying Tip:** More expensive than other types of pipe.

About Tubular Goods

Tubular goods are drain pipes used underneath sinks, basins, and tubs. They have their own type of joining system, using slip nuts, and are easy to work with.

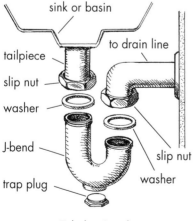

Tubular Goods

Tubular Goods

Also Known As: Drainage fittings, drain pipes, drain fittings, drainage pipes, slip-joint pipe.

Description: Large diameter, variously shaped lightweight brass or plastic pipes. Those that are exposed to view are often chrome-plated or nickel-plated brass. Others are satin-finish brass (unpolished chrome-plated) or plastic, including chrome-covered plastic. Kitchen-sink tubular goods are usually 1$^1/_2$"; lavatory tubular goods are 1$^1/_4$". All are usually held together and made watertight by hexagonal slip nuts and plastic or rubber washers called *slip-joints*—though some tailpieces that attach to sink strainers have threaded ends. Washers may be called *cut sj washers*.

The long piece with an L-bend at one end is often called a *waste ell* for kitchen piping (1$^1/_2$") and a *slip ell* for bathroom basin piping (1$^1/_4$"). *Corrugated flexible drain* is plastic tubular goods that can be bent with the bare hands and is an option if there is more than the usual distance to cover between the sink and the drain line, particularly if precise alignment is difficult.

Types: Typical parts are tailpiece, tail pipe, branch tailpiece, extension piece (also known as *extension tube*), trap, repair trap, offset, waste ell, waste bend, J-bend (also known as *trap bend, replacement trap bend, kitchen-sink drain bend*), P-trap, S-trap, continuous waste line. The most common is the tailpiece (descends from the sink) and the P-trap (from the tailpiece to the drain).

Use: To route waste water from a sink, disposer, or tub to other drain pipes. *Traps* (J- and P-bends) retain water in their curved part, which acts as a seal against sewer odors and vermin.

Use Tips: A variety of configurations are possible with tubular goods; it is a simple matter of assembling the right shapes so that everything fits together. Occasional rinsing with extremely hot water helps clear debris from the trap. This pipe and especially the chrome finish is delicate, so use a **strap wrench** and special tools such as **spud wrenches** instead of regular **pipe wrenches (Part VIII, Chapter 63)** or **tongue-and-groove pliers (Part I, Chapter 7)** and extra care when handling. Forcing one of these pipes might crush it.

A reducing slip nut with an extra large rubber washer can connect $1^1/_2$" to $1^1/_4$" tubular goods if necessary. If for some reason you are using galvanized piping in the drain line, a slip joint nut and washer can be "borrowed" from tubular goods and used on galvanized. You can also use a device called a **flexible coupling (Part VIII, Chapter 55)**, which consists of soft rubber fittings in various sizes that are clamped onto the pipes.

Buying Tips: Plain plastic is the cheapest material, but not the best-looking. If the lines will be out of sight, then plastic or rough brass is suitable. If it is visible, chrome-plated brass is recommended; chrome-covered plastic is new and relatively untested. Some brands come with fittings and others do not; be sure to check before leaving the store. Because a J-bend (trap) comes off easily for cleaning, the more expensive model with a cleanout plug is unnecessary. Parts for P- and S-traps are sometimes sold in kits, though this can be more costly than buying parts individually.

Water Supply Tubes

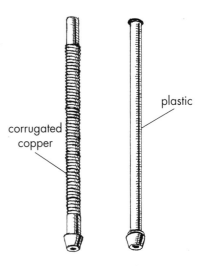

corrugated copper

plastic

Water Supply Tubes

Also Known As: Speedies, Speedees, basin tubes, sink supply tube, lavatory supply tubes or pipe, lav supply tubes, water connectors, water supply pipe, inlet pipe, flex line, toilet supply tube, tank tube (latter two for toilets)

Description: Short $3/8$" diameter tubes made of plastic, rough brass (raw copper), chrome-plated copper or brass, copper, corrugated copper, nylon weave in clear plastic, and nylon covered with stainless-steel weave. Corrugated is plain or chrome-plated copper and may be corrugated in a central section or for its entire length for bending ease.

Use: Makes the connection between the **water supply valve (Part VIII, Chapter 59)**—the water supply—and the sink faucet or toilet tank.

Use Tips: Always get tube longer than needed and trim the excess. Plastic is easiest to connect, cut, and bend; the metal types, except for corrugated, may kink. Nylon can withstand any kind of bending—pretzel shape if you want—and attaches like a garden hose.

Buying Tips: Nylon is five or six times as costly as other plastics. Nylon supply tube is usually sold in kit form, i.e., with necessary connectors attached.

Pipe-Hanging Tape

Pipe-Hanging Tape

Also Known As: Hanger strap, pipe hanger, band iron, band clamp

Description: Steel or copper band with holes at regular intervals, sold in coils.

Use: Suspending pipes of all sizes from walls and ceilings. Infinitely adjustable to fit. Tightened with a **machine screw (Part III, Chapter 21)**.

> **Use Tip:** Use copper tape on copper pipe, not steel.

Pipe Strap and Tube Strap

Description: Pipe strap is a U-shaped piece of galvanized steel with two holes in flanges; tube strap is similar but made of copper for copper tubing.

Use: Screwed or nailed to wall to hold small pipe.

> **Buying Tip:** Serves the same purpose as *pipe hanging tape*, but only when the pipe can be snug against the wall or ceiling.

Hose Clamp

Hose Clamp

Description: Stainless-steel band with notches and a closing gear. The gear is in the form of a $5/16$" nut.

Use: To apply even pressure around pipe or hose; in particular to clamp a hose or a gasket onto a tube or pipe. Also used with **insert fittings (Chapter 55)**.

> **Use Tips:** Don't overtighten. If you have many to do, use a $5/16$" **nut driver (Part I, Chapter 8)** or a **T-handle torque wrench (Chapter 63)**.

> **Buying Tips:** New plastic types—one brand is Speedy Clamp®—are becoming available. No tool is required. Instead of a worm gear, they have sawtooth-edged ends that lock in when you squeeze them together and come apart when you twist them. *Spring-type clamps*, used on cars and appliances such as clothes dryers, are just thick wire loops, and are harder to use.

Floor and Ceiling Plates

Description: Chrome-plated split doughnut-shaped flat metal piece. A tiny rivet acts as a hinge for the two halves, which open up for installation.

Use: Goes around radiator pipes for decorative purposes where they enter a ceiling or a floor.

Radiator Air Valve

Radiator Air Valve

Also Known As: Steam vent, air vent, vapor equalizing valve, air eliminator

Description: Small round or cylindrical metal device that screws into small hole on top or side of a steam radiator or at end of run of steam pipe. Comes in various sizes, 1–5 and C–D, for placing different distances from the boiler.

Use: Allows cold air to escape steam-system radiators as steam enters, closing automatically when steam fills the radiator or pipe.

> **Use Tip:** Boil valves in vinegar from time to time to remove scale.

> **Buying Tips:** Choose category carefully in order to balance system. Be sure you get the technical brochure that is usually packaged with the valves.

3-in-One Radiator Repair Tool

3-in-One Radiator Repair Tool

Description: Metal, three-armed tool with a tap, a screw extractor, and a die.

Use: Repairing worn-out holes in radiators where an air vent has broken off or stripped the threads. Extracts broken air valves, retaps radiator, rethreads air valve.

Use Tip: Make sure radiator valve is closed when removing vent.

Radiator Air Bleeder Valve Key

Description: Tiny metal key with square opening, similar to a roller skate key.

Use: Opens air bleeder valve on hot-water-system radiators to let air out.

Radiator Air Bleeder Valve Key

Buying Tip: These are inexpensive and important enough to warrant buying several to ensure that you can find one when you need it.

Flexible Gas Hose

Also Known As: Gas range or dryer connector

Description: Brass (old style) or gray epoxy-coated (new style) flexible, corrugated hose with brass hex fittings on the ends. Comes in a range of sizes from 18" to 6' in $1/2$" or $3/4$" diameter. Modern appliances have $1/2$" fittings but typical supply lines are $3/4$". Adapters for reducing the connection are available with the hose.

Use: Connects gas supply line to kitchen gas stove or clothes dryer.

Use Tips: Use plenty of **pipe dope (Part VIII, Chapter 60)**—not tape—and care. Make sure no kinks are in the line. Test by brushing with soapy water and examining connection for bubbles.

Fitting Types

About Fittings

Fittings are devices that allow pipe to be connected to increase length and to change direction. For each kind of pipe there are fittings made of the same material, wall thickness, and sizes, with a few exceptions. For quality check to make sure that there are not too many rough edges.

Galvanized, plastic, and copper fittings come in two variations, for *water supply* and for *waste,* or drainage. Waste fittings have recessed threads that leave a smooth inside—when connected they do not impede the flow of waste and thereby avoid causing blockages. They are not available in all sizes. They may also be called *Durham fittings,* after an old manufacturer. Supply fittings are also known as *malleable steel fittings.* When purchasing fittings you should, of course, specify if they are for water supply or waste lines. *Black iron fittings* come either for gas or for steam. *Cast iron* is made for waste only.

Fittings are made of copper, plastic, galvanized steel, black iron, cast iron, brass, and so on to go with pipes of the same material and wall thickness. All fittings have similar functions, shapes, and names but have notable differences as to type. Entries for both types and shapes follow. An almost infinite total of combinations are manufactured, so these represent the basic ones.

Some terms are shorthand for one style in a variety of fitting shapes. For example, the term *reducer* refers to any fitting that will go on to one size of pipe at one end, and another size pipe at the other end, but may be incorrectly used to refer to such items as a *reducing bushing, reducing coupling, reducing nipple*, or *reducing wye,* etc. For example, you would use a *reducing tee* to branch off a 1½" water pipe to two 1" pipes. And an *adapter* can mean almost anything, but we make an attempt to define them in Chapter 55.

Threaded Fitting

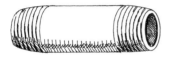

Nipple

Description: The most common type of fitting, with male (exterior) or female (interior) threads at each opening. Comes in most materials and sizes.

Use: Connecting water supply, waste, steam, and gas piping systems in all kinds of threaded pipe.

> **Use Tips:** Use plenty of *pipe dope* or **Teflon® pipe tape (Part VIII, Chapter 60)** on the threads of metal pipes to prevent leaks and reduce corrosion.

Sweat-Soldered Fitting

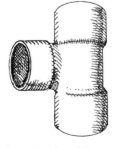

Sweat-Soldered Fitting

Also Known As: Copper fitting (incorrect), sweats

Description: Smooth-ended (no threads) copper pipe fitting with a slightly enlarged end that receives copper pipe.

Use: Connecting copper pipe or tube.

Use Tips: Ensure that fittings are clean before soldering and that plenty of **flux (Part VIII, Chapter 60)** is used. Soldering *copper pipe joints* is not all that difficult. Do not use lead solder on water supply lines.

Buying Tip: Now available with solder pre-applied.

Compression Fitting

Description: Two-piece copper or plastic device that uses a nut and a metal or plastic ring on the end of a pipe that is inserted into a fitting. As the nut is tightened the ring presses into the fitting and the pipe, making a watertight seal.

Use: Connecting water supply tubes under faucets, or wherever one wants to avoid using a torch and sweat fittings. *Plastic grip fittings* are for use with **flexible plastic (PB) pipe (above)**.

Buying Tip: The small rings and nuts can be bought individually in case one is lost.

Compression Fitting

Flare Fitting

Also Known As: S.A.E. flare

Description: Similar to a **compression fitting (above)** but with an end that is expanded, or flared, and that fits against the beveled end of the fitting.

Use: Mostly for refrigeration and oil heating systems and small appliance lines. Similar to *sweat-soldered fittings* but installed without using a torch, which can be important in areas where fire would be a risk. Prohibited by some codes.

Solvent-Welded Fittings

Also Known As: Glued fittings, cemented fittings

Description: Plastic fittings with slightly enlarged, threadless openings designed for use with special solvent, sometimes called *glue*. They look similar to **copper sweat-soldered fittings (above)**. Considered the best joining method for plastic pipe and fittings.

Use: Rigid plastic plumbing connections.

Insert Fitting

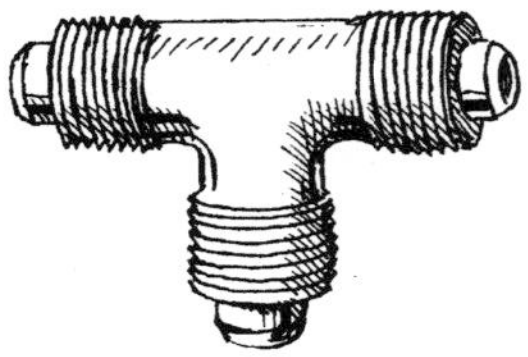

Insert Fitting

Also Known As: Insert

Description: Ridged plastic or metal piece that is inserted into the end of flexible plastic pipe and clamped in place with a stainless-steel **hose-type clamp (Chapter 54)**. Made of nylon, polypropylene, or polystyrene.

Use: To connect flexible plastic pipe to other pieces or fittings, including to standard female threads. Common on lawn sprinkler systems.

Hubless Fitting

Also Known As: No-Hub®, no-hub clamp, no-hub band, clamp, banded coupling

Description: A neoprene (black rubber) sleeve, or gasket, covered by a corrugated metal sleeve, or *clamp band,* with hose-type clamps on each end.

Use: Connecting hubless or No-Hub® cast-iron pipe sections and fittings. Also cast iron-to-plastic.

Hubless Fitting

Use Tips: Clamp nuts can be tightened down with a small wrench, screwdriver, a $5/16"$ **nut driver (Part I, Chapter 8)**, or a special tool called a **T-handle**, or **No-Hub® torque wrench (Part VIII, Chapter 63)**. The latter tool contains an internal mechanism that prevents overtightening and speeds the job.

Adapter

Also Known As: Transition fitting

Description: Common term for virtually anything that helps connect two normally incompatible things—hoses to pipes, or whatever. As for fittings, though, it is a type of coupling or union with a different type of joining method on each end, i.e., thread/sweat, thread/solvent weld, etc.

Adapter

Types:

> *Transition union adapter:* Special fitting designed to compensate for thermal differences in expansion and contraction between metal and plastic pipe.
>
> *Dielectric adapter:* For connecting galvanized to copper.

Use:

> *Transition union:* Allows connecting different kinds of pipe, such as plastic to galvanized, or copper to plastic, etc.
>
> *Dielectric fitting:* Allows connecting dissimilar metals and prevents destructive *galvanic* or *electrolytic* action, a major cause of rust and corrosion. Typically used under faucets where copper pipe connects with galvanized. Suitable for water and waste.

Flexible Coupling

Also Known As: Fernco Coupling (brand name)

Description: Length of soft plastic (elastomeric PVC or polyurethane) that slips over the outside ends of waste pipe and is secured by hose clamps. Heavier yet more flexible than **hubless fittings (above)**. Comes in a variety of dimensions and shapes as a **reducer coupling (Chapter 56)**.

Use: Waste lines only, but fits over any kind of pipe. Especially useful where precise alignment is not possible or where some flexibility is needed and where connecting two pipes of different diameters. A "forgiving" fitting.

Tap-On Fitting

Also Known As: Saddle valve

Description: Short nipple with heavy saddle end and a U-bolt. Comes with a **sillcock (Chapter 57)** or similar valve.

Use: Clamps onto a copper, brass, or galvanized supply line with the U-bolt and, after a hole is drilled and the valve installed, provides a new source of water. Typically used in small sizes to install an ice-maker.

Fitting Shapes and Forms

About Fitting Shapes and Forms

These shapes, or forms, are made in all the various pipe materials, but regardless of the material, they resemble each other (the illustrations show galvanized fittings). The nomenclature is the same.

Cap

Cap

Also Known As: End, end cap

Description: A short piece with female threads on one end and the other closed.

Use: Seals male end of pipe at the end of a run or when a fitting or valve has been removed.

Coupling, Reducing Coupling

Coupling   Reducing Coupling

Also Known As: Straight coupling, reducing bell (reducing coupling), reducer (reducing coupling)

Description: Short length of pipe with female threads, generally no longer than the threaded area itself. Reducing couplings have two different-sized openings.

Use: Connects lengths of pipe that are not intended to be disconnected. Reducing coupling connects pipes of different sizes up to 3". Can also be used in combination with **bushings (below)** when there are large differences in pipe diameters.

$ **Buying Tip:** When buying a reducing coupling state the larger dimension first—2 × 1½" etc.

Cross

Cross

Also Known As: 4-way tee, straight cross

Description: Four female threaded openings of the same size set at 90-degree angles (straight cross); a side-outlet cross has a fifth opening on the side, in the center, and is extremely rare.

Use: Joining four (or, with a side outlet, five) pipes.

 Use Tip: Using a fitting with five openings is extremely difficult and unusual.

Dresser Coupling

Also Known As: Mender coupler, slip fitting, "no-thread" fitting, mender dresser

Description: Similar to a *nipple* with hex or ribbed nuts on each end, inside of which is a compression fitting containing rubber and metal washers. Available in copper, steel, and plastic.

Use: Slips onto unthreaded pipe ends to make a convenient connection, often used to cover a leaking section (after the pipe has been cut through) or where a very slight flexibility is needed.

Dresser Coupling

 Use Tips: May be used on supply or waste lines. Helpful where threading is impossible, such as when replacing a damaged section.

Elbow

Types:

90-degree elbow

45-degree elbow

Drop-ear elbow

Side-outlet elbow

Also Known As: Ell, L, S.O. ell (side-outlet ell)

90-Degree Ell

45-Degree Ell

> **Note:** Similar to and easily confused with cast-iron fittings $1/4$ bend (90-degree) and $1/8$ bend (45-degree).

Description: Female threads at both ends, or in the case of side-outlet ells, all three, with openings at angles corresponding to the type of elbow. *Drop-ear* (also known as *drop ells*) have a *flange* for attaching to a wall. The ell that brings water from a toilet tank to flush a toilet bowl is known as a *closet bend.*

Use: Joins pipes for corners at 90- and 45-degree angles.

> **Use Tips:** Side-outlet ells are useful in corners of construction or for making railings or fences. If placed outdoors, protect exposed threads to keep from rusting.

Flange

Also Known As: Floor flange

Description: Round, female-threaded fitting that can take pipe up to 2", surrounded by flat flange with holes that permit attaching to a floor or a wall with screws or bolts.

Use: Often a nonplumbing use, such as making a railing or a table. Pipe just screws into the flange and is relatively solid.

Hex Bushing, Flush Bushing

Also Known As: Bushing

Description: Short plug (threaded, with hexagonal top) or nipple (flush)-type piece with female threads inside.

Use: Joining pipe of dissimilar size. Bushings fit inside other fittings, especially couplings, and can be combined to reduce pipe as required.

Hex Brushing

Nipple

Also Known As: Close (if threads from each end of a straight nipple meet or almost meet in the middle), straight nipple

Description: Any piece of pipe that is less than 12" and male threaded on both ends. Generally stocked in lengths from *close* (minimum) to 12"; lengths beyond this are usually considered *cut pipe* and are available in 6" intervals. Diameters are standard nominal pipe sizes, from $1/8$" to 4". *Reducing nipple* has different diameter ends. Reducing nipples are particularly short, available only up to 2" maximum diameter, and are very rare.

Use: Links longer pipe sections where the final "fit" is being made, such as the span between two fittings in a run of pipe. Reducing nipple connects different sizes of pipe in place of a **bushing** and **coupling (above)** combination. Provides a smoother, neater connection.

threads

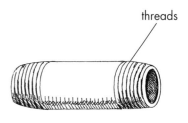

Nipple

Pipe Clamp, Repair Plate

Also Known As: Often the two items above are confused and considered the same thing.

Description: A *hinged pipe clamp* consists of two concave stainless-steel pieces a few inches long with a hinge on one side and flanges with two carriage bolts on the other. It comes with a rubber gasket that fits over the pipe when the clamp is bolted down. A *repair plate* is one concave steel piece a few inches long with two flanges and two U-bolts, also supplied with a rubber gasket.

Use: Covering small holes and cracks in drain pipes.

> **Use Tips:** Not for use on supply lines. Pipe usually has to be replaced where leaks occur on any line with pressure.

Plug

Plug

Also Known As: Hex head plug, square head plug, round head plug

Description: A short, solid piece with male threads and a hexagonal, square, or round head. A large cleanout plug has a square protrusion in the middle for a wrench to grab.

Use: Seals female ends of fittings or valves and the like.

Street Ell

Also Known As: Street elbow

Description: 90- or 45-degree elbow with male threads on one end and female threads on the other.

Use: Joins pipes at corners with the male end going into a fitting or valve.

Street Ell

Sweep

Description: Similar to an elbow in that it consists of two openings at 90 degrees or 45 degrees to each other. Comes in "long" version as well as normal to create a longer curve to fit different situations.

Use: Same as elbows, but with longer dimensions and more gradual configurations.

> **Use Tips:** If replacing an existing piece of plumbing, be sure to measure the sweep to see if it is "long" or normal.

Tee

Also Known As: T, straight tee, reducing tee, sanitary tee

Description: Three openings, two in a line and one on the side, in a T shape. *Straight tees* have the same size openings; *reducing tees* have one opening of a different size. *Sanitary tees,* used in waste lines, have a curved branch that is slightly offset for a cleanout plug and a smooth inside.

Tee

Use: Connecting three pipes. Sanitary tees are for waste lines where lack of obstruction is important.

$ **Buying Tips:** When ordering a reducing tee specify the lateral, or horizontal, dimensions first, followed by the vertical branch. Keep the letter T in mind. For example, 1" × 1" × 1$\frac{1}{2}$". Be sure to mention the use you have in mind, as there is some variety in sanitary tees.

Union

Also Known As: Ground joint union

Union

Description: An assembly of one (sweat) or three (threaded) hex nuts. Its two halves are separated and screwed onto the ends of the pipes to be joined, then the larger, central hex nut is tightened down to join them.

Use: Connecting pipe sections of similar size that are expected to be disassembled or that are being fit into a position between two fixed pipes.

X **Use Tip:** Because this is a sort of compression fitting the surfaces must be clean to avoid leaks.

Y Branch, Reducing Y

Wye (Y)

Also Known As: Y bend, wye

Description: Three openings, with two in a line and one at an angle, that can be the same or a different size in the case of a reducing Y.

Use: Bringing together two pipes from similar directions.

Faucets and Faucet Parts

About Faucets

Kitchen sink, laundry, and lavatory faucets come in a tremendous array of styles and colors. Some have separate handles for hot and cold water, while others—mixing, or combination, faucets—have a single lever. Materials include chrome-plated brass, chrome-plated plastic, plain plastic, and pot metal.

When buying a faucet the key dimension to specify is center-to-center, or "centers"—the distance between the center of one handle and the center of the other. Kitchen sinks usually have 8" centers but may be 6". Lavatory faucets mounted on the basin are called *deck-mounted* and are usually 4" apart but 8" is not uncommon. Wall-mounted lavatory faucets are usually on $4^1/_2$" centers but may be 6".

Selecting a faucet can be a complicated exercise, dependent on a variety of factors, but one thing that experts suggest is buying a good-quality, name-brand model. It will be more expensive, but it will work better, and replacement parts, which are generally unique to each brand, will be available when needed.

Faucet types include ledge- or deck-mounted (exposed, on the countertop; concealed (plumbing is below countertop), shelf-back (on vertical splash back of counter). And all can be dual or single knob-controlled, with or without spray.

There can be no doubt about sizes or types when repairing or replacing faucet parts. Always take the old parts into the store, or at least the brand and model names.

> ### $ General Buying Tips:
>
> - Avoid pure plastic or chrome-covered plastic faucets, often known as "builder's specials." They can deteriorate rapidly. Also avoid pot-metal faucets.
>
> - Cast brass is much better than tubular brass; chrome-plated pot metal is inferior. Both metals look similar, but brass is much heavier.
>
> - Avoid faucets manufactured in the Far East. They are generally of inferior quality. Again, some German-made faucets are very good.
>
> - If you are a reasonably handy do-it-yourselfer, you can install any kind of standard faucet. Some come with installation kits and don't even require tools.
>
> - Major, advertised name brands of kitchen and bathroom faucets such as Moen, Delta, and Kohler can be much more expensive than their average counterparts but worth it.

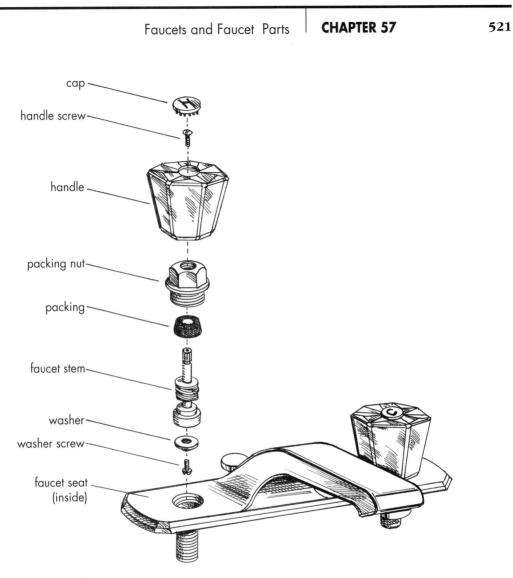

cap

handle screw

handle

packing nut

packing

faucet stem

washer

washer screw

faucet seat
(inside)

Compression Faucet

Compression Faucet

Also Known As: Basin faucet (in lavatory)

Description: Common faucet that has a threaded *spindle* or
stem, with a washer on the end that presses against a hole,

the *faucet seat,* where the water emerges from the supply pipe.

Use: Controls water flow into basins or sinks.

Use Tips: Leaks are usually due to a worn-out washer or a pitted, corroded seat.

Buying Tips: Get faucets with a replaceable or renewable "seat"—the part that the washer presses against. If a nonreplaceable seat goes bad, the entire faucet may have to be replaced or perhaps saved by regrinding the seat with a **faucet seat reamer (Chapter 65)**.

Washerless Faucet

Description: Regular faucet operated by an internal mechanism, either a cartridge or a ball, controlling the water flow. Strictly speaking, a washerless faucet is not without a washer—there has to be some soft substance between the cartridge or ball and the faucet seat. In a washerless faucet this may be a gasket, O-ring, or a rubber diaphragm. Manipulating the faucet handle moves the cartridge or ball over the hole where the water emerges. Single-handled mixing faucets, such as those invented by Moen, are always washerless; those with two handles may be washerless or compression type.

Use: Controls water flow into sinks and basins, especially in single-handled, or mixing, faucets.

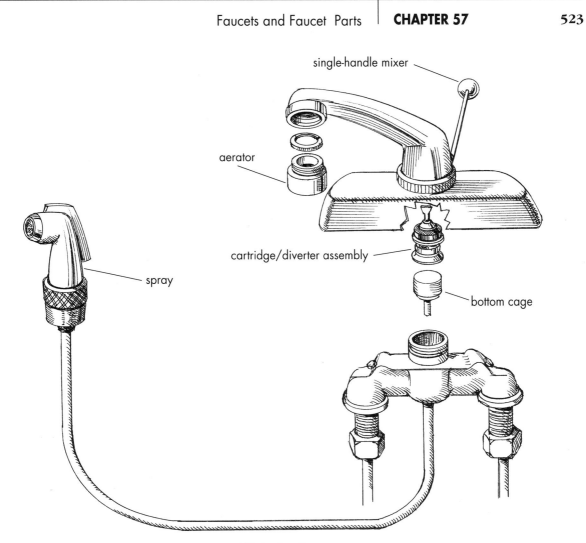

single-handle mixer

aerator

spray

cartridge/diverter assembly

bottom cage

Washerless Faucet

Use Tips: Parts vary quite a bit from brand to brand, but repair of parts or replacement of the whole internal mechanism is possible. Leaks are usually due to worn gaskets or springs in the ball type or the O-ring in a cartridge type.

Faucet Stem

Faucet Stem

Also Known As: Stem (not to be confused with cartridge), spindle

Description: Metal or plastic bar fluted at one end. The **faucet handle (below)** is attached to one end and the **faucet seat washer (below)** to the other end. Sold as "hot" or "cold" with threads corresponding to the way a handle is turned to open or close the faucet.

Use: The internal mechanism of a compression faucet and a common replacement part.

Use Tips: On some models the screw that holds the handle to the stem (always smack in the center) is concealed by a small decorative cap that must be pried up to gain access to the screw.

$ Buying Tips: Stems vary greatly from brand to brand and model to model, so you must take the old one in to get a duplicate. Don't hesitate to replace old, corroded, leaky stems if replacing washers and cleaning and greasing the threads doesn't work. They are inexpensive, especially third-party (non-name) brands. Be sure to specify hot or cold.

Faucet Washer

Also Known As: Gasket (incorrect)

Description: Doughnut-shaped part usually made of neoprene plastic or rubber, flat or beveled, black or red. Fits into a cup on the end of the stem and is held with a brass screw.

Use: Seals off the supply of water by pressing against the faucet seat when a **compression faucet (above)** is closed.

Flat Faucet Washer

Beveled Faucet Washer

No-Rotate Washer

> **Use Tips:** Keep a supply of various sizes of washers and stainless-steel or brass screws on hand because washers are the most common part of a faucet to wear out.

> **Buying Tips:** Beveled washers are usually better for repair than flat ones as they seal better if the seat is worn and pitted. Neoprene is better than rubber. Even nominal sizes vary by manufacturer; a quarter-inch washer of one make may actually not fit where another manufacturer's "quarter-inch" washer did. The only way to ensure that a washer fits is to try it. Keep an assortment on hand so you'll have one that fits an old faucet just right. Washers are commonly sold in boxes of 12 and 20 assorted sizes, with brass screws included, as well as singly.
>
> If the cup or rim on the end of the stem where the washer goes is worn or missing, the washer will not seat properly. You can try a new rim that attaches with a screw or a *no-rotate washer* or *5-year faucet washer*, which snaps into place and, in effect, has its own rim built on. However, these are not long-lasting. You may end up having to replace the whole stem.

Faucet Seat, Removable

Faucet Seat, Removable

Description: Small, doughnut-shaped brass device that screws into the top of the water supply pipe; water flows through its center hole, which is either hex-shaped or square (in the case of removable seats).

Use: The part against which the *faucet stem washer* presses in order to seal off the flow of water.

> **Use Tips:** If the seat is worn, the faucet will leak. To remove a worn seat use a **faucet seat wrench (Part VIII, Chapter 63)**, or if not replaceable, grind it down so the washer will fit snugly against it with an inexpensive **faucet seat reamer (Chapter 65)**. You can use a **screw extractor (Part III, Chapter 22)** if it is difficult to use a wrench.

> **Buying Tips:** Seats rival stems in the number of different sizes available. While packages of assorted sizes are available, buying this way is poor economy as the ones that don't fit will never be used. Take the old one into the store to get the exact size and make needed.

O-Rings

O-Ring

Also Known As: Gasket (incorrect)

Description: Rubber ring that comes in various diameters.

Use: Fits over spindle of some faucets to make a seal.

> **Buying Tips:** If difficult to remove, use a dental tool or other small, pointed tool for getting underneath the O-ring.

Aerator

Aerator

Also Known As: Spray diffuser

Description: Small barrel-like metal or plastic part that screws onto the end of a spout with either inside or outside threads and a screen inside. Made in a variety of sizes and types.

Use: Makes the stream of water coming from a faucet spout smooth and prevents splashing.

> **Use Tips:** Unscrew occasionally and clean debris from screen. If it doesn't unscrew by hand, use **tongue-and-groove pliers (Part I, Chapter 7)** with a rag to protect the chrome finish of the aerator.

> **Buying Tip:** Universal aerators are available that fit most faucets.

Lavatory Faucet Handle

Lavatory Faucet Handle

Also Known As: Faucet handle

Description: Plastic or metal piece that attaches to faucet stem. Available in an almost infinite number of shapes and styles.

Use: To open and close faucet.

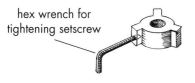

hex wrench for tightening setscrew

Universal Faucet Handle

Use Tips: On some handles the screws that hold the handle on the stem are concealed under a decorative cap, often marked "Hot" or "Cold." These must be pried up to gain access to the screws.

Buying Tips: For the best fit buy a duplicate replacement handle. Failing this, buy a *universal handle.* Types with two setscrews are more secure but may still slip and damage the stem.

Bathtub and Shower Faucets

Also Known As: Valves, diverters

Description: A variety of types: three-valve faucets have hot- and cold-water faucets with another faucet in the middle for diverting water to the shower. Two-valve faucets have hot- and cold-water faucets with a lift-up device on the tub spout for diverting the water to the shower. Two-valve shower fittings have hot- and cold-water faucets only. Two-valve tub fillers have faucets that fill the tub only. Single-control faucets have one lever that controls the flow and mix of hot and cold water.

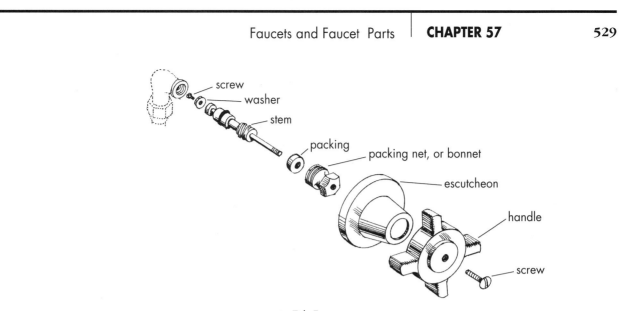

Tub Faucet

The standard center-to-center measurement on tub faucets is 8", though 6" and 11" centers are also used. The center measurement on old-style free-standing tubs with exposed plumbing is $3^1/_2$". Tub faucets are available in chrome-plated brass or plastic, pot metal, and plain plastic.

Use: Controlling water flow and temperature in a shower or bathtub.

Use Tips: To remove the stem after the handle is removed, a bonnet nut must be removed. This is usually best done with a **deep-throat socket wrench (Part VIII, Chapter 63)**.

> **Buying Tips:** Same as for sink and lavatory faucets except that kits are usually not available. Five brands stand out: Delta, Kohler, Moen, Powers, and Symmons.

Tub Faucet Parts

> **Note:** Same as sink and lavatory faucets.

Tub and Kitchen Spouts

Also Known As: Tub-filler spout, over-the-rim spout

Description: Chrome-plated brass piece that screws onto the water pipe in the tub or is part of faucet assembly in the kitchen.

Use: Routes water from faucets into tub or sink.

> **Use Tip:** Before unscrewing tub spout (easily done by hand) remove the faucet handles if they interfere.

> **Buying Tips:** Finding a duplicate kitchen spout is difficult and expensive. It's better to replace the whole faucet.

Shower Arm and Head

Shower Arm

Description: A shower arm is a chrome-plated pipe threaded on both ends if new type or threaded on one end if old type. The newer one has a removable shower head, while the arm and head are permanently attached with a ball joint in the old style. Shower heads are made of chrome-plated brass or plastic.

Use: The shower arm carries water from supply pipe to shower stall, and the head directs and sprays it.

Shower Head

> **Use Tips:** Shower arms are removable, but care must be exercised when removing. You don't want to lose anything inside the wall.

> **Buying Tips:** Plastic shower heads are less expensive than metal ones and may be of lesser quality. Many water-saving characteristics have been developed and incorporated into the better models. Massaging shower heads provide a pulsating stream; continental shower heads are attached by flexible hose and hand-held, as in Europe.

Sillcock

Also Known As: Outside faucet, hose bib, male hose faucet

Description: Bronze faucet with valve handle and a flange to go against a wall and a male-threaded spout for connecting to hoses ("plain" faucet has no threads). Frostproof version

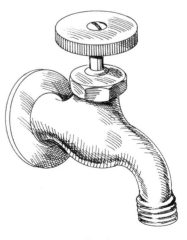

Sillcock

has a pipe connected to valve to keep water inside the house and unfrozen.

Use: Exterior water supply, especially to hoses.

> **Use Tips:** Old-style can be unscrewed; new-style sillcocks are usually soldered in place and are therefore unremovable. Leaks can be repaired the same ways as other faucets. If you are concerned about unauthorized people turning on the sillcock, such as on the exterior of public buildings, remove the handle and open or close the faucet with a **sillcock key (below)** that you carry with you.

> **Buying Tips:** If a difficult-to-repair leak occurs, a small **Y connector (below)**, can be screwed on to act like a new valve. This is handy anyway, as it creates two faucets in the place of one. Cast-brass decorative handles are also available.

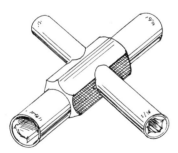

4-Way Sillcock Key

4-Way Sillcock Key

Description: Crisscross metal bar with hex-shaped openings at each end.

Use: For opening sillcocks without handles.

> **Use Tip:** Helpful when it is inconvenient to leave handles on faucets, such as in public buildings.

Y Connector

Also Known As: Siamese connection

Description: Female threads at base with two male-threaded legs that have small shut-off valves built in. Bronze or plastic.

Y Connector

Use: Screws onto **sillcock (above)** or other hose connection and provides two hose connections in the place of one, with individual valves. Useful when supplying cold water to a washing machine and a garden hose from the same pipe, for example, or when a sillcock valve is broken.

> **Use Tip:** Make sure only the side you want open is open when turning on the main valve.

> **Buying Tip:** Avoid plastic—it is not strong enough.

Drains and Accessories

Tub Drain Mechanisms

Types:

Spring drain

Weight drain

Also Known As:

Spring type: Pop-up drain, rocker arm

Weight type: Trip lever

Description:

Spring type: Consists of a chrome-plated escutcheon, or decorative faceplate, through which a trip lever sticks. Connected to the lever, inside the overflow pipe behind the tub wall, is a linkage that presses against a rocker arm assembly that controls a chrome pop-up stopper with an O-ring.

Weight type: Similar to the spring type but the linkage terminates in a weight that lifts up or down out of a drain hole, depending on whether the lever is flipped up or down.

Use: Controls tub draining.

> **Use Tips:** Most of the problems associated with tubs concern clogging, usually caused by hair. It is simple to unscrew the escutcheon, lift out the linkage, and clear away the debris. The mechanism itself rarely fails, but the spring behind the lever and escutcheon often loses its tension due to corrosion. This is easily replaced. The O-ring on a spring type must also be replaced from time to time.

> **Buying Tip:** If repairing the weight type seems too difficult, just use an inexpensive rubber drain plug instead.

Pop-Up Drain Assembly

Also Known As: P.O. drain

Description: Metal stopper and linkage found on the interior walls of a sink.

Use: Controls the pop-up drain in a lavatory basin or bathroom sink to plug or unplug the drain.

> **Use Tips:** When removing the drain itself or the piping, use a **P.O. plug wrench (Part VIII, Chapter 63)** or a pair of pliers inserted into the drain to hold it stationary while the nut is turned with pliers or a wrench underneath.

> **$ Buying Tips:** The top part, or insert, on a basin pop-up assembly comes in a large variety of styles and sizes. Only the manufacturer's replacement insert will do, so buying a complete linkage is recommended if replacement is required. Or use a simple rubber drain plug.

Basin and Tub Drain Strainer

Basin and Tub Drain Strainer

Description: Cylindrical chrome metal basket, either 1 $^5/_{16}$" in diameter for bathtubs or 1" in diameter for wash basins.

Use: Catches hair, toothpaste-tube caps, and other things that you don't want down the drain, like the occasional errant earring.

> **Use Tips:** Easily kept on hand even if drain plugs are in use—simple to toss into place when desired.

Kitchen Sink Strainer

Kitchen Sink Strainer

Also Known As: Strainer cup, strainer, duo strainer, duo cup strainer, basket strainer

Description: A perforated, cup-shaped metal device that fits into the drain opening of a kitchen sink. The strainer insert usually has a rubber washer on the bottom.

Use: Catches debris from water. The insert acts as a stopper when its rubber washer is snug against the bottom.

Use Tips: When installing or removing a strainer an **internal spud wrench**, or **basket strainer wrench**, may be used from above to resist the turning of a **spud wrench (Chapter 63)** below. A hammer and chisel or screwdriver may also be used to turn the spud nut that holds the strainer. The rubber washer on the bottom of the strainer insert may need replacement regularly.

Valves

About Valves

Valves, like faucets, control the flow of water or steam, but they are stronger and have more specialized characteristics than faucets. Valves and sillcocks are found on plumbing; faucets are simply valves that are used on fixtures such as sinks. Valves are made in all the sizes and types that pipe is made and in most of those materials as well, although cast brass is most common. The type of fitting must be specified, such as "threaded" or "sweat."

Ball Valve

Description: Large lever controls an interior plastic ball that covers or uncovers an opening for water.

Use: Controls water flow where quick action is a premium—one quick, easy twist of the lever and the valve is opened or closed.

> **$ Buying Tips:** Best valve available—shuts water off quickly and it's easy to see if valve is open or closed, unlike other valves.

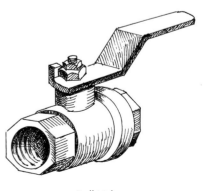

Ball Valve

Check Valve

Description: Regular and swing type, some for installation on vertical lines. Handle-less valve with loose flap inside that closes when water flows the "wrong" way and swings open when it flows properly, allowing water to flow in one way only.

Use: To prevent backflow.

> **Use Tips:** Models designed for use on vertical lines will not work if installed upside down; arrow on body denotes basic "open" direction.

Drainable Valve

Also Known As: Stop and waste valve, bleeder valve

Description: Essentially a globe or gate valve with a drain opening.

Use: Draining pipe (on the nonpressure side) to prevent it from freezing in cold weather.

Gate Valve

Description: Faucet-like handle controlling a metal wedge that slides up and down into a seat. A *connector gate valve* has a union fitting on one side, handy when connecting to a radiator.

Use: Controls water flow where total, unimpeded opening is required, such as on a water main, and is recommended wherever a constant flow is expected.

> **Use Tips:** Usually best to keep completely, rather than partially, open or closed. Leaks from the stem sometimes can be fixed by tightening the outside hex nut or else removing it and adding **stem packing (Part VIII, Chapter 60)**. Repair is not usually possible, though, so replacement is your only course if there are problems.

> **Buying Tips:** Buy only the very best quality, especially for a water main. No other valve in a residence is so important.

Gate Valve

Globe Valve

Also Known As: Compression valve

Description: Rounded body with a seat on its bottom that a stem with a replaceable washer presses against. Rounded body is what gives this valve its name. Comes in most pipe sizes. Also available with openings at right angles to change the direction of the flow 90 degrees, known as an *angle*

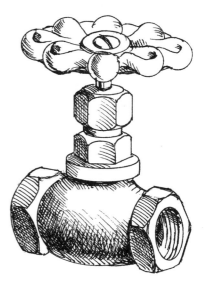

Globe Valve

valve (regular is called *straight*). A *connector globe valve* has a union fitting on one side, which, like the **gate valve (above),** is handy for connecting to radiators.

Use: Controls water or steam flow, especially suitable for high pressure and frequent use.

> **Use Tips:** Washers and seats can be replaced, as is necessary on radiators. Leaks from the stem can usually be fixed by tightening the hex nut or else removing it and adding **stem packing (Chapter 60).**

> **Buying Tip:** Search out the better quality brands.

Water Supply Valve

Also Known As: Speedy valve, angle stop, shutoff valve, lavatory straight valve, cutoff valve, stops

Description: A small globe-type valve, usually chrome-plated, made of plastic or metal. Can be 90-degree (angle) or straight.

Use: Controls water flow of the **water supply tubes (Part VIII, Chapter 54)** to toilets and sinks. The tubes are often called *speedies* (they have built-in fittings and are quickly installed).

Angle Speedy Valve

Speedy Valve

> **Use Tips:** The handle has great leverage, making it all too easy to strip the plastic kind. Take care.

> **$ Buying Tip:** Using metal-stemmed valves limits the risk of stripping.

Gasket

Description: A generic term for soft material that fits between two hard items in order to make a seal. It may be made of rubber, plastic, or strong paper and is shaped for each particular use.

Use: Seals joints in fittings, between parts of valves, and so on.

> **$ Buying Tips:** Formed gaskets as well as sheets for making your own are available. In some low-pressure cases you can form your own small gasket in between parts of leaking radiator valves and the like by using a liquid (sold in tubes) made for that purpose.

Joint and Fitting Materials

Pipe Joint Compound

Also Known As: Pipe dope, thread sealant

> **Note:** Do not confuse with **drywall joint compound (Part VII, Chapter 50)**, which is a totally different material.

Description: Thick, oily paste applied to pipe threads before assembly. Sold in containers as small as 1-ounce tubes.

> **Note:** Different types of compound are available for pipes carrying oils and gases.

Use: Helps prevent leaks and makes for easier disassembly; also helps prevent corrosion of exposed threads where the zinc coating has been removed during the threading process.

> **Use Tips:** Use gloves—some kinds of pipe dopes are extremely difficult to clean off of hands. Apply liberally.

> **$ Buying Tip:** Works well, but **Teflon® pipe tape (below)** is neater and faster for the same job.

Teflon® Pipe Tape

Also Known As: Pipe tape, Teflon® tape

Description: Extremely thin, white tape sold in rolls from $1/4$" to $3/4$" wide and in various lengths.

Use: Applied to pipe threads before assembly, same as **pipe joint compound (above)**. Not for use on gas pipes.

> **Use Tip:** Do not overwrap; once around is sufficient.

Epoxy Repair Material

Also Known As: Epoxy putty, epoxy

Description: Two-part putty material mixed together just before use. May be a long package resembling a candy bar, or a tube, or a small package resembling a packet of chewing gum. You break off as much as you need of this clay-like substance and massage it a bit, mixing the two parts together.

Use: Repairs small leaks in pipes.

Use Tips: While epoxy cannot be depended on 100 percent to stop a leak, it may work for years. Some kinds work even when applied to a wet pipe.

Solder

Description: Soft, silver-colored wire sold on a small reel; 95-5 solder is the most common type, made of 95 percent tin and no lead.

Use: Used in sweat-soldering of copper pipe joints.

Use Tip: Parts to be soldered must be very clean.

Buying Tips: The old-fashioned kind with lead was outlawed nationally in 1986; use 95-5. If you can't find 95-5 at your hardware store, try a plumbing supply store.

Flux

Description: Jelly-like paste.

Use: To ensure proper fusion of solder to copper sweat-solder joints.

Use Tip: Use liberally.

> **Buying Tip:** Use the *noncorrosive* type, sometimes called *self-cleaning* or *nonacid* type.

Flux Brush

Also Known As: Acid brush, utility brush

Description: Light $1/4$" wide metal-handled brush with short bristles, about 6" long.

Use: Applying solder to copper fittings or for cleaning threads.

> **Buying Tips:** Very cheap. Buy a large number and use for touch-up or anything else around the shop and dispose of after use.

Copper Fitting Cleaning Brush

Also Known As: Sweat fitting wire cleaning brush

Description: Wire handle with cylindrical black bristle brush on the end. A *combination brush* has $1/2$" and $3/4$" brushes on either end.

Use: For scrubbing copper fittings clean prior to soldering.

Plumber's Putty

Description: Soft putty.

Use: Applied to sink rims, drain plugs, and faucets before installation to ensure seal.

> **Use Tip:** Remove all old putty before applying fresh material.

> **Buying Tip:** Buy only what you can use right away as it tends to dry out. Use **caulk (Part IV, Chapter 32)** to seal sinks and countertops.

Stem Packing

Also Known As: Faucet packing, packing, gasket rope, plumber's twine

Description: Graphite or Teflon®-impregnated string.

Use: Wrapped around valve stems to prevent leaks.

Stem Packing

> **Use Tips:** If a slow leak at a handle stem cannot be stopped by tightening the nut, just back it off and add more packing—but first make sure the water is off!

Oakum

Description: Short lengths of shredded rope or hemp fiber, sold dry or tarred (oiled). White oakum has a thin woven coating and is impregnated with a type of cement powder.

Use: Originally used mostly for sealing old-fashioned hub-and-spigot cast-iron waste pipe along with molten lead, but useful for packing any kind of large gap. For example, it could be stuffed into a crack and used as a base for caulking. White oakum, which has dry cement in it, swells when brought into contact with water. Interestingly, oakum and tar were the traditional materials used to caulk the planks of ancient ships' hulls.

Use Tip: Wear gloves to avoid a nasty clean-up job.

Toilet Parts

About Toilets

The mechanism for operating a toilet hasn't changed much since it was invented in the nineteenth century. It is a marvel of ingenious operation. Improvements have been made only on some parts, but not on the concept.

Many toilet part names still reflect the first name for a toilet—water closet. Hence, a *closet bend* is the pipe that brings the water from the tank to the bowl, a closet, or closet floor, flange sits over the drain opening, etc. Additionally, probably because the openings between the tank and bowl are very big, they are often called *spuds,* so related tools and parts have spud in their names—spud pipe, spud wrench, etc. Confusing and inconsistent but not impossible.

A toilet works simply. When you push the handle a trip lever it is attached to inside the tank lifts the tank ball or the flapper off the flush valve seat by means of two linked rods or a chain. Clean water in the tank then rushes out the hole and into the bowl, flushing out its contents.

The float ball, which floats on the tank water (that's the big thing you see first when you take the top off the tank), goes down as the water level goes down. The end of the rod is screwed to the ballcock mechanism and its movement opens a valve in the ballcock that lets new water into the tank. Think of the ballcock as the faucet that fills the tank. At the same time some water is routed down a *refill tube* into the bowl.

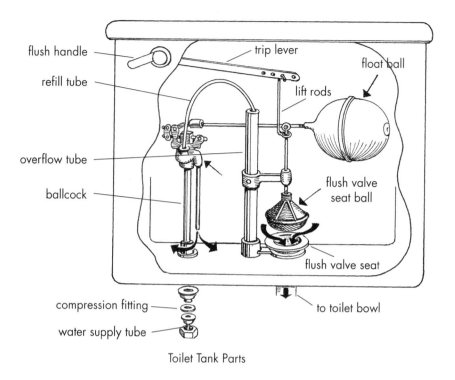

flush handle

refill tube

trip lever

float ball

lift rods

overflow tube

ballcock

flush valve
seat ball

flush valve seat

compression fitting

water supply tube

to toilet bowl

Toilet Tank Parts

As the water level rises the end of the float-ball rod gradually closes the ballcock valve and when the tank is full—and the float is again at the top of the tank—it shuts down completely, ready for the next flush. In fact, if you have a tank leak or a flood while you are working on the tank, just lift the float ball and arm up to the top position, which will shut off the water that is flowing into the tank (you can hold it up with **duct tape [Part IV, Chapter 38]** in an emergency). Best is to shut off the water supply, of course, at the water supply valve or main line.

Toilet Flush Handle

Description: Chrome-plated lever on side or front of tank. Usually supplied with the lever or arm attached.

Use: Raises *flush valve ball* to start flushing process.

> **Use Tips:** Unlike most things, to remove the handle unscrew in a clockwise direction. It is held on by a *left-hand threaded nut.*

Float Ball

Also Known As: Float

Description: Plastic or copper ball $2^1/_2$" to 3" in diameter, sometimes ribbed, attached to the end of the float arm.

> **Use Tips:** Ball sometimes develops small holes (caused by corrosion) and water enters. It should be replaced if you can hear water inside.

> **Buying Tip:** Plastic is recommended but copper works well too.

Lift Rod, Upper and Lower

Also Known As: Upper or lower lift chain or wire

Description: Metal rod with eye in the end.

Use: Connects tank ball to trip lever; this is the part that lifts the tank ball out of its seat and starts the water flushing.

> **$ Buying Tips:** Available individually or as part of pre-packaged assemblies. Often replaced by the new flapper-type mechanism.

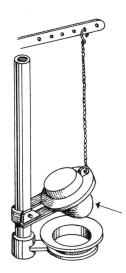

Flapper

Flush Valve Ball

Also Known As: Tank ball, flush ball, valve seat ball

Description: Rubber ball-like device, suspended by lift rods or wire, which fits into flush valve seat. The older models are called *Douglas flush valve balls*.

Use: Controls water flow from bottom of tank. When it is lifted the tank water rushes out and flushing is started.

> **$ Buying Tips:** The traditional flush valve ball design is frequently the culprit when a tank leaks. It is easily replaced by a new design called a *flapper* or *flapper ball*. The flapper is connected to the float arm by a chain, and one size fits all toilets—$2^1/2$". Very easy to install; just be sure to adjust the height until it seals properly. It eliminates the easily jammed wires or rods, guide or guide arm, and the cursed tank ball.

Flush Valve Seat

Also Known As: Valve seat, flush ball seat, tank outlet, seat

Description: Round rubber seat at bottom of tank that "lines" tank outlet to bowl. Two types exist: one for toilets connected to but separated from the tank by a short elbow, called a *closet bend*, and one for tanks that sit directly on the bowl.

Buying Tips: Replacing a seat is difficult. Better to leave it in place and use a modern replacement, such as the Fluidmaster Fixer Kit. This consists of a stainless-steel cup, which is epoxied to the old seat, and a flapper ball.

Ballcock

Also Known As: Ballcock assembly, inlet valve

Description: Tubular valve device that has a main pipe that screws onto the water supply piping and has a smaller, parallel tube called a *filler tube* attached. Newer *float-cup ballcocks* have just one big shaft.

Use: Controls water supply to the tank and bowl. Activated by the float ball arm or float cup.

> **§ Buying Tips:** Although replacement ballcock parts can be bought, this may be a problem for older toilets. The solution is to install a complete new ballcock. Standard ballcocks are easy to install. Newer ones that operate by water pressure and have no float ball are best, such as the one made by Fluidmaster. Both regular and "antisiphon" types are made, but the antisiphon is better because it protects against toilet water backing up into the water supply lines.

Refill Tube

Also Known As: Bowl refill tube

Description: Small tube that screws into the ballcock mechanism and empties into the overflow tube. Made of plastic, brass, or aluminum.

Use: Fills bowl with water after flushing to keep sewer odors out.

> **§ Buying Tip:** Plastic is normally better than metal as the metal tubes tend to break off at the threads.

Overflow Tube

Also Known As: Douglas valve, Douglas flush valve

Description: Copper, brass, or aluminum tube 1" or $1\frac{1}{8}$" in diameter that screws into flush valve seat.

> **$ Buying Tips:** Sold with *flush valve seats* or individually. Get the largest thickness, or gauge, available and avoid aluminum, which corrodes quickly.

Tank-to-Bowl Attachment Hardware

Description: Long brass bolts with large rubber washers and a very large foam-rubber washer. These items are usually available in small packages. Standard size for all brands.

Use: The two items necessary to secure a close coupled standard tank to the toilet bowl. The two brass bolts and nuts go in small holes for that purpose in the bottom of the tank, and the large (bagel-sized) washer fits around the open drain hole that the water goes through on its way into the toilet bowl.

> **$ Buying Tips:** Make sure the connections are clean and don't hesitate to add **caulk (Part IV, Chapter 32)** or **plumber's putty (Part VIII, Chapter 60)** to ensure a seal. Stand ready with sponge and bucket when testing as you can't tell if the seal is good until you actually flush the toilet.

Closet Flange Bolt

Also Known As: Closet bolt, toilet bolt, hold-down bolt

Description: Bolt with flanges at middle and one end; a *closet screw* screws into a wooden floor and thus has screw threads on one end.

Use: Secures toilet to floor and flange to toilet base.

Wax Ring and Closet Flange

Description: Literally a wax ring and a metal ring with inside diameters the size of the drain pipe and toilet bowl bottom opening.

Use: Sealing toilet bowl to drain piping.

> $ **Buying Tip:** Buy and use a double wax ring for the best seal.

Special Products for Boilers and Furnaces

Boiler Cleaner

Also Known As: Boiler liquid

Description: Liquid or powder chemical sold in convenient containers for steam, hot water, or both kinds of heating systems.

Use: Cleans out and prevents rust and sludge deposits in boilers of heating systems; may help prevent additional wear and tear on the system. Poured directly into the boiler.

> **Use Tips:** The liquid form is easier to use if you must pour it through a small opening, such as a *pressure relief valve*.

Boiler Solder

Description: Liquid chemical sold in convenient containers for either steam or hot-water heating systems.

Use: Settles into and plugs hairline cracks or pinholes in boilers of heating systems. Poured directly into the boiler.

Oil Tank Treatment

Also Known As: Sludge treatment

Description: Powder or liquid chemical.

Use: Dissolves dirt and sludge and absorbs water found in the bottom of oil tanks. Apply just prior to being refilled with oil.

Soot Destroyer Stick

Description: About 1"× 8" cylinder of chemical that is merely tossed into the active hot chamber or firebox of oil, gas, coal, or wood heating units. Similar material available in aerosol spray can as well.

Use: Removes soot and creosote from flues.

Furnace Cement

Description: Heat-resistant premixed patching cement.

Use: Cementing furnace or boiler flues into masonry.

> **Use Tips:** Amazingly gooey and sticky. Very hard to use neatly but good to use for simple and important repairs. Helps prevent exhaust gas leaks.

Plumbing Wrenches

About Plumbing Tools

Following are some commonly needed tools for plumbing. You needn't buy many of them—perhaps only the plunger and a snake or other drain-cleaning tool. But you should be aware of them so you can purchase or rent them on the occasion when you decide to do without a professional plumber. Sometimes even the purchase of a fairly specialized tool for a one-time use can be worthwhile, considering the price of a plumber's visit.

About Plumbing Wrenches

A wrench is not always a wrench, because sometimes a wrench is a *plumbing wrench*, as described here, and other times it is a *combination wrench*, or an *adjustable wrench*, or one of many other specialized machinist's or carpenter's wrenches, as described up front in **Part I, Chapter 8.** Also, some folks in the British Isles tend to refer to all wrenches as *spanners*. When you are ordering a wrench, be specific.

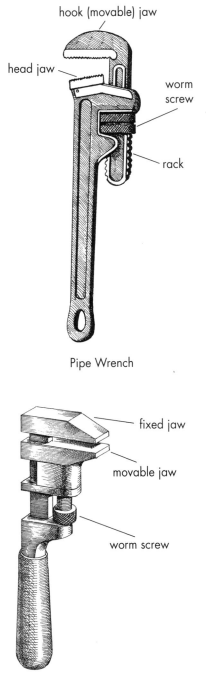

hook (movable) jaw

head jaw

worm screw

rack

Pipe Wrench

fixed jaw

movable jaw

worm screw

Monkey Wrench

Pipe Wrench

Also Known As: Stillson (or Stilson) wrench

Description: Heavy metal tool with serrated jaws—one fixed and one adjustable and slightly offset. Comes in *straight pattern* (standard), *end-pattern* (slightly offset), and *offset* (jaws at 90 degrees to the handle). The teeth of the jaws dig into steel pipes. Another type, a *compound pipe wrench,* has a head that is a combination of **end-pattern and chain wrench (below)**.

Uses: Turning steel pipe and fittings, or, in a pinch, anything round.

> **Use Tips:** Pipe wrench jaws can leave marks on metal so use only where this is not a concern, or use tape or cloth to protect the finish. Two pipe wrenches are needed when working with pipe, one for holding the fitting and the other for turning the pipe, so keep two on hand. Turn toward the lower jaw to "set" the teeth firmly.

> **Buying Tips:** Wrenches come in various lengths, with the jaw capacity increasing as the wrench gets longer. Two wrenches, one 8" and one 10", should serve well.

Monkey Wrench

Also Known As: Ford wrench, automotive wrench, auto wrench

Description: Large wrench with parallel smooth jaws, one fixed and one adjustable, that are always parallel. Unlike a pipe wrench, jaws are smooth. Some manufacturers call a thin, large-opening, smooth-jawed pipe wrench a **spud wrench (below)** for large spud nuts—but it looks like the classic monkey wrench.

Use: Turning nuts or fittings wherever there are flat sides for the wrench to grip. Good on chrome because the jaws won't mark it.

> **Use Tips:** Stronger than a pipe wrench. Always pull the wrench toward you rather than pushing it.

> **Buying Tips:** These days large, **smooth-jawed, tongue-and-groove pliers, adjustable wrenches (Part I, Chapters 7 and 8)**, or **pipe wrenches (above)** are generally used in place of monkey wrenches. No longer commonly available.

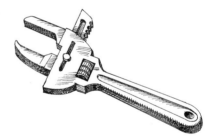

Adjustable Spud Wrench

Spud Wrench

Types:

> *Fixed spud wrench*
>
> *Adjustable spud wrench*
>
> *4-in-1 combination spud wrench*
>
> *Closet spud wrench*
>
> *Internal spud wrench*
>
> *Radiator valve spud wrench*

Also Known As: *Adjustable:* sink wrench

4-In-1 Spud Wrench

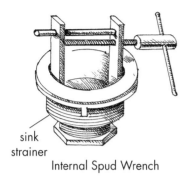

sink
strainer

Internal Spud Wrench

Radiator Valve Spud Wrench

Description: Metal tool, various models of which have large, flat-sided jaws, except for the *radiator valve spud wrench,* which is a long, solid metal tapered rod with angular sides for turning with a pipe wrench.

Use:

Fixed: To turn large spud nuts, i.e., the nuts that hold the toilet tank to the toilet, or the locknut under a kitchen sink strainer, or really any large nut.

Adjustable: Jaws are especially notched for use on various sizes of strainer nuts or any large nut. All-purpose adjustable locknut wrench. Available in a combination model.

4-in-1: For turning large locknuts on closet, or toilet tank, spuds and basket strainers, similar to the fixed model.

Closet: Especially for spuds on toilet tanks and bowls.

Internal: Removing and installing closet spuds, large and small sink strainers, pop-up plugs, bath strainers. Holds strainer in place while you are turning locknuts below with a wrench.

Radiator valve: For removing or tightening radiator spud nut.

> **Buying Tips:** The adjustable spud, or sink, wrench is the handiest for general purpose use.

Spanner Wrench

Also Known As: Duo strainer wrench, hook spanner, strainer nut wrench

> **Note:** Many Britishers call all wrenches *spanners*, and indeed any flat, open-end wrench that fits only particular devices can be referred to as a spanner by U.S. manufacturers.

Description: Flat metal handle with a half-circle jaw with one or two hooks at either end. A *face spanner* (also known as a *pin spanner*) has two pins perpendicular to a full C-shaped arc.

Use: Tightening or loosening large nuts especially designed for this wrench, usually found under a kitchen sink drain or strainer.

Duo Strainer Wrench

Strap Wrench

Description: Wrench-like handle on one end of which is an adjustable fabric strap.

Use: For turning chrome-plated or polished pipe while avoiding scratches.

Strap Wrench

> ✗ **Use Tips:** Never force tubular goods—they are thin-walled and might crush.

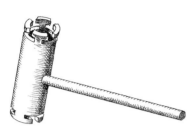

Basket Strainer Wrench

Chain Wrench

Description: Wrench-like handle with a chain on one end.

Use: Turning pipe, tubing, or fittings, particularly where there is limited space for a conventional wrench and great turning power is required.

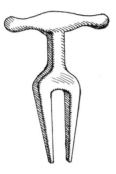

P.O. Plug Wrench

Basket Strainer Wrench

Description: Hammer-shaped steel tool with notched cylinder for a head and short rod for a handle.

Use: Keeping kitchen sink or tub strainer in place during installation.

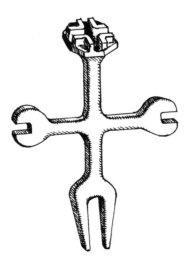

P.O. Plug Wrench

Description: Small cast-metal wrench with a fork-like end and a T-handle. A 4-way model has two arms.

Use: Removing P.O. ("Pop Up" or "Pop Out") plug from basin drain opening. Holds plug stationary in basin while nut is turned underneath.

4-Way P.O. Plug Wrench

> **Use Tip:** 4-way model is for use with a variety of strainer types, including basket strainers.

T-Handle Torque Wrench

Also Known As: No-Hub® torque wrench

Description: Ratchet tool consisting of T-handle, bar coming off to side, and a hex opening at the bottom.

Use: For tightening fittings on hose clamps, such as on No-Hub® fittings.

> **Use Tips:** Easier to use than a nut driver or screwdriver as it has an internal mechanism that prevents overtightening. The T-handle provides more torque, or force.

Deep-Throat Socket Wrench

Also Known As: Plumber's wrench, wall socket set, tub/shower valve nut socket wrench, tub-and-shower valve wrench

Description: Short, hex-shaped hollow steel tube. Usually sold in sets of five graduated sizes.

Use: Removing and driving nuts and valves, especially on bathroom faucets, such as are found in showers.

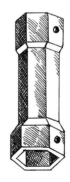

Deep-Throat Socket Wrench

Eccentric Nipple Extractor

Also Known As: Internal pipe wrench, tube extractor, nipple puller, nipple extractor

Description: Hexagonal cylinder with a serrated floating (loose), offset (eccentric) part on one end.

Use: Removing pieces of pipe or tube that have broken off or corroded inside fittings. It is inserted inside the pipe and turned with a wrench.

Eccentric Nipple Extractor

Basin Wrench

Also Known As: Faucet wrench, faucet nut wrench, crowfoot faucet wrench

Description: Bar with a rod through one end and knurled hook on the other.

Use: Essential, unique tool for loosening and tightening the nuts that hold a faucet in place.

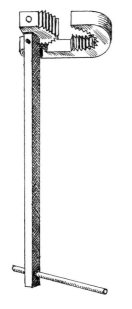

Basin Wrench

Faucet Seat Wrench

Also Known As: Faucet seal tool, seat wrench

Description: L-shaped or straight bar of metal with one end machined to four flat sides and the other to five.

Use: Removing **faucet seats (Part VIII, Chapter 57)**.

Use Tips: Check with flashlight to see if hole (faucet seat) has four or five sides. Press firmly into place before unscrewing seat. If it has a round hole, it is not replaceable, and either the entire faucet must be replaced or the seat reamed out instead with a **faucet seat reamer (Part VIII, Chapter 65)**. If it is difficult to use this wrench because it can't "grab," try a **screw extractor (Part III, Chapter 22)**.

Faucet Seat Wrench

Handle Puller

Also Known As: Faucet handle puller, faucet valve handle remover

Description: Two hook-like parts with a rod down the center and a turning handle.

Use: For freeing frozen faucet handles.

Use Tip: Applying a little **penetrating oil (Part IV, Chapter 37)** to the parts first helps loosen them.

Faucet Spanner

Description: Flat metal bar with various-sized wrench openings at each end and along its length. Actually a simple wrench.

Handle Puller

Use: Tightening or loosening faucet parts during installation or removal.

> **Buying Tip:** These are supplied along with some brands of new faucets.

Drain-Clearing Tools

About Drain-Clearing Tools

Tools are better for clearing drains than chemicals. Try the plunger first, then a small snake, then renting a *power snake* if these other options have failed. Among other reasons, the power snake might work just because it is longer and can go around corners more easily.

Drain Opener

Also Known As: Drain line opener

Description: Chemical product in powder or liquid form. Often strong acid or caustic, though some natural products that dissolve hair are available. Lye is a common component of this product.

Use: Poured into slow drains to dissolve whatever might be blocking the line.

Use Tip: Follow directions carefully if using any of the acids or caustics.

Note: Exercise caution when you deal with chemical drain openers. While chemicals can be useful, they can be problematic if they don't work—they may solidify and leave you with a caustic, clogged line. If you do call a plumber after having poured caustic chemicals into the drain, you must tell him so—he might be putting his hands in the water or splash his face by accident and get serious chemical burns. Also, certain chemicals may damage plastic piping and solvents.

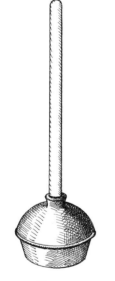

Plunger

Plunger

Also Known As: Plumber's friend, force cup, force pump, handyman's helper

Description: Short, broomstick-like handle on the end of which is a cup-shaped piece of rubber. Some models, called *combination plungers,* have two cups, one inside the other. Typical diameter is $2^1/_2$" to $5^1/_2$". Another type has an accordion-like bellows for pushing massive amounts of air.

Use: For clearing blockages in sinks, tubs, and toilets.

Use Tips: Make sure that the edges of the plunger are immersed in water for a good seal. Rubbing the edge with petroleum jelly helps. The models with a smaller cup inside a larger one are for toilets; the extended smaller cup fits snugly in the bowl hole. It can be retracted for use on sinks.

Bellows Type Plunger

Snake

Also Known As: Auger, drain auger, trap auger, drain-clearing or -cleaning tool, plumber's snake, drain snake

Description: Coiled spiral cable, about $1/4$" thick, in various lengths up to 25', with a removable or fixed handle on one end and a slightly open coil at the business end. Another type, which is much more efficient, has a crank mechanism in a wide funnel-shaped container. Professionals use power versions with power supplied by an electric drill-like tool. The best DIY model has no handle but instead an end that goes into a portable electric drill.

Use: Clearing sink and basin drain lines. (For toilets, see next item, **closet auger**.)

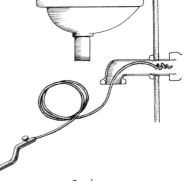

Snake

Use Tips: Feed snake in gradually. Don't push too hard or you might kink it. If you have no success, try renting a heavy-duty power snake. Not only can they clear tough obstructions, but it is easier for them to turn corners in pipes, and they are longer.

Buying Tips: Get a top-quality snake as a low-quality one can kink at turns in the pipes.

hose connection

Drain Unclogger

Drain Unclogger

Description: Oblong rubber bulb a few inches long, with openings on either end. One end is threaded to receive a garden hose, and the other is an open nozzle.

Use: Forcing obstructions from pipes by using water pressure from the garden hose. The bulb expands with the hose water to prevent backflow.

 Use Tips: Beware of creating problems with delicate plumbing when using high pressure.

Closet Auger

Also Known As: Auger, toilet auger, closet snake

Description: Short, thick, spiral cable with a hooked end in a rigid tube; has a crank handle.

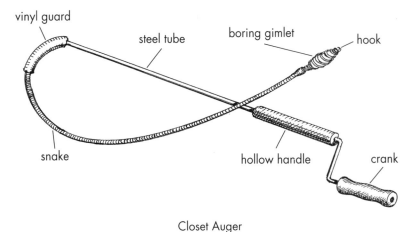

vinyl guard • steel tube • boring gimlet • hook • snake • hollow handle • crank

Closet Auger

Use: Clearing clogged toilets. Better than a regular snake because of its rigidity.

Sewer Tape

Also Known As: Drain-clearing tool, sewer rod

Description: Flat metal band 40 or 50 feet long, sold in a coil, with a coiled hook or point on one end.

Use: Clearing blockages located between the main house trap and the sewer or other disposal area.

> **Use Tips:** If the tape doesn't work, a rented *heavy-duty auger* or *power rooter* is recommended. These are sharper and stronger and longer. If this fails, call a plumber.

Special Plumbing Tools

Faucet Seat Reamer

Also Known As: Valve seat grinding tool, faucet seat dressing tool, cone bibb reamer, faucet reseater, seat dresser, T-handle reamer, taper reamer (one version), seat-dressing tool

Description: Comes in various versions but essentially consists of a turning handle and metal shaft on the bottom of which is a cutter, either replaceable or fixed.

Use: Smoothing a faucet seat that has become rough with wear, corrosion, or calcium deposits.

Faucet Seat Reamer

Use Tips: Work slowly and carefully. Be sure to cut perfectly horizontally or else the washer may not seat well.

Flaring Tool

Description: Two bars that clamp closed and form openings for various sizes of copper tube, and a vise-like part called a *yoke* with a drive screw and cone that slides along the bars and locks in place.

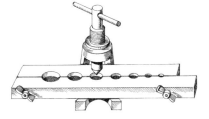

Flaring Tool

Use: Flaring the ends of copper tubing prior to joining with flare fittings.

> **Use Tip:** Proceed slowly and carefully when flaring pipe.

Lever-type Tube Bender

Also Known As: Hickey, pipe bender

Description: A clamp-type device with two legs and a gauge showing angle of bend.

Uses: Bending rigid copper, brass, aluminum, steel, and stainless-steel tube up to $5/8$" outside diameter ("O.D.").

> **Buying Tips:** Tubing heads can be purchased separately. Hickeys can be rented.

Reamer

Also Known As: Pipe reamer

Description: Metal fluted cone with sharpened edges and a handle or chuck for turning.

Use: Removing burrs from the ends of various kinds of metal pipe after cutting.

Pipe Reamer

Tube Bender

Also Known As: Spring bender, tubing bender, copper bending spring

Description: Tightly coiled length of spring in various diameters.

Use: Bending copper tube without kinks.

Use Tips: Bend very slowly; don't force it, or you risk getting kinks.

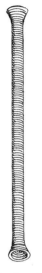

Tube Bender

Tubing Cutter

Also Known As: Tube cutter

Description: Metal device with a cutting wheel and a knurled knob for bringing the cutting wheel into snug contact with the tube. Comes in midget size for tubing up to $1/2$" outside diameter and another size for larger pipe.

Use: Cutting copper tubing.

Use Tips: Just as easy to cut small pipes with a hacksaw or *PVC saw* and file off ends, but the cutter does it at perfect right angles and leaves a cleaner cut than a saw.

Tubing Cutter

$ **Buying Tips:** Cutters also available for cutting steel and plastic pipe. Some models have reamers attached for taking burrs off pipe after cutting. Larger size can cut tubular goods.

Electrical Products and Tools

About Polarized Plugs and Receptacles

Electrical devices manufactured nowadays are polarized to minimize the chances of electric shock. This means that the "hot" wires (carrying the current) and "ground" wires must remain consistent through the entire electrical circuit—hot wires must be linked only to hot wires and ground wires only to ground. In practice today's appliances are polarized to keep them consistent with receptacles. To do this one prong of a plug is made larger than the other; one slot of each receptacle is made larger than the other. The result is that the device can't be plugged in any way but correctly.

About Grounding

The third prong on plugs is the *grounding plug,* which is a safety feature that routes errant electrical current to the ground instead of letting it go through your body when an electrical malfunction occurs. It is therefore recommended that grounding plugs be used wherever possible, and that **adapters (see 3-to-2 adapter, below)** are used properly in two-slot receptacles.

Taps, Adapters, and Plugs

About Taps and Adapters

Receptacles and light sockets are not always where we need them, nor are there even enough, it seems. Happily, a whole array of household devices exists that convert and multiply receptacles and sockets to bring power—whether an outlet or a socket—to where we want it by tapping into the current.

Each manufacturer calls their items by different names, and the terms they choose are not always very descriptive. Following, then, are our terms, which we think will help your understanding. There are two groups of devices—those that plug directly into a receptacle, or outlet (*extension cords*, *outlet strips*, and *outlet adapters*), and those that screw into lightbulb sockets (*socket* or *lamp-holder adapters*).

Thoughout this section the terms *male* and *female* are used to denote whether a device has prongs or threads that protrude on the outside (male) or slots or openings with springs and threads on the inside for receiving male prongs and threads (female).

About Extension Cords and Outlet Adapters

The following six items can be extremely convenient, but one cardinal rule must be followed: do not ever overload the circuit by plugging in many different adapters on top of one another. You might find yourself blowing fuses and circuit breakers unnecessarily and dangerously.

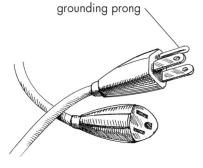

grounding prong

Extension Cord Ends

Extension Cords

Description: Available in various lengths from 3' to 100' and in various colors; wire may be two- or the heavier three-wire (grounded) type (recommended). Extension cords are typically supplied with a female plug on one end and a male plug on the other. Latest innovations are a cord with three female receptacles and another with a receptacle box with six female receptacles and a built-in *circuit breaker* or **GFI (Chapter 69),** sometimes called a *portable outlet center.*

Use: Provides power at a remote location.

> **Use Tips:** Extension cords are sized to handle a certain amount of current and should be matched to the device at hand. Most cords will be marked for the kinds of items they should be used with, such as air conditioners and hedge trimmers. For safety use only highly visible yellow or orange cords for gardening devices and in the workshop. A triple female plug is convenient when you are switching between several power tools on a job—but not for using them all at once.

Multiple Outlet Strip

Description: Rectangular plastic strip containing multiple receptacles and a long cord to plug into a nearby outlet. Available in different sizes from a few inches long with two outlets to 18" long with a dozen outlets and in two- and three-wire types. Some surface-mounted types are specially adapted for mounting on walls. Newer models may have **built-in circuit breakers (Chapter 68)**.

Surface-Mounted Multiple Outlet Strip

Another version is the *power strip,* which is a 6" to 12" long plastic device that has two slots along its length instead of individual receptacles and can take as many as 15 plugs. In any case, this is still a sort of multiple-outlet extension cord.

Still other models of this and other taps may have a *surge protector* built in, a device that protects your electronic equipment from sudden surges in electricity due to lightning or power supply malfunctions. These are generally not sophisticated enough to protect computer equipment from minor fluctuations, though.

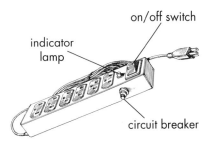

Power Strip with Circuit Breaker and On/Off Switch

Use: Provides power for a variety of items at a distance from one receptacle.

Table Tap

Also Known As: Plug-in strip, plug-in outlet adapter, outlet tap

Description: One-piece plastic unit containing two to six pairs of slots for plugs. Comes either with third grounding prong or not.

Table Tap

Use: Plugs into any outlet to provide multiple receptacle capacity.

Cube Tap

Cube Tap

Also Known As: Cube adapter, plug-in outlet adapter

Description: Small plastic or rubber device with one set of prongs (either two or three if grounding type) and two or three female receptacles for other plugs. Smaller version of **table tap (above)**.

Use: Provides extra capacity at a receptacle.

6-Outlet Tap

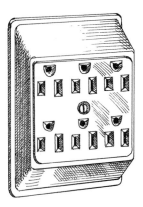

6-Outlet Tap

Also Known As: Multioutlet, multiple tap

Description: Plastic receptacle shaped roughly like a truncated pyramid that plugs into an existing duplex outlet and can accommodate four or six plugs, depending on the model. Comes polarized and/or grounded; some models contain circuit breakers or surge protectors.

Use: Converts a two-plug receptacle to six.

 Buying Tip: Small surge protectors are not necessarily sufficient for delicate computer equipment.

Outlet-to-Lamp-Holder Adapter

Outlet-to-Lamp-Holder Adapter

Also Known As: Outlet adapter, socket adapter (manufacturer's terminology is unclear)

Description: Lightbulb socket with prongs on end for plugging into standard receptacle or extension cord.

Use: Creates an extra light source, generally for temporary use only.

About Socket Adapters

Socket adapters, sometimes called *current taps,* differ from the taps described above in that they screw into sockets rather than plug into outlets. They also should be used sparingly and are generally intended for temporary use, although if used appropriately, they work as well as permanent products.

The term *lamp-holder* is the manufacturers' term for a socket, the device that holds a lightbulb ("lamp"), as well as for the larger porcelain or metal device that serves as a base to attach a socket to an electrical box. This latter item is described in **Chapter 67**.

Socket-to-Lamp-Holder/Outlet Adapter

Also Known As: Current tap, socket adapter (often confused with other outlet-to-lamp-holder adapter, above), socket switch

Description: Round, ivory or brown plastic device with lightbulb-like threads on each end (male on one, female on the other) and receptacle slots on each side. Some models have a *pull chain* or *toggle switch* that turns off the bulb but not the outlets. If it has no pull chain, it is called a *keyless adapter*.

Socket-to-Lamp-Holder/Outlet Adapter

Use: Provides two outlets wherever there's a light socket without sacrificing the bulb.

> **Use Tip:** Plugging in numerous extension cords risks overloading the socket.

Lamp-Holder-to-Outlet Adapter

Lamp-Holder-to-Outlet Adapter

Also Known As: Plug body

Description: Single receptacle with lightbulb-type threads on one end.

Use: Creates a single receptacle wherever there's a light socket.

Single-to-Twin Lamp-Holder Adapter

Single-to-Twin Lamp-Holder Adapter

Also Known As: Twin light adapter

Description: Siamese (V-shaped) device that holds two lightbulbs at an angle to one another, with one threaded end that screws into a regular socket.

Use: Provides a double socket in the place of a single one.

About Plugs

Electrical plugs come in two basic forms, male or female. Male plugs have prongs while female plugs have slots. Male plugs may also have either two or three prongs (one U-shaped prong for grounding and two flat ones).

Male plugs are either *open construction* or *dead-front* type. The former, popular for years, has an insulating disk covering the screw terminals inside the plug; the disk can be pried up to access the wires' ends. It is no longer being manufactured and should be replaced as necessary. Dead-front plugs are safer. To get at wires in the dead-front type a thick cap must be unscrewed; wires are looped around terminal screws on the cap or mounted in pressure slots.

Like other electrical devices, plugs are rated in terms of amperage to handle particular currents.

Open Construction-Type Plug   Dead Front-Type Plug

Standard Plug

Also Known As: Plug

Description: Male plug with two or three prongs as described in **About Plugs (above)**. Plugs may be of light or heavy construction, such as black rubber (for appliances) or light plastic in brown, black, and/or ivory. Side-outlet plugs have the wire coming out the side. A plug is technically a **male receptacle (Part IX, Chapter 69)**. Nonstandard currents, such as for major appliances, may require different shapes and types of prongs.

Use: Terminal device on wire that plugs into **receptacles (outlets) (Chapter 69)** to provide power for whatever device it is connected to. Black rubber plugs are used on appliances while plastic plugs are used on lamps and other devices with minimal electrical consumption. Side-outlet plugs can be used effectively where there is little clearance, such as behind furniture.

> **Buying Tip:** Plugs are available in ivory, brown, black, and white for decoration purposes.

3-to-2 Adapter Plug

Also Known As: Grounding adapter

Description: Small, cube-shaped plastic or rubber plug with two prongs on one end and three openings in the other, with a small, U-shaped metal piece (lug) attached directly to the plug. Older models have a 3" grounding wire (lead)—usually green in color—coming directly out of the middle with the U-shaped lug on its end.

3-to-2 Adapter Plug

Use: Allows use of three-pronged (grounded) plug in a two-slot receptacle.

> **Use Tips:** Be sure to attach the grounding metal (U-shaped piece) to the screw in the middle of the receptacle. Failure to do so exposes you to a potentially severe electric shock. You will have defeated the purpose of the safety grounding system. Best to avoid using this kind of plug except for temporary situations; better to install three-hole grounded receptacles.

Clamp-On Plug

Also Known As: Snap-on

Description: Comes in various forms. A common one is a plug with a hole in the back for wire; there are prongs that have small teeth for making electrical contact that can be removed and spread apart. Other types are *cam* and *squeeze*.

Use: Clamp-on plugs are used to replace damaged plugs on lamps or similarly small electrical devices.

Clamp-On Plug

Use Tips: Clamp-on plugs are quick and easy to use but some electricians question their safeness. If you have any doubts, you can use a standard type as described above.

Female Appliance Plug

Description: Black or ivory plastic plug that can be separated in half by unscrewing the screws that hold the halves together.

Use: Plugs into small appliances to make electrical connection at one end of electrical wire; the male end plugs into the wall outlet.

Female Appliance Plug (shown open)

Lighting Fixtures and Bulbs

Fluorescent Fixtures

Types:

Rapid start: Goes on the instant the fixture is turned on.

Starter: Flickers a bit before going on.

Instant: Goes on after a momentary pause.

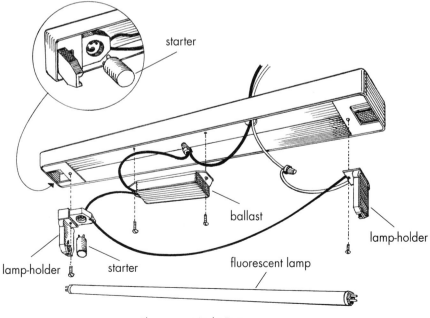

Fluorescent Light Fixture

Description: Fluorescent fixtures are rectangular or circular and contain *sockets*, or lamp holders, which house the ends of the bulbs used, and a *ballast*, a heavy black metal box that is a kind of transformer that reduces the regular high voltage so it can be used by the fixture, which operates on a lower than normal voltage. Rapid start types have a starter and ballast in one piece. Starter types contain a smaller ballast and a small aluminum barrel, the starter, a special type of automatic switch.

Use: Holding fluorescent tubes or bulbs.

> **Use Tips:** Almost all the parts of a fluorescent fixture are replaceable, including the ballast, starter, and lamp holders. Of course new parts must match those being replaced.

> **Buying Tip:** Fluorescent fixtures are much cheaper to operate than incandescent ones.

Fluorescent Lamps

Also Known As: Fluorescent lightbulbs

Description: Fluorescent lamps or tubes are available in a variety of lengths from 6" to 96". They are mercury-filled tubes of white glass with capped ends that have two pins extending from them. Fluorescents come in varying light intensities, from giving off a rather harsh light to one that's much warmer. A mixture can create a daylight effect; special intensities are available for uses including examination of color

Compact Fluorescent Electric Bulb

printing and growing plants indoors. 9,000-hour bulbs, or *compact fluorescent bulbs* have a screw-in base and screw into regular sockets like incandescents—a unique design. They are squat cylinders.

Use: All bulbs supply light. Tubes are for use only in fluorescent fixtures, except as noted above.

> **Use Tips:** Fluorescents are designed to be left on—they last much longer if you don't keep turning them off and on.

> **Buying Tips:** Fluorescent lamps supply the same light at much less cost than incandescent bulbs. They are simply rated at less wattage for the same luminosity.

About Incandescent Light Fixtures

There are a large variety of light fixtures available. Styles vary tremendously—there are entire stores devoted to nothing but light fixtures of different design—but all have essentially the same internal mechanism and one simple purpose—to hold lightbulbs.

When hanging any fixture make sure the hardware used is strong enough to support it.

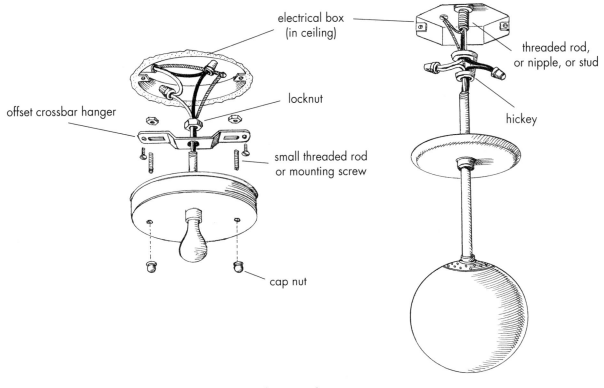

electrical box
(in ceiling)

threaded rod,
or nipple, or stud

locknut

hickey

offset crossbar hanger

small threaded rod
or mounting screw

cap nut

Incandescent Light Fixtures

Incandescent Ceiling and Wall Fixtures

Description: There exist an almost infinite variety of styles and shapes of lighting fixtures, but they usually have three wires and are mounted on an **electrical box (Part IX, Chapter 71)** that accepts the shape and size of the fixture. Mounting is either to an existing threaded *stud* (threaded rod) with a device called a *hickey* or, if there is no stud, a *crossbar hanger,* or *strap,* may be used. These are available flat, offset, and adjustable. Or a Rube Goldberg arrangement of various mounting parts—mixing *nipples* (short lengths of threaded rod) straps, hickeys, and *locknuts*—may be required to hang the fixture. Hickeys and nipples come with ends of different sizes. There is even a part called a *crow's foot,* which provides a stud where there is no electrical box. *Track lighting* is a series of fixtures mounted on a metal track that contains wiring. Fixtures can be moved along the track to any position without rewiring.

Use: Holds lightbulbs.

> **Buying Tips:** Don't be afraid to look for miscellaneous individual items for mounting a fixture to an electrical box. In old houses, especially, each location may be different. All parts are available loose. There are various sizes of nipples and studs, so bring in the old piece or buy several to be sure of getting the right fit.

Indoor Incandescent Light Bulbs

Also Known As: Lamps, bulbs

Description: Glass spheres with necks and screw-in metal bases, containing a delicate wire element that glows when electricity flows through it. Various-sized bases are available; *Edison-base* is standard. Socket reducers are available for fitting small bases into large sockets. 130 volt bulbs and other *energy-saving bulbs* look just like regular incandescent bulbs but have a heavier, stronger filament. *Appliance bulbs* are similar, designed for use in ovens and refrigerators. *Construction grade bulbs* (also called *coated lamp* and *rough service* or *extended service*) are more resistant to breakage. They are made with a slight "skin" for protection and have stronger filaments than normal bulbs.

Use: To supply light. Construction grade bulbs are suitable for portable work lights that must "take" some vibration. For more intense light, use interior high-intensity lamps known as **halogen lamps (Part I, Chapter 15),** which require their own special fixtures and transformers.

> **⚡ Buying Tips:** The energy-saving bulbs will not save money at time of purchase but will, because they use less energy, save money over a long period of time. Some will last 5 years at 8 hours per day.

Outdoor Fixture

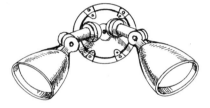

Outdoor Light Fixture

Also Known As: Weatherproof fixture, weatherproof lamp holder

Description: A variety is available, some round and others square. They are made of cast aluminum or galvanized steel. Many weatherproof fixtures have $1/2$" pipe threads for screwing into covers or boxes; others, the *canopy* type, screw onto the box and cover it at the same time.

Use: Provides light outside the home.

Outdoor Bulbs

Types:

Incandescent

High-intensity—mercury, sodium vapor, metal halide

Also Known As:

Sodium vapor: Sodium

High-intensity: HID (high-intensity discharge)

Description:

Incandescent: These are regular bulbs designed for outdoor use. Types include yellow-colored, spotlights, floodlights, etc., that are flat or teardrop shaped. Spotlights and floodlights, often called just *spots* or *floods*, have a reflective coating on the back of the inside. They may be referred to as *reflector* spotlights or floodlights.

High-intensity: Vapor-filled bulbs of various shapes that give off strong, intense light.

Various types of high-intensity bulbs include

Mercury: Yields twice the light of an incandescent of the same wattage. Oval shape.

Sodium: High-wattage bulbs—250 to 1,000 watts—many times more efficient than incandescents. Light cast has a yellowish hue.

Metal halide: Emits a greenish light; available in various wattages from 50 to 1,000 watts.

Use:

Incandescent: Yellow bulbs are used because they don't attract insects. Spots are chiefly for decorative purposes to highlight detail. Floods are for security and to illuminate entrances.

High-intensity: Security.

Use Tips: Handle broken high-intensity bulbs with extreme care because they contain toxic materials. High-intensity bulbs take about 15 minutes to reach full brightness when turned on and are often used with timers.

> $ **Buying Tip:** High-intensity bulbs last much longer than incandescents.

outdoor floodlight

Bulb Changer

Bulb Changer

Description: Suction cup or basket made of springs mounted on a handle with a release mechanism.

Use: Holding bulbs in order to change them without having to use a ladder.

> $ **Buying Tip:** Note that some brands have different models for different styles of bulbs, i.e. regular incandescent lamp bulbs or outdoor floodlights.

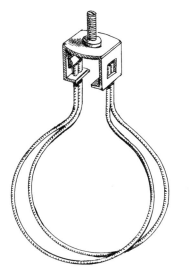

Clip Adapter

Lamp Parts

Part:

Clip adapter

Coupling

Finial

Harp

Locknut

Reducing bushing

Socket

Threaded rod (also known as *all-thread*)

Wire (also known as *lamp cord* and *flexible cord*)

Description:

Clip adapter: Two oblong wire forms with stems in a metal piece that has a short threaded rod.

Coupling: Small, tube-like fitting threaded on the inside.

Finial: Small, decorative cap with female threads in one end.

Harp: Oblong-shaped wire form around six inches high and several inches wide, with a connecting fitting at the narrow end.

Locknut: Small, flat metal ring, sometimes with an opening and a slight spiral shape, sometimes hexagonal.

Reducing bushing: Small, round fitting threaded on the inside and outside.

Socket: Cylindrical metal part with electrical switch, two screws for securing wires, and inside threads for screwing in the bulb.

Threaded rod: Hollow metal tube threaded along its entire length. It is available with $1/8$" internal diameter and an outside diameter of $3/8$".

Wire: Lamp wire is 18-2 SPT-1 **(see wire, Chapter 70)** and may be bought with or without a plug.

Use:

Clip adapter: Clips onto bulb and is used when a lamp has no harp to hold the lampshade.

Coupling: For joining two lengths of rod.

Coupling

Finial

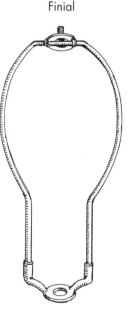

Harp

Locknuts

Reducing Bushings

Threaded Rod

Socket Reducer

Clamp-on Lamp

Finial: Screws on to secure lampshade to top of harp.

Harp: Holds lampshade.

Reducing bushing: Reduces the inside diameter of rod from $1/4$" to $1/8$"; to change from one rod size to another.

Socket: Electrical heart of lamp, containing switch mechanism, where the bulb is screwed in.

Threaded rod: The spine of the lamp. The lamp wire runs through it and all the lamp parts—the "head" of the lamp—are supported by it.

Wire: Provides electrical power.

> **$ Buying Tips:** Lamp parts are sold in kit form but it is more economical to buy individual parts. Socket parts may also be bought individually and can result in slight savings for repair **(see socket, below)**. *Socket reducers* are available that screw into a larger socket and permit use of bulbs with small *candelabra bases.*

Clamp-On Lamp

Also Known As: Utility lamp

Description: Normal socket, but with a large metal reflector and a spring clamp about 8" long. Reflectors come in a small variety of styles.

Use: Clamp allows temporary placement anywhere, especially at a worksite.

> **Use Tips:** Deep, large, bell-shape reflector is most efficient. Cord set and clamp can be purchased separately from the reflector.

Lamp Holder

Also Known As: Porcelain fixture, outlet-box lamp holder

Description: Round porcelain or Bakelite® fixture with socket, either with screw terminals or prewired with leads—white and black wires—ready for connecting. Porcelain fixtures come 3", 4", and 5¼" in diameter. Available in three styles—with pull chain, with pull chain and receptacle for plugging into, and without a pull chain, or *keyless*.

Incandescent Lamp-Holder
(Rear View)

Use: Lamp holders are mounted on electrical boxes so they are exposed. They are normally used in garages, shops, and other areas where just lighting function rather than fixture good looks is the key.

> **Use Tip:** The two-separate-lead-type fixture is easiest to install.

> **Buying Tip:** *Pigtails*, sockets with two wire leads, are used for temporary installations, as well as for testing.

Socket

Socket
Mechanism

Standard Socket

Also Known As: Incandescent lamp holder

Description: Metal cylinder with a threaded portion (female threads), which lightbulbs (male threads) are screwed into, and a switch mechanism—toggle or chain. Despite their various on-off actions, the wiring is the same—there are two screws, one copper and the other nickel, for each electrical supply wire.

Use: To control on-off action of incandescent lightbulbs. Some sockets have simple on-off actions while others provide three levels of light—30, 70, and 100 watt.

> **Use Tip:** When securing two wires to a socket it does not matter which wire goes to which screw.

> **Buying Tips:** All parts of a standard socket—shell and switch mechanism—are replaceable. To save money you can buy either part, though some users say that fitting a new part to an old socket can be difficult because machining is not precise.

Dimmer Socket

Description: Looks like a **standard socket (above)**.

Use: Used to change a standard socket to a dimmer, which can be adjusted to provide graduated levels of light.

Fuses and Circuit Breakers

About Fuses

A fuse can be considered the weak link in an electrical circuit. When an electrical malfunction occurs and passes too much current through the wires, the linkage inside the fuse heats up and melts—"blows"—and the flow of electricity is stopped—it has no more wire to "ride" on. It's like part of a road, a bridge, dropping away—vehicles can't continue.

There are a variety of fuses available. You must make sure that before installing a new fuse the reason for blowing has been corrected. Usually, if the fuse window is blackened, it indicates a short circuit; if the metal linkage just melted, then it indicates an overload.

The most common fuses screw into sockets in fuse boxes. Such fuse boxes are usually found in the basement of a home. Each fuse protects one circuit; circuits have different switches and outlets on them and are distributed in different rooms. Circuits may go through several rooms and floors, particularly in older homes.

Fuses are rated according to amperage, or "amps," and are designed to protect electrical devices whose total amperage is equal to the fuse's amperage rating. Hence, when selecting a fuse never select one bigger than specified—too big and the wire will heat up and possibly start a fire before the fuse blows.

Fuses are simple to replace: just unscrew or remove the bad one and screw or push in the good one. For convenience, it's good to have some spares on hand, plus a flashlight in case the lights are out or if the lighting in the area of the fuse box is very dim.

Many fuses have been replaced by **circuit-breakers (below)**. These have a metallic strip inside that heats up in case of a problem and trips a switch from on to off. As mentioned earlier, it's a simple matter, after correcting the electrical malfunction, to flip it back on. If need be, circuit breakers can also be replaced.

Plug Fuse

Plug Fuse

Also Known As: Edison base fuse, plug-in fuse, glass fuse

Description: This used to be the most commonly used fuse. It is a round device about 1" long with a small window on one end for viewing a tiny metal linkage and a threaded base like a light bulb's.

Use: Safety device in electrical circuits **(see About Fuses, above)**. Screws into panel in fuse box.

> **Use Tips:** If the window of the blown fuse is blackened, it likely means that a short circuit is the problem; a broken linkage (no blackness) usually means a circuit overload.

> **Buying Tips:** Electricians favor plug-in fuses over circuit breakers, whose internal mechanism can malfunction. Plug-in fuses are available in 5-, 10-, 20-, 25-, and 30-amp sizes; the amperage is stamped on the top of the fuse. In a pinch, plug-in fuses can usually be bought at supermarkets and drugstores.

Type "S" Fuse

Type "S" Fuse

Also Known As: Nontamperable, nontamp, Fustats®

Description: Consists of two parts—a narrow, threaded adapter, which screws into the fuse box, and the fuse proper, which screws into the adapter. Adapter and fuse are color-coded and should be the same color. Has become one of the most common types of fuses.

Use: Used where there is fear of someone accidentally using the wrong fuse, such as in rental property, because these fuses are tamperproof. For example, only a 15-amp type S fuse can screw into a 15-amp adapter, whereas different *plug-type fuses* can be screwed into the same opening because all are the same physical size.

> **Use Tips:** Good for replacing all your existing plug-type fuses. Type S fuses are available in the same amp ratings as plug-in fuses and are interchangeable with them. Be sure to tighten them down as far as possible when inserting them. May be required in new construction.

Cartridge Fuse

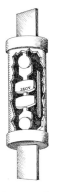

Knife-Blade Contact Cartridge Fuse

Also Known As: If for a circuit above 60 amps, known as *knife-blade cartridge* or *knife-blade contact fuse;* for 60 amps and below, known as a *ferrule contact* type.

Description: Looks like a rifle cartridge casing with metal caps, or *ferrules,* at the ends, or else blades that stick out. Cartridge fuses for 60 amps and below have the plain capped ends; those for above 60 amps have blades and are, as noted above, known as **knife-blade cartridge fuses**.

Use: Works like any fuse but for larger devices such as air conditioners and appliances. Unlike plug-type fuses, you cannot tell if it is "blown" by looking at it.

Ferrule Contact Cartride Fuse

> **Use Tips:** Be sure to observe safety precautions when removing and installing fuses. If installing them in an appliance, make sure the device is turned off. There is a special pliers, a **fuse puller (Chapter 73)**, available for installing and removing cartridge fuses.

> **Buying Tips:** Both *one-time* and *renewable* cartridge fuses are available. One-time fuses melt and must be replaced; renewable fuses have a linkage that can be replaced. The ends of the fuse are unscrewed to get at it.

Time Delay Fuse

Time Delay Fuse

Description: Similar to a **plug-in fuse, above**, but contains a different element.

Use: Protects circuits for motor-operated devices that cause momentary high surges of electricity when turned on. A regular fuse would blow needlessly.

Circuit Breaker

Also Known As: Breaker

Types:

Push button circuit breaker

Toggle circuit breaker

Description: Typically a small, narrow, black plastic box that resembles a switch and is activated by either a *push button* or a *toggle* switch. Circuit breakers are plugged, snapped, or clipped into place on the house electrical panel—the metal cabinet found near where the power supply enters the house. An average house might have as many as a dozen circuit breakers on a panel.

Other than the typical models described here, circuit-breaker mechanisms are found in small **multiple outlets (Chapter 66)** and also in fuses with **plug-type bases (above)**.

Use: Circuit breakers serve the same function as **fuses (above)**. They cut the circuit off—"break" it—if there is a "short" or other hazardous malfunction that would possibly cause a fire. Like fuses, they are sized in terms of amperage to handle from 15- to 100-amp circuits. 15 to 20 amps are commonly used—20 in modern construction. Unlike fuses, they do not need to be replaced after functioning. The switches merely "trip," or "flip," and you just push or flip them back to reset once the offending problem has been eliminated.

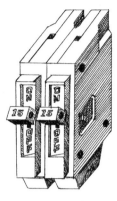

Circuit Breaker

Plug-Type (Screw-In) Circuit Breaker

Use Tips: When replacing a circuit breaker make sure the main power supply is off. Also, take the old breaker to the store to ensure getting the correct replacement—one manufacturer's breaker will not necessarily fit where another's did.

Buying Tip: Much easier to use than fuses.

Switches and Receptacles

About Switches

Switches function by interrupting electrical flow. There are many types of switches but they can be divided between those linked to the main house wiring and those that are used elsewhere, such as on wires of electrical devices. Within the category of house-wiring switches there are some that are commonly used and some that are uncommonly used; this distinction is observed when describing them below.

Regarding house-wiring switches, terminal screws—the screws that wires are connected to—may come on one side or both sides of the switch and this can make installation more or less difficult depending on the situation. The screws are color-coded for correct wiring—check your manuals.

All house-wiring switches have some sort of mounting attachments for installation in **electrical boxes (Chapter 71)**. Mounting is usually done with No. 6-32 machine screws but sometimes No. 8-32. If unsure, buy both—they cost only a few cents each.

Single-Pole, Duplex Switch

Common House Switches

Types:

Single-pole switch

Double-pole switch

Three-way switch

Four-way switch

Dimmer switch

Fluorescent dimmer switch

Also Known As:

Single-pole: S.P.

Dimmer: Rheostat

Description: All come in a variety of voltage and amperage ratings, which must be specified.

Single-pole: Identified by the presence of two brass terminal screws.

Double-pole: Has four terminal screws.

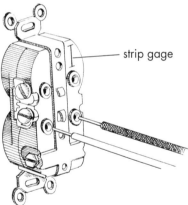

Clamp-Type Switch (Rear View)

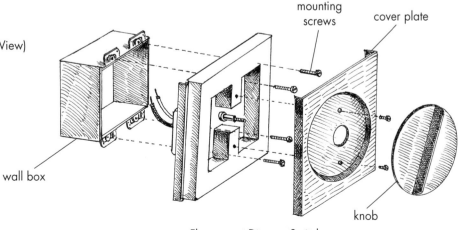

Fluorescent Dimmer Switch

Three-way: Has three terminal screws—there may also be a green grounding screw.

Four-way: Has four terminal screws—and possibly a green grounding screw.

Dimmer: Looks like a regular switch but may have a turning or sliding knob instead of a toggle, and wire leads instead of terminals.

Fluorescent dimmer: Three times the size of a standard dimmer switch but with a knob instead of a toggle.

Single-pole, three-way, and four-way switches come with three types of on-off action:

Snap: Flip a switch and there is an audible click.

Quiet: A slight click is heard when the switch is flipped.

Mercury: This toggle is controlled by a tilting tube of mercury and no sound at all is heard when the switch is flipped.

Switches may also be obtained with illuminated toggles.

Use: Controlling light or, in the case of dimmers, the level of light.

Use Tips: Most models are available in a *push-in* or *clamp-type* style, which means you can just slide the end of a wire into them without having to wrap the wire end around the terminal screws, making for a much simpler job.

> **$ Buying Tips:** Like other electrical devices, switches come in *standard* or *spec* (specification) grade. For normal house use standard grade is fine. The least expensive switches are those with the loudest action—mercury, the quietest, is the costliest. Switches, like receptacles, can be bought in bulk by the box for less money than if bought individually.

Switch with Pilot Light

Specialized House Switches

Types:

> *Combination switch*
>
> *Pilot light switch*
>
> *Nontamperable switch*
>
> *Timer switch*
>
> *Outdoor switch*
>
> *Safety switch*
>
> *Miniaturized switch*
>
> *Photoelectric switch*

Also Known As: *Miniaturized:* Despard®

Description:

> *Combination:* Regular switch that also contains a receptacle.
>
> *Pilot light:* Regular switch but with a light to indicate if the switch is on.
>
> *Nontamperable:* Regular switch that must be turned on and off with a key.

Timer: Like an oven timer with a spring-loaded rotary knob.

Outdoor: Consists of a turning lever built onto a weatherproof box cover and a regular toggle switch. The regular switch is mounted inside the box and the box cover over it.

Safety: Also built like a regular switch but may or may not have a fuse; remove the fuse and the switch will not work.

Miniaturized: Small self-contained toggle switch.

Photoelectric: Contains a light-sensing "eye" that operates the switch according to whether there is daylight present.

Use:

Combination: Use wherever a switch and receptacle are required at one location.

Pilot light: Alerts you to when an electrical device is on. Particularly good when the device it controls is in a remote location, such as an attic fan or light.

Nontamperable: Good on machines, particularly where children are around, such as near swimming pools, or in offices.

Timer: For turning lights on automatically, for security or for safety's sake, or for preventing an iron or other appliance from being left on.

Outdoor: Where convenient power is needed outside the house.

Miniaturized: Allows installation of as many as three separate switches in a normal wall box, often in combination with a pilot light and a single receptacle.

Photoelectric: Turns lights on at sundown and off at dawn, for security, especially outdoors.

About Line Switches

Line switches are those that are installed in the electrical cord. They interrupt the flow of electricity in the same way as regular and specialized switches.

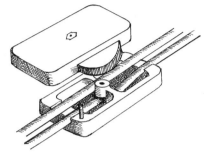

In-Line Cord Switch

Canopy Switch

Line Switches

Types:

Cord switch

Canopy switch

Rotary switch

Toggle switch

Push-button fluorescent starter switch

Push-button momentary on-off switch

Also Known As:

Cord: In-line, feed through

Toggle: Tumbler

Description:

Cord: A typical cord switch is made of two small, separable plastic halves that have prongs inside that push through the wire's insulation when the halves are screwed back together, making electrical contact.

Canopy: Small switch with knurled metal pushbutton and wires stripped ready for attaching to the existing wires.

Rotary: Similar to canopy, but with turnbutton.

Toggle: Similar to canopy, but with toggle lever.

Push-button fluorescent starter: Small, round switch with a push button and four wire leads.

Push-button momentary on-off: Small switch with leads for wiring into power-tool circuits. Inch-long switch that looks like a bell.

Use:

Cord: For installation on a lamp cord for convenience, such as for bedside lamps or radios.

Canopy: Also for use on floor and lamp cord.

Rotary: A variety of uses including controlling table and floor lamps and small appliances; for controlling two individual or built-in units in an appliance or for controlling two circuits.

Toggle: For use on table and floor lamps and small appliances. Toggles are also available for heavy-duty appliances such as vacuum cleaners, portable tools, and motors.

Push-button fluorescent starter: This switch has a starter built in and its small size makes it good for use where space is cramped. Typical use is to operate fluorescents under hanging kitchen cabinets.

Push-button momentary on-off: Operates only when it is pressed—spring action closes it—so it can be used anywhere intermittent power is required.

Timers

Description: Timers vary in shape and function. They can be simple box-like affairs that plug into a wall outlet, or designed to be linked to house wiring, or they can be tabletop models. They can be bought with capacities up to 1,000 watts. In all cases they contain clock mechanisms.

Uses: Various. One is for turning on lights at certain times for security. Another is for turning on appliances such as televisions or air conditioners.

> **Use Tip:** Like other electrical devices, the wiring of the timer must be heavy enough to do the job required.

> **Buying Tips:** Basic kind tends to wear out and make noise. Electronic types are superior but much more costly.

Thermostats

Description: A form of electronic or electromechanical switch sensitive to temperature and time settings, depending on the model. Generally powered by a low-voltage circuit (24 volts). Many different types: the more advanced models have some computerization and can be programmed for different temperatures at different times in different rooms on different days; the most basic ones are set manually for minimum temperature.

Use: Turns a heating or cooling system on and off in response to a chosen temperature and time setting.

Use Tips: Remember that the temperature of the room containing the thermostat determines the temperature of the rest of the house. Therefore you should place a thermostat in an average room, away from any drafts or heat sources. Wiring is usually done with a special lightweight wire called a *thermo*, or *thermostat wire*, and uses a transformer to reduce the house electricity to 24 volts. Each model comes with specific wiring diagrams.

Buying Tips: Recent advances in computers have spawned a whole range of elaborate thermostats; some are too sensitive to be useful, though, and we highly recommend a thorough study of magazine articles and the like prior to purchasing one of the newest electronic models.

About Receptacles

Receptacles, commonly called *outlets,* come in a variety of styles. Like other electrical devices, they are rated to handle a specific amount of current. Capacity is stamped on the receptacle. For lights, receptacles rated at 15 amps and 125 volts are used. Receptacles that are designed for different devices may have different shapes but they are all geared to do one job—provide a link between the plug of a particular device and the house power supply.

Although some may be linked to room switches, most receptacles are always on, so exercise caution when plugging something in. Above all, be sure to turn off the power to a particular receptacle before working on it. Check to see if it is off with a **test lamp (Chapter 73)**.

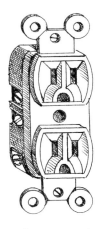

Duplex Receptacle

Standard Receptacle

Also Known As: Outlet (technically incorrect)

Description: Plastic device with two pairs of vertical slots for plugs or two vertical slots and a third hole, in the standard "duplex" model, for a grounding prong of a plug. Available in a single model too. Comes with metal attachments for mounting in an electrical box. Standard receptacles are usually ivory or brown plastic. (An outlet is technically just the point at which current is supplied—i.e., where the receptacle is installed.)

Use: Provides connection with current when a plug is inserted.

Use Tips: Like switches, terminal screws are mounted in different side positions. You may want to try using a new, more convenient clamp type with no terminal screws for wires to be wrapped around—just push wire in holes in back and it is clamped in.

Buying Tips: If you want top-quality receptacles, get *spec* (for specification) *grade receptacles;* the term *spec* will be stamped on the receptacle. Spec grade receptacles are costly, however, and for around-home use would not seem to be warranted; use *standard* grade. If you are going to need a number of receptacles, buy them in bulk to save money.

Appliance Receptacle

Description: Contains one pair of vertical or slanted slots and one vertical or U-shaped slot. Designed to be surface-mounted.

Use: For heavier-duty plugs and appliances, such as dryers and air conditioners.

Appliance Receptacle

Ground Fault Circuit Interrupter

Also Known As: GFI, GFCI, ground fault interrupter

Description: Comes in three different kinds but basically resembles a standard grounded receptacle, usually with a small reset button in the middle.

Use: The GFCI's job is to sense hazardous leakage of electricity instantaneously and shut off the circuit. It works far faster than a standard circuit breaker or fuse. One type of GFCI is designed to be installed in the circuit breaker box, another kind is installed in a standard electrical box in place of a standard receptacle, and the third kind is portable—it plugs into a grounded outlet.

Ground Fault Circuit Interrupter

Use Tips: GFCIs are useful (and, in many cases of new construction, required) in kitchens, bathrooms, and around pools or wherever electrical hazards are magnified.

Wall Plates

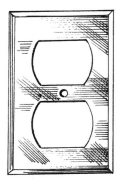

Duplex Outlet Wall Plate

Also Known As: Faceplates, covers

Description: Flat metal, wood, or plastic piece with openings for receptacles or switches; generally a couple of inches across and four or five inches long. Available in a wide range of colors and shapes. Supplied with screws for attaching to an electrical box. Available to go over "ganged" boxes for groups of switches—up to a dozen.

Use: Covers switches and receptacles in electrical boxes. Mounts with a No. 6-32 machine screw.

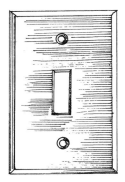

Toggle Switch Wall Plate

Use Tips: Some wall plates are available in oversized dimensions, especially in wood, and are handy for covering a too-large opening that a receptacle or switch is housed in or to cover a gap in wallpaper around the box.

Buying Tips: Fancily packaged wall plates can be very expensive. It's cheaper to buy them loose or in plain cellophane wrappers. They can easily be painted or covered with wallpaper.

Electrical Wire and Connectors

About Electrical Wire

The term *wire* is a misnomer because wire actually means metal conductors—lengths of metal—encased in some sort of insulation—perhaps plastic, rubber, or cloth composition.

Conductors are made of copper and will either be solid or stranded. Strands are easier to bend than the solid material.

Wire is characterized according to gauge number and runs from 0000 to No. 40, with the numbers getting smaller as the wire gets thicker—a No. 38 wire would be about the diameter of a human hair while a No. 2 wire would be the diameter of a pencil. The most common gauges used in the home range from 10 to 20.

Wire is also described by letters according to the kind of insulation (covering) and electrical capacity; for example, lamp wire is SPT-1, as in strippable, pendant thermoplastic. But technical nomenclature is not required—you should simply specify your intended use for the wire. The descriptions below are a guide to what is commonly available.

When wire is temporarily run around walls it should be protected from possible damage. It may be held in place by insulated staples, which are driven in with a small hammer. Regular house wiring requires conduit or other special material, discussed in **Chapters 71 and 72**.

Heat-Resistant appliance Cord Set

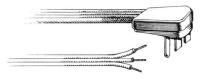

Large Appliance Cord Set

Lighting and Small-Appliance Wire

Types:

> *Bell, or hookup wire*
>
> *Conductor, or Thermo (for thermostat) wire*
>
> *SJ wire*
>
> *SPT-1 wire*

Also Known As: SPT-1

Description: Insulated copper wire in a range of gauges.

Use:

> *Bell:* For doorbells, thermostats, and low-voltage hobby work.
>
> *Conductor:* For thermostats.
>
> *SJ:* For appliances and power tools.
>
> *SPT-1:* For lamps, chandeliers, and commonly used hanging lighting fixtures.

> **$ Buying Tips:** There are a variety of wires available for many uses, such as making your own extension cords, heat-resistant cord, and more. Such cord can be identified by letter according to the insulation used, but this can get complicated—just ask the dealer for it by use. For example, ask for a cord for a toaster. If you wish, you can also buy cord sets in which the cord comes with a plug on one end and bare wires or leads on the other for attaching to a large electrical device, such as an air conditioner.

House Wire

Types:

BX

Romex®

THHN, THWN, and *MTWN*

Also Known As:

BX: Armored metallic cable, armored electrical cable, armored electrical cable, bushed armored cable, spiral armored cable

Romex®*:* Nonmetallic sheathed cable, NM cable, loom wire

Description:

BX: Two or three individually insulated wires, each wrapped with spiral layers of tough paper (bushing), running inside a galvanized-steel spiral casing. Two-wire BX has one black and one white wire. All BX has a bonding wire that runs along its length. The casing acts as the ground wire; the bond wire serves as a backup in case the casing breaks.

BX (Armored Cable)

Romex®*:* Consists of a flat, beige thermoplastic jacket with two or three wires, each covered with insulation and wrapped with spiral paper tape and a paper-covered copper wire. Type NM is for indoor use; NMC for damp indoor or outdoor use; and UF for underground outdoor use.

Romex (Nonmetallic Cable)

THHN, THWN, and *MTWN* are heavy-duty insulated copper wires.

Use: All are used for standard interior house wiring. BX is one of the most enduring and common items found in house construction. THHN, THWN, and MTWN are used inside **conduit** and **greenfield (Chapter 72)**. *Service cable,* which is not included here, is used outside the house to bring power from the municipal supply to your house.

Use Tips: BX is cut either with a hacksaw (works best in a vise) or a special cutting tool that clamps onto the cable and has a cranked circular blade. Cutting Romex® is simpler using a special tool called a **splitter (Chapter 73)**. It is held to walls and joists by nonmetallic cable straps, similar to **conduit straps (Chapter 72)**. Romex® and BX connect to electrical boxes with their own individual type of connector fittings, called *connectors,* or *cable clamps.*

Buying Tips: Romex® and BX are sold in precut lengths of 25' and 50' per box and in bulk, cut to the length you require. Buying by bulk is usually less expensive because you buy only exactly what you need.

About BX, Greenfield, and Romex® and Where Their Names Came From

As I researched this book I encountered terms that intrigued me as to what their origins were—how various items got their names. I figured out most, but the names for three very common items kept defying explanation—Romex®, which is plastic-covered cable; greenfield, which describes a hollow steel cable through which electric wires are pulled; and BX (armored cable), which is really greenfield with the wires already in place. Romex is just one of the most popular brands—that was easy. But for the others, I asked at many, many hardware stores, I asked at electrical supply stores, I asked electricians, I even asked executives at wire companies... No one knew. A real mystery.

But I finally found the answer from James C. Dollins, a vice president of AFC (American Flexible Conduit), in New Bedford, Massachusetts, which makes armored cable. Dollins brought the terms to ground, as it were, a few years ago. He explained that he learned from an old-timer that around the turn of the century there was a company run by two men, Harry Greenfield and Gus Johnson. They made this hollow metal product called—what else—*greenfield*. End of mystery one.

One day, while manufacturing greenfield, there was a problem with a cord used to bind the material and the cord accidentally was run all the way through it. An idea was born. What if they could do that with wire—sell the greenfield with the wires already in place? They worked up an experimental batch of the stuff and gave it to an electrician they knew to try it out.

His response was a rave—it saved him many hours of pulling the wire through the usual hollow cable. He wanted more of it—all they could get to him. But he had one question: What do you call it?

Up to that point they had made only one product, so they hadn't given a name any thought. "BX," said one of the quick-thinking partners. "B because it's our 'B' product line, and 'X' because it's experimental."

And that's how greenfield—and BX—got their names.

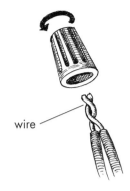

wire

Wire Nut

Wire Nuts

Also Known As: Scotchloks®, solderless connectors, twist connectors, wire connectors, connectors, spring wire locks, screw-on wire connectors

Description: Plastic caps with threaded insides; come in various colors according to size.

Use: Connects and insulates the ends of wires that have been twisted together, generally inside an electrical box or lighting fixture.

Use Tip: Specific size nuts must be used with specific size wires.

Crimp Connectors

Description: Small metal wire connectors that are crimped (squeezed) onto the ends of small-gauge wires. Color-coded for wire gauge—red is for 22 to 18; blue is for 16 to 14 gauge.

Use: Connecting small-gauge wires.

Use Tip: Easily used with a special **crimping,** or **combination, tool (Chapter 73)**.

Electrical Boxes

About Electrical Boxes

No bare wires secured to receptacles or in other junctions can be left exposed—the wires must be enclosed for safety, and this is the job of the electrical box.

Boxes come in dozens of different shapes and sizes but can generally be broken down into boxes for walls, boxes for ceilings, and outdoor boxes. Most boxes are made of galvanized metal, but plastic wall boxes, for interior use only, are coming on strong because they cost a lot less than metal. Before using plastic make sure your local electrical code allows them. Using something that isn't allowed and then having it cause a fire could result in your fire insurance being invalidated.

Boxes are made with open holes or holes plugged with easily-removed *knockouts* that can be either pried out (if they have little slots for screwdrivers in them) or (guess what) knocked out with a hammer. For whatever kind of cable or conduit you are passing through **(BX, conduit, or plastic sheathed, Chapter 70)**, there are specialized connectors and cable clamps either built in or sold separately under the catchy name of *connectors*, complete with setscrews or locknuts and various bushings (sleeves). Similarly, there is a whole set of elbows, couplings, and other fittings for the various types of conduit available. Make sure you get everything you need the first time you go to the hardware store.

Some wall boxes have plaster *ears,* which are metal brackets or tabs for mounting the box in existing construction. The ears grip the wall and keep the box close to the surface. If the box does not have ears, it will have holes for nailing to studs. Most components are attached to boxes with 8-32 **machine screws (Part III, Chapter 22)**.

Boxes must be installed with holes in gypsum wallboard that match their size exactly. Take care to mark holes for accurate cutting.

knockouts

threaded hole for attaching cover

cable clamps

4-Inch Square Electrical Box

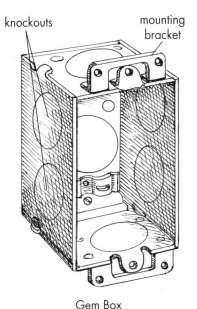

knockouts

mounting bracket

Gem Box

Wall Boxes

Types:

Four-inch square box

Gem box

Handy box

Plastic box

Sheetrock® box

Stud box

Also Known As:

Four-inch: "1900" box

Handy: Utility, surface-mounted

Sheetrock®: Drywall

Stud: nail-on

Wall box (general): Outlet box, junction box, switch box

Description: Most are made of either galvanized steel or aluminum. Some are made of plastic.

Four-inch square: Four-inch square box but only $1^1/_2$" or $2^1/_8$" deep.

Gem box: Gem is a term used to describe a commonly used box made by various manufacturers. It is metal and commonly 2" wide, 3" high, and $2^1/_2$" deep, but it does come deeper.

Handy: Small rectangular box with rounded corners.

Plastic: Various sizes, made of plastic.

Sheetrock®: Various-shaped metal box with expandable arms.

Stud: Various-sized box with a nailing bracket for attachment to studs.

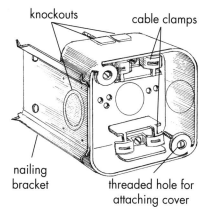

Stud Box

Use: All wall boxes are for housing switches and receptacles, sometimes referred to as *outlets*. However, please note the following differences:

Four-inch square: In some cases the wall will be too shallow to mount a gem box. Here the shallower four-inch box can be used because it still has the cubic-inch capacity to accommodate the wires. May also be used on the ceiling.

Gem: Standard box for mounting switches or receptacles.

Handy: Surface-mounted. Its rounded corners make it a safer box.

Plastic: This comes in various sizes but is basically for use on new work because it must be nailed to studs, an impossibility if wall material is present.

Sheetrock®: Designed to be mounted on gypsum wallboard.

Stud: Metal boxes designed to be nailed to framing members in new construction.

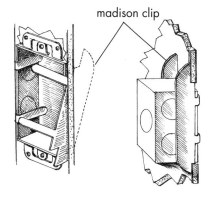

Gem Box with Madison Clips

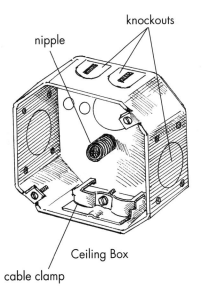

nipple

knockouts

Ceiling Box

cable clamp

> **Use Tips:** Many boxes can be *ganged*—sides taken apart and the boxes linked together—if you have many outlets or switches to accommodate. If you use plastic boxes, make sure the wires are properly grounded. A simple way to mount gem boxes in walls is with *Madison clips,* also known as *battleships, bracket set,* or *switch box supports* because of their shape; they bend around the box's side and pull it up against the wall. Sheetrock® boxes are easier to mount.

> **Buying Tips:** Plastic boxes cost far less than galvanized, but as mentioned in the **About section** are not permitted by some local building codes.

Ceiling Box

Also Known As: Junction box, splice box

Description: Comes in two different forms—4" octagonal or round—and in two depths—$1^{1}/_{2}$" and $2^{1}/_{8}$". It may have *extendable* or *adjustable* mounting hangers (also called *bars, box hangers, barhangers,* or *brackets*). Hangers, which can be purchased separately, provide the short threaded rod (the *stud* or *nipple*) that fixtures attach to. Flat, shallow boxes may be called *pancake boxes.*

Use: Anchors ceiling fixtures or serves as a junction box where any wires meet, are connected, and then run to some other area of the home.

Weatherproof Box

Also Known As: Outside box, outdoor box

Description: Usually round or square box in double ("duplex") or single form with threaded holes in sides to accept correspondingly threaded light fixtures. Rubber gasket between box and cover keeps moisture out; receptacles have either screw- or snap-type covers. Slightly thicker than interior boxes.

Use: Housing exterior switches, receptacles, and mounting fixtures.

Use Tips: Covers that screw in place on weatherproof boxes should be used only where you do not need ready access to the receptacle or outlet; use the snap-type cover instead.

Weatherproof Receptacle
with Snap Covers

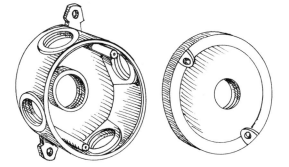

Weatherproof Box

Switch Box Cover

Box Covers

Description: Covers of boxes for inside use are metal or plastic in a variety of shapes—round, square, octagonal—to fit over boxes. Covers may be solid or have cutouts to accommodate switch toggles or receptacles. Covers are secured to the box by **machine screws,** usually No. 8-32 **(Part III, Chapter 22)**. Weatherproof (exterior use) box covers also vary in shape but many have threaded holes to accommodate light fixtures, or snap covers to protect receptacle slots when not in use, or a lever switch that operates an inside toggle switch. A lidded type houses GFCI receptacles. Partial covers, called *collars* or *plaster rings,* have a shoulder design and provide additional depth to the box.

Use: Both inside and outside covers protect wiring and devices; outside covers have a gasket that makes the box weatherproof too. Collar-type covers serve as a base for **wall plates (Chapter 69)** and also provide a border for applying plaster.

Blank Box Cover

Duplex Receptacle Box Cover

Collar-Type Box Cover

Conduit

About Conduit

Conduit comes in a variety of types but you will be required to use whatever your local electrical code specifies.

Thin-Wall Conduit

Also Known As: EMT (electric metallic tubing)

Description: Light steel thin-wall pipe that comes in inside diameters of $\frac{1}{2}$" to 4", and even larger, and in 10' lengths; the $\frac{1}{2}$" size is most common.

Use: For carrying house wiring in areas where it must be left exposed, such as along unfinished garage or basement walls or for outdoor lighting.

> **Use Tips:** Thin-wall pipe should not be used underground, nor is it practical to use in an existing house because walls and the like would have to be removed to accommodate it. It is used for new construction but even here much sawing of framing members has to be done. Once installed, however, new wires can easily be pulled through it.

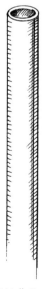

Thin-Wall Conduit

Heavy-Wall Conduit

Heavy-Wall Conduit

Also Known As: Rigid conduit

Description: Comes in the same length and diameters as **thin-wall (above)** but is galvanized and has thicker walls and is threaded for connections. Also available in plastic.

Use: For carrying wire outdoors, underground, where it is exposed to elements or perhaps subject to physical abuse, such as in a lawn where it might be run over by a mower. Typical use is to extend wiring between a house and room addition.

> **Use Tip:** Like thin-wall, not for use in existing construction, but may be used for new construction.

Electrical Cable and Conduit Connectors

Description: They come in a wide variety of shapes, some resembling plumbing fittings (elbows, couplings, and the like), some galvanized for exterior use, called *condulets*. Exterior fittings have covers and gaskets. Made in three versions—for **BX**, **EMT**, and **Romex® (Chapter 70)**.

Use: Connecting conduit of various kinds so that longer runs can be made and to enable it to turn or do whatever else is required for a particular installation.

> **Use Tip:** Be sure to use antishort collars on BX wherever you cut it to protect it from damage through vibration.

Conduit Fasteners

Types:

Cable Staples

Conduit Straps

Also Known As:

Straps: One-hole: Conduit half strap; Two-hole: Conduit full strap

Description:

Staples: U-shaped metal piece with sharp points, either plain or covered with plastic insulation.

Straps: Formed metal pieces with either one (for one-hole strap) or two holes (for two-hole strap).

Use: Plain metal staples and straps secure *conduit* and *greenfield* to walls, ceilings, or framing members. *Plastic-covered,* or *insulated,* staples are used to secure extension-cord wire and the like to walls inside the house.

Cable Staple

One-Hole Conduit Strap

Two-Hole Conduit Strap

⅄ Use Tips: Straps (one- or two-hole) work best for securing thin-wall, heavy-wall, and plastic conduit. The general rule electricians have is that they use straps outside the house and staples inside. The two-hole strap makes the most secure job.

Plastic Conduit

Description: Rigid plastic pipe.

Use: Housing wire inside and outside the home.

> **$ Buying Tip:** Simple and easy to use where permitted by code.

Greenfield

Greenfield

Also Known As: Flex, flexible metal conduit

Description: Consists of a fairly flexible hollow spiral metal jacket and resembles **BX (see Part IX, Chapter 70)** but is available in larger diameters to allow wires to be pulled through it. Specialized fittings and connectors are available.

Use: Housing wire running inside the home.

> **Use Tip:** Greenfield may be installed the same way as BX, requiring small holes to be drilled in the wall.

Wire Channels

Also Known As: Raceway, wire mold

Description: Metal or plastic channels about $1/2$" square designed to contain house wiring; switch and receptacle boxes are designed to work with each specific brand or type of channel.

Use: Housing wiring on the surface of masonry or other walls in the place of conduit. Enables house wiring, both permanent and temporary, to be installed without piercing walls.

> **Use Tip:** Metal channels have an advantage over plastic in that they ensure a grounded circuit if installed correctly.

Electrical Tools

About Electrical Tools

Only a few tools are needed for everyday electrical jobs, but if you get into large home improvements or repair jobs there are others that can serve one well. Following is a roundup that should handle all but the basic needs.

Test Lamp

Also Known As: Circuit tester, neon lamp tester, neon tester, testlight, voltage tester, line tester, neon circuit tester

Description: Basically a plastic housing with a small neon bulb with two 6" insulated wire probes. Large variations in design.

Use: To see whether there is electricity in an electrical circuit (if it is "live") or whether a circuit is properly grounded.

> **Use Tips:** A test lamp is a very important safety device and no one working on electrical projects, no matter how small, should be without one.

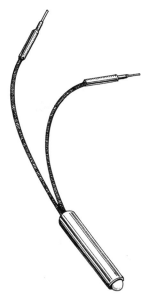

Test Lamp

Continuity Tester

Description: Usually a slender plastic housing about half a foot long containing batteries, two probes (one may be an alligator clip), and a small indicator light; works off battery power. Comes in various forms.

Use: To check if wires, such as appliance cords, or any circuit can carry a flow of electricity from one end to the other. Also used to check fuses.

 Buying Tip: Better to get a combination tool called a *multitester* then such a specialized item.

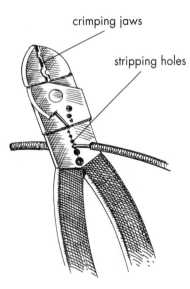

crimping jaws

stripping holes

Combination Tool

Combination Tool

Also Known As: Wire crimper and cutter, wiring tool, crimper, wire crimper-stripper, multipurpose tool, combination stripper-crimper, combination stripper-pliers, sheath stripper

Description: Similar to flat pliers, jaws have different-sized holes and notches for insertion of corresponding sizes of wire, allowing the insulation to be stripped off without touching the wire when the jaws are closed. Other parts of jaws have flat lips for crimping and pulling wire.

Use: For cutting and stripping wires of various diameters, or gauges, but also for crimping solderless wire connectors. Can cut screws without damaging threads too.

Buying Tips: Combination tools that have multiple holes are of better quality than tools with only hole.

Fish Tape

Also Known As: Fish wire, snake, electrician's or electrical snake

Description: Stiff, flat wire, $1/2$" to $3/4$" wide, with a hook on one end, which is coiled in a case and comes in 25' and 50' lengths.

Use: For pulling the wire through conduit or greenfield tubing as well as for probing wall cavities to determine the best paths for wire.

> **Use Tip:** Before using a fish tape to probe walls, try to calculate as much as possible where framing members are so that you avoid hitting them.

Wire Cutter/Stripper

Description: Two flat metal bars that crisscross and have sharpened ends, with a small notch for stripping wire.

Use: Cuts and strips small-gauge wire.

> **Use Tips:** If you need to cut something thicker than wire, such as a bolt, a lock hasp, chain, or cable, use a **bolt cutter (Part II, Chapter 6),** a huge version of a wire cutter—$1 1/2$" to over 3' long—with great mechanical advantage.

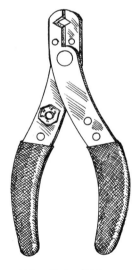

Wire Cutter/Stripper

> **$ Buying Tips:** Much the same work can be done with various pliers designed to serve this purpose, such as **diagonal side cutters, etc. (Part I, Chapter 7)**.

Splitter

Also Known As: Cable ripper

Description: T-shaped galvanized piece about 6" long with triangular cutter notches and holes in the handle to measure wire gauges. A similar item with a hand crank and a small blade, is a *cablesplitter*.

Use: Strips outside insulation from Romex® cable. The bladed model splits BX.

> **Use Tips:** This tool saves much time. Stripping Romex® or splitting BX without it is difficult.

Electrical Tape

Types:

> *Friction tape*
>
> *Plastic tape*

Also Known As: Electrician's tape

Description: Both types sold by the roll.

Friction: Cloth-like material impregnated with chemicals, usually ¹/₂" to ³/₄" wide.

Plastic: Thin black plastic usually ³/₄" wide.

Use: Various uses, but in electrical work tape is mainly used to cover bare wire after it has been stripped of insulation.

> **Buying Tips:** Friction tape has largely been outmoded by plastic tape, which is actually much less costly, works better, and lasts longer, but some people find it is harder to tear.

Fuse Puller

Also Known As: Cartridge fuse puller

Description: Plastic pliers-like tool with hinge in the middle and with rounded jaws.

Use: Removing cartridge-type fuses.

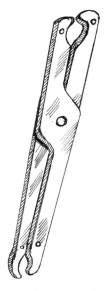

Cartridge Fuse Puller

P A R T

X

Masonry Materials, Products, and Tools

Masonry Materials

About Masonry

The term *masonry* is generally understood to mean any of a variety of products made with cement or cement-like substances. Most masonry jobs are best left to professional masons, but for small repair jobs the following items will help orient you to the basics.

Brick

Types:

> *Face brick*
>
> *Fire brick*
>
> *Used brick*

Also Known As:

> *Face:* Common, facing, paint-grade common
>
> *Used:* Reclaimed

Description: Standard building brick comes about 8" long, $3^3/_4$" wide, and $2^1/_4$" high, but it is made in a wide variety of dimensions both wide and thin—8" × 8", 4" × 8" pavers, for terrace patterns, and so on. It may be *cored* (have holes) or *frogged* (have a shallow depression) and comes in a variety of colors—red, cream, brown, yellow, white, pink—and with the surface glazed, smooth, enameled, or rough. In short, brick types exist to fit different jobs. Dimensions may include the intended thickness of the mortar joint, or the "nominal" versus the "actual" dimensions, incorporating the $1/2$" mortar joint.

> *Face:* Standard, finished brick used in exterior walls. ("Construction" brick is a slightly lower grade used for basic construction of walls.)
>
> *Fire:* A light yellow brick that has been fired to stand high heat.
>
> *Used:* Literally used brick—recovered from demolished old buildings. Varies as much as brick itself varies and has absolutely no manufacturing standard.

Use: Brick may be used for a variety of building projects inside and outside the home. A typical exterior wall is known as a *masonry* or *brick* veneer wall.

> *Fire:* Lining fireplaces. Fire clay is used instead of regular mortar. Dimensions are different from common brick, such as $4^{1}/_{2}$" × 9" and so on.
>
> *Used:* Any of a variety of building projects where the aesthetic appeal of oldness is desired; also may be cheaper to buy.

Use Tips: Any brick used outside the house may be designated SW, for *severe weathering* capability, or MW, *medium weathering,* for more moderate climates. NW, for *no weathering,* is used indoors only. You'll often find these marks, which refer to how the brick reacts to the seasonal freeze-thaw cycles, on the brick. Brick dimensions are proportional so that they may be used conveniently in patterns—a brick is approximately a third as high as it is long and half as wide. Experienced masons will remeasure bricks on site and refigure the quantity needed for a particular job no matter how many calculations have been made beforehand.

Brick—SW grade only—is often laid on a bed of gravel and sand to make walks and terraces. Gravel is graded according to the maximum size of each stone, though it is mixed with smaller stones and some sand. Item 4 gravel is best for this kind of use (6" to 8") and on top of that a 1" to 2" layer of sand; bluestone chips are highly recommended instead of sand, though. 4" × 8" pavers, solid bricks available in both regular and half, or "thin," thickness, are recommended, especially if you want to make the traditional basket-weave pattern, which requires that bricks be twice as long as they are wide.

> $ **Buying Tips:** As the many brick types exist to match type to job, ask questions of your supplier about as many characteristics of the brick as possible before delivery. The more new bricks you buy, the cheaper they are—the smallest unit being a *strap,* or 100 bricks bound with a metal strap. A *cube* is 500 bricks. Dimensions and terms vary by region of this country.
>
> Before buying used brick make sure that it is not heavily coated with mortar, as removing it could add hours to the job. To test used bricks for quality, tap them together—they should ring. Also, rap each brick with a hammer—it should not crumble or crack. You can sometimes buy brick from nonuniform runs at a discount price if dimensions are not important to you.

Concrete Block

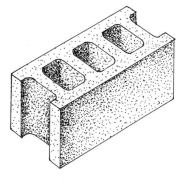

Concrete Block

Also Known As: Block, cinder block

Description: Concrete block comes in a variety of styles, sizes, materials, and colors. The standard concrete block is made with cement, sand, and small stones as aggregate, while others use light aggregates such as volcanic cinders or pumice. Some are made of slag clay or shale. All are graded as to water resistance and therefore as to use above or below ground, interior or exterior, load- or nonload-bearing.

The standard, common, hollow-core block, called a *stretcher,* is just under 8" × 8" × 16" and weighs around 40 pounds. Other kinds (slag, clay, shale) can weigh as little as 25 pounds.

Most blocks have voids but some are solid, and all come in various shapes, such as bullnose, corner (or pier), or half units to facilitate building. Depth ranges from 2" to 12", and height either 4" or 8". Other block is strictly decorative—*split*, *slump*, and *screen* block are examples. And some block comes with special finishes—marbelized, glazed, and so on.

Use: Depending on the type, could be used for building privacy walls, foundations, or as a decorative element outside the house.

> **Use Tips:** Do not use concrete blocks outdoors—they don't stand up to moisture well. They are also so heavy to work with that we recommend avoiding their use altogether. Use a pro.

Stone

Terms:

Dressed stone

Semidressed stone

Undressed stone

Rounded stone

Veneer stone

Mortar stone

Brick or stone veneer panels

Types: Limestone, bluestone, granite, marble, and other materials, depending on the local quarries.

Description:

Dressed: Stones cut and trimmed to set sizes.

Semidressed: Rough-cut stones that need to be trimmed before use.

Undressed: Rough, just the way they are cut from the quarry.

Rounded: Local fieldstone, just the way it is found, rounded by glacial or river action.

Veneer: Various types of stone that are cut 2" to 3" thick, leaving front as is and back flat.

Mortar: Veneer stones composed of grindings of some sort of rock chips.

Brick or stone veneer panels: Made of plastic and stone or brick dust embedded in the surface. There is one grade for outdoor use and one for indoor use.

Use: All stone is used for walks, walls, retaining walls, barbecues, and a wide variety of other projects, with some specialties:

Veneer: Installed outside a home on steel studs and lath.

Mortar: Also used as siding.

Brick or stone veneer panels: Used outside or inside, as the grade permits.

> **Use Tips:** Larger stones are more difficult to handle than small- or medium-sized ones but quicker to install. Stones can be laid without mortar, but usually only for landscaping projects and walks. If you feel you need a **mortar (below)**, use regular sand **mix (below)**, as mortar will tend to dry out and crumble.

Premixed Cement Products

Types:

Concrete mix

Mortar mix

Sand mix

Description: Premixed cements are available in 10- to 80-pound bags and are mixed only with water. Cement refers to Portland cement, a mixture of different types of crushed and treated rock. Cement is mixed with gravel to form concrete and with lime to form mortar, and with sand for general use. *Portland cement* is readily available in 94-pound bags (1 cubic foot), which you can mix yourself with clean, moist sand, generally in a 1 to 3 ratio, but for most small projects it makes sense to buy it premixed. There are five types, but type 1 is general purpose, the others being for winter work or for bridge pilings.

Concrete: Comes as a powder containing cement and gravel, or aggregate, which is available in various sizes that must be specified.

Mortar: A special cement powder containing lime and sand. Various types available for special purposes. Strength rated according to type M (strongest), S, N, O (weakest).

Sand: Comes as a powder containing cement and sand.

Use:

Concrete: Used for projects calling for concrete as well as for repairing large holes in concrete.

Mortar: Used for repairing (tuck-pointing) or making mortar joints in brick and block. Use type S for brick walls and type N for concrete block.

Sand: Used for repairing cracks, holes, and other small masonry patching jobs.

Use Tips: When mixed with water a seemingly large bag of material can be reduced to a surprisingly small amount. Before buying calculate your needs carefully so you don't over- or underbuy. Cement and concrete "cure" very slowly, and should even be kept moist at first. *Latex masonry adhesive* or *emulsion* can be added to sand mixes to increase bonding ability and curing quality. Avoid inhaling the dry dust when mixing and moving cement products. Clean excess mortar off bricks with *muriatic acid* diluted 1 to 5. And watch your back—a solid model, two-wheel luggage carrier does nicely for transporting those bags. A large plastic or metal *mortar tub* is best for mixing.

Buying Tips: In comparison to buying separate components and mixing material from scratch, premixed cement is expensive. On the other hand, it is very convenient—just mix with water. Most do-it-yourselfers are willing to pay the extra cost for this convenience.

Cement and Concrete Patchers

Types:

Anchoring cement

Epoxy cement

Hydraulic cement

Latex cement

Standard cement

Vinyl patching cement

Also Known As:

Anchoring: Expansion cement

Hydraulic: Water-stopping cement

Description: Cement mixed with a bonding agent and other additives that increase adhesion strength, and allow for thin-setting ability. Some are ready-to-use, others need water.

Anchoring: Slightly expanding, fast-setting cement, ready to use, although some brands need water added. Slower setting than hydraulic cement.

Epoxy: Comes as a bag of dry cement, hardener, and emulsion that is mixed together before use.

Hydraulic: Comes as a powder. Similar to anchoring, but faster-setting. Expands as it cures to fill cracks tightly.

Latex: Powder is mixed with a latex liquid before use. Can be troweled to $1/16$" thickness. Excellent adhering power.

Standard: Blend of cement and sand that is mixed with water for use.

Vinyl: Comes as a powder that is mixed with water for use. Can be troweled to $1/8$" thickness. Excellent adhering power, more than regular cement and sand mixtures.

Uses:

Anchoring: Anchoring wrought-iron rail and gate posts, fences, and bolts.

Epoxy: May be used to patch any kind of material, including glass and steel, particularly where strength is important, and may be used to set flagstone and other patio-paving materials.

Hydraulic: Applied directly to a water leak in masonry and quickly hardens in place.

Latex: Smoothing rough surfaces as well as repairing hairline cracks.

Standard: Repairing small holes and cracks; cracks need to be undercut first.

Vinyl: Used to repair small cracks in concrete, glass, marble, tile, and brick. Vinyl bonding is strong.

Use Tips: Generally, for patchers, surface should be well cleaned before application with a *concrete cleaner, etching material,* or *de-greaser.* Latex sets very quickly, so no more than can be easily applied at one time should be mixed.

Buying Tips: Epoxy is the most expensive patcher. Acrylic, resinous, or latex bonding agents or adhesives are also sold separately as additives or primers.

Masonry Sealers

Types:

Acrylic resin sealer

Bituminous sealer

Cement latex sealer

Cement mortar

Epoxy resins

Silicone

Also Known As: Masonry waterproofers, waterproofers, waterproof cement paint

Description: Many proprietary formulations. Most common are:

Acrylic resin: Rubber and Portland cement mixture applied by brush.

Bituminous: Thick black tar-like material that can be applied hot or cold.

Cement latex: Cement-based with latex additives.

Cement mortar: Composed of one part water and one part cement.

Epoxy: Synthetic material that sets very quickly.

Silicone: Highly viscous material that goes on like paint.

Uses: To seal masonry walls against moisture penetration, dusting, staining, spalling, and the effects of weather. Decorative as well. Bitumonious may be used as a *roof coating*.

> **Use Tips:** Before using a waterproofer make sure that the problem is moisture intruding through the walls and not condensation. Always try to cure the source of the moisture. Follow surface preparation directions exactly. Note if product requires use of *etching* and *cleaning compound*. Most won't work over old paint. Take precautions to avoid eye and skin irritations as specified on the label.

$ **Buying Tips:** Quality sealers penetrate and swell to become an integral part of the masonry, not just a surface coating. Some products contain a mildewcide too. Some are better whites than others; check regarding colors. May require special additives.

Masonry Tools

About Masonry Tools

It pays to buy quality tools here unless you will only be doing a very simple or small patching job. Using a cheap, low-quality bricklaying tool for an extensive job is the sure route to frustration. After all, masonry is rough, heavy work to start with. Poor-quality tools have lightweight handle connectors and thin, low-quality steel. Good-quality tools are not that much more expensive, nor do they cost much to begin with. Handles have brass ferrules, and will often be attached by parts that are integral to the tool—forged in one piece—rather than spot-welded. Materials are magnesium, bronze, stainless steel, and the like. All specialized large tools are available to rent.

Despite their differences as described below, tradesmen call many of these tools merely by their basic types, such as *trowel* or *float,* without more precision. Be sure to know the specific uses intended when purchasing these items. And it is highly recommended that the first-time user practice on small brick or concrete jobs prior to tackling anything large.

Bricklayer's Hammer

Description: Narrow head with slightly curved, long claw.

Use: To break brick to size.

Masonry Trowel

Pointing Trowel

Types:

Bucket trowel: 6", blunt, stiff blade for scooping mortar out of buckets or mortar boxes and onto hawks, etc.

Buttering trowel: Triangular, wide, and slightly curved sides, about 7" long, for "buttering" the mortar directly onto individual bricks and general use by nonprofessionals. About the right size for digging anything out of 5-gallon buckets.

Duckbill trowel: Rectangular, about 2" × 10", rounded tip, for special shaping. Similar to margin trowel.

Margin trowel: Rectangular, about 2" × 5" or 8", for small patching, cleaning other tools, very useful.

Pointing trowel: Triangular, typically about 5" long, for small patching jobs.

Also Known As: Brick trowel

Description: Triangular-shaped flat metal blade with a wooden or metal handle. 5 or 5¹⁄₂" wide by 11" long, the most popular length; minimum length should be 8".

Use: Handling wet mortar.

> **Use Tips:** Clean thoroughly after use; if dried mortar accumulates on bottom it causes problems when you use the trowel for smoothing.

$ Buying Tips: For the average amateur the buttering trowel is the best all-round choice, though the margin trowel is useful. A pointing trowel tends to be too small and cheaply made—a bad choice for your one trowel. For regular trowels the *Philadelphia pattern,* with a square heel, is handier and more popular than the *London* type, with a rounded heel. Buy only the very best—this item gets rougher use than most tools.

Tuck-Pointing Trowel

Also Known As: Joint filler, tuck-pointer, pointing trowel, caulking trowel

Description: Long, narrow flat blade secured by a dogleg to a handle, like other trowels, usually $1/4"$ to 1" wide and $6^3/4"$ long.

Use: For repointing—applying fresh mortar to existing brick joints.

$ Buying Tips: Quality models are stiff and of one-piece construction. Flexible ones tend to cause the mortar to drop off as you apply it.

Hawk

Description: A flat, thin metal platform with a perpendicular handle in the middle of the bottom. Usually square, about 14" on a side.

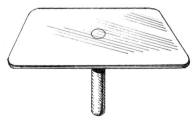

Hawk

Use: Holding "working" amounts of plaster, drywall compound, or mortar in one hand while applying it with a trowel with the other hand.

Brick Jointer

Also Known As: Jointer, jointing tool, striker, slicker, square brick jointer

Description: Narrow, S-shaped piece of metal about a foot long with differently curved, half-round ends. The ends are different widths, such as $1/2$" and $5/8$". Typical style is concave, but convex, V, and colonial (grapevine) styles are available too. May also be straight, with a wooden handle, called a *sled runner,* which is often used for long concrete-block joints.

Use: Smoothing fresh mortar in brick joints.

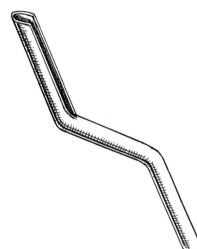

Brick Jointer

> **$ Buying Tips:** A jointer receives a lot of abrasive wear, so get one that's heat-treated and will therefore take the abuse. Any bent metal rod may be used on smaller jobs.

Joint Raker

Also Known As: Joint rake, skate, scratch jointer

Description: Of the two types the most convenient is a long-handled, metal device with two 1" to 2" diameter wheels and a specially hardened nail between them. A simpler model is a bent, narrow piece of metal with an offset tooth.

Use: Scraping old mortar out of a brick wall prior to tuck-pointing and recessing fresh mortar joints before the mortar sets up.

Tuck-Pointer Tool

Description: 14" to 16" long metal bar with a point on one end and a wedge on the other, both turned 90 degrees. A similar tool is the *plugging chisel,* or **flat joint chisel (below)**.

Use: Scraping old, loose mortar out of brick walls prior to tuck-pointing (filling in with new mortar).

 Buying Tip: Some people prefer to use an old screw driver and a hammer for this job.

Line Blocks

Also Known As: Corner blocks, line dogs, dogs, chicken legs, line stretchers

Description: Line blocks are small wooden or plastic devices that fit on brick corners; all the other names are for variations on blocks that may be used in the middle of a wall without touching the corners.

Use: Anchoring a line stretched across a new row of bricks that is used as a guide for bricklayers.

Masonry Chisels

Description: Short, hexagonal tempered-steel bars with chisel points shaped according to type and use. One solid piece of steel.

Types:

General use:

> *Cape chisel:* Flat, small wedge-shaped tip for making grooves and cleaning out mortar joints.

> *Star drill:* Long, narrow, fluted; driven with a hammer to make a small hole in masonry for anchoring a fastener.

Brick:

> *Bricklayer's, also known as wide, brick, brick set, plumber's, mason's, nail, long brick chisel:* Very wide blade, about 4", for cutting bricks to size and cleaning mortar off used brick.

> *Plugging chisel:* Narrow, flat pointed blade for cleaning out mortar prior to tuck-pointing.

Stone mason's:

> *Plain chisel:* Wide blade, plain edge for cutting stone; concrete chisel is similar but with longer handle.

> *Point (also known as bull point chisel):* Hex bar beveled to a point for cutting and shaping stone, or just breaking up masonry.

> *Tooth chisel:* Wide blade, approximately 2", with toothed edge for cutting stone.

Star Drill

Bricklayer's Chisel

Use Tips: Always wear safety goggles when using masonry chisels. Heavy gloves are recommended too. Star drills tend to shatter bricks; **electric drills with masonry (carbide) bits (Part II, Chapter 16)** are much, much better. Many masons prefer narrower chisels than the 4" wide bricklayer's model, especially if they come with longer handles, which afford more control. Hold chisels with your thumb and first two fingers instead of your whole hand—the pain and damage will be much less if you miss the chisel with your heavy hammer. And strike these chisels only with a heavy hammer made for this purpose: a **hand drilling hammer (Part II, Chapter 16)**. Don't use a regular *claw hammer.*

About Cement Tools

Large-scale cement and concrete work is beyond the domain of the usual do-it-yourselfer, but we know some of you will attempt a small job now and then. We therefore include here some of the basic tools used, but this is by no means exhaustive. There are entire catalogs of nothing but tools for cement work. These are presented in approximate order of use.

Screed

Also Known As: Strike-off board

Description: Wood or metal plank, often just a 2 × 4, 3' to 5' long.

Use: Scrapes off the top of freshly poured concrete.

Darby

Description: Several-foot-long wood or metal plank with two handles on top.

Use: Smoothing concrete after first smoothing with a screed, prior to floats. Used with a *puddling* or spading tool sometimes to consolidate the concrete.

Float

Float

Description: Flat, rectangular piece of wood, metal (magnesium is common), cork, or wood with rubber bottom, often 5" × 12" or 3½" × 16". A *bull float* is an extremely long float—4' and even 5' long by 8" wide—with a long handle secured to it. Handle may be composed of linked sections in order to get an extreme length, up to 20'.

Use: For the first smoothing of wet concrete or plaster. If a rough surface is desired, this may be the last smoothing as well. Bull floats are used for finishing very large areas. Plaster is often smoothed with a wood float with a sponge-rubber surface. Smaller floats with rubber bottoms (*rubber floats*) are for pushing grout into ceramic tile.

Finishing Trowel

Finishing Trowel

Also Known As: Cement finishing trowel, cement trowel, plasterer's trowel

Description: Rectangular, flat metal piece with a hardwood handle attached to a rib down its middle. Typically 10" to 20" long and 3" to 4" wide.

Use: Finishing, or final, smoothing of wet cement or plaster surface. Plasterers tend to use a shorter model when building walls.

> **Use Tip:** When smoothing a patch draw the trowel across it so that the trowel edges overlap the patch edges.

Edger

Description: Metal blade, usually 3" × 6", with one end curved downward and ends flat or slightly curved up, with a handle.

Use: Rounds off edges of wet concrete slabs.

Edger

Groover

Also Known As: Cement jointer, hand jointer

Description: Flat, rectangular metal tool with curved ends usually about 6" long, with a raised projection along the bottom up to 1" deep and a handle.

Use: Cutting grooves in wet concrete slabs.

Groover

Safety Equipment

About Safety Gear

Accidents for the do-it-yourselfer can be as serious as those for professional construction workers. Risks of losing an eye or inhaling highly toxic material are present with many of the most common tasks. Top pros won't work without their safety gear, which they consider as important as quality tools, and neither should you. The key to safety is to identify potential hazards so you will know what safety gear to use and be sure to get the right equipment for the job.

Pay special attention to the chemicals you use. Certain chemical products can cause extreme allergic reactions, affect long-term health, or cause reproductive problems. Most toxic products should be avoided during pregnancy. Always refer to the label because it should tell you the hazards of use and how to protect yourself. If a product label is not specific, call the manufacturer.

Safety gear is easily obtained. Check under Industrial Safety Equipment in your commercial Yellow Pages for suppliers in your area. If you have questions about how to protect yourself, consult your federal or state OSHA (Occupational Safety and Health Administration) office or check with an industrial hygienist, found in the commercial Yellow Pages. In the cases involving the removal or disturbing of asbestos, consult a professional since it might be illegal for a nonprofessional to do the job.

Safety Clothing and Other Gear

Earplugs, Ear Protectors

Also Known As: Hearing protectors

Description: Wide range of types, from soft wax to small round rubber plugs, to ear protectors that resemble earmuffs or old-fashioned headphones.

Use: Limiting noise of power tools reaching eardrums.

Ear Protectors

> **Use Tips:** With good earplugs you may not be able to hear someone calling to you. Keep your eyes open for possible warnings from others.

> **Buying Tips:** Get earplugs that provide maximum amount of noise reduction (described in decibels). If ear protection is used frequently, get reusable rather than disposable protectors.

Hard Hat

Description: Hat made of metal or impact-resistant or reinforced plastic with a web lining. Some are *dielectric* (insulated against electric shock).

Use: Protects head from falling objects or from hitting against hard surfaces.

> **Use Tips:** Extremely helpful not only during any demolition but when working near an uneven ceiling, such as an attic or basement, with low beams that may have nails protruding dangerously.

> **Buying Tip:** Large variety of hardness and internal webbing available.

Protective Gloves

Also Known As: Work gloves

Description: Gloves made out of heavy material such as vinyl, leather, or canvas.

Use: Rubber gloves prevent chemicals like paint thinner or remover from entering your bloodstream through your skin. Heavy canvas and leather gloves are for handling rough or heavy objects like stone or brick or scrap lumber with random nails exposed. Heavy work gloves also prevent splinters when handling clean lumber and provide a better grip when handling materials in general.

Use cheap, lightweight cotton or plastic gloves only for painting to avoid having to clean your hands with strong chemicals.

> **Use Tips:** Treat yourself to some peace of mind with a good, big pair of the thickest, toughest gloves you can find. For chemicals be sure to get the kind that will stand up to what you are using; black neoprene with a fabric lining is a good general choice.

> **Buying Tips:** Invest in a variety so you can use what's appropriate. Disposable plastic gloves are a great time-saver and keep chemicals off your skin.

Protective Goggles

Also Known As: Safety goggles

Description: Plastic glasses with large front and covered sides large enough to fit over regular eyeglasses.

Use: Protects eyes from splashes of dangerous chemicals such as paint thinner or stripper. Also helpful when painting ceilings or doing demolition. Some makes are suitable for protection from impact but most aren't.

Protective Goggles

> **Use Tips:** Don't forget to clean dust off goggles often. Obscured vision can cause accidents too—it's easy to get used to a diminished view.

> **$ Buying Tips:** Get goggles with replaceable lenses and that meet ANSI (American National Standards Institute) or OSHA standards.

Protective Glasses

Also Known As: Safety glasses

Description: Regular-looking glasses frames with shatterproof lenses. Available in plain or prescription. Many have additional shields on the sides, which are recommended. Polycarbonate lenses are strong.

Use: Protects eyes from projectiles when hammering or using tools of all sorts—not from splashes.

About Respirators

Unfortunately most small respirators commonly found at hardware stores do not provide the maximum protection required. Many are unreliable at best. We recommend, as part of your tool box, a reusable (or dual) cartridge-type half-face respirator as described below.

In choosing a respirator you should keep four things in mind:

1. Get the appropriate filter for the job.

2. Be sure the respirator fits you properly.

3. Use only a government-approved respirator.

4. Regularly clean and maintain your respirator and change filters.

Respirator

Also Known As: Breathing mask, dust mask, gas mask, painter's mask

Description:

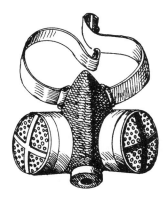

Respirator

Reusable (or dual) cartridge-type respirator: Large rubberized piece that holds two filter cartridges over mouth and nose; half-face model covers most of face; full-face model has face shield that covers entire face—necessary for anyone who must wear glasses. Special frames are required, available from the respirator manufacturer. Both are held on the head by double-wide rubber straps. Each filter cartridge should be government-approved for specific uses as marked on the package: dusts (toxic and nontoxic), mists, vapors, fumes, pesticides, radon, gases, etc.

Plastic dust (or filter) mask with replaceable filter: Small triangular plastic cup that holds a paper-like triangular filter. Fits over mouth and nose, held on the head by rubber band. Usually not government-approved.

Disposable Paper Dust Mask

Disposable paper dust mask: Small pyramid-shaped white paper cone that fits over mouth and nose, held on the head by rubber band. Also known as a painter's mask (incorrect—most do not stop paint vapors) or pinch mask. Only a few makes are government-approved.

Use:

Reusable cartridge type: Special cartridges are available to filter out a large array of dusts and toxins, ranging from serious dirt dust to chemical odors to asbestos. Must be chosen for the specific use intended, such as paint and organic vapor, pesticides, etc.

Replaceable filter type: Similar to above, and also for sanding operations. Minimum protection. Not for anything toxic or for painting.

Disposable paper type: Most brands provide below-minimum protection; possibly okay for light amounts of dust such as during housecleaning, although some newer models exist for more efficient filtration of a variety of toxins or home insulation particles.

Use Tips: In all cases, masks that fit improperly are not only useless but dangerous, especially if you get closer to poisons than normal, thinking you are protected. Respirators must be carefully, snugly fit to your face. *Disposable masks should be discarded after each use.*

Buying Tips: To emphasize: get the type of mask you need for the job being done. It is a dangerous waste to use anything too lightweight. Check packaging to see if cartridges are for the categories of dusts, mists, vapors, or fumes. And always check for the government approval from NIOSH or MSHA. If not available through your local hardware store, try the Yellow Pages for Safety Equipment or Industrial Supplies.

Fire Extinguishers

About Fire Extinguishers

Fires are characterized according to type: *Type A fires* are those involving wood, trash, cloth, and similar materials. *Type B fires* are those involving oil, gas, paint thinners, and other flammable materials. *Type C fires* are those involving electrical equipment.

Fire extinguishers are labeled with the letter or letters of the type or types of fires they can extinguish. *It is crucial that you use a fire extinguisher only on the fire types it is designed to handle.*

Extinguishers are also rated according to the size of the fire they'll put out. For example, an extinguisher rated *1A* could extinguish a burning stack of twenty-five 40" long sticks. One rated *2A* could put out a fire twice that size.

Fire extinguishers contain either pressurized water, a dry chemical propelled by nitrogen, or a gas.

$ General Buying Tips:

- Buy a good-quality fire extinguisher, and if you can't find one in your local hardware store, try a fire equipment dealer in the Yellow Pages—they generally carry quality equipment.

- Only buy an extinguisher approved by a testing agency, either Factory Mutual (FM) or Underwriters Laboratories (UL).

- Buy an extinguisher that is rechargeable.

- Some extinguishers don't have pressure gauges and are not as good as those that do.

- Water remains one of the best fire-fighting "chemicals" around. Small dry-chemical extinguishers only work for a matter of seconds anyway.

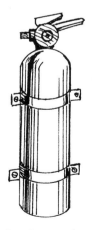

Fire Extinguisher

Multipurpose Dry Chemical Fire Extinguisher

Description: Steel, aluminum, or plastic canister, red or white, with a hand-operated valve and a gauge for reading pressure. Supplied with a strap and bracket for wall mounting. Comes rated according to types and sizes of fire it can handle, either types A, B, or C, and 1 to 10 indicating proportion of ingredients. (*A* is ordinary combustibles, *B* flammable liquids, and *C* is electrical equipment.)

Use: Extinguishing fires around the house.

Use Tips: Hang extinguishers away from stoves and near escape routes—stairwells, doorways, hallways, and the like. Also—very important—read the instructions that come with the extinguisher and make sure all family members understand them. Note that dry chemicals leave a sticky residue after use. And they spray for only a matter of seconds.

Buying Tips: While different extinguishers can be bought for different types of fires, a fire is an emotionally convulsing event that leaves little time for thought. Get a universal type that will put out anything. For the kitchen a 1A 10BC type would be good. That rating means that it handles all three types of fires, being especially strong against flammable materials. Something twice that strength against Type A fires—2A 10BC—would be good where water is not accessible and where there is lots of fire fuel, such as a basement workshop. Put several 10-pounders around your house.

Halon or CO_2 Fire Extinguisher

Description: Similar to dry chemical, above, although can be just as effective in smaller-sized canisters. Colorless, odorless, and evaporates after use. Leaves no residue.

Use: An extinguisher containing halon or CO_2 won't damage delicate electronic equipment like a **dry chemical extinguisher (above)** will.

Use Tips: Normally, halon can extinguish Type B and C fires and in the larger sizes is effective against Type A fires too. Sucks up oxygen.

Buying Tip: More expensive than the dry chemical type but generally more compact.

Metals and Metal Finishes

About Metals and Metal Finishes

It's not hard to get confused about all the finishes and metals used for hardware, tools, and materials. Following is some information that should clarify the picture and help you make more informed buying decisions.

Blued: Not really a treatment but a light coating given to items like nails to keep them from rusting in the box while waiting to be sold.

Brass: Many hardware items are made of pure brass. It is a soft metal (mostly copper and zinc) but weatherproof, though salt water or salt air will turn it green, a form of corrosion. (This condition is not serious and will not affect the integrity of the metal.) Brass screw slots are easily stripped because the metal is so soft.

Brass-Plated: Steel coated with brass. It is used when good looks count and strength is needed too. It provides a measure of protection against corrosion but is not really weatherproof.

Bright: A term meaning that hardware is not coated with anything.

Bronze: An alloy mostly made of copper and tin. Pure bronze is very strong, does not corrode, and can be used inside and outside the house. It is a favorite in marine applications. Bronze is harder than brass.

Bronze-Plated: Steel plated with bronze. Unlike pure bronze, it is not considered weatherproof, though good-quality plating can last for a number of years before corroding. Generally, though, bronze plating is just designed to add good looks and a small measure of protection against moisture.

Cast Iron: Iron made in such a way that it is more brittle than malleable iron.

Chromed: When an item is described like this it means that chrome has been added to the steel—it is an integral part of it.

Chrome-Plated: A material, say steel or even plastic, coated with chrome. It serves a decorative as well as an anticorrosive protective function. Bath items are typically chrome-plated. Items with chrome plating are not as durable as those where chrome has actually been added to the steel.

Chrome Vanadium: Steel that has had vanadium and chrome added to it. Makes a tool or other item stronger without becoming brittle.

Forged: Refers to items that have been heated and shaped to give great strength. Drop-forged items are made by pouring molten metal in a form and then dropping a great weight on it to distribute the metal in the form.

Galvanized: Most outdoor items are galvanized, which means the item has been given a zinc coating to make it weatherproof. There are two kinds of galvanizing—coated and hot-dipped. Items that are hot-dipped have a characteristically rough finish. It is by far the superior of the two finishes.

High-Carbon Steel: Also known as *tool steel*—hardened in a hot-and-cold manufacturing process. Very common, nothing special.

Hollow-Ground and Tapered: Usually refers to the way saw blades have been shaped to reduce binding—they are thinner in the middle. Hollow-ground circular saw blades are dish-shaped—the outer cutting edge is thicker than the middle to reduce binding. Hollow-ground handsaws are thicker at the cutting edge but taper to the spine, or back. Hollow-ground taping knives flex in the middle rather than at the handle, giving greater smoothing ability.

Machined: Refers to items that have been cut and shaped by grinding and polishing; simply describes the way steel is worked.

Malleable Iron: Iron that has been made so that it still has some bendability—or some capacity to be hit without cracking—without loss of strength.

Oiled: Many items such as bolts are oiled, but this in no way affords them any permanent protection, but rather, like blued items, helps them resist rust while stored.

Stainless Steel: Totally corrosion-resistant steel that contains nickel and chrome. Generally very strong and hard steel too.

Tempered: Steel that has been heated and cooled in a certain way for strength.

Zinc- or Cadmium-Plated: These two terms mean the same thing and refer to a plating given to hardware items that makes them rust-resistant rather than rustproof. Though also treated with zinc, **galvanized items (see above)** get a much thicker shield of zinc, which makes them more weatherproof.

Basic Tools and Materials Every Homeowner Should Have

Here are some suggestions for essentials for common repairs and maintenance tasks, plus a number of things that just make it all easier, in alphabetical order. Those few with an asterisk are so basic that even an apartment dweller would do well to have them.

While it is always nice to have a fully-equipped workshop with an in-depth supply of tools and materials, it seems that most of us need to rely on a semiportable collection of things for minor and typical repairs around the house. Keep the small stuff in an open plastic tool box or canvas bag that won't scratch floors, and the larger stuff in something like a 5-gallon plastic bucket. If weight is still a problem, get a second plastic tool box that is stored empty and fill it only with the tools needed for each job. In a big house, it is also a good idea to store a few pliers, hammers, and screwdrivers (and a small container of various fasteners) in places like a kitchen drawer and an upstairs bedroom. Combination tools are no substitute for the real things, but good-quality ones can be convenient for small repairs.

Better, more pleasurable results will be yours if you keep a couple of things in mind: Always use the right tool for the job, and always try to get good-quality tools. I might add to that, *always* have some duct tape handy and *always* wear a painter's hat (request a free one along with some paint mixing sticks when you buy paint. Besides protecting your hair from paint splatter, it could just possibly make you look semiprofessional as you wander around a worksite). But that's just my thing.

Hand Tools

- 5-in-1 tool (page 393)
- adjustable wrenches* (page 56)
- allen wrenches (set) (page 63)
- awl (page 90)
- C-clamps (2 small or 2 quick-action clamps) (page 65 or 69)
- carpenter's level (24") (page 78)
- caulking gun (page 289)
- claw hammer* (page 3)
- cold chisel (page 13)
- combination wrenches (set) (page 58) or socket wrench set (page 61)
- curved jaw locking pliers (10") (page 51)
- fasteners*: various finishing nails and drywall screws (pages 174 and 184)
- four-in-hand rasp/file (page 96)
- grip light (page 112)
- hacksaw (page 34)
- Japanese saw* (ryoba) (page 30)
- latex gloves (page 678)
- long-nose pliers* (page 51)
- nail claw (page 18)
- nailsets (page 11)
- nut driver ($^5/_{16}$") (page 60)
- offset screwdriver, ratchet combination style* (page 25)
- paint and varnish scraper (page 394)
- painter's hat (above)

Absolute basics.

- Phillips head screwdrivers*: 3 sizes (Nos. 1 to 3 or at least 1 and 2), all normal length, plus one stubby (page 22)
- pipe wrenches (page 564) (if you don't have copper or plastic piping)
- pry bar (6 to 10") (page 17)
- putty knife* (flexible) (page 454)
- razor blade scraper (page 394)
- shave hook (page 393)
- slip-joint pliers* (page 47)
- slotted screwdrivers*: 3 sizes (extra-narrow, $^3/_{16}$" and $^1/_4$", plus one stubby and wide) (page 21)
- square: try or combination (page 74 or 75)
- tape measure* (page 71)
- taping knife (6" or so wide, flexible, hollow ground) (page 453)
- test lamp (page 645)
- tongue-and-groove pliers* (page 48)
- torpedo level (page 79)
- utility knife* (page 37)
- wood chisels* (set of 3 or 4 bevel-edged, $^1/_4$" to 1" wide) (page 14)
- worklights* (page 111)

Power Tools

- belt sander (page 153)
- circular saw (page 143)
- cordless drill/driver and full set of bits (page 126)
- extension cord (page 586)

Absolute basics.

Materials

- caulk*: neoprene, rubber adhesive (small tube) (page 286); general-purpose latex caulk with silicone; and 100% silicone caulk (page 286)

- damp patch roof cement or other roofing repair material (page 295)

- duct tape* (page 330) — an absolute necessity

- electrical tape (page 330)

- epoxy repair material (page 548)

- glues*: cyanoacrylate glue (page 282) and wood glue (page 279)

- joint compound* (page 442)

- penetrating oil* (aerosol form) (page 326)

- sandpaper (variety of grits) (page 99)

- spackling compound* (page 448)

- synthetic steel wool (page 101)

- teflon tape and/or pipe dope (page 547) (if you don't have copper or plastic piping)

- water putty* (page 416)

Absolute basics.

Index

THE COMPLETE ILLUSTRATED GUIDE TO EVERYTHING SOLD IN GARDEN CENTERS

(EXCEPT THE PLANTS)

ILLUSTRATIONS BY ROBERT STRIMBAN

Acknowledgments

The principal research for this book was done by Robert S. Coleman, of the Brooklyn Botanic Garden, Brooklyn, New York. He proved to be ideally qualified for this work by his background as a professional gardener and research librarian as well as that of a dedicated and enthusiastic teacher. He also conceived the sections on garden ornaments (chapter 11) and appendix D ("Mail-Order Catalog Guide"). I gratefully acknowledge his hard work and long hours, which helped make this book happen. I am also grateful for the helpful comments made by other members of the staff of the Brooklyn Botanic Garden who reviewed the manuscript for accuracy and otherwise encouraged and helped me.

· · ·

The following organizations, individuals, and garden center personnel are among the many who were open and generous with their time and expertise, granting interviews, reviewing parts of the manuscript, providing leads for further research, or giving me run of their garden centers, without which this book would not have been possible:
Longacre's Nursery Center, Lebanon, New Hampshire; Agway Farm, Home and Garden Supplies, Holden, Massachusetts; Silver Fox Nursery, Worcester, Massachusetts; Jay Dubrofski of Midtown Garden Center, Brooklyn, New York; Fred Hicks and Vinnie Drzewucki of Hicks Garden Center, Westbury, New York; Tom Durkin of Cedar Grove Garden Center, Cedar Grove, New Jersey; Russell Ireland, Bill Simmeral, Elizabeth Stout, and Wayne Bourdette of Martin Viette Nurseries, East Norwich, New York; Bruce Butterfield of the National Gardening Association; P. Whitney Yelverton of the Fertilizer Institute; Beverly C. and Dr. Eliot C. Roberts of the Lawn Institute; the American Association of Nurserymen; the Garden Council; the Office of Pesticides and Toxic Substances, Environmental Protection Agency, Washington, D.C.; the National Pesticides Hotline; Susan Cooper of the National Coalition Against the Misuse of Pesticides (NCAMP); Melba Davis of the California Association of Nurserymen; Wally Patterson of Frank's Nursery and Crafts, Inc.; Anne W. Markle, gardener; Henry Handler, gardener; Edward Ettlinger, gardener; Alex L. Dommerich, Jr., gardener; Ann Marie Thigpen, garden ornament expert; Professor James B. Beard, Texas A & M University; and John Ameroso.

A note of thanks is due to the many garden

centers around the country which I visited anonymously, poking around the aisles while surreptitiously taking notes. I made a point to buy at least one thing on each of these visits, in case you wondered.

Thanks are due to the many different manufacturers who so kindly sent their catalogs, and a special thanks to those who also answered detailed queries for technical information over the phone. Some individuals employed by these companies provided invaluable expertise by reviewing certain parts of the manuscript. This effort went well beyond the normal range of their work, and I appreciate the time they took for this book.

The general support and enthusiasm of my colleagues at Macmillan is gratefully acknowledged, especially that of Pam Hoenig (my editor), Susan Richman, Barry Lippman, and Bill Rosen. For all those who supported my work on *The Complete Illustrated Guide to Everything Sold in Hardware Stores,* especially David Wolff, a second round of thanks. The success of that book encouraged me to work even harder on this one.

Debbie Steele and Whitney Hanscom assisted me on the error-free preparation of the final manuscript and illustrations with unflagging enthusiasm and energy.

Though this is not the kind of book that usually has strong personal roots, it should be noted that I was lucky enough to have my mother, an avid gardener (and orchidist) who was on the staff of the Chicago Botanic Garden, assist in the research and editing. Her perceptive thoughts and razor-sharp opinions helped shape the book in numerous essential ways. I was helped on my earlier book on hardware by my father, who has a wonderful affinity for the stuff. I am delighted to have their extensive contributions. More importantly, and more relevant to the journalistic approach to research required by this kind of book, my father taught me to question experts to the third degree while my mother taught me to be observant. They have both given me the urge to try to figure everything out, for which I am ever thankful and because of which I am, of course, still unsatisfied. Stand by for more books.

This book is also dedicated in part to my son, Dylan Alexander, born as this went to press, who will certainly show me a thing or two about growing. I would also like to thank and further dedicate this book to my wife, Gusty Lange, who has always supported my need to work long hours, who has amazingly accurate editorial judgment, and who inspires me in so many different ways.

Steve Ettlinger

Contents

Preface

WHY THIS BOOK

You could say that this book is the sequel to *The Complete Illustrated Guide to Everything Sold in Hardware Stores,* but that would be too simple.

However, there is no doubt that the reasons for this book are the same as for that one: All of us, at one time or another, have gone into a hardware store or garden center slightly unsure of what it is that we need and have found ourselves intimidated by the vast array of similar-looking items on the shelves. They all turn into whatchamacallits and thingamajigs. The clerks are often just not available to explain comparative points well (especially in the large self-service stores), or if they are, they may use terms that are unfamiliar. That leaves much of the decision making to you.

Most of us want to know what the difference is between the various choices we are confronted with so that we can make our own intelligent decisions, but it is all complicated by the bold claims made in the advertisements and on labels and compounded by the assertion that certain products replace all others, do everything, and do it perfectly, no less. On top of that, labeling is often inconsistent.

Furthermore, to the uninitiated, differences may not seem important. Probably the most common request a garden center clerk hears is, "I'd like some fertilizer, please." Now one thing you will learn from this book is that there is no such thing as "just plain fertilizer." Nor is there *just* a trowel—there are long and short, narrow and wide, curved and straight ones, each designed for specific uses. And when you ask for a hoe, for example, you'll most likely be offered the choice between a solid-socket or tang-and-ferrule model. Terms have to be understood and decisions made. This book will help you make those choices.

Despite all the books on gardening, there is no one book that lists all the stuff you have to buy—there are plenty of books explaining *how to,* but none saying *what with,* across the whole spectrum of products. This book was conceived to address that problem. I hope it helps you get what you need without fear of being intimidated by the daunting displays at your garden center.

—Steve Ettlinger

Introduction

ABOUT THIS BOOK

The chapters of this book correspond roughly to the areas of the front "store" sections of a typical large garden center, though there are plenty more items listed here than you would normally find there.

The chapters themselves fall into two basic groups, just like the items in the garden center: Part 1 is supplies, or *packaged goods,* and part 2 is tools, equipment, and accessories, or *hard goods.* Unfortunately, it isn't possible to make this an absolutely clean division and you will find some overlap. For example, you'll find fencing that is used as a pest barrier in the chapter on pest control products in part 1 and fencing that is used for other purposes in the chapter on growing products in part 2.

Items are grouped by association, and alphabetically within each chapter. Make good use of the index—it lists much more than you might expect, including all cross-referenced and associated items, as well as, and perhaps more importantly, the various names by which things are called from the "Also Known As" sections.

Please note that some of the names listed in the "Also Known As" sections may be incorrect. Listing doesn't assure correctness: Certain aka's are just plain wrong, corruptions that have found their way into print or the mouth of a professional by any of a number of ways. As a matter of fact, many of them are taken from the distributors' and manufacturers' catalogs, where the use of poetic license is in widespread practice, sometimes fueled by quite imaginative translations of descriptions of imported items. Furthermore, right or wrong, a number of different tools are called by the same name—it is up to you to fully describe what you want when you go to the garden center. The illustrations should help you get what you want. In any case, aka's have been included so you can find something in the index even if you have been given an incorrect or colloquial name.

No reference book would be complete without a disclaimer, so here is ours:

Brand and trade names are used here as an aid to the consumer, and are in no way meant as an endorsement of any product or manufacturer; likewise their omission is in no way meant to be a negative comment. In some cases, brand names are used by the public in a generic way, and we have made every effort to note when this is so. Trade names and trademarks are noted to the best of our ability; we will be glad to make any corrections necessary if a manufacturer should find us in error. All in all, the items listed in this book are simply meant to be representative of what you might be able to buy in a garden center. Nothing is implied to be essential or even beneficial by its inclusion.

WHAT IS NOT INCLUDED IN THIS BOOK

First of all, as per the title, no plants or flowers (the "green goods") are listed here, although appendix A has some general advice about shopping for them. This book lists only the supplies, tools, equipment, and accessories (the "packaged goods" and the "hard goods") that an average home gardener might find in a well-stocked garden center; you should not expect every garden center to have everything listed here.

Furthermore, items that fall in the broad "outdoor living" category—such as furniture and recreation equipment—are not included. Nor will you find pet supplies or farming equipment or landscaping materials or general home improvement items that are found at some garden centers. The line had to be drawn somewhere. Regular home gardening, with a slight nod to decoration, is the limit.

Some of the items listed (or some you might find in catalogs) are intended for professionals. Most garden centers will be glad to special-order these items for you, and in fact they probably already sell to a small group of local professionals (landscapers, tree surgeons, or groundskeepers) on a special-order basis. This is especially true of garden centers that also have their own nurseries, which is quite common (and a good sign), because their own growers need these professional products. So don't be shy about asking for products that you don't see on the shelves.

You may find that we don't list certain chemical products that you know of, especially pesticides. There are so many, including some that are mixtures, that it is impossible to be complete. Also, some chemical products, even well-known commercial ones, are sometimes abruptly removed from the market as tests determine that they are much more dangerous than previously thought. Legislation that was pending for many years may have suddenly become effective, or regulations that vary from state to state may lead you to search out something that is unavailable where you live. Another reason some chemical pesticides go off the market is that the pests become resistant to them, rendering them ineffective. As in all related matters, checking with your local Cooperative Extension agent (see appendix B) is the best way to go.

A PERSONAL NOTE TO READERS

I am always glad to hear from readers who have found items or "Also Known As" aliases that were not included in this edition. Suggestions for use tips and buying tips are always welcome, too. Please write me c/o Macmillan Publishing Company, 866 Third Avenue, New York, NY 10022.

P A R T   I

Supplies

Growing Media and Soil Conditioners

ABOUT SOIL

Dirt is what you track into the house. *Soil* is a complex growing medium that holds moisture and nutrients for plants. It is composed of microorganisms and bacteria—organic, or living, matter—and mineral particles—nonliving matter. It has structure and chemical balance. Some soils are better than others for growing plants, and some types are better than others for particular plants. For a variety of reasons, your soil may need help. You can improve the soil in your garden, both in terms of chemical makeup and in terms of structure, if need be, with *garden soils, soilless mixes, pro-mixes, topsoil, soil amendments,* or *conditioners,* all sold at garden centers. To better understand what these products are and how to use them, it is important to understand the three primary soil types, *clay, sand,* and *silt,* each of which has differently sized mineral particles and different texture.

TYPES OF SOIL

• *Clay soil* is composed of the smallest particles found in soils. It also is referred to as a *heavy* soil. When wet, the particles in clay stick to each other, making it impervious to water and, for that matter, plants. When dry, it becomes hard and often cracks. Clay soil contains little air, and water does not drain easily through it: It needs to be loosened or opened up. Humus (decayed organic matter), peat moss, or other organic matter or gypsum can be added to clay soil to make it lighter, counteract its tendency to stick together and pack down, and allow water to drain through it.

• *Sandy soil* is composed of the largest particles found in soil. It is referred to as a *light* soil. When wet, the particles do not stick to each other and water, along with fertilizers and other nutrients, flows easily. Because it has such good drainage, sandy soil may not retain enough moisture to aid good plant growth. Sandy soil can be improved by adding peat moss or humus or organic matter that will become humus to help it retain more moisture. This humus needs to be replenished every few years, as it has a tendency to wash away.

• *Silt soils* are composed of particles in sizes between those of sand and clay.

• *Loam* refers to soils that are composed of a desirably balanced mixture of the particles found in clay and sand along with organic matter. Loam is good for plant growth because it is open, retains moisture well, and has a crumbly structure, or good *tilth*. Loam is what every gardener wants. Surprisingly, loam consists of about 50 percent open pore space that can be filled with air and water.

A NOTE ABOUT SOIL TESTS: A *soil test,* in which a few tablespoons of soil in solution are chemically analyzed, determines the composition of your soil: the exact type of soil, the percentages of various nutrients in the soil, and the pH of the soil.

The *pH* (potential hydrogen) is the term used to express relative acidity (low pH, or "sour") or alkalinity (high pH, or "sweet") of soil on a scale of 0 to 14, with 7 being neutral. Each level of pH represents ten times the concentration; a pH of 5.0 is ten times as acid as a level of 6.0. This is probably the most important test you'll take in your garden. The range for the average garden is 6.0 to 7.5, and experts disagree as to what is the absolute best range, though most nutrients are available to the plants in a range between 6.0 to 6.8. Essentially, pH level affects the solubility of the nutrients, which allows them to travel through the soil and into the plant roots. An extreme pH on either end of the scale prevents the plants from getting the nutrients they need.

Soil tests can be done with a variety of meters or kits (see pages 237–38) for free or at a nominal fee by your local Cooperative Extension (see appendix B), or by a private laboratory (often listed in the Yellow Pages under "Laboratories—Testing"). Lab tests are more accurate than kit tests, of course.

If you have not had your soil tested, you might want to do so before adding any fertilizers or additives to your garden. A soil test is one of the few ways of determining the amount of phosphorus, potash, and nitrogen in your soil, as well as its acidity. This is important information when choosing fertilizers as they will raise or lower the pH, depending on their ingredients. Consider tests a one-time effort, or at most something to be done every three or four years, usually in the autumn or spring, as a search for the basis of specific problems.

If you know your soil pH and the level that is optimum for the plants you are growing, you can then choose fertilizers (see chapter 3) that will maintain a good pH level for your plants. For example, plants like azaleas, rhododendrons, heaths, and heathers prefer a more acidic soil (with a lower pH) so you will want to buy fertilizers that will keep the pH lower. Without a soil test, though you may be able to judge the soil's needs from the appearance of your lawn or plants, you could be paying a lot for special fertilizers that contain trace elements or nutrients that are already present in your soil, or worse yet, not buying the fertilizers that could provide the nutrients lacking in your soil.

The most typical choice for *raising* the pH of soil is to add lime, and to *lower* it, to add a soil acidifier like sulfur in one of its various forms, such as aluminum sulfate. The amount you need to add is noted on the package of whatever kind of product you are using. For example, to raise the pH of sandy soil by one pH level, you need to add 7½ ounces of ground limestone per square yard, but for clayey soil, you need to add 15 ounces. To lower it by one pH level, that is, to increase the acidity, approximately 2¾ ounces of aluminum sulfate are needed per square yard (1 pound of sulfur per 100 square feet), or 6 pounds of manure. There are many other products and measures that you can use; these examples are provided just to give some perspective. All these additives will take different lengths of time to achieve their effects, from a few days to a few months. Check the labels and general gardening reference books.

ABOUT PACKAGED SOILS

Few gardeners have soil in their gardens that is suitable for houseplants or seed starting. Indoor gardening, with its intensive watering, puts a strain on soil, necessitating various requirements that are met by the specialized soils listed here. Some are mere refinements of a suitable all-purpose blend, so choice becomes just a matter of personal preference. Mixing your own can be fun also and sometimes better. Growing media, soils, and conditioners are sold in packages ranging from a few ounces to 100 pounds. Buy larger packages; smaller ones always cost much more per pound. They are also sold by the quart and by the cubic foot, depending on the manufacturer.

Growing media are literally anything you can grow a plant in, and are generally used to refer to those media that do not contain soil.

General Use Growing Media

HUMUS

ALSO KNOWN AS: Compost (incorrect), composted topsoil, peat muck

DESCRIPTION: Humus is a general term for decomposed and decayed organic matter and is an ideal, stable part of rich soil with little nutrient content. It looks like soil and is sold in bags (typically 40 pounds) just like topsoil (see page 8). Some gardeners consider compost and leaf mold (see page 14) forms of humus.

TYPES: *Peat humus* (also known as *organic peat):* Humus derived primarily from decomposed reed-sedge peat (see page 16) and other decomposed organic matter. Mined from bogs in Michigan, New England, Pennsylvania, and a few other states.

Pine bark humus (also known as *pine bark conditioner):* Humus derived from decayed pine bark, i.e., mined from the forest floor. Consists of "woods matter" and leaves and can be either gathered in the wild or produced commercially (composted).

USE: Building up soil in containers, lawns, or flower beds, or replacing topsoil that has been removed in building construction. Can also be used as a conditioner to enrich soils and improve their drainage and friability, but it is essentially a growing medium.

USE TIP: Doesn't hold water or nutrients as well as topsoil. Mix with soils or use straight; often used as a growing medium for potted plants and in greenhouses.

POTTING SOIL

ALSO KNOWN AS: Houseplant soil

DESCRIPTION: Ready-to-use soil that is a mixture of organic and inorganic ingredients such as peat moss, compost, sand, and vermiculite. Sold in packages that range in size from 9 to 40 quarts or 2 to 40 pounds. Some contain small amounts of slow-release fertilizer and trace elements and some are sold in bags that are meant to be used as planters. *Sterile* potting soils have been heated to over 180° F to kill bacteria and weed seed.

USE: Good for houseplants and for starting seeds because of increased drainage and the decreased chance of rot and a variety of fungal problems, especially damping-off, soil-borne fungal diseases that kill seedlings. Gardens need the bacteria and microorganisms found in nonsterile or partially pasteurized soils.

USE TIP: Good potting soil rewets better than plain soil. If it dries out, it won't pull away so much from the sides of the pot.

BUYING TIPS: Soils intended for interior use can be sterilized, but it is not necessary for general exterior use for mature plants. Also, if you are using organic fertilizers, you must *not* use sterilized soil, as it lacks the microorganisms needed for the fertilizer to work.

SOILLESS MIXES

ALSO KNOWN AS: Light potting mix, peat-lite mix, seed starting mix, soil-less mix (see chapter 9)

POPULAR BRAND NAMES: Pro-Mix®, Peat-Bark Mix

DESCRIPTION: Growing medium for potting mixes formulated from all organic material that contain no grit soil (mineral particles). These mixes are extremely water and nutrient retentive. They have been sterilized so they contain no bacteria or weed seed. Available in sizes that range from bags of 8 quarts to compressed bales of 5½ cubic feet.

The most common types sold contain peat moss, perlite, vermiculite, and gypsum, along with nutrients and trace elements. Some are specifically formulated for container gardening, and include good-quality sphagnum moss and composted softwood bark, which increase water retention—loss of water being a major problem in container gardening.

USE: Seed-starting growing medium, for both potted plants (indoors and out) and gardens. They can also be mixed with soil. Because some are sterilized, they prevent damping-off, soil-borne fungal diseases that kill seedlings. (See also seed starting products, chapter 9.)

USE TIP: If soilless mixes are used in containers or tubs on terrace gardens, mix in sand or soil to make the mix heavier. This is particularly important if you are growing trees or shrubs in a container as soilless mixes alone do not hold up the heavier plants very well.

BUYING TIP: This is a convenient packaged item to buy, but you can mix your own very easily if you want, which might also be less expensive. Typical mixes include peat moss (2 parts), vermiculite (1 part), perlite (1 part), fertilizers, a small amount of ground limestone, and a wetting agent, all of which are sold individually and all of which are described later in this book.

TOPSOIL

ALSO KNOWN AS: Loam, garden loam, top soil

DESCRIPTION: A rich, dark soil with a high quantity of organic matter. Topsoil is the rich top layer of soil created naturally when leaves and organic matter weather and decompose completely. Most often sold in natural form, with microorganisms, or sterile, with none.

USE: Topsoil is an excellent additive when building up the quality of the soil in a garden. It can be used when creating your own soil mixes, and as part of a soil mix for use in containers and tubs. Often during the construction of new homes the topsoil is removed by bulldozers during the grading process. If this rich soil is not replaced by the contractor, the new homeowner has to replace it in order to have a garden.

USE TIP: Sterile topsoil is preferable for potting soils used for starting seeds and rooting cuttings, as there is less likelihood of rot or damping-off, a soil-borne fungal disease that kills seedlings. Once the seedlings have grown this is no longer necessary.

BUYING TIP: Look for soils with a lot of organic matter.

Specially Formulated Growing Media

AFRICAN VIOLET SOIL

DESCRIPTION: A prepackaged soil mix composed of sterile organic ingredients that holds moisture extremely well but still has excellent drainage. Sold in sizes from 2 to 8 quarts. Typically contains peat moss, ground limestone, vermiculite, and perlite.

USE: Specifically prepared to be used for African violets.

BUYING TIP: Though regular potting soil should be adequate for African violets, the special African violet soil mixes are usually the same price and formulated to be better for the plants, containing slightly more perlite or vermiculite for increased drainage and aeration. African violets seem to attract a good number of specialized products, which actually may have more to do with their popularity as houseplants and the vast market that creates than with their horticultural needs.

CACTUS SOIL

DESCRIPTION: Porous blend of sterile sand, organic matter, and sometimes nutrients. Products may vary in color from white to reddish brown, depending upon what types of sand are used. Most often cactus soil is sold in 4-quart sizes. Has more perlite and less peat moss than other potting soils.

USE: For cactus and other succulent plants.

ORCHID BARK

DESCRIPTION: Chips of redwood bark or a mixture of chips of redwood and pine barks. Despite its name, it is not made from gigantic orchid plants.

USE: Growing medium for orchids.

OSMUNDA FIBER

DESCRIPTION: A coarse, reddish brown fiber that is made from the roots of the *Osmunda* fern. *Tree fern fiber* is similar, but darker.

USE: As an anchoring medium for some epiphitic orchids and other plants that get their moisture and nutrients from the air, collectively known as *air plants*.

USE TIP: Moisten, squeeze out excess moisture, and attach to wood, bark, or cork block with wire.

BUYING TIP: Tends to be sold as an expensive specialty item, so shop around for the best price.

SHEET AND SPANISH MOSSES

ALSO KNOWN AS: Decorator moss

DESCRIPTION: Either of two types of long, fibrous moss in its natural state: *Sheet moss,* which is harvested from South Carolina forests in sheets and is very green, or *Spanish moss,* which is lighter and more bulky, and light gray.

USE: Sheet moss is used primarily for lining wire hanging baskets, and both are used in a variety of decorative arrangements and wreaths.

USE TIP: Birds may nest in a well-watered sheet moss basket.

TERRARIUM SOIL

DESCRIPTION: Special mixes of organic and inorganic ingredients. Often these soil mixes contain some ground charcoal to absorb salts and other chemicals that tend to build up in an enclosed environment.

USE: Terrarium soils can be used as a medium for growing plants in terrariums, jars, and other closed containers and pots with no drainage.

USE TIP: If you have a decorative pot without drainage that you wish to grow plants in, this would be a good choice of soil, though it is always better to provide drainage.

Soil Conditioners and Additives

ABOUT SOIL CONDITIONERS

Most gardens are planted where the gardener likes them to be, rather than because of a perfect soil. Gardeners usually find that their soil is lacking in some character of structure, as well as in nutrients, either because of inadequate soil care in the past or because of the special requirements of the plants you intend to grow. Fertilizers can add nutrients, but soil conditioners, often called *soil amendments,* improve the ability of the soil to hold water and to deliver nutrients to the roots, as well as improve aeration, drainage, and structure. Some conditioners are more often found as components of fertilizers, but are also sold separately. Others merely raise or lower the pH, depending on whether they are soil sweeteners or soil acidifiers, respectively.

ALUMINUM SULFATE

ALSO KNOWN AS: Aluminum sulphate, sulfate of aluminum

DESCRIPTION: Powdered bauxite that has been treated with sulfuric acid. Sold in bags from 5 to 100 pounds.

USE: Soil acidifier for acid-loving plants. Brings out the color, especially the blue, in hydrangeas. Can also be used as a coagulant for home swimming pools.

COW MANURE

DESCRIPTION: Dried and ground-up cow manure that has been aged in such a way that it has rotted, losing its smell and increasing its concentration of nutrients. More often considered a fertilizer (see its more extensive entry in chapter 3).

USE: Makes the soil friable, adds organic elements, and generally improves all soils. Also contains nutrients. Mixed into any soil, but routinely mixed into soil that is being put into tree holes or new gardens.

EARTHWORM CASTINGS

ALSO KNOWN AS: Worm castings

DESCRIPTION: Coarse brown powder sold in small, convenient bags (2-pound size is typical). Consists of ground-up earthworm castings, an imaginative euphemism for worm manure. Odorless. A similar product is *cricket castings.*

USE: A general soil amendment that increases the friability of soil, acting as a soil builder that increases water retention.

USE TIP: Ideal for potted plants.

GARDEN CHARCOAL

ALSO KNOWN AS: Soil freshener

DESCRIPTION: Chunks of charcoal that range in size from $\frac{1}{16}$ inch to $\frac{1}{2}$ inch. It is usually sold in 2-quart bags.

USE: When added to soil mixes, charcoal helps absorb odors, acids, salts, and other impurities. It also eliminates odors in terrariums and containers having no drainage and holds moisture. Especially good to have at the bottom of a container. Helpful as well in the water of vases containing cut flowers.

USE TIP: When planting in a terrarium or in a container without drainage, place a layer of gravel on the bottom, followed by a layer of charcoal, and then the soil or growing medium.

BUYING TIP: If you cannot find garden charcoal in your garden center, try pet stores, where it is sold as aquarium filter material.

GYPSUM

ALSO KNOWN AS: Land plaster, sulfate of lime

DESCRIPTION: Light-colored, finely powdered rocks or pellets containing calcium sulfate. Similar products that are blends of calcium and sulfur are *gypsite* (crystalline form of gypsum) and *lime sulfur* (which is sold as *calcium polysulfide).* The latter may have a wetting agent that makes for deeper soil penetration.

USE: Improves packed-down and clayey soils for water penetration (drainage) and aeration by making the fine particles of clay stick together and neutralizing the salt in salty (high-sodium) soils, without raising the pH as lime (see page 14) does. The process is a chemical one, whereby sodium ions are exchanged for calcium ions, which separates the clay particles enough to create "pore space" for air and water. Because it is a mild soil acidifier, gypsum may be used where the use of lime would pose a problem to acid-loving plants. Also supplies calcium and sulfur, both secondary nutrients (see pages 46–47).

USE TIP: Can be used in great quantities if warranted. Has been used since the days of the early Greeks.

BUYING TIP: The pelleted form is easier to use than the powder form.

HORTICULTURAL SAND

DESCRIPTION: Pure sterilized sand often sold in 2-quart bags. May vary in color, depending upon what type of sand is used. Contains no salt or other impurities that might bother plants.

USE: Mixed with potting soil to aerate and help with drainage. It can be used for rooting succulents and cacti, and as the primary base in a cactus soil mix.

BUYING TIPS: Regular *builder's sand,* which can be purchased at hardware stores or construction sites, is cheaper and works just as well as horticultural sand. Do not use ocean beach sand for plants, as it contains salt. Look for sharp and relatively coarse particles. Avoid fine, rounded ones.

IRON SULFATE

ALSO KNOWN AS: Iron sulphate, copperas, ferrous sulfate

DESCRIPTION: Granular product commonly sold in 5-pound bags or as small containers of liquid. Often sold as *iron chelate*.

USE: Contains 20 percent iron and 11.5 percent sulfur. Provides iron and acidifies the soil. Assists in the production of chlorophyll and corrects iron deficiencies (yellowing, or chlorosis, and green veins). Aids in blooming.

USE TIP: Make sure that your plant is definitely deficient in iron before applying, and if you do, apply carefully and strictly according to the directions. Too much iron can damage a plant. Yellow leaves are the usual sign of an iron deficiency, but the problem might lie elsewhere as well. Check your books or with experts.

BUYING TIPS: The standard granular product is for application to the soil and takes awhile to affect the plant. The liquid form, used as a foliar spray, tends to give quicker results (2 or 3 days).

LEAF MOLD

ALSO KNOWN AS: Woods soil, compost (when sold commercially)

DESCRIPTION: Shredded flakes of partially decomposed leaves and forest litter, usually an attractive dark brown. When a local nursery sells its own leaf mold as compost, it is usually sold by the cubic yard or small truckload. Often considered a mulch (see chapter 2), it also has fertilizing characteristics; some gardeners consider it a form of humus (see page 6).

USE: A particularly good source of humus and a general organic soil conditioner for vegetable gardens, as it opens up the soil, making it friable. Encourages development of fibrous roots. Also a good mulch for any area of the garden, because as it breaks down and turns into compost, it can be mixed into the soil to become a soil conditioner.

USE TIPS: Enriches and fertilizes the soil where it is used. It can be worked into soil to help build up the humus. Not effective if it is powdery. Lightens clayey soils. Can be turned into the soil after use as a one-season mulch to go to work as a soil conditioner.

BUYING TIP: Leaf mold is a bargain at about $1.50 a cubic foot, considering what it does for the garden. Very difficult to find for sale, though.

LIME

ALSO KNOWN AS: Ground limestone, limestone, liming material, pulverized limestone, agricultural lime, garden lime

CHEMICAL NAME: Calcium carbonate ($CaCO_3$) in a number of forms; commonly mixed with magnesium carbonate ($MgCO_3$)

DESCRIPTION: A fine, white powder, pellets, or granules of ground limestone. When mixed with magnesium (which is quite common), it may be called *dolomitic, dolomite,* or *magnesium limestone.* Lime is often incorrectly considered a fertilizer, probably because calcium is a secondary nutrient and magnesium is a micronutrient that all plants need. *Marl,* a natural mixture of weathered shells containing clay and calcium carbonate, is another source of lime.

USE: Primarily to raise the pH of soils—to make them more alkaline, or sweeter, which means essentially to neutralize soil acidity—so that microorganisms can help break down organic matter into the all-important humus. However, it is helpful in many other ways as well. Though it is not a fertilizer, lime is a catalyst for the release of nutrients and improves the structure of clayey soils by increasing moisture retention and drainage. Lime is also helpful in the control of club root, a disease found in plants of the cabbage family Cruciferae. Also prevents moss growth, disinfects, and can be used for both whitewashing and pickling vegetables.

USE TIPS: Most lawns require annual liming, especially in areas of the country with acid rain, such as the Northeast. Fall or spring is the best time to do this, depending on where you live, although fall is usually better. Be sure to water it in well. In acid soils (those with a low pH), liming is necessary to grow many perennials and vegetables. Do not apply at the same time as manure, or else they will combine and release ammonia gas, wasting valuable nitrogen and killing plants. Refer to your soil test to determine how much to apply (that is your *lime requirement),* and be patient: Trying to raise the pH of your soil by more than one point a year can be harmful to your plants, as it ties up the nutrients. Hydrated lime acts faster, but it can burn the plants—measure carefully and apply lightly.

BUYING TIPS: Though there are several forms of lime sold, be sure that you are buying a *dolomitic* or *ground* limestone (dolomitic is better because of the magnesium it contains); the general term used from time to time is *agricultural lime.* This type minimizes the risk of "burning" the foliage of plants, particularly grass. Most soils can use the magnesium and are not harmed by a slight excess. *Hydrated,* or *slaked, lime* is a third choice, though it must be applied carefully because it is very caustic and therefore dangerous to handle, and leaches out quickly. Other types of lime, such as *builder's lime,* are designed to be used in construction materials such as mortar and plaster. They are much more concentrated and will burn plants. Do not use *quicklime* in your garden—it will damage the soil. Pelletized limestone has less dust than fine ground limestone.

OYSTER SHELLS

DESCRIPTION: White material consisting of coarsely ground oyster shells, which are full of calcium carbonate ($CaCO_3$).

USE: As a liming material to raise the pH of soils (to make them more alkaline), although sometimes used as a fertilizer to add calcium, a secondary nutrient (see page 46).

USE TIP: Better used as a way to raise the pH of soil than as a fertilizer.

PEANUT HULL MEAL

DESCRIPTION: A tan to brown meal obtained from ground peanut hulls.

USE: In the South, often used as a soil conditioner to help open up packed soil. Also used as an additive or filler in fertilizers.

BUYING TIP: Generally less expensive and more commonly found in areas where peanuts are grown.

PEAT

ALSO KNOWN AS: Peat moss, peat muck, peat mulch, sphagnum peat moss, sphagnum peat, sphagnum moss

DESCRIPTION: Dried and partially to fully decomposed roots, leaves, stems, moss, and other plant debris that have been harvested from wetlands. Light brown to black. Compressed up to half the normal volume and roughly ground up for commercial packaging, peat is light, loose, and fluffy when unpacked, though some types are granular. Peat moss is much more commonly available than peat muck, which contains more mineral and fully decomposed plant matter.

TYPES: *Reed-sedge peat* (also known as *reed, fibrous,* or *sedge peat):* The product of partly decomposed plant residues (reeds, rushes, cattails, grasses, and the like) that grew in a water-saturated environment. *Michigan peat* is reed-sedge peat from Michigan, and is a bit darker and denser than the regular Canadian peat moss, having decomposed slightly. Sometimes sold as *humus.*

Sphagnum peat moss (milled and unmilled): Partially decomposed sphagnum moss and other bog plants that grow well in parts of Maine, Minnesota, and Canada. Most packages from Canada—the source of 90 percent of sphagnum peat moss sold in the United States—are also labeled in French, *Tourbe de spaigne.* It is the most common type of peat moss available.

Milled peat is dark to light brown in color and is simply sphagnum peat harvested by a mechanical milling process. May be sold as *organic seed starter.* Sold compressed to half its normal volume and packaged in heavy-gauge plastic bags. Usually not labeled as "milled." The most common form of peat, sold in large plastic packages of 1 to 6 cubic feet. Also available in super-compressed plates that expand when wet.

Unmilled peat (also known as *floral sphagnum moss)* is a greenish light brown material that looks more like you would expect dried moss to look: fibrous, with small branches and leaves visible. Usually sold in small plastic bags. Not readily available as it is harvested by hand.

Note the difference between two confusing uses: Sphagnum *moss* is gray and stringy, harvested before it has decomposed. Sphagnum *peat moss* is brown and is made of partially decomposed plants.

USE: As a soil additive, particularly when the pH needs to be lowered (mix it with lime if you don't want to lower your pH). Its main characteristic is its great water-holding capacity: Peat absorbs between five and fifteen times its weight in water (good-quality air-dried sphagnum will absorb up to twenty times its weight). It aids in opening up clay soil for better aeration and supplies organic matter to poor soil. Besides these special qualities, it improves all soils in terms of water retention and porosity. Though it is not recommended (see Use Tips, below), sphagnum peat is commonly used as a mulch (see chapter 2) for acid-loving plants, breaking down after about three years. Unmilled peat is used as a growing medium for orchids and other epiphytic plants and bromeliads, as well as a lining for wire baskets to hold soil. Milled peat is used not only as a conditioner but as a seed starting medium, and mixes well with perlite and vermiculite for container gardening.

USE TIPS: Moisten and work the peat into the soil well; if it gets packed down it might block water from reaching the plant. Use wet as a soil amendment. Peat does not make good mulch because if it is allowed to dry out, it will block water like a thatched roof. Also, remember that peat tends to lower the pH of soil as it breaks down.

BUYING TIPS: Peat moss is sold in cubic foot bales. Usually, the larger the bale, the lower the cost per cubic foot, so don't hesitate to buy more than you might need right away. It keeps well. Buy in the fall, slash the packaging, and allow to absorb water over the winter. Try to buy name brands of peat from reputable dealers, as good peat is over 95 percent organic fiber.

PERLITE

ALSO KNOWN AS: Horticultural perlite

DESCRIPTION: White, light, hard, porous, gritty material similar to vermiculite (see page 19) in appearance. Formed when lava (volcanic rock) is heated, which causes it to expand. Nontoxic, sterile, and odorless. *Construction grade perlite* is made of smaller, lighter particles.

USE: Increases drainage (loosens heavy soils), improves aeration (gets oxygen to the plant roots), and decreases the weight of potting soils, an important consideration for planters on decks. Also helps retain water, which attaches to the particles' surface. Can be used as a rooting medium on its own. Construction grade perlite is used as loose fill insulation and as a light aggregate with concrete where weight is a factor, such as on roof decks.

USE TIP: Use the finest ground forms of perlite for seed starting mixes; if it is not finely ground, it tends to go to the top of a mixture. Coarser grades combine well with peat moss for lightweight container mixtures.

SOIL SULFUR

DESCRIPTION: Granular or powder form of the basic garden chemical, sold in 5- to 80-pound bags.

USE: Acidifying and breaking up (or *flocculating*) the soil, as does gypsum (see page 12–13). It causes clay soil to form small particles, allowing air and water to accumulate and making the soil friable, or better for growing things. The sulfur actually breaks down into sulfuric acid, which reacts with the natural calcium carbonate in the soil to make calcium sulfate, the basic stuff of gypsum.

USE TIP: Use carefully—follow all precautions on the label. It is caustic, and most people are sensitive to sulfur. Its use is the fastest way to lower your pH, but can be toxic if overdone—apply no more than 1 pound per 100 square feet in any one application, and no more often than every eight weeks. Work into the soil and water in thoroughly to avoid burning leaves in the sun.

VERMICULITE

ALSO KNOWN AS: Horticultural vermiculite

DESCRIPTION: A gray or white, extremely lightweight granular substance, with grains about 1/16 inch in diameter (known as no. 3 grade). It is formed when mica chips are heated and expanded to many times their original size. Contains some potassium, magnesium, and calcium, which are slowly released in soil. *Construction grade vermiculite* is larger, and is used for loose fill insulation.

USE: Used in soil mixes to increase the water and fertilizer retention of the mixture, as well as to lighten and open it up. Considered a soil amendment and a rooting medium as well as a mulch (see chapter 2).

USE TIP: It is a very light material, lighter than sand, and is an important additive to container soil mixes. Avoid adding to clayey soils as the clay bonds with the vermiculite, instead of the vermiculite breaking up the clay.

WATER RETENTION CRYSTALS

ALSO KNOWN AS: Water release crystals, root-watering crystals, water retention granules, water-retaining soil additive, hydrogel crystals, super absorbant

POPULAR BRAND NAMES: Agrosoke™, Water Gels, P-4, Water-Grabber®, Aquagel

DESCRIPTION: Fine, translucent white granules that absorb many times their own weight of water (some brands claim five hundred times) in about thirty minutes. They swell up to form moist, sticky beads of gel that then release almost all the absorbed water evenly over a long period, increasing the time between waterings, depending on the brand. A nontoxic, nonbiodegradable, and pH-neutral polymer. Lasts about five years. Sold in packets as small as 2 ounces.

USE: Reduces the frequency of plant watering. Mixed with soil in lawns but especially in containers to maintain an even distribution of moisture; sort of a moisture reservoir that acts like a sponge. Plant roots actually attach themselves to the water-swollen crystals, stimulating the production of feeder roots. The increase in the size of the crystals aerates the soil, too. Minimizes transplant shock and reduces the need for watering by up to 50 percent, according to some manufacturers—one good soaking may last three weeks, for example. Can be mixed into small containers, placed around specific plants, or spread over entire gardens. Helpful if you find it hard to water regularly.

USE TIPS: Add the crystals to the soil after they have absorbed water (or been hydrated) so you can mix in the right amount. A 6:1 ratio of soil to hydrated crystals is typical. Most brands are compatible with fertilizers, but check the label to be sure. Helps prevent overwatering, the scourge of houseplants, to a certain extent. Don't overload a container with this, though, or you will end up holding so much water that you'll create a swamplike condition and rot your plant roots. Test before using regularly—some critics claim these don't work.

BUYING TIP: The amount of water that crystals soak up varies tremendously by brand. Be sure to compare labels. Avoid starch-based versions, which do not last long. Popularity greatly the result of the interest shown in container gardening by otherwise capable young urban professionals who can't seem to take responsibility for even the simplest domestic chores.

WETTING AGENT

DESCRIPTION: Granules or liquid sold in 10- and 50-pound or quart and gallon containers. Larger containers are available to professionals.

USE: Granules are mixed into soil and soilless mixtures (see pages 7–8) used for potting plants. Reduces watering needs and speeds up delivery of fertilizers by improving water penetration and drainage of growing media, especially hard soils. Liquid is more often used by professionals on lawns and flower beds.

Mulches and Grass Seed

ABOUT MULCHES

Mulches are organic and inorganic substances that are placed in planting beds and around plants because they are not only decorative (they are often called *decorative ground cover),* but more importantly because they retain moisture in the bed by shielding it from the drying effects of the sun, help cool the bed during the warm seasons, help insulate it during winter (the general term is *temperature fluctuation protection),* attract earthworms, and above all, help keep down weeds. They also act as an erosion control. Mulches are sold in a wide range of package sizes, measured by weight or volume. Mulching is one of the essential gardening practices in low-maintenance gardening.

Organic Mulches

ABOUT ORGANIC MULCHES

Organic mulches are simply those derived from natural material, meaning that they are able to break down and decompose over a period of time, improving soil structure and enriching it. Many gardeners find organic mulches more attractive and natural-looking (naturally!) than inorganic mulches. They are not permanent, though a breakdown over several years is certainly not hard to deal with. You merely need to add some new mulch annually. Their decomposition slowly adds nitrogen to the soil; however, most organic mulches initially deplete some of the nitrogen in the bed because as organic matter breaks down, the microorganisms that aid in decomposition utilize nitrogen in the initial stages of the process. It is therefore necessary to add extra nitrogen to beds where you are using organic mulches that decompose rapidly, that is, over a year or two. Apply most to a depth of 3 to 4 inches.

Listed here are the most common organic mulches sold nationally; some very good mulches may not be listed here because of their general unavailability. For example, the by-products of regional agricultural crops, such as various nut shells or rice hulls, are often sources of unusual and excellent mulches. These are often available only from local food-processing plants. There are also some good homemade mulches, such as shredded newspaper, which are not sold commercially and of course are not listed here either.

BARK CHIPS AND SHREDDED BARK

ALSO KNOWN AS: Bark nuggets (bark chips)

DESCRIPTION: Pieces of chipped or shredded tree bark. Both items are a pleasant brown color, and texture varies from medium to coarse. Generally three types are available: *hardwood bark, cedar* or *cypress bark,* and *pine bark nuggets* or *mulch,* which may come from any kind of pine. In all cases, these mulches should contain no more than 15 percent wood (as opposed to bark). *Shredded bark* is made of thin, light pieces less than 1½ inches long. *Nuggets* are larger, as big as 3½ inches in diameter, and more decorative. *Mini-nuggets* are ¼ to 1½ inches in diameter. *Pine bark mulch* is made of particles ⅛ to ¼ inch long, though all these terms and sizes vary considerably from manufacturer to manufacturer. In the West, bark is sold as *West Coast large* (or *Western*) and *West Coast medium nuggets;* the fine stuff that is left over from the chopping and screening is called *West Coast pathway,* but in the rest of the country it is called *fines.* Western red cedar, redwood, and driftwood barks are also popular. Domestic cedar bark is reddish brown and has a distinct cedar aroma. Canadian cedar is lighter in color and does not have as much aroma. Cypress mulch has similar characteristics and is light gray. A popular alternative found in the Northeast is *root mulch,* often made of shredded licorice root.

Oddly, *orchid bark* (see page 9) is not made from extremely large orchids but is a mixture of pine and redwood barks, and is used for growing orchids.

USE: Bark is an excellent natural-looking mulch that, depending on the size of the chips, takes about three to four years to break down, longer than most organic mulches. It can be used for flower beds, around trees and shrubs, and even in the vegetable garden. Shredded bark is more efficient as a mulch, but nuggets are more decorative. Root mulch may be used as a soil conditioner to provide humus.

USE TIPS: Use as you would any mulch. A depth of about 3 inches is sufficient to ensure weed control and moisture retention. Hardwood bark lasts longer and is usually heavier, so it doesn't blow away; pine bark nuggets might float away in a heavy rain if the garden is on a slope. Thirteen bags of 2 cubic feet cover about 100 square feet to a depth of 3 inches. Barks are often placed over a layer of plastic sheeting, called *bark base mulch,* to keep it from decomposing into the soil.

BUYING TIPS: Bark is usually easy to find at most garden centers, selling for around $2 per cubic foot. Your local parks department may also offer shredded bark as a public service, though you must check with them as to whether any diseased trees of the same species as yours were shredded into the mulch, in which case, avoid their mulch like the plague. Of course, you can get bark directly from sawmills if you live near a cooperative one. Cedar bark is more expensive but lasts longer (it resists both insects and rot) and is better for the garden, though it tends to acidify the soil. Shredded cypress bark lasts the longest, as it is basically inert. Root mulch is usually expensive.

BUCKWHEAT HULLS

DESCRIPTION: A fine-textured, dark brown mulch that comes from the hulls of buckwheat. Resembles cocoa shells (see next entry) in appearance, but is much lighter.

USE: An attractive, natural-looking mulch well suited for any area of the garden or on houseplant pots. It is particularly pleasing in a perennial border.

USE TIP: Because they are so light, buckwheat hulls will blow away if placed in exposed, windy areas. They will stay in place after aging a bit and if they are kept well wet down. Put down about 2 inches and add new mulch after two or three years, when it begins to break down.

BUYING TIP: Buckwheat hulls, like many organic mulches, are cheaper where buckwheat grows. They are more expensive than cocoa bean hulls and tend to blow away more, but if you like the look, they are well worth the extra cost.

COCOA SHELLS

ALSO KNOWN AS: Cocoa bean hulls, cocoa hulls, cocoa mulch, cocoa shell mulch

DESCRIPTION: Crushed dark brown hulls of the cocoa bean. They have a pleasant texture composed of particles sized ¼ to ½ inch. If they are fresh, they smell like chocolate when they are first put down, but unfortunately soon lose this delightful fragrance. Usually sold in large, 3– or 4–cubic foot bags.

USE: An attractive mulch for almost any area of the garden. The dark brown color is a natural complement to most plant material. Breaks down after a couple years, adding nutrients at the grade of about 2.5-1-3 (see page 48 for an explanation of *grade).

USE TIPS: When first put down it may be necessary to add extra nitrogen to the soil to compensate for the nitrogen taken out in the initial stages of decomposition. Very good for rose beds. Don't expect it to stay put in windy areas—it is too light. Rinse off any mold that appears in the process of decomposition. Apply to a depth of 3 to 4 inches for best results.

BUYING TIPS: In areas of the country where there are chocolate factories cocoa hulls are less expensive and readily available, sometimes for free directly from a candy factory. In other areas they may be more expensive, if available at all, costing as much as $3.50 a cubic foot, which makes them one of the more expensive organic mulches.

PEAT MOSS

Though this is often used as a mulch, it is more commonly and more effectively used as a soil conditioner. See its entry on pages 16–18.

SALT HAY

DESCRIPTION: Dried salt marsh grasses, light brown or tan in color and thin textured. Available in bale form in the coastal parts of the country, though it is sometimes sold in other areas at a higher cost.

USE: An all-purpose organic mulch. Like straw (see next entry), it is popular as a winter mulch for protecting tender perennials and bulbs.

USE TIP: Salt hay is particularly good for winter protection of vegetable and flower gardens because, unlike straw, if properly stored, it does not contain any seed (that is, any that would germinate in your garden—they need salt water to germinate). Salt hay breaks down during one growing season and needs to be replaced each year, although if it is in good shape, it can be stored for a season. Put it down to a thickness of about 4 inches for good weed control. Watch out for wind and fire, both of which are enemies of this mulch.

BUYING TIP: Prices fluctuate from year to year, but it is usually more expensive than plain straw. The fact that it is seed-free makes it a better buy than straw.

STRAW

DESCRIPTION: Straw, a long, dry grass, is tan to yellow in color and differs from hay in that it is composed of the stems of grain crops, whereas hay contains both stems and leaves. Much of the straw sold for mulches comes in rectangular cubic bales weighing from 30 to 50 pounds a bale.

USE: Straw is an attractive and useful mulch for most areas of the garden, but it is commonly used in the vegetable garden or even on garden paths to keep down weeds. Most popular as a winter mulch for its insulation quality.

USE TIP: Straw tends to blow around a lot and is very flammable when dry. Don't use it or store it where a careless smoker might drop a cigarette or you might see your garden go up in flames. As straw comes from the stems of grain crops, grain seed is often present. These can germinate and become weeds; oat straw is particularly notorious for its seed content. Because of this, straw is not a highly recommended mulch for repeated use, but will do in a pinch, or when price is the biggest problem.

Breaks down in one season. Depth of application varies from a light scattering over newly seeded lawns or construction sites to 6 inches on walks (it packs down nicely).

BUYING TIP: Straw is one of the least expensive organic mulches. It sells for under fifty cents a cubic foot. Make sure it is *weed-free*.

WOOD CHIPS

DESCRIPTION: Small, odd-shaped pieces of wood created when tree limbs are chipped and shredded. They form a coarse-textured mulch that is white, yellow, and brown, darkening to gray and brown as it ages. It may be colored and sold in small bags for indoor use; it is bagged or sold in bulk for outdoor use.

USE: Wood chips are a good mulch for weed control on path areas of a garden. They can be used around plants, but their texture is often too coarse for the flower bed or the vegetable garden. They are better suited for trees and shrubs than for regular plants. Wood chips break down after about three to six years, making them one of the longest-lasting mulches.

USE TIPS: Be sure that you are getting wood chips that have aged at least a few months. Fresh wood chips that are compacted may actually absorb nitrogen and heat up as they oxidize, damaging your plants. You can mix them with fertilizer in storage to avoid this. Additional chips can be added every few years. Try to verify that no diseased trees were included in the chipping. Apply at least 3 inches deep. Your garden will require additional nitrogen as this mulch decomposes.

BUYING TIPS: Wood chips can be purchased for as little as fifty cents a cubic foot. They can also be purchased or had for free from many municipal parks throughout the country that shred tree limbs as part of a normal pruning and maintenance program. They are often given free to community gardening programs and projects in large cities.

Inorganic Mulches

ABOUT INORGANIC MULCHES

Inorganic mulches are those that are not derived from living organisms. Being inorganic, they do not break down or decompose. This can be an advantage because they do not have to be replaced: They are as long-lasting as any landscape accessory. They do not, however, have the more natural appearance of organic mulches, and they add no nitrogen to the soil as organic ones eventually do. They also get "dirty" over time, if that is a concern from a decorative point of view.

FIBERGLASS BATTING OR MAT

ALSO KNOWN AS: Weed control mat, erosion preventer, erosion cloth, geotextile

DESCRIPTION: Woven fiberglass matting the color of which varies from manufacturer to manufacturer. Sold in sheets or rolls.

USE: Placed in a bed or on a border. Holes for plants can be cut in them. Great for insulation and temperature control, if that is an important concern.

USE TIP: It is easy to cover a fiberglass mat with an attractive organic mulch like bark or straw. If it is not porous, use a soaker hose underneath it to irrigate your plants.

BUYING TIP: Fiberglass mats sell for around $1.25 to $1.50 a square yard.

LANDSCAPE FABRIC

ALSO KNOWN AS: Weed-blocking fabric, weed mat, ground cover

POPULAR BRAND NAME: Typar®

DESCRIPTION: A number of porous woven or nonwoven, spun-bonded permeable sheet products made from plastics and natural, and inorganic fibers that come in colors including white, off-white, redwood, brown, and black, and range in size from 3 to 6 feet wide by 15 to 50 feet long. Larger sizes are available to professionals. Biodegradable versions are available, too, made of cloth or peat paper. Available with various degrees of porosity.

USE: Landscape fabrics allow moisture and water to penetrate through to the plants, but prevent weeds from growing. Not considered suitable for landscaped gardens (unless covered with a thin layer of organic or decorative stone mulches as they are very unnatural looking, but quite useful in a vegetable garden, where they also warm up the soil for early-season planting. Cut holes for plants to grow through. Open-weave fabric is also useful for covering newly seeded lawns to keep the seed from washing or blowing away, and to encourage germination, if not treated with weed preventative chemicals.

USE TIP: Some fabric is made from fibers (such as peat moss and recycled paper) that break down—a good product for annual use in a vegetable garden, as it does not have to be removed but can be plowed into the field at the end of the season.

BUYING TIP: This is usually an expensive product: A roll 3 by 100 feet might sell for around $60.

POLYETHYLENE SHEETING

ALSO KNOWN AS: Black polyethylene, black plastic mulch, black poly sheeting weed shield, weed barrier

DESCRIPTION: Rolls of black plastic, usually 3 or 6 feet wide and 25 to 100 feet long, although it can be found in sheets 40 feet wide by 100 feet long; commercial growers use rolls 3 and 4 feet wide by 1,000 feet long. Comes in thickness ranging from 1.5 to 6 mil; for comparison, a sturdy garbage bag is about 3 mil thick (a mil is one-thousandth of an inch); 4 mil is considered average strong sheeting, while 6 mil is used under stone mulches. Some brands have millions of microscopic holes that allow water to penetrate while still preventing weeds from growing.

USE: A good mulch for vegetable gardens, but not suited for landscape mulching, though it is often placed under sand and brick patios to prevent weeds from growing. Also used under decks and concrete for the same reason. Because of its color, it absorbs the sun and helps warm up a vegetable bed and speeds up seed germination. This is particularly useful for plants that need warm soil when they begin growth. Cut holes in the plastic for the plants to grow through.

USE TIP: If you are using solid plastic sheet, water cannot penetrate, so you must get water underneath by using a soaker hose (see chapter 8) or other means of irrigation. Although it can be placed under a decorative mulch, it may eventually show through.

BUYING TIP: Black plastic is a good vegetable crop mulch and is not very expensive at twenty-nine cents a square yard.

STONE MULCHES

ALSO KNOWN AS: Landscape chips, landscape stone, garden stone, decorative stone mulch

DESCRIPTION: Pebbled, chipped, or crushed rock of varying sizes, shapes, and colors. Pebbles may be sorted into colors as different as pink, yellow, and brown.

TYPES: *Brick nuggets:* Deep red pieces of brick in three sizes, ¼ to 1½ inches across.

Granite chips: Chips of granite, red or black in color. As with all stone mulches, the texture varies according to "grind."

Limestone chips: White stone chips of varying size and texture.

Marble chips: Usually white, sometimes red or black chips varying in size from pea-sized to 3 to 4 inches in diameter. Texture varies, depending on how the stone is chipped.

River gravel (also known as *river pebbles):* White or off-white rounded pebbles available in different textures.

Volcanic rock (also known as *lava rock* or *volcanic stone):* A red or black rock mulch created when volcanic rock is chipped into different-sized particles. One-third the weight of regular stone products.

USE: Low-maintenance mulch. Often seen in commercial landscaping around fast-food places, industrial buildings, and shopping malls, but generally not around homes where gardeners are not willing to make the trade-off of convenience versus aesthetics: This type of mulch does not rot, decompose, harbor termites or other insects, burn, fade, or erode—but it is not natural. Some people find the starkness of white stone mulch pleasing in contrast to the colors of their plants, even though it is an unnatural pairing.

USE TIPS: Use as you would any mulch, applying to a depth of about 1 to 3 inches. For extra weed control, chips can be placed over landscape fabric or a polyethylene sheeting mulch (see pages 27–29). Marble chip mulch raises the pH slightly, and therefore should be avoided with shallow-rooted, acid-loving plants such as azaleas. Lightweight volcanic rock is likely to float off slopes in rainstorms.

BUYING TIPS:

Granite chips: Like other stone mulches, this is more available in areas of the country where the stone is found naturally. Prices vary according to availability. Granite chips are generally among the more expensive mulches, going for around $4 per cubic foot.

Limestone chips: Considerably cheaper than marble chips. Selling for around $1.50 per cubic foot, it is one of the less expensive inorganic mulches, especially in areas of the country where it is mined.

Marble chips: One of the most expensive mulches, retailing at around $7 a cubic foot.

River gravel: A moderately priced inorganic mulch selling for around $2 per cubic foot.

Volcanic rock: Where it can be found, volcanic rock is a moderately priced inorganic mulch, retailing for about $2 per cubic foot. Easier to handle in quantity, due to its lighter weight.

Grass Seed and Sod

ABOUT GRASS SEED

Purchasing the right seed for your site is one of the most important steps in seeding and reseeding lawns. To help you make an informed decision about which grass seed to buy, a number of factors have to be considered, but they are not too complicated. Typical among them are

- How sunny or how shady is your site?
- How much time do you have to spend maintaining your lawn? Some grasses and combinations of grasses demand more care and maintenance than others.
- How much traffic will your lawn encounter? Will children be playing on it?

- How much water is available and how often will you be able to water the lawn?
- How quick-growing does the grass need to be? Is it being planted on a slope?
- What climatic zone you are in—do you need a *Southern, (warm-season)* or *Northern (cool-season)* grass?

There is a strong tradition in America of having a beautifully maintained lawn, and that tradition is not about to die; a "perfect," uniformly green lawn remains a basic element of suburban life. It is, however, likely to evolve somewhat as its high costs—environmental, monetary, and labor—become unacceptable. In some parts of the country, water alone is a major cost. More and more homeowners are choosing to conserve water by using less water-intensive landscaping than lawns, such as a plan that emphasizes trees and shrubs.

Most people cannot afford to be so picky about lawns resembling perfectly manicured outdoor carpets as professional "turf managers" who care for golf courses and the like. After all, the model for perfect lawns is British, and few places in this country have the ideal growing conditions that the British do (indeed, grass is native to few of our settled areas), let alone the years it took for them to get their lawns going right. Just pouring chemicals and other products onto the ground every weekend does not make a perfect lawn. A little thought and planning can solve problems better than lots of money and products, and a beautiful lawn can be had if the idea that it must be absolutely perfect is put aside.

Today's sensible approach to lawns includes such notions as:
- A well-prepared and maintained site will produce a healthy lawn more able to resist diseases, pests, and weeds without the need for reliance on natural or synthetic chemicals.
- Chemical herbicides are not the only way to a weed-free lawn (and the possible threat to the environment of herbicide abuse makes a few weeds seem quite tolerable). Ninety percent of all weeds can be controlled through proper mowing and fertilization, according to some experts.
- Fertilizing twice a season will produce an acceptable turf cover, though some synthetic fertilizer manufacturers still recommend four or more feedings a year.
- The choice of the right grass seed and mixtures to fit the site has as much to do with how well the lawn will grow as anything else.
- We should break the typical American habit of overdependence on chemicals, especially new "convenience" blends that may duplicate others or include unnecessary products.

Synthetic chemicals should be used for what they do best: curing specific problems. Nontoxic methods should be explored and adopted wherever possible.

The best time to reseed or seed a lawn of cool-season grasses in the North is the early fall. This allows the grass to establish a good root system before winter. In the South, late spring is best. Look for the grass seed mixtures long before you are ready to plant to assure yourself that you will be able to get just what you want. Settling for whatever is available after the prime planting season will result in a poorer lawn that needs much more work.

You can't just throw the seed onto the ground and expect it to grow well. Soil preparation for a new or renovated lawn involves a fair amount of work. The soil should be tilled to a depth of 3 to 6 inches. All rocks, weeds, and old grass clumps should be removed. Hard soil should be opened up by incorporating peat moss, humus, and fertilizers as needed. Finally, the area should be leveled, rolled, and raked. After seeding according to directions, the lawn should be kept moist for the first few weeks and covered with a light, biodegradable lawn netting (see pages 283–84) or a thin layer of salt hay to protect the seeds a bit from birds, wind, rain, and excessive sun.

ABOUT SEED TYPES AND MIXTURES

In the North, many manufacturers offer premixed seed specifically developed for certain types of lawns, or the garden center may have its own mixture, or you can mix your own from the single types available. It is always important to know the types and amounts of seed in the mix to determine if you are really getting what you need. To do this, you need to know a little about the types of grass you can grow and what situations they are suited for, which is what this chapter is about.

Usually the *Northern,* or *cool-season,* mixes contain the ever-popular, hard-wearing Kentucky bluegrass, some turf-type fast-germinating, narrowleaf perennial ryegrasses (as opposed to the common broadleaf type), and some fine fescue. The actual mix depends entirely on the part of the country where it is sold and, of course, on your taste, budget, and needs. *Southern,* or *warm-season,* grasses are generally not mixtures but rather one single type of grass, most of which are sold as sod, plugs, or sprigs (individual plants) instead of seed.

Some mixtures are described in general terms, such as *play* (for high traffic), *sun* (for more than four hours of sun daily), *shade* (for less sun), and *sun/shade* (for the typical mix of areas). The local garden center quality mixture is sometimes a good bet, if the ingredients are listed so you can judge for yourself.

Should you go with one variety of grass or a mixture of several? Particularly in the North, if you use just one variety of seed for your lawn (monoculture), you may be courting disaster. Lawns of a single variety may be badly injured by diseases that affect that variety, whereas lawns that contain a blend of types of grasses are more likely to have only some affected by the disease while the others survive. Nothing is sadder than a completely browned-off and dead lawn of a single type of grass, while surrounding lawns of mixed types survive! A mixture of grasses also produces a lawn with a more interesting texture than the single-variety lawns. Southern grasses are unfortunately not usually seeded (sod is laid down), nor are they compatible aesthetically in mixes.

As already mentioned, it's important to know what you're getting when you buy grass seed. The label on a mixture lists the types of *grass seed, crop seed, inert matter,* and *weed seed.* You want the lowest levels of the latter three items, of course, no more than 1 percent of each (in fact, there should be no crop seed or, at most, a few tenths of a percent). Note the percentages of grass seed types and see if that meshes with your needs and desires. This chapter should help you decide what's best, or check with your local Cooperative Extension for help (appendix C). The *percentage of seed germination* should be 80 to 90 percent and the seed should have been tested *during the year of purchase.* The state of origin should not affect its growth. All of this information should be on the label.

The listing of the types of grass seed can be a little confusing, though the following pages should help explain this. *Cultivars* (or *cultivated varieties* or *named varieties* or *proprietary types)* and *hybrids* (types that are the result of crossing or breeding plants of different species or varieties to respond to needs, ranging from pure aesthetics to better disease and insect resistance) are specific types of grass that tend to perform well; most are new and improved types, and new ones are constantly being added to the market. Look for these when buying grass seed. There are over three hundred of them now, biologically different (they are even patented or registered by the developers—the symbol is *PVP,* for Plant Variety Protection), but only some of the essentially similar and more commonly found ones are listed in this chapter as an example. There are many more that are perfectly fine but that are not listed.

Manufacturers may swear by one or another variety, but the differences are subtle and the ultimate performance of all grass seed is influenced by weather, fertilizer, watering, and soil to a great extent. No miracles should be claimed by the manufacturers. Be leery of any that do. Price generally reflects quality, and national brands are dependable.

Most of the grass seed in a mix should be of the fine-textured type, and should be cultivars rather than "unnamed" or "common" types. For example, "Adelphi Kentucky bluegrass" is better than "Kentucky bluegrass." Much like wine, the generic types are not as good nor as expensive as the ones with more specifics on the labels—region, year, etc. The common, unnamed variety is often listed as "variety not stated." This is the kind of seed labeled "red fescue" or "perennial ryegrass." Try to find named seed for a more vigorous, disease-resistant, and longer-lasting quality lawn. Unnamed varieties are better for a special use such as a quick cover crop to prevent erosion or mud or to solve a particular overwintering problem. The more named seed in the mixture, the better the buy.

As to which specific cultivar is best for you, get all the advice you can, experiment, and keep in mind that almost any of the new ones are bound to do better. The fact that they are named is sufficient to set them a cut above the unnamed kind and to make them worth a little bit more in price.

State land grant universities and the U.S. Department of Agriculture evaluate turf grass types by characteristic and by overall performance on a state-by-state basis, providing yet another way to decide which type is best for you. Check with your Cooperative Extension (see appendix C) for more information. With gene transplants entering the picture, we may yet find the "perfect" grass seed—but don't hold your breath.

SOD

DESCRIPTION: Grass sheets, like pieces of a grass rug, typically 2 by 4 feet and 2 to 4 inches thick (including the grass), that have formed a thick root mass. Type of grass depends on where grown and is the choice of the supplier.

USE: Provides an instant lawn on well-prepared sites. Sod is particularly useful on sloping sites as erosion control, where the time that grass takes to grow from seed is a problem.

USE TIPS: Best installed in the spring through early fall, provided there is ample water. Sod should not be laid if the ground is too wet to be prepared correctly, but it must be moist soil. Soil preparation for sodding is similar to that for seeding. Sod is laid down in a pattern that looks like brickwork; this staggering ensures that horizontal seams do not meet. The strips are laid perpendicular to a slope. If installed properly, seams do not show and the sod appears to be one continuous lawn.

Most sod contains grasses that do well in the sun and not so well in shade. A few sod growers do provide a shade-tolerant type, but it will probably have to be specially ordered by your garden center.

BUYING TIPS: Sodding is initially more expensive than seeding, but offers the possibility of instant gratification for those who can pay for it or need it for erosion control. After all, it is essentially an instant lawn. Most sod sold in garden centers does not have a label that tells you what grasses are in it. *Ask!* If your garden center cannot provide this information, it is best to go somewhere else. Much of the sod sold in the North today contains Kentucky bluegrass or blends, which are better than those that contain only one type. Using a sod that contains a blend is wise as each variety has its own strengths, with some able to resist diseases and pests better than others. On the other hand, Southern grasses are sold in the South unmixed, such as Bermudagrass or St. Augustinegrass. In either case look for thin-cut sod, which roots faster. Roots and soil should be ½ inch thick. Three- to 4-inch thick-cut sod can tear easily because of the weight and is harder to handle.

Northern Grasses

ABOUT NORTHERN GRASSES

The following cool-season grasses grow well in the Northern climates and at higher altitudes in the South. Wherever there is a winter snow, they should thrive, growing especially vigorously in the spring and fall.

COLONIAL BENTGRASS

BOTANICAL NAME: *Agrostis tenuis*

SAMPLE AVAILABLE CULTIVARS: 'Exeter,' 'Highland'

DESCRIPTION: Bentgrasses are finer in texture than Kentucky bluegrasses and require more care; they are therefore more likely to succumb to disease. These grasses usually spread by rhizomes (a below-ground-level spreading branch) and have thin, erect blades.

USE: A grass that does well in shade and sun and in acid soils that won't support other grasses; mixes well with fine fescues. Bentgrass helps produce a thick, rich lawn in areas of the country that are seasonally moist, such as the Northwest and Northeast coastal regions, and some areas around the Great Lakes. Fares well in inland New England, too. Avoid using in hotter, drier areas.

USE TIP: Colonial bentgrass needs frequent mowing to a height of ¾ to 1 inch, which often means mowing twice a week in areas where it grows rapidly.

CREEPING BENTGRASS

BOTANICAL NAME: *Agrostis palustris*

SAMPLE AVAILABLE CULTIVARS: 'Emerald,' 'Penncross,' 'Prominent'

DESCRIPTION: Creeping bentgrass is a beautiful fine grass that spreads naturally by lateral stolons to produce a thick, green carpet. *Creeping* is a term used interchangeably with *spreading*.

USE: This is the incredible stuff you find on putting and bowling greens, mowed to as short as ¼ inch—or even less.

USE TIP: These grasses need lots of moisture, fertile soils, and much attention. Not recommended for homeowners, unless your home is a country club and you have (or are) a full-time groundskeeper.

BUYING TIP: Avoid any mix containing this seed for the reasons stated earlier, though this is unlikely to be found in a typical seed mixture.

FINE FESCUE

SAMPLE AVAILABLE CULTIVARS:
> *Red type:* 'Boreal,' 'Dawson Red,' 'Flyer,' 'Fortress,' 'Pennlawn,' 'Ruby'
> *Chewings type:* 'Agram,' 'Banner,' 'Cascade,' 'Highlight,' 'Jamestown,' 'Koket,' 'Shadow'

Hard type: 'Aurora,' 'Biljart,' 'C-26,' 'Reliant,' 'Scaldis,' 'SR 3000,' 'Waldina'

DESCRIPTION: Thin-leaved and olive to dark green in color, with a thinner and finer blade than that of bluegrass. Often found in mixtures with bluegrass because it is particularly suited to Northern areas of the country and faster to establish itself.

TYPES: *Red fescue (Festuca rubra*—also known as *spreading* or *creeping red fescue):* Though it spreads slowly (by rhizomes, a sort of swollen underground stem), it establishes itself quickly in the first season and is therefore often mixed with slow-to-establish bluegrass.

Chewings fescue (Festuca rubra 'Commutata'): Tends to form dense clumps; named after the man who developed it, a Mr. Chewings of New Zealand. Can be cut shorter than red.

Hard fescue (Festuca longifolia or var. *duriuscula):* Developed for an increased tolerance to heat and drought.

Sheep fescue (Festuca ovina): Very clumpy. Better used as an ornamental border plant than for turf. Usually very blue. Not commonly available.

USE: Most often found in mixtures with other grass seed. Grows under drier and shadier conditions than many other grasses—hardier in general than bluegrasses. Fine fescues are tough grasses that wear well in traffic areas.

USE TIPS: Give this grass sun or dry shade and it does well even in poor soil. Does not require as much nitrogen as bluegrass and can be mown to a minimum height of 1½ inches, though 2 inches is better for the health of the grass in the heat of the summer.

BUYING TIPS: Buy in a mix with other grasses rather than alone. The best shade grass. The varieties 'Highlight' and 'Jamestown' are good Chewings types for thick lawns.

KENTUCKY BLUEGRASS

BOTANICAL NAME: *Poa pratensis*

SAMPLE AVAILABLE CULTIVARS: 'Abbey,' 'Adelphi,' 'America,' 'Arboretum,' 'Baron,' 'Bensun,' 'Birka,' 'Bonnieblue,' 'Bristol,' 'Chateau,' 'Classic,' 'Delta,' 'Derby,' 'Eclipse,' 'Enmundi,' 'Estate,' 'Flyking,' 'Freedom,' 'Glade,' 'Gnome,' 'Huntsville,' 'Liberty,' 'Majesti,' 'Merion' (developed from a single plant found on the course of the Merion Golf Club in Ardmore, Pa.), 'Merit,' 'Monopoly,' 'Nassau,' 'Nugget,' 'Plush,' 'Ram I,' 'Rugby,' 'Sydsport,' 'Touchdown,' 'Vantage,' 'Vieta,' 'Windsor'

DESCRIPTION: An attractive, fine-textured, dark green, perennial grass. It is often in sod because it spreads from rhizomes (underground stems) to form a thick carpet. Over eighty cultivars have been developed, making this one of the most common and popular grass seeds. Some are listed here; researchers continue to develop better ones constantly.

USE: Kentucky bluegrass seed produces a thick, good-looking lawn. It is your basic Northern grass. In order for it to be able to compete with weeds and withstand heavy traffic or play, and because it takes a while for bluegrass to establish itself, it is often mixed with *fine fescues* or *perennial ryegrasses* (see preceding and next entries, respectively), which establish themselves much faster and are a little hardier or shade-tolerant. Does best when mowed to a height of at least 1 ½ inches (higher in shady areas) and needs a fair amount of feeding, moisture, and light, though types vary in their needs. 'Glade,' 'Bensun,' and 'Eclipse' are excellent performers in shade. 'Adelphi' is one of the most popular types.

USE TIPS: Do not overwater during the hotter months. Mow grass often so that it does not grow more than 2 to 3 inches in height, but without cutting more than one-third of the length of the blades. Grows best in sun, but some varieties tolerate shade better than others.

BUYING TIPS: Select varieties and blends that include disease-resistant cultivars. Specialized publications will tell you which diseases each grass resists. Avoid mixes of bluegrass and turf-type tall fescues, as the fescues tend to overwhelm the bluegrass.

PERENNIAL RYEGRASS

ALSO KNOWN AS: Turf-type perennial ryegrass

BOTANICAL NAME: *Lolium perenne*

SAMPLE AVAILABLE CULTIVARS: 'All*Star,' 'Applause,' 'Blazer,' 'Citation,' 'Delray,' 'Derby,' 'Diplomat,' 'Fiesta,' 'Gator,' 'Loretta,' 'Manhattan II' (developed from a single plant found in New York City's Central Park), 'NK-200,' 'Omega,' 'Ovation,'

'Pennant,' 'Pennfine,' 'Prestige,' 'Regal,' 'SR4000,' 'Tara,' 'York-town II'

USE: Provides quick cover and is tough and clean-mowing during the summer (it will cut well only with a very sharp mower blade during the late spring). However, it often does not come back or does not do well the second year after it is planted in locations with severe winter cold and little snow cover. Found in mixtures because it provides coverage while the slower-germinating spreading grasses fill in, and it looks good, to boot.

USE TIPS: Ryegrass needs the same care as Kentucky bluegrass (see preceding entry) and should be mown as frequently. Grows best in full sun with plenty of water. Mow to 1 to 2 inches.

BUYING TIPS: When mixing or buying in a mix with bluegrass and fine fescue, make sure there is no more than about 20 percent ryegrass in the mixture. Used in higher percentages, the ryegrass crowds out the slower-growing grasses. Look for varieties that are new *turf-types* with endophytes (insect resistance). 'All*Star,' 'Manhattan,' and 'Pennfine' are good choices. Avoid annual or Italian ryegrasses.

REDTOP

BOTANICAL NAME: *Agrostis alba*

DESCRIPTION: A coarse grass that forms a thin turf.

USE: Primarily as an erosion control or cover grass along highways and open lands. Not a permanent grass, and too thin and unattractive for use as a lawn.

USE TIPS: Redtop requires minimum care and maintenance, and does well in wet, cool sites. Does not require much fertilizer and grows in poorly drained soils. Moisture is its primary requirement.

BUYING TIP: Avoid mixes with redtop in them. It is not at all suited to use as a lawn grass, though it was once found in grass mixes.

ROUGH BLUEGRASS

BOTANICAL NAME: *Poa trivialis*

SAMPLE AVAILABLE CULTIVAR: 'Sabre'

DESCRIPTION: Prostrate (meaning it lies down) light green grass, similar to the bentgrasses. It spreads by surface stolons, but is not a very hardy grass.

USE: Does well in moist, cool shade but is not as drought-resistant as other grasses as it is shallow-rooted.

USE TIPS: Does not grow well in sun or under dry conditions. 'Sabre' is a cultivar that grows well in the North; in the South it is used as a winter grass to overseed lawns after Bermudagrasses go dormant during the winter season. Mow to 1 to 2 inches.

BUYING TIP: Buy this grass seed in shade mixtures with fine fescues and other seed.

TALL FESCUE

BOTANICAL NAME: *Festuca arundinacea*

SAMPLE AVAILABLE CULTIVARS: 'Arid,' 'Bonanza,' 'Carefree,' 'Chesapeake,' 'Falcon,' 'Galway,' 'Houndog,' 'Kentucky,' 'Mustang,' 'Rebel II,' 'Tempo,' 'Titan,' 'Trident'

DESCRIPTION: A coarse-textured bunchgrass (one that does not spread), but once established, its deep roots allow it to be persistent. Relatively disease-, wear-, heat-, shade-, and drought-tolerant. Good winter recovery and spring green-up. New cultivars, known as *turf-type tall fescues,* have much finer texture owing to their thinner leaves.

USE: Particularly suited to difficult sites in the central United States between Northern and Southern regions—transition areas. It can be used in areas that get little attention, as it does well in poor soils without needing maintenance, and is often used wherever bluegrass or the fine fescues have failed. Often considered a weed in Northern areas where it is difficult to remove from bluegrass lawns. It does, however, prove useful in areas where nothing else grows well. If it is found in a mixture with Kentucky bluegrass, it should be the main component— over 90 percent. Developed for use in the transition zones that fall between the Northern and Southern areas of the United States.

USE TIPS: Tall fescue requires basic care, though it keeps its color better if fertilized in the spring and fall. Mow 2 to 3 inches high.

BUYING TIP: In a major exception to the rule, this is not good to have in a seed mix, especially if appearance is important to you. It doesn't spread, but it does persist. Use it alone, and use only improved varieties.

Southern Grasses

ABOUT SOUTHERN GRASSES

Most of the following warm-season grasses will grow only in the South, though some can be grown in the so-called transition areas at the lower altitudes. Therefore most will be found for sale only in the South. Also, unlike the Northern grasses, these are not aesthetically compatible and thus are used alone and not in mixtures. They are, however, more resistant to weeds, heat, and drought than Northern grasses. Generally only the common types are available as seed—all, except Bahiagrass,* are propagated vegetatively, so they must be planted as sod, plugs (small clumps of sod), or sprigs (individual grass plants).

BAHIAGRASS

ALSO KNOWN AS: Bahia grass

BOTANICAL NAME: *Paspalum notatum*

SAMPLE AVAILABLE CULTIVARS: 'Paraguay,' 'Pensacola,' 'Wilmington'

DESCRIPTION: An easy-care, coarse-textured grass. Considered a weed if mixed with other grasses. Has unattractive seed heads. Commonly available as seed.

USE: Bahiagrass is an inexpensive, low-density, coarse grass that grows well in the South, especially along the Gulf Coast. A few varieties can grow in cooler regions where the temperatures get as low as 5° F. Bahiagrass grows in poor conditions, such as sandy soils, where little else will grow. Drought-tolerant.

USE TIPS: This is a relatively low-maintenance grass. It tolerates some neglect and poor conditions, but of course looks better if

---

*Throughout the industry, on packages and in books and magazines, these grasses are written as one word, i.e. Bahiagrass. Unfortunately, the correct form according to Webster's is to use two words, i.e. Bahia Grass. Because this is a guide to what you find in stores, and because at least one Northern grass is written as one word in Webster's (Bluegrass), they are listed here as used, that is, one word. Both forms are acceptable.

at least some care is given. Mow high, between 2 and 3 inches. Needs frequent mowing.

BUYING TIP: Bahiagrass in a mix with fine fescue produces a quick cover, but the fine fescue dies out as the Bahiagrass fills in.

BERMUDAGRASS

ALSO KNOWN AS: Common Bermudagrass

BOTANICAL NAME: *Cynodon dactylon*

SAMPLE AVAILABLE CULTIVARS: 'Cheyenne,' 'Guymon,' 'Midiron,' 'Sahara,' 'Sunturf,' 'Tifton,' 'Tifgreen' ('Tifton 328'), 'Tiflawn' ('Tifton 57'), 'Tifway' ('Tifton 419'), 'Tufcote,' 'U-3,' 'Vamont'

DESCRIPTION: Medium- to fine-textured grass with dark green color. Some types are sterile hybrids that must be planted as sod, plugs, or sprigs—they do not come as seed. The first three listed above are the newest, improved seeded types.

USE: Easy-to-grow, wear-resistant grass that responds well to good care in areas where the temperature remains high. Common seeded types are found in mixtures for Southern or warmer areas of the country, intended for lawns as well as golf courses. The best sportsfield turf.

USE TIPS: Unlike Bahiagrass (see preceding entry), some Bermudagrasses demand much attention. They generally require much fertilizing to look good, though some varieties are hardier than others. They only stay green where the temperature is above 55° F. They turn brown at the first frost and remain so until the return of summer. Lawns in frost areas must be winterseeded or overseeded with cool-season grasses (such as perennial ryegrass) to keep weeds from invading. Mow to ⅔ to 1¼ inches.

BUYING TIP: Often included in mixes sold in hospitable areas. Because it is a high-maintenance grass, buy only mixtures with a lower percentage of Bermudagrass seed.

ST. AUGUSTINEGRASS

BOTANICAL NAME: *Stenotaphrum secundatum*

SAMPLE AVAILABLE CULTIVARS: 'Bitter Blue,' 'Floralawn,' 'Flora-tam,' 'Floratine,' 'Raleigh'

DESCRIPTION: Attractive, wide-leaved, rapid-spreading, shade-tolerant, medium green grass with flat-tipped leaves. The leaves are in bunches and give the lawn a thick appearance. Not available in seed form—it must be planted from sod, plugs, or sprigs.

USE: One of the most widely used Southern grasses. Grows well in shade and sun, and tolerates salty soils. It is often used in sod or sold in small clumps (plugs) to be set out in a grid pattern to fill in, as this grass spreads rapidly.

USE TIPS: Though normally it should be relatively easy to care for, St. Augustinegrass has been affected by several severe diseases and pests in the last few years. Unfortunately, these problems require high chemical maintenance, and if it were not for these plagues St. Augustinegrass would be easier to grow. Also needs lots of water. Does best in neutral to alkaline soils. Mow to 1½ to 2 inches.

BUYING TIP: A very good grass for Southern lawns, but given the problems recently with pests and diseases, try to buy more resistant varieties. Check with your local Cooperative Extension agent (see appendix C) for advice.

ZOYSIAGRASS

ALSO KNOWN AS: Japanese carpet grass

BOTANICAL NAMES: *Zoysia japonica, Z. matrella, Z. tenuifolia*

SAMPLE AVAILABLE CULTIVARS: 'Belair,' 'El Toro,' 'Flawn,' 'Meyer,' 'Midwestern' (all *Z. japonica)* and 'Emerald' (a cross between *Z. japonica* and *Z. tenuifolia)*

DESCRIPTION: The thickest and most attractive of the Southern turf grasses. Its most distinguishing characteristic, unfortunately, is that it turns brown during its long off-season. Certain varieties have been developed that will grow in the Midwest and other areas of the country. Similar in appearance to Bermudagrass. Very slow to establish—it may take up to four years to form a lawn. *Z. japonica,* also called *Meyer zoysia,* is the most common improved species, and has medium width leaves. *Z. matrella* has the widest leaves (and is very rarely available) and *Z. tenuifolia* has the finest. Common seed is available in limited quantity; most is sold as sod, plugs, or sprigs.

USE: Used in Southern lawn mixtures where density is desired, mixed in with a good companion cover grass such as turf-type tall fescues. It grows well in sun but not as well in shade. Thickest and most resilient cover of all grasses. Best used in transition zones.

USE TIPS: Though not as high-maintenance as Bermudagrass, zoysiagrass is slow to germinate and mature. It does not recover as well as Bermudagrass does against pests or damage by soil compaction. It should be mixed with other grasses to provide a quick cover and crowd out weeds. You may need a heavy-duty mower to cut this. Mow to a height of 1 to 2 inches. Avoid planting in poorly drained, moist areas. Remove thatch regularly.

BUYING TIP: Zoysiagrass seed is good in a turf mix in areas of the country where it will grow. It should, however, be mixed with grasses that mature more quickly. Unfortunately, seed is rare and costly—sprigs are more common.

CHAPTER 3

Fertilizers and Plant Care Products

ABOUT FERTILIZERS

Fertilizers may very well be the most common product purchased in garden centers—and the one that causes the most confusion. Here's an extended introduction to help orient the average beginning gardener who wants to know the background for the terms used on fertilizer labels and found in gardening advice. If you want to get right to the essential listings, just skip over the next few pages and start in with the first item, on page 55.

Though often referred to as *plant food,* fertilizers are just a part of the plant food creation process. Green plants actually make their own food through photosynthesis, the process whereby green plants use sunlight, water, and carbon dioxide to produce the carbohydrates that nourish the plant. Sixteen elements, or *nutrients,* are essential in order for green plants to do this. The first three elements needed are carbon, hydrogen, and oxygen, and they come from water and air. Whenever any of the thirteen other nutrients are lacking in the soil (or just need to be replenished as they are naturally used or leached out of the soil by water), they can be provided by fertilizers.

The most important basic nutrients, commonly known as *primary nutrients* (or *macronutrients,* or *essential,* or *major nutrients),* are *nitrogen* (chemical symbol N), *phosphorus*—also referred to as *phosphate, phosphoric acid,* or *phosphoric oxide* (chemical symbol P, also P_2O_5), and *potassium*—commonly referred to by its soluble name, *potash* (chemical symbol K, also K_2O).

Each of these elements affects plant growth differently (and each plant a bit differently) and must be chosen according to what you have determined the plant needs. In general, though, the primary nutrients work as follows:

- *Nitrogen* promotes the growth of green leaves and stems. (Grass is a big consumer of nitrogen.)
- *Phosphorus* aids in the production of roots, flowers, and fruit. (This is most desirable for ornamentals, vegetables, and especially bulbs.)
- *Potassium* aids in the flowering and fruiting, as well as the sturdiness, of the plant in terms of disease and stress resistance (like winter weather).

All plants and soils require these nutrients in a particular balance, and providing too much of one nutrient over another will cause stress and problems for the plant. For example, plants getting too much nitrogen will have plenty of green leaves, but they will be soft, the root system will be underdeveloped, and the blooms for flowers or fruit will be retarded. Read your detailed gardening guides carefully to determine what your plants really need.

The three primary nutrients described above work in conjunction with three *secondary nutrients* and at least seven *micronutrients,* which ultimately help the plant function, much as vitamins and minerals do for humans. Just as we need a balanced diet with different vitamins to turn our food into energy, plants cannot process the macronutrients without a proper amount of micronutrient minerals in the soil. Macronutrients also tend to balance out the pH of the soil, pH being the term used to describe the relative acidity or alkalinity of soil (see page 4 for a discussion of pH).

The secondary nutrients are *calcium, magnesium,* and *sulfur,* and are sometimes lumped with the macronutrients. Under normal circumstances, these occur naturally in soil in sufficient quantity but need to be added to correct a deficiency or to cure a particular problem—much as with humans and vitamin pills. And too much can be a bad thing. Here's what they're needed for:

- *Calcium* is needed for the cell-manufacturing process—particularly important for early root growth. It is usually supplied by lime or other soil conditioners.
- *Magnesium* is a prime element of seed development and development of chlorophyll. It is usually found with calcium.

• *Sulfur* is a primary element of plant proteins and helps give plants a dark green color. It is supplied by most fertilizers and nature (including rain from polluted skies!), often in some form of sulfate. (*Sulphur* and *sulphate* are alternative terms.)

Micronutrients include *iron, manganese, copper, boron, zinc, chlorine,* and *molybdenum.* As fertilizers, they are usually applied to specific plants to cure specific conditions of deficiency. They occur sufficiently in normal, pH-balanced soils, although houseplants, being in an unnatural environment, may need a boost sometimes via special products (see chelated micronutrients, page 68). They should be added only when you know your soil needs them, otherwise you may damage your plants—just as humans can overdo it with vitamin supplements. In most cases, though, it is easier to change the pH of your soil in order to get your micronutrient levels where they should be. They are needed in very small quantities, so small that the amount is called a *trace,* giving them the alternative name *trace elements;* iron is needed in larger quantities to promote chlorophyll production and the resulting green color.

One important thing to keep in mind when using fertilizers is that only the right amount will do. It helps only when the nutrients are needed; more is not better and may be quite harmful (in fact, overfertilizing is more harmful than underfertilizing), so do not overapply. With many plants, such as fruit trees, you can reduce the need for fertilizer by pruning and mulching, among other good gardening practices. Finally, no amount of fertilizing can make up for serious environmental problems, such as poor soil, rampant disease, extreme acidity or alkalinity, lack of moisture or sunlight, or (and this is the hardest to accept for so many of us) an inappropriate climate. Plants cannot be forced to grow where they really don't want to just by pouring on more fertilizer.

ABOUT FERTILIZER LABEL TERMS

Fertilizer packages are labeled with a host of confusing terms, the most common of which are defined here. Note that some items are mixed together to provide a balance of characteristics; the most important thing to understand is that certain ingredients make the fertilizer fast- or slow-acting. All nutrients are absorbed by the plants via osmosis when in solution, so you always need water with fertilizers. The details you find on product labels are required by laws that vary from state to state.

COMPLETE FERTILIZER: Fertilizers intended for general use which contain significant amounts of the three primary nutrients (N, P, and K). Hundreds of these formulations are marketed for use as "plant food," "vegetable food," or for specific plants, as explained later in this chapter. The percentages of these three elements contained in any mixture (and their sources) are required by law to appear on the package label. N, P, and K percentages are stated as three numbers separated by dashes—5-10-5, 8-6-4, 22-3-3, etc. This is called the *grade, ratio, rating, guaranteed analysis,* or *NPK number.* The first number is always the percentage of nitrogen, the second number is always the percentage of phosphorus, and the last is always the percentage of potash. The grade tells you how much of each nutrient is in the package, by weight, which is what you are ultimately concerned with—fertilizer is usually applied at a rate of so many pounds per 1,000 square feet. Obviously, these same numbers tell you the ratio, or proportion, of one nutrient to another as well.

Keep in mind when comparing prices that you pay for the nutrient concentration, not the weight per se. Once you have determined the square feet of the area you wish to fertilize (most helpful if rounded off to the nearest 1,000 square feet) and what your fertilizer needs are, purchase the fertilizer with the appropriate grade for the amount of nutrients you want, while taking into account the size of the bag. For example, a common lawn fertilizer, Scotts Turf Builder, is rated at 29-3-4. A 15.5-pound bag contains 29 percent nitrogen, or 4.5 pounds. If you bought a fertilizer rated 15-3-4 instead, you would need almost twice as much fertilizer—30 pounds—to obtain the same 4.5 pounds of nitrogen. And always note how much of it is going to be released quickly and how much released slowly, according to the information on the types of nitrogen noted later on in this chapter.

INCOMPLETE FERTILIZER: If a fertilizer contains only one or two of the primary nutrients, it is called *incomplete.* This is not to say that it is of lower quality, but simply to identify it as a fertilizer to be used in a specific way to treat a specific deficiency. An almost infinite variety of mixes are made for specific applications, which are explained later in this chapter. Keep in mind when shopping that the unit cost of each nutrient increases as the package size decreases.

ORGANIC FERTILIZER: Any fertilizer produced by natural, once-living or live sources—animals or plants—is *organic, natural organic, natural, bio-organic,* or *naturally derived.* These products all contain carbon compounds. (The opposite of natural organic is *synthetic,* or man-made, fertilizer—manufactured products made from nonliving sources—called *inorganic, chemical,* or *petrochemical fertilizers.)* If a natural product is mined and then treated in some chemical process, it is no longer considered purely organic. The nitrogen in organic fertilizers is the *water-insoluble,* slow-release type, meaning it lasts longer in the soil before leaching out and probably will not "burn" the plants. Some well-known organic fertilizers are manure, blood meal, and fish tankage, all expanded upon later on in this chapter. They nourish the plants as they decay naturally with the help of microorganisms.

However, and this is terribly important, a fertilizer may be labeled "organic" even if part of it is from manufactured sources, as long as a certain percentage of it is from water-insoluble materials (most synthetic chemical products are almost 100 percent soluble, which is why they work and then wash out of the soil so quickly). Standards for use of the word *organic* in fertilizer labeling are determined by each state and can vary quite a bit. *Natural organic* is the most precise term, and the one generally used in this book, though in labeling it is used interchangeably with just plain *organic.* The fact that a product may be labeled by its manufacturer as organic or partly organic when it contains man-made chemicals or is chemically treated is confusing at best and downright misleading at worst, especially in this day when there is a certain cachet attached to the word *organic* by many consumers. *Caveat emptor.*

WATER-INSOLUBLE NITROGEN (WIN): This is a slow-release form of nitrogen. A certain amount is desirable, especially when mixed with faster-acting nitrogen sources like those noted here. A higher percentage of this kind of nitrogen in relation to the fast-acting kind means that the plant does not receive much nitrogen right away, but it does eventually; this is usually desirable because the plant has time to get the nitrogen in a useful way. Check your gardening guides to determine how much to apply, as the size and frequency of the applications will be dictated by the percentage of insoluble nitrogen. More than 50 percent means fewer applications. The presence of water-insoluble nitrogen tends to make the fertilizer more expensive, but less likely to burn the plant or to leach out, like the fast-acting nitrogen sources. Organic fertilizers are high in this kind of nitrogen. Container plants that are watered frequently need this kind of nitrogen.

AMMONIACAL, UREA, AND NITRATE NITROGEN: Fast-acting

("quick-release"), inexpensive, synthetic, water-soluble sources of nitrogen, derived from the salt of an acid. These may lower the pH of the soil (acidify) various degrees, depending on the type of nitrate compound used. Various nitrates are usually mixed in complete fertilizers to lessen their effect on pH. They act quickly (they can even burn the plant) and are generally inexpensive, but also tend to leach quickly from the soil. Synthetic fertilizers are high in this kind of nitrogen, and because it is caustic, it should be handled very carefully. Too much too fast, and your plants may weaken, making them susceptible to fungi.

Included in this group are *ammonium nitrate, ammonium sulfate (sulfate of ammonia), calcium nitrate,* and *nitrate of soda* (though one brand of nitrate of soda is organic: Bulldog, from Chile). While these are usually components of complete fertilizers, most are also available separately—they have up to 46 percent nitrogen—if you want to mix your own fertilizer (not a great idea, by the way) or cure a particular major deficiency in extreme conditions, such as cool weather, when nutrients move slowly. Their labels indicate whether they acidify or alkalize the soil; most acidify the soil (lower the pH), as indicated in the *potential acidity equivalent,* explained below.

UREA-FORM, UF, OR UREAFORM, OR METHALINE UREA: Urea reacted with formaldehyde to make it partially water-insoluble, resulting in a slow-releasing, nonburning source of nitrogen, containing 35 to 40 percent nitrogen. Urea is a man-made form of nitrogen derived from natural gas products, and even though it is synthethized, because it contains carbon it is sometimes labeled "organic" or "synthetic organic." It is not organic, according to all but the broadest definition of the term. It competes with organic fertilizers in the marketplace, offering more slow-release nitrogen per pound, in general.

COATED SLOW-RELEASE UREA NITROGEN: This is the earlier-mentioned quick-release nitrogen coated with sulfur to delay its release, adding sulfur to the soil at the same time (which reduces the pH, meaning it acidifies the soil) and reducing the tendency of the chemical burn. Sometimes abbreviated SCU, for sulfur-coated urea. Each coated granule is called a *prill,* or *sprill.* Another form of synthetic, slow-release, treated nitrogen is IBDU, or isobutylidene diurea, which has about 30 percent nitrogen that releases at low temperatures over a long period of time.

POTENTIAL ACIDITY EQUIVALENT: This tells the degree to which a synthetic fertilizer will change the pH of a soil (natural organic fertilizers are not obliged to list this), expressed in terms of pounds of calcium carbonate per ton, that is, the amount of $CaCO_3$ needed to neutralize the acidifying effect of the fertilizer, and can range from 0 to over 2,200 pounds, with anything over about 400 being considered acidic, and a range up to about 1,000 being common. Most gardeners can ignore this—it is only important if a soil test indicates a pH problem or you are concerned about plants that are fussy about pH, such as hydrangeas. The actual degree of effect is not acute and really depends on many other factors. It's really more a question of building up acidity over time. Check your how-to books to find out if your plants need an acid or alkaline soil, and take soil tests to determine where you stand. Organic fertilizers do not create this problem as much as synthetic fertilizers, which tend to be acidic, especially the faster-acting, less expensive ones.

CHELATES OR CHELATED SECONDARY AND MICRONUTRIENTS: Water-soluble compounds of metals that are made readily available to the plants. Usually in the form of a foliar spray (one that is sprayed directly onto the leaves), they can also be applied to the soil like any other fertilizer. These nutrients would not be available to the plants unless they were chelated. Micronutrients may be aided in their becoming rapidly available by a chemical catalyst called a *chelating agent.* Iron, magnesium, manganese, copper, and zinc are the most common ones sold individually, although some products include more. Many gardeners consider these to be professional products only.

FORMS OF FERTILIZERS

LIQUID: Concentrations of either water-soluble powders or liquids that need to be diluted with water. Liquid fertilizers, also called *nutritional sprays,* may be used as a *foliar spray* (applied to the leaves—also called a *nutrient leaf spray)* or as a *ground spray* (applied to the ground to be absorbed through the roots). They are more easily applied (especially in small quantities) and usually more readily available to the plant than other forms, making them popular for houseplants. However, they are less practical for large areas and easy to overapply by mistake, which may burn the plant, and they are also easily leached from the soil. Most are meant to provide a special boost to plants in difficulty, and usually contain more micronutrients than the other forms of fertilizer.

SOLUBLE POWDERS: As the name suggests, these are plant nutrients in powder form that are dissolved in water before use. They offer quick sources of nutrients to plants suffering nutritional disorders, but are easily leached out of the soil. They may be blown away by the wind and can cake in storage, but generally cost less than other forms.

TIME-RELEASED OR CONTROLLED RELEASE: Fertilizers in capsule form (sometimes called a *prill* or *sprill),* covered with a resin membrane that dissolves slowly when the plant is watered and as the soil temperature rises, thus releasing the nutrients over a period of time. Often a sulfur coating, it lets water in through osmosis or just breaks down slowly. Some brands may last in the ground up to nine months, releasing fertilizer as the plant needs it. *Osmocote* is a well-known brand name of this sort.

PELLETIZED OR PELLETED: These are powders that have been compressed into pellets, in some cases containing uniform amounts of each nutrient. As it takes longer for the pellets to break down, the easily leached nutrients are released more slowly. They can be applied through spreaders, aren't affected by wind as powders are, and resist caking. Very large pellets may be called *tablets,* and are used mostly by professionals for planting shrubs and trees when they want the fertilizer to last up to two years.

SPIKES: Sticks or stakes, 2 to 3 inches long, made from a compacted fiber impregnated with fertilizer. These are often used for houseplants but are also available in larger sizes for trees and outdoor shrubs. The fertilizer is released slowly as the spike disintegrates in the soil. Some spikes also contain pesticides. This is the most convenient form for houseplants and small gardens, but expensive in terms of the amount of nitrogen.

GRANULAR OR GRANULATED: Granules, designed to be applied with spreaders, consisting of larger particles than found in powders but generally smaller than pellets. The granules break down over time with exposure to moisture, releasing the chemicals slowly. This is the most common form for *top-* or *side-dressing* (applying fertilizer directly to the soil surface).

TRIONIZED: Homogeneous granules, usually containing vermiculite or other lightweight material to which the three primary nutrients have been bonded, making for a very even distribution of nutrients. Each granule contains all three nutrients.

SIMPLE-MIX: Variously sized granules of nutrients which, though blended, may be unevenly distributed in the bag because of their different weights and textures; therefore fertilizer may be delivered unevenly to a lawn or plant.

POLYFORM: The lightest, most concentrated form of fertilizer. The nutrient granules have been screened, so they are all the same size.

GENERAL BUYING TIPS

Fertilizers are sold in packages ranging from a few ounces to 100 pounds. As with many products, the larger the package, the cheaper the fertilizer is per pound, often dramatically so. Keep in mind that the grade—the three numbers on the label—indicate the percentage of the package by weight of each major nutrient, and that therefore you need less of a fertilizer with a higher grade than of one with a lower grade to obtain the same results.

Most gardeners can get by with the general mixes of the 5-10-5, 10-6-4 (for lawns, evergreens, and trees), and 10-10-10 varieties. As for specialized fertilizers, these are for fine-tuning when you know precisely what kind of problem you are addressing, and for personal preference in brands, forms, price, and the like. One thing is sure: Gardening is far from an exact science. It is quite amusing to hear people (sellers and consumers alike) absolutely swear by or about one product or another—with totally opposite conclusions.

An alarming aspect of fertilizer merchandising which takes advantage of this manic search for the one perfect product is the common practice of manufacturers (particularly those among the best known and most widely distributed) to sell the exact same fertilizer labeled in different ways, for example, *flower* as well as *shrub, tree,* and *ground cover* fertilizer, or *lawn food* and *garden food.* This may help the gardener who needs to be told as a convenience or reassurance that a particular product is OK for his or her garden or lawn or flowers, but it also might encourage that same gardener to buy twice as much as needed, that is, two containers when one would do. It is not difficult to read the labels to see if they are any different from one another.

Natural Organic Fertilizers

ABOUT NATURAL ORGANIC FERTILIZERS

Technically known as *naturally derived fertilizers,* these are made from nutrients taken from plants or animals; they are not manufactured (see "About Fertilizer Label Terms," pages 47–51). Some manufacturers argue that any carbon-based or mined material is organic, but in gardening terms this definition is not narrow enough, as it allows the inclusion of synthesized or treated materials. However, for the sake of brevity here, the term *organic* is used to mean "natural organic."

Organic fertilizers help build up the soil, in terms of both structure and microorganisms. Over time, organic fertilizer use builds up the micronutrients and the earthworms in a soil. Some gardeners claim that after regular use of organic fertilizers, you may need to use less, a persuasive argument for their use; the opposite is considered true of synthetic fertilizers by these same gardeners. All soils need organic matter, if only to encourage earthworms and other organisms to do their work, and synthetic fertilizers add none. Organic fertilizers generally do not harm the environment in manufacture nor in use, and need only renewable sources of energy for their "production." While synthetic fertilizers may cost less per bag in the short run, they require huge factories and vast amounts of nonrenewable energy sources for their manufacture. The essential characteristic of organic fertilizers is that they act as soil conditioners (see chapter 1) as well as low-nutrient fertilizers. The basic idea of organic fertilizers is to build up the soil, as well as to fertilize the plant.

However, organic fertilizers have some drawbacks: They are usually not complete fertilizers, in that they do not contain a conveniently balanced mix of the primary nutrients (N, P, and K). Typically, each kind of organic fertilizer is a particularly good source of one or two of the primary nutrients, and other types of fertilizers must be used to provide the balance, meaning more work for the gardener. They also release their nutrients slowly, which may not be fast enough to solve an acute nutrient problem. They need warm temperatures for the microorganisms to do their work, while chemical fertilizers need only water. And some are hard to store, owing to their bulk. Finally, you may have to apply many pounds more than you would of a synthetic fertilizer in order to achieve the same effect, because they are less concentrated, making for more work. Synthetic fertilizers are usually more convenient, precise (that is, packaged for particular needs and plants), and easy to store.

Much has been written and argued about the value of using organic instead of synthetic fertilizers; your final decision will probably involve your perception of the merits of short-term versus long-term effects on the environment and your attitude toward chemicals in general. A balanced approach of mixed use is a typical solution, though promoters of the strictly organic approach to gardening make good sense, especially for the home gardener. After all, gardening is essentially a natural operation, and they suggest you keep it that way.

General Use Organic Fertilizers

COTTONSEED MEAL

DESCRIPTION: Cotton seeds ground or powdered after the oil has been extracted from them (the seeds are left over from cotton production). *Soybean meal,* rated at 6-2-2, is a similar product.

USE: Rated at 6-2-1 or 7-2-2, it also contains some trace elements and micronutrients. Good for acid-loving plants and shrubs. Nutrients more available to plants in warm soil.

USE TIP: Often used as cattle feed as well as a fertilizer.

BUYING TIP: A good grade of meal is deep yellow; fermented meal is red-brown; ground meal containing the hull of the cottonseed is dark brown.

GUANO

DESCRIPTION: Guano is the decomposed, aged manure of seabirds and bats. (The word *guano* is from the Quechua language of the Incas, and originally referred only to the droppings of seabirds.)

TYPES: *Peruvian guano:* The decomposed manure of cormorants and other fish-eating birds found on certain extremely dry desert islands, making it both concentrated and rare. Rated at around 12-11-2.

Phosphatic guano: A now rarely found bird manure that has been leached by rain and is rated at about 10 to 14–8 to 10–2. It was popular in the United States before the 1960s, at which time rock phosphate (see page 62), which provides a less expensive source for phosphate, started being processed commercially in South Carolina and Florida. Very strong and difficult to use.

Bat guano or *desert bat guano:* The dried, decomposed manure of bats, and a complete fertilizer rated from 2-8-.05 to 8-4-1 with the phosphorus and the potash immediately available to the plants; also contains most micronutrients, including iron, calcium, magnesium, boron, and sulfur. It is an odorless, fine, brown powder.

USE: A good source of phosphate and a generally balanced and complete fertilizer supplying both fast- and slow-release nutrients. Bat guano is one of the best organic fertilizers (and soil conditioners) around, particularly suited for flowering ornamental trees and shrubs.

USE TIP: Organic fertilizers such as these do not usually burn plants, so the amount used does not have to be exact, but the recommended quantities on the label should be used in any case.

BUYING TIP: Because the term *guano* has been loosely used to describe animal manures, fish scrap, or tankage containing feces, check to see that you are purchasing bat guano or Peruvian guano. If it is hard to find bat guano in garden centers near you, try a mail-order source. Not inexpensive.

MANURE

DESCRIPTION: A finely ground, dry, soillike material with a very slight or no manure (ammonia) odor. Sold in bags ranging from 5 to 100 pounds.

The term *green manure* refers to succulent crops, such as mustard, buckwheat, annual ryegrass, and winter rye, that are grown specifically to be plowed right back into the ground before they ripen, thus enriching the soil. *Fresh manure* comes straight from a local farmer, or more accurately, from the farmer's horse, cow, or other animal. This is usually not found for sale in garden centers; if you want to use it, beware of weeds: You should heat it up and decompose it for about one season in your compost heap in order to kill the weed seeds.

All manures fall into two general categories:

Hot manures: These are high in nitrogen and come from chickens, crickets (yes, crickets), horses, sheep, and rabbits. They range from 1 to 4 percent in nitrogen at the very most; chicken and cricket manures contain the most primary nutrients, up to 4-4-2. Some manufacturers label mixtures of these manures as "supreme" or "super" manure. (The term *hot manure* is also used colloquially to mean any fresh manure that is decomposing.)

Cold manures: These are lower in nitrogen than the hot manures and come from cattle and hogs. They usually have no more than 1 or 2 percent nitrogen. Dehydrated and composted cow manures are rated as high as 5-5-5 and as low as .2-.1-.2; pH tends to the balanced range; dehydrated manures are more concentrated.

TYPES: *Composted* (also known as *decomposed, rotted,* or *aged):* Aged with compost and exposed to microorganisms over a period of time, which has caused it to break down.

Dehydrated (also known as *dried):* Similar to composted manure, but pasteurized (heated up to 180° F) and reduced to about 17 to 30 percent moisture, killing all the weed seeds and plant pathogens, and ground into a fine, soillike texture. Some companies heat the manure naturally, in a giant compost pile, without the use of fossil fuels.

Fresh-milled: Shredded, usually with straw or other "bedding litter." Fresh-milled manure is not treated in any way other than being chopped up ("milled") and it is drier than manure fresh from the animal.

USE: A source of nitrogen in a form that is not as concentrated and is less likely to burn than chemical fertilizers. Cow manure is also a very effective soil conditioner (see page 11), and many gardeners think of it as one, instead of as a fertilizer, because it is so low in nutrients (it may also be labeled as such, though because it is really a fertilizer, it has an NPK number). This makes it better for mixing in with soil when planting rather than as top-dressing fertilizer. Manures both add and stimulate essential microorganisms in the soil and build humus. All good-quality manures contain sufficient macro- and micronutrients to maintain healthy soil, though they are more concentrated in dehydrated manure. Composted cow manure is best for turning into the soil of an entire garden with the use of a power tiller, while dehydrated is better suited to mixing into bedding or container soil mixes with hand tools. A must for roses.

USE TIPS: Cattle manures are often low in nutrients, but when used in sufficient quantities do provide enough to make a difference. They also improve soil condition by adding organic material humus, which opens up the soil to air and water (improves the tilth). If too much manure is used, or if it is insufficiently decomposed, even it may burn plants; fresh cow manure may burn your plants and introduce weeds from the straw in it. Furthermore, the bacteria that breaks down fresh manure needs extra nitrogen to do so and competes for it with your plants. And besides, it smells! Chicken manure should be used with care and then only after it has been sufficiently rotted, or else it will burn your plants.

BUYING TIPS: Dehydrated cow manure is much more expensive than composted cow manure, as it is more concentrated per pound—so you use less. That lower price of composted manure includes a lot of water. Dehydrated cow manure is also easier to spread. Check with local stables or zoos for sources of different kinds of manure.

SEWAGE SLUDGE

ALSO KNOWN AS: Activated sewage sludge

POPULAR BRAND NAMES: Milorganite®, Electra

DESCRIPTION: Created from municipal sewage that has been treated with microorganisms, heat dried, and aerated in a special process. Looks like a rich soil mix. Depending on the source, it may vary from dark gray to black in color. Rated at about 5-2-5, with iron. *Does not smell of sewage.*

USE: As a fertilizer and a soil conditioner, usually on lawns and in ornamental gardens. Particularly well suited to houseplants. It is a good substitute for fish emulsion (see page 60) as it smells less, not only to humans, but to domestic cats.

USE TIPS: Sewage sludge may contain pesticides, industrial chemicals, and heavy metals that may be harmful to you or the environment, so it is not recommended for use in the vegetable garden. Even when it is used on a lawn or ornamental garden (it is commonly used on golf courses), you could possibly be adding harmful chemicals to the water table. Experts are quite divided on this question.

BUYING TIP: Avoid buying sludge that does not identify all the chemicals contained in it. With more and more municipal sewage contaminated by the often unlawful disposal of heavy metals and industrial chemicals, it is worth checking to see if any of these chemicals are present in sewage sludge before purchasing or using it.

TANKAGE

DESCRIPTION: The dried, ground, and rendered by-products of slaughtered animals—what's left over after the meat has been processed for commercial food consumption. Rated at 7-10-0. Some specialized forms are *hoof and horn meal,* with a grade of 14-2-0, and *leather meal* or *leather dust,* rated at 5-0-0. A more specialized, but similar product, bone meal (see below), is made from bones only.

USE: Tankage is a common fertilizer ingredient and is sometimes available in pure form to be used as a fertilizer. It was more available pure in the past, before it became popular as an additive to animal food.

Specialized Organic Fertilizers

ABOUT SPECIALIZED ORGANIC FERTILIZERS

Fertilizers can be blended, or simply occur naturally, in ways that are particularly well suited to specific purposes and plants. Organic fertilizers tend to occur with concentrations of one of the major nutrients, as you can see by the entries that follow.

BONE MEAL

ALSO KNOWN AS: Steamed bone meal

DESCRIPTION: As the name suggests, this product is obtained from the animal bones left over after processing for meat (renderings); they are steamed and ground. It is sold in powder form, has a mild smell, and is white in color. Slightly alkaline, a typical grade is 4-12-0. *Raw bone meal* is harder to find but is slower acting and longer lasting.

USE: A natural source of phosphorus, usually a minimum of 12 percent. Especially helpful for giving bulbs a boost.

USE TIP: Commonly placed in the bottom of the planting holes for bulbs, shrubs, and trees.

BUYING TIPS: The phosphorus level in bone meal today is lower than in the past, owing to more efficient slaughterhouses. Today, bone meal contains fewer additional animal parts (meat, marrow, or blood) than previously because they are being used as additives to pet food. Superphosphate (see pages 73–74) might be a better source of phosphorus, especially when it is used for the fall planting of spring bulbs, as might a commercial mix called something like *bulb booster.*

DRIED BLOOD

ALSO KNOWN AS: Blood meal

DESCRIPTION: Dried and ground blood from slaughtered animals, containing on the average about 12 percent nitrogen, and no other primary nutrient (12-0-0). May be red or black in color, and is kiln-dried or spray-dried.

USE: A good source of nitrogen sold as a powder, which may be applied as a diluted liquid as well. The nitrogen in dried blood is readily available to the plant.

USE TIPS: Has a strong smell that sometimes attracts rodents and some people find unpleasant. Capable of burning plants.

BUYING TIPS: Spray-dried blood meal is finer and faster acting. Blood meal is more expensive than many other organic fertilizers.

FISH EMULSION

DESCRIPTION: Sold in a concentrated liquid form, fish emulsion is a thick brown liquid with a decidedly fishy smell, though some brands are now deodorized. It is sold in plastic bottles ranging in size from a few ounces to a gallon. Usually 5-1-1 or 5-2-2.

USE: A popular organic form of nitrogen, as it is easy to use and widely distributed. The nitrogen in fish emulsion is released slowly to the plant roots. Can be used as a foliar fertilizer (applied to and absorbed by the leaves) when diluted and sprayed on.

USE TIPS: Neighborhood cats may be attracted to the garden when fish emulsion is used. Be sure to follow the dilution rates on the bottle, as there is no standard rate.

BUYING TIP: The nitrogen level of fish emulsion is often not listed on the label as it varies from manufacturer to manufacturer.

FISH SCRAP

ALSO KNOWN AS: Fish tankage, dry ground fish, fertilizer grade fish meal

DESCRIPTION: Dried and ground parts of rendered and unrendered fish, crab meal, and fish manure. (Rendered fish contains the parts that are left after the primary commercial food products have been processed.) Typically made from such fish as menhaden and dogfish and the leftovers from fish canneries. Usually contains the primary nutrients in percentages of 9-7-0. Fish scrap, especially the manure, is sometimes treated with sulfuric or phosphoric acid to break it down and called *acid fish* or *acidulated fish tankage;* its percentages of primary nutrients are 6-6-0.

USE: As an organic source of nitrogen and phosphate.

USE TIP: Acidulated or plain fish scrap can be used interchangably.

BUYING TIP: An excellent, easily procured source of nitrogen.

GREENSAND

ALSO KNOWN AS: Glauconite

DESCRIPTION: A *pulverized rock powder* of sandy clay material (iron-potassium silicate) with 6 to 7 percent potash (K) and up to thirty trace minerals, magnesium, and silica. Mined from natural marine deposits found near the New Jersey coast. *Granite dust,* or *granite meal,* which is just crushed granite, is a similar item with 3 to 5.5 percent potash. Its potash comes from the feldspar and mica in the granite.

USE: Adding a natural source of potash to vegetable garden soil as well as lawns and orchards. Retards soil compaction and holds moisture. Some people consider it and granite dust soil conditioners because of these qualities.

USE TIP: Often recommended for roses and greenhouse potting mixtures where moisture retention and drainage are issues.

LANGBEINITE

POPULAR BRAND NAMES: Sul-Po-Mag, K-Mag

DESCRIPTION: Mineral mined in the Southwestern United States, usually composed of 20 to 22 percent sulfur, 20 to 22 percent potassium oxide, and 10 to 18 percent magnesium oxide.

USE: Potassium source rich in secondary nutrients.

ROCK PHOSPHATE

ALSO KNOWN AS: Phosphate rock, rock powder, pulverized rock powder

DESCRIPTION: Pure mined phosphate rock, most likely from South Carolina or Florida, with 20 to 30 percent phosphoric acid. When treated with sulfuric acid, becomes superphosphate (see pages 73–74). *Colloidal phosphate,* or *soft rock phosphate,* is a similar product from Tennessee rated at about 18 to 20 percent phosphate and which contains calcium and trace minerals. Quicker acting than rock phosphate.

USE: An organic source of water-insoluble, very slow-release phosphorus, but also a general soil conditioner. Good source of many trace elements.

USE TIP: Because it is a natural mineral source it does not leach away as fast as superphosphate. However, it may have no effect at all on soils with a pH over 6.2, and is most effective on pea family plants and compost, rather than on lawns.

BUYING TIP: Must be exceedingly fine ground to be of use; superphosphate is much more effective, but not an organic product. Has largely replaced bat guano (see page 56).

SEAWEED EXTRACT

ALSO KNOWN AS: Kelp, kelp meal, liquid seaweed, liquefied seaweed

DESCRIPTION: Brown liquid in concentrate form made from ocean kelp, rated around 1-0-1.2, with up to 33 percent trace minerals.

USE: Good but expensive source of micronutrients and potash, which are necessary for root development and overall stress resistance, especially for seedlings, for which nitrogen is not so important.

BUYING TIP: The amount of nitrogen is often not given on the label as it varies.

Organic Plant Care Products

ABOUT ORGANIC PLANT CARE PRODUCTS

There are many products sold in garden centers alongside the fertilizers. These products promise to take care of your plants in more direct ways, such as maintaining a good moisture level.

ANTITRANSPIRANT

ALSO KNOWN AS: Antidesiccant

POPULAR BRAND NAMES: WILT-PRUF®, Vapor-Gard®, ForEver-Green®, Cloud Cover®

DESCRIPTION: Most are made of a natural pine oil emulsion or natural, latexlike, biodegradable polymer in ready-to-spray liquid, concentrate, or aerosol form, sold in a wide range of sizes. Nontoxic. Some contain chemicals that cover the stomata (tiny openings in the leaves) through which moisture escapes. Dries to a clear, glossy film and does not affect the natural breathing and growing processes of a plant.

USE: Sprayed on ornamental plants, especially evergreens such as pine trees, dormant tubers, bulbs, and bare root stock to prevent excessive moisture loss after transplanting, during shipment, over winter, and during storage. Small plants may be dipped in it. Also effective against windburn and drought, or any other condition that dries out plants. One spraying lasts for about three months. Also used as a fungal preventive on annuals.

USE TIPS: These products should be used only during periods when there is excessive evaporation of moisture—otherwise you can harm the plant by preventing some needed transpiration. Because some plants may be sensitive to an antitranspirant, test some first on a small part of the plant. Be sure to dilute it correctly if necessary.

BUYING TIP: Read the label on the product to see that it will do what you wish it to.

LEAF POLISH

ALSO KNOWN AS: Leaf gloss, leaf shine, shine and cleaner, leaf shiner and cleaner, leaf cleaner

POPULAR BRAND NAMES: Moonshine, Ortho Leaf Polish

DESCRIPTION: Liquid chemical mixture sold in small hand-pump spray containers or regular bottles. Normally does not contain any fertilizer. Usually organic, but not necessarily, so check the label. Most are made with mineral oil, but some are made of a surfactant that breaks up dirt without clogging the plant's pores.

USE: Shining and cleaning leaves of hard surface houseplants and decorative arrangements.

USE TIPS: The myth behind the desirability of polished foliage may very well be similar to the one about a fat baby being a healthy baby—hard to prove. Even if these products claim no harm to plants, some brands may leave residues on the foliage that clog pores and prevent or slow down the natural processes of the leaves, as did the buttermilk your grandma may have used to clean her plants.

BUYING TIPS: A clean leaf may be healthier than a polished leaf. Stick to tepid water to wash the foliage of houseplants as harmful dust does build up, or try to find those cleaners that really lift off the dirt or wash it away. You can use a lamb's wool ball made for this purpose, or put your plants in the shower (really!).

Synthetic Fertilizers

ABOUT SYNTHETIC FERTILIZERS

Please note that some manufactured brands of fertilizer contain organic matter as well, and in fact may be labeled in a way that leaves you confused as to whether this is a natural or manufactured product. For example, "rich in organic matter" means that it contains both natural and artificial ingredients. There is nothing wrong with this; on the contrary, it means that the mixture takes advantage of the qualities of both kinds of ingredients. However, products that contain anything artificial or that are chemically treated are included in this section rather than the preceding one. Most fertilizers label organic sources as such, but not chemical sources; anything in a fertilizer not noted as natural can be assumed to be synthetic.

Notation of the breakdown of sources and percentages of types of nitrogen is required on the labels of synthetic fertilizers but not on those of natural organic ones in most states. If you like to have a well-balanced mixture of nitrogen sources, look for more *water-insoluble nitrogen* than *fast-acting* sources (see "About Fertilizer Label Terms" on pages 47–51).

Synthetic fertilizers are man-made. Most are combinations of chemicals that form a complete fertilizer as defined in "About Fertilizers" (see pages 45–47). They are mixed to fit many needs, including some quite specialized ones. Convenience and price are their trademarks. However, there are definitely some trade-offs for that convenience. The end result of complete dependency on and overuse of synthetic fertilizers is that you may need more chemicals to counteract the first chemicals and their side effects, ultimately harming the environment through water pollution and soil depletion, which is added to the environmental cost of their industrial manufacturing. Pound for pound, organic fertilizers may be more expensive than synthetic ones, but over time, you will probably need to put more synthetic fertilizer in your garden than if you use organic fertilizer, and in any case more often, because the very characteristic that makes synthetics act so fast—water solubility—also makes some of their nutrients wash out of the soil with the rain. They add nothing to the soil permanently and may actually harm the soil's microorganisms and valued earthworms.

Many gardeners choose to use chemical fertilizers sparingly, in coordination with naturally derived (organic) fertilizers. More and more gardeners, in fact, are becoming organic gardeners. And now even the National Academy of Sciences has begun to recommend the use of biological interactions instead of agricultural chemicals for many tasks. This said, there are more chemical products than organic ones on the market, proving their popularity and wide acceptance.

Specialized Synthetic Fertilizers

ABOUT SPECIALIZED SYNTHETIC FERTILIZERS

To make life easier, special fertilizers are available for use on specific plants or types of plants. Fertilizers can be purchased for foliage (typical for houseplants), flowering and fruiting plants, acid-loving plants, container plants, African violets, roses, geraniums, tomatoes, cacti, lawns, vegetables, and so on. Also, certain formulations that have just about nothing other than one of the primary nutrients are available, such as potash (0-0-60) and urea (46-0-0). These latter items are used to solve specific plant problems, such as building up an aspect of disease resistance. They are sometimes called *simples.*

Using these products does raise the problem, however, that you may be giving the plant more than it needs of certain nutrients, particularly micronutrients. Some minor trace elements or micronutrients, such as water-soluble salts (borates and sulfated forms of copper), iron, manganese, and zinc, are helpful to plant growth in small quantities, while others, such as boron and molybdenum, can be harmful—even toxic—in excess. A garden plan and a complete soil test (see pages 237–38) should indicate how much and which trace elements and/or micronutrients are already present in your soil and which you need. Reading the fertilizer labels will tell you if it contains just what you need or whether you are paying more for extra, unwanted nutrients.

Many manufacturers make complete lines of fertilizers, creating a lot of duplication on the shelf. Some specialize in liquid fertilizers, others in granular, for example, making the choice more one of which form you find most convenient rather than of product performance. The plant doesn't care about the form of nutrients as much as you do. The choice is large and encourages experimentation—it is very much a question of personal preference or "feel" for a particular line of products that governs a final choice.

ACID-LOVING PLANT FERTILIZERS

POPULAR BRAND NAMES: Holly-tone®, Miracid®, Ortho Azalea, Camellia, and Rhododendron Food

DESCRIPTION: Granular or liquid fertilizer, often containing chelated iron and other micronutrients and soil acidifiers. Other ingredients that may be found include aluminum sulfate (bauxite that usually has been treated with sulfuric acid), ammonium sulfate (or sulfate of ammonia) that has 20.5 percent available nitrogen, and iron sulfate, which helps correct iron deficiencies. A grade of 4-6-4 is common, as is 5-10-10, 7-7-7, 10-7-7, and 4-12-12, depending on the plant it is intended for, and 30-10-10 is also available. Aluminum sulfate (see page 11) is packaged pure as well, as a soil acidifier. Sold in bags from 5 to 20 pounds.

USE: Fertilizing hollies, azaleas, rhododendrons, evergreens, and the like, all plants that crave acid soils, by promoting growth and good color. Aluminum sulfate imparts a blue color to hydrangeas.

USE TIPS: Spring and fall feedings, depending on the particular brand. Follow the directions on the bag for each type of plant.

BUYING TIP: Sulfate of ammonia is slow acting but long lasting.

AMMONIUM NITRATE

DESCRIPTION: Granular form of rapidly available nitrogen, usually in a 33-0-0 concentration.

USE: Fast-acting source of nitrogen for quick greening of turf grasses such as fescue, bluegrass, and Bermudagrass, especially during cool seasons.

USE TIP: Extremely concentrated; may burn. Most people are better off with traditional sources of nitrogen.

BUYING TIP: Considered a professional product—not necessarily available in small packages.

AMMONIUM PHOSPHATE

DESCRIPTION: Granular source of fast-acting nitrogen and phosphorus, usually rated at 16-20-0.

USE: For fast growth of lawns, especially in the South.

USE TIPS: Reapply every sixty days—this goes fast. Not recommended for dichondra, a grass substitute used in the Southwest. Difficult to use accurately.

BULB FOOD

ALSO KNOWN AS: Bulb booster

DESCRIPTION: A complete fertilizer that contains more phosphorus than nitrogen or potassium, typically in a 4-12-8 or similar grade. Often blended natural organic (bone meal, for instance) and synthetic materials. Sold in small bags or boxes for the home gardener.

USE: Encourages healthy root development so essential to bulbs.

USE TIP: Place in the bottom of each bulb's planting hole.

BUYING TIP: Cheaper than bone meal with a comparable phosphate rating, but just as effective.

CHELATED MICRONUTRIENTS

DESCRIPTION: Powdered, granular, or liquid form of water-soluble compounds of the metallic nutrients made with organic chelating agents that make these micronutrients available to the plants when they normally wouldn't be. Very similar to vitamin pills for humans—in fact, some are sold mixed with vitamin B-1. Micronutrients include iron, manganese, zinc, boron, copper, chlorine, and molybdenum.

USE: Treating certain deficiencies of micronutrients in soil.

USE TIPS: Use only as directed, and only when you are quite sure that you need them. Normally balanced and well-fertilized soils should not be lacking in micronutrients, and a major deficiency should be thoroughly analyzed. Iron is the most commonly deficient micronutrient, causing leaf yellowing (chlorosis). May be very fast-acting.

BUYING TIP: Professionals have more use for these items than amateurs. If you must absolutely buy them, and have trouble finding them in a garden center, try to find a professional source through a landscaper or botanic garden.

FLOWERING OR FRUITING PLANT FERTILIZER

DESCRIPTION: Complete fertilizer heavily weighted to supply nitrogen and potash or, most often, equal amounts of all three primary nutrients. Commonly rated at 12-12-12.

USE: Encouraging normal growth and fruiting of fruit-bearing woody plants.

USE TIPS: Sprays are not useful on fruit trees except when a superficial fix is desired; ground application in the fall or early spring is the best. Applications to large trees such as apple trees last longer when accompanied by hay or straw mulching and heavy pruning.

BUYING TIPS: Keep in mind when deciding on a particular grade that large fruit trees, such as apple and pear trees, may not require much phosphorus or calcium or micronutrients, which many of these fertilizers may contain. Pay special attention to the tips on the package label.

HOUSEPLANT FOOD

POPULAR BRAND NAMES: Liquid Miracle-Gro® House Plant Food, Stern's Therapy for House Plants, Schultz Instant Liquid Plant Food, Granny's Bloomers, Granny's Jungle Juice, Jobe's Houseplant Spikes, Peters® Concentrated Liquid Plant Food, Ra-Pid-Gro, Ortho Plant Food

DESCRIPTION: Concentrated liquid applied directly to soil, powdered concentrate mixed with water, or spike, specially formulated for houseplants, containing chelated iron and other micronutrients usually lacking in indoor growing media. Normally should not lead to buildup of salts. Liquid sold in small bottles ranging from 2 ounces upward. Grades tend to be 8-7-6, 10-8-7, 10-5-10, and the like.

USE: Providing nutrients not otherwise available to potted plants.

USE TIPS: Usually formulated to be quickly available to the plant. Often very concentrated so that it can be sold in small containers, it must be diluted according to instructions or else it might harm the plant. Note whether acidic or not.

BUYING TIPS: There is lots of competition for this market, so experiment until you find a product that gives you the best results. Each plant may react differently to the various formulations available. Furthermore, this is an intimate process, and your selection may have as much to do with the way you like to care for your plants as does the actual effect of the fertilizer. Ultimately, houseplant food is not that different from garden fertilizers except in the degree of concentration and the packaging or form.

LAWN FERTILIZER

DESCRIPTION: Sold in all possible forms: pellets, granules, liquids, powdered concentrates to be mixed with water, or powders to be applied dry. Whether synthetic or organic, they come in two general types: *slow-acting* and *fast-acting*.

Many specialized products are made for starting new lawns or greening up old ones in the spring. Starter fertilizers have a higher percentage of phosphorus to promote root development. "Green-up" fertilizers feature extremely high nitrogen content for the leaves.

TYPES: *Starter Lawn Food (10-18-12):* Particularly good for building roots during fall and winter. Added iron prevents leaf yellowing.

Lawn and Tree Food (10-6-4): Good both spring and fall, for both new and established lawns, and for any other leaf crops.

Lawn and Garden Food (10-10-10): Good general use fertilizer.

USE: Keeping lawns healthy and green. This is not just for aesthetics or impressing the neighbors: A healthy lawn is better able to compete with weeds and is more resistant to pests and diseases.

USE TIPS: Follow label directions carefully. Too much fertilizer or too high a concentration of liquid fertilizer will burn and brown off a lawn. Excessive application of nitrogen can cause thatch buildup and poor drought tolerance, and make your lawn vulnerable to diseases. Almost all lawn fertilizers need to be watered in well; failure to do so evenly will result in dead areas where the fertilizers were not watered in and thus did not enter the soil. Lawn fertilizers may be broadcast by hand, applied with a hose attachment (see page 237), or applied with a spreader (see pages 252–53).

Slow-acting lawn fertilizers are best applied only once or twice a year. Organic forms are less likely to burn the lawn. Fast-acting lawn fertilizers produce greener lawns within hours of application, but generally do not continue to fertilize a lawn for more than four to eight weeks, making it necessary to reapply them as often as every month or so during the growing season. This is a case of a choice between instant and delayed gratification, but if you go for the instant kind, you have to have the time and the money to repeat the application often.

Lawns should be fertilized in the spring and in the fall. Most experts recommend early fall fertilizing of lawns to ensure good growth and root development, especially in areas of the country where winters are below freezing. As a general rule, fall is the best time for many other lawn care practices too, such as seeding and sodding.

Remember that rain is going to leach out the chemicals you

put on your lawn, and therefore the repeated, excess application of certain chemicals may pollute your water supply or harm your soil. Caution and moderation are the way to go here.

BUYING TIPS: Which form of fertilizer to buy is pretty much a question of your own preference. Some people prefer to use a dry fertilizer that they then water in well. Others enjoy the practice of liquid feeding. Avoid a fertilizer in which *all* of the nitrogen is supplied by ammonium nitrate or ammonium sulfate—the fast- or quick-release, synthetic, water-soluble forms of nitrogen which act so fast that they break down very soon after application.

MAGNESIUM SULFATE

ALSO KNOWN AS: Epsom salts

DESCRIPTION: White powder containing 9.6 percent magnesium and 14.5 percent sulfur.

USE: Source of magnesium when need is indicated by a soil test or foliage. Most concentrations are spread at a rate of ½ pound per 100 square feet.

USE TIPS: Usually applied as a foliar (leaf) spray to fruit trees in foliage; mix with a spreader-sticker (see page 117). Dolomitic limestone (see pages 14–15), a good source of magnesium, is more often applied to the soil when you have time—this is a quicker treatment.

MURIATE OF POTASH

DESCRIPTION: Granular fertilizer that consists of soluble potash in concentrations of 0-0-60 or 0-0-55. Made from potassium chloride, a potash salt, which actually ranges from 48 to 62 percent soluble potash. Another similar source is sulfate of potash, or potassium sulfate, which has no less than 48 percent soluble potash.

USE: Potassium supplement for accelerating root and tuber growth; typical component of fast-acting, acidic, synthetic complete fertilizers.

USE TIPS: Add only when your soil test tells you that your soil is quite deficient in potash. Also good for melting ice and snow on driveways and sidewalks.

NITRATE OF SODA

ALSO KNOWN AS: Sodium nitrate, Chile or Chilean saltpeter

DESCRIPTION: White, granular substance sold in bags. A salt traditionally mined from natural deposits in Chile or, more recently, produced synthetically by reacting nitric acid with sodium carbonate. Pure nitrate of soda ($NaNO_3$) contains 16 percent nitrogen (16-0-0) and 27 percent sodium (Na). One brand from Chile—Bulldog—is considered natural organic.

USE: Concentrated, highly water soluble source of quickly available nitrogen. Encourages rapid leaf and stem growth.

USE TIP: Use carefully, or you may burn your plants.

BUYING TIP: Old source of nitrogen that was more common before the development of modern synthetic ammonia fertilizer plants.

ROSE FOOD

POPULAR BRAND NAMES: Ra-Pid-Gro®, Peters®, Miracle-Gro® for Roses, Bandini Rose Food®, Osmocote® Plant Food, Verdi-Sol®, Sequestrene® 330 Fe, Rose-Tone®, Ortho Rose Food, Gro-Well Rose Food

DESCRIPTION: Premixed liquids, liquid concentrates, powder concentrates to be mixed with water, pellets, and all of the other forms that fertilizers can come in. Sold as complete fertilizers, rose foods usually have equal or higher percentages of phosphorus, such as 20-20-20, 6-12-6, 8-12-4, or 18-24-16, although there are some exceptions, such as Ra-Pid-Gro® at 23-19-17 and Osmocote® at 18-6-12.

USE: Promoting foliage growth, especially bloom set of roses. Specialized formulations encourage brilliant color.

USE TIPS: Read labels carefully, because many are concentrates that if not diluted properly could easily damage the plants. Others may contain unneeded micronutrients that could change the pH of your soil in a damaging way. If you know your soil conditions, you will be wise to avoid fertilizers that contain additives you may not need.

BUYING TIPS: These products are usually reliable, but at a price. Roses grow best in a soil with a pH around 6.5. To help you maintain this pH level, note the potential acidity equivalent on the label. Liquid rose fertilizers (concentrates and pre-mixed) are readily available to the plant roots and leaves, while pellet and granular fertilizers are not as available but may have the advantage of working over a longer period of time, eliminating the need to fertilize more frequently. Make your choice based on the time you have to spend fertilizing. Sometimes the convenience of application (as with preformulated fertilizers) is worth the extra cost. Roses usually need a yearly dose of cow manure, too.

SULFATE OF AMMONIA

ALSO KNOWN AS: Ammonium sulfate

DESCRIPTION: Granular, acidic fertilizer made from ammonia treated with sulfuric acid, with 20.5 percent available nitrogen (20-0-0). Generally sold in 5-pound bags. Sometimes considered a soil conditioner, as an acidifier.

USE: Fertilizing acid-loving plants; often blended into complete fertilizers as noted earlier in the chapter in the entry for acid-loving plant fertilizers on pages 66–67. Longer lasting but not as quickly available as nitrate of soda (see page 72), but still considered fast-acting. Acidifies the soil (lowers the pH) and feeds sulfur to the plants immediately.

SUPERPHOSPHATE

DESCRIPTION: Bagged white or gray granular fertilizer. During the nineteenth century, superphosphate was made from bone black, a product derived from charred bones, but since then has been manufactured almost exclusively from phosphate rock. Superphosphate is created when rock phosphate, a subtropical mineral deposit found in South Carolina in 1867 (mined in huge open pits there and in Florida, Wyoming, and Tennessee), is treated with either sulfuric acid or phosphoric acid or a combination of the two, making this a synthetic product. A very common kind of phosphorus fertilizer. (Pure mined rock phosphate is an organic fertilizer and is discussed on page 62.)

TYPES: *Normal:* Contains up to 22 percent phosphorus. Made from natural phosphatic material that has been exposed to sulfuric acid. Formerly known as *regular, single, stan-*

dard, simple, or *20 percent superphosphate.* Typical grade is 0-20-0.

Enriched: Derived from natural phosphatic material treated with sulfuric and phosphoric acids. Graded from 0-22-0 to 0-40-0.

Concentrated (also known as *double, treble, triple,* or *multiple superphosphate):* Any grade that contains 40 percent or more available phosphorus, which is the highest percentage of available phosphorus sold. Commonly graded 0-46-0.

USE: Rapidly available source of phosphorus.

USE TIP: Particularly useful when planting bulbs and seeding in lawns.

BUYING TIPS: Superphosphate may be a better buy than bone meal (see pages 59–60) and bulb food (see pages 67–68), at similar phosphate levels.

UREA

DESCRIPTION: Inexpensive source of synthetic nitrogen, derived from natural gas products. Granular, with at least 35 percent but commonly with 46 percent available nitrogen (46-0-0). Acid-forming, nonstaining, and noncorrosive. Sold in bags of all sizes, including 5 pounds. Another similar but slow-release product is *nitroform,* at 38 percent nitrogen.

USE: Foliar feeding and side-dressing of all plants. Also melts snow and ice. Is water-soluble and fast-release.

BUYING TIP: Confusingly called "synthetic organic" by some manufacturers.

VEGETABLE FERTILIZER

ALSO KNOWN AS: Garden fertilizer, garden food, tomato food, vegetable food, etc.

POPULAR BRAND NAMES: Miracle-Gro® All-Purpose, Ra-Pid-Gro®, Gro-Well Garden Fertilizer 5-10-5, Gro-Well Tomato Food 5-10-10

DESCRIPTION: Concentrated powders, pellets, liquids, and granules, with an equal or higher percentage of phosphorus than nitrogen or potash. Perhaps the most common type of fertilizer purchased. Typically 5-10-5 or 10-10-10. Often fortified with micronutrients, including chelated iron. Sold in bags or boxes from 4 to 20 pounds.

USE: To promote the early development of fruiting vegetables, and to help with the bloom set (when the blooms fall and fruit appears). Slightly different formulation than those for blooming ornamental (nonfood) plants.

USE TIPS: Too much fertilizer is worse than too little: Excess nitrogen promotes leaf and stem development at the expense of blooms or fruit, for example. Vegetables benefit from fertilizer at the young seedling stage and again just before bloom set. When fertilizing at these times, follow label directions carefully.

BUYING TIPS: A general purpose 5-10-5 or 10-10-10 is a good garden fertilizer and cheaper than special vegetable foods with their added micronutrients. In fact, some micronutrients, like chelated iron, lower the pH of the soil, and that may be unnecessary in your case. Don't buy it if you don't need it.

WEED AND FEED MIXTURE (LAWN FERTILIZER/HERBICIDE MIX)

POPULAR BRAND NAMES: Twinlight Lawn Food Plus Balan®, Lawn Pro Weed and Feed, Turf Builder Plus 2

DESCRIPTION: Bagged fertilizers that contain both fertilizer and herbicides, and in some rare cases, insecticides.

USE: Promoted as a convenient, labor-saving one-time application, allowing the user to promote lawn growth and fight weeds at the same time.

USE TIPS: This is one instance where convenience can come at a high cost and risk. The government has even issued a warning. The USDA says, in part, "CAUTION: Combinations of [such] materials may be ineffective or even harmful. Their misuse can kill desirable plants or make the soil unproductive. Apply combinations of fertilizer and insecticides or herbicides only on the recommendation of your state agricultural experiment station." Spot control is usually more efficient.

BUYING TIPS: Mixes of fertilizers with weed killers or insecticides are almost always more expensive than the individual products sold separately. Furthermore, performance usually doesn't measure up to the products' claims because the proper time to use pesticides may not be the same as the proper time to fertilize, thereby wasting at least one part of the mix. That makes it even more expensive.

Synthetic Plant Care Products

GRAFTING SUPPLIES

DESCRIPTION:

Grafting wax: Wax compound that is heated, either in a double boiler or by kneading in your hands. Sold in 1/4- to 10-pound boxes. *Trowbridge's* is the oldest and best-known kind.

Rubber budding strips: Small rubber strips of different sizes, ranging from 3/16 to 3/8 inch wide and 4 to 8 inches long, and from .010 to .020 gauge thick. A wider version with a fastener is made, called a *bud tie.*

Grafting thread: Fine waxed line sold in rolls of hundreds of feet.

Grafting tape (also known as *nurseryman's tape):* A type of adhesive tape that decomposes to prevent damage from girdling. Available 1/2 to 1 inch wide, in 60-yard rolls.

USE: Holding freshly made grafts in place and protecting them. Covers exposed plant tissue until new tissue grows in. Grafting most commonly done on fruit or nut trees and roses.

USE TIP: This is a difficult process—follow directions carefully.

ROOTING HORMONE

ALSO KNOWN AS: Rooting powder

POPULAR BRAND NAMES: Rootone®, Hormo-Root, Dip 'N Grow, Hormex

DESCRIPTION: Powder containing growth regulators and sometimes fungicides.

USE: Rooting cuttings faster and without rotting or loss to disease.

USE TIP: Dip just the first inch or so of a cutting into the powder and shake off the excess.

BUYING TIP: Because you dip only the end of a stem into the container, even small amounts last a long time.

SOIL INOCULANT

DESCRIPTION: Powder containing live bacteria of the *Rhizobium* genus.

USE: Mixed with legume (bean family) seed prior to planting in order to facilitate the conversion of nitrogen into a readily available source. This process is known as *nitrogen fixation,* and is a primary characteristic of legume plants.

USE TIPS: A little bit of vegetable oil mixed in with the seed helps the inoculant adhere better. Make sure you are matching the correct bacteria to your particular type of plant. Do not use on seed that has been treated with fungicide: The bacteria you just bought will be killed along with the bacteria that the fungicide was intended for.

BUYING TIPS: Especially helpful in soil never planted with legumes before; not usually all that helpful in soils that have already been treated.

STUMP REMOVER

DESCRIPTION: Potassium salt of nitric acid (potassium nitrate), usually in powder form.

USE: When poured onto tree stumps accelerates the natural rotting process, making the stump and roots porous throughout. Holes then can be easily drilled into the rotted stump, filled with kerosene, and the stump set afire, if local laws permit this.

USE TIP: Generally not dangerous to other plants. Check label to be sure.

TREE PAINT

ALSO KNOWN AS: Tar, tree wound dressing, pruning seal, sealer, tree wound spray, tree paint

DESCRIPTION: Black petroleum asphalt base liquid sold in either aerosol form or as a liquid to be brushed on. Some brands contain an antiseptic fungicide, such as copper naphthenate, to help prevent disease.

USE: Seals the stump of a pruned limb or branch against weathering, drying out, decay, pests, and infection.

USE TIPS: We now know that it is unnecessary to paint over the stump of a normally, cleanly pruned limb, as the tree isolates the area and seals it itself, providing a scar tissue that does not allow decaying to advance into the tree. Also, the USDA Forest Service has found that wound dressing does not prevent rot. However, tree paint may be of value to help seal damaged bark or wounded trees, preventing insects or diseases from entering the tree through the wound. It also fills an aesthetic function when a tree has sustained a large prominent scars.

BUYING TIPS: Can also be used to waterproof wooden tubs and planters. Though sold for use after pruning roses and shrubs, it is not needed if the branches are properly pruned at an angle—the slanted cut allows water to run off.

Pest and Disease Control Products

ABOUT PESTICIDES

Synthetic chemical pesticides, which are so familiar to us and so prominently featured in garden centers, are only one set of tools you can use to manage pest problems. Other tools include regular weeding, crop rotation, mechanical control (traps, barriers, and hand picking), biological controls (introducing predator insects or diseases that infect only the pests), naturally derived (organic) products, and cultural controls such as companion planting methods, planting resistant varieties of plants, proper fertilization, and regular watering. In fact, there are so many alternatives that there is a name for them, *integrated pest management (IPM)* (see pages 81–83 for a fuller discussion). Gardeners who practice IPM have come to think of pesticides as only one alternative among many other gardening practices.

Pesticides cannot replace the good gardening habits and techniques mentioned above, despite the constant din of advertising to the contrary. Strong chemicals treat symptoms; good gardening corrects the sources of the problem. It's just not as simple as the ads would have it. Synthetic products can help, but they are no cure-all, by a long shot. In fact, while 224 insect species were listed as resistant to pesticides in 1970, by 1984, 448 were. That's *double*. And now even the Department of Agriculture is reporting that we rely too much on agricultural chemicals. They are good for solving specific acute problems, but many other products that are not synthetic and are every bit as effective, if not more, are available.

Pesticides come in a wide array of types and forms, all of which are explained in the pages that follow. The terms can be confusing, so if you are unfamiliar with them, read the following pages first. Otherwise, go right to the items, starting on page 93.

ABOUT DEFINING PESTICIDES

Garden centers sell a variety of chemical products to rid the garden of the insects, fungi, diseases, animals, or weeds that threaten plants. These include chemical products that are either naturally derived (organic) or synthetically produced. These "garden chemicals" are usually collectively referred to as *pesticides.*

Several specific pesticides are designed for particular types of pests, while others deal with problems that are not pest-related per se. The former group includes chemicals to control insects *(insecticides),* chemicals to control spiderlike mites *(miticides* or *acaricides),* chemicals to control mice, rats, and other rodents *(rodenticides),* and even specific chemicals to control microscopic worms called nematodes *(nematicides).* All of these specialized garden chemicals are sold under the collective term *pesticides.*

In addition to this group of pesticides, a second group sold as pesticides includes garden chemicals or similar products specifically designed to deal with fungal problems *(fungicides)* and other chemicals that help control weeds and unwanted vegetation *(herbicides).* This is how the term *pesticides* refers to both a family of chemicals and to specific ones that do specific jobs.

Many chemical products exist that are not commonly available to consumers and therefore are not listed here. In some cases these products are not available because they are too dangerous to be used by noncertified individuals; in other cases they are hard to find simply because they are generally marketed only to professionals for commercial use. Such items include chemicals for antibacterial use *(bactericides)* and many products for the control of slugs and snails *(molluscicides).* Diseases and viruses are usually controlled through garden management or IPM techniques.

Finally, this is one area where there are so many products available that are new, or new formulations, or slightly different mixtures of the same ingredients, that it would make this book unwieldy to include them all. What are listed are the basic building blocks of pest control. Undoubtedly, some useful items may have been omitted. If you don't see what you want, check with your local Cooperative Extension agent (see appendix C), your garden center manager, or call one of the major manufacturers whose number or address is easily found on similar products. Your local garden center manager will surely be able to assist you, if only to contact the local representative.

ABOUT USING PESTICIDES

Over the last few decades, there has been an enormous increase in the amount of chemicals, in the form of both pesticides and fertilizers, that Americans put on their gardens and lawns. There is no doubt that this has been costly to the environment, and this misuse can cause harmful injury and death. There are now civil and criminal penalties for misuse of synthetic pesticides. Using chemicals safely means taking the time to read and understand the labels and rigorously following the instructions for mixing, application, and disposal. Much information exists on alternatives to this garden chemical dependency, and the alternative products can be found in the same garden center where you buy the chemicals. Remember, garden chemicals are like prescription drugs: They are very helpful in curing specific unusual problems, but may cause their own problems if relied upon on a regular reflex basis.

Finally, keep in mind there is no such thing as a "safe" pesticide, because by definition a pesticide is toxic to *something*.

ABOUT INTEGRATED PEST MANAGEMENT (IPM)

Using chemicals alone as a method of controlling pests is a relatively recent approach to this perennial gardening and farming problem, driven to a certain extent by the development of our consumer- and advertising-oriented society. However, since the advent of popularly available chemical products forty or fifty years ago, we are more knowledgeable about the effects of chemicals on our environment, on natural pest predators, and on public and personal safety. In fact, safe, intelligent use of pesticides and other chemicals need not pose a threat to the environment, animals, or people.

What we are learning about the effects of some toxic chemicals has caused many people to take a new look at how we use them, how we combine them with natural methods of pest control, and to seek methods of pest management that take into consideration the overall effect on the environment and people. The result is *IPM: integrated pest management.*

Rapidly emerging as the most sensible approach to pest control, IPM incorporates the use of chemicals or toxic pesticides into a system designed to utilize natural and physical controls along with the chemical controls. IPM is neither proorganic nor prochemical, though some may call it ecological pest management: It is instead an approach that seeks the best method of controlling garden pests *using all available resources,* though it does generally mean choosing chemicals only after all other methods have been tried. Furthermore, emphasis is placed on finding the *least toxic* method at every stage.

The following are some of the basic building blocks of the IPM system:

- *Planting resistant plants:* It is possible to select food crops that have been specially bred to be resistant to viral problems. For example, tomato plants labeled VF or VFN are resistant to the common diseases verticullium and fusarium wilts and, with the designation VFN, nematodes. Planting resistant varieties is often easier than doing battle with the pests.
- *Good gardening practices:* A healthy plant is less affected by diseases and pests. Good gardening practices such as doing regular soil tests, maintaining appropriate pH levels for each type of plant, using the right fertilizers, planting to ensure sufficient sun and moisture, weeding, choosing the right plant for the right place, and paying attention to general habitat conditions, like humidity and air circulation, produce plants that are more likely to survive an occasional pest problem.
- *Physical controls and traps:* Physical measures can be taken that include things like hand picking (or even vacuuming!) pests from plants, installing barriers (ranging in form from plastic collars made from coffee cups to elaborate fences and row covers), or such simple practices as flushing pests off foliage with water, mulching well, and installing traps.
- *Biological controls and beneficial insects:* Insects such as the ladybug, lacewing, and the praying mantis are natural predators of harmful insects, and can be introduced to your garden (you can purchase them from mail-order catalogs) or conserved. Unfortunately, these insects are usually more sensitive than the pests to the broad-spectrum insecticides in common use.
- *Oils and soaps:* Highly refined horticultural oils are low in toxic chemicals (though they can be dangerous) and act by

smothering the pest without the use of poisons, while soaps both smother and destroy some insects and weeds.

• *Research and development:* This ranges from scientists taking products designed to deal with one problem and trying them for others to genetic engineering. A recent example is antitranspirants, which were originally developed to prevent the loss of moisture from evergreen leaves during winter and which are now used to help prevent fungal problems.

• *Choosing toxic chemicals carefully:* Selective use of synthetic insecticides, fungicides, and herbicides can be made in integrated pest management programs, but only if these chemicals work together with the other components in the system, such as the introduction of beneficial insects. For example, you would want to avoid using a pesticide that might kill the ladybugs and praying mantis which are being used to control aphids and other pests. The least toxic chemical is sought out first and its reuse considered carefully; no chemical is used routinely.

• *Analysis of the problems and the solutions:* Much time is given to the positive identification of pests, monitoring of the pest population, level of plant injury, and evaluation of the effect your strategy is having.

ABOUT THE MOST COMMON PROBLEMS WITH HOUSEPLANTS AND GARDENS

COMMON INSECT PESTS: There are over two thousand insects that are considered pests; add to that the fact that many pests exist in different forms at different stages of development, causing different types of damage. Immature beetles, for example, are known as larva, and leafhoppers at the stage just prior to adulthood are nymphs. Many books are available that identify these pests; they should be consulted thoroughly in order to figure out what plagues you. Proper identification of the pest is the most important first step. Here are descriptions of the most common insect pests:

• *Aphids* are small sucking insects that are teardrop in shape, winged or wingless (depending on their life stage), and range in color from light green, gray to dark brown, to black. Aphids are often found on the tender growing tips of plants and flower buds. They are of particular concern as they often carry plant viruses.

- *Spider mites* are small, almost microscopic, sucking animals that are black, orange-green, or red in color. The red spider mite is one of the more common ones. It lives on the underside of plants, thriving when the weather is hot and dry. Often the mite is not visible to a casual observer, but in large numbers their fine webs are evidence of their presence.
- *Scale* are also small sucking insects that may be hard or soft, oval or round in shape, and slow moving in juvenile stages (they are immobile in their adult stage). Types include cottony taxus, oleander, brown soft, oyster, and white peach scale. Many resemble small brown turtle shells attached to the stems and veins of plant leaves. The presence of scale is often indicated by a sticky syrupy substance on the plant. This is actually the honeydew that the scale excretes.
- *Mealybugs* are common sucking insects that are oval and soft-bodied. Their presence is indicated by cottony masses in the axis of leaves, stems, and branches. These masses are actually the nests or egg masses of the reproducing pests.
- *Nematodes* are microscopic sucking worms, some types of which produce hard swellings on plants. Symptoms include slow growth of plants and yellowing leaves. If nematodes are present in container-grown plants or houseplants, it is best to discard the soil and replant in sterile soil.
- *White flies* resemble small moths and can be found on the underside of the infested plants. When the leaves or plant is shaken, the white flies fly around the plant in numbers. White flies are sucking insects and are often a perennial problem on many vegetable crops, such as squash, beans, and tomatoes, as well as begonias, citrus trees, fuchsias, and geraniums.
- *Grubs* are little wormlike creatures that actually may be any of a number of insects, especially Japanese beetles, which spend part of their life cycle as wormlike grubs during their larval stage in the soil. They can do extensive damage to roots and turf. Fortunately, this is usually a vulnerable stage for them, during which controls are quite effective.
- *Beetles* are hard-shelled insects that damage leaves, stems, and roots.
- *Caterpillars* are moths and butterflies in a wormlike stage. They often do major damage to plants, especially the leaves, during their short life stage.

FUNGI: Fungi are plants without chlorophyll. Because they cannot make their own food, they often live as parasites on plants and animals. The garden fungi include *rusts, mildews, molds, smuts,* and a variety of *blights* (athlete's foot and yeast infections are common fungal infections that plague humans). Of the common fungi, the following are likely to be encountered by most gardeners:

- *Powdery mildew:* A fungal problem endemic to many roses, euonymus, lilacs, and garden phlox. It appears as a white film on the leaves late in the season or after particularly wet spells. Since this is hard to prevent and cure and will not kill a healthy plant, it is often wise to learn to live with the problem.
- *Black spot:* A very common fungal problem, particularly on roses. It appears on leaves as yellow spots with brown or black centers.

Fungi are spore-borne, with the spores germinating in the presence of water and the absence of light. A good garden practice to reduce the spread of fungal problems is to avoid watering in the evening or at night. There is no absolute cure for fungal problems on plants once infected, and at best fungicides only prevent the spread of the fungus, though recent experiments with antitranspirants (see page 63)—substances that coat the leaves and prevent spores from attaching or growing—promise hope.

ABOUT TYPES OF GARDEN CHEMICALS

Pesticides are sold in many different forms, which determine the way in which the chemical is applied and how it works.

- *Systemics* are pesticides that are taken into the system of a plant and ingested by insects that suck or eat the plant, therefore working from within the plant. Available in dry, liquid, powder, granular, and concentrated forms, they are absorbed by plants and cannot be leached away by rain or watering. The conscientious gardener should be aware that some systemics can remain in the soil and water table for long periods of time before breaking down, possibly becoming a serious threat to you and the environment, and of course they can remain in food plants.
- *Nonsystemic* pesticides are not absorbed by the plants but instead are ingested directly by the pest, or else work on contact with the insect.

- *Contact* pesticides are those that kill the insect on contact.
- *Selective* chemicals are specifically designed to kill or attack certain insects or weeds without harming other creatures or plants.
- *Nonselective* chemicals are not particular in what they destroy—they kill whatever they touch, and thus can destroy desirable plants (in the case of herbicides) or beneficial insects (in the case of insecticides) when applied incorrectly. Recent gardening wisdom encourages the specific identification of the problem and the use of more selective methods of control. The point is to avoid the indiscriminate use of nonselective chemicals.
- *Baits* contain some type of pesticide and usually a pest attractant, which the pest eats, while others are used as lures with traps.

ABOUT THE FORMS OF GARDEN CHEMICALS

Pesticide packages range in size from a few ounces to 100 pounds, depending on the form and manufacturer.

SPRAYS: Some chemicals are sold to be used as a nonaerosol spray, either prepackaged in a pump or spray container or sold for use in a sprayer (see pages 232–34). These chemicals include:

- *Emulsifiable concentrates,* or *emulsions,* solutions sold as liquids that must be diluted with water (follow label directions carefully). They are produced when the toxicant (the toxic substance) and an emulsifier (a substance that keeps the chemicals together) are dissolved in an organic solvent. The amount of the toxicant in relation to the rest of the mixture is noted on the label as a percentage. The strength of the product is sometimes described in terms of pounds of toxicant per gallon of concentrate.
- *Wettable powders,* very fine powders that are applied after being mixed with water. They remain suspended in the water, not dissolved, so you have to keep shaking the solution as you use it to keep it evenly distributed. Wettable powders, abbreviated *WP* on labels, are made up of an active ingredient (the actual pesticide), often a wetting agent (the substance that causes it to become more easily wettable), and some inert or filler (carrier) ingredients. The amount of the pesticide relative to the filler is shown on the label as a percentage, such as "50W" or "50WP" for a 50 percent concentration. Wettable powders are applied with a sprayer

just as emulsifiable concentrates are. Be sure to keep nozzles and filters clean, as they tend to clog up quickly with this kind of material. Mix into a paste and then dilute, rather than just dumping the powder into the water.

• *Flowable liquid* (also known as *flowable powders, flowable formulations, flowable wettable powders,* or *water-dispersible suspensions),* creamy fluids whose active ingredients are suspended in a flowable liquid or paste. They need to be diluted with water to be used as a spray. Flowable liquid is a fairly recently developed form of pesticide, similar to wettable powder in its properties, but it forms a more stable suspension when mixed with water. It still eventually settles out in a sprayer, but more slowly than a wettable powder. Available in a dry form, called *dry flowable powders* or *DF.*

• *Horticultural oils* (also known as *sprayable* or *miscible oils*) contain an emulsifier (see emulsifiable concentrates on preceding page) and can therefore be mixed with water before application. These are often sold with an insecticide added, though not always. They are applied to the plant and work by smothering the insects, such as aphids, mites, and scale. These oils have been particularly helpful in the control of scale on ornamental trees and shrubs.

SPRAY CANS AND AEROSOLS: These are ready-mixed formulas that are sold in spray cans. There are two types and are distinguished by the insects they are intended to control. Many contain oil as a solvent. *Space sprays* produce a fine mist or fog and help control flying insects. *Surface sprays* produce a spray of droplets larger than the former and fall from the air quickly. These are used to control crawling insects.

DUSTS: Powders that are usually made up of particles larger than those of wettable powders. They are applied with shakers and dusters and are not wet when applied. They stick to the surface of the leaves and stems.

BAITS: Food substances to which poison has been added.

GRANULES: Like dusts but are made up of even larger particles. They are applied dry. Watering and rain make them available, but the large particle size makes them slower acting.

ABOUT READING A PESTICIDE LABEL

Pesticides must, by law, include a whole range of information on their labels, telling you clearly what it is, how, when, why, and

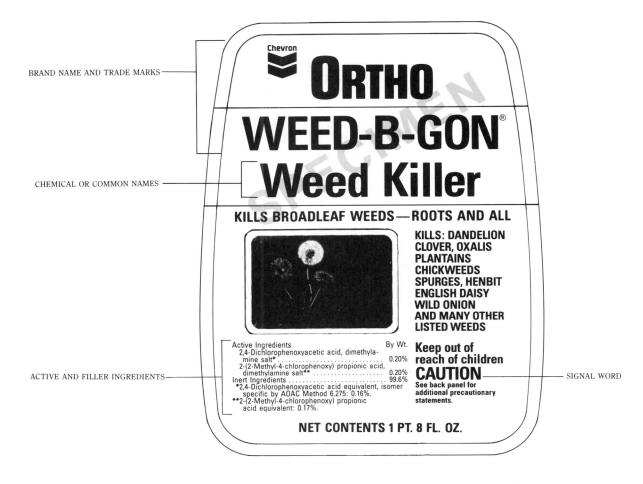

BRAND NAME AND TRADE MARKS

CHEMICAL OR COMMON NAMES

ACTIVE AND FILLER INGREDIENTS

SIGNAL WORD

where to use it, and who made it. The sample label above is typical. This information is officially grouped in the following categories: *product and brand name and identification; active and filler ingredients; precautionary statements* (including the signal word and first aid instructions); *directions for use; directions for storage and disposal; manufacturer's name and address;* and *EPA code numbers.*

PRODUCT AND BRAND NAME AND IDENTIFICATION: The manufacturer's name for this product may suggest its use or it may be the official common name of the chemical. Some formerly trademarked names have become common names, such as diazinon, malathion, and ferbam, all of which are described later on. It is often stated here what type of chemical it is, too, such as "sys-

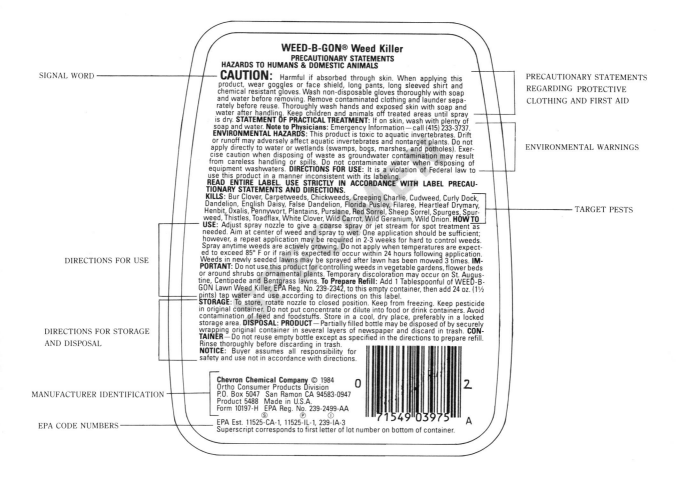

SIGNAL WORD

PRECAUTIONARY STATEMENTS REGARDING PROTECTIVE CLOTHING AND FIRST AID

ENVIRONMENTAL WARNINGS

TARGET PESTS

DIRECTIONS FOR USE

DIRECTIONS FOR STORAGE AND DISPOSAL

MANUFACTURER IDENTIFICATION

EPA CODE NUMBERS

WEED-B-GON® Weed Killer
PRECAUTIONARY STATEMENTS
HAZARDS TO HUMANS & DOMESTIC ANIMALS
CAUTION: Harmful if absorbed through skin. When applying this product, wear goggles or face shield, long pants, long sleeved shirt and chemical resistant gloves. Wash non-disposable gloves thoroughly with soap and water before removing. Remove contaminated clothing and launder separately before reuse. Thoroughly wash hands and exposed skin with soap and water after handling. Keep children and animals off treated areas until spray is dry. **STATEMENT OF PRACTICAL TREATMENT:** If on skin, wash with plenty of soap and water. **Note to Physicians:** Emergency Information—call (415) 233-3737. **ENVIRONMENTAL HAZARDS:** This product is toxic to aquatic invertebrates. Drift or runoff may adversely affect aquatic invertebrates and nontarget plants. Do not apply directly to water or wetlands (swamps, bogs, marshes, and potholes). Exercise caution when disposing of waste as groundwater contamination may result from careless handling or spills. Do not contaminate water when disposing of equipment washwaters. **DIRECTIONS FOR USE:** It is a violation of Federal law to use this product in a manner inconsistent with its labeling.
READ ENTIRE LABEL. USE STRICTLY IN ACCORDANCE WITH LABEL PRECAUTIONARY STATEMENTS AND DIRECTIONS.
KILLS: Bur Clover, Carpetweeds, Chickweeds, Creeping Charlie, Cudweed, Curly Dock, Dandelion, English Daisy, False Dandelion, Florida Pusley, Filaree, Heartleaf Drymary, Henbit, Oxalis, Pennywort, Plantains, Purslane, Red Sorrel, Sheep Sorrel, Spurges, Spurweed, Thistles, Toadflax, White Clover, Wild Carrot, Wild Geranium, Wild Onion. **HOW TO USE:** Adjust spray nozzle to give a coarse spray or jet stream for spot treatment as needed. Aim at center of weed and spray to wet. One application should be sufficient; however, a repeat application may be required in 2-3 weeks for hard to control weeds. Spray anytime weeds are actively growing. Do not apply when temperatures are expected to exceed 85° F or if rain is expected to occur within 24 hours following application. Weeds in newly seeded lawns may be sprayed after lawn has been mowed 3 times. **IMPORTANT:** Do not use this product for controlling weeds in vegetable gardens, flower beds or around shrubs or ornamental plants. Temporary discoloration may occur on St. Augustine, Centipede and Bentgrass lawns. **To Prepare Refill:** Add 1 Tablespoonful of WEED-B-GON Lawn Weed Killer, EPA Reg. No. 239-2342, to this empty container, then add 24 oz. (1½ pints) tap water and use according to directions on this label.
STORAGE: To store, rotate nozzle to closed position. Keep from freezing. Keep pesticide in original container. Do not put concentrate or dilute into food or drink containers. Avoid contamination of feed and foodstuffs. Store in a cool, dry place, preferably in a locked storage area. **DISPOSAL: PRODUCT**—Partially filled bottle may be disposed of by securely wrapping original container in several layers of newspaper and discard in trash. **CONTAINER**—Do not reuse empty bottle except as specified in the directions to prepare refill. Rinse thoroughly before discarding in trash.
NOTICE: Buyer assumes all responsibility for safety and use not in accordance with directions.

Chevron Chemical Company © 1984
Ortho Consumer Products Division
P.O. Box 5047   San Ramon CA 94583-0947
Product 5488   Made in U.S.A.
Form 10197-H   EPA Reg. No. 239-2499-AA
EPA Est. 11525-CA-1, 11525-IL-1, 239-IA-3
Superscript corresponds to first letter of lot number on bottom of container.

0   2   A
7 1549 03975

---

temic insect control," and what it is most often used for, such as "kills broadleaf weeds" or other general statements.

ACTIVE AND FILLER INGREDIENTS: Listed, with percentage of volume or weight, by both common and/or chemical names, many also have registered trademarks. These names are found in the entries on the following pages. Many people, even experts, confuse the common or chemical names with trademarked names, such as carbaryl (a chemical name) with Sevin® (a trademarked name). Chemical names are technical terms that describe the composition of a substance. These are the names that you would want to give a doctor in the case of an accidental poisoning. Filler ingredients, usually labeled as inert ingredients, are not necessarily inert in regard to the user or the environment—just trade secrets that are not required to be divulged.

PRECAUTIONARY STATEMENTS: This statement is found on various parts of the label. One of three *signal words*—DANGER, WARNING, or CAUTION—is written in large type on the front of the label and often repeated on the back or sides. Toxic garden chemicals must, by law, include these signal words, or *indicators,* which clearly state the level of toxicity as indicated by the *LD 50 value,* a test that determines the dosage required to kill 50 percent of laboratory test animals, such as mice, rats, or rabbits. Neither chronic toxicity nor whether the chemical might be a carcinogen is indicated. The chemicals available in garden centers are known as *general classification chemicals;* more toxic or difficult to handle chemicals are available only to licensed professionals and are known as *restricted chemicals.* The most toxic restricted chemicals are labeled DANGER—POISON, in red, along with a skull and crossbones.

The most toxic chemicals available over the counter to consumers are marked with the signal word DANGER and are extremely poisonous to humans and animals. May be fatal if swallowed.

Chemicals that are somewhat less toxic carry the signal word WARNING. They are toxic, but kill fewer lab animals at higher dosages than those marked DANGER. Some of these can be fatal if swallowed. Handle carefully.

The rest of the chemicals, which are still less toxic, carry the signal word CAUTION on the label. The warning CAUTION does not mean that a chemical is not toxic; it just means it will take more of it to kill you, your family, or your pets than the more toxic chemicals.

All chemicals, even the less toxic ones, carry the warning "Keep Out of Reach of Children." Handle as if it were very toxic to be on the safe side.

The rest of the precautionary statements include information on hazards to humans and domestic animals, first aid instructions (or "Statement of Practical Treatment"), a "Note to Physicians" with suggestions of more advanced treatment and antidotes (and what *not* to give), "environmental hazards" (actually warnings about where not to use it), and "physical or chemical hazards," such as flammability. If the product is intended for use on food crops, then the amount of time you must wait after application before harvesting fruit or vegetables may be indicated here if it is not noted in the directions for use. The label may also indicate here if any special clothing or safety equipment is required.

DIRECTIONS FOR USE: This is the part you should reread until you are absolutely certain of how to use the product, and above all, how much of it to use. Labels on larger containers of a given product might contain additional useful information, such as an extended list of which pests it kills instead of a general grouping. "Days to Harvest" is the number of days after application you must wait in order to eat fruit or vegetables treated with this product. Whether or not this product can be combined with others would be shown here too.

DIRECTIONS FOR STORAGE AND DISPOSAL: Varies surprisingly from product to product. Most urge you not to reuse the container, among other things.

MANUFACTURER'S IDENTIFICATION: Provided so that you can write or call for more information. Many manufacturers have an 800 number for your convenience and good literature that they willingly send out.

EPA CODE NUMBERS: Both the manufacturer and the EPA give these products identification numbers for additional accuracy when you are inquiring about them. They refer to the chemical and the manufacturing plant and batch, among other things.

GENERAL BUYING AND USE TIPS FOR GARDEN CHEMICALS

Because pesticides are usually poisonous, they must be used sparingly and correctly, both in terms of common sense and with respect to the law. You should make every effort to do so, no matter how small your problem. Should you decide to go with pesticides after trying alternative strategies, you should always proceed cautiously.

- Use the least toxic method of pest management first. It is easier to advance to a more toxic substance if the first does not work than it is to eradicate the effects of a too toxic solution. If there is a safe organic method, you may wish to try that first. If it does not work, go to the next least harmful method. Many books and magazines offer information on this problem. If at all possible, use chemicals no stronger than those that contain CAUTION on the label and avoid those labeled WARNING, DANGER, and POISON (you need a license to apply DANGER—POISON products). Few home gardening problems are so threatening that you need to risk using the more toxic and dangerous chemicals. Each of those words denotes a jump to the next higher level of poison. Stick with CAUTION level poisons whenever possible.

• Identify the pest and determine how destructive it actually is, before deciding what to do. Most Cooperative Extension Services (see appendix C) are more than willing to help with the identification of pests and plenty of literature is available. Many insects, while a nuisance, may not be all that harmful to you or your garden, and in fact the chemicals introduced to deal with them are often more destructive than the discomfort of living with nuisance pests. Try to avoid a knee-jerk reaction to kill all pests.

• Know your chemical. If the specific pest affected or purpose for using a chemical cannot be found in the directions on the label of a product, *do not use that product.* Use only those products that specifically treat the problem you have and nothing else, and only use it on the plants indicated. Read and then reread the instructions. Follow them religiously, including dilution, application, and "Days to Harvest" directions in the case of use on food crops. Pay attention to whatever other chemicals you may be using, including fertilizers, and check with the manufacturer or your Cooperative Extension agent to see if they are compatible. Also check to see if the chemical can be mixed with other pesticides.

• Figure out exactly how much of a material is needed to handle the problem and buy only that amount. It is easier to buy more if it is needed than it is to dispose of unused chemicals. Furthermore, some chemicals lose their effectiveness in storage. Plus, storage can be dangerous too. Overapplication rarely kills more pests (it may even increase some types) and can harm you or your garden. Don't pour excess chemicals down the drain. Never reuse a pesticide container. Most can be wrapped in several layers of newspaper and put in the trash; others have special instructions for disposal on the label.

• Apply toxic chemicals wisely and safely. Do not apply sprays on a windy day. Do not eat, chew gum, or smoke while using pesticides, as this can lead you to ingest the chemical. Wear rubber gloves and clothing that covers your whole body, but avoid natural fiber clothing and shoes (cotton, wool, linen, or leather) because they act as natural wicks and carry the chemical to your skin. Respirators are recommended in some cases. Some gardeners use only one set of clothes for applying toxic chemicals and wash them separately from other clothes. Never use or store pesticides near food, utensils, toys, or children. Never use food utensils for measuring toxic chemicals. Instead, designate one particular measuring cup for this purpose. Remember that small children or pets may eat baits.

● Do not mix two or more chemicals, whether pesticides alone or pesticides with fertilizers, unless you are absolutely sure that no harm will result. In most cases this should not be done. You should really mix only when it is specifically suggested on the label.

IMPORTANT NOTE

The popular brand names listed here are by no means the only names under which these items are sold. Many excellent brands have been omitted. There are over six hundred active ingredients and fifty thousand formulations to choose from. Many new ones are announced daily and old ones removed. A listing here—or omission—is in no way an endorsement of or comment on these products. Dilution rates are indicated as a guide and are by no means to be considered definitive. Only the directions on a pesticide's label should be followed. This book is intended only as a guide and not as the authority on how a chemical should be used or the risks of using it. Neither the authors nor the publishers are responsible for any consequences of using any of the products noted here.

Organic Pesticides

ABOUT ORGANIC PESTICIDES

Pesticides derived from natural sources, while often toxic, are particularly useful in IPM programs. Most of them break down with little residual toxicity, meaning that the toxic chemical does not linger in the soil, water, or atmosphere. Some are based on soap and others on plants, which may be the oldest pesticides around. Remember, just because it is a natural pesticide does not mean it is entirely safe: Some are quite toxic.

Organic Insecticides

DIATOMACEOUS EARTH

ALSO KNOWN AS: Diatom flour, D.E., fossil shell flower

SIGNAL WORD: None—not officially registered as a pesticide.

DESCRIPTION: A white powder composed of finely ground, sharp-edged fossilized shells of diatoms—small-shelled, water-dwelling creatures of the algae family. Can be used as a spray when mixed with water, or used as a dust. Nontoxic.

USE: The microscopic prism-shaped particles' razor-sharp edges easily penetrate many insects on contact, causing them to dry up (desiccate). Sprinkle a band of it around plants that slugs attack. Also used in swimming pool filters and as the abrasive material in scouring cleansers as well.

USE TIP: Use a mask when applying and avoid breathing the dust or getting it in your eyes. Can be fatal to pets if ingested.

BUYING TIP: This is not an expensive product when you consider what it can do relatively safely. Sold in 10-pound bags. Try your local swimming pool dealer if your garden center does not carry it.

INSECTICIDAL SOAPS

POPULAR BRAND NAMES: Safer® Insecticidal Soap, Orthomite Insecticidal Soap

SIGNAL WORD: CAUTION

DESCRIPTION: Products that contain (or are) salts of fatty acids mixed with water and alcohol. They are a direct alternative to synthetic chemical pesticides. Most are sold in liquid concentrates to be mixed and sprayed on the plant, though some are sold in premixed solutions in sprayer bottles. Different formulations of various fatty acids are available for different plants and their pests, such as one for roses, flowers, and houseplants, and another for fruits and vegetables. Gentle to beneficial insects and animals (the birds and the bees); compatible with many biological controls (beneficial predators and the like) and a good number of chemical and organic pesticides; it is incompatible with certain ones that are listed by the manufacturer.

USE: Killing aphids, spider mites, mealybugs, rose slugs, psyllids, earwigs, scales, and whitefly on both garden plants and houseplants, depending on the formulation, which is clearly indicated on the label.

USE TIP: Insecticidal soaps are a contact spray—they kill the insect when they come in contact with it. However, they kill insects only in a certain stage in the life cycle (such as during some juvenile stages before the insects have formed a hard shell). Because of this, it is often necessary to repeat the application at intervals of seven to ten days. Safe to use on food crops right up to harvest.

BUYING TIP: Insecticidal soaps are safe and easy to use, especially those that are premixed and come in easy-to-use pump sprayer bottles. Ivory soap, when mixed with water, often works as well, but you should experiment as it might damage your plants.

NICOTINE SULFATE

ALSO KNOWN AS: Nicotine sulphate

POPULAR BRAND NAME: Black Leaf 40

SIGNAL WORD: DANGER

DESCRIPTION: Alkaloid extract of tobacco, mixed with sulfuric acid when sold as an aqueous solution concentrate, or with lime as a dust, containing 40 percent nicotine. Often combined with an alkaline water or soap solution. Also sold as a smoke for fumigation when combined with a combustible material, and as a wettable powder.

USE: Nonselective contact spray, sometimes a fumigant, for a wide range of insects—none are immune! Its efficiency as a fumigant is increased by a high temperature.

USE TIPS: Leaves little residue, but by the same token has a short shelf life. Can be washed off plants. May harm flower petals. Increase effectiveness by adding a few teaspoonfuls of dormant oil spray (see pages 119–20) per gallon. Nicotine is extremely toxic to humans and nicotine products are usually labeled POISON. A few drops can kill a horse!

BUYING TIP: Selective insecticides are preferable to nonselective ones, as their toxic effects are more predictable.

PYRETHRUM

ALSO KNOWN AS: Pyrethrins, pyrethrin

SIGNAL WORD: CAUTION

DESCRIPTION: Considered a broad spectrum natural botanical

insecticide that works as a contact or stomach poison, it is organically derived in oil form from the ground dried flowers of the African daisy, or oriental chrysanthemum, *Chrysanthemum cinerariaefolium,* grown in Kenya, Rwanda, Tanzania, and Ecuador (and now, as a test, in New Jersey). Sold in pressurized cans or as an oil concentrate for sprays, though can be found in dust form, too. Sometimes mixed with liquid rotenone (see next entry). In use since the mid-nineteenth century. *Pyrethrins* refers to the active ingredients of the plant. *(Permethrin* is a synthetic version.)

USE: In spray form for controlling flies, mosquitoes, springtails, aphids, and whiteflies. Follow label directions carefully so as not to harm plants. Often sold as a household spray for use on insects directly.

USE TIPS: Pyrethrum has a low toxicity to most nonallergic people and animals and leaves no harmful residues on food crops or vegetables ("low residual toxicity"), but skin contact or contamination of water should still be avoided. Some formulations contain petroleum distillates that can be carcinogenic or cause allergic reactions. Use as a last resort after other natural controls have failed. Dispose of empty container according to instructions on the label.

BUYING TIP: Look for the pure dust form if petroleum distillates present a problem for you.

ROTENONE

POPULAR BRAND NAMES: Chem Fish, Derris, Nicouline, Rotacide, Tubatoxin, DX, Prentox®, Noxfire®

SIGNAL WORD: CAUTION (in some formulations); DANGER (in some formulations)

DESCRIPTION: Organic, biodegradable insecticide made from the roots of several types of pea plants in the legume family. Generally sold as a dust or a wettable powder, though sometimes as a spray, to be used as a selective contact insecticide. Moderately toxic to animals (very toxic to swine and fish) but leaves no harmful residues on food or vegetable crops. Sometimes mixed in liquid form with pyrethrum (see preceding entry).

USE: For control of beetles, caterpillars, and other chewing insects. Some mixes may be used as a flea and tick spray for pets, and would be marked as such.

USE TIPS: Tends to break down after a week, which is helpful around harvest time. Avoid contact with skin and keep away from bodies of water, such as fish ponds, and bees. Do not store spray mixture—buy or mix only what you can use right away.

RYANIA

POPULAR BRAND NAMES: Ryanicide®, Triple-Plus (mixture), R-50

SIGNAL WORD: CAUTION

DESCRIPTION: Ground stems of *Ryania speciosa,* a South American shrub. Available as a dust or a wettable powder, often as a mixture with rotenone (above) and pyrethrum (see pages 95–96).

USE: Very effective against European corn borer.

SABADILLA

POPULAR BRAND NAME: Red Devil®

SIGNAL WORD: CAUTION

DESCRIPTION: Dust made from the seeds of a South American lily, sold as a wettable powder or a dust. In use at least since the sixteenth century.

USE: Controlling a wide range of tough pests, especially squash bugs, stink bugs, harlequin bugs, and blister beetles—all hard to control in their adult stage with other pesticides. Commonly used on turnips, collards, and cabbage.

USE TIPS: Can also be used as a spray. OK to use up to the day of harvest. Irritating to mucous membranes, so wear a mask when applying.

BUYING TIP: May no longer be registered with the EPA.

TOBACCO DUST

SIGNAL WORD: CAUTION

DESCRIPTION: Fine granular dust sold in small and large bags. Consists of approximately 5 percent nicotine and 95 percent inert matter in most formulations for consumer use. An old standby, a less refined version of nicotine sulfate (see page 95).

USE: Control of leafhoppers, thrips, plant lice, and other soft-bodied insects.

USE TIPS: Rinse leaves with water after application to avoid burning. Very potent: Use prior to release of beneficial insects in your garden. May turn roses black! May also affect growth and flowering in some plants, so experiment first.

Organic Herbicides

MOSS AND ALGAE KILLER

POPULAR BRAND NAME: Safer® Moss and Algae Killer (previously Cryptocidal Soap)

SIGNAL WORD: WARNING

DESCRIPTION: Liquid concentrate mixed with water and used as a spray. Nonstaining, noncorrosive, with a natural fatty acid base. Similar to insecticidal soap (see pages 94–95). Available in formulations for lawns or for decks, patios, and walls.

USE: For the control of algae, lichens, mosses, etc.

USE TIPS: Can be safely used on roofing, siding, walkways, fencing, trees, and greenhouses. Even works on bathroom fixtures and tiles. Do not spray on plant foliage to control insects.

BUYING TIP: At around $9 a quart, this product may be more expensive than a more toxic substance, but it may be worth the cost if you want an entirely nontoxic product.

WEED AND GRASS KILLER

POPULAR BRAND NAME: Safer® SharpShooter™

SIGNAL WORD: CAUTION

DESCRIPTION: Biodegradable spray made from naturally occurring saturated fatty acids. Works on contact.

USE: Killing weeds and unwanted grass.

USE TIPS: Leaves no residue after forty-eight hours, which means you can plant whatever you actually want in that soil then. Must be applied under the exact conditions specified on the label in order to work.

Organic Fungicides

ABOUT ORGANIC FUNGICIDES

A number of different products are considered organic fungicides that are not necessarily labeled as such, nor listed here. One prime example is antitranspirants, or antidesiccants—used for maintaining the moisture in evergreens and shining houseplant leaves—which also happen to be effective at smothering various types of fungal infestations. See page 63 for a more lengthy discussion.

LIME-SULFUR SOLUTION

SIGNAL WORD: DANGER

DESCRIPTION: Liquid compound of calcium polysulfide sold by the quart, gallon, or 5-gallon container.

USE: Controlling powdery mildew, cane blight, brown rot, and the like on fruit and nut trees, ornamentals, and flowers. Can also be used as an insecticide against scale and as a miticide.

USE TIPS: Apply as a dormant spray as well as in the growing season. Best if used as buds are just starting to swell, but before they break open. More caustic than sulfur—wear a mask and avoid contact with skin when applying.

SULFUR

ALSO KNOWN AS: Wettable sulfur, wettable dusting sulphur, garden sulfur

POPULAR BRAND NAMES: Safer® Garden Fungicide, Flotox® Garden Sulfur, Cosan, Sul-Cide, Magic Dusting Sulfur, Elosal, Kumulus S., Thiolux

SIGNAL WORD: CAUTION (in some formulations)

DESCRIPTION: Fine powder consisting mostly of ground-up sulfur rock. Available in either a wettable micronized powder (extremely small particles) form for use as a dust or in liquid, both as a ready-to-use mixture in a spray bottle or as a concentrate. Sulfur is one of the oldest known garden pesticides (it has been used for thousands of years), and a relatively benign one, though it does smell bad during application.

USE: Controlling powdery mildew, black spot, scab, brown canker, leaf spot, rust, and other diseases on fruits, vegetables, flowering trees, roses, and ornamentals. Like most sulfur products, this works as an organic miticide, too, and kills thrips. Sometimes combined with acephate (see page 117) to control other insects (see labels for details). Also used as a soil acidifier (see page 5). Do not use within one month of using an oil spray.

USE TIPS: No residue. Safe for use on food crops. Extra-fine size of granules makes for better adhesion. Can cause skin irritation, may acidify soil, and may harm beneficial microorganisms and beneficial insects.

BUYING TIPS: *Micronized sulfur* has the smallest possible particle sizes, which makes it cover better. Also, check the label to be sure you are getting pure sulfur.

Organic Miticides

MITE KILLER

POPULAR BRAND NAMES: Safer® Mite Killer, Orthomite Insecticidal Soap

SIGNAL WORD: CAUTION

DESCRIPTION: Liquid spray sold in concentrated as well as ready-to-use strengths, in 8- and 24-ounce plastic bottles. Made from salts of fatty acids, as are the insecticidal soaps. Rapidly biodegradable.

USE: Kills mites once an infestation has begun, especially red spider mites, two-spotted mites, and most sucking insects. Intended for use on houseplants.

USE TIP: Use a flashlight and a magnifying glass to make sure you have covered every area, especially where webbing is found. Most problems are on the undersides of leaves.

BUYING TIP: Other controls include wiping or rinsing off leaves.

Organic Rodenticides

CASTOR BEAN

DESCRIPTION: Seed of the castor bean plant, about the size of a lima or pinto bean. Speckled brown and white, it is often used in necklaces. Though in a tropical climate the plant can grow to become a 40-foot-tall tree with leaves 3 feet across, in the United States it usually grows to a height of only 8 to 12 feet.

Like its seeds, the plant is poisonous to humans and domestic animals. Oil made from the castor plant seed is toxic, too.

USE: The seed, placed in a mole tunnel, is a toxic bait for moles and voles. A repellent spray can be made from a tablespoon of castor oil mixed with 2 tablespoons of liquid detergent and sprinkled over mole-infested areas.

USE TIPS: Do not use if a child might pick up and eat the bean (though it is not toxic to handle). Remove after a month if not eaten by a mole so that a castor plant does not grow. Repellent sprays work best if applied just after a rain shower, for increased penetration.

BUYING TIP: Generally not sold as a rodenticide but sold in seed catalogs for the castor bean plant.

RED SQUILL

POPULAR BRAND NAMES: Scillirocide, Death Diet, Red Quill, Rodine

SIGNAL WORD: CAUTION

DESCRIPTION: A powder or liquid extract made from the bulb of red squill, *Urginea maritima,* which grows in the Mediterranean. It is often used as an additive in rodent baits because it is toxic to rats but not to other animals when used in recommended dosages.

USE: For the control of Norway rats.

USE TIP: Not as harmful to the environment or humans as many similar products.

BUYING TIP: This is not commonly available, but it could become more popular if consumers keep requesting it. An imported item.

STRYCHNINE

SIGNAL WORD: DANGER—POISON

DESCRIPTION: White crystalline powder, somewhat soluble in water and alcohol, extracted from the seeds or berries of the tropical tree and vine family *Strychnos nus vomica.*

USE: Common ingredient in poison baits for moles and gophers in concentrations of less than .5 percent.

USE TIP: Keep baits out of reach of children, pets, and wildlife.

VITAMIN D-3

POPULAR BRAND NAMES: Quintox™, Rampage™, Ortho Rat & Mouse-B-Gon™

CHEMICAL NAME: Cholecalciferol

SIGNAL WORD: CAUTION

DESCRIPTION: Granular bait, pellets, meal, or parafinized blocks, often sold wrapped in disposable paper or cardboard traps. Usually in a mixture containing only .075 percent active ingredients.

USE: Natural rat and mouse control with low toxicity. Causes death in about two to four days.

USE TIPS: Dead rodents are not poisonous to other animals, so this is a fairly safe item to use around pets and domestic animals that might eat them. Good for rodents that have developed resistance to warfarin (see page 133).

Biological Controls

ABOUT BIOLOGICAL CONTROLS

Insects succumb to diseases just like plants and people, and these products increase the naturally occurring disease organisms. Many *microbial control agents, biorational pesticides,* or *microbial insecticides*—which are inherently organic—are on the market and are very easy to use.

BACILLUS POPILLIAE

ALSO KNOWN AS: Milky disease spores, milky spore powder, milky spore disease, milky spores, BP

POPULAR BRAND NAMES: Doom, Japidemic, Grub Attack™, Safer® Grub Killer

DESCRIPTION: A powder of spores applied directly to the soil, usually on lawns, and watered in well.

USE: For the control of Japanese beetles in the larvae stage (grubs), although some brands claim to control oriental beetles, rose chafers, and some May and June beetles as well. Allow one to three years for it to spread completely through your soil.

USE TIPS: Not known to be toxic to humans, nor does it produce any health threats. Harmless to animals, birds, fish, plants, and beneficial insects. Remains active in the lawn only as long as there are sufficient grubs in the lawn for it to feed on. Will not work as a preventive—it only works if grubs are present.

BUYING TIPS: Container should be kept in a cool, dark place. Don't buy it if you think it has been stored improperly—the spores may have become inactive.

BACILLUS THURINGIENSIS

ALSO KNOWN AS: Bt, B.t., BT

POPULAR BRAND NAMES: Dipel, Thuricide, Bactur, Mosquito Attack™, Safer® Caterpillar Killer, Caterpillar Attack™, Bacthane, Biotroe, SOK-Bt, Biotrol, Vectobac (some of these products are meant to control certain insects only—read the labels)

SIGNAL WORD: CAUTION

DESCRIPTION: Microbial insecticide usually sold as a wettable powder and sometimes as a liquid. It contains the spores and toxins produced by the bacteria *Bacillus thuringiensis Berliner,* variety *kurstaki.* Also sold as a dust and bait.

USE: For control of some leaf-eating caterpillars, pupating larvae, cabbage loopers, armyworms, imported cabbage worm, and gypsy moths. Bt is considered one of the most significant biological controls because it is harmless to humans, animals, food crops, and useful insects, and it stops caterpillars instantly. Used on crops such as tobacco, cotton, alfalfa, soybeans, vegetables, shade trees, forested areas, fruit trees, and ornamentals. The bacillus interrupts the digestive cycle of certain larvae, making it a *larvacide* as well as an insecticide. A new variety, 'San Diego,' is being tested to combat the Colorado potato beetle, and another type, var. *israeliensis,* or *Bti,* attacks mosquito and black fly larvae (not adults) on water.

USE TIPS: Compatible with most insecticides, fungicides, and nutritional sprays. Plants must be thoroughly covered, especially the undersides of leaves. Can be mixed with a soap-based solution so it sticks to both sides of leaves. Can be used up to the day of harvest. Apply only when you see insects present—it has no residual effect.

BUYING TIP: Target insects are noted on the label.

BAT HOUSE

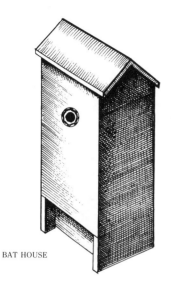

BAT HOUSE

ALSO KNOWN AS: Bat box

DESCRIPTION: Wooden box 17 to 27½ inches high, 8 to 11 inches wide, and 3½ to 7 inches deep, with a slanted roof and an open bottom through which bats enter and leave. The bat house is made of natural finished western red cedar. A single house usually holds twenty to thirty bats, though some models, *macrobat dwellings,* can hold up to one hundred.

USE: Provides a shelter for bats, thus attracting them to your garden. Bats prey on insects, consuming thousands each evening (actually, any birdhouse can be considered an insect control product).

USE TIP: Place the box high up, in a sheltered location near a pond or stream. If there are no bats in your area to begin with, it is unlikely the bat house will attract any, but if you have seen bats flying around at dusk or in the evening, you may want to coax them closer to your garden with a bat box. Especially helpful in areas where bats have lost their natural tree shelters.

BUYING TIP: Bat houses have become extremely popular in the last few years.

BENEFICIAL NEMATODES

POPULAR BRAND NAMES: Scanmask, BioSafe™, Bio-Logic, Grub-Eater

DESCRIPTION: Biologically active insecticide made of microscopic worms called nematodes (principally the beneficial Nc type, *Neoaplectana carpocapsae),* which feed on damaging insects in the soil. May be shipped in a semidormant state, mixed into a gel on a screen that you dissolve with an activator powder mix, or in topsoil or peat mosslike media. Eventually the worms are mixed into a water-based solution that is sprayed or watered onto lawns and gardens.

USE: Controlling insects in lawns, gardens, and houseplants; different nematodes are effective against different pests—check the label.

USE TIPS: Apply directly to the soil in the root zone, not on the leaves of the plants. Follow storage and mixing directions very carefully, as you are dealing with living organisms that are easily affected by sunlight and moisture and soil structure. Keep refrigerated before use, and be sure to use whatever you mix right away. Moist soil is necessary for success.

NEMATICIDE

POPULAR BRAND NAME: Safer® ClandoSan

SIGNAL WORD: CAUTION

DESCRIPTION: Ground and treated crab shells and shellfish waste full of naturally occurring chitin proteins that stimulate the growth of beneficial soil microorganisms, fungi, and bacteria.

USE: Controlling unwanted nematodes by producing enzymes that destroy them as well as their eggs.

NOSEMA LOCUSTAE

ALSO KNOWN AS: Grasshopper spore

POPULAR BRAND NAMES: Nolo, Grasshopper Attack™

DESCRIPTION: Organic insecticide powder made of protozoa spore.

USE: Controlling grasshoppers of the Malanoplus family. Even the eggs laid by the infected grasshoppers infect young nymphs.

USE TIP: Apply by hand or with a seeder. Takes about a year to have maximum effect.

Physical and Mechanical Controls

Traps

ELECTRONIC INSECT KILLER

ALSO KNOWN AS: Bug zapper

DESCRIPTION: Fluorescent or incandescent light inside an electrified metal grid. Some brands are shaped like a lantern. Typical wattage of current in grid is 4,500 to 6,000. Lights are either yellow or black light, a type of ultraviolet light that appears to us as a dull blue. Fluorescent bulbs may be normal ones covered with a *black light blue filter (BLB)*. Higher-wattage models are self-cleaning, meaning that they actually burn off the bugs that hit the grid. Another version uses the same light to attract insects, but has a fan instead of an electrified grid. The fan blows the insects into a container of water with detergent on top of it, and the insects drown. All models come with a variety of brackets and hangers for use indoors and out.

USE: Controlling flying insects in an area about 25 to 70 feet square, although larger models are available. Can be operated twenty-four hours a day, but most effective at night.

USE TIP: Keep grid clean.

BUYING TIPS: There is no doubt that the higher-wattage units are more effective, as are the black light fluorescent bulbs—not the ones with the filters. Nonselective, this device tends to kill many insects that are not pests.

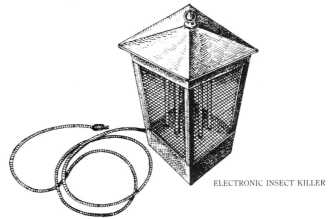

ELECTRONIC INSECT KILLER

MOLE TRAP

POPULAR BRAND NAMES: Victor®, Out-of-Site®

TYPES: Skewer type, scissor type

DESCRIPTION: Metal device about a foot high with spring-loaded blades that is set above a mole burrow and anchored by two

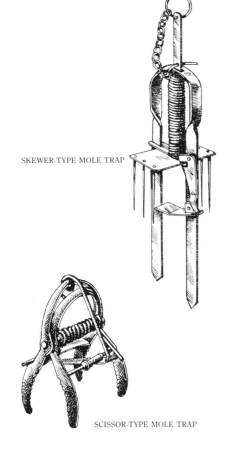

SKEWER-TYPE MOLE TRAP

SCISSOR-TYPE MOLE TRAP

spikes stuck in the ground on both sides of a mole tunnel. When the mole comes along, it sets off the sensitive device and is skewered to death by three sharp spikes, in the case of the Victor trap, or squeezed to death by four scissorlike blades with the Out-of-Site trap.

USE: Control of tunneling moles in the garden or lawn.

USE TIP: With the scissor-type design it is easy to tell if a trap has been triggered. When a trap has done its deed, just remove the trap and pat the soil back down with your foot. It is better not to look at what you have done to the mole, as this is not a scene for the fainthearted. On the other hand, it is entirely nontoxic.

BUYING TIPS: The choice between the two types pretty much depends upon your personal taste: Do you prefer your moles skewered or squeezed? This kind of trap has been around for a while, and is time-tested to be a nontoxic way of killing one mole at a time, but if you have a real infestation you might want to look into putting out castor bean seed (see pages 101–102). Check your local game trap laws—they may dictate what you can do about small animals.

MOUSETRAPS AND RAT TRAPS

DESCRIPTION: Mousetraps and rat traps are the same, except that rat traps are bigger.

TYPES: *Spring-loaded trap* (also known as *spring* or *snap trap):* These are the classic mouse and rat traps that have been around forever. A spring device is set when a U-shaped wire is pulled against the tension of the spring and a short wire is placed over it and onto a flat tin trigger. Cheese or some other bait (including dental floss or a small piece of cloth that a mouse might like for nesting material) is placed on the trigger, and when the mouse or rat goes for it the animal is caught under the U-shaped wire and held there (and if the spring is strong enough, killed there) by the pressure of the spring.

Box trap (also known as *live trap.* Popular brand name: Victor Smiling Cat Repeating Mouse Trap): This is the better mousetrap we've been waiting for! Consists of a metal box with small apertures on either end. When the mouse enters the trap it cannot find its way out again. Available as single models or larger ones that are

REPEATING BOX TYPE MOUSETRAP

reputed to capture as many as a dozen mice at one time without resetting, and without killing them (though they may kill each other or die of loss of body heat).

Glue trap (popular brand name: Tanglefoot): Nontoxic, 3-inch-square up to 7-by-12-inch plastic trays that contain a sticky bait substance. They are placed where rats and mice travel, and the animal is trapped when it walks on the glue, where it dies slowly.

USE: For the control of mice and rats. These are nontoxic and time-tested ways of catching mice and rats. The box type is for areas with an extreme problem.

USE TIPS: Be careful that you don't set off a spring-type trap when you try to set it. Many a finger has been hurt this way. It is also a good idea to put the bait material on the trap before trying to set it, because once the trap is set, you might catch your finger if you press the bait trigger. The only problem with the box-type trap is the problem of what to do with a box full of live mice, although this is a challenge that might appeal to some of the more mischievous gardeners among us. Glue-type traps must be placed where mice travel, usually around the edge of rooms. Both the spring and glue types can be dangerous to inquisitive pets and small children. Disposal of the pest is simple with these two types, as it is just a matter of throwing the trap in the garbage along with the animal stuck to it.

BUYING TIP: All these traps are safe, nontoxic ways of trapping mice. The spring- and glue-type traps are especially inexpensive and efficient; killing a mouse instantly may be more humane than trapping for later dispatch.

PHEROMONE TRAP

ALSO KNOWN AS: Sex traps, Japanese beetle trap, pheromone lures

POPULAR BRAND NAMES: Bag-A-Bug, Japanese Beetle Attack™

DESCRIPTION: Plastic bag or metal or cardboard container underneath a bug-attracting strip containing female Japanese beetle sex pheromone and sometimes floral scents. Trapped bugs fall into container. Strips are yellow and about 15 inches high.

USE: To attract and capture Japanese beetles and other flying insects.

USE TIP: Because the pheromone attracts more insects to the garden than it can kill at once, be sure to place it away from plants that can be eaten by the pest, such as roses and zinnias. This problem makes pheromone traps particularly ill-suited to small urban gardens. In fact, some folks say that the best location for a Japanese beetle trap is in your neighbor's garden—that way the bugs will leave you alone and head over there. Lasts one season.

BUYING TIP: The yellow color of the trap itself is an attractant, but models with both pheromones and floral lures *(double lures)* are better—you just increase your chances.

SLUG TRAP

SLUG TRAP

DESCRIPTION: Plastic cup with lip and a plastic, mushroomlike roof. A *slug barrier* can be made from a strip of copper, which somehow reacts with slug slime to produce an electric shock.

USE: When trap is filled with beer or some other liquid slug-attracting bait, slugs climb into the cup and drown. A safe alternative to placing highly toxic slug bait in your garden or lawn, where it can be eaten by birds.

USE TIP: Stale beer is cheaper and works as well in the traps as the more expensive slug baits. We recommend discount domestic brands over the finer, imported beers. We are sorry to report that no recent studies indicate which brand, in particular, slugs prefer.

BUYING TIP: Cat food and tunafish cans can also be used as slug traps, but at under $2, the slug trap is not that expensive and is slightly more effectively designed, as the cover keeps rain from washing away the beer.

STICKY INSECT TRAP

ALSO KNOWN AS: Flying insect trap, sticky whitefly trap

DESCRIPTION: Small flat piece of yellow material coated with a sticky material that attracts certain insects, such as whiteflies and aphids. May be sold as cards to be placed in holders or hung from hooks. This trap coating (popular brand name: Tanglefoot Tangle-Trap Paste) is also sold separately for making your own traps in aerosol spray, paintable, or spreadable formulations. The color yellow is an attractant.

USE: Not only does this kind of updated flypaper trap insects, it provides an opportunity to identify and count whatever kind of pest is arriving on the scene, acting as an early warning and identification system. Labels identify which insects are attracted to each particular trap, such as flying aphids, thrips, leaf miners, gnats, fruit flies, and leafhoppers.

BUYING TIP: Check out the type of insect each trap attracts.

WIRE CAGE ANIMAL TRAP

POPULAR BRAND NAME: Havahart

DESCRIPTION: Galvanized wire mesh cage that comes in several sizes, from 10 by 3 by 3 inches for mice and shrews, to 42 by 11 by 11 inchs for raccoons. Standard trap for rabbits and squirrels is 30 by 7 by 7 inches.

USE: To capture small animals without harming them. Often used when populations of some animals, like rabbits and squirrels, are particularly high. The animals are released in areas where their populations are lower.

BUYING TIP: Check your local game trap laws—they may dictate what you can do about small animals.

WIRE CAGE ANIMAL TRAP

Barriers

CATERPILLAR TAPE

DESCRIPTION: Plastic silicone tape, 5 inches wide by 40 feet long, with sticky substance on the top part. When attached to a tree, pleats are made every few inches, creating a "skirt" effect. Another type is 3 inches wide by 500 feet long and is completely sticky.

USE: Prevents gypsy moth ("tent") caterpillars from climbing trees—they cannot climb over the smooth surface of the tape. The sticky kind merely traps the caterpillars.

USE TIP: Install carefully.

BUYING TIP: Proven nontoxic control of gypsy moths.

ELECTRIC FENCING

ALSO KNOWN AS: Deer fencing

DESCRIPTION: Thick lengths of wire which conduct pulses of low-voltage electricity; any animal that touches it receives a harmless but unpleasant shock. Wires are attached to fence posts by *insulators;* lightweight custom *fence posts* are available too, as are *insulated gate handles.* Electricity is supplied by house current, a storage or solar battery, and conducted to the fencing by a variety of *fence chargers* or *condensers,* the transformers that change regular electricity into pulsating, low-voltage surges of a fraction of a second—and harmless—duration. Strands are approximately 2 feet apart and usually three strands constitute the fence; they are placed much closer together and closer to the ground when used for protection against smaller animals.

USE: Keeping cattle or horses contained or to prohibit animals such as deer from entering a garden area. Also effective against rabbits, raccoons, and other smaller animals, but this requires more strands of wire.

USE TIP: Deer can make considerable pests of themselves, and electric fences are useful in keeping them at bay. However, deer are also impressive jumpers and may jump over a low electric fence.

GALVANIZED STEEL FENCING

ALSO KNOWN AS: Welded wire fabric

DESCRIPTION: Welded and woven, galvanized 16-gauge steel fencing with various types of mesh. *Rabbit guard, rabbit fencing,* or *garden fencing* has 1-by-4-inch or 1-inch-square mesh on the bottom 12 inches, then 2-by-4-inch mesh on the next 4 inches and 4-inch-square mesh on the top, whether the fencing is 24, 28, 36, 40, or 50 inches high. Sold in 50-foot rolls. Others have just the small mesh on the bottom and 2-inch hexagonal mesh on the top, for economy. Standard *yard fencing,* or *utility fencing,* is usually 14 gauge (thicker than 16 gauge and thinner than 12½ gauge) and has a 2-by-4-inch mesh. *Hexagonal netting,* or *chicken wire,* is sold in 24-, 36-, and 48-inch heights and 75-foot rolls and is made of lightweight 20-gauge wire. Fourteen-gauge steel *fence posts* are sold separately (13 gauge for heavy duty), usually with a green baked-enamel finish, 3 to 8 feet long. Made in either a T shape or a U shape. Packed ten to a bundle.

USE: Barrier for rabbits, pets, and other small animals (and sometimes people).

USE TIP: Where there is a will in the animal world, there is a way. These critters are persistent and will dig under or jump over almost any kind of fence if they possibly can. Try to extend rabbit fences below ground level at least half a foot.

PROTECTIVE NETTING

PROTECTIVE NETTING

ALSO KNOWN AS: Anti-bird net, bird control net, bird netting, garden net, tobacco netting

DESCRIPTION: Nets made from synthetic material such as polypropylene in a range of sizes from 20 by 20 feet to 4½ by 75 feet. A ¾-inch mesh is typical.

USE: Placed over fruit trees, fruit shrubs, or plants such as strawberries to protect the crops from birds. Can also be used to cover a lily pond or fish pool to catch falling leaves in autumn. Lasts a few seasons. A heavier version is now available for protecting crops from deer, although it can also be used to keep leaves out of pools, as a snow barrier, and for transporting large quantities of pruning debris. This latter model has a ½-inch mesh, and is also known as a *garden utility net* or a *garden net.* A finer mesh is made for *insect netting,* used primarily on fruit trees.

USE TIPS: Be sure that the net is secured well at the bottom, as birds can get in underneath it. When placing the net over thorny plants like blackberries or raspberries, prop the net up above the plants with a frame to prevent it from becoming stuck on the thorns. Cover tree after fruit set but before ripening starts.

BUYING TIP: Buy a size that is a little larger than you think you need. It is better to have too much than too little.

TREE TANGLEFOOT®

DESCRIPTION: Viscous goo sold in 6-ounce tubes, 1- to 25-pound cans and pails, caulking cartridges, and aerosol cans. Sticky and nontoxic, made from castor oil, gum resins, and vegetable waxes.

USE: Banding trees and vines to protect against climbing pests such as cankerworms, gypsy moth caterpillars, and ants. The pests get stuck and suffocate.

USE TIPS: Lasts three to four months. Apply a band about 3 to 4 inches wide at 5 to 6 feet above the ground. Put Tanglefoot on banding material for small young trees. Though some people use it, it is not recommended for sealing pruning wounds. If you insist on painting tree wounds, Tanglefoot makes a specially formulated tree paint.

Repellents and Scarecrows

ABOUT REPELLENTS AND SCARECROWS

This is an area of products which contains more folklore than most others. It is very hard to prove the effectiveness of scarecrows and the like, and in fact, some government studies have indicated that the more high-tech devices used to scare animals, such as ultrasonic gopher repellents, are not particularly effective. Some of these items seem to work more on personal faith than scientific principle. And they are nice to have around, out of tradition.

ANIMAL REPELLENT

POPULAR BRAND NAMES: RO-PEL®, Deer Guard®, Hinder®, Hot Sauce Animal Repellent®, Rabbit & Dog Chaser®, Dog and Cat Granular Repellent®, Scent-Off Pellets®, Scent-Off "Twist-On" Buds®, Repel® Dog and Cat Repellent, Repel® Liquid Animal Repellent, Chaperone Squirrel & Bat Repellent®, Scram® Dog & Cat Repellent

DESCRIPTION: Extremely vile-tasting, bitter chemical, either granular or aerosol or powders mixed with a solvent base for spraying. Smells offensive to sensitive animals but not to humans. Also comes in wax buds that are hung from the lower branches of trees and bushes.

USE: Discouraging specific pest animals (ranging from deer to pet cats) from gnawing, nibbling, licking, or biting plants, trees, fences, garbage cans, siding, and furniture. Works without harming the animal—they merely find the odor offensive and move away from it.

USE TIPS: Some brands contain toxic chemicals that must be handled exactly as the label instructs, in terms of both application and storage and disposal. Test on plants or furniture before application. Many need to be reapplied often.

BUYING TIP: Check the label carefully. Some animal repellents carry environmental hazard warnings on the labels. You may find that the environmental condition you create by using the product is worse than the pest you wish to repel. Furthermore, some brands may repel generally beneficial animals, such as bats, along with the pests.

SCARECROWS

ALSO KNOWN AS: Bird repellents, decoys, natural enemy scarecrows, bird scarers, pest scarers

DESCRIPTION: Natural-looking decoys in the form of natural predators of certain garden pests. The inflatable items are made from heavy vinyl, others from molded plastic. All are painted or printed with lifelike detail, with the exception of the scarecat and the monster.

TYPES: *Garden monster:* An unclassifiable model, consists of eight plastic film "tentacles" attached to a stake. Monstrous-looking to pests only.

Inflatable and *plastic owl:* Great horned owl, 18 to 22 inches tall; big orange eyes. Plastic molded type is amazingly lifelike and beautiful.

Inflatable scarecrow: More than 6 feet tall. Resembles a straw man.

Inflatable snake: Six feet long and an inch or two in diameter.

Scarecat (also known as *Le chat* or *cat's head bird scarer):* Either a silhouette of an entire cat or a silhouette of a cat's head. A French product made from flat, black metal, with two clear marbles for eyes. It is hung on a

PLASTIC OWL SCARECROW

GARDEN MONSTER

SCARECAT

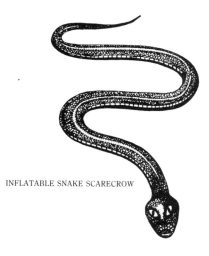

INFLATABLE SNAKE SCARECROW

wire in the garden where it blows in the wind; the movement causes sunlight to glance off the glass eyes. A similar, and perhaps more effective, version is a mobile of highly reflective chrome-plated disks suspended from a hanger or yard-high stake.

USE: The owl and the snake are supposed to scare rodents, such as rats, mice, and rabbits as well as some birds, from the garden and around the house. The snake and the cat are designed to scare birds (especially pigeons), squirrels, and other small animals away from berry patches and vegetable gardens. And the scarecrow is for scaring birds from grain crops.

USE TIPS: Change the position of the snake every few days to aid in its effectiveness against your more cynical pests. Be sure to warn any fainthearted visitors about the snake's presence before they discover it on their own.

BUYING TIPS: It is not entirely clear if these work well or not, but they are generally fun, and certainly traditional, to have in the garden. The solid plastic model owl is more realistic looking to humans and makes for a more decorative object. The cat is probably the least effective and most expensive, considering that a tin can lid performs the same function. However, it is quite nice looking and very popular in France, so maybe that doesn't matter so much.

Synthetic Pesticides

ABOUT SYNTHETIC PESTICIDES

Much has been said in preceding sections of this book about alternatives to the following chemical products. There is no doubt that they provide an excellent service and convenience, but nonetheless, they are very dangerous, not only to the environment but to the consumer, especially if precautions and directions are not followed to the letter. If you should ever have an accident or misuse any of these toxic products, be sure to call your local poison center with the information provided on the label, especially the Note to Physicians. If you go to see a doctor, be sure to take the label or the container with you—the prescribed treatment may be on the label. Also note the code and EPA numbers for positive identification with the authorities.

You can also call the NPTN, the National Pesticide Telecommunications Network, at 1-800-858-7378, twenty-four hours a day, 365 days a year, for information on pesticides and help in responding to pesticide poisoning. Ortho, one of the major manufacturers of these products, requests that you call them collect at 415-233-3737 twenty-four hours a day if you ever have an emergency or accidental spill.

Please note that some garden centers unwittingly sell professional products—that is, *restricted use* chemical products for which the EPA requires that you obtain a pesticide permit or applicator's license number. Be careful. There is a reason for those licenses. These products are very strong, and may be hazardous to you and your environment. This is not to say that the off-the-shelf chemicals are not dangerous: Some were approved for consumer use long ago, when our standards were less demanding and our knowledge less comprehensive. Once-common products disappear from the shelves from time to time as regulations change and research grows in sophistication and the chemicals are discovered to be much more dangerous than originally thought—such as DDT (one of the most popular and widely used pesticides, it is now banned because although harmless to humans, it caused enormous damage to birds). Some of the items listed here will come to the same fate.

For an explanation of the common terms and labels of pesticides, see pages 87–91.

General Use Synthetic Pesticide Products

SPREADER-STICKER

ALSO KNOWN AS: Sticking agent, wetting agent (though not the same as the wetting agent described on page 20)

DESCRIPTION: Highly concentrated liquid petroleum product typically sold in 4- and 8-ounce bottles. A sort of *wetting agent, surfactant,* or *emulsifier.* Also available in an organic formulation. Part of a family of products that are mixed with pesticides to improve or modify their action, called *spray adjuvants.* Another similar product more oriented to the professional market but available to the consumer is a *sticker-extender.*

USE: Increases the efficiency of pesticides (or fertilizers) by reducing surface tension so they can more thoroughly cover plant surfaces (hence, *spreader)* and leaving a film that encapsulates the pesticides, drying to form a shield against rain (hence, *sticker).* An *extender* protects the active ingredients from degradation by the sun, like a sun block, prolonging its effectiveness.

USE TIP: Use at least one hour before rainfall. Note that some additives are quite toxic, even though they are not listed as pesticides.

BUYING TIP: This product is often included in many quality pesticides.

Synthetic Insecticides

ACEPHATE

CHEMICAL NAME: O,S-dimethyl acetylphosphoramidothioate

POPULAR BRAND NAMES: Orthene®, Ortran, Tree and Ornamental Spray

SIGNAL WORD: CAUTION

DESCRIPTION: White, 75 percent soluble powder made for use as a spray, when mixed with water, or an aerosol. Also available as a 9.4 percent emulsifiable concentrate. Works both as a contact and as a systemic insecticide. Absorbed within about twenty-four hours; rain-fast.

USE: Controlling aphids, caterpillars, leaf miners, scale, whiteflies, and many other bugs on potted, flowering, bedding, and ornamental plants and cut flowers. Especially good in combatting fire ants. Sometimes used on roses, trees, and shrubs, too.

USE TIP: Stays in the plant about fourteen to twenty-one days when applied to the leaves as recommended.

CHLORPYRIFOS

CHEMICAL NAME: O,O-diethyl O-(3,5,6 trichloro-2-pyridyl) phosphorothioate

POPULAR BRAND NAMES: Brodan, Dursban®, Eradex, Lorsban®, Pyrinex, d-Con Home Pest Control Killer, Raid Home Insect Killer

SIGNAL WORD: WARNING or CAUTION (granular products)

DESCRIPTION: White granular crystal or fine powder, emulsifiable concentrate, or diluted household spray. Contained in many common household insect sprays.

USE: Insecticide for use against ants, ticks, cutworms, chinch bugs, earwigs, grubs, cockroaches, silverfish, spiders, fleas, dog ticks, and mosquitoes. Also used to control termites, against which it may be effective for up to eighteen years.

USE TIP: One of the most common sources of organophosphate poisoning because it is extremely toxic to fish, aquatic invertebrates, and birds—keep away from water supply.

DIAZINON

CHEMICAL NAME: O,O-diethyl O-(2-isopropyl-6-methyl-4-pyrimidinyl) phosphorothiate

POPULAR BRAND NAMES: Spectracide, Basudin, D-264, Dazzel, Diagran, Dianon, Diaterr-Fos, Diazajet, Diazatol, Diazide, Diazol, Dizinon, Drawizon, Dyzol, D.zn., Fezudin, G-24480, Gardentox, Kayazion, Kayazol, Neocidol, Nipsan, Sarolex (and many ant and roach killers)

SIGNAL WORD: WARNING (spray form) or CAUTION (granular form)—varies with formulation

DESCRIPTION: Comes as an emulsifiable concentrate, wettable powder, granular mixture, or prediluted ready-to-use household spray. A member of the organophosphate family. Extremely toxic to birds feeding on treated lawns. One of the most commonly used insecticide ingredients since the early 1950s, and one of the most toxic available to the consumer. Often mixed with other chemicals, such as fertilizers.

USE: Lawn and garden control of aphids, leafhoppers, leaf miners, sawflies, scale, cutworms, grubs, chinch bugs, and other soil insects. Household uses include cockroaches, ants, fire-brats, silverfish, fleas, sow bugs, springtails, spiders, crickets, earwigs, carpet beetles, and brown dog ticks.

USE TIPS: This is a pretty toxic chemical that has not been tested in every way it is used, because it is in so many consumer products for which it is hard to develop reliable data. However, the EPA recently banned its use on sod farms and golf courses owing to the number of deaths it caused in bird populations. Watering it in thoroughly after application helps some, but then that brings earthworms to the surface which attract birds. It also persists in the insects that birds eat. You should consider this before putting it on your lawn. Try not to use old or improperly stored pressurized containers, as they may explode. Also, certain compounds that are even more toxic are sometimes formed as this product breaks down in storage.

BUYING TIPS: This is such a toxic product that you may want to find alternatives to whatever it is that you think needs it. Check labels of mixtures to see if diazinon is included.

HORTICULTURAL OIL

ALSO KNOWN AS: Dormant oil, dormant spray, summer oil, growing season spray, oils, sprayable oils, miscible oils, white oils, petroleum oils, insect spray, superior oil, oil spray, superior horticultural spray oil, scale oil

POPULAR BRAND NAMES: 90-Par, Volck®, Scalecide

DESCRIPTION: A high-grade, highly refined, light viscosity petroleum product not unlike mineral oil that is sprayed on ornamentals, shrubs, and trees either in early spring (known as *dormant oil)* or late spring–early summer (known as *summer, verdant,* or *growing season oil).* New technical improvements allow it to be used on more plants and for a wider range of seasons. Usually mixed with water—contains an emulsifier for this purpose. May also be made from fish oils or a mixture of borax and kerosene (brand name: Ced-O-Flora). The difference between dormant and summer oils is the viscosity—dormant is thicker, summer is thinner—which may just be the rate at which it is mixed with water by the gardener. Some are sold just as *dormant oils,* the old name. Considered an organic pesticide by many gardeners.

USE: Suffocates certain pests, such as mites, mealybugs, and scale. Dormant oil sprays are applied in March, before new leaves have appeared, for the control of scale, aphids, and spider mites on the stem and trunk. As a summer oil, it is applied in late spring or early summer for the control of aphids, mites, and scale in their crawling stages. Sometimes used as a contact herbicide and, when greatly diluted, as a leaf polish. Can be mixed with compatible pesticides as a spreader-sticker (see page 117), to enhance the pesticide's performance. It works by coating and suffocating the pest.

USE TIPS: Toxic to fish. Flammable—do not store or use near heat or flame—and harmful if swallowed. Wash your hands thoroughly after use. This has been in use for many, many years and no oil-resistant strain of insects has developed. A weak, 2 percent mixture can be used on vegetable crops, but overwintering insects need a strong dose: 3 to 5 percent. Do not try to make your own with mineral or motor oil—they may damage the plants.

Summer oil can be applied when there is little wind or breeze during late spring. Dormant oil must be sprayed on shrubs and trees before new leaves appear, when it is not windy, and when the temperatures are above freezing and are expected to stay there for a few days.

BUYING TIPS: The better-quality oils are light and highly refined, as indicated by a high percentage—87 to 90 percent—of *sulfonation.* The rate at which the oil can pass through a sprayer is noted in its *viscosity,* stated in seconds (sixty to seventy is good). The more refined oils pass through sprayers more easily, and are therefore easier to apply.

MALATHION

CHEMICAL NAME: O,O-dimethyl dithophosphate of diethyl mercaptosuccinate

POPULAR BRAND NAMES: Calmathion, Celthion, Cythion, Detmol MA 96%, Emmatos, Emmatos Extra For-mal, Fyfanon, Kop-Thion, Kypfos, Malaspray, Malamar, Malatol, Home Orchard Spray, Bonide Rose Spray, No-Roach Spray

SIGNAL WORD: CAUTION

DESCRIPTION: Wettable powder or emulsifiable concentrate that makes a clear to amber liquid with a garlic odor. Broad spectrum insecticide, only slightly toxic to mammals.

USE: For the control of aphids, leaf miners, mealybugs, white-flies, scale, and lace bugs.

USE TIP: Harmful if swallowed, comes into contact with your skin, or is inhaled. Wash well after using.

METHOXYCLOR

CHEMICAL NAME: 2,2-bis (p-methoxyphenyl)-1,1,1-trichloro-ethane

POPULAR BRAND NAMES: Marlate, Methoxyclor 25

SIGNAL WORD: CAUTION

DESCRIPTION: Developed as a substitute for DDT; is less harmful to the environment and has very low toxicity to animals and humans. Comes as a wettable powder or emulsifiable concentrate, as well as a dust or aerosol.

USE: For control of chewing insects that attack flowers, shrubs, vegetables, and fruit and shade trees, as well as mosquitoes, ticks, and flies.

USE TIPS: Store in a cool, dry place. Long residual effect.

SEVIN

CHEMICAL NAME: Carbaryl (1-naphthyl N-methylcarbamate)

COMMON BRAND NAME: Sevin®

SIGNAL WORD: CAUTION or WARNING—varies with formulation

DESCRIPTION: Dust or spray, generally containing 5 to 10 percent carbaryl, or a stronger liquid concentrate.

USE: Very broad spectrum insecticide for combating armyworms, cutworms, squash bugs, tomato hornworms, fleas and ticks, certain varieties of beetles, leafhoppers, and numerous other vegetable pests.

USE TIP: Despite the commonness of this product, use it very carefully, following the directions as with all pesticides and taking precautions to keep it out of the home (when using it on animals) and away from bees, to which it is very toxic.

Synthetic Herbicides

ABOUT SYNTHETIC HERBICIDES

Herbicides are products that kill plants or interrupt their growth, and are used to control weeds, brush, or unwanted grass. Most gardeners never need to use herbicides. If you have a weed problem that does not respond to cultivation, hand picking, or other methods of eradication, then you may want to consider using an herbicide that has little or no residual toxicity. There are not too many on the market, as the really effective ones are far too toxic to be used safely: Remember Agent Orange?

TYPES: *Preplanting herbicides:* Used after the soil has been prepared for planting, but before the seed is sown.

Preemergent herbicides: Used after seeding but before germination, to control weeds that might compete with the crop or planting, such as crabgrass.

Postemergent herbicides: Used after a crop or planting is established.

Sterilant (nonselective) herbicides: Kills nonselectively all plants that are treated with it, and is commonly used on walks and patios.

2,4-D

CHEMICAL NAME: 2,4,-dichlorophenoxyacetic acid

POPULAR BRAND NAMES: Agrotect, Aqua-Kleen, BH, "D," D50, Dacamine, Debroussaillant 600, Ded-Weed, Desormone, Dinoxol, Emulsamine, Envert, Envert 171, Super D Weedone, Estone, Fernesta, Fernimine, Fernoxone, Ferxone, Formula 40, Greensweep Weed & Feed, Hedonal, Herbidal, Lawn-Keep, Manccondray, Miracle, Netagrone, Pennamine, Planotox, Plantgard, Salvo, Scotts Lawn Weed Control, Transamine, Tributon, Tuban, U 46, Weedone, Weed-Rhap, Weedtrol, Weed-B-Gon®, Gordon's Dymec Turf Herbicide, Acme Amine 4, Acme Butyl Ester 4, and many others

SIGNAL WORD: CAUTION, WARNING, or DANGER—varies with formulation

DESCRIPTION: In any one of a number of forms, but most often a flowable liquid. A selective herbicide that may be the most common home product of its type in the United States, but also may be reevaluated for cancer risk by the EPA. Often mixed with *MCPP* or *dicamba*.

USE: Postemergent control of most broadleaf lawn weeds, such as dandelions, clover, and plaintain.

USE TIPS: Dilute according to the label, as concentrations may vary. Do not allow this product to contaminate food, feed, or water, and be careful when applying it not to let the spray drift over onto any other plants that may be damaged by it, especially, of course, food crops. May not be compatible with lime-sulfur or oils, and depending on the formulation, should not be used in weather over 80° F.

EPTAM®

CHEMICAL NAME: EPTC (ethyl dipropylthiocarbamate)

SIGNAL WORD: CAUTION

DESCRIPTION: Granular, preemergent herbicide sold in 1- to 20-pound containers and bags.

USE: Control of nutgrass, Bermudagrass, quackgrass, sandburs, and other weeds in lawns and gardens.

USE TIP: Apply within two or three days of cultivation, before weeds germinate.

BUYING TIP: Dacthol (DCPA) is a common alternative product that controls crabgrass as well. Comes as a flowable liquid or wettable powder in addition to the common granular form.

GLYPHOSATE

ALSO KNOWN AS: Grass killer, weed and grass killer

CHEMICAL NAME: Isopropylamine salt of N-(phosphonomethyl) glycine

POPULAR BRAND NAMES: Roundup®, Glifonox, Glycel, Kleenup®, Rodeo, Rondo, Vision

SIGNAL WORD: WARNING or CAUTION—varies with formulation

DESCRIPTION: Sold most often as a concentrated aqueous solution. Nonselective, postemergent, broad spectrum, systemic, foliar spray. Also available in aerosol foam that leaves a residue that indicates where it has been sprayed.

USE: Controlling over fifty types of grasses, brush, vines, and broadleaf weeds after they are grown. Can also be used to control some trees and woody brush. It is one of the safest herbicides on the market because it has little residual toxicity, meaning that it breaks down quickly after application. However, it does kill most plants it touches for up to four weeks.

USE TIPS: Because this product is nonselective, care should be taken so as not to spray desirable plant material around the weeds. Keep people and pets away for any treated area for at least six hours, or overnight. It translocates, meaning that it goes into the roots after killing the leaves. Mix only what you need: The concentrate has a shelf life of many years, but once mixed, it begins to degrade.

TRICLOPYR

POPULAR BRAND NAMES: Brush-B-Gon®, Poison Ivy & Oak Killer

CHEMICAL NAME: Triclopyr (3,5,6-trichloro-2-pyridinyl-oxya-cetic acid) as triethylamine salt

SIGNAL WORD: CAUTION

DESCRIPTION: Postemergent aerosol spray, commonly mixed to a .5 percent acid. Contains foam to help you see where you have sprayed. Largely replaces use of ammate (ammonium sulfa-mate).

USE: Controlling bushy and woody plants, especially poison ivy and poison oak, in noncrop areas. OK for use on poison ivy in apple and pear orchards. Applied as a spray to the foliage of the offending plant; translocates to the plant roots after killing the foliage. Also kills stumps.

USE TIPS: Takes two to six weeks to show results. Apply to mature foliage. Not hazardous to animals and people when used according to directions. One of the few items on the market that controls poison ivy. Avoid applying directly to lakes, streams, or ponds, or disposing cleanup rags in them.

Synthetic Fungicides

ABOUT FUNGICIDES

Fungi are plants that actually feed on other plants. Contrary to what one might think, fungicides cannot get rid of an established fungus. They are used to prevent fungi from becoming estab-lished or to control their spread. Fungi are quite common in all kinds of gardens and especially with fruit trees, which need to be sprayed routinely. Unfortunately, many of these items break down into products that are suspected carcinogens. Some may be removed from the market as studies progress; others will be proven safe.

BENOMYL

CHEMICAL NAME: Methyl 1 -(butylcarbarmoyl)-2-benzimidazolecarbamate

POPULAR BRAND NAMES: Benex, Benlate, Tersan 1991

SIGNAL WORD: CAUTION

DESCRIPTION: General purpose systemic fungicide. Usually a white crystalline solid, practically insoluble in water and oil. Sold in concentrated forms in small plastic bottles for the home gardener. Used as a spray.

USE: For the prevention of a variety of fungal problems in the garden, including black spot and powdery mildew on roses, phlox, and lilacs.

USE TIPS: Be careful not to let the spray drift into water or water sources, as it is harmful to fish and other aquatic animals. This is a relatively safe fungicide for the prevention of fungal infection, but it requires intensive application practices. It must be sprayed on the foliage before a fungal problem is apparent and application must be repeated every fourteen days or more frequently if there is rain. Store container in a dry place with the cap securely tightened. Benomyl's effectiveness is lessened if the stored product becomes wet. Keep shaking container so the chemical remains in suspension.

BUYING TIP: Fairly dangerous in case of misuse—may cause nonmalignant tumors.

BORDEAUX MIXTURE

ALSO KNOWN AS: Copper-Fixed, fixed copper, Bordeaux mix, copper dust, liquid copper

POPULAR BRAND NAMES: Kocide, Bordo-Mix, Tri-Basic, CPTS, Copper Bordeaux 22

SIGNAL WORD: WARNING or CAUTION—varies with formulation

DESCRIPTION: Comes in different formulations, but usually sold as a concentrate in wettable powder form. Basically a mixture of copper sulfate and hydrated lime which gets its names (Bordeaux) from years of use in the French vineyards. Low toxic residue—may be considered organic. When copper sulfate is sold in liquid form without lime, it may be called *copper fungicide,* an organic product used in season as a corrective control (applied as disease appears).

USE: Controlling fungal and bacterial diseases such as leaf spots, anthracnose, rusts, molds, and fruit rots found in flowers and small fruit and shade trees. Possibly acceptable for use on organic farms. Considered a general preventive garden fungicide, often used as a dormant spray (meaning not during the growing season).

USE TIP: Dilution rates vary, so follow label directions closely.

BUYING TIP: A relatively safe fungicide that has been around for a long time, but now largely replaced by ferbam (see page 128) and zineb (see page 130).

CAPTAN

CHEMICAL NAME: N-trichloromethylethio-4-cyclohexene-1,2-dicarboximide

POPULAR BRAND NAMES: Orthocide, Captanex, Captaf, Merpan, Vondcaptan, Ortho Home Orchard Spray, Orthocide Captan Garden Fungicide, Bonide Rose Spray, Gro-Well Fruit Tree Spray, Vancide 89

SIGNAL WORD: DANGER or CAUTION—varies with formulation

DESCRIPTION: A protectant-eradicant fungicide, that is, one that prevents fungus from attacking, sold as a wettable powder concentrate that must be diluted. One of the most popular broad-spectrum fungicides in use on crops and seeds of all kinds.

USE: For the prevention of a variety of fungal problems in the garden, including black spot on roses and powdery mildew on phlox and lilacs, and damping off on seedlings. Add a tiny bit to a seed packet of untreated seeds and shake the packet.

USE TIPS: This is a relatively safe fungicide for the prevention of fungal infection, but it requires intensive application practices, similar to benomyl (see page 125). Avoid contact with skin or clothing. Store in a cool, dry place. Wear protective clothing when using. Keep shaking container so the chemical remains in solution.

BUYING TIPS: Not permitted for use on vegetables because it has caused cancer in laboratory animals. It may be used on apples and some other fruit trees. The EPA legislation on this chemical, a probable human carcinogen, has been changed a number of times over the years, so check with the EPA or your local Cooperative Extension agent for the most recent findings.

CHLOROTHALONIL

CHEMICAL NAME: Tetrachloroisophthalonitrile

POPULAR BRAND NAMES: Bravo, Daconil 2787

SIGNAL WORD: WARNING or DANGER—varies with formulation

DESCRIPTION: White crystalline solid usually sold as a wettable powder or liquid concentrate. Also available as a smoke or vapor.

USE: Controlling a wide range of fungal diseases. Considered a broad-spectrum fungicide for use on most vegetables, melons, and much fruit, as well as ornamentals.

USE TIP: Use with care. This is a probable human carcinogen.

DYRENE

ALSO KNOWN AS: Anilazine

CHEMICAL NAME: 2,4-dichloro-6-(O-chloroanilino)=s-triazine

SIGNAL WORD: DANGER or WARNING—varies with formulation

DESCRIPTION: White to tan crystalline solid sold as a wettable or flowable powder. Applied as a spray.

USE: Controlling fungal diseases of turf. Many other uses have been prohibited recently.

USE TIPS: This is a skin irritant—wear protective clothing. Keep away from fish and aquatic invertebrates.

FERBAM

CHEMICAL NAME: Ferric dimethyldithiocarbamate

POPULAR BRAND NAMES: Fermate, Carbamate, Ferbam, Ferberk, Hexaferb, Knockmate, Trifungol

SIGNAL WORD: CAUTION

DESCRIPTION: Wettable powder.

USE: Controlling fungal diseases, such as apple scab, cedar apple rust, peachleaf curl, tobacco blue mold, and others that are common to ornamentals and popular garden flowers. Often applied for general protection against other diseases.

USE TIP: Sometimes recommended as part of a combination spray for apples.

MANCOZEB

CHEMICAL NAME: Zinc ion and manganeze ethylene bisdithiocarbamate

POPULAR BRAND NAMES: Dithane M-45, Manzate 200, Fore, Dithane

SIGNAL WORD: CAUTION

DESCRIPTION: Wettable powder, a mixture of two chemicals (zinc and manganese) that are not normally considered pesticides but which works because it is a *coordination product:* They are effective only when mixed together.

USE: Controlling a wide variety of fungal diseases such as anthracnose, early and late blights, rust, scab, and downy mildew in fruit, vegetable, nut, and field crops, pretty much replacing maneb (see next entry).

USE TIPS: Caution should be taken that it does not get into water, food, or feed. Empty containers should be buried away from water supplies or sources. Store in a dry, dark place with good air circulation.

BUYING TIP: Currently under review by the EPA. Many homeowner products will be affected if it is banned.

MANEB

ALSO KNOWN AS: Akzo Chemie Maneb

CHEMICAL NAME: Manganese ethylene bis-dithiocarbamate

POPULAR BRAND NAMES: Dexol Maneb Garden Fungicide, Security Maneb Spray, Dithane M-22, Manzate

SIGNAL WORD: CAUTION

DESCRIPTION: Wettable, odorless yellow powder that has been replaced in most uses by mancozeb (see preceding entry).

USE: Controlling fungal diseases of vegetables and fruit.

USE TIP: Open dumping is prohibited, so bury empty containers away from all water.

BUYING TIP: Currently being reviewed by the EPA.

TRIADIMEFON

POPULAR BRAND NAMES: Bayleton®, Amiral™

SIGNAL WORD: WARNING (as wettable powder) or CAUTION (depending on formulation)

DESCRIPTION: Dry, flowable (may be abbreviated DF) systemic fungicide in powder form. Also available as granules and liquids of various concentrations.

USE: Fighting majority of diseases of turf and ornamental plants, outdoors and in greenhouses, including flower blight, leaf blight and spots, powdery mildew, and rusts. Particularly good on greenhouse plants such as African violets, carnations, geraniums, and roses.

TRIFORINE

CHEMICAL NAME: Triforine

POPULAR BRAND NAME: Funginex®

SIGNAL WORD: DANGER

DESCRIPTION: Liquid (emulsifiable concentrate) sold in small bottles.

USE: Controlling fungal diseases such as black spot, powdery mildew, and rusts on roses and other flowers.

USE TIP: May be combined with certain insecticides as noted on the label.

ZINEB

CHEMICAL NAME: Zinc ethylene bis-dithiocarbamate

POPULAR BRAND NAMES: Parzate, Dithane

SIGNAL WORD: CAUTION

DESCRIPTION: Wettable powder.

USE: Controlling fungal diseases of vegetables, fruits, and flowers. Applied as a foliar protectant, before disease appears.

USE TIP: Dispose of very carefully away from all water (follow directions on label).

BUYING TIP: Currently being reviewed by the EPA.

Synthetic Miticides

DICOFOL

CHEMICAL NAME: -1,1-bis (chlorophenyl)-2,2,2, trichloroethanol

POPULAR BRAND NAME: Kelthane

SIGNAL WORD: WARNING or CAUTION—varies with formulation

DESCRIPTION: Wettable powder or amber-colored emulsifiable concentrate.

USE: For the control of mites.

USE TIPS: Avoid contact with skin, and wash thoroughly after using. Should be used with a mask if applied as a mist. Harmful if swallowed. Toxic to fish, and should be kept away from water sources.

BUYING TIP: Currently under review by the EPA and therefore hard to find.

TETRADIFON

CHEMICAL NAME: -4-chlorophenyl 2,4,5-trichlorophenyl sulfone

POPULAR BRAND NAME: Tedion

SIGNAL WORD: CAUTION

DESCRIPTION: Wettable powder or emulsifiable concentrate.

USE: For the control of mites and spiders.

BUYING TIP: Vendex® is a similar product.

Synthetic Molluscicides

SNAIL AND SLUG BAIT

POPULAR BRAND NAMES: Slug-Geta®, Bug-Geta®

SIGNAL WORD: CAUTION or WARNING, depending on the brand

DESCRIPTION: Potent, toxic, granular, pelletized, or thick liquid bait, made of a number of chemicals, such as metaldehyde or Mesurol®.

USE: Poisoning slugs and snails as well as crickets, millipedes, and sow bugs (depending on the brand). Granules are made to be spread across a lawn, but may be placed in special slug traps (see page 109), as may the pellets, which is how they are intended to be dispensed. Liquid form is placed in a chain of drops between berry and vegetable plants—not directly on them—and around flower beds or lawn edges.

USE TIPS: Do not use around food crops or bodies of water. Toxic to fish and wildlife, and, of course, to pets and people. All labels carry the warning to "keep children and pets out of treated areas," which makes it an unlikely choice for a family garden. Certain formulations are actually attractive to dogs, and are marked as such in the label's fine print. Birds that feed on a treated area may be killed. Safer to use in small slug traps than to apply directly.

BUYING TIP: Alternative baits are yeast and water mixtures or stale beer, which are nontoxic, to say the least, although some beer connoisseurs may claim certain inferior brands of beer to be toxic.

Synthetic Rodenticides

CHLOROPHACINONE

ALSO KNOWN AS: Liphadione, LM 91

CHEMICAL NAME: 2-(p-chlorophenyl) phenylacetyl-1,3-indadione

POPULAR BRAND NAMES: Caid, Drat, Microzul, Ramucide, Ratomet, Raviac, Rozol, Topitox

SIGNAL WORD: CAUTION

DESCRIPTION: Chlorophacinone is a pale yellow crystalline material that is sold as a concentrate in oil and dust forms. It is also sold as bait in the form of paraffin blocks and pellets, and as a ground spray (one that is sprayed right onto the soil).

USE: For the control of rodents.

USE TIP: Be sure to check the label for the recommended cautionary practices for application, such as using masks and gloves when handling concentrates of this chemical, and for the most effective form to use for your problem.

CLORECALCIFEROL

POPULAR BRAND NAMES: Mouse-B-Gon™, Rat-B-Gon™

SIGNAL WORD: CAUTION

DESCRIPTION: Bait usually manufactured in paper traps.

USE: Rat and mouse control.

USE TIP: Maintain bait for at least ten days. Do not place any bait where children have access.

COUMAFURYL

CHEMICAL NAME: 3(a-Acetonylfurfuryl)-4-hydroxycourmarin

POPULAR BRAND NAMES: Fumarin, Kill-Ko Rat, Mouse Blues

SIGNAL WORD: CAUTION or DANGER—varies with formulation

DESCRIPTION: A powder that is mixed with cornmeal, rolled oats, or other cereals, is ingested by the rodents, and causes death by internal bleeding.

USE: Used to kill common rodents such as mice and rats.

USE TIP: Should be put out in three to five doses daily for no more than every two days.

PINDONE

CHEMICAL NAME: 2-Pivalyl-1,3-indandione

POPULAR BRAND NAME: Pival

SIGNAL WORD: CAUTION

DESCRIPTION: Sold as a powder concentrate and a premixed bait.

USE: For the long-term control of mice, rats, and other rodents.

USE TIPS: Because it is tasteless and odorless, rodents do not develop bait shyness, making this a popular choice where there is a chronic rodent problem. As with most rodenticides, it is advisable to keep it away from children, pets, and wildlife.

WARFARIN

ALSO KNOWN AS: Wafarin

CHEMICAL NAME: 3(a-Acetonylbenzyl)-4-hydrozycoumarin

SIGNAL WORD: CAUTION or WARNING—varies with formulation

DESCRIPTION: Sold to general public as a ready-to-use bait, but available to exterminators in a concentrated form for mixing with cornmeal. It acts as an anticoagulant (it causes internal bleeding) and has no color or odor.

USE: For the control of mice and rats.

USE TIPS: Keep away from children, pets, and wildlife. Do not store near food or feed. Avoid contact with skin, eyes, or mouth. Use baits only in areas where larger animals cannot reach them. It often takes a couple of weeks before a reduction in the number of rodents is noticed.

Tools, Equipment, and Accessories

Digging Tools and Wheel Goods

ABOUT DIGGING TOOL DURABILITY

These tools are designed to be used for digging as well as turning soil in the garden and include shovels, spades, trowels, and forks. You will find a wide range of digging tools in your garden center, with an even wider range of quality. How durable a digging tool is depends primarily on how the "business end" is attached to the handle, since this is the part of a digging tool that is put under the most stress when the tool is being used. There are three ways in which the tools listed here can be attached to their handles.

TANG-AND-FERRULE: A *tang* is a projecting shank or tongue, in this case, one that comes out the rear end of a shovel or rake head; a *ferrule* is a metal ring or collar that is fitted over the end of a wooden handle after a tang has been inserted into it. Often

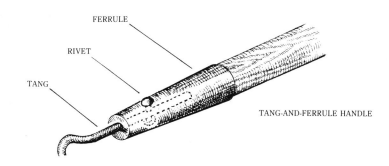

FERRULE

RIVET

TANG

TANG-AND-FERRULE HANDLE

SOLID-SOCKET HANDLE

SOLID-STRAP HANDLE

a rivet or bolt is inserted through the ferrule and the tang to ensure a secure attachment. The tang-and-ferrule method is common in garden tools, but is not as secure a fit as the solid-socket method described next. It is, however, easier and therefore cheaper to manufacture this type of tool. The ferrule should be one long piece; those with a small "extra" collar about 1 inch wide at the end are actually not as good, because the small collar is doing the work that a foot-long piece should do. This kind of tool also may be called a *tanged* or *shank tool.*

SOLID-SOCKET: With this method, a handle is attached to a tool blade via a solid collar that is actually part of the tool blade, having been forged or stamped from the same piece of steel (not welded on). It is wrapped around the first foot or so of the handle or, on the better models, the handle is actually driven into the socket; they may also have a pin or rivets driven through the shaft to hold the handle in. This is sturdier than the tang-and-ferrule method and less likely to bend or break where the handle meets the blade, especially with very long collars. Long, forged solid-sockets are a sign of top quality. However, it is more costly to manufacture because the entire tool must be made from a larger piece of metal than the tang-and-ferrule method just described, and forged versions require hand labor. It is still the best value and recommended for the sturdiest forks, shovels, and spades. May also be called, confusingly, *solid-shank,* or *chucked.*

SOLID-STRAP: In the solid-strap method of attaching the tool blade to the handle, a metal part called a *strap* is extended from the socket up toward the tool handle. The blade, socket, and strap are all forged from one piece of steel, making this kind of tool the sturdiest and most durable. As you might imagine, this is a rare form of manufacture but an excellent find and a highly recommended purchase if you have plenty of heavy work to do, such as digging up shrubs or trees.

All metal tools should be wiped dry after use and coated with a little oil to prevent rust. You can wipe them with a slightly oily rag or spray them with an aerosol lubricant.

Many manufacturers make their most popular models in two sizes, the smaller of which is often called a "ladies' " tool, such as a "ladies' spade," although their "floral" models serve the same purpose. These generally, but not always, are of the same quality and refer only to a lighter weight and smaller head and handle (for working in flower beds), ranging from 15 to 40 percent less. As any tool is an extension of your body, it should fit properly, and these so-called ladies' tools are the way to go to get your fit, if need be. These and children's tools should be of the same quality as the larger tools, but some manufacturers seem to think that smaller tools can be of lesser quality. They are wrong, and these tools should be avoided.

Some manufacturers are now making tools with interchangeable handles, including both hand- and full-sized (one popular brand is Twools™, another is Scotts). This is certainly convenient and may be economical, but be sure to check the balance and the feel of these tools—in some combinations, they may not be as comfortable to use as those that have been specifically designed with a handle of a certain length in mind.

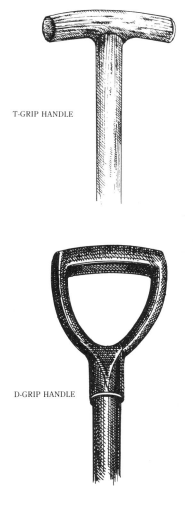

T-GRIP HANDLE

D-GRIP HANDLE

ABOUT GRIPS AND HANDLES

Digging tool handles, or "hilts," come in three types: *straight, T-,* or *D-grip.* Generally speaking, straight handles, just long rods, are useful in longer length (40 to 48 inches) tools where a lot of lifting is done, while D- and T-grips are found in shorter lengths, like 26 to 30 inches, where control or prying is more important, or you're maneuvering in tight quarters. The longer straight handles make it easier to dig deeply and throw farther (the soil, not the shovel!), while T handles are a bit slippery to use as they are awkward to grip, and are not recommended.

D-grips should be made of wood and may be covered with metal for extra protection; heavy-duty models have a reinforcement in the V of the neck while lightweight models are plastic. If the grip is an all-metal piece that is attached to the blunt end of the handle, be sure to check the quality, as this can loosen with time. The best ones are made entirely of wood; the handle is split and formed into a Y, making for a solid and beautiful handle, sometimes reinforced at the narrow part. The *cob* (the crosspiece on the D-grip) should be sturdy, and not turn at all when you grip the tool. Some manufacturers call this a *Y-D grip,* and it is traditional and good.

Ash is the material of choice for wooden handles, though hickory is as good and as common; only the cheaper tools use Douglas fir, which should generally be avoided by the serious gardener. Wooden handles should be free of knots and flaws, and the grain should run lengthwise in even, continuous lines. The closer or tighter the grain of the wood in the handle, the stronger it is. Tubular steel handles are usually too heavy for the average consumer to enjoy, but lighter alloys (usually plastic covered) are found on some fancy models. Replacement handles are available with the end adapted for solid-socket style or ferrule style.

Digging Tools

ABOUT DIGGING TOOLS

There is a wider variety in style and quality among these products than almost any others. Your choice depends largely on the type of gardening you do and the type of soil you have. Acquire slowly and look for quality wherever you can—it will pay off in the long run in terms of comfort and utility for you, and longevity for the tool. As with all metal tools, make an effort to keep these clean, dry, and sharp. See the note at the beginning of this chapter about shovel handle construction.

BULB LIFTER

DESCRIPTION: Wide, two-pronged hand fork with a 6-inch steel blade and a 12-inch wooden handle.

USE: Lifting bulbs out of the garden for division or overwintering, and for transplanting flowers.

USE TIP: Make sure you dig below the bulb to avoid damaging its storage cells.

BULB LIFTER

BULB PLANTER

DESCRIPTION: Tapered metal cylinder from 6 to 10 inches tall, with a D-grip handle right above it or with a long handle (approximately 30 inches long—abbreviated often as an *L.H. bulb planter)* and a foot rest. The hand-held bulb planter is used in a kneeling or stooping position, while the long-handled ones can be used from a standing position. Long-handled bulb planters are often made from a single piece of metal. They all should have

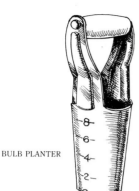

BULB PLANTER

depth markings in inches on their sides. May be confused with the narrow trowel made for this purpose, as they are often called by the same name. A similar model is made for planting zoysia-grass plugs. Another version, called a *sod planter,* is made for planting sod plugs. It has a 2-inch-square cutter and extractor.

USE: Planting bulbs singularly in confined spaces or where there are other plants close by.

USE TIP: The cylinder is pushed into the soil and removed, taking a plug of soil with it, as long as the soil is not completely dry. The bulb is placed in the hole and the plug replaced. Many of these tools have depth markings on the side to help make the correct depth hole for each bulb.

BUYING TIP: Many gardeners prefer a trowel to the hand-held bulb planter, but the long-handled versions are extremely useful for people who cannot kneel or stoop easily.

CROWBAR

ALSO KNOWN AS: Prybar, pinch bar, axle rod, curb-setter, bull prick, bar (*Note:* The term *crowbar* is often used incorrectly for a *gooseneck wrecking bar,* which has a curved end and is 18 to 36 inches long)

DESCRIPTION: Long, straight high-carbon steel bar, about ¾ inch in diameter and about 4 to 5 feet long. Approximately two-thirds of the bar is round, with the working (lower) third square and tipped with either a wedge (triangular) point or pinch point (like that on a chisel). A digger bar, or a fencing crowbar, has a flat end. Crowbars weigh either 12 or 18 pounds.

CROWBAR

WEDGE POINT   PINCH POINT

USE: Prying large rocks or root-balled trees out of holes, or maneuvering large stones for fences or curbs (or removing chunks of busted-up sidewalks). It can also be driven into hard soil to start a hole, whether for digging or inserting a tomato stake or bean pole. Some people even use a crowbar to measure the temperature of a compost pile (left in the center of a large "ripe" pile, the tip will heat up to the point where you can't hold onto it).

USE TIPS: When using as a lever to pry out a rock or stump, put a large sturdy piece of scrap wood at the edge of the hole under the crowbar to act as a fulcrum; the bar will otherwise sink right into the soil. Heavier models work best in hard soils and clay, with the weight doing much of the work for you.

BUYING TIP: These things don't age. They make for nice buys at flea markets or auctions.

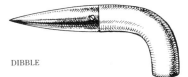

DIBBLE

DIBBLE

ALSO KNOWN AS: Dibber, dibbler, planter

DESCRIPTION: The original dibble was just a cow's horn. Now they are made of solid plastic or cast iron, steel, or metal-covered wood or plastic and are about 8 inches long, pointed and round with a curved, T-, or D- handle just above it, though one with a waist-high handle is also made.

USE: Quick way of making holes for transplants and bulbs.

USE TIP: This is a handy tool if you are setting out numbers of plants or bulbs, but if you are just doing just a few, a trowel will suffice. This is really a tool for large gardens. When planting bulbs, note that the bulb may not rest completely flat in the deep indentation made by the point, thus leaving an air pocket under the bulb. Push the bulb down to nestle it into the soil.

BUYING TIPS: Look for a smooth, comfortable grip. Dibbles are not indispensable tools for most gardeners. A couple of good trowels generally do the job just as well.

EARTH AUGER

ALSO KNOWN AS: Landscape auger, bulb drill

POPULAR BRAND NAMES: Earth Auger, Daffodrill™

DESCRIPTION: Large steel spiral drill bit, 18 to 24 inches long and 1½ to 2½ inches in diameter, designed to fit into a standard power drill (both ¼- and ⅜-inch sizes). Professional models are made for ½-inch drills. Other models are long, open-sided cylinders rather than spirals.

USE: Drilling small holes in the ground for direct access to roots (to install a root feeder, take a soil sample, fertilize, or apply a hose for soaking a newly planted tree or shrub), for installing large stakes, or for planting bulbs and seedlings, in which case the 2½-inch-wide model is used.

USE TIPS: This is the occasion for a cordless drill to shine, owing to the dearth of electrical outlets in your typical garden. Heavy clay or thick sod will require a larger, heavier model. Watch your hole depth when planting bulbs.

BUYING TIP: Definitely a help when planting large quantities of bulbs or small seedlings.

EDGER

EDGER

ALSO KNOWN AS: Turf edger, half-moon edger, semicircular edger, edging knife, lawn edge trimmer, hand edger

DESCRIPTION: Flat, semicircular blade, about 8 inches across, attached to a handle that may be long and straight or end in a T- or D-grip. The straight top of the edger often has a rolled footrest. Top of the line models have solid-socket construction, and some are made of mirror-polished stainless steel. The rotary edger (see page 203) is for trimming grass borders.

USE: Cutting a sharp edge along garden or lawn walks, borders, driveways, buildings, and sidewalks.

USE TIP: Place the edger about 1 to 2 inches from the walk or area to be edged. Press down by stepping on the footrest. A sharp edge is cut when you pull the handle back toward yourself, creating a slight angle.

BUYING TIPS: Because of the amount of tension that is put on the edger at the shank, it is wise to pay more for a solid-socket type. Highly polished stainless steel slices more easily through the soil than other metals.

FORK

DESCRIPTION: Simply a large steel fork, the size of a shovel, with three to ten tines (or more), depending on the type of fork. Most are tang-and-ferrule construction, but top-of-the-line models are solid-socket type (see "About Digging Tool Durability," pages 137–39, for an extended discussion of methods of

MANURE FORK

PITCHFORK

joining). The shape of the tines also depends on the type of fork.

The four types actually fall into two broad categories, *garden* and *pitch (spading* and *manure* forks are respective subcategories). There is much confusion surrounding the terms *garden, digging,* and *spading. Digging* is a general term that applies to both kinds, but is only accurate as a name for the garden fork. Many well-known and widely distributed manufacturers lump all their forks together under the category of "digging" forks, an error that adds to the confusion. May have lightweight plastic handles or handles that are reinforced with *straps* running from the tines to three-quarters or all of the way up the handle. The plastic handles of high-quality tools are usually filled with a steel alloy and epoxy bonded for extra strength and to exclude moisture. Made of regular or stainless high-carbon steel; the top of the line stainless models are highly polished and the seams of the solid-socket are welded (seam welded), but only in the garden and spading models. A *ladies' fork* is merely a smaller and lighter version (weighing about 1 to 3 pounds) of any model, and some special smaller designs with curved heads and long handles, sometimes called *cultiforks,* are designed for wheelchair gardeners.

Handles are usually D-grip or straight, depending on the type (see "About Grips and Handles," page 139).

TYPES: *Garden fork* (also known as *digging, English garden, English pattern, English digging,* or *English style fork):* A 7- to 8-inch-wide head with four thick rectangular or square tines approximately 12 inches long and a 30-inch-long handle ending in a D-grip, although available with a 5-foot-long straight handle. Most common model. Available in heavy-duty versions that are slightly larger. The square tines may be called *English tines.*

Manure fork (also known as *stable fork* or *apple picker):* Four to ten 12-inch-long, curved, round, fine tines spaced closely together. A similar model with longer tines is a *mulch fork.* The term *stable fork* is usually applied to lighter, almost rakelike models with even more tines, usually sixteen, and may at that point be called a *bedding fork.* Handles are usually 4 feet long.

Pitchfork (also known as *farm, hay,* or *Kansas header fork):* Three to five round, tapered tines about 12 inches long, usually with a 4-foot-long, straight handle attached

SPADING FORK

by either a solid-socket or a tang-and-ferrule. Shorter handles with D-grips are also available. A *Scottish composting fork* is a lighter and smaller version.

Spading fork (also known as *turning, border,* or *digging fork,* though this last is incorrect terminology): Four flat tines, sometimes with diamond or triangular backs. Slightly lighter and smaller than garden fork; sometimes the term *border fork* refers to a lighter, narrower version with wider tines. Usually 42 inches long overall.

USE: The garden and spading forks are used to turn over garden soil, while the other two—pitch and manure—are used to lift and throw light, loose material, such as hay. Forks are often easier to use than shovels for turning and cultivating because it is easier to insert the tines into the ground than it is to shove in an entire shovel blade, particularly if the soil is compacted.

Garden fork: Best suited for turning unbroken soil, breaking up clods, and for heavy cultivation. Use a heavy-duty model for rocky or clayey soils.

Manure fork: Good for lifting manure and other fine material without sifting. More suited to farm use than home garden use.

Pitchfork: Used to lift hay, straw, and leaf mold. Essentially for farm or large garden use.

Spading fork: Turning over already-broken, loose soil for cultivation. Often used for lighter digging, such as lifting out bulbs and perennials, and for harvesting vegetables that grow under the soil surface, such as potatoes and beets.

USE TIP: When cultivating or turning the soil, the fork should be perpendicular to the ground, pushed in with your foot on the footrest, and then pried up.

BUYING TIPS: As with all digging tools, it is important that the length of the handle be comfortable. It should come up just to your waist when fully inserted in the ground. The tool should have good balance and not be too heavy. Unfortunately, American companies no longer manufacture solid-socket or solid-strap garden forks, but many are imported from England. And watch your weight—that is, get a fork that is not too heavy for you to use.

Generally, a spading fork is not as good a buy as a garden fork, if you want only one fork. The flat tines on a spading fork may bend if you hit a rock, and it is difficult, if not impossible, to straighten them. The square tines of the garden fork are less likely to bend, and the fork will do most of the same work of the spading fork. It may not work as well when trying to turn a fine-textured soil, but a spade can then be substituted. Look for high-carbon, tempered steel with a slight "spring" to it. Smaller, hand-sized versions are made, listed under hand forks (see page 164).

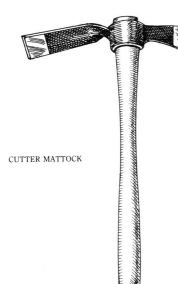

CUTTER MATTOCK

MATTOCK

ALSO KNOWN AS: Grubbing hoe, grub hoe

DESCRIPTION: Sort of a combination serious hoe (see pages 160–63) and ax (see pages 194–95), or pick (see next entry), but with a wider, thicker, duller blade and a heavier wooden handle, larger at the tool end.

TYPES: *Pick mattock* (also known as *trencher* or *trencher pick, garden pick):* Pick on one end, heavy-duty hoe on the other. Weighs about 5 pounds. A smaller, 2-pound model is called a *pick-a-hoe.*

Cutter mattock (also known as *grubbing* or *garden cutter mattock):* Ax on one end, heavy-duty hoe on the other. Weighs about 3½ to 5 pounds.

Garden mattock: Lightweight version of a cutter mattock.

Single-bladed mattock (also known as *adze hoe* or *grubbing mattock):* Rarely available, resembles a wide-bladed adze, with only one flat blade perpendicular to the handle.

USE: Breaking up hard ground and grubbing out roots and rock. Very helpful tool for digging trenches when laying electrical or water lines in a garden, or for removing tree stumps. Mattocks and picks are used for many of the same jobs, but the pick is more useful in initially breaking up very hard soils while mattocks are more useful in lifting rocks and cutting through roots because of its wide blade.

USE TIP: Swing as you would a pick, described below.

BUYING TIP: If you are gardening in a long-neglected garden where the soil is very hard or there is hardpan (a soil that is so hard water cannot drain through), a mattock is indispensable. The lightweight garden mattock should suffice for normal use. Mattocks remain sharp on jobs that would quickly dull an ax or hatchet, such as cutting roots that are surrounded by soil.

PICK

ALSO KNOWN AS: Clay pick, railroad pick

DESCRIPTION: Slightly curved, heavy metal blade from 16 to 20 inches long, with about a 30-inch-long wooden (usually hickory or ash) or fiberglass handle attached in the middle. One end of the pick blade is pointed while the other has a 1- to 2-inch-wide chisel head. When the chisel end is a few inches wide, it may be called a *pick-a-hoe* (pick and hoe), which is sold with a short handle. A *pick axe* (or *pickax)* has a full ax blade on one end and a short pick blade on the other.

PICK

USE: Breaking up hard ground or working rocky or root-laden areas. Once the area has been broken up by the pick, the earth is easier to pick up with a shovel or work with a fork. Picks are also helpful in reclaiming long-abandoned urban gardens, some of which may even have solidified coal cinder piles.

USE TIP: A pick can be used by swinging the tool in a circular motion at the side of the body, or in an over-the-head motion in which the tool lines up with the center of the body on the down stroke. Allow the weight of the tool to complete the motion as this will require less of your energy and strength, because the weight of the tool does most of the work.

BUYING TIP: Find a pick that is comfortable for you to lift over your head. If the pick is too heavy, just lifting it can be tiring. Picks are not indispensable gardening tools, but for larger gardens and some urban gardens they can be worth the investment.

POSTHOLE DIGGER

DESCRIPTION: Hinged digging blades attached to two long handles.

TYPES: *Clamshell digger:* The most easily found. Consists of two wooden handles, each of which is attached to a curved blade about 12 inches long. A pivot joint is placed between the two blades where they attach to the handles. The blades are plunged into the ground in an open position (that is, when the handles are parallel). The handles are then pulled apart, causing the blades to come to-

CLAMSHELL POSTHOLE DIGGER

gether like a clamshell to scoop up soil that is then lifted from the hole.

Manual auger (also known as *earth auger, posthole auger,* or *posthole borer):* Has two stationary blades that are bent at angles. These are attached to a wooden handle that ends in a crossbar about a yard long. A manual auger works by the blades being screwed into the ground as the crossbar is turned in a clockwise direction. When the blades are full, they are lifted from the hole and emptied. *(Note:* The term *earth auger* also refers to a spiral drill bit that is used with an electric drill for making small holes, described on pages 142–43.)

Lever-action digger (also known as *Canadian, Canadian style, scissor type,* or *universal digger):* One stationary blade attached to a wooden handle with a moving blade attached to a lever about 3 feet up on the handle. The blades of this digger are plunged into the soil and the lever is pulled down, causing the two blades to scoop up soil that can be lifted from the hole and released when the lever is pulled up.

LEVER-ACTION POSTHOLE DIGGER

USE: Digging narrow holes for fence posts and footings for garden structures such as gazebos, arbors, shelters, porches, and the like. Manual augers are effective only in soft soil, not for hard or rocky soil.

USE TIP: Clean digger blades after each use with an oiled cloth. Be sure to oil all moving parts before storing in a dry place.

BUYING TIPS: A must for large estates and farms, but less important in small gardens. If you are installing a fence or garden structures that are supported by posts anchored in the ground you may want to consider purchasing a posthole digger, as these structures usually require some repair maintenance in the future. However, posthole diggers can be rented or borrowed from a neighbor. Lever-action diggers are the most efficient; clamshell models require more energy to use and make a wider hole, but give you more direct control.

The clamshell digger is a durable, reliable tool. With proper care it can last a long time. If you are digging a hole more than 2 feet deep, this is probably the tool for you. Manual augers work well only in loose soil and can make holes only up to 12 inches wide. They work less well, or not at all, in hard or rocky soils. The advantage of a lever-type digger is that it can dig a deep hole that is narrower than one dug by a clamshell digger, the latter always digging a hole as wide as the handle spread required to close the clamshell.

SHOVEL

DESCRIPTION: Probably the gardener's most familiar tools, shovels have a good deal of variety of detail and type. (Spades are a different item and are listed on pages 151–53.) Blade tips may be rounded, pointed, or blunt, depending on the type. Handles vary in length and shape, ending in either a D-grip, a T-grip, or just a slight taper (see "About Grips and Handles" on page 139). The degree of cant, or the angle of the handle from the ground when the blade is flat, varies from model to model.

Steel shovel blades are made one of two basic ways: *stamped* or *forged*. Stamped shovels are stamped out of a large sheet of metal, and contain a crimp, or fold, called a *frog*, near the top of the blade by the handle, to make the blade stronger. These shovels are referred to as *hollow-backed* or *open-back* if the frog opening is left as formed. When a triangular piece of metal is welded over the frog to close and reinforce it, the shovel is referred to as a *closed-back* or *fast-back shovel.*

Forged shovels are rolled out and forged from a single thick piece of steel. They are naturally strong, stronger than stamped shovels, so there is no need for the frog in the blade. Forged shovels, sometimes called *solid-shank* shovels, may be either of solid-socket design or solid-strap design (see "About Digging Tool Durability" on pages 137–38). Top-quality models are made of epoxy-coated, heat-treated, high-carbon steel. Most manufacturers also offer a chrome-plated ceremonial shovel for ground-breaking ceremonies.

TYPES: *Round point shovel* (also known as *pointed, dirt, round-nose, round-point,* or *American pattern shovel):* Pointed, curved blade with an almost 4-foot-long wooden handle;

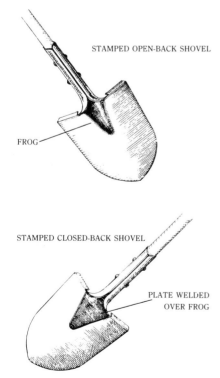

STAMPED OPEN-BACK SHOVEL

FROG

STAMPED CLOSED-BACK SHOVEL

PLATE WELDED OVER FROG

ROUND POINT
SHOVEL

FORGED
SQUARE
POINT
SHOVEL

SCOOP SHOVEL

a less pointed model is called *medium point* and may be broader. The top of the blade, nearest the handle, is often rolled over to form a tread, or footrest. About 8½ inches wide by 11 or 12 inches long. A rare model is the *narrow-blade shovel,* about half the normal size. Some models have serrated front edges to assist in cutting through roots and compacted soil.

Square point shovel (also known as *square-nose* or *square-mouth shovel):* Blunt-ended, flat blade with up-turned sides. May have long plain handles or shorter handles with D-grips. About 9½ by 11 inches.

Scoop shovel (also known as *coal, coal and street,* or *barn and snow shovel):* Much like the square-nose shovel but larger and much lighter. May be made of aluminum or plastic. Almost twice as big as the other types. *Eastern scoops* are smaller than *Western scoops,* which usually have reinforcing ribs in them. Some are more specialized, such as *grain scoops.*

USE: General purpose models are used for digging and moving loose soil or other materials like sand, cement, and gravel from one place to another. The round nose holds more—the wide, slightly curved blade allows you to pick up a good-sized load. Gardeners need at least one of these for tasks such as digging up beds, planting trees and shrubs, and working in compost. The narrow-blade model can be used to dig small trenches or simply as a smaller shovel for smaller gardeners. Square-nose shovels are an excellent construction for when you have to lift material like sand off a sidewalk. Scoop shovels are not for digging but rather for moving loose and light material like snow, sawdust, or trash.

USE TIPS: Clean shovels with an oiled cloth after using and store in a dry place. Shovels are not really designed for lifting light plant material such as straw or uncomposed compost—spades (see pages 151–53) and forks (see pages 143–46) are more appropriate. Though a long-handled shovel has good leverage for lifting, many a handle has been broken when a shovel was used to lift a plant by prying it out.

BUYING TIPS: The lightweight, stamped, hollow-backed shovel is a good purchase for most gardeners, and is the most popular and least expensive. The closed-back models are a bit stronger and generally more expensive. If you want to purchase a higher quality tool that will really last, a forged shovel is worth the investment—the top of the line of any brand is forged. The gardener with a small garden probably does not need a scoop shovel or square-nose shovel, which are used primarily for moving material, but the estate gardener will find these useful—the exception being for snow removal, when either one is a help. In any shovel, look for a good cant, or angle, of the handle to the ground, for ease of use—the larger the angle the less you'll have to bend over. Longer handles also avert bending over. Sockets should be riveted to the handles. Seam-welded sockets are typical of top-quality shovels. Don't buy a large shovel if you have trouble lifting heavy loads—buy the size that's comfortable for you to work with.

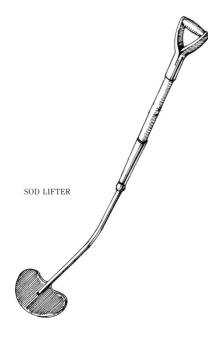

SOD LIFTER

SOD LIFTER

DESCRIPTION: The first cousin of the edger (see page 143). It looks similar, but the sod lifter has a long solid steel shank that is bent at an angle and has no footrest. The handle of the sod lifter often ends in a D-grip.

USE: Lifting sod pieces from a lawn prior to reseeding. Also helpful when cutting a hole in a lawn to plant a tree or to create a bed. When sod is lifted with a sod lifter, less damage is done to it than when a spade or shovel is used, and the sod can be used elsewhere in the lawn.

USE TIP: This tool, which relies on leverage to work, can be a back breaker if used incorrectly. If working on a large area, rhythm and a pattern of motion make using this tool less painful. Use the curve of the handle as a fulcrum to pry up the sod— don't lift with your forward hand.

BUYING TIP: This is not an essential garden tool, but for the gardener who is putting in a border or flower bed or planting trees in a sodded area, it may be worth purchasing. An edger, however, may do a small job just as well.

SPADE

DESCRIPTION: Similar to a shovel (see pages 149–51) but with an almost flat, rectangular blade (or head), usually a shorter handle, and usually a D-grip (see "About Grips and Handles," page 139). The blade is straight or slightly tapered, depending on the type, and may have a small section of the top of the blade bent over to form a footrest, or tread, depending on the model.

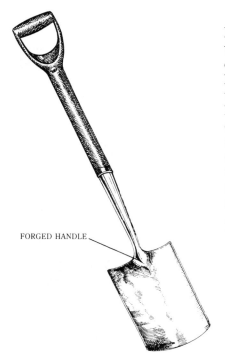

FORGED HANDLE

FORGED STAINLESS STEEL GARDEN SPADE

Professional brands have models that are even further differentiated, by purpose, such as *shrub, drain,* or *balling spades.* For example, drain spades can be as narrow as 5 inches. Spades may have handles that are reinforced with steel straps running from the blade three-fourths or all of the way up the handle, or lightweight plastic-coated hollow steel handles. They are made of regular, high-carbon, or stainless steel; the top of the line stainless models are polished to a mirror finish and the seams of the solid-socket types are welded (referred to as "seam welded"). The plastic handles of high-quality spades are usually epoxy bonded to the socket for extra strength and to keep out moisture.

TYPES: *Border spade:* The smallest, an easy-to-use spade that gets its name from having been used in border gardening, where narrow beds are common. A modified version is sometimes called a *poacher's spade,* with a curved blade and a rounded tip; a *Dutch spade* is a bit shorter and has a slightly curved blade and a T-grip. All are about 5½ inches wide by about 10 inches long, with an overall length of about 36 inches, though the Dutch spade is often longer.

Garden spade (also known as *digging spade):* Medium to large-sized, general purpose spade. The flat or slightly curved blades are usually 8 inches wide and 12 inches long. The top edge of the blade near the handle should be folded over to make two *footrests* (also known as *treads* or *step treads).* Overall lengths range from about 3½ to over 5 feet (on the straight handle models). A smaller, lighter model (about 1 to 3 pounds less) is commonly offered, called a *ladies' spade,* as is a heavy-duty model, with a longer socket and perhaps a more angled blade.

Irish garden spade (also known as *Irish spade):* Longer, more tapered blade than the border spade, with a T-grip handle.

Tree-planting spade (also known as *tree spade, sharpshooter, trenching tool,* or *transplanting spade):* Longest, tapered blade, about 16 inches long, with a very wide footrest at the top of the blade.

USE: Digging, cutting, turning, and lifting soil, especially heavy soil and sod, often when making a lawn edge. Spades are particularly well-suited for cutting through roots and compacted soil when digging planting holes or turning beds. The flat blade is helpful when edging or digging a trench. Border spades are popular with children or older gardeners who appreciate their light weight, as well as for transplanting. Irish garden spades dig deep holes and are the choice of gardeners who like to double-dig their gardens (digging up the soil to a depth of two shovel blades). The extra-wide footrests on a tree-planting spade make it easier to dig deep holes for planting trees and shrubs.

USE TIPS: Keep the cutting edges of spades sharp with an emery wheel, file, or whetstone. Clean spades with an oiled cloth and store in a dry place.

BUYING TIPS: Many gardeners consider the spade to be a more essential gardening tool than the shovel (see pages 149–51), as it can help with so many specific gardening tasks. The length of the handle is important. For the best leverage, the D-grip should be just below waist level when the spade is inserted in the soil. Avoid spades with T-grips, as they are awkward to use, unless you find yourself using two hands for lots of edging, in which case a T-grip has more room to hold on than a D-grip. Look for treads, or footrests on the top edge of the blade. Some of the most amazing spades are made of surgical-quality, mirror-polished stainless steel. They can cost around $100 and are terrific gift items, plus a little easier to use, but a heat-treated carbon steel spade (or even an epoxy-coated one) is just about as good and should last for a few generations—long enough for most of us.

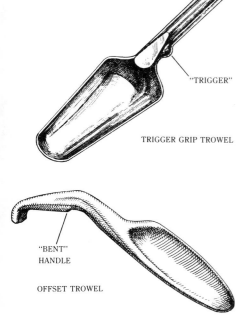

"TRIGGER"

TRIGGER GRIP TROWEL

"BENT"
HANDLE

OFFSET TROWEL

TROWEL

ALSO KNOWN AS: Hand trowel, garden trowel

DESCRIPTION: Small, narrow, hand-held metal scoop, either made from one piece of cast metal or a metal blade with a plastic or wooden handle of one of a variety of colors. Some newer models have specially curved and foam-padded handles or *trigger grip handles* with "triggers" on the bottom side which make them easier to use for people with arthritic joints. Handform manufactures an ergonomic design for arthritis or carpal tunnel syndrome sufferers that features a sideways offset blade and "bent" handle, making it easier to push or scrape without bending or forcing the wrist (it rests against your palm so you don't need to grip it). A curved handle is offered in a one-piece cast aluminum model as a way to avoid blisters, called, unsurprisingly, the *no-blister trowel.* Several makes now come with long handles that can be attached as desired in place of the hand-sized handle, and some manufacturers offer *long-handled trowels,* with 2- or 3-feet long, lightweight handles for use by those gardeners who have trouble bending over, or by children. *Houseplant trowels* are made in an almost miniature style, with extremely small blades for use in container gardening.

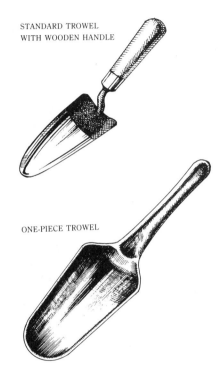

STANDARD TROWEL
WITH WOODEN HANDLE

ONE-PIECE TROWEL

TYPES: *Standard trowel:* Two-piece hand tool with a wooden, metal, or plastic handle and metal blade, and a sharp edge.

One-piece trowel: Made from cast lightweight aluminum or other metal alloy or forged heavy-gauge steel. Usually the handle is covered with a colorful plastic grip. The blade on a one-piece steel trowel is often V-shaped rather than curved (adding strength), and the edge is not sharp.

Planting or *bulb trowel:* Constructed like either of the above two, but with a narrower blade, usually 2 inches but no more than 3 inches wide at the top, tapering down to about 1 inch at the tip, and as much as 6 inches long, although some are made even narrower for delicate indoor work with seedlings. The smaller blade allows you to dig a small hole suitable for planting bulbs, bedding plants, or seedlings. Most models have measuring lines stamped into the blades for your convenience when determining how deep to plant each bulb, leading some people to call them *graduated trowels.* May also be called a *bulb planter* (though this is incorrect usage—see pages 140–41), or *planter, transplanter,* or *transplanting trowel.* The narrowest can be known as *rockery trowels,* for use in rock gardens.

USE: Planting, transplanting, and moving soil in garden beds or into containers. They are essential tools, especially for gardening in small spaces such as containers on terraces and roof gardens. Narrow and V-shaped blades are best for digging out weeds and planting bulbs; wider and flatter blades are better for general use with loose soil. Long handles are convenient for gardeners who have trouble bending over or kneeling.

USE TIPS: When transplanting with a trowel it is not always necessary to actually *dig* a hole. Simply insert the trowel into the soil and *open* a hole by moving the trowel from side to side; the curve of the blade forms the hole. Standard metal garden trowels should be cleaned with an oily cloth after use and stored in a dry place to avoid rusting.

BUYING TIPS: Colorful or bright metal trowels are easier to find in the garden. One-piece aluminum or steel trowels are more durable than the standard garden trowels where the blades are attached to a handle by the tang-and-ferrule method (see pages 137–39 for the discussion on handles). Standard trowels with blades made from chrome-plated steel are better buys than those with other metals. Among one-piece trowels, those made from steel are among the strongest and most durable sold. V-shaped blades are strong and less likely to bend. Aluminum trowels are lightweight, a consideration for people with arthritis or some other disability affecting their ability to grip, but the edge of the blade is not as sharp as on other trowels and cannot be sharpened. By all means, get a trowel that won't bend, and of course one that feels comfortable to grip—after all, that's what you do with it. Try all the various grip designs, because they fit individual hands differently from one another. Usually, the larger the grip, the easier the tool is to use. Interchangeable handles are sometimes not well-balanced—try them out before you buy. Finally, you may want to buy several sizes of trowels for use in different jobs.

WIDGER

ALSO KNOWN AS: Nitpicker, nit-picker, everything tool, potted-plant tool, double-ended widger

DESCRIPTION: Plain convex stainless steel strip, ½ inch wide and 7 inches long.

USE: Digging out small seedlings for transplanting and removing small potted plants by pushing the plant down along the side of the pot. Also good for seeding and applying small doses of fertilizer.

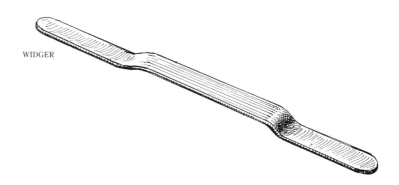

WIDGER

Wheel Goods

ABOUT WHEEL GOODS

The choice between a cart and a wheelbarrow is largely one of personal preference, or feel, though a cart is a bit less maneuverable and needs more room than a wheelbarrow. On the other hand, there are more innovative features to be found in a myriad of makes and models of carts than with wheelbarrows, which remain simple in design. Here is another tool category where it is quite worthwhile to buy the better quality item, or else you will need to replace it sooner than you think.

GARDEN CART

GARDEN CART

ANGLED
FRONT END

ALSO KNOWN AS: Yard cart, utility cart

DESCRIPTION: A cubish, deep-sided container (the "bucket"), about 20 by 40 inches by a foot high, on two wheels, with a metal loop handle, making it larger and deeper than a wheelbarrow (see next entry). Made of sheet metal or wood. Some wooden carts are open on the handle end, and the front end is a board that can be removed for dumping loads (on folding models, all panels are removable). Others can tilt on their axles for easy dumping. Some are designed with an angled front that lies on the ground when tilted down for easy loading. Capacity ranges from 4 to over 13 cubic feet, holding over 300 pounds with ease, but capable of carrying up to 450 pounds. A hybrid version is available that looks like a wheelbarrow with two wheels and a single handle, called a *yard buggy*. Many have spoked bicycle-type wheels for greater weight capacity and maneuverability.

YARD BUGGY

USE: Hauling heavier and larger loads than most wheelbarrows, but because of their double wheels they are not quite as maneuverable. Tilting feature allows for easier unloading and loading than with wheelbarrows.

USE TIPS: Position loads in carts closer to the front of the bucket, balancing them over the wheels to make hauling easier. Keep carts clean and bearings oiled.

BUYING TIPS: Metal carts and the metal parts of wooden carts should be made of heavy-gauge steel that is well protected from rust (zinc-plated is best). Look for large (20-inch) spoked wheels with pneumatic tires, a front panel for unloading, top grade, exterior-stained plywood, and a sturdy, adjustable handle. Choose the size that is right for you—there is quite a range. The yard buggy dumps easily like a wheelbarrow but is able to balance a heavy load like a cart.

WHEELBARROW

DESCRIPTION: A shallow, scooped container (the "tray") about 2 by 2½ feet made of wood, metal (assembled or one piece, seamless aluminum or 18-gauge steel), or heavy plastic (high-density polyethylene), attached to a single 10- to 16-inch wheel. Two long handles made either of metal or 2-inch-square wood are used for pushing the wheelbarrow around the garden. Wheels may be either inflatable or solid rubber, or wooden with a steel surface. A deep model with heavier, wider supports, a sturdier wheel, and higher sides is called a *contractor's* or *concrete wheelbarrow.* Sizes are measured in cubic feet (helpful when you plan to use this for mixing cement): 3 or 4½ cubic feet is a typical small size; the deep models hold as much as 6½ cubic feet. Capacity ranges from 150 to 700 pounds.

WHEELBARROW

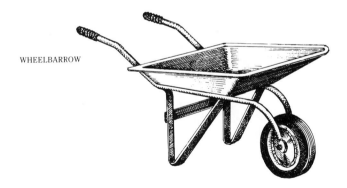

USE: Moving heavy loads around the garden, though not as large and heavy as can be moved with a garden cart (see preceding entry). The single wheel makes for easier maneuvering. An essential piece of equipment for any larger garden, and one that should last for years. Deep models are used for mixing concrete as well.

USE TIPS: Keep wheelbarrows clean when not in use. Do not allow water to stand in metal wheelbarrows, as this might cause them to rust. Oil wheels for easier movement. Semirounded front makes for easier dumping. The front brace that connects the two handles immediately in front of the wheel can catch on the ground as you move the barrow along, especially if you hold the handles high and are moving over irregular terrain—and if it does, you and it will come to an immediate and painful stop. Be careful.

Watch out for overloading: If the load shifts, you might injure yourself trying to save it. Better to let it go or just set it down whenever it starts to become unwieldy. Remember, too, that you have to lift half of the weight yourself.

BUYING TIPS: The better wheelbarrows are made of one piece of heavy steel with extra braces on the legs, which are set wide apart for stability. They also have heavy wooden handles that are attached with countersunk bolts. Check the wheelbarrow out for feel and balance. Wide, inflatable tires give the smoothest ride and are a bit easier to use, but can flatten out or puncture under heavy use. Wooden barrows with wooden wheels are great looking but may be a bit rough to use. Plastic models are maintenance-free, of course. In all types, look for good bracing on the legs.

Cultivating, Weeding, and Raking Tools

ABOUT ALL TOOLS

As with shovels (see pages 149–51), cultivating, weeding, and raking tools are generally made either in a tang-and-ferrule or solid-socket style, though smaller tools are also made as one piece. The tang-and-ferrule style is not as strong as the others, but while tools of this design which are intended for light use may work fine, the better-quality tools that are built to endure generally do not use it (see the explanations and illustrations on pages 137–39 under "About Digging Tool Durability").

Metal shaft handles that end with a grip at a slight angle are generally more comfortable to use. The British term for this is *cranked handle.* Hand tools should be designed so that there is clearance for your knuckles when working close to the soil, so check your angles carefully. When investigating tools with interchangeable short and long handles, be sure to check the balance and feel of the tools with *both* handles. Some sacrifice balance for this convenience.

Remember that metal tools should always be wiped dry after use and coated with oil from an oily rag or an aerosol spray, and that their moving parts should be kept lubricated. Cutting edges should be filed sharp from time to time.

Some individual power tools can be duplicated by attachments to multiuse tools; these are not discussed here but are indeed available.

Cultivating Tools

ABOUT CULTIVATING TOOLS

Veteran vegetable gardeners hold cultivating—the loosening of soil around plants—to be one of the most important gardening tasks. Regular cultivating opens up the soil to allow water to reach the roots easily, destroys small weeds, or prevents weeds from getting established in the first place.

There seem to be more types of tools sold in garden centers specifically designed to help with this garden task than any other. It is an ancient job that has provided much grist for the mills of inventors and marketing folks, resulting in a wide array of inventions. Their names may reflect the way they function, the manufacturer, region of origin, or most common use. Some are good, some will disappear after one season, and all are touted as the absolute best. What works for one gardener might not for the next. One thing is sure: There is no one "right" cultivating tool.

GARDENING HOE

ALSO KNOWN AS: Draw hoe

DESCRIPTION: Small, flat metal blade attached at an angle—70 degrees is considered ideal—to a long wooden handle, typically 50 to 70 inches long. The blade of a hoe may be square, rectangular, or triangular in shape, depending upon the type of hoe. The edge may be quite sharp, but not always; corners may be sharp or rounded. The blade is attached to the handle via a long curved shank called a *gooseneck* or *swan neck,* and is held either by the tang-and-ferrule or solid-socket method. Grubbing hoes, or mattocks (see page 146), are sometimes considered types of hoes, too. There are *wheeled hoes* that look like small plows, but they are not commonly found (see pages 167–68).

There are many manufacturers and each may call a slightly different-sized hoe by a different name, and with not much consistency. A typical grouping of specialized hoes that resemble the homeowner type of garden hoe but are a bit larger includes *southern* (also a general category for all of these), *cotton, light cotton, cotton chopper, barn, field, blackland,* and *planter hoes. Note:* Although these hoes can be used for a variety of jobs, including heavy weeding, hoes especially designed for weeding are listed under *weeding hoes* on pages 173–76.

TYPES: *Garden hoe* (also known as *common, general gardening, draw, mounding,* or *digging hoe):* Rectangular blade measuring about 6 inches wide and 4¾ inches high, often with a rounded or scalloped top. Garden hoes are the most common ones sold in garden centers and hardware stores. A slightly larger version, about 7 inches wide and not as high, and with an angular, tapered top, is called a *nurseryman's, nursery,* or *beet hoe.* There is also the *floral hoe,* a narrow, lightweight model suitable for people who don't want the standard weight, or for children. Some models have holes in the blade for the soil to flow through to help pulverize it or for mixing cement *(mason's* or *mortar hoe).* An even larger version, 12 inches wide, is called a *raised bed builder.*

Eye hoe: The heavy-duty hoe. Has a short, thick handle inserted into an eye in the blade, sort of like a mattock or ax, and is made in a number of similar but slightly different patterns: two normal-looking models, the *American* (7 to 8 inches wide by 6½ to 7 inches deep, available in small, medium, and large models, all with curved shoulders) and the *Scovil* (6½ to 9 inches wide by 5½ to 7½ inches deep, with square shoulders, and either flat or slightly curved—*Scovil* is an old Japanese brand name that may soon be a thing of the past); and more specialized versions such as the larger *grape hoe* (7 inches wide by 10½ inches deep, with almost no shoulders and with an oval eye, developed for working in vineyards), the narrow *grub hoe* (4½ inches wide by 7¾ inches deep, with square shoulders, the heaviest, for compacted or stony soil), and others that vary from

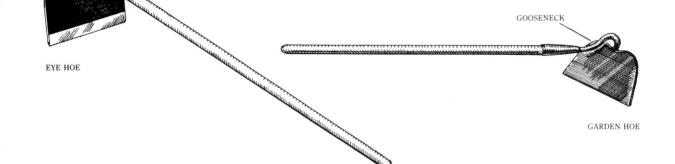

EYE HOE

GOOSENECK

GARDEN HOE

brand to brand, such as the lighter *southern meadow hoe.* All are imported, mostly from Austria and Japan. Handles are 54 inches long, except for the grape hoe, which is 41 inches long.

Onion hoe (also known as *square top onion, nursery, colinear,* or *beet hoe):* Has a wider, higher, narrower blade than the common garden hoe, running about 7 inches wide and 2 inches high. The blade is sharpened on the bottom and the sides, allowing it to be used in two directions. Nursery and beet hoes, according to some, are simply garden hoes with angular sides, like large onion hoes. Available in a hand-sized version, too.

Warren hoe: A pointed blade bent in the center with two smaller points, or ears, near the handle. One model with much larger ears is called a *garden row zipper.*

ONION HOE

WARREN HOE

USE: Basically for moving small quantities of soil when planting (hilling and tilling) and cultivating soil, but also for chopping small weeds just below the soil surface, and for very light digging. The broad head is good for moving or tamping down soil. This is the gardener's most basic tool: Break the earth and you can garden. Everything else is extra. Used most often by drawing the hoe toward you, hence the name *draw hoe.* The various types with specialized uses are

Garden hoe: Working around flowers in beds and other confined spaces; general lightweight use for gardeners who find other models too heavy.

Eye hoe: Serious chopping of roots or compacted soil, agricultural and heavy-duty farming work. Subtle differences of models due in large part to tradition—some by crop, others by ethnic group.

Onion hoe: Cultivating in confined spaces, such as between closely planted vegetable crops. Can be used to disturb the soil just under the surface, cutting small weeds, or to just skim the surface of the soil when control is very important.

Warren hoe: Creating rows and furrows. The smaller ears can be used for filling in furrows after the seeds have been laid down. Also good for digging up weeds.

USE TIPS: Only when digging is there a need to use a chopping motion with a hoe; otherwise, just pull it toward you and under the hardened, unworked soil. And keep the inside edge sharp.

BUYING TIPS: If you can find them, hoes with solid-socket handles are better buys for the money than the common tang-and-ferrule type, although the heavy-duty eye hoes are the strongest. Look for forged construction, not welded. The onion hoe is one of the best all-purpose hoes available, and is a wiser choice over the common garden hoe. As with other tools with long handles, the grain of the wood should be tight and run lengthwise. Longer-handled tools are more comfortable to use—they reduce the need to bend—than shorter ones. The head should be the same piece as the tang (forged) or else solidly welded; avoid spot-welded hoes. Replaceable blades are available for some of the more unusual designs. In hand-sized hoes, look for a comfortable shape in the handle, such as an hour-glass design, and good balance. Some of the heavier, more specialized hoes are difficult to find in stores but are carried in the professional catalogs. There seems to be a hoe designed for each hoeing task.

HAND CULTIVATOR

HAND CULTIVATOR

ALSO KNOWN AS: Three-prong cultivator

DESCRIPTION: Commonly three but sometimes more prongs or tines attached to a short wooden or plastic handle. Tines may be flat and pointed, or round, or with angular *harrow-toothed tips,* shaped like arrowheads. Head is attached to handle in either the solid-socket or tang-and-ferrule method (see pages 137–38), although some tools are made that can snap into long or short handles as you want. Prongs may be spring-tooth type, which means they are somewhat flexible.

Grubber is used by some manufacturers to describe a slightly narrower or more lightweight version with no special tips, more like a simple claw; however, this is incorrect: A grubber is used to dig out roots, and is either a knifelike weeder (sometimes called a *soil knife* or *farmer's weeder)* or a type of mattock (see page 146), called a *grubber hoe.*

USE: Hand cultivators are indispensable to gardening, just like hand-held trowels. They are particularly useful when gardening in raised beds, containers, and terrace gardens, especially when working a conditioner or fertilizer into the soil or weeding next to established plants.

USE TIPS: When weeding with a cultivator, be sure to get under the roots of the weed. Clean with an oiled rag for storage.

BUYING TIPS: Hand cultivators should have sharp tines to dig into the soil, a comfortable grip, and a solid-socket construction handle. Using handles that are too small for you may cause blisters. Those that snap into long handles as well may not be well-balanced, so check them out thoroughly before purchasing. Tines should be angled back slightly toward the handle and extend a bit below the line of the handle, enabling you to cultivate the soil by just pulling the tool toward you and be spared having to jam it down, with your fingers hitting the ground each time it enters the soil.

HAND FORK

HAND FORK

ALSO KNOWN AS: Hand-held fork, flower fork, weed fork, digging fork (incorrect)

DESCRIPTION: Head of three or four straight, flat, metal tines attached to either a wooden or plastic handle, or a single piece of cast or stamped metal, such as lightweight aluminum. Hand-sized to a maximum length of 20 inches, though some manufacturers offer *long-handled forks* with 2- or 3-foot-long, lightweight handles for use by those gardeners who have trouble bending over, or by children.

USE: Cultivating in confined spaces, such as small gardens or in containers.

USE TIP: Use as you would a garden fork (see pages 143–46).

BUYING TIPS: Though popular in other countries, hand forks are not considered an indispensable garden tool in this country. This is probably because there is little you can do with a hand fork that cannot be done as well with a good trowel. Though some manufacturers make their hand forks of lesser quality than their full-sized forks, there is no reason for this. Get something sturdy and comfortable.

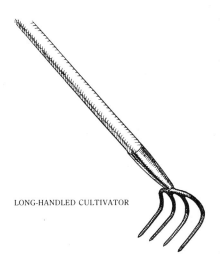

LONG-HANDLED CULTIVATOR

LONG-HANDLED CULTIVATOR

ALSO KNOWN AS: Tined hoe, garden cultivator

DESCRIPTION: Similar to the hand cultivator (see pages 163–64), usually with three, four, or five curved tines and a handle 4 or 5 feet long. Heads are forged or welded, and the tines may have wide, diamond-shaped, harrowtooth-type tips. The handle is attached either by tang-and-ferrule or with a solid-socket (see pages 137–38). A *hook* is a slightly larger and heavier version intended for specialized farming uses, such as harvesting potatoes (called, unsurprisingly, a *potato hook* or *potato hoe),* spreading manure, removing stones and roots, refuse (called a *refuse hook),* and so on. Some models have a U-shaped blade, like an oscillating hoe (see page 174), and are called *cultivator/weeders.* Many brands now are made with handles that snap on and off, and can be interchanged with short handles for hand-held use.

USE: Excellent general cultivation and weeding tool that can be used without stooping.

USE TIPS: Easier to use if you pull the tool toward you. Because the tines of this tool are sharp, you may want to store it with corks on the sharp points. Clean with an oiled cloth before storing.

BUYING TIPS: Among serious gardeners this is an indispensable tool. Look for one with nice weight and balance; forged tools are stronger but welded ones will do in lightly packed soil. Handles attached with a solid-socket are more durable than others. Hooks are often a better buy, because they are heavier and bigger, and some gardeners prefer them for general garden use. Those with snap-on handles may not be well-balanced, so try them out before buying.

POWER TILLER

ALSO KNOWN AS: Rotary tiller, rototiller, tiller/cultivator

DESCRIPTION: A gas or electric motor attached to a tined wheel or a series of tined wheels, with long, straight, or plow-type handles. The smallest tillers have only one or two blade wheels, and the larger tillers have four blades or more; small electric models may be called *power cultivators,* or *tiller/cultivators.* Some models come with special blades that can furrow, aerate, dethatch, or make raised planting rows, or with attachments for

SMALL GAS-POWERED
FRONT-TINED TILLER

snow removal, edging, or trimming. Electric tillers generally have a single shaft or handle, and the tined wheels are below the motor, while gas-powered models tend to be bigger and usually have two regular rubber wheels in addition to the tined wheels. Power tillers come in a wide range of sizes up to 5 horsepower, and dig at adjustable depths up to 8 inches. Tillers come with three basic kinds of tines or tined wheels: *bolo,* which are sort of a universal design for deep tilling; *slasher,* for thick vegetation and roots in soft ground; and *pick and chisel,* or *spring steel,* for general use on hard, rocky ground.

TYPES: *Front-tined tiller* (also known as *front-tine* or *front-end tiller):* Gasoline or electric motor on top of tined wheels (the parts that do the cultivating), sometimes with rubber stabilizing wheels behind, and plow-type handles; the tined wheels propel the machine. Many are 6 to 9 inches wide—smaller and lighter than rear-tine tillers.

Rear-tined tiller (also known as *rear-tine* or *rear-end tiller):* Largest power tiller, with blade wheels located at the rear of the machine, often propelled by the load-bearing front wheels. Gas-powered motor is above front wheels.

USE: Tilling or cultivating medium or large gardens when the job is too hard to do by hand. Electric and front-tined tillers are more suited to easier-to-work soils, such as in established beds and gardens and soils that have been previously cultivated, and for regular cultivation prior to seeding or for working in soil amendments. Electric, lightweight tillers are for the easiest jobs. Heavier, rear-tined tillers are for areas that may never have been tilled; heavier machines of this type can cultivate even hard-packed, rocky soils that the smaller front-tined models cannot handle.

USE TIPS: Be sure the ground is moist enough to work, but not so moist that it is unable to support the weight of the tiller. Always check the oil before operating—many mechanical problems stem from not doing this. Do not attempt to till soil with tall weeds on it—they will only wrap themselves around the tiller tines; rather, cut weeds before tilling. Remember that this is a powerful machine that can be dangerous if not used carefully. Don't overoil the blades after use. Use it several times a year, spring, summer, and fall, turning in compost and green manures (grasslike plants grown only to be turned into the soil for enrichment), as well as for planting and cultivating. Don't expect a small machine to do heavy-duty work.

BUYING TIPS: Shop around and rent one or two (and try out your neighbors'), because this is one of the more expensive garden tools you can buy. Rear-tined tillers can cost twice as much as front-tined models. Determine if your space is large enough to justify the expense of a tiller. In the past, front-tined tillers were for smaller gardens and rear-tined for larger ones, but many models now overlap a bit. In the larger models, the rear-tined tillers are still easier to control than front-tined. Rear-tined tillers are regular workhorses, doing more than front-tined models, and their wheels do not pass over and compact freshly tilled soil, a problem of front-tined tillers. Light, small tillers of both types are great for churning up the top layer of soil to combat weeds. On any model, see how easy it is to turn. Buy the machine that can take all of the extra attachments you might need. The capability of any tiller is determined largely by the size of the engine and the weight of the machine. The engine should be almost directly over the tines of a front-tined tiller to aid the digging. Look for high-quality, high-carbon steel tines that are adjustable for width, chain drives, easily operated controls, a shielded muffler, and adjustable handles, and try to see how much noise and vibration the motor produces. Rear-tined tillers should have hinged tine covers for safety. If you are using the machine only once a year, consider renting one instead of buying. And if you send away for information, beware: The manufacturers try to outdo each other with volumes upon volumes of brochures. They almost claim to have replaced the hoe and the shovel.

WHEELED CULTIVATOR

DESCRIPTION:

High-wheel cultivator (also known as *big wheel cultivator):* Sort of a miniature plow designed to be pushed by you rather than pulled by mules. The larger models have wheels as big as 22 inches in diameter and wide, bicycle-like handles, while the smaller ones have a wheel about 8 inches in diameter and a single shaft with one handle. Both have cultivating tines, weeding knives, or plow blades attached just behind the wheel.

Spiked-wheel cultivator (also known as *hand rotary cultivator* (small version), *rotary cultivator, star harrow, star tiller, spin tiller,* or *soil miller):* A popular design among major manufacturers—a set of tined wheels with a long, straight handle. Each brand is slightly different, but two of the more popular brands are the Weasel® and

HIGH-WHEEL CULTIVATOR

the Crumbler™, which are about 6 inches wide. Others are as wide as a rake (10 inches) with as many as sixteen revolving, spiked disks and resemble reel-type lawn mowers. Some models include an attachment that resembles the U-shaped blade on an oscillating hoe (see page 174) which is dragged through the soil surface, followed by the tines that break up the clods of earth. Others have only two wheels with a foot-long handle, for use in containers. These are all actually miniature tillers (see preceding entry). Large models resemble old rotary lawn mowers with a single crossbar handle. Instead of a leading wheel, there is a barrellike contraption with pointed blades. Cultivating blades can be attached behind this spiked drum.

SPIKED-WHEEL CULTIVATOR

USE: Breaking up, aerating, and mixing soil in place when preparing seedbeds, or for mixing in fertilizer or peat. Particularly useful for laying out long garden rows or breaking ground for a new and large garden site. Functions somewhere between a hand cultivator and a motorized tiller. Also offers an alternative for those gardeners who find it physically difficult to handle a regular cultivator, which (like a hoe) you have to lift up and down in a hacking motion. These require only a push-pull motion, or just a push or a pull in the case of the larger models. The spiked-wheel type is for smaller gardens and requires less energy to use than the high-wheel model.

USE TIP: Wheeled cultivators are somewhat less work than hand cultivators. Clean well after using with an oiled cloth.

BUYING TIP: High-wheel cultivators can usually be purchased for under $50. If you garden in long rows or hills, and your soil is fairly loose, it might be worth looking into one. Try to find one that's self-cleaning.

Weeders and Weeding Hoes

ABOUT WEEDERS

Weeds are the plague of most gardens and gardeners. The pervasiveness of weeds leads to an enormous variety of weeders in garden centers throughout the country. These products promise to rid the garden of weeds through prodding, poking, digging, scraping, cutting, slicing, lifting, and more. Probably as much energy and thought has been put into designing a better weeder as that expended for a better mousetrap. What follows are but a few of the weeding tools you will find on the shelves of garden centers, as new ones come out each season.

When using any of these tools, keep in mind that sharp blades make for more effective weeding. Also, once an area has been weeded, allow the disturbed weeds to dry in the sun before removing and composting. Hand-held weeders are designed for small or raised-bed gardens.

ASPARAGUS KNIFE

ALSO KNOWN AS: Fishtail weeder, garden weeder (incorrect), weeder (too general), dandelion digger (incorrect—refers to a larger model, described on page 171)

DESCRIPTION: A metal shaft about 14 inches long with a flat, V-slotted fishtail head and a wooden or plastic handle, like a big screwdriver. The shaft is slightly bent and the head has sharp cutting edges. As the name suggests, this was originally used to cut the tender shoots of asparagus, but it has become a popular weeding tool. A larger version, over 3 feet long, is the dandelion digger. A rarer version has three V slots, instead of one, for pulling, rather than prying weeds out.

ASPARAGUS KNIFE

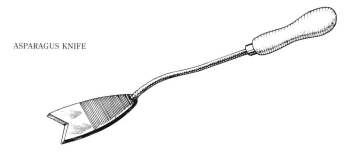

USE: Designed to reach into the soil and cut off or lift deep-rooted weeds with little disturbance to the area where they are growing, a particular concern with lawn weeds such as dandelion and dock.

USE TIPS: Insert the tool a few inches away from the weed you wish to lift and at a slight angle. Keep the points and cutting edges sharp for better cutting.

BUYING TIPS: Buy a solid, well-constructed asparagus knife. A colorful handle prevents loss when you put it down on the lawn.

CAPE COD WEEDER

DESCRIPTION: Hand tool with a long-necked, L-shaped metal blade attached to a wooden handle. The short part has the cutting edge and is at an angle that varies according to brand. Another similar version, in which the cutting edge is aligned with, not at an angle to, the neck, is known as a *crack weeder* or *joint scraper.* This is sometimes called a *pin point weeder,* or confusingly referred to as a *weeder knife.*

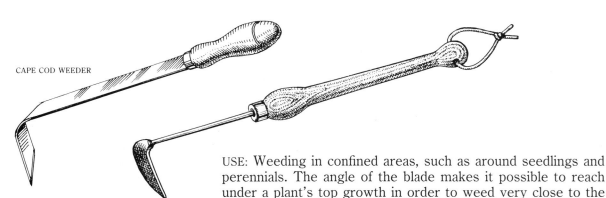

CAPE COD WEEDER

CAPE COD WEEDER

USE: Weeding in confined areas, such as around seedlings and perennials. The angle of the blade makes it possible to reach under a plant's top growth in order to weed very close to the stems. The crack weeder is good for going after weeds or moss in the space between bricks, stones, or slabs.

USE TIPS: Pull the blade toward you just under the surface of the soil. Keep blade sharp for easier weeding.

BUYING TIPS: Because the blade of the Cape Cod weeder curves to the left, this is primarily a tool for right-handed gardeners. It would not appear difficult to manufacture this in a left-handed version, but none seem to be on the market. Crack weeders are not as efficient as you might want, because they can rarely get under the larger weeds.

SPRING-OPERATED WEED PULLER

DANDELION DIGGER

ALSO KNOWN AS: Lawn weeder, weed puller, back-saver weeder

DESCRIPTION: Just a larger (it's over 3 feet long) version of the asparagus knife (see pages 169–70) with a fishtail tip. The handle is attached with a tang-and-ferrule design (see pages 137–38). Another version is the *yard arm weeder,* with a yard-long handle and two long, slightly curved, barbed hooks on the tip, sold under a variety of trade names with a play on the words *easy* or *handy,* or under the brand name Weedigger. Other brands use a small fork and fulcrum design. Finally, there are 5-foot-long spring- or lever-operated models that cut, grasp, and pull weeds.

USE: Removing deep-rooted weeds, especially dandelions, and other garden debris without the gardener having to bend over or leave a wheelchair.

USE TIPS: Same as for asparagus knife. Very helpful if you have a bad back or other handicap.

BUYING TIP: The length of the handle provides more leverage than is possible with the asparagus knife, but the tool works the same. If you have trouble with the leverage in the asparagus knife, these are good alternatives.

HEART HOE

ALSO KNOWN AS: Single-tined cultivator, finger hoe, single-finger hoe, one-prong cultivator

DESCRIPTION: Hand tool, generally with a 12- to 18-inch-long wooden handle, with one large (4½-inch diameter) C-shaped, pointed claw with a small heart-shaped blade tip. Not unlike a miniature double-edged plowshare. Also available with a 5-foot-long handle, usually with a C-shaped claw about 9 inches in diameter, and may be called a *biocultivator.*

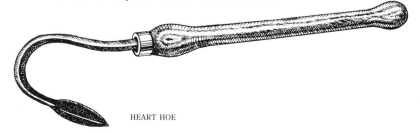

HEART HOE

USE: Cultivating small gardens and window boxes where precise control is needed. Extremely versatile tool. Narrow blade allows for working in tight, difficult-to-reach spaces, and curved neck lets you lift weeds out of the soil. Does not mix up levels of the soil unless you intend for it to do so, making it sort of an *aerator*.

USE TIP: Actually quite useful in a wide variety of situations.

HOTBED WEEDER

HOTBED WEEDER

ALSO KNOWN AS: Ideal weeder

DESCRIPTION: Short-handled, C-shaped, with ¾-inch-wide flat blade, with all three edges sharpened.

USE: Weeding in tight areas, such as greenhouses—hence the name.

USE TIP: Because the hotbed weeder has cutting edges on three sides and straight and curved parts, it can be used in three positions, making it slightly more versatile than the Cape Cod weeder (see page 170).

BUYING TIP: Versatile, but not great with large weeds.

THE ORIGINAL WEEDER

ALSO KNOWN AS: Magic weeder, spring-tooth weeder

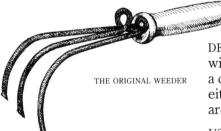

THE ORIGINAL WEEDER

DESCRIPTION: Resembles a hand cultivator (see pages 163–64) with three round curved prongs or tines, but the middle tine has a curl, or spring, in it. The tines fit directly into a wooden handle either 5, 14, or 32 inches long. Venerable design that has been around for years.

USE: Hand weeding and cultivating. The spring in the middle prong gives it an added flexibility and makes it more effective than plain versions.

USE TIP: The plain wooden handle makes it easy to lose in the garden, so paint it a vivid color.

BUYING TIP: Any tool that has remained as popular as this one has over such a long period of time has got to be one of the best. Versatile, easy to use, and effective.

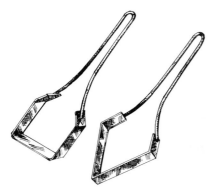

UOO AND VEE WEEDERS

UOO AND VEE WEEDERS

ALSO KNOWN AS: U and V weeders

DESCRIPTION: A short metal blade in the shape of a U or a V attached to a plastic, hand-sized handle. Lightweight (4 ounces!) and less than a foot long. Made of spring steel.

USE: Hand cultivating or surface weeding around crops, and thinning vegetables and plants. They work by cutting roots just below the surface of the soil.

USE TIP: Put sturdy tape on the handle to prevent blisters and give a better grip. Open handle ends provide a convenient design for hanging up when not in use.

BUYING TIPS: Inexpensive weeding tools that are easy to use on young weeds. They are used quite often by commercial growers, which is a good recommendation for the home gardener, but some people find them a little difficult to handle.

WEEDER/ROOTER

WEEDER/ROOTER

ALSO KNOWN AS: Pronghoe

DESCRIPTION: A small hoe with two heads: One resembles a narrow garden hoe, and the other has two, three, or four small prongs. Made as a hand-sized tool, as well as with a long handle.

USE: Particularly well suited for weeding around transplants and seedlings, but also a good general purpose hoe.

USE TIP: The prong side is for getting close to plants, tipping to one side and using just one prong in tight places if need be.

BUYING TIP: One of the most versatile hand tools.

WEEDING HOE

DESCRIPTION: Long-handled tool with metal blade of various designs, with sharp edges on two, three, or four sides, or all around in the case of a curved or round hoe. Designed to be pushed, pulled, and moved from side to side, as opposed to merely pulled, or drawn, through the soil, like the gardening hoes (see pages 160–64). Many different brands make similar items under slightly different names—this is an area of intense competition, artisanal ingenuity, and nuanced designs—which is to say that it is hard to pin down all the various types and names here. And most can cultivate as well as weed, too, just to add to the confusion.

TYPES: *Cavex hoe:* Sharply curved or rounded blade.

Dutch hoe (also known as *Dutch scuffle hoe, push-pull weeder, push hoe,* or *thrust hoe):* Open triangular blade, with a cutting edge on the inside.

Oscillating stirrup hoe (also known as *hula hoe, oscillating hoe, action hoe, pendulum weeder, stirrup hoe,* or *scuffle hoe):* Four-edged blade that looks like a stirrup, hinged so it moves back and forth when pushed and pulled through the soil. This rocking motion gives it the name *hula hoe.* A relatively new design, introduced in 1958.

Rockery hoe: British hand tool with a forged, 4-inch-wide semicircular blade attached to a 7-inch-long handle by a curved metal shank. Designed for use in small, tight areas, such as in rock gardens, which the British insist on calling "rockeries" for some reason.

Scuffle hoe (also known as *glide groom hoe, push-pull hoe, root-cutting hoe,* or *Dutch hoe*—this last term is incorrect): Comes in the widest variety of blade shapes. Blades can be triangular, curved, diamond shaped, or rectangular, with sharp edges on several sides. Some variations have special names, such as *floral* (smaller), *garden* (large rectangular), and *orange grove* (triangular). Other brands are simply called by their shape, such as *crescent hoe* or *colinear hoe. Note:* Almost all multi-edged weeding hoes that use a push-pull motion to cut weeds just below the surface (at their roots) might be called *scuffle hoes.*

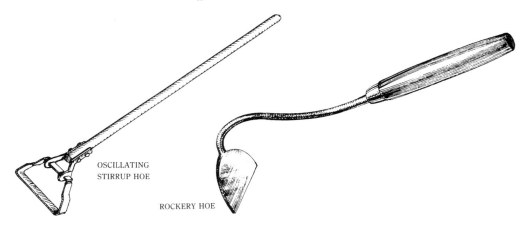

CAVEX HOE

OSCILLATING
STIRRUP HOE

ROCKERY HOE

Swoe (also known as *shuffle, scuffle,* or *cultivation hoe):* Odd rectangular, about 5 by 3 inch, almost triangular blade, sharp on three sides, in either a hand-weeding version with a foot-long handle, or a longer, stand-up version that looks like a golf club. The blade of either model is at an angle to the handle, attached by a long tang. True Temper calls their hand version the *Swoe Jr.* and the stand-up version *Swoe Sr.* Basically a modified scuffle hoe.

Weeding hoe (also known as *rabbit ears, planting hoe,* or *three-prong cultivator):* Double-headed blade. One side resembles the blade of a narrow garden hoe, while the other is made up of two or three long prongs or points,

SCUFFLE HOE

SWOE

or a triangular blade. The prongs break up crusty soil and rip up weeds, such as dichondra. Another version is triangularly shaped, with no ears, called a *triangular hoe,* and if it is on the end of a long, curved neck, it is called a *gooseneck hoe.* Still another version is the *Southern Belle,* with a rectangular blade on one side and a triangular blade on the other, sort of like a mattock (see page 146). In fact, it might be called a *mattock hoe.* Hand-sized versions are available, too.

USE: Cutting off and removing small weeds in frequently cultivated beds before they become established, especially those found just below the surface. The multi-edged design allows for cutting in any direction; the large oscillating models work well in heavy soil while the basic scuffle designs work best in light, sandy soils and under mulches—in fact, they don't disturb mulch as they work. Hand-held models are useful in cold frames and greenhouses. Swoes (and some of the other models, depending on the gardener) can easily be used for traditional hoeing chores, such as making furrows and general cultivation.

USE TIPS: Keep all blade edges sharp. Dry off tool after use, and do not leave it lying about—someone might step on the business end and get clunked in the face with the handle.

BUYING TIPS: A good second hoe to have, in addition to a regular gardening hoe. As for which type, this is really a case of personal preference, though of course the smaller blades are handier in confined gardens. The variety of designs reflect the industry-wide effort to develop the ideal weeder. Oscillating hoes work just below the surface and are a little bit less work because less soil is being displaced. The swoe is available in stainless steel, for truly serious weeding. Always look for one-piece forged blades and necks instead of spot-welded ones.

WEED SLICER

ALSO KNOWN AS: Hand weeder, gooseneck hoe

DESCRIPTION: A 6-inch-wide triangular blade attached at an angle to a 5-inch-long wooden handle by a curved metal shank (called a swan neck) about a foot long. Usually a sturdy, forged steel item. Left- and right-handed versions available.

USE: The razor-sharp blade slices through weeds just under the soil surface. Especially good for hard-to-reach places in a small garden, and "intensive" gardening. Design lends itself to a variety of detail work.

USE TIPS: Keep blades sharp for easier weeding. This is another hand tool that is easy to lose in the garden, and because of the sharp blade, it can be dangerous with children around. Be sure to paint the handle a bright color.

WEED SLICER

Rakes

BOWHEAD GARDEN RAKE

GARDEN RAKE

DESCRIPTION: A row, over a foot long, of solid steel tines a few inches long, set perpendicular to a long, usually wooden, handle. Lightweight handles are made of tubular aluminum. Most garden rakes are attached to the handle in the tang-and-ferrule way, but a few can be found attached using the solid-socket method (see page 138). Small versions, as small as 6 inches wide, may be called *floral* (or *flower), children's,* or *ladies' rakes.*

TYPES: *Flathead rake* (also known as *level head rake):* Made of forged, high-carbon steel. A long center tine is bent back to form the tang that is used to attach the rake to the handle, causing the rake head to fit flush with the handle to form a T. Hand-held, "miniature" models are available, too.

    Bowhead rake (also known as *bow* or *bow holder rake):* Attached to the handle by way of two steel rods or tangs that run from each end of the rake head, bow out, and are inserted into the handle. Traditional design.

USE: Leveling out soil for lawn or garden seeding. The hard teeth help break up soil and remove debris. Also useful for spreading gravel, sand, or topsoil. An essential garden tool. When pressed into a seedbed, makes small holes about 1 inch apart, for planting seeds.

USE TIPS: When using the rake for leveling a bed, allow the rake handle to slide freely through the forward hand while pulling and pushing it with the hand nearest the far end of the handle, gripping firmly. If you grip it firmly with both hands, the rake head follows only the present contours of the bed and will not level it. The straight back of the rake can be used for final smoothing. Always leave the tines facing down when not in use in your garden.

BUYING TIPS: If you can find a garden rake with solid-socket construction, definitely buy it. Some gardeners feel that the slightly lighter bowhead rake adds a desirable spring to the raking motion. If you want to buy one of the smaller versions, make sure the handle is long enough for you to use comfortably.

LAWN RAKE

LAWN RAKE

ALSO KNOWN AS: Broom rake, leaf rake, fan rake, sweep rake, spring lawn rake

DESCRIPTION: Long wood, flat steel, bamboo, rubber, or plastic tines fanned out from the wood or aluminum handle of the rake so that it resembles a wide broom, about 20 inches or so wide. The tips of the tines are bent slightly downward. The width of some metal models can be adjusted for easier raking around shrubs and in flower beds. Steel rakes may have a spring brace on their backs for additional strength. Bamboo rakes are available in a large range of sizes, including a small one with a 6- or 8-inch fan for raking in beds and around shrubs. The width on some brands is adjustable from 7 to 24 inches. Recently a rake with wheels like a reel-type lawn mower (see pages 248–49) was introduced for people with back problems (it works on both the push and pull strokes). There has long been a model with a bend in the handle, called a *back-saver rake,* which is easy to use without bending your back. Other versions have a rectangular shape, often with rubber tines. *Floral* and *shrub rakes* are simply narrower and of lighter construction.

USE: Raking leaves, twigs, grass clippings, and other light debris. A basic, indispensable garden tool. Rubber tines are used where their flexibility is desirable to prevent damaging shallow-rooted plants.

USE TIPS: Store in a dry place. To make bamboo rakes pliable before use (if they have dried out in storage) they should be soaked briefly in soapy water. This should be done especially at the beginning of a season. Don't use stiff wire-tined rakes on a lawn, or you may rip up your grass.

BUYING TIPS: Although any well-made model is a good buy, this is one of the few cases where the cheaper product—bamboo rakes—is as good a buy as others, because they can be so easily and cheaply replaced, and some gardeners even prefer the feel of the natural material of the bamboo rakes. They are also gentler on the lawn than metal, though rubber tines are the most gentle and flexible in regard to the terrain. Plastic rakes don't rust, but check to see that the handle is securely attached to the head with a screw. Steel rakes must be of top quality only, or they are likely to come apart.

LEVELING RAKE

LEVELING RAKE

ALSO KNOWN AS: Grading rake, lawn rake, hay rake

DESCRIPTION: A 2- to 2½-foot-long board with a series of holes in it, through which sharpened 4-inch dowels (usually of ash) protrude to form the tines. The handle is stuck into a hole in the rake head and secured with metal braces. Resembles the old wooden *hay rakes,* though those intended for raking grass or hay usually have more closely spaced teeth. Also made in aluminum and magnesium, for professionals. Although the term *lawn rake* is used correctly here, this more often refers to the fan-shaped bamboo rake described in the preceding entry.

USE: Particularly useful in creating a level surface on a seedbed or lawns in preparation for seeding, just after spading has left large clumps of soil. Lighter models are used to remove grass clippings and clumps of leaves, fallen fruit, and, of course, cut hay.

USE TIP: Same as for garden rake (see page 177). This rake is not as strong as the garden rake and is intended for kinder, gentler jobs.

BUYING TIP: Be sure that the handle and the wooden tines are secure.

THATCHING RAKE

ALSO KNOWN AS: Cavex rake, multipurpose rake, lawn rake, adjustable rake, dethatching rake

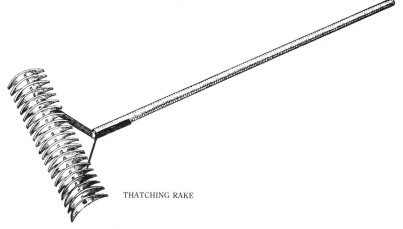

THATCHING RAKE

DESCRIPTION: A specialized design composed of about twenty crescent-shaped blades attached 1 inch apart with the curved side of the crescents pointed out. The angle of the bladelike tines is usually adjustable to fit the height of the grass. Some brands have a tilting head for self-cleaning.

USE: Removing dead and matted grass (thatch) from a lawn, permitting better growth.

USE TIPS: When removing thatch, adjust the head of the rake so that the tines ride above the soil and do not cut into it. You can clean tines easily by pushing with the head down a bit. Be prepared to work hard—when this rake cuts into thatch, it takes some effort to pull it through.

BUYING TIP: Make sure that the rake is well constructed and the rake head is attached securely to the handle. This is a specialty tool, and not every gardener needs it.

Pruning, Cutting, and Trimming Tools

ABOUT PRUNING, CUTTING, AND TRIMMING TOOLS

All cutting tools perform better if they are kept sharp. This is not just a case of being professional or perfectionist; it also makes them safer. Sharpen each one according to its size and design: Use a hand-held whetstone or a file, or take them to a professional sharpener (look them up in the Yellow Pages under "Sharpening Services"). The best blades are "hollow ground" (slightly concave) and are more difficult to sharpen yourself.

Be sure to wipe cutting tools dry after each use, coat them with oil from either an oily rag or an aerosol spray, lubricate the moving parts or hinges, and store them in a dry place.

Pruners and Shears

ABOUT PRUNING AND HEDGE SHEARS

This is the kind of tool where good quality is immediately apparent to the user: Good ones cut better. Ones made of top-quality steel cut and last longer, too. Good gardeners know when to use pruning shears instead of hedge shears—the former is for removing whole branches, and the latter is for superficial cutting. Each type of cut affects the plant differently. Keep both kinds of shears clean and wiped with an oily rag or sprayed with a penetrating lubricant aerosol such as WD-40.

Shears made especially for trimming grass are listed in their own section (see pages 202–204).

FLOWER GATHERER

ALSO KNOWN AS: Cut-and-hold shears, flower shears (also see next entry), flower gathering scissors

DESCRIPTION: Very closely resembles regular kitchen scissors, except that one blade is thick and serrated and the other is a small, sharp, blunt-ended blade that slices into it. Other types have a setback over the cutting blade which holds the cut stem. Some brands are designed with a thorn remover and stem crusher in the handles. Large handles should allow use by both left- and right-handers. Made with a 28- or 31-inch-long pistol grip as well as hand-sized.

USE: Cutting flowers for display. Cuts and holds the bloom in the same move. Long-handled models are excellent for gardeners who have difficulty bending and reaching, such as wheelchair gardeners. Handy also in rock gardens, for hanging plants, climbing plants, or reaching over greenhouse benches.

USE TIP: Blunt ends mean you can drop these into your pocket.

FLOWER SHEARS

FLOWER SHEARS

ALSO KNOWN AS: Freehand snips, Japanese flower shears, Japanese flower arranging shears

DESCRIPTION: Extra sharp and sturdy scissors, some models of which have giant loops called *butterfly handles,* for the insertion of your entire hand. Other models, called *flat-end scissors,* have one broad, blunt-ended blade and one slightly hooked one. Japanese models with butterfly handles are called *Ikebana shears* and have a black, Parkerized finish; they come in either the short-bladed *Koryu* style or the thin, long-bladed *Ashinaga bonsai hasami* style (see page 306).

USE: Trimming or cutting flowers and small plants. Models with large loops are for use with gloves on, or more importantly, if you have trouble gripping, because of arthritis or other conditions.

USE TIPS: Try not to cut too much woody or extra-thick material, a job more appropriate for pruning shears. If the rivet becomes loose, see if you can tighten it by hammering it down on a metal surface.

BUYING TIPS: Better than kitchen scissors because they make a cleaner cut, helping the flower stem draw water in a vase. Flat-end scissors can go in your pocket or tool kit without danger. Butterfly handles are good for gardeners who have difficulty gripping.

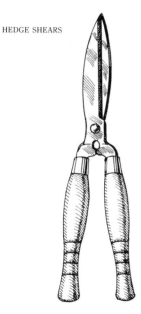

HEDGE SHEARS

HEDGE SHEARS

ALSO KNOWN AS: Hand hedge shears, hand shears

DESCRIPTION: Large scissorlike device 12 to 28 inches in length overall. The long, straight handles may be wooden or metal with rubber grips, and the blades can be straightedged, curved, serrated, or wavy. Most shears have a notch in one blade close to the pivot that allows you to cut larger branches. (The curves, serrations, or waves hold branches in place as the blades are closed; without this design feature, branches tend to spring out of the blades' grasp.) Forged and occasionally stainless steel blades are available in better models. Rubber bumpers at the pivot point absorb the shock of the two handles coming together. Light models are available, as are long-handled versions.

USE: Trimming hedges and cutting branches up to ½ inch thick. A notch near the pivot point is for slightly larger branches. Hedge shears are not intended for general pruning, where branches and limbs should be cut individually. Hand hedge shears cut through thicker branches than power shears.

USE TIPS: Hedges should be trimmed so that the top is narrower than the bottom, and not squared off. Tapering allows the sun to reach the entire surface of the hedge so it fills in evenly. Longer blades are best for cutting evenly. You can hang shears that have a hole in a blade on a nail.

BUYING TIPS: Hedge shears are not for general pruning, so buy a pair only if you have a hedge. Rubber bumpers, which should be replaceable, make the shears less taxing to use, as does a lighter weight. Shears with serrated or wavy blades hold the branches better and are easier to use. Handle shape and finish vary from brand to brand and model to model, so pick them up and try them out first. Look for those with an adjustable locknut at the hinge, so you can adjust the tension of the cutting motion.

LONG-REACH FRUIT AND FLOWER PICKER

DESCRIPTION: A 5-foot-long aluminum pole with a squeeze grip handle on one end and scissorlike blades on the other (anvil style, where one blade has a cutting edge while the other has a flat surface against which the cutting blade works). Attached to these blades are two metal strips that come together when the blades meet in order to hold the stems of the fruit or flowers so they can be lowered after cutting. Another basic version of a fruit picker is a simple wire or cloth basket with tines on one side, on a 15-foot-long handle. This is also known as a *fruit harvester* or *fresh-fruit picker*. Head sold separately.

LONG-REACH FRUIT AND FLOWER PICKER

USE: A helpful tool for cutting dead stems, spent rose blooms, and general garden cutting in beds and places not easily reached with pruning shears. Because the cut material does not drop into the bed (it is held between the metal strips on the blade), it is very helpful for people who have trouble bending over to pick things up or for cutting from thorny plants. It is also useful in water gardening, allowing you to reach into a pool to pick out, for example. dead lily blooms or debris. The basket-style fruit picker is used just for that: picking ripe fruit. The basket holds the fruit as long as it is larger than the openings in the mesh.

USE TIP: Be sure that whatever is being cut is grabbed by the clamping side of the blade, or else it will drop.

BUYING TIP: At under $50, this is a good investment for most gardeners. Even small gardens have areas that are difficult to reach with hand pruners, and where using a ladder is not a good solution.

LOPPER

ALSO KNOWN AS: Lopping shears, two-handed pruning shears, two-handed shears, clopper

DESCRIPTION: Long-handled pruning tool that looks like pruning shears (see next entry) with arm-length handles (12 to 28 inches long), and comes with either a curved bypass cutting head or an anvil-type cutting head (see description at pruning shears, page

186). Loppers may be made entirely from one piece of steel or have wooden handles and high-quality steel blades. Recently some constructed from other materials, such as fiberglass, have appeared, and still other new models have gears *(geared* or *gear drive loppers)* or *ratchet* devices that look like an offset hinge, for cutting thicker branches than those possible with standard models. These may be referred to as *multilevel* or *compound action loppers,* versus the normal *single-level* type. *Two-handed pruning shears* often refers to loppers that have extraordinary cutting capacity. *Vine pruners* are lightweight models, and specially designed long, telescopic-handled models are available, such as the *pulley lever lopper.* Better models have shock absorbers.

LOPPER

USE: Pruning branches that are thicker or tougher than those that can be cut with pruning shears easily, that is, those between ¾ and 1½ inches thick. Loppers' longer handles give more leverage for heavier cutting than the short handles of pruning shears, and compound action loppers can cut still thicker branches.

USE TIPS: Do not twist loppers when cutting, as this will bend the blades, preventing clean cuts in the future. If you are having trouble cutting through a branch with loppers, don't force them; go for the pruning saw (see pages 192–93). Place the anvil blade on top when cutting with anvil-type loppers.

BUYING TIPS: The choice between wooden or metal-handled loppers depends upon the feel of the tool and your own preference, but the anvil type should be avoided in favor of the bypass type with forged blades. Bypass loppers make cleaner, closer cuts. Try them out and see how they feel. Many gardeners like the balance of the newer all-metal loppers, but if you are cutting branches over your head, you may feel that they are too heavy for you, and many find the fiberglass handles not quite as durable as those made of wood or metal. As with pruning shears, the longer the blade, the thicker the limb they can cut. Most loppers are graded by weight, with the heavier ones capable of doing the heavier-duty jobs and being usually of better quality. Ratchet models give you more force, which is a consideration if you don't have the strength for heavy pruning with regular models. Chrome alloy steel resists rust better than other types. Hinges that are slightly offset keep the branch being cut from slipping out of the blades, as does a hooked end.

PRUNING SHEARS

ALSO KNOWN AS: Pruners, hand pruners, secateurs, pruning snips

DESCRIPTION: Resembling pliers or short, heavy-duty scissors, pruning shears consist of hand-sized handles, a pivot point with a spring, and one or two strong cutting blades. The spring causes the cutting end to remain open when the handles are not squeezed together. The shears usually have a lock for storage in a closed position. Usually sized by the maximum thickness of the branches they can cut, such as ½, ⅝, or ¾ inch. Some smaller ones are made with short handles, sometimes called *pocket pruners,* and are often recommended for women's smaller hands. *(Pocket pruner* also refers to a plain scissors design with blunt ends that can be carried in your pocket.) The more exotic-looking designs have blades at a slight angle to the handle, or offset, for easier access to branches and reduction of wrist fatigue (it is easier to get the right cutting angle). The most refined design has one grip that rotates to fit the angle of your hand as it moves through the squeezing motion, reducing friction and the possibility of blisters as well as fatigue (the manufacturer claims a 30 percent reduction in effort). Better quality shears also have small shock absorbers, sap grooves (slots in lower blades for draining sap), wire-cutting notches, ergonomically shaped handles, and replaceable blades or other parts. Left-handed versions are available, as are *long-reach extensions* that enable wheelchair-bound gardeners to prune with ease thanks to an added lever. *Pneumatic shears,* operated with one hand and powered by compressed air, are also available from professional sources.

TYPES: *Anvil shears:* One cutting blade and one solid, flat-faced "anvil" that the cutting blade touches when squeezed shut. The cutting blade is straight, made of cast or stamped steel, and may be coated for longer life and less sticking. The anvil is usually brass, which is softer than the cutting blade, and may be replaceable. Some have a "swing" anvil that is hinged in such a way as to give the pruner a wider opening and also produces a slicing action to the cut. Many models have a ratchet device for additional force and are called, not surprisingly, *ratchet anvil pruners.*

Curved bypass shears (also known as *blade-on-blade, double-cutting,* or *hook-and-blade shears):* Two slightly curved blades that cut when their surfaces pass each

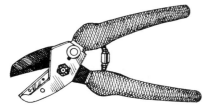

ANVIL PRUNING SHEARS

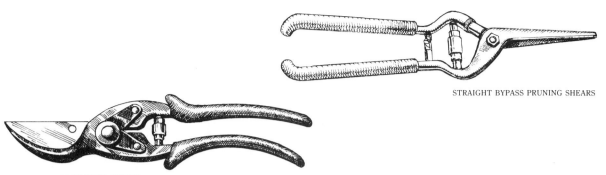

STRAIGHT BYPASS PRUNING SHEARS

CURVED BYPASS PRUNING SHEARS

other, just like a pair of scissors. Some manufacturers call the lower blade the anvil blade. Made of cast, stamped, or forged steel, including stainless steel. May be coated. May also have a convenient *wire-cutting notch* near the hinge. Left-handed versions available, but not from many manufacturers. Lightweight version may be called *floral pruner.*

Straight bypass shears (also known as *grape shears, thinning shears, minishears* or *houseplant minishears*— if small—*all-purpose snips,* or *utility shears):* Cut like curved bypass shears, but the blade edges are straight, rather than curved, resembling stubby kitchen scissors. Cast, stamped, or forged steel, including stainless steel. A particularly pointed model may be called *needle-nose pruners.* Usually smaller than the other shears.

USE: Cutting small branches up to approximately ¾ inch thick (though generally for diameters less than ½ inch thick) and twigs from woody plants. Smaller pruning shears are designed to be used on less woody plants and small green wood. An essential tool for any gardener. Anvil types are generally used for casual or light pruning and bypass types for serious and closer pruning, though *ratchet anvil pruners* have more force for thick or tough woody plants, and there is less risk of bending, or springing, the blade than with bypass pruners. Straight pruners are good for detail work on flowers.

USE TIPS: Keep blades sharp. Pruning shears work best when the spring and the pivot area are oiled before or after each use. Don't twist them when you have difficulty cutting through something—you'll bend the blades, and they can't be bent back. Never try to cut a branch that is too thick for the shears or you will bend the blade (anvil types can cut a bit thicker branches with less danger of bending). If you can't squeeze through with one hand, the branch is too thick—use your loppers (see preceding entry). Cut at a diagonal to the grain for less resistance. This and the trowel are the most often lost tools: Paint the handles bright orange or yellow or buy them with brightly colored grips so they are easier to spot in the garden, or use a holster (some brands of shears, such as Felco, make their own). Curved blades keep the branch from slipping out as you squeeze. Making good clean cuts is essential to preventing disease.

BUYING TIPS: Anvil-type shears smash the branch when cutting and leave a stub when cutting off branches or sprouts. They are better suited to cutting up branches that have already been pruned from the tree or shrub. However, they are quite common and usually the cheapest; unfortunately, they are also often cheap in quality, though high-quality ones can be had. Look for the kind that have offset pivots which cause the blade to slice along the anvil, and for replaceable anvils. Try to find those with hardened and tempered edges.

Curved bypass shears are the most efficient type, as they give the cleanest and closest cut, right down to the trunk or branch, leaving no stub. Wire-cutting notches are very convenient if you have lots of plant ties, and if you prune for long periods of time, the rotating grip is helpful. Look for a pivot adjustment that allows you to align the blades perfectly. Felco of Switzerland makes ergonomically designed, red-handled shears that are the industry standard; they are often referred to as "Felcos" without any more description (Felco has been making them for over forty years). They have hollow-ground, replaceable blades, as a top-quality shear should have. Models 9 and 10 are left-handed. Straight bypass shears are good for light work where the space may be confined, such as with houseplants and small shrubs.

Many concerns for any type of pruning shear are similar. Ratchet-style shears have more strength in their cut and require less effort from the gardener, an important consideration for arthritic gardeners. Small shock absorbers are also helpful. Pruning shears are sold in a variety of grades determined by weight, design, and the overall quality of the tool, and you can generally bet on getting what you pay for. Left-handed shears are manufactured and very advantageous if you need them. It is unclear if Teflon®-coated blades are an advantage, though they may reduce sap buildup, but then so does a regular wiping or a "sap groove" in the blade.

Shears with thumb-operated locks are easier to use, as they allow you to lock and holster or pocket the tool between cuts.

Make sure the lock is in a place where it doesn't give you blisters, especially at the heel of your hand; it is more convenient if you can operate it with one hand while holding the shears. Shears that come apart for sharpening or blade replacement are a good idea. The longer and wider the blade, the thicker the limb the shears will cut. Look for stainless or forged steel, as opposed to cast or stamped, which are slightly rough. Buying quality pruning shears means more than buying a tool that is durable and will last; quality pruning shears produce a clean cut that is better for the shrubs and trees you are pruning. Get good ones.

Saws

BOW SAW

ALSO KNOWN AS: Buck saw (usually in context of carpentry), tubular saw, log saw

DESCRIPTION: Metal frame in the D shape of a bow, with a thick blade connecting the two ends. Available in a small range of sizes, and in two D shapes: tapered to a point at one end, and a basic, even D shape. The variously sized teeth are slightly offset to accommodate green wood. Some blades are disposable, others are longer lasting and sharpenable hardened steel. Wooden-framed bow or buck saws, now known as *frame saws,* were indispensable tools for cutting firewood in the past.

BOW SAW

USE: Cutting firewood or branches 10 to 20 inches in diameter. Each cut can only be as deep as the bow frame.

USE TIPS: Keep blades sharp and well oiled. Because of their thin blades, bow saws cut faster and easier than other handsaws. When cutting heavy branches, make a cut from the bottom of the branch about 2 inches closer to the trunk than where the final cut will be made. This prevents the bark from skinning beyond this point when the branch falls. If you intend to do a lot of light pruning, buy a tapered bow saw rather than a basic D-shaped one. This prevents the end from hitting other branches while cutting; however, a tapered saw is not good for cutting thick firewood.

BUYING TIP: A bow saw is a good investment for those people with large gardens and many trees, and especially for those who cut their own firewood.

CROSSCUT SAW

TYPES: *Two-person* (or *two-man) saw*
One-person (or *one-man) saw*

DESCRIPTION: The two-person crosscut saw has a 6-foot-long blade with a combination of two kinds of incredibly large teeth, both pointed and rectangular (called "rakers") and two 11-inch-long wooden, removable handles attached to the ends of the blade with nuts and bolts. The one-person model is similar, but only about 3 feet long, and has a vertical grip attached to the top of the blade.

USE: For serious and quick tree-felling and log-cutting. A very efficient tool with two people sharing the labor.

USE TIPS: Never push on a two-person crosscut saw, as this will bend the blade and cause it to bind in the log or tree. Wait until your partner has finished his or her pull, then *pull* the saw back toward yourself. When cutting a log on a buck (an X-shaped log stand) it is better to start the movement of the saw before the blade makes contact with the log. This gets the mutual movement of the partners going and gently lines up the cut.

BUYING TIP: Such a saw makes sense only if you have a wood-burning stove, lots of firewood to cut, and a partner to help you saw. If you are doing some log construction as a one-time activity only, then try to rent one.

CROSSCUT SAW

HIGH LIMB CHAIN SAW

ALSO KNOWN AS: Chain blade high-limb cutter

DESCRIPTION: A linked chain (like a bicycle chain) with carbon steel blades on each link, attached to long pieces of rope, one

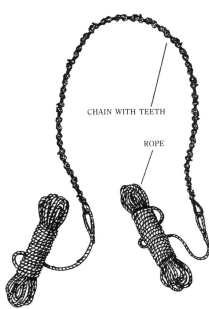

CHAIN WITH TEETH

ROPE

HIGH LIMB CHAIN SAW

of which has a weight on the end. The chain and one rope are thrown over a limb with the chain positioned on the limb itself. When the cords are pulled back and forth, the blades of the chain cut through the limb.

USE: Cutting branches that are hard to get to by ladder or beyond a long-reach pole saw (see next entry).

USE TIPS: Add your own rope for really high limbs (and good luck throwing the saw up there). Do not stand directly under the limb that is being cut. This may seem obvious but is a common mistake.

BUYING TIP: Though not something you would need often, if you have many trees it may be worth purchasing for a rare use that would otherwise mean calling in expensive professionals.

LONG-REACH POLE SAW AND LOPPER

ALSO KNOWN AS: Pole pruner, long-reach pruner, telescoping tree pruner, pole tree-trimmer, tree pruner, pole pruning saw, telephone tree-trimmer, tree trimmer, pole pruner/trimmer, pole pruner/saw

DESCRIPTION: A long sectional or telescoped pole made of wood, metal, or fiberglass, with a 16-inch or so long pruning saw or a pruning shear or lopper (may be called a *clipper),* or a combination of both, depending on the brand, on one end. Can be as much as 20 feet long. The shear is operated by a large lever attached to a long cord that is pulled by the operator at the tail end of the

LONG-REACH POLE SAW AND LOPPER

tool. The leverage on this tool comes from the cord being run through a pulley by the blade; it is spring-loaded to return to the open position automatically. Other versions have a pump-style mechanism, with a round grip that is slid up and down the handle. Older models of this tool had wooden handles that were in sections, but today most are light, telescopic poles made of metal or fiberglass which are easily extended by twisting the pole.

(Names are used differently by each manufacturer, and some products with the same name may be quite different, i.e., one may have only a pruning shear while another might have only a saw, while a third has both.)

USE: Pruning limbs and branches that cannot be reached by hand-held tools or are inconvenient to trim by standing on a ladder. The shear cuts branches up to ¾ inch diameter. The pump-style pole pruner is excellent for the wheelchair gardener. A good telescopic handle enables you to prune branches up to 18 feet high.

USE TIPS: Stand to the side of branches you are cutting or sawing, not below them. If you try to prune a branch that is too large for the blade to cut, the blade may become stuck in the branch. Check the label to see the maximum-size branch the shear or lopper can cut. Remember to look down and around from time to time, or you'll get a crick in your neck. And wear goggles.

BUYING TIPS: Fiberglass poles are often preferable to metal ones, especially when pruning near electrical wires (metal poles are illegal in some states). If you have trees or tall shrubs in your landscape, this is an indispensable tool. Teflon-coated saw blades—a very good idea—are now available. Double pulleys are a definite advantage with the shear. Tie a handle to the end of the rope to make it a bit easier to grip.

PRUNING SAW

ALSO KNOWN AS: Tree saw, gardener's saw

DESCRIPTION: The most common pruning saws are curved steel blade saws about 14 inches long with amazingly large, sometimes razor-sharp triangular teeth and straight, pistol-grip, or D-grip handles. Some steel blades are Teflon coated. One model, a *duplex saw,* is straight, with tapered blades 18 inches long that have teeth on both sides: one side is for coarse cutting and the other for fine cutting. The teeth are usually angled so that you cut on the "pull" stroke, enabling them to be designed with more aggressive teeth than if they cut on the "push" stroke. They also cut faster and don't get gummed up with green wood. Four to 8 teeth per inch is standard, with the lower number better for green woods and the higher number better for hard or dry woods. Available in either *fixed,* sometimes called *rigid,* or *folding* models (in which the blade folds back into the handle like a big

FOLDING PRUNING SAW

DUPLEX PRUNING SAW

pocketknife), sometimes called *collapsible saws.* Rigid models are sometimes called *single-* or *double-sided,* depending on their design.

USE: Cutting branches from 1½ to 10 inches in diameter.

USE TIPS: When pruning large branches, it is a good idea to make an initial cut 1 to 2 inches deep into the bottom side of the branch closer to the trunk than where the final cut will be. This prevents the branch from ripping the bark beyond this point, should it fall before the final cut is completed. Use the folding type if you are working on ladders, so you can put the folded saw in your pocket or holster when not in use. Folding saws are a bit safer and more likely to hold their extreme sharpness because the blade is protected when folded up.

BUYING TIPS: Many gardeners have found pruning saws with the double-sided blade a good investment because they need both fine and coarse cuts (more teeth per inch yields a finer cut; fewer teeth, a coarser cut). The curved blade saws, however, are easier to use as the curve allows for a smoother sawing rhythm. A medium tooth gauge of around 8 to 10 teeth per inch does most of the work required in home gardens. Tooth edges should be beveled for sharpness. Check out the saw for balance and the feel of the grip before purchasing. Look for a saw with a small hang-up hole near the tip.

Knives and Other Hand Cutting Tools

ABOUT KNIVES AND OTHER HAND CUTTING TOOLS

Every gardener should have at least a good pocketknife for jobs such as opening plastic bags, sharpening stakes, cutting cords and string, and many similar jobs that pop up while gardening.

However, garden centers usually carry many specialized knives that are in some cases invaluable.

Before using any large cutting tool that you swing, such as an ax or machete, take note of surrounding objects that you might hit by mistake. Bushes or low branches might deflect a tool into you, or there may be some garden furniture in the way. Above all, keep children and pets away; because you are focused on your work, you might not notice them until too late.

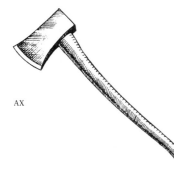

AX

AX

ALSO KNOWN AS: Axe

DESCRIPTION: Wedge-shaped cutting tool, approximately 4½-inch-wide, 8-inch-long, made from tempered steel with a handle 20 to 36 inches long, usually of hickory or white ash, though available in fiberglass. The handle is attached to the head through the eye (a hole or socket in the butt end of the ax head). Some newer models, called *splitting axes,* have spring fingers on the sides that help split wood more easily.

TYPES: *Single-bit ax:* Only one cutting edge with a flat butt end. The handle is curved and saddle-horn shaped at the end for leverage and to prevent your hands from slipping off. Most popular model is the *Michigan-style ax,* with a head weighing about 3½ pounds. Other similar popular patterns are *Dayton,* with a slightly flared cutting edge, and *Jersey.*

Double-bit ax: Two curved cutting edges instead of one and a straight handle.

USE: Cutting down trees, removing their limbs ("limbing"), cutting roots, sharpening stakes and poles, and for chopping and splitting logs. The blunt end of the head can be used for driving wooden stakes.

USE TIPS: Move your hands correctly to ensure that the momentum of the ax head does the work and not your back. Spread your hands at either end of the handle at the top of the swing and slide the forward hand back down the handle during the swing so that both hands are at the base when you hit the wood. *Hammer wedges* (small triangular bits of metal) should be driven into the head end of handles if the head is loose. Do not use the "heel" end of the head for driving metal objects.

BUYING TIPS: Buy only axes with heads made of tempered steel, as these hold an edge better than those that are not tempered. Avoid axes with painted handles, because imperfections in the wood or the grain of the wood may be covered up. The grain of the handle should run lengthwise and be thin and close together. Knots or swirls in the wood mean the handle is weak; you should avoid tools with these imperfections. An ax is an impact tool, so the handle, which takes the impact, is as important as the cutting head. Newer fiberglass handles do not necessarily give the tool the proper balance between head and handle. Finally, a double-bit ax is a loggers' tool and not recommended for the home gardener—it is very dangerous to use.

BUSH HOOK

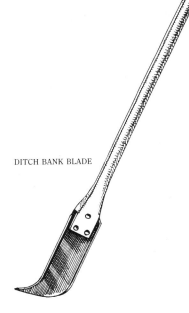

DITCH BANK BLADE

ALSO KNOWN AS: Bush ax, bush knife, bush hog, brush knife, brush hook, brush cutter, bank blade, slashing hook

DESCRIPTION: A heavy-duty tool consisting of a short, wide blade with a hooked end. The blade may be *single edge* (sharpened on only one side) or *double edge* (sharpened on both sides). The blade is attached to the handle with a heavy metal collar forged onto the blade, though one version, a *ditch bank blade,* is usually bolted to the handle (it has the same blade but with a cutting edge on its entire circumference). Handles are heavy and from 35 to 40 inches long. Sort of a large, heavy alternative to the machete (see page 198). A smaller version, called a *bill hook,* is used to harvest sugarcane or for the rough pruning of bushes; other versions are used to harvest corn (they may be called *corn knives)* and still more versions are called by whatever a manufacturer might invent, which allows for a fair amount of imagination.

A smaller version is a *weed* or *brier hook,* which is simply a hook with a sharp inside cutting edge and a long handle. It cuts when the hook is pulled toward you; handy for wheelchair-bound gardeners. Another variation is a sort of hybrid of an ax and a bush hook, called a *clearing ax.* It has a steel bow with a short, replaceable blade instead of the solid blades noted here.

USE: Clearing heavy weed bushes and shrubs, as well as trees up to 1½ inches thick. They are particularly useful in clearing overgrown lots or wooded areas in preparation for a future garden.

USE TIP: Keep the blades sharp because, like machetes, a dull bush hook is more dangerous than a sharp one as it can bounce off the brush it's cutting and possibly inflict you with a nasty gash.

BUYING TIP: This is an item to rent if you have an unusual clearing job ahead of you.

FOLDING PRUNING KNIFE

FOLDING PRUNING KNIFE

DESCRIPTION: Usually a slightly curved, wooden or plastic handle about 4 or 5 inches long into which folds a curved blade with a hawkbill hook in its tip.

USE: A well-cared-for folding pruning knife is a valuable tool for cutting twigs, small woody shoots, and any other cutting job that requires a small knife. The curved tip of this knife holds the limb and makes it easy to cut when the knife is pulled toward you.

USE TIP: Keep the blade sharp and clean.

BUYING TIP: A folding pruning knife is not just a cheap pocket-knife—a good one costs from $40 to $50. Quality here goes up pretty much with cost. Wooden handles are preferable to plastic. Check the tool out for feel and balance.

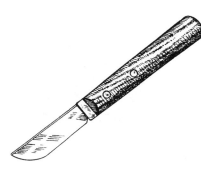

GRAFTING KNIFE

GRAFTING KNIFE

ALSO KNOWN AS: Horticultural knife, gardener's knife

DESCRIPTION: Folding or stationary (nonfolding) pocketknife with an extremely sharp blade less than 3 inches long. The plastic or wooden handles are approximately 4 inches in length, and the blades generally have a straight cutting edge with a curved top side, although curved blades are available. Some models have a stubby brass blade called an *opener,* which is used to hold bark open for the insertion of a graft. A wide range of similar types of horticultural knives are made for professionals, such as *nursery knives.* A smaller bladed knife with a blunt or stubby point is a *budding knife.*

USE: Taking cuttings from plants, called *scions,* which are then grafted onto other plants or root stock, or for budding.

USE TIP: Good clean cuts produce the most successful grafts, so keep grafting knives particularly sharp.

BUYING TIPS: Grafting is not done casually, and a sharp grafting knife is definitely required. The criteria for buying a grafting knife are the same as for buying any knife—good feel and balance, a comfortable grip. A wooden handle is preferable to a plastic one. Also, the highest quality steel is more easily kept razor sharp. Look for a combination model with two different blades and a small brass opening blade, for spreading bark apart at cuts. This is probably not something needed by the beginning gardener.

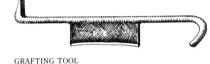

GRAFTING TOOL

GRAFTING TOOL

DESCRIPTION: Heavy steel rod, from about ½ to 1 foot long, in either of two versions: with a 2¼-inch-wide convex blade on one end (which may be called a *grafting chisel),* or with a 4-inch-long concave blade in the middle (of the longer version); both have hooked ends (two, in the case of the larger model).

USE: Splitting and holding open trees for grafting.

USE TIP: Make sure you know what you are doing before attempting to graft trees, or you may easily damage them.

BUYING TIPS: The smaller version may be included in a *grafting kit,* which might also include a *grafting knife, grafting wax, grafting tape, rubber budding strips* (for holding the graft together), and instructions for making grafts (see page 76 for information on grafting equipment).

HATCHET

HATCHET

ALSO KNOWN AS: Camp ax or axe, kindling ax or axe, hand ax

DESCRIPTION: Hammer-sized single-bit ax (see page 194), usually with a wooden handle, or one solid piece of metal. Heads are about 6 inches long and 3 to 3½ inches high.

USE: Many garden uses, such as cutting poles, trimming stakes for flowers and vegetables, driving stakes into the ground for row covers and cloches. The name *camp ax* comes from its earlier common use for setting up camp, chopping wood for the campfire, and chopping and driving the tent stakes.

USE TIP: Leather holsters make the use of hatchets easier and have saved many a hatchet from being lost in the weeds where it could be stepped on.

BUYING TIPS: Similar to the regular ax. Look at the grain of a wooden handle and, whether you buy a hatchet with a wooden handle or one that is solid steel, check for weight and balance. The head should be of tempered steel.

MACHETE

DESCRIPTION: Huge knife, around 18 to 27 inches long and 3 inches wide, with wooden or plastic riveted handle; weighs 2 to 2½ pounds. The blade is curved at the tip and is tapered toward the handle, making it tip-heavy and therefore giving momentum to the swing. Blade should be high-quality carbon steel.

USE: Excellent for cutting tangled vegetation, thick grasses, vines, bamboo, saplings, and thin, woody weeds, as well as for harvesting sugarcane, one of its most common uses. It is perfect for clearing an overgrown lot or garden, tropical or not. In a jungle or other tropical setting, it is more common and more useful than shoes. Short, thick blades can be used for chopping almost anything.

USE TIP: A machete with a dull blade is more dangerous to use than a sharp one—it might bounce or glance off woody material and inflict a serious cut on the user. Extra-sharp machetes also don't seem as heavy.

BUYING TIPS: Heavy steel machetes found at army surplus stores may be a better buy than those that have been manufactured to be sold as garden tools. Wooden handles wear better and are often more comfortable than plastic ones.

MACHETE

MAUL

ALSO KNOWN AS: Splitting maul

DESCRIPTION: Looks like a heavy-headed ax (see page 194), and it is—almost twice as heavy. Made of high-quality steel. The cutting edge is much more flared and curved than an ax's, and the "heel" side is quite thick—just like a sledgehammer. Thirty-six-inch-long handle (wood or fiberglass) is typical; *Oregon maul* is a common style, named after an old brand. Weighs about 6 to

MAUL

8 pounds. Some makes have a straight triangle for a head, instead of the modified ax style. An enormous cast-iron model with a hammerlike head 6 inches wide and 6 inches long is called a *fence post maul.*

USE: Splitting firewood and pounding stakes. Its extreme wideness makes it excellent for splitting wood along the grain, and the weight makes it easier to take advantage of its momentum than that of an ax. The wider the head, the faster it splits logs (but the heavier it is to heft). A fence post maul is used only for pounding wooden posts.

USE TIPS: Be careful when using a maul to pound something, as you can cut yourself with the cutting edge on your backswing—this is a very heavy tool. Eliminates the need to use a wedge—you can use the maul's extra width to cut all the way through a log lengthwise.

SCYTHE

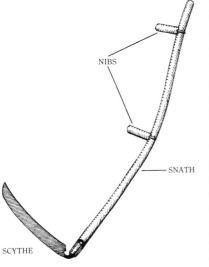

NIBS

SNATH

SCYTHE

DESCRIPTION: You may recognize this tool as the one carried by Father Time. It has a long, slightly curved wooden or aluminum handle, known as a *snath (snaith,* in England, as well as *snade, snead, sneathe,* or *batt),* to which are attached two short, straight wooden hand grips called *nibs.* The steel blade is 24 to 34 inches long and just barely curved, with the sharp cutting edge on the inside; a short metal rod called a *grass nail* crosses the inside corner of the blade and handle junction to prevent grass from catching there. Replacement handles, or those designed for specific jobs, such as lighter or heavier cutting, are available separately. Straight-handle models are made, too, and are a matter of personal preference. Blades are available in three weights: *grass, weed,* and *bush* (grass blades are the longest and heaviest). Many fine blades come from Germany and Austria. A lighter model with a straight snath and only one nib is called a *scythe hook.* A similar lightweight English version is called a *scythette,* and its handle has no grips; it may also be called a *grass hook,* which is actually a long-handled sickle (see next entry).

USE: These days, used to cut areas with tall grasses, weeds, or light brush. The scythe is an old farm tool, used for centuries to harvest hay and grain crops.

USE TIP: Swing the blade by rocking your entire body back and forth. Using the arms alone to move a scythe will quickly tire you; farmers who used the scythe for harvesting grain developed a rhythm that made using this heavy tool easier.

BUYING TIPS: Look for fine, high-carbon steel and heat-treated blades. This beautifully shaped and balanced tool can also be rented, which is a good thing to do because these days most gardeners do not have much use for one. However, you may enjoy owning a cutting tool that looks as if it came from an old farm or a museum. A lighter, cheaper alternative is the swing blade or grass whip (see below).

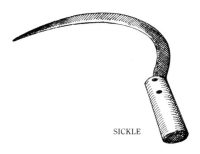

SICKLE

SICKLE

ALSO KNOWN AS: Hand scythe, grass hook, reaping hook, bagging hook

DESCRIPTION: A sharply curved blade, sharpened on the inside (also may be finely serrated), with a short, usually wooden handle. It may be familiar to you, shown with a hammer, as the symbol of the USSR. Models with long, straight handles are available, but rare, and have straighter blades.

USE: Excellent for cutting weeds or grass too high for a lawn mower or in areas that a mower cannot reach. A *rice sickle* is made for particularly heavy grasses.

USE TIPS: The sickle is easy to use when moved in an elliptical pattern with the pulling motion at the bottom of the movement doing the cutting. Keep in mind that you have to bend over to use this; if you have a lot of ground-level cutting to do, use a scythe (see preceding entry).

BUYING TIP: Look for a heavy steel blade and a comfortable wooden handle.

SWING BLADE AND GRASS WHIP

ALSO KNOWN AS: *Swing blade*—weed cutter; *grass whip*—grass cutter, stand-up grass cutter, weed whip, grass hook, grass trimmer, weed cutter, weed hook

GRASS WHIP

SWING BLADE

DESCRIPTION: The blades on both of these tools are about 14 to 18 inches long, 2 to 4 inches wide, double-edged, and usually slightly serrated. The blade of the *grass whip* is attached at only one end to a metal handle with a plastic or rubber grip, making it look like a giant golf club. A heavier-duty version is called a *brush cutter* (as are a few other different tools). The wooden handle of the *swing blade* is attached with two metal strips, or brackets, to both ends of the blade, forming a D. Some manufacturers consider a modified model with a short hooked blade and a 45-inch handle in lieu of the 36-inch handle a *bean* or *soybean hook;* it is quite similar to the *weed* or *brier hook* (see at bush hook, page 195), or even the same thing.

USE: Both of these tools are used for cutting weeds and grasses, but the swing blade is heavier and made for heavier plants. The grass whip is for woody or hard-to-reach weeds, or thorny bushes, and is helpful for those who cannot bend and reach easily.

USE TIPS: The grass whip is held in one hand and moved in a 75-degree arc with the power of the downstroke doing the cutting. The swing blade is used similarly with either one hand or two, though many experienced gardeners prefer to use it with only one hand. Keep blades clean. A good, cheap alternative to lawn mowers for small lawns. Watch out for surrounding bushes, furniture, trees, lights, and of course, children: Your swing is very, very wide, and you're bound to cut things you don't mean to, even if you are experienced. Take a good look at the distance of your swing when you start, and by all means keep inquisitive children away; they have a way of sneaking up on you when you are concentrating on your work.

BUYING TIPS: Grass whips can be found with smooth-edged blades, but the serrated edges cut better as they give a greater cutting surface. The swing blade is a standard farm tool, but may not be as indispensable to most gardeners. This is a tool that can be rented if needed only once. Consider it a lighter-duty, less expensive version of the scythe (see pages 199–200), easier to handle and keep sharp. Look for high-carbon steel blades.

Grass and Weed Trimmers

ABOUT GRASS AND WEED TRIMMERS

Trimming has always been one of the more arduous garden chores (second only to weeding), and grass and weed trimmers have proven essential in this task. They allow you to cut where lawn mowers can't go, such as up close to buildings, trees, or paths. The manual trimmers are relatively easy to use in small gardens, but for a garden with many areas to trim, the new power trimmers are a blessing.

GRASS SHEARS

ALSO KNOWN AS: Hand shears, grass trimmers, hand trimmers, floating blade grass shears, vertical grip hand trimmers, garden shears (this last term is incorrect and misleading)

VERTICAL SQUEEZE GRASS SHEARS

DESCRIPTION: Scissor-type blades that cut by passing over one another like household scissors, but the handles are arranged so they are squeezed in a vertical position, called *vertical squeeze* or *pump action* style, with the blades cutting horizontally. The top blade "floats" over the fixed lower blade on most models. Most handles are plastic coated. The blades of some new designs can be swiveled so that they cut in a vertical direction as well as horizontally, and are Teflon coated. Some new models designed for people with gripping problems have a hand-sized trigger grip.

USE: Trimming grass or weeds around trees or structures.

USE TIP: Wear gloves to prevent blisters.

BUYING TIPS: A comfortable grip is the most important feature to look for, and the better models have handles that are plastic or rubber coated. The new designs that swivel or use large triggers may be easier for an arthritic gardener. Floating top blade is the sign of a better shear, but the choice is largely one of personal "feel."

LONG-HANDLED GRASS SHEARS

LONG-HANDLED GRASS SHEARS

ALSO KNOWN AS: Long-handled hand trimmers, border shears, lawn shears, lawn trimmers, light edgers, edging shears

DESCRIPTION: Quite similar to grass shears (see preceding entry) but with a metal handle about a yard long. On some models, two wheels at the rear of the blades allow these trimmers to be rolled along the ground and operated from a standing position. Seven- to 9-inch blades. True *edging shears* have blades that cut in line with the handles (vertically) for edging; those with blades that cut horizontally are true *lawn shears.*

USE: Trimming grass and weeds from a standing position.

USE TIPS: Keep blades sharp and wear gloves to prevent blisters. Clean blades after use. Remember not to trim the grass too closely.

BUYING TIPS: Check for comfort of grip, above all. Plastic-covered grips are easier to use. These shears are particularly helpful if you have trouble bending and stooping, or even kneeling, and can even be used from a wheelchair. Quality shears are edge-hardened and hollow-ground.

ROTARY EDGER

ALSO KNOWN AS: Rotary turf edger, lawn edger, single-wheel edger, two-wheel edger

DESCRIPTION: One or a pair of hard rubber or plastic wheels attached to a metal wheel with sharp, pointed cutting teeth. Made with a 4- to 5-foot-long handle. When the wheels are rolled along the ground, the movement forces the teeth to cut. This edger works by cutting, unlike the semicircular plain edger (see page 143). Also available in a power version that works like either a string trimmer (see pages 208–209) or a small gas-powered lawn mower with a vertical blade.

USE: Trimming grass and weeds along paths and plant beds and the like. May be adjustable to cut a trench ⅝ to 1½ inches deep.

USE TIP: Keep wheels cleaned and oiled.

BUYING TIP: Models on which the blade depth can be adjusted for deep-rooted weeds are more expensive and not always necessary.

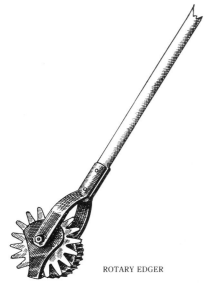

ROTARY EDGER

SCISSOR-TYPE GRASS SHEARS

DESCRIPTION: Resemble a pair of heavy-duty household scissors, with the blade and handles being made from one piece of metal. The handles are usually plastic-coated and spring-loaded to force the shears open after each cut. Blades cut by crossing over each other.

USE: Trimming small amounts of grass and weeds around trees or structures.

USE TIP: Wear gloves, as these shears are prone to cause blisters.

BUYING TIP: The horizontal squeeze action required to operate these shears is more difficult than the vertical squeeze movement required by regular grass shears (see page 202), but they are less expensive and good for use as standbys in small areas.

SHEEP SHEAR TRIMMER

SHEEP SHEAR TRIMMER

ALSO KNOWN AS: Grass shears, sheep shear pattern trimmer, singing grass shears, English clipping shears, English garden shears, short-handled grass shears

DESCRIPTION: Commonly made from a single piece of fine carbon steel, sheep shears consist of two 5½-inch-wide triangular blades at the end of a bent metal loop, with straight handles. The bent loop acts as a spring, holding the shears open when not cutting. The simplicity of the design—one piece of metal, and self-sharpening at that—is part of the charm of owning these shears. These blades cut with a scissorlike action when the handles are squeezed. This design has been around at least since the nineteenth century, and was originally designed to shear wool from sheep. Available in a left-handed version. Makes a pleasant ringing sound when used.

USE: Trimming small areas of grass. As there are no pivoting parts—only bending ones—these are easy to maintain if kept free from rust.

USE TIP: Extended use may cause blisters if you don't wear gloves when trimming.

BUYING TIP: This is a simple, straightforward tool, but people with difficulty gripping may find these hard to use.

Power Trimming and Cutting Tools

BATTERY-OPERATED
HAND TRIMMER

BATTERY-OPERATED HAND TRIMMER

ALSO KNOWN AS: Cordless hand trimmer, electric grass shears, electric shears

DESCRIPTION: Plastic-housed motor with two metal blades having sharp triangular teeth extending horizontally from it, about the size and shape of an eggbeater. The teeth on the top blade move over the bottom blade, which is stationary. Uses rechargeable batteries and is cordless. Cuts a swath about 3 to 4 inches wide.

USE: Designed only for light trimming jobs, such as the grass around trees, not for heavy weeds or woody plants. Useful for someone who has difficulty gripping. Charge lasts 30 to 55 minutes.

USE TIP: Do not try to force these trimmers to do heavier work than they are designed to do. The blades should be replaced when they become dull.

BUYING TIP: Cordless electric trimmers are relatively inexpensive, at under $50. These trimmers are helpful for light trimming or as an aid to someone with difficulty gripping.

BLADE-TYPE POWER TRIMMER

ALSO KNOWN AS: Combination edger and trimmer, power edger, brush cutter

DESCRIPTION: A variety of blade types have appeared over the years for this popular item, including a straight piece of metal similar to a miniature rotary mower (see page 249), a double blade with triangular teeth similar to the battery-operated hand trimmer (see preceding entry), or a circular, serrated blade like a circular saw. The gas or electric motor may be mounted above the blade or at the end of the handle. These trimmers have long metal handles for operation from a standing position. They were among the first power tools introduced.

USE: Heavy lawn trimming work along walls, such as brush or thick and woody weeds.

USE TIPS: The model with the spinning metal blade is capable of flinging stones and other objects, so it is necessary to wear protective clothing and goggles when using it. For the same reason, it is a good idea not to use these machines near other people, especially small ones, or pets. Most of these should be used with a lunging, chopping motion for larger branches.

BUYING TIP: Metal blades can cut woody material that the string trimmers (see pages 208–209) cannot. If you are cutting only green weeds and grass, the string trimmers are better suited to the job and safer to use.

CHAIN SAW

DESCRIPTION: Gas- or electric-powered saw with a wide, 10- to 20-inch-long blade called a *guide bar* surrounded by a continuous cutting chain that revolves around its edge. Gasoline-powered saws tend to be heavier duty and are available in a wide range of sizes and capabilities, from those for home use to production models used in professional logging operations. Gas engines are rated by displacement (measured in cubic inches, running from about 1.6 to an enormous 8.3), with the higher numbers indicating more power. Chain saws have four types of teeth: *chipper* (most common), *chisel* (typical on professional models), *semi-chisel* (a good combination of chipper and chisel), and *automatic sharpening* (for specially equipped saws). Replacement guide bars are available, as are chains.

Electric chain saws are powered by electric motors. They are quiet, do not use volatile fuels, are easy to start, and emit no exhaust fumes. *Gasoline chain saws* are powered by gasoline engines. The range in size is from small and lightweight to the large heavy logger machines. Pull-cord or electronic push-button ignition.

CHAIN SAW

USE: Heavy pruning, felling unwanted or overgrown trees, and cutting up firewood. The latter is the most common use of chain saws among homeowners.

USE TIPS: This is one of the most dangerous tools you might own, so be absolutely sure to use it correctly and carefully. Double-check the manufacturer's instructions. The contact point of the blade and the tree or log should be right up near the motor—otherwise the moving chain might pull you and the saw into the tree, causing you serious injury. Be especially careful when felling a tree over 4 inches thick: Make sure the saw does not bind in the cut, and be prepared to get back quickly when the cut goes through and the tree begins to fall. Be sure to keep the chain tension properly adjusted. Keep your blade sharp; *saw sharpener kits* are available. Keep well-lubricated with special oils.

BUYING TIPS: Be sure to consider your needs carefully before buying a chain saw. A small bargain saw that cannot stand up to the work you need it for is no bargain in the end, especially the bottom-of-the-line electric ones. A good electric chain saw that can do the job well should cost as much as a comparable gasoline one. A chain brake that stops the saw automatically should it become bound (or if your hand hits it) is a feature definitely worth paying for, but it is unfortunately not usually found on the smaller models. Look for a toothed cutting guide where the blade meets the motor on the larger chain saws and better small ones. This is used to anchor and stabilize the saw at the cut. Also look for solid-state ignition, a tip guard, antivibration devices, an automatic oiler, a nose sprocket (to reduce friction at the tip), and a compression release button, which makes for easier starting of gas models. The grip and oil button should be comfortable to you; the location of the oil button is of particular concern to left-handed people, as it is often designed to be pressed with the operator's right thumb. Electric chain saws are fine if you are no further from an electrical source than 150 feet; the advantage of gasoline saws lies in their portability and power, but they are noisy and fuel is volatile. They are the way to go, however, if you have lots of firewood to cut.

POWER HEDGE SHEARS

ALSO KNOWN AS: Power shears, garden trimmers

DESCRIPTION: Two back-to-back sets of blades about 2 to 3 feet long, with many large, moving, pointed teeth, with a gas or electric motor and handle. Resembles the beak of a swordfish. Normally cuts from both sides.

USE: Trimming hedges with branches up to ¼ inch thick, though some professional models will cut up to ½ inch thick.

USE TIPS: Trim the top of a hedge so it is narrower than the bottom, allowing sunlight to reach the bottom branches. When

POWER HEDGE SHEARS

working with an electric trimmer, be careful not to cut the power cord.

BUYING TIPS: Electric trimmers are lighter and quieter to use than gasoline-powered ones but are limited by the length of the cord. Look for double-insulated, UL-approved makes. Look also for an adjustable handle, for better balance when cutting in different positions. Blades may be made from stainless steel or forged steel, but while stainless steel is slightly better than forged steel, the advantage is so slight that the cost difference makes forged steel a better buy.

STRING TRIMMER

ALSO KNOWN AS: Rotary trimmer, nylon cord trimmer, nylon string trimmer, grass trimmer, weed trimmer, flexible line grass trimmer, line trimmer

POPULAR BRAND NAMES: Weed Eater®, Weed Wacker, Weed Wizard®

DESCRIPTION: A long-handled tool, either straight or slightly curved, with one, two, or three heavy nylon monofilament strings on a spool that are spun at high speed by an electric (regular or battery-operated) or two-cycle gas engine. They weigh upwards of 3 pounds. The strings act as a blade. The heavier-duty models are usually gas powered and have straight shafts. The cord is reeled out as it becomes frayed or broken, either by a button on the handle *(push button feed)* or by bumping the head on the ground *(bump feed),* although some *automatic feed* models are available. String trimmers are a revolutionary form of power trimming created in 1974 by George Ballas. Some gas-powered models can also take a metal sawtooth blade for heavy brush cutting. Trimmer line is available by itself in various thicknesses from .040 to .130 inch and in lengths from 40 to over 1,000 feet (that's just a 1-pound box of the thinnest line). Curved shafts are found on most light-duty models.

A recent variation is a nylon trimmer that mows as well as trims. This is a traditional-looking gasoline-powered mower

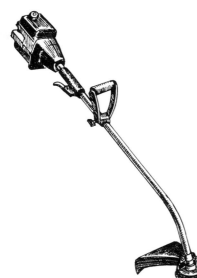

STRING TRIMMER

with the motor mounted behind the nylon reel and between two large wheels. This "nylon mower" may in time replace the classic rotary mower.

USE: Cutting weeds and long grass but not woody material. Particularly good for trimming near buildings, trees, and other solid structures in the garden. Some models double as edgers when turned on their sides; others are designed specifically as edgers. Cuts a path from 7 to 20 inches wide, depending on the model.

USE TIPS: While generally safer to use than metal blade trimmers, nylon cord trimmers are not without hazard. The nylon cord can sling stones and debris, so appropriate clothing, heavy boots, and goggles should be worn, and no pets or people should be in the area. Some manufacturers even offer shin guards. Though string trimmers do less damage to trees than ones with metal blades, they are still capable of knocking off tree bark or damaging flowers and shrubs through carelessness. A plastic or metal tree guard (see page 288) is recommended for young trees. Don't try to work a multiple-line trimmer with only one line.

BUYING TIPS: There is a large choice of makes and models on the market today. The tool should feel comfortable to use: Check the handle length, controls, and overall feel, and above all, the balance. Note if it is easy to replace the string. Models with the engine mounted on the upper end of the handle are slightly better balanced, and this position keeps the engine clean; straight shafts are more easily handled and a bit more powerful and durable. Models with more than one "whip" have a larger cutting capacity. Larger models carry more string. A built-in clutch that prevents the cord from turning when the motor idles is an important safety feature. Look for models with "bump feed," which means that the head of the tool is simply bumped on the ground to release more cord while the motor remains on. Other models require that you shut them off in order to hand-feed new cord. Automatic release models often release more than you might need, wasting cord. Electric trimmers are generally preferable to gasoline ones if your area is not so large, as they are so much more quiet (gas models are actually banned in some areas) and vibrate less. A 20 to 25 cubic centimeter gas engine is usually sufficient for most lawns and gardens; electric models have a narrow range of $\frac{1}{8}$ to about $\frac{3}{4}$ horsepower. Look for the most amperage. This is fast becoming considered a basic homeowner tool.

Maintenance Tools and Equipment

ABOUT GENERAL MAINTENANCE TOOLS AND EQUIPMENT

This is one area of the garden center where there is plenty of overlap, so here is a broadly inclusive category for lawn and garden items. Although it could be argued that shovels (chapter 5) can just as easily be used for maintenance as for planting, this is how these items are usually arranged.

Watering Equipment

ABOUT WATERING EQUIPMENT

Every garden, large or small, needs to be watered. While this is a simple and usually relatively passive task, figuring out your needs can be daunting. Garden centers sell a confusing variety of watering equipment and accessories (collectively known as *watering goods),* but basically all you need is a good hose, a watering can, a good nozzle, and if your space demands it, a sprinkler. The many other watering accessories can be purchased as you discover a special need for them.

Watering should be done on a regular and careful basis. Most gardens (especially a vegetable garden) require at least 1 inch of water a week. However, too little water is often worse than none at all, because shallow watering causes plants to be shallow-rooted, leaving you with plants that will not survive periods of drought. *When* you water can be as important as *how much* you water, since fungal infections are spread by spores that develop in the presence of moisture and in the absence of light—so it is best not to water at dusk or at night. Plants that are particularly susceptible to fungal problems (such as roses, lilacs, zinnias, and phlox) should be carefully watered at soil level, taking care not to wet the foliage. It is wise to choose watering accessories that can help you garden with this type of concern in mind.

Plumbing fittings, including garden hose accessories, are described in terms of *male* and *female,* which refers to the screw threads. Female threads are on the inside, while male threads are on the outside. Female threaded parts seem bigger because they actually house the threads, while male threads seem smaller because all that is present is the threads. Another way to remember which is which is to remind yourself that male threads *go into* other fittings, while female threads *receive* other fittings.

BUBBLER

BUBBLER

ALSO KNOWN AS: Soaker, irrigator, bubble soaker

DESCRIPTION: Rounded, fist-sized nozzle that mixes air with water which is dispersed in a gentle flow.

USE: Watering trees and large plants one spot at a time, when you want to give a well-targeted, good soaking. The bubbler is left on the ground wherever the water is needed.

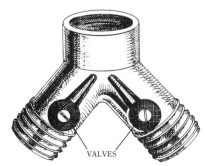

VALVES

DOUBLE HOSE SHUTOFF

DOUBLE HOSE SHUTOFF

ALSO KNOWN AS: Y-connector, 2-way hose shut-off, dual shutoff coupling, Siamese shutoff, two- or 2-hose adapter, twin shut-off, Siamese coupling with shutoffs

DESCRIPTION: Brass, zinc, or plastic accessory that screws onto a male-threaded faucet and into two female hose couplings; contains two shutoff valves in each leg of the Y, similar to the shutoff valve (see page 223).

USE: Separate control of two hoses from one faucet.

BUYING TIP: Get the best heavy-duty quality make you can find.

DRIP IRRIGATION SYSTEM

ALSO KNOWN AS: Spaghetti-type irrigation system, landscape or garden watering system, drip watering system, microtube system, emitter system

DESCRIPTION: Network of small hoses—¼ to ½ inch in diameter—with numerous small *dripper heads,* or *emitters,* tiny spray heads, and associated accessories designed to be custom assembled for each individual garden layout. They are usually made of black plastic, to prevent sun penetration and algae formation. Each brand is sold with its own accessories of *dripper heads, hose adapters, T-couplings* and *connectors* (for tapping into the supply line), *elbow connectors, hole punches, hole plugs, clamps* or *mounting clips, spikes* or *support stakes,* and *distributors,* complete with several built-in valves, and of course, *tubing,* or *line.* You may also need (or the kit may include) a *vacuum breaker, filter, pressure regulator* with hose bib connector, and *wall clips.* Usually you can find these bundled into a one-package starter kit. Smaller diameter (¼ inch) kits are for containers, and larger (⅜ and ½ inch) for gardens. Should come with appropriate connectors for a spigot or indoor faucet, and an antisiphon device. A sort of miniature version is a *drip ring,* which fits around the trunks of potted trees or plants; models are made for 6- to 16-inch diameter containers.

USE: Slow, even, efficient watering system that delivers water only to planted areas, and then only to the root zone, a drop at a time (though some accessories include misters and small sprinklers). Minimizes evaporation and delivers water at the prescribed rate and amount for your plants. Also used for application of fertilizers. Cuts wasted water dramatically. Used on potted plants, hanging baskets, planters, trees, shrubs, and vegetable gardens of all types.

USE TIPS: The latest systems are easily assembled, and the component parts should be readily available from a display at your local garden center. In cases where a part of the system is higher than the faucet, or when fertilizing, be sure to use an antisiphon *backflow preventer* or *vacuum breaker* (a common plumbing device) to prevent fertilizer from being drawn back into the home water system should there be a drop in pressure. You may also require a *pressure regulator* to lower the pressure to an ideal level. Both of these should be sold along with the other parts of the system; they are relatively small valves that screw into the hose line near the faucet. If your water source is a pond or other body of water where algae are present, use a *filter,* which should also be a readily available component, to trap the algae. Drip irrigation is particularly useful with vegetable gardens, but less so with flower gardens.

BUYING TIPS: Start with a small system and experiment, because you can always add to your system as you become more familiar with it. Look for systems that promise to deliver uniform flow and clog-free operation through the use of devices such as a pressure- (or flow-) regulation valve (PRV), or large, specially designed dripper openings. They should be unaffected by temperature.

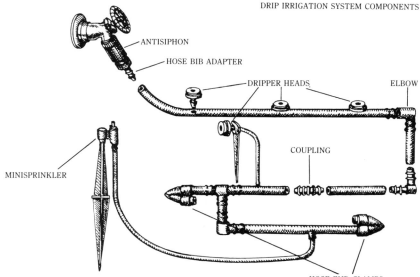

DRIP IRRIGATION SYSTEM

DRIP IRRIGATION SYSTEM COMPONENTS

ANTISIPHON

HOSE BIB ADAPTER

DRIPPER HEADS

ELBOW

MINISPRINKLER

COUPLING

HOSE END CLAMPS

FAN HEAD SPRAYER

FAN HEAD SPRAYER

ALSO KNOWN AS: Fan sprayer, fan spray, flaring rose

DESCRIPTION: Metal or plastic nozzle, wide and triangular in shape. It has a very wide spray head with many small holes with a narrow, threaded end that attaches to a hose. Some models have a spike attached which allows them to be left on in a particular area for deeper soaking, like a stationary sprinkler.

USE: Delivering a large quantity of water in a gentle spray. Ideal devices for watering in seeds and seedlings, as well as roses and other delicate flowers.

USE TIP: Be sure that the area is well soaked when watering in seedlings; shallow watering encourages transplants to be shallow rooted.

BUYING TIP: These are inexpensive devices, but the slightly more expensive ones with built-in valves that shut the water on and off are easier to use.

GARDEN HOSE

REINFORCING MESH

GARDEN HOSE

DESCRIPTION: Plastic, rubber, nylon, or vinyl flexible tubing ½, ⅝, or ¾ inch in diameter, usually available in 25-, 50-, or 75-foot lengths. Most often green in color, but also found in red or black. Most are made of several plies of materials and many include an integrated reinforcing mesh. Hoses are rated by the amount of pressure required to burst them, indicated in pounds per square inch (psi). Ratings run from 50 to 600 psi. Lengths of hose can be joined together with threaded brass, steel, or plastic couplings that screw into each other. Two-ply vinyl hoses are sold that are lightweight and consist of a vinyl core with an additional outer vinyl layer. Those with plastic couplings may feature a grip design that makes tightening and loosening the connection easier by providing a flange to push with your thumb.

A *flat hose* is made of a vinyl or other plastic weave that collapses when empty and can be reeled up in a more compact space than a regular hose. A miniature version for use with houseplants, called a *house hose,* is designed to be hooked up to the kitchen sink faucet (in place of the aerator) and has a trigger at the foot-long wand end.

USE: Carrying water throughout the garden.

USE TIPS: It is a good practice to roll up hoses when not in use, because leaving them out exposes them to the deteriorating rays of the sun. Be careful not to damage plants when dragging the hose through the garden; stakes or hose guides (see page 216) help prevent this from happening. And don't bang the couplings against stone, or you'll have some leaks.

BUYING TIPS: Price determines quality when purchasing garden hoses, and you should buy the best quality possible; 500-pound (psi) burst strength is a main criterion for the best. Hoses with larger diameters deliver more water faster to the garden, making ⅝-inch-diameter hoses a good buy. As most leaks occur at the couplings, look for good crush-resistant couplings of heavy-duty cast brass. Only the best-quality vinyl is both flexible, kink-resistant, and durable. The best rubber or vinyl hoses are reinforced with a synthetic mesh layer, or ply. The higher the number of plies to the hose, the better the quality; 4 is tops, though 3 is good if the mesh is thick.

Note that nylon and vinyl are more sensitive to the sun, and deteriorate after much exposure. They generally have lower pressure capacity ratings than rubber hoses; some are rated as low as 50 psi, which indicates a hose of very low quality. Two-ply vinyl hoses are lightweight and are some of the cheapest on the market, but they kink easily and are not very pliable, making them very annoying to use; they are not worth the money saved. In all hoses, look for ones sold with a 4-inch plastic *hose collar* to keep the hose from kinking at the faucet, or buy one as an accessory. At least one manufacturer offers a lifetime guarantee, which is hard to beat. Rubber hoses are more expensive and heavier, but they are more durable, resisting sun, cold weather, and kinks, and are generally considered the best—quite worth the extra expense.

GOOSENECK COUPLING

ALSO KNOWN AS: Gooseneck hose swivel connector, gooseneck connector, gooseneck swivel connector

DESCRIPTION: Brass coupling with female threads on one end and male on the other, which is at a 45-degree angle and, in most brands, swivels. Simply an extension of a spigot, but one that puts the threads on an angle and allows it to move with the hose.

GOOSENECK COUPLING

USE: Allows for easier connection of a hose and may save on hose wear at the spigot.

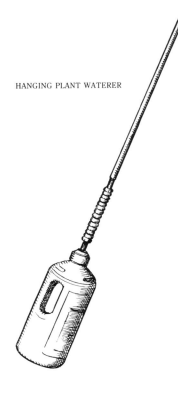

HANGING PLANT WATERER

HANGING PLANT WATERER

DESCRIPTION: Quart or half-gallon plastic bottle with a small, J-shaped, yard-long tube. Either one of two types: one that you squeeze, or one that has a sliding pump grip, like a trombone.

USE: Watering and fertilizing hanging plants up to 9 feet above the floor. Excellent for wheelchair gardeners.

USE TIP: Practice over a sink to see how much water comes out with a squeeze, or else you may find yourself taking an impromptu shower.

BUYING TIP: Inexpensive, handy item.

HOSE GRABBER

DESCRIPTION: Simple loop of heavy-gauge steel wire that is stuck into the ground; loop is a double ring that springs apart to hold a hose by tension.

USE: Holds nozzle end of a hose in a position for spraying one spot you wish to soak, such as a newly planted shrub. Easily set up and removed.

BUYING TIP: An inexpensive alternative to a sprinkler.

HOSE GUIDE

HOSE GUIDE

DESCRIPTION: Metal or wooden rods, which may be plain or encircled by a large roller or made of three small rollers, designed to be inserted into the ground. Some models have a hook or curved top that prevents the hose from riding up and over the guide. Others are quite ornamental, with sculpted leaf tops and the like.

USE: When placed in the ground near plant beds and plants, prevents the hose from being pulled over the bed and damaging plants as it is dragged through the garden. The hose just rubs against the guides.

BUYING TIP: Though excellent hose guides are sold in garden centers, they can also be made easily by the gardener. Strong bamboo stakes or metal rods driven in the ground can suffice.

HOSE HANGER

HOSE HANGER

DESCRIPTION: Basically a large hook or double hook with a wide, partially curved support designed to be attached to a wall, though there is a wide variety of models available. Made from galvanized, epoxy-coated, or painted metal as well as plastic. Capacity ranges from 50 to 150 feet.

USE: Garden hose storage. The hose is coiled over the hook. The curved support holds the hose in a coil form instead of pinching it, as a simple hook would do.

USE TIP: Ideal for winter storage of hose in a garage or shed.

BUYING TIP: Make sure you get a model sturdy enough to support the weight of your hose.

HOSE REEL CART

HOSE REEL

DESCRIPTION: Large spool, or reel, that is either attached to a wall or is part of a cart with two wheels. The *hose reel cart,* or *trolley,* allows you to move the hose from place to place in the yard. Capacity is about 150 feet of ⅝-inch hose, more of smaller hoses. *Estate* models hold up to 400 feet and have four wheels, like a wagon; other, fancy models have an accessory storage tray for nozzles and couplings. Reel carts usually have a 4- to 6-foot leader hose that attaches to the water supply. Made of galvanized or enameled steel, or heavy plastic, or a combination of materials. There are few alternative designs, though attractive ceramic pots with an interior cone (known as *hose pots)* can be found; the hose is coiled within.

USE: Storage of hoses in a coiled position off the ground and out of the sun (presuming they are installed under shelter), avoiding sun damage as well as garden tripping hazards. In the case of the cart type, also provides convenient transport of a heavy hose to distant gardens and out-of-sight storage.

USE TIPS: When reeling in the hose, be sure that it does not kink. Install it out of the sun's reach. Cart type may offer some relief to gardeners who do not have the strength or ability to carry a heavy coil around the garden.

BUYING TIPS: Buy a reel that is large enough for the length of hose you wish to store. Cart-type hose reels are complicated and are available in a range of styles and qualities; buy the sturdiest you can afford. Poorly constructed hose reel carts do not last long and often bend after normal use.

MALE HOSE COUPLING

HOSE MENDER

HOSE REPAIR ACCESSORIES

DESCRIPTION: A variety of items are available to replace or repair most parts of garden hoses.

TYPES: *Couplings:* Sets of male or female threads that are secured to a hose end with two screws, or an expanded collar (known as a *clincher coupling)* that is pinched down with pliers for one of three reasons: to attach two lengths of hose to one another after a damaged section is cut away (male and female threads); to a nozzle (male threads); or to a faucet (female threads). Usually made of nylon or other plastic, top-quality models are made of brass and a metal ring with a clamp for tightening that is then screwed down upon them. A specialized version of a coupling, called *mender,* has clamps on both ends and is used for patching two pieces of hose together where a leaky section has been cut out, and can be the clinch or the clamp type (sometimes called the *clam shell* type), or a new quick-connect style (see page 221).

Tape: Plastic tape with strong adhesive for temporary repairs of small leaks.

Patch kit: Small package containing rubber patch material and cement for patching pinholes.

Washer: Small package of flat donut-shaped rubber pieces that fit inside the hose fitting and help seal the connection made when the parts are screwed together.

USE: Replacing or repairing damaged hose parts.

USE TIPS: Clincher-type couplings need to be pinched down very carefully, sometimes with the aid of a hose clamp. The clamp types are easier to use. Replace washers often, as they tend to wear out. It is a good idea to keep a few on a small wire attached to a spigot.

BUYING TIPS: A good-quality hose can be repaired easily and for less money than is required to replace it. None of the replacement coupling parts are very expensive, and sturdy, top-quality plastic (not rubber) may work as well as solid brass parts. Experiment to find out which replacement parts are easiest for you to use.

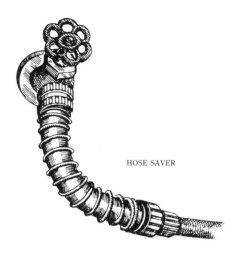

HOSE SAVER

HOSE SAVER

DESCRIPTION: Short length of hose wrapped in heavy steel spring, with couplings on either end. Attaches to faucet and hose end.

USE: Prevents kinking of hose at faucet by maintaining a gentle bend.

BUYING TIP: Excellent accessory that is often part of newer hoses, sometimes in an all-plastic version.

NOZZLE

DESCRIPTION: Hand-sized plastic or metal devices that attach to the male end (the smaller end, with external threads) of a hose. Various settings control the shape and force of the spray or stop the water altogether; many ingenious devices are available.

TYPES: *Twist-type nozzle* (also known as *spray* or *straight nozzle):* Straight shaft made of metal or plastic. Spray is controlled by twisting the shaft. Most common kind.

TWIST-TYPE NOZZLE

Pistol-grip nozzle (also known as *spray gun nozzle):* Water is turned on or off by squeezing or releasing a trigger. In most models, the spray is adjusted by screwing a knob at the top of the trigger to control how far the trigger can be compressed when it is squeezed. Others have a rotating or twist-type spray head that is adjusted by twisting the shaft of the head. A modified version, called a *trigger nozzle,* looks like a gun and is very comfortable to use.

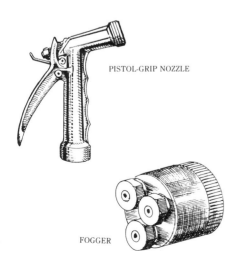

PISTOL-GRIP NOZZLE

Cleaning nozzle (also known as *sweeping, sweeper,* or *power nozzle):* Not adjustable. A small aperture causes water to spurt out with extreme force.

Water Breaker™ *nozzle:* Large, round aluminum or plastic nozzle with many small holes, like a kitchen sink aerator. Reduces a full volume of water to a soft, rainlike spray without increasing pressure. Smaller ones are made for low-pressure sources. A trademark (held by the Dramm Company) that aptly describes what it does to water: breaks it up into a fine, gently spray.

Fogger nozzle (also known as *misting head, fog nozzle,* or Fogg-It—a brand name): Finely machined brass nozzle with three small holes that create a fine mist. Four degrees of spray fineness available.

FOGGER

Seedling nozzle: Finely machined, cadmium-plated brass nozzle with one small hole that produces an extra-fine mist.

USE: Controlling the shape, volume, and force of the water coming out of a hose.

Twist-type nozzle: Can be set at a particular spray pattern and left on, such as when watering beds or transplants.

Pistol-grip nozzle: Excellent for quick spray jobs where spray consistency is not important and where quick on-and-off action is needed.

Cleaning nozzle: High-pressure tool intended to be used for cleaning patios, driveways, or sidewalks, and is not at all suitable for watering plants or gardens.

Water Breaker nozzle: Normal watering of plants, particularly in greenhouses. Popular with professional growers.

Fogger nozzle: Watering delicate flowers such as orchids, or wilting plants.

Seedling nozzle: Watering delicate seedlings.

USE TIPS: Nozzles are helpful hose attachments for washing off foliage or when light watering is required for seedlings and transplants. Hand-watering a lawn with a hose and nozzle is wrong, though; a sprinkler is the best way to achieve the 1 inch of water necessary to avoid shallow watering.

BUYING TIPS: The best nozzles are made of solid brass, which can last a lifetime. Less expensive nozzles are made of plastic or brass-plated zinc, which can rust where scratched, and are not as sturdy, although some recent designs of top-quality, thick plastic are very good. Cleaning nozzles are usually an unnecessary investment, as the other, adjustable nozzles can produce a spray almost as hard. It is not unwise to have both the twist and the pistol types of nozzles on hand. Look for pistol types that can be set to hold a particular spray pattern.

PAIL

ALSO KNOWN AS: Bucket, utility pail

DESCRIPTION: Hot-dipped galvanized metal or plastic container, open on one end, with a slightly curved, hooplike wire handle. Plastic versions may have one or even two specially channeled lips, or spouts, for easy pouring. Some fancier models actually have two lips. Extra-fancy models have plastic grips in the middle of the wire handles for carrying comfort, and a molded grip on the bottom of the pail to aid in pouring. Plastic models also come in a variety of colors, such as red, black, white, beige, brown, and green.

USE: Carrying water of all kinds and styles, including frozen water if need be, as well as fertilizers, pesticides, fruit, vegetables, compost, sand, and gravel. Secondary uses include carrying tools and even toys.

USE TIPS: Bend your knees when lifting. Carrying a full pail of water while in a hurry is generally conducive to a condition known as "wetfoot." Even if you do manage to transport the water without a spill, the abrupt stop when it is set down often sends a small wave over the edge. Practice, and carrying smaller quantities, rather than caution, is the best solution to this ancient problem. Drain metal pails completely when not in use.

BUYING TIPS: Plastic pails with reinforced shoulders can carry a heavier load that those without. In metal pails, look for a wire-reinforced top, hot-dipped galvanized finish, double-locked welded seams, and riveted ears.

QUICK-CONNECT HOSE SYSTEM

ALSO KNOWN AS: Snap-together watering system, Gardena® system, snap adapters

DESCRIPTION: Plastic devices based on a small connector that snaps onto garden hoses or accessories (like sprinklers) quite easily. Some models have a built-in valve that automatically shuts off water flow when accessories are removed. Invented in Germany a number of years ago by Gardena, a West German company, there are now quite a few manufacturers with their own similar products. Systems include adapters for attachment to conventional accessories, taps or faucets, more hose, two other hoses (Y-coupler), 4-tap distributor, and other accessories of the same manufacturer, such as sprinklers and nozzles—the entire range of hose accessories. It can also serve as the basis for an entire drip irrigation system (see pages 212–13).

USE: Quick connection of hose accessories without force or having to turn off the water at the faucet.

BUYING TIP: This is an inexpensive item and makes for a very easy-to-use system. Look for shock-resistant plastic that won't break if you step on it accidentally.

RAIN DRAIN

ALSO KNOWN AS: Rain spout lawn protector, downspout drain, downspout control

DESCRIPTION: Heavy-duty vinyl tube with many small holes that is installed, coiled up, at the foot of downspouts (or drains or leaders); the vertical pipe that leads down from gutters. Recoils automatically when rain has stopped. Similar item is a permanent stone or plastic (solid or water-filled) flat triangle called a *splashblock* about 28 inches long.

USE: Rainwater forces the device to unroll and is sprinkled over the lawn instead of gushing out and eroding it. The splashblock merely diverts water a few feet away from the bottom of the downspout.

RAIN GAUGE

DESCRIPTION: Plastic or metal cylinder with measurement markings along the side. Some types have a colored ball that floats inside. Made to be attached to a fence post or a stake away from buildings. A smaller version with a stake is made for measuring sprinkler output—it is easy to move from location to location.

USE: Measuring the amount of rainfall or sprinkling water a garden receives, particularly over a period of time, like a week. Bright floats allow you to read them from afar.

USE TIPS: Make sure you position the gauge for the most accurate reading. Remove during cold weather when water might freeze and damage the gauge. Keep it clean of insects and debris. Determine the goal of water per week that you need, such as 1 inch, and add what the rain doesn't supply.

BUYING TIP: The most accurate gauges have tiny calibrations and small capacities, at least at the bottom, and may be tapered for this purpose.

ROOT WATERER

ALSO KNOWN AS: Root irrigator, root feeder, tree feeder, tree feeding needle, deep root waterer

DESCRIPTION: Steel tube, just under a yard long, with holes in

ROOT WATERER

the end, which is inserted into the soil; the other end is attached to a hose. Some root waterers come with fertilizer chambers at the top for cartridges that allow you to fertilize as you water trees and shrubs. The cartridges are supplied by the waterer manufacturer.

USE: Delivering water and fertilizer directly to the root areas of trees and shrubs where it is needed most. Ideal when compacted soil is a problem.

USE TIP: Insert the probe at the edge of the circle around the tree where the branches end, known as the *drip line.* Move the waterer about 6 feet every hour or so until you've gone around the entire tree, using moderate water pressure. Particularly useful during drought periods.

BUYING TIP: Root waterers are excellent devices that deliver the water where it is needed most, eliminating the problem of shallow-watering trees and shrubs as well as mud puddles. Models with handles are easier to insert into the soil. If you want to use the waterer for applying fertilizer, look for one that has a chamber at the top for this purpose.

SHUTOFF VALVE

ALSO KNOWN AS: Shutoff coupling, hose accessory

DESCRIPTION: Brass, zinc, or plastic accessory that screws into female hose couplings and contains a small twist piece. One particular make is a short rubber nozzle that shuts off whenever it is dropped onto the ground, called a *water miser.*

SHUTOFF VALVE

USE: Allows you to stop the water flow without having to go back to the spigot when you want to change nozzles or other accessories. Y connectors allow you to run two separate hoses from a single water source, controlling the water flow in one or both of the attached hoses independently of one another.

USE TIP: Shutoff valves save time and labor when they are attached between hoses that are connected together. When connected to the spigot, though, shutoff valves are no easier to use than turning the faucet knob.

BUYING TIP: Brass is usually the best quality and most durable. If you have extremely good water pressure, plastic may not be sturdy enough.

SOAKER HOSE

ALSO KNOWN AS: Soil soaker, leaky pipe system, porous pipe, weeping watering system, drip hose, oozer

DESCRIPTION: A hose that contains thousands of small holes or is made of porous material so that water seeps out of it along its length rather than just at the end, as with a conventional garden hose. Sort of a hose that "leaks" over its entire length. The first types of soaker hoses were made from canvas, and can still be found in some garden centers. Others are made from plastic with small holes along one side, while some of the newer models are made from porous foam, vinyl, or rubber (often recycled rubber). Designed to be buried as deep as 14 inches or laid in a garden bed, and can be left there indefinitely—freezing should not bother it. Sold in 25- to 500-foot lengths. Accessories include *feeder sets* and *flow regulators.* Should be rated in number of gallons per hour per foot. A similar product is a two- or three-tubed flat garden hose with small holes throughout one side, sometimes called a *sprinkler hose* or a *sprinkler soaker hose.*

USE: Even, gentle watering of plants that ensures that the root area receives the most water. Watering with a soaker hose is healthier for most plants than using a conventional hose and nozzle or sprinkler as it avoids the problem of spreading fungal diseases caused by wet foliage. It also makes better use of water, as there is less runoff—it just seeps into the ground alongside the hose.

USE TIPS: Adjust the water pressure to avoid bursting the hose. If you are using a buried soaker hose, wrap the open end with a plastic bag. This prevents dirt from clogging up the hose. If you are using a flat soaker hose with holes on one side, face the holes toward the ground to avoid wetting foliage.

BUYING TIPS: A good-quality soaker hose may cost more, but lasts longer. The newer rubber or vinyl hoses are more expensive, but they are more durable in general and do not rot or decay when buried, making them good buys. In either a soaker hose or a sprinkler hose, look for one with removable end caps so that you can flush them out occasionally.

SOAKER HOSE

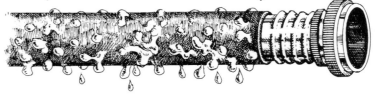

SOIL CORE SAMPLER

DESCRIPTION: Hollow aluminum rod about 1 inch or less in diameter and about 3 feet long, with a T-handle. Eight inches from the open end is a short step sticking straight out.

USE: Taking 8-inch core of soil from your lawn to check the moisture content (to see if you are watering properly) as well as the texture. Other things you can check for are turf quality, the presence of pests, root depth, and thatch buildup, and of course you can use the soil for testing (see soil test kit, pages 237–39).

USE TIP: Can also be used to plant tiny crocus bulbs.

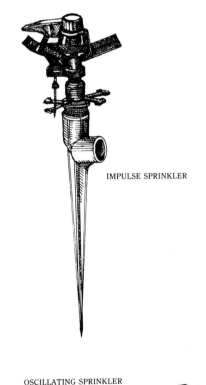

IMPULSE SPRINKLER

SPRINKLER

DESCRIPTION: Metal or plastic device that attaches to the end of a water hose and disperses a gentle spray of water over the garden or lawn. There is a wide array of types and models, rated by the square foot or dimensions of the area they can water, such as 2,600 square feet, or a diameter of 30 to 80 feet.

TYPES: *Impulse sprinkler* (also known as *impact, pulsating, pulsator,* or *pulse sprinkler):* A small nozzle shoots water straight out, which is then deflected by a spring-loaded arm. The arm bounces back and forth, breaking up the stream of water into droplets and moving the sprinkler head slightly each time. The radius can be adjusted to cover full or partial circles up to 100 feet in diameter— well over 5,000 square feet. Usually designed to be staked into the ground, whether at ground level or on a stand as much as 6 feet high. Mechanism made of brass, bronze, plastic, or stainless steel; the base is made of the same materials and is a stake, a ring, or a platform. Rainbird is the most common brand used by professionals, who sometimes use this brand name as if it were a generic term.

Oscillating sprinkler (also known as *oscillator sprinkler):* Curved sprayhead tube, 8 to 20 inches long, which oscillates slowly from side to side as it is driven by water power. May have a built-in timer for automatic shutoff and a stationary setting. Typically waters from 2,600 to 3,600 square feet in an area 55 by 66 feet. Usually on a "sled" base.

OSCILLATING SPRINKLER

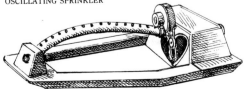

Pop-up sprinkler: Small impulse or stationary sprinkler head inside a plastic or metal cone which is designed to be permanently buried in the lawn surface as part of a permanent built-in lawn watering system. Water pressure pops the head up over the surface a few inches.

Revolving sprinkler (also known as *whirling, whirling head,* or *rotating sprinkler):* Two or four arms, parallel to the ground, that revolve and disperse water through nozzles at the tips of the arms. Most have simple sled bases and must be moved from area to area of the garden; some have spikes of various heights up to 4 feet. Most models can water a circle (some can do a square) up to about 50 feet in diameter (and down to a few feet, if you keep the water pressure low). *Traveling sprinklers,* revolving sprinkers on a wheeled base, have water-powered motors that move the sprinkler along as it waters, either following the hose pattern laid out and coiling up the hose as they go *(wind-up type)* or dragging the hose behind them *(tractor type).* These can water areas as large as 20,000 square feet.

Stationary sprinkler (also known as *fixed, hose-end,* or *static sprinkler):* No moving parts; the simplest model. There are some that resemble the rose heads found on the spouts of watering cans (see pages 228–29) called, if they protrude a bit, *turret sprinklers,* or showerhead-like *ring sprinklers;* others are simple devices that merely deflect the water coming out of a hose and have a 6-inch-long metal spike for staking in the ground, and may be called *spike sprinklers* (some spikes have steps for pushing them into the ground with your foot). The simplest models are either a 3½-inch-diameter cast-iron piece with a small hole in its top, called a *centrifugal sprinkler,* or a spray head made of two circles with eyelets for spiking the sprinkler in place, called a *double eyelet, twin dome,* or *twin spot sprinkler.* These all can

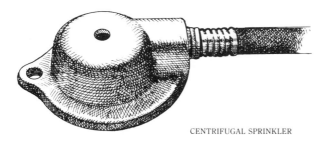

REVOLVING SPRINKLER

CENTRIFUGAL SPRINKLER

DOUBLE EYELET SPRINKLER

water an area from a few feet to 30 feet in diameter and in square or rectangular patterns, depending both on their design and on the water pressure.

USE: Watering lawns. Much better than hand-held nozzles, but not as efficient as soaker hoses or underground systems. With the wide variety of sprinklers on the market, it is easy to find one that sends out water in the same shape as the area to be watered. Stationary sprinklers are for the smallest areas.

USE TIPS: Sprinklers should be drained of water (or as much as can be drained) and stored in areas that do not freeze at the end of the season. Holes should be cleaned regularly to prevent clogging and assure an even spray. Adjust the volume of water that your sprinkler puts out to that which the soil can absorb easily. If it is delivered in too high a volume, much is not absorbed and the excess just runs off. On the other hand, too little water coming from the sprinkler just means that it takes longer to water the garden. Buy a rain gauge specifically designed for this or place a large open can, like a coffee can, in the range of the sprinkler as a measuring guide, and try to give your garden or lawn 1 inch of water per week. Be careful not to water foliage of plants susceptible to fungal problems.

BUYING TIPS: The better sprinklers are made of brass and stainless steel, while the cheaper plastic sprinklers are not as durable. Traveling sprinklers (the revolving type) are good for people who are unable to move the sprinkler around the lawn as needed or are not going to be present to do their own watering. However, these are among the more expensive models on the market. Some traveling sprinklers even shut off when the job is done. With oscillating sprinklers, look for those that have brass nozzles that screw into the holes along the oscillating tube. They can be easily cleaned, and replaced if they break; the end plug should be removable for cleaning, too. And they should have a filter to prevent clogging. Cheaper oscillating sprinklers hesitate at the extremes of each watering cycle, putting excess water down and causing puddles to form; make sure you get a model that is engineered to avoid this. The impulse type is the one most often used by professional gardeners. Look for models with many points of adjustment, such as a baffle plate to limit height, and part circle operation. Know the measurements of the areas you wish to water before buying—some can cover many thousands of square feet. If need be, look for one with an adjustable pattern. Try to find sprinklers that use as little water as possible, called *low gallonage sprinklers.*

WATER CONTROLLER

ALSO KNOWN AS: Water timer, water computer, water meter

DESCRIPTION: Small plastic box containing a meter that measures the volume of water flowing through, or the amount of time a faucet is open. Designed to be attached to a faucet with a female coupling end and to a hose with a male coupling end. Depending on the model, contains electronic or mechanical dials and indicators of settings.

USE: Automatic watering. Settings control turning on and shutting off water at predetermined times and/or volumes. Particularly useful for people who travel often. Electronic models can be set for multiple tasks over a long period of time; mechanical models are more like glorified oven timers and can be set only at the time of each watering to shut off automatically, usually within a range of two hours.

USE TIPS: The accuracy of a water controller is easily affected, so check the device by using buckets or a rain gauge (see page 222). The type of sprinkler you use may also affect the accuracy of the water meter settings. It is a good idea to get a *moisture sensor* as well, to prevent watering on rainy days.

BUYING TIPS: Better water meters have a bypass or override setting that allows you to set them for a continuous flow for manual watering, or to stop them on rainy days. Top models should have an *antihammer device* that prevents hammering (the knocking or rattling of pipes that occurs when water is suddenly shut off), which can damage your pipes.

WATERING CAN

ALSO KNOWN AS: Sprinkling can

ROSE

WATERING CAN

DESCRIPTION: Plastic or metal cans of a wide range of sizes (from 2 pints to 2 gallons) with a spout on one end and a handle on the other. The spout end is usually capped with a round or oval sprinkling head with many small holes, known as a *rose,* which can point either up or down; it either screws or slides on. *Long-reach watering cans* have spouts as long as 36 inches. A variation on this style, called a *watering box,* is a large boxlike container with a short, flexible hose. Handles and roses are sometimes made of brass.

USE: Light watering, such as that needed when setting out trans-

ROSE

LONG-REACH WATERING CAN

plants or watering in seeds. Also useful for applying liquid fertilizers. An oval rose that points up provides a gentle sprinkle for delicate seedlings and plants; it points down for other watering. A round rose that faces forward is an all-purpose head for watering established plants. A variation made for hanging plants is called a *hanging plant waterer* (see page 216). Watering boxes are for watering difficult-to-reach plants. Long-reach cans are useful in greenhouses, wide beds, or wherever plants are a bit hard to reach, or where you want to avoid watering the foliage and just get to the roots with fine spray.

USE TIPS: Metal cans, particularly those made of galvanized metal, should be dry when stored, as most eventually corrode if stored with water in them. Watering cans should not be used for applying any kind of pesticide—they should be used for water and fertilizer only. Plastic cans in particular might absorb any toxic chemical put in them. If you must apply pesticide this way, designate one watering can just for that purpose. The capacity of English-imported cans is noted in imperial gallons, which are about 1 pint larger than ours. Smaller cans are easier to use for hard-to-reach plants, especially those that are high up. Watering boxes are easily stored owing to their efficient shape.

BUYING TIPS: Plastic watering cans are usually cheaper than metal ones, and do the job well. Watering cans made from heavy-gauge galvanized steel (the best are treated with zinc chromate), which last very well when cared for, have been manufactured for more than fifty years and are still the most popular. Check to see if the seams are reinforced. Rose heads, especially brass ones that screw on, can be replaced with different types, and are therefore more desirable. Cans with long spouts tend to be better balanced; a crosspiece helps when carrying a full load. Brass and copper watering cans are attractive and very durable when they are kept clean and dry during storage, but are much more expensive. Always look for a well-balanced can that has a solid spout, the end of which should be at a higher point than the water level in order to prevent spilling. A collar around the top opening is further insurance against spilling. Unless you have only one or two plants to water, get something that holds at least a couple of quarts. Remember that large cans are quite heavy when filled and that they may not fit under your faucet for filling, so measure first.

WATER SIGNAL

DESCRIPTION: Small paperlike marker, about an inch high, with a point.

USE: Stuck in container soil to indicate if moisture is present or if the soil is dry, i.e., needs watering. Changes color accordingly from green to yellow.

WATER WAND

ALSO KNOWN AS: Spray wand, rain wand, garden soft spray, soft spray wand, soft sprayer, hose extender, hose extension, extension wand, showerhead nozzle, shower arm, water breaker, trigger-release lance, lance

DESCRIPTION: Watering and fertilizing device made of a lightweight metal pipe, from 1½ to about 3 feet long, that attaches to the end of a hose. On one end is a type of nozzle or spray head (or *rose),* and on the other is a grip with some type of water shutoff valve, often a pistol grip. Those designed for fertilizing as well as watering contain a clear plastic chamber on the grip end which delivers fertilizer diluted with the water that flows through the wand. Fertilizer is usually supplied by a solid *fertilizer tablet,* sold for a particular type of plant. Many water wands, such as the Gardena Watering System, have a variety of attachments that control the type of spray. The shortest models—16 inches—may be called *patio plant wands.*

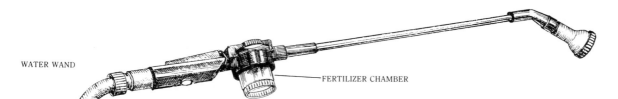

WATER WAND

FERTILIZER CHAMBER

USE: Watering hard-to-reach bed plants at soil level; applying foliar fertilizers.

USE TIPS: Keep the holes in the spray heads clean and unclogged. Drain water from the wand when storing. Change rubber washers in the connectors frequently to prevent leaks.

BUYING TIP: This is one gardening device where plastic does not signal poor quality.

WATER WICK

DESCRIPTION: Small, porous clay cone with length of wick material attached. Other versions incorporate a wick in a reservoir-type pot, or include cones as part of an irrigation network, like a drip irrigation system (see pages 212–13). On the other extreme are plain wicks (soft woven line not much different from a shoelace) that have one end hardened with a little plastic (again, like a shoelace).

USE: Continuous and unsupervised watering of houseplants. Wick end is placed in a bowl of water and the cone in the soil of a small plant container. Water is wicked into the soil as needed.

USE TIP: Start with moist soil. The amount of water that a wick can deliver is sufficient for maintenance, but not for soaking a whole pot of soil.

Fertilizing and Pest Control Equipment

ABOUT FERTILIZING AND PEST CONTROL EQUIPMENT

Keep in mind that the toxic chemicals in pesticides of all kinds should not be mixed with fertilizers or, in some cases, with each other. Equipment should be kept thoroughly cleaned and, in many cases, dedicated exclusively to the use of a particular pesticide (mark the containers well). Measuring cups used for pesticides should be treated with the same respect (some are made especially for this purpose). Nozzles, either *hollow cone* (circular spray pattern) or *flat fan* (flat oval spray pattern), should be removable for cleaning. Remember that dusts are applied with dusters, while wettable powders are dissolved in water to be applied as a liquid spray.

Most sprayed products, whether liquid or dust, should be applied only when there is very little wind. Always wear appropriate protective clothing and determine if a respirator or face mask is necessary.

BACKPACK PUMP SPRAYER

BACKPACK PUMP SPRAYER

ALSO KNOWN AS: Knapsack sprayer

DESCRIPTION: A metal or plastic rectangular tank worn on the back just like a backpack. Capacity ranges from 3½ to 5 gallons. Similar to the compression sprayer (see pages 233–34), but designed to be carried on your back instead of lifted by hand, permitting a larger capacity. A hose and wand with a nozzle on the end come out of the top, and a pressure lever comes out the bottom on one side or the other. The user holds the wand with one hand while pumping the pressure lever with the other hand.

USE: For heavy chemical application over large areas. Often used by professional foresters who need to spray large areas of forest and do not wish to be constantly refilling a smaller sprayer.

USE TIPS: Clean nozzles and tank well before storing. Because backpack sprayers hold more solution than others, do not put in more chemical than you really need for a given job. To do so is obviously wasteful and may even be dangerous, as the disposal of such a concentrated chemical is very difficult to do safely (the liquid is concentrated because it was intended to be sprayed, or dispersed lightly over a large area). If poured in one place, it may enter the water supply.

BUYING TIPS: Heavy duty—not often needed by home gardeners. You might consider this item if you have large wooded areas that require regular spraying, because it is more convenient than a compression type that you have to put down and pick up every time you change locations. Look for a large pumping handle, which is easier to use. Don't get too large a size: A gallon of water weighs about 8 pounds. Look for a model that can be easily converted to be used by either left-handed or right-handed people.

BARK SPUD

BARK SPUD

DESCRIPTION: Hand tool with a 2-by-4-inch flat metal blade, sharpened on its three sides, and a short wooden handle; overall length is about a foot. Usually solid-socket construction.

USE: Removing bark from dead or old trees or fence posts to eliminate insect attraction. Heavier models can be used like a big knife to hack off small branches and the like.

CAN SPRAYER

CAN SPRAYER

ALSO KNOWN AS: Bottle sprayer, hand sprayer, plunger duster, piston duster

DESCRIPTION: Hand-held sprayer consisting of a metal tube about 10 to 12 inches in length, into which a plunger is inserted, much like a bicycle pump. At the other end of the sprayer is a can or bottle that holds the chemical to be sprayed. Works with a pumping action, much like an atomizer. Some are *intermittent sprayers* (spray only on the forward motion) and others are *continuous sprayers* (spray steadily because of pressure built up from pumping).

USE: Spraying liquids, be they pesticides, fertilizers, detergents, water, or any other household or garden liquids.

USE TIPS: If the sprayer is used for toxic chemicals it should not be used for other things, especially not fertilizer or any foliar spray. Only oil-based sprays should be used in intermittent sprayers.

BUYING TIP: Look for models with adjustable nozzles that are easily cleaned and corrosion-resistant.

COMPRESSION SPRAYER

COMPRESSION SPRAYER

ALSO KNOWN AS: Pump sprayer, pump-type sprayer, compressed-air sprayer, pressure sprayer, sprayer/mister, hydraulic hand sprayer

DESCRIPTION: Metal or plastic tank, usually about 2 feet tall and about 8 inches in diameter, equipped with some kind of pump. Capacity ranges from 1 to 4 gallons of liquid, but 1½ gallons is typical. A short hose is attached to a wand with a spray head with an adjustable nozzle and a squeeze handle. Chemicals are mixed to the correct dilution rates before being poured into the tank. The sprayer is then closed and the pressure in the tank is pumped up by hand. Perhaps the most common type of sprayer. A smaller version, a *pressurized hand sprayer,* is a sturdy quart-sized plastic bottle in which compression is provided by a vertical hand pump knob on top, and a cordless electric model is now available as well.

USE: Applying chemicals to the garden or lawn, or in the case of the smaller ones, misting plants. Because of their light weight and portability, compression sprayers are used in areas of a garden beyond reach of a hose.

USE TIPS: Toxic substances should not be used in sprayers that are also used for fertilizers. Fine mist spraying should be done only on a windless day. Mix only the amount of chemical that you need and use it up completely before washing out the sprayer. Many plastic compression sprayers use a leather plunger cup (the disk that builds up the pressure when the sprayer is pumped) that needs to be kept oiled to ensure a tight fit and good pressure. If possible, take the sprayer apart to clean it. Don't ever leave a compression sprayer in the sun or near a heat source—it might explode, or in any case release its contents with much more pressure than you intend. Always let the pressure out when you are done using it.

BUYING TIPS: Plastic tanks can absorb chemicals; metal tanks do not. Plus, metal wears better. If you have a need for a compression sprayer only infrequently, or for very small amounts, the cheaper plastic types will probably be satisfactory, though there are a few excellent plastic makes on the market with permanently fused couplings and removable filters. Look for a nozzle with a setting that produces an extremely fine mist—you'll use less chemical. High pressures (up to 150 pounds) are helpful in creating fine mists.

HAND-CRANKED DUSTER

DUSTER

DESCRIPTION: Small plastic or metal housing with a container for pesticide and a pump or crank handle.

TYPES: *Pump duster* (also known as *hand pump* or *plunger duster):* Looks like a bicycle air pump, with a rigid tube instead of a hose. Capacity ranges from a few ounces to a few pounds.

Hand-cranked duster (also known as *crank, hand crank,* or *rotary duster):* Plastic or metal hopper with a crank on one side and a long, wide barrel. Squirrel-cage type fan. Capacity ranges from less than 1 to over 9 pounds. Tubes have flat ends for dispersal of dust, and may be supplied in various shapes and models.

USE: Dispersing dusts over foliage at close range (around 2 feet) in small gardens and greenhouses. Pumps are used for the most accurate applicators.

USE TIPS: Simple to operate, as most pesticide dusts can be used without mixing, especially as opposed to a sprayer, where they must be mixed with water for each use. However, dusters are not as accurate or efficient as liquid sprayers. Make sure you use them only when a wind is not blowing. Pump-type dusters can spray the undersides of leaves

BUYING TIP: Generally inexpensive. All parts should be noncorrosive.

FERTILIZER SIPHON

ALSO KNOWN AS: Hose-on

DESCRIPTION: Small metal or plastic device with female threads on both ends. Designed to be screwed onto a faucet and connected to a garden hose, with a small hose that comes out its side that is placed in a container of liquid fertilizer. The force of the water running from the faucet through the garden hose draws the fertilizer mixture into the flow through natural siphon action.

USE: A simple way to fertilize while watering. Especially useful when applying concentrated fertilizers, as it eliminates premixing.

USE TIPS: Should be clean of all products and dried for storage. Sometimes siphon devices can be used for applying pesticides, but those used for this purpose should never be used for fertilizing. The water to fertilizer ratio can range from 16 parts water to 1 part fertilizer, to 1 tablespoon of fertilizer per gallon of water that is being applied to the garden—so read the directions.

BUYING TIP: Siphons made of brass are usually better than those of plastic.

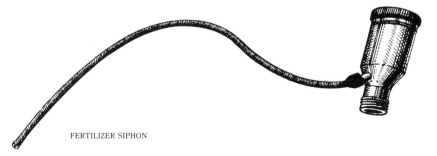

FERTILIZER SIPHON

HAND SPRAYER

HAND SPRAYER

ALSO KNOWN AS: Utility sprayer, pressure mister, sprayer/mister, plant mister, plant sprayer, trigger sprayer, sprayer dispenser, all-purpose sprayer

DESCRIPTION: From pint- to quart-sized plastic or metal bottle with trigger spray head, adjustable from a wide, fine mist to a coarse spray to a steady stream of liquid. An adjustable model that makes mist only is called a *mister.* The pumping action of the trigger sucks up the liquid from the bottom through a small tube. Triggers and longer tubes are sold separately for dispensing from your own gallon containers.

USE: Spraying water or anything mixed with it, such as fertilizers or pesticides, in small quantities and at targeted areas. Good for misting tropical plants. Not bad for wetting clothes when ironing, either (just make sure that there are no unwanted chemicals inside when you start on your fine garments).

USE TIPS: Don't mix fertilizers and pesticides. If you ever use these for strong chemicals, note this on a label and try to use the container for this only.

BUYING TIPS: Prices vary widely—this should be an inexpensive item. However, better ones can be taken apart for cleaning.

HERBICIDE APPLICATOR

POPULAR BRAND NAME: Killer Kane

DESCRIPTION: Yard-long plastic tube with small plunger on one end. Herbicide tablet is inserted into tube that is then filled with water; when plunger is pushed in by pushing the tube down onto it, herbicide is released. The amount that is released with each "hit" is adjustable.

USE: Accurate application of herbicide to dandelions and crabgrass in a lawn.

BUYING TIP: One of the safer and more economical ways to apply herbicide, as nothing is likely to go astray of the intended target.

HERBICIDE APPLICATOR

HOSE-END SPRAYER

HOSE-END SPRAYER

ALSO KNOWN AS: Hose sprayer, lawn and garden sprayer (incorrect—too general)

DESCRIPTION: Glass or plastic container with spray nozzle (usually made of plastic) built into a top designed to be attached to the male end of a hose. Like a big atomizer, the container holds the product to be sprayed. There is some type of valve to control the outflow, and while most nozzles on these sprayers are set to disperse the mixture only at a certain ratio, some nozzles can be adjusted to change the ratio of the product to water. The nozzle usually controls the type of spray as well. Should contain an antisiphon backflow-preventer device so chemicals don't get sucked back into the home water supply should there be a drop in water pressure. The container may hold only a pint or two, but the solution is made from a concentrate that can be diluted to make up to about 100 gallons of chemical spray. Many chemical products are now available in plastic containers with caps that act as disposable hose-end sprayers. Those designed for use with fertilizers are larger than those intended for pesticides.

USE: Spraying concentrated fertilizers or pesticides, depending on the design.

USE TIPS: Sprayers that are used for pesticides should not be used for fertilizers. Containers and nozzles should be washed thoroughly and dried after each use. Follow the dilution ratio carefully for the sprayer and chemical product you are using.

BUYING TIPS: Inexpensive and efficient product. Determining the correct dilution rate is often the most difficult part of using these sprayers, so purchase a sprayer with clear instructions and measurement marks on the container that are easy to read. Sprayers that have nozzles which can change the dilution ratio cost more, but may be worth the price. Glass containers may be breakable, but they do not absorb the chemicals that are put into them. Inexpensive and very helpful. Products in disposable hose-end sprayers are very convenient but, because they are prediluted, are likely to cost more per use.

SOIL TEST KIT

DESCRIPTION: A wide variety of kits are on the market, with an equally wide range of prices and types. Some are electronic probes *(pH meters)*, some are paper products (usually *litmus tests)*, some are elaborate portable laboratories with test tubes, filters, funnels, and testing chemicals for over five hundred tests, and some are low-priced kits that test only for one nutrient at a time. A professional accessory is a *soil probe* or *soil core sampler*, a long tube with a large T-handle for taking core samples of soil.

USE: Testing soil for pH (degree of acidity or alkalinity) and, in the cases of the more advanced kits, nutrients. The end result guides you in your choice of fertilizers and soil conditioners in your effort to build the right soil for your garden. Directions are supplied with each kit, but typically you dig out a small sample of soil and mix it with water and the various chemicals supplied, then watch for it to turn a particular color. Litmus paper tests are made by simply putting the paper in contact with the soil and waiting for it to turn a color that indicates a particular pH level.

USE TIPS: Follow directions carefully, and take soil samples properly. Most tests require that you dry out your soil first, which may take a few days. The most inexpensive probe-type meters may be inaccurate—back up your readings with a full test.

BUYING TIPS: For the average gardener, it is easier and more accurate to send a soil sample to your local Cooperative Extension office (see appendix C), though some of the tests, like the meter or litmus paper roll, are very simple to use.

TROMBONE SPRAYER

ALSO KNOWN AS: Slide-type sprayer, slide sprayer, slide pump sprayer, lance, spray lance

DESCRIPTION: A type of pump consisting of two tubes, one inserted in the other, which are pushed and pulled apart. (The British term for the spraying tube is *lance.*) One end of the

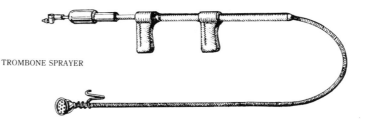

TROMBONE SPRAYER

sprayer is attached to a hose that is placed in the container of the chemical being sprayed. The pushing and pulling of the cylinders builds up pressure that then propels a long stream out of the sprayer. The pump works with both the push and pull stroke, making for an even spray. The nozzle can be adjusted to emit anything from a fine mist to a long jet.

USE: Spraying trees or tall shrubbery. These have the longest reach of all the sprayers.

USE TIP: Keep nozzles cleaned and moving parts well oiled. Empty and clean completely before storing.

BUYING TIPS: The best of the trombone sprayers is made of brass, with the nozzles also of brass. Some models have a grip-type handle attached to both of the sliding tubes that makes it easier to pump.

Composting and Mulching Equipment

COMPOST
AERATOR TOOL

ABOUT COMPOSTING AND MULCHING EQUIPMENT

The following products are sold at many garden centers to help the gardener recycle organic material that all too often is simply thrown away or to process material into an easily decomposable state.

COMPOST AERATOR TOOL

ALSO KNOWN AS: Compost tool, aerator

POPULAR BRAND NAME: Compostool

DESCRIPTION: A 30-inch metal shaft with a T-handlebar about 12 inches long, usually with vinyl grips. The tip has small hinged paddles that fold up flat when the tool is inserted into a compost bin or pile. The paddles open up to turn the compost as the tool is pulled and twisted out of the bin.

USE: To open, aerate, and turn a compost pile. The tool is considerably easier to use than a fork.

USE TIP: Keep clean and dry when not in use. Use every few days.

BUYING TIP: Check around, as the same tool may be sold at different places at prices ranging from $13 to $20.

COMPOST BIN

COMPOST BIN

ALSO KNOWN AS: Composter

DESCRIPTION: Wood, solid metal, wire, or plastic container where organic material, such as leaves, grass clippings, and kitchen garbage, is kept during the process of decomposition. Many ingenious designs have been developed around the world for the purpose of making compost. Some plastic bins resemble barrels or large garbage cans with vented sides. A drum version, called a *compost tumbler,* is mounted on a metal frame, allowing the drum to revolve and turn the compost, which speeds up the decomposition action without your having to use a fork or other tool. The simplest model is just a large, vented, heavy-duty garbage bag. Composters usually are covered to keep out rain, and have holes that ensure air circulation and ventilation, a necessity for proper decomposition. Sides afford an element of insulation, increasing the heat within, and have some sort of opening for easy removal of compost.

USE: Contains both compost and the heat compost generates (from the bacteria breaking down the organic matter); certain designs (the drum models) facilitate the composting process with movement and any design with a cover helps keep the compost dry. Most can make compost in around twenty-one days.

USE TIPS: Place on a level surface, and make sure it is located in a place convenient for the continuous addition of raw material. Core temperatures may be over 160° F, so be careful to keep it away from any materials, organic or inorganic, that should not be exposed to such levels of heat.

BUYING TIPS: Because of all the competition and innovation in this field, be sure to shop extensively for the best deal. Drum-type models should revolve easily; some of the better models hold as much as 18 bushels. Popular commercial models go for around $100, but many garden books have designs for bins you can build yourself. Perhaps the easiest are either made from a cylinder of wire mesh or by cutting holes in a 30-gallon garbage can. Still, the more refined models do speed up the process and require less room and effort than the cruder homemade versions. Look for something that is easy to remove the compost from, and easy to stir up.

COMPOST STARTER

ALSO KNOWN AS: Compost maker

DESCRIPTION: Bacteria and other microscopic soil organisms in a powder form, sold in containers (2 pounds is typical) as well as tablets. Some brands are for composting specific materials only, such as for leaves or grass clippings.

USE: Added to the compost pile or bin to speed up the process of decomposition and to assure a balanced blend of essential nutrients.

USE TIP: Use the appropriate amount for the size of your compost bin and wet in well.

BUYING TIP: Compost starters are available under a variety of trade names, so shop around. Prices vary a great deal, and smaller packages may or may not be a bad deal, depending on how much compost can be created per pound of the product used—some 2-pound boxes make half a ton of compost, others make 2½ tons; one brand's 6-ounce package is good for "tons" of compost, and so on.

GARDEN SIEVE

GARDEN SIEVE

ALSO KNOWN AS: Soil sieve, riddle (British term)

DESCRIPTION: A steel mesh screen strung over a rectangular or round frame, with legs in the case of larger models, or merely a plastic tub with an open grid for a bottom. The frame may be made of plastic, metal, or wood. Before they were commercially manufactured, gardeners made their own sieves from ¼ inch galvanized mesh (such as hardware cloth) nailed to a wooden box frame. One type, called a *Roto-Sieve,* has a crank on its top, sort of like an oversized flour sifter/turntable.

USE: Sifting out large particles from compost before using it in flower beds or soil mixes.

USE TIP: If compost is too wet, it is sticky and does not sift well. Compost should be moderately dry and crumbly for sifting.

BUYING TIPS: Look for a sturdy, well-made sieve constructed from material that will not rust. You may wish to have a couple of sieves with different mesh sizes. On the other hand, it is not difficult to make your own, and a flour sieve is good for small quantities of very fine soils, needed for indoor seed starting.

SHREDDER

SHREDDER AND CHIPPER

ALSO KNOWN AS: Mulcher, grinder

DESCRIPTION: Gasoline or electric motor with a cutting mechanism contained inside a chute, into which you feed leaves or branches.

A *shredder* has a spinning interior drum with small *hammers* (known as the *hammer mills system)* or nylon lines called *flails* that break up organic material when it comes in contact with them. Shredders work well on leaves, small twigs, and other light plant material. They tend to be small, consisting of a plastic or metal tube, about a foot and a half in diameter, on legs that make them waist high, with a ¼ or ½ horsepower electric motor. Some popular models weigh about 15 pounds and can be placed directly over a plastic bag, garbage can, or compost pile. They can reduce eight large trash bags of leaves to one.

Chippers are armed with a blade or many blades that transform heavier woody material, including large branches, into a load of chips. These tend to be large and some models can be enormous, almost industrial machines.

Shredder/chippers are machines that shred leaves and other plant material as well as chip woody material. Machines that are sold as shredder/chippers usually work with some type of blade mechanism, but some machines have two separate chutes, one for shredding and one for chipping, with both hammers and blade(s).

USE: Shredding and chipping garden debris, both to rid the garden of large piles and to create raw material for compost (the smaller pieces) or mulch (the larger pieces). Shredded compost material decomposes much more rapidly than if left whole.

USE TIPS: Shredders and chippers can be hazardous machines, and safety precautions should be followed strictly, such as using goggles and gloves and keeping hands away from the blades and hammers. Wear tight-fitting clothes to prevent anything from getting caught in the mechanism. Don't force a machine to chip larger branches than it is intended to accommodate.

BUYING TIPS: Most gardeners can get by with one of the smaller electric shredder/chippers unless they have a large estate. Shredder/chippers at bargain prices are probably not a good buy—expect to pay $100 to over $200 for a well-built, versatile, reliable machine. Twelve- to 16-gauge steel is a sign of quality, as opposed to sheet metal. Look for safety features such as lids and baffles or feeding chutes that make it impossible to insert your hand near the cutting devices (these features include small diameter chutes, or chutes longer than your arm, and the like). Check out the size of the shredding hopper, the height of the shredder section, and the maximum diameter wood it can take—in short, the ease of feeding. Narrow feeder chutes are safer but slower to use. This is a major purchase, so ask for a demonstration of the machine you are considering. Wheeled units are more convenient to use. Look also for cleaning access.

WORMS

ALSO KNOWN AS: Red wigglers, *Lumbricus rubellus,* bed run worms

DESCRIPTION: Red earthworms, usually around 6 to 8 inches in length.

USE: Help break down kitchen scraps and other compost material rapidly. Result is known euphemistically as *worm castings* (see page 12) and is an excellent soil conditioner.

USE TIP: Prepare a tub with plenty of vegetable scraps and composting material before purchasing these worms. Check a book on organic gardening for information on raising them.

BUYING TIP: Though available through mail-order firms, the survival rate of the worms is higher if you can purchase them from a garden center. Fish bait shops are an alternative source.

Lawn and Yard Care Equipment

AERATOR

ALSO KNOWN AS: Soil digger

DESCRIPTION: A long-handled metal tool with two or four hardened steel spikes on the working end and a crossbar grip. The spike end is forced into the soil by stepping on the tool, much as one would a shovel.

TYPES: *Sod coring aerator:* Spikes are hollow tubes that remove plugs of earth when forced into the lawn.
   Spiked (or *spike) disk* (or *disc) aerator:* Consists of a disk with numerous spikes protruding from it that is

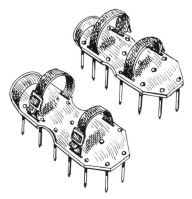

LAWN AERATOR SANDALS

rolled over a lawn by pulling or pushing, by hand or with a small tractor.

Lawn aerator sandals: Spiked platforms that are strapped onto your shoes like roller skates and worn while you walk around the lawn (such as while mowing).

USE: Opening up sections of lawn where the soil has become compacted by traffic or nature, or for cultivating heavy soils without disturbing the soil structure. Also may kill some grubs.

USE TIPS: Hollow tube spikes should be kept open; remove any plug of soil that becomes trapped in them. Remember to remove aerator sandals from your feet before entering your house—they're not great for floors.

BUYING TIP: If the entire lawn is in need of aeration, it is time to consider tilling and reseeding or sodding. The spiked disk aerators cost more than most gardeners can justify.

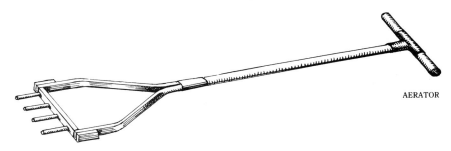

AERATOR

BAGS AND ACCESSORIES

ALSO KNOWN AS: Lawn and leaf bags, garbage bags

DESCRIPTION: Large black, gray, white, brown, or green plastic bags, varying in thickness from 1 to 4 mil and with an average capacity of about 6 bushels or 30 gallons, the size of a standard large garbage can. Available up to 55-gallon capacity. Some brands are enormous, up to 45 by 96 inches, sometimes called *banana bags*. Now available in biodegradable plastic. Accessories include a plastic hoop, about 2 feet in diameter, which clamps onto the edge of the opening of the bag to hold it open for loading, and a stand or small two-wheel cart, or caddie, similar to a baggage cart, which holds the hoop and bag. Enormous plastic bins that look like giant garbage cans are used by professional landscapers, but can be found in some garden centers, especially those that have their own landscaping business. They are usually green.

USE: Bagging leaves, grass, or garden clippings for disposal. Hoops and carts make the process more efficient, especially for people who have trouble lifting large objects. Biodegradable bags are required in some communities where they are trying to cut down on landfill debris.

USE TIPS: If you are planning to use plastic bags for hedge trimmings, be sure to cut the branches into very small pieces or they will pierce the bags and prevent you from filling them with any appreciable quantity. When disposing of concrete or plaster rubble, or gravel fill, just put a little in each bag so you can handle them easily.

BUYING TIP: Professional bins are not all that expensive. 1.5 mil bags are light and tear easily; 3 or 4 mil is heavy duty. Look for bags with no seams. A reusable alternative to bags is a 7- or 10-foot-square piece of reinforced plastic or burlap, with handles, which lays flat on the ground while you sweep or rake leaves and garden refuse onto it; the corners are easily gathered together for transportation. These are often sold in packages as *totes,* or *burlap squares* (see page 284).

BLOWER

BLOWER

ALSO KNOWN AS: Leaf blower, blower/vac

DESCRIPTION: Electric- or gasoline-powered 5 to 10 horsepower motor with a large tube or accordion hose attached, much like a powerful canister vacuum cleaner with the hose attached to the outflow vent. Some of the smaller blowers are designed to be hand held and are more often powered by electricity (some also may have shoulder straps). Cordless models are available, and may be called *electric brooms.* Larger (usually gas-powered) blowers designed to fit on the back with straps are known as *backpack blowers.* The largest are wheeled contraptions resembling lawn mowers. A number of attachments that resemble large vacuum cleaner heads fit onto the hose; some work as misters or sprayers. A variation of the blower is the *power wand,* a multipurpose tool with the motor at the ground end that has a blower attachment, though certain models have *gutter cleanout* attachments. Some are convertible to vacuums, complete with a cart for the leaf bag.

USE: Blowing away leaves, debris, water on patios and tennis courts, and even light snow, as a substitute for a vigorous sweeping, shoveling, or raking. Vacuums can pick up light debris like leaves and some models shred them for mulch. Replaces both rake and broom for the handicapped or gardeners with bad backs.

USE TIPS: Wear goggles and ear protectors when operating a blower. The latter are especially important if you are operating a powerful gasoline-driven blower, which is quite noisy (and is banned in some areas). Never point the nozzle of a blower toward people.

BUYING TIPS: If you want to blow debris and leaves from beds but leave the mulch, look for one of the less powerful blowers, probably an electric one. If you have heavy leaf work to do, consider the more powerful gasoline-powered blowers. Look for a 16-gauge cord on electric blowers, and adjustable speed. The throttle should fit your hand; some models are adapted for left-handed users. Air speed is one feature by which to measure blowers, if you need to compare. Those who garden in small spaces can find little justification for the expense of this power tool in any case. Test them to get the feel, first. Certain models have the power unit at ground level, which may be harder to use because of clogging with leaves. Electric models are much quieter and vibrate less than gas-powered models. Shop around—there is much competition here. Prices can range from $25 to $75 for average models up to over $150 for very powerful ones.

LAWN ROLLER

ALSO KNOWN AS: Roller

DESCRIPTION: Large metal or plastic drum, usually from 14 to 24 inches in diameter and from 2 to 3 feet wide, with a handle attached so it can be pushed or pulled. Today's rollers are hollow and are designed to be filled with water when they are used, making them lighter to transport and store. Old-fashioned ones were filled with cement, and were often homemade.

USE: Preparing a lawn for seeding or sodding or for rolling out sod after it is planted to ensure good root contact with the soil.

USE TIPS: Roll a seedbed both horizontally and vertically to ensure a smooth, level surface. Adjust the amount of water to a weight that compacts the soil properly—when walking on the lawn after rolling, you should leave slight footprints.

BUYING TIP: Rent a roller instead of buying one, unless you are likely to reseed a lawn or seedbed regularly.

LAWN ROLLER

LAWN SWEEPER

LAWN SWEEPER

ALSO KNOWN AS: Push-type lawn sweeper, lawn sweep

DESCRIPTION: A long drum about 8 inches in diameter and 20 to 30 inches long, fitted around an axle, with rows of bristles and two wheels on either end. A canvas hopper trails behind to catch leaves or grass clippings that are thrown back by the bristles when the sweeper is pushed over the lawn. The handle holds or is part of the hopper and may be attached directly to the wheels. Hoppers hold 6 to 9 bushels of debris. Some larger models are designed to be towed behind a riding mower or lawn tractor.

USE: Cleaning up grass clippings and leaves.

USE TIPS: Keep all metal parts cleaned and oiled. Sweepers work best on level and dry lawns.

BUYING TIPS: A good lawn sweeper is a definite labor advantage over raking and much quieter than a blower. Sweepers with handles attached directly to the wheels are sturdier. The hopper floors of better sweepers are made of steel or fiberglass to reduce wear and friction. Narrower models do a better job on uneven terrain.

PUSH BROOM

DESCRIPTION: Push-type brooms with large bristled heads mounted to long wooden or fiberglass handles.

TYPES: *Heavy-duty broom* (also known as *street, street sweeper type, barn,* or *outdoor broom):* Fourteen- to 18-inch-wide head, usually with two sets of five rows of tough fiber bristles, sometimes over 6 inches long. This is what you see used by professional street sweepers. Bristles made of African basswood, palmyra stalks, or plastic, and are suitable for wet or dry use.

Sidewalk-and-garage broom: At 18 to 24 inches, wider than the heavy-duty model, with shorter palmyra fiber bristles about 4 inches long. A steel version with plastic bristles is available for caked-up dirt or debris, in models up to 36 inches wide. Made for wet or dry use.

Floor broom: More finished wooden head than the above types, with Tampico fiber or plastic bristles usually around 3 inches long. Eighteen to 24 inches wide.

Porch-and-patio broom (also known as *lawn broom):*
One-foot-wide steel head with stiff 3-inch-long plastic
bristles.

USE: Sweeping patios, terraces, garages, walks, and driveways.
Also for sweeping clippings and leaves from thick, well-mowed
lawns.

USE TIPS: Store brooms with the bristles up to prevent them
from getting bent. Move the handle to the opposite side if the
bristles are worn on one side.

BUYING TIPS: A good push broom is reinforced where the handle
is attached to the head, usually with a metal shank screwed to
the handle. Handles that are just stuck into a hole in the head
are likely to work loose. Braces can be purchased separately.

REEL MOWER

ALSO KNOWN AS: Push mower; push-reel, hand-reel, hand-push-
reel, or power-reel mower; beater bar type mower; cylinder
mower

DESCRIPTION: Five to eight curved blades, 14 to 18 inches long,
mounted on a reel approximately the same size as the large
wheels found on either of its ends. The blades rotate as the
mower is moved, cutting grass as they are drawn over a stationary blade (the "bed knife"), like a pair of giant scissors. This was
the conventional design for all home lawn mowers before rotary
power mowers were introduced after World War II. The reel
mowers available today are lighter than ever and the handles are
made from metal instead of wood. The power reel mower has
the same basic design, but is driven by a gasoline engine above
the reel. Most models are easily adjusted to different cutting
heights.

USE: Cutting grass that is not too long. Manual reel mowers are
ideal for cutting small lawns, such as those in urban areas. And
they are quiet. Models with fewer blades are fine for mowing
bluegrass and creeping fescues; more blades are suggested for
Southern types, such as Bermudagrasses.

REEL MOWER

USE TIPS: The reel mower works quite well if the blades are kept sharp, producing a superior, more efficient cut than that provided by a power rotary mower, which cuts only with the tips of its blades. The bed knife should be adjusted so that the entire length of the cutting blade makes contact with it when the mower is pushed. To check the bed knife, insert a piece of paper between the blade and the bed knife. It is well adjusted if the paper is cut the full length of the blades when the reel is turned. Reel mowers are better suited to lawns that are mowed regularly, as they do not cut tall grass well.

BUYING TIPS: Look for a reel mower that is lightweight but still well made. Power reel mowers are preferred by many gardeners and turf specialists because they cut grass cleaner than rotary mowers (see next entry) owing to their scissorlike cutting action. Make sure that the mowing height can be adjusted. Manual reel mowers are more easily stored than power mowers, and use no fuels—other than refreshments for the person doing the pushing. Look for all-steel construction.

ROTARY MOWER

DESCRIPTION: Either an electric or gasoline motor mounted on a metal casing below which rotates a propellerlike blade with a diameter of 18 to 24 inches. Mostly gasoline powered, rotary mowers are the most common design of power mowers today. Electric mowers may be either battery-driven or plugged into an outlet by a long cord. Battery-powered mowers run for about forty-five minutes on a charge. Gasoline mowers are driven by either a two-cycle or four-cycle engine with an average strength of 3 to 4 horsepower.

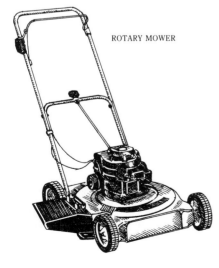

ROTARY MOWER

TYPES: *Walk-behind* (also known as *walking mower):* The most common type. The higher-priced gasoline rotary mowers are usually self-propelled (that is, the motor not only turns the blade but drives the wheels as well), while the less expensive ones must be pushed. Smaller models have flip-over handles, which save you from having to turn the mower around at the end of each pass. Mowing height on most models can be adjusted. Some models either can be converted to or are *mower-mulchers* that cut the grass clippings very finely so they can settle down on the soil where they act as a mulch that decomposes and returns nitrogen to the soil. If you don't cut your grass often, however, you may want to rake them up or bag them because long clippings tend to mat. Two basic bagging designs are made: *rear bagging,* in which the grass clippings are spewed into a bag that hangs from the handles of the mower, or *side-discharge,* which spews them onto the lawn or a side-mounted bag.

Riding mowers (also known as *lawn tractors):* Self-propelled mowers that you sit on and drive. Often rotary types and usually feature the blade housing, or *mower deck,* under the seat, but some, called *front-cut mowers,* have the blade housing in front, making for a more maneuverable mower that can also cut underneath fences, bushes, and trees. The width of cut usually ranges from 26 to 42 inches. In all cases, a *grass catcher,* usually a canvas and metal or plastic container that trails along behind the mower, is a recommended accessory for catching the clippings. There is as much competition among manufacturers of riding mowers as there is for automobiles, it seems—with as many features to choose from: width, clutch, automatic transmission (hydrostatic drive), control panel, steering (wheel or levers), diesel engine, engine access for maintenance, four-wheel steering, warranties, and the number of optional attachments, like snow blowers. These are a matter of personal choice.

Nylon string mower (also known as *trimmer/mower):* The newest type of mower is quite different from standard rotary models. This is a large string trimmer (see pages 208–209) on wheels, and may be either gas- or electric-powered. It does not have a metal blade but rather a rapidly spinning nylon cord. This design may prove to be a safer lawn mower to use. Another new string type is a *floating mower,* which actually floats on a cushion of air and has no wheels. After a long, hot day mowing a large lawn with a heavy, conventional mower, many gardeners wish to float, too, for which a large swimming pool is recommended; at that point, they themselves might be considered yet another type of "floating mower."

USE: Cutting lawns, especially larger lawns with long grass (stemming from extended time between mowings). Riding mowers are helpful when you have more than ¾ acre to mow.

USE TIPS: Keep the blades of rotary mowers sharp, or else the grass will be beaten and bruised instead of cut. The oil in gasoline-powered mowers that have reservoirs is essential to their operation, and should be checked regularly and changed completely once during the mowing season. The rotating blade is extremely dangerous and capable of slinging stones, so safety precautions should be followed when using these mowers such as wearing shoes, long pants, and keeping children away. Rear bagging–type mowers allow you to maneuver a bit more easily, but leave the grass catcher off if you mow often: Grass clippings are a good source of nutrients. Always determine the best length for your grass, and keep in mind that much damage comes from cutting it too short.

BUYING TIPS: The electric or battery-powered rotary mowers are best suited to small lawns that are mowed regularly. Gasoline-powered rotary mowers capable of cutting tall or tough grasses are generally heavier duty than electric mowers. Self-propelled mowers are helpful for large hilly areas or for people who have trouble pushing. Some gasoline-powered mowers come with push-button electronic ignition instead of pull-cord starters, but you pay dearly for this convenience. Check to see how comfortable the controls are. When buying any model, but especially the larger ones, be sure that you understand which attachments are standard and which must be purchased as extras. *Leaf shredders* are one of the most useful attachments for those gardeners who have lots of trees. Look for blades that are attached to the drive shaft with a *half-moon key,* or *Woodruff key*—it will shear off if you hit a big object, instead of severely damaging the entire drive shaft and engine. Although two-cycle engines are better for hilly terrains owing to their lighter weight, the choice is largely one of size: of lawn and of mower, as well as of the person doing the work. Two-cycle engines are smaller and lighter, but four-cycle engines are more efficient.

Look for the following safety features: a rear deflector, which is a hinged flap on the rear of the mower that stops flying rocks and sticks from hitting you; a similar deflection guard at the grass-clipping discharge opening; and a well-placed exhaust system and muffler—namely, away from the grass catcher bag. All-steel construction is best.

Wide selections of riding mowers may be found at specialized outdoor equipment dealers; many garden centers do not sell riding mowers because this requires another expertise and maintenance capability, as well as a lot of space. Be sure to buy equipment from a reputable dealer with a well-known service department. Avoid buying from dealers who are only into power equipment a little bit: They may not be able to service you promptly or well. Front-cutting riding mowers are more expensive. With all riding mowers, check to see what other attachments, such as snow blowers, are available, and how easy it is

SOD TAMPER

to attach or remove them. The turning radius is an important point of comparison (less is better). Above all, test-drive the mower to see how it feels.

SOD TAMPER

ALSO KNOWN AS: Lawn tamper, tamper

DESCRIPTION: Heavy, flat metal square of about 8 to 10 inches, with a 4-foot-long perpendicular handle in the middle. Models vary in weight from around 11 to 25 pounds.

USE: Leveling and tamping down sod after it is planted, seedbeds before seeding, or sand and gravel before pouring concrete or laying brick. Does many of the same jobs a roller does (see page 246).

USE TIP: Work in an overlapping pattern to ensure a smooth and level surface.

BUYING TIP: Unless you are a professional sod layer, or doing it for a lot of neighbors, this tool may be better to rent than to buy.

SPREADER

ALSO KNOWN AS: Seed sower, seeder (these two names are used only when the spreader is used to broadcast seed), lawn spreader

DESCRIPTION: Hand-operated device carried like a front pack, or a cartlike device pushed over the lawn like a lawn mower, both of which have hoppers made of steel, structural foam plastic, regular plastic, or canvas.

TYPES: *Broadcast spreader* (also known as *rotary* or *rotary broadcast spreader):* Canvas or metal hopper that holds material to be broadcast, below which is a ridged, revolving, circular disk. There are two basic types—hand-driven and wheeled. The hand-driven broadcast spreader, also known as a *shoulder* or *hand spreader,* is suspended from the shoulder by straps and the broadcast platform is turned by a hand crank on the side as you walk along. The wheeled model, called a *push* or *rotary broadcast spreader,* is similar (and much more common), except that the hopper is on a metal cart and the broadcast platform is turned by the movement of the wheels as it is pushed. Hoppers on wheeled spreaders can be tall

BROADCAST SPREADER

DROP SPREADER

cylinders, holding as much as 5 gallons or 60 pounds. Spreads material as wide as 30 feet.

Drop spreader (also known as *wheel drop spreader):* Two-wheel cartlike device that drops the material through an opening in the bottom as the spreader is pushed over the lawn. A control lever that opens (to a particular size) and closes the drop mechanism is located on the handle of the spreader. Spreads material only to the width of the hopper, about 20 inches. Capacity of the hopper ranges up to 75 pounds.

Organic spreader (also known as *manure spreader):* Perforated steel drum, about 2½ cubic feet capacity, that holds manure or other organic material. Holes are cut so there is either 48 or 63 percent open space through which the material falls as you roll it over your lawn or garden.

USE: Spreading fertilizer, seed, lime, pesticide, or other powdered or pelleted materials over a garden, field, or lawn.

USE TIPS: Broadcast spreaders tend to concentrate the material near the spreader. Because of this, it is important to overlap when broadcasting to get an even coverage. Drop spreaders disperse material more regularly and evenly than the broadcast spreaders, so it is important *not* to overlap. On the other hand, drop spreaders cover less ground with each pass than broadcast spreaders; they are more accurate but more work. Spreaders should be cleaned and oiled after each use.

ORGANIC SPREADER

BUYING TIPS: Broadcast spreaders are more efficient for large areas because they scatter seed and other material over a wider space. However, drop spreaders are more reliable in the amount and the evenness of material dispersed, making them a marginally better buy. Be sure to check that the spreader you purchase can handle the types of material you are using. Plastic spreaders are more rust-resistant. Many larger professional models are available for gardeners with extremely large areas to cover. Look for models with easily operated gates. Steel bargain models are likely to corrode very quickly and should be avoided.

Starting Products and Gardening Aids

Seed Starting Products

ABOUT SEED STARTING PRODUCTS

In late winter and early spring, about the same time that the seed displays begin to make their annual appearance, garden center shelves contain bags of starter soils, seed flats, seed flat heaters, light units, peat pots, soil blockers, and myriad other products to help you start your own plants from seed. Most gardeners find growing plants from seed a fun, not to mention therapeutic, activity in late winter. Perhaps because it is often done in the house, or because it is more of a hobby than a utilitarian job, there is enormous competition in this area, resulting in a bewildering variety of types and models and packaged sets. Chances are there is a specialized product for any problem you might encounter in this delicate work.

AUTOMATIC TIMER

DESCRIPTION: Clock mechanism that is plugged into an electrical outlet. Many different types are available. The simplest are mechanical—just a twenty-four-hour clock dial and box with a plug—and the most sophisticated are electronic, capable of controlling a number of devices at once.

USE: Remote, automatic control of electrical devices, such as growing lights. Turns the light unit on automatically in the morning and shuts it off in the evening.

USE TIP: If you are using light units for growing seedlings, set the timer to simulate the day length at the time of the year that the seeds would germinate and grow outdoors. For example, if you are growing seed indoors in February that would normally be sown outside in April or May, set your timer for the April and May day length and not the shorter February time.

BUYING TIP: Check around before purchasing a timer. Good timers may not cost as much as bad ones, so be sure to ask for advice before making your choice.

CAPILLARY WATERER

DESCRIPTION: Variety of designs that consist of a large reservoir of water that is delivered as needed to pots by capillary action via a spongelike mat *(capillary matting)* or wicks. Most waterers have a tray covered with channels for the water; the mat sits on top of the channels and the pots are set on top of the mat. The reservoir may look like a coffee urn.

USE: Long-term, consistent watering of seedlings.

USE TIPS: Make sure the tray is on a level surface. Experiment to determine the rate and volume of water your plants require.

BUYING TIP: Often used with houseplants by people who travel for long periods.

HEATING CABLE

ALSO KNOWN AS: Heating wire, soil cable

DESCRIPTION: Electrical wire, covered with lead and hooked into a thermostat, that is pluged directly into a grounded electrical outlet.

USE: Placed under soil in seed flats (see page 262) to control the temperature when starting delicate seedlings.

USE TIPS: Though the wire is covered with lead to protect it and you from electrical shock, you should be careful when digging near a heating cable with metal tools. It is important that the heating cable be attached to an electrical plug with a third prong for grounding, and that this be plugged into a properly grounded outlet. Note that if a grounding adapter is used, the short green wire must be screwed into the wall outlet. Be sure to bury the thermostat in the ground.

BUYING TIP: The less expensive heating cables have thermostats that are part of the cable, while the more expensive ones have thermostats that are separate from the cable. The latter is the safer design.

HEATING MAT

ALSO KNOWN AS: Heat mat, propagation heat mat

DESCRIPTION: Two rubber mats with electric heating wires sandwiched between them. The heating wires are attached to a thermostat that is in turn plugged into an electrical outlet. Supplied with transformer for low-voltage current. Usually rectangular, but available in long and narrow shapes for windowsills.

USE: Providing consistent, gentle bottom heat, essential to good seed germination.

USE TIP: Thermostats may not be accurate. It is a good idea to insert a thermometer into the seed flat itself to check the temperature of the flat and adjust the thermostat accordingly. Check your gardening books for ideal temperatures.

BUYING TIP: Do not buy a heating mat that does not come with a thermostat. Many gardeners have grown plants from seed for years without a heating mat with thermostat, but many experienced gardeners swear by them. If the conditions under which you are growing plants from seed do not provide a uniform temperature, or temperatures vary greatly, a heating mat is worth investing in.

LIGHT AND MOISTURE METERS

DESCRIPTION: Small, hand-held meters. Sometimes both functions are combined in a single unit, but more commonly they are sold separately. Moisture meters have a probe, either on the end of a cable or as part of the meter body.

USE: Estimating light and moisture content in soils and growing areas; particularly useful under artificial conditions, such as with light units or greenhouses. May also help discover problem conditions that affect especially sensitive plants. The primary use of a light meter is to check the difference in intensity of light from the center to the edge of an area lit by fluorescent tubes. One way to compensate is to rotate the position of the plants. Some moisture meters, usually sold as part of a system, are connected to water computers that turn the water supply on and off as needed, their prime purpose being to prevent automatic sprinkler systems from going on when it's raining.

USE TIP: Always wipe off the tips of the probes after use.

BUYING TIP: Once you have learned the proper level of moisture for your plants, you may find that your finger can replace the probe.

LIGHT UNIT

ALSO KNOWN AS: Growing light, growing lamp unit, plant light, propagation light

DESCRIPTION: Basically a standard fluorescent light fixture that has been adapted to the special needs of indoor plant growing. Typically a two-lamp fixture, mounted in a reflective metal hood. Some models come as part of a unit that includes one or two shelves for plants, and a frame that holds the light at the right distance above them. Twenty-four to 48-inch-long 20 or 40 watt *wide spectrum* (or *full spectrum* or *continuous spectrum)* fluorescent tubes, sometimes called *grow lights,* are used, though one "cool white" and one "warm white" is recommended by some experts. Some brands claim to last 24,000 hours.

USE: Providing the light required for plants to make their own food, or photosynthesize, indoors and away from sunny windows. Light units are also ideal for starting plants indoors, as they provide consistent light that can be controlled at this delicate stage in a plant's life.

USE TIPS: The amount of light produced from fluorescent lamps diminishes toward their ends, and as the plants must be close to the fixture, you must place the plants with this in mind. You must also change the height of the fixture as the plants grow to keep them at the same distance. Plants also need a period of darkness, so plant light units should not be on all the time. An automatic timer (see pages 254–55) is useful to control the amount of light the plants receive. It is important that the period of light the plants and seedlings receive be fairly consistent and mock natural day length conditions. Units can be covered with plastic to help retain humidity, the lack of which is often a problem during the winter heating season. Specialized grow lights work best with flowering houseplants; vegetables are less fussy. Do not use *white* or *daylight* tubes.

BUYING TIPS: Light units are more efficient if there are two 4-foot fluorescent tubes. Units sold specifically for plants are more expensive than the same unit sold for general lighting use, but you usually still need to get the "wide spectrum" lamp at a garden center. Because they are a bit costly it is a good idea to use them in tandem with a regular "cool white" lamp. If you buy a regular fixture, you need to make the frame and shelves yourself—not a difficult task for some people, but for those with little time or inclination to build or assemble, the ready-made unit is a big advantage.

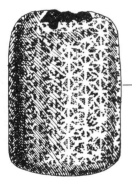

EXPANDED
PEAT PELLET

PEAT PELLET

PEAT PELLET

POPULAR BRAND NAME: Jiffy-7®

ALSO KNOWN AS: One step disk, growing cube

DESCRIPTION: Small brown disk, about 1½ inches wide and 1/16 inch thick, made from compressed peat and wood fibers, that is sterile and pH balanced. Expands on contact with water to become a combination small pot of peat and growing medium. Peat pellets are encased in a light plastic netting that keeps the peat intact. Jiffy-7s expand to 1⅔ inches square, but a deeper Jiffy-7 (extra-depth pellets, no. 727) expands to 2⅜ inches square. Another version is a block of cubes stamped out of a whole sheet of this material; some brands include fertilizer and use a gel instead of a net to hold it all together.

USE: Self-contained pots and planting medium all in one, for starting slow-growing annuals and vegetables from seed. Once the seedlings have grown and have been thinned to only one plant per "pot," the pot itself is set directly in the garden, avoiding transplant shock.

USE TIPS: Tepid water causes disks to expand more quickly. To allow the gel to work best, allow the disks to sit for a few hours after expanding. Once seeds begin to germinate, the medium should be kept evenly moist, and any pot material above the soil line should be trimmed off so it does not wick water away. Sow several seeds per pot to compensate for poor germination; thin to one seedling.

BUYING TIPS: A real convenience if you are just starting to grow plants from seed, as there is no soil to mix nor pots to fill. The plastic nets on Jiffy-7s do not decompose, and because they remain in the soil some gardeners prefer other types that decompose over time.

PEAT POT

PEAT POT

POPULAR BRAND NAMES: Jiffy-Pots®, Fertil Pots

DESCRIPTION: Small pot made from compressed peat and wood fiber and sometimes fertilizer. Standard sizes include 2 inches square, 2¼ inches round or square, and 3 inches round or square. One hundred percent biodegradable. *Dwarf pots* are a bit wider and less tapered than normal; *Long Tom* pots are taller.

USE: Starting seeds, particularly with sterile soilless mixes. The pot is planted directly into the garden when the seedling is ready, avoiding transplant shock as well as the work of repotting. Especially suitable for bedding plants and vegetables that normally may be hard to transplant.

USE TIPS: Remove any small part of the pot that sticks above the soil level when setting the plants into the garden—otherwise it acts as a wick, drawing water away from the plant and into the air. Sow several seeds per pot and thin to one after germination.

BUYING TIP: Peat pots are about the same price as the peat pellets (see previous entry) but you need to fill peat pots with a growing medium, making them ultimately just a little more expensive.

PLANTING LINE

DESCRIPTION: Length of cord with a stake at either end and a winding mechanism, usually a reel. Many different lengths offered in the range of 50 or 100 feet. Stakes made of metal, wood, or plastic. Line may be natural hemp or plastic coated, and is often sold on a convenient reel, like kite-flying string.

USE: Laying out a garden: This allows planting row crops in a straight line. Pull line taut above the soil surface.

USE TIP: Keep your line relatively clean by trying to use only on dry soil; moist soil sticks to planting lines.

BUYING TIP: This is the kind of item that is manufactured as a convenience only. It is very easy to make yourself.

PLANT MARKER

ALSO KNOWN AS: Flower markers, plant labels

DESCRIPTION: Plastic, metal, or wooden stake just under a foot long with a flat area, about 1 by 3 inches, which can be written on. Metal markers have one or two long wire prongs that are stuck in the ground, with an angled top that has an etched zinc band for writing on with a special black carbon pencil. Others, often called *pot labels,* are thin, flat plastic or wood pieces from 4 to 12 inches long and ⅝ inch wide, angled to a point for insertion in the soil; sometimes the longer ones are called *garden stakes.*

USE: Labeling plants, either as a marker of a freshly seeded row of vegetables or to identify prize flowers. Also handy as a reminder of when something was fertilized or treated with a pesticide. Small wooden pot labels are good for seedling pots.

BUYING TIPS: Top-quality metal markers are made of zinc, aluminum, or galvanized steel. Plastic may look good, but it is breakable. Wooden ones tend to rot in a season, and are more suitable for temporary jobs, such as indicating where seeds have been planted.

SECTIONED FIBER SEED TRAY

POPULAR BRAND NAME: Jiffy Strip®

DESCRIPTION: Compressed 2¼-inch-square fiber pots attached at their tops to form a tray, or strip, of twelve units, like a large ice cube tray. Commonly sold with plastic trays that they fit into perfectly and that contain drainage holes for excess water. Some are designed especially to fit onto windowsills, called *windowsill sets.*

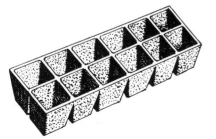

SECTIONED FIBER SEED TRAY

USE: Growing seedlings, when filled with a growing medium.

USE TIPS: Growing medium should be premoistened before sowing seed. Sections can be cut apart and completely buried in the garden (where they will disintegrate naturally) instead of transplanting. Trim off any part of pot above soil line. Sow several seeds in each section to compensate for poor germination; seedlings should then be thinned to one seedling per section.

BUYING TIP: Fiber planting trays are as inexpensive as individual peat pots (see page 259), and more convenient to use.

SECTIONED STARTING TRAY

SECTIONED STARTING TRAY

ALSO KNOWN AS: Compartmentalized tray, seedling flat, seedling tray, growing tray, plug tray, planter flat, plug seedling tray, cell pack, cell tray

DESCRIPTION: Lightweight plastic or biodegradable paper tray divided into separate cubes, like a muffin tin, for growing individual seedlings. Cells are 2 to 3 inches deep and up to 3 inches square or round; round ones are also available as small as 1 inch deep and 1 inch in diameter. Trays vary in size from small six packs (approximately 4 by 8 inches) to approximately 12 by 20 inches. Some have a flat tray underneath to catch excess water.

Some more elaborate *self-watering* models, with drainage holes and capillary matting (see capillary waterer, page 255), are sold with outer trays without drainage holes that they fit into like a sleeve. The seedlings are watered indirectly—water put in the bottom tray is pulled up into the starting tray. A high, clear plastic cover is provided for extra climate control at the germinating stage in the case of *propagating trays.* The plainest version is a *seed pan,* which looks like a casserole dish.

USE: Growing seedlings for transplanting.

USE TIPS: Sow a couple of seeds in each compartment to compensate for poor germination. If more than one seed germinates, they should be thinned out, leaving only one seedling in each section. Remove the clear plastic cover as soon as the seeds germinate. All the plants in each tray should have the same watering requirements and planting times for ease of maintenance.

BUYING TIPS: Sectioned trays are more expensive than the single flats often used by many professional growers. Sectioned trays, however, are worth the extra money because they prevent root competition among seedlings, as roots can develop only within the confines of each section—thus reducing transplant shock. Plastic trays are a good investment, as they can be reused year after year. The self-watering trays are easy to use and worth the extra cost. Look for stiff, solid fabrication that will not easily break. Using your old coffee cups or yogurt containers is good for recycling, but not as easy. And they are hard to carry out to the garden for transplanting.

SEED FLAT

ALSO KNOWN AS: Seed tray, nursery flat

DESCRIPTION: Shallow, rectangular plastic or fiberglass tray approximately 12 by 20 inches and about 2 to 3 inches deep, with ribs and usually drainage holes. When sold with a clear plastic top, may be considered a *propagator,* which is then usually packaged with other seed starting products, such as the pots and other items listed here.

USE: A place to put peat pots or other small containers. Can also be filled directly with soil and seeds, though this is not recommended. Some are sectioned to hold small pots.

USE TIPS: Avoid overwatering, especially if your flat has no drainage holes. When peat pots of seedlings are placed in a seed flat, apply no more water than the pots can absorb in less than one half hour. Professional growers with little greenhouse space to waste plant seeds directly into seed flats, but seedlings' roots can then intertwine, and there is considerable transplant shock when they are cut apart and moved into larger containers.

BUYING TIPS: Look for seed flats that are sturdy and do no bend if the weight of the pots is unevenly distributed in the flat. Foam plastic has greater structural rigidity, making it easier to carry a loaded flat. Plastic resists rot, mildew, fungi, and other damage.

SEED GROWING KIT

ALSO KNOWN AS: Seed starter kit, seed starting kit

DESCRIPTION: Prepackaged group of products containing all of the necessary items for starting plants from seed. They often contain pots, flats, planting medium, a thermometer, labels, and fertilizer. The number of seedlings you can produce with one of these kits depends upon the size of the kit.

USE: Simple and sure germination setup.

USE TIP: Follow the general directions for growing plants from seed. If your kit does not have directions, use a gardening book.

BUYING TIP: It is usually cheaper to buy these prepackaged kits than it is to purchase each item separately. If you prefer peat or fiber pots to plastic, or peat disks, look for seed growing kits that have just what you want.

SEED SCOOP

SEED SCOOP

ALSO KNOWN AS: Seed planter, seed sower

DESCRIPTION: Small hand-held scoop that resembles an ice cream scoop with a divider across the middle that has a small open space at the bottom for seeds to pass through. The space behind the divider serves as a hopper for the seeds, which pass underneath the divider one at a time. Smaller versions look like big test tubes, palm-sized powder compacts, giant hyperdermic needles, or long and narrow shoehorns. This last item is an English import known as a widger (see page 155)—some people call it the *everything tool* because it is not limited to seed planting, but is more often used for digging.

USE: Planting small quantities of seeds evenly.

USE TIP: Can also be used for applying small amounts of granular fertilizer.

BUYING TIP: The least expensive version is the clear plastic tube, though it could be argued that this is only one small step up from using seed packets or pieces of cardboard folded into a V shape, which are, of course, still less expensive.

SEED STARTING MIX

ALSO KNOWN AS: Soilless mix (see pages 7–8)

DESCRIPTION: Lightweight soil substitute, usually light brown in color with white specks. The white specks are either vermiculite or perlite (see pages 19 and 18), and the brown is peat (see pages 16–19) and other organic material. Contains no soil, and is sterile, having been exposed to high temperatures to kill off the bacteria. Retains moisture extremely well.

USE: Starting seeds. Constant moisture is essential to the germination and growth of seeds. The sterile soil prevents the problem of damping-off, a fungal disease that kills seedlings.

USE TIP: Wet thoroughly before using. It is more difficult to moisten after seed has been sown than before sowing. Tepid or warm water is absorbed more quickly than cool or cold water.

BUYING TIPS: Mixes that contain perlite are preferred to those that contain vermiculite, because vermiculite, which is lighter than perlite, tends to rise to the surface when water is applied. Most sterile starter mixes on the market are fairly reliable, so just look for those within your budget. Even cheaper is mixing your own from milled peat and perlite, or any recipe found in a good general gardening book.

SEED-SPACING TEMPLATE

DESCRIPTION: Large, lightweight plastic sheet with large holes in a regular pattern, such as every 6 inches.

USE: Placed over the ground, provides an accurate guide for planting seeds in an exact pattern.

USE TIP: Mark where the edge of your template falls so that you can maintain your pattern when you move the template over to cover the adjacent area.

BUYING TIP: It is just as easy to mark off measurements on a line, or to make a similar item from a large sheet of cardboard or a notched piece of wood.

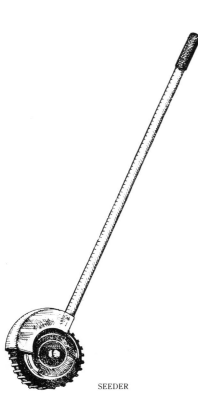

SEEDER

SEEDER

ALSO KNOWN AS: Row seeder, garden seeder

DESCRIPTION: Single wheel with a long handle and a large hub; the hub contains a hopper and a release device for seeds. A larger, two-wheeled model simultaneously furrows, covers, and marks the next row.

USE: Sowing row crops. As you walk along your garden, the seeder releases seeds at a preset rate, so you don't have to bend over or kneel.

USE TIPS: Be sure to set the rate and walk at the pace necessary for the proper dispersion of each kind of seed.

BUYING TIPS: Reduces the need for thinning, and of course is much faster than hand planting.

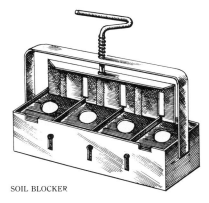

SOIL BLOCKER

SOIL BLOCKER

ALSO KNOWN AS: Soil block, soil block maker

DESCRIPTION: Small metal device that compresses soil or planting medium to form four tight 2-inch soil blocks. Another version, a *soil cuber,* makes twenty ¾-inch cubes at once. Four plastic blocks, called *cube attachments,* make ¾-inch holes in the large blocks in which the small cubes can be dropped. A spring-held lever forces the soil or medium out of the blocker neatly.

USE: Makes cubes that are both the planting medium and the transplant container, an efficient way to grow plants from seed without transplant shock. Once the seed has sprouted in small cubes it can be dropped into the larger cube made by the soil blocker.

USE TIPS: The moister the growing medium, the tighter the cubes, and the more likely they will hold together while the seed germinates and grows. Seed germinates better in the smaller cubes than in the soil blocks. Special blends of peat, humus, and vermiculite are available that make ideal blocks.

BUYING TIP: Not many different makes are available, but prices do vary.

THERMOMETER

DESCRIPTION: Dial or small mercury-filled tube with calibrations in centigrade or Fahrenheit degrees suitable for indoor or outdoor use. Some are mounted alongside a barometer or *hygrometer* or *humidistat* or *humidity meter* (for measuring humidity). A *soil* or *garden thermometer,* a large specialized version with a long spike like a meat thermometer, is made for measuring the temperature of compost piles (one brand is called a *hot bed soil thermometer,* and it is over a foot long). A *minimum-maximum* (or *min/max) thermometer* has markers that show the low and high temperature points each day. A special accessory is a *temperature alarm* that you can set for minimum or maximum temperatures.

USE: Measuring air temperature or, in the case of soil thermometers, soil temperature. Both help you avoid planting your vegetable garden too early in the season or leaving certain plants in too late in the fall. Humidistats help you maintain the proper level of humidity in your home or greenhouse.

BUYING TIP: Make sure you get one that is easy to read in relation to where you intend to place it—on a greenhouse wall, outside a window, or whatever. A must for greenhouses.

Planting Containers and Accessories

ABOUT PLANTING CONTAINERS

Most garden centers devote a large area to planters, pots, and containers made of clay, wood, plastic (many of recycled plastic), metal, cement, and ceramics. Which material is best for pots and planters depends primarily on personal taste. The most notable point of comparison is this, though: The more porous the material a pot or planter is made of, the more quickly the soil or planting medium dries out. That is, if two pots are the same size, one made of clay and the other of plastic, the soil in the clay pot needs to be watered more often than the soil in the plastic pot, although now some terra-cotta planters have a self-watering feature, like many plastic ones. This is particularly important when gardening in dry and hot places, like roof gardens. And clay pots are harder to clean than plastic pots. Still, the old debate over whether clay pots are better than plastic ones remains unsettled for many gardeners.

Beyond their inherent qualities is the question of weight. Outdoor pots and pots for larger plants must be heavy enough to resist wind. Hanging plant pots need to be light. You may want to put a heavy planter on a *plant dolly* (or *plant caddy, planter base,* or *coaster),* a small platform with four sturdy casters, so that it can be moved.

Remember that all planting pots must have drain holes so excess water does not rot the plant's roots. You may want to use a saucer to catch any water that flows out. Pot dimensions are given as the diameter at the top, and sometimes the height as well, though some dimensions are not given if the design is extreme, such as with the flat planter used for forcing bulbs or starting seedlings, called a *bulb pan.*

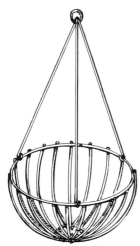

BASKET PLANTER

BASKET PLANTER

DESCRIPTION: Half- or quarter-sphere frames constructed from concentric circles of wire connected by perpendicular wires, or of solid plastic. Quarter-sphere models may be called *wall baskets* or *English hayrack flower baskets.* Other items that do the same job with much charm are unglazed pottery faces and other decorative shapes with one flat side that goes against a wall.

USE: Lined with peat moss or other fibrous material and filled with soil for hanging plants. Quarter-sphere models hang from a wall, like a picture, while half spheres hang free. Those made of solid materials, like plastic and pottery, do not need a moss lining.

USE TIPS: Fill the basket with a growing medium that holds moisture well (one with a lot of humus). Plants can also be placed through the wires from the outside, inserted into the peat moss on the sides of the basket to produce a fuller planter, usually a very striking effect. If possible, water by submersing the basket completely, which gives it a really thorough soaking.

BUYING TIP: Wire frames provide a suitable base for hanging baskets, but only if you can supply ample water. Look for sturdy construction, and if it is made of painted metal, an even, solid paint job.

CERAMIC PLANTER

DESCRIPTION: Cast terra-cotta in a wide range of sizes and designs, both freestanding and wall hanging. Some have a vitreous glaze, adding an even wider range of colors. Some are fired in such a way as to be frost-proof, meaning they can be left out over the winter, with no danger of cracking.

USE: Typically used as an accent piece on a terrace, patio, or in the home.

USE TIP: May add just the right focus to a deck or terrace, so one or two are better than a whole collection.

BUYING TIP: Good-quality ceramic planters, especially those with beautiful decorative detail and a nice glaze, are more expensive than other types, so choose carefully. Those with drainage holes are more desirable than those without, as holes cannot be added, though a layer of gravel can be placed in the bottom if need be.

FIBERGLASS PLANTER

ALSO KNOWN AS: Tub

DESCRIPTION: Lightweight containers in all kinds of shapes and sizes, from small urns to large tree containers. Many are painted to look like wood, stone, or ceramic material. Some are designed to match furniture or architectural detail.

USE: Substitute for heavier containers, especially where weight is a consideration, such as on a roof or balcony. Will not weather, chip, or peel. The great variety of design possibilities makes these fit into specific decors, unlike other kinds of containers.

USE TIP: Drainage holes can be drilled in fiberglass planters if they do not have them.

BUYING TIP: What fiberglass container you should buy depends largely upon your taste, need, and ability to pay. Those that most closely resemble wood or stone are usually more expensive. Try to buy one with drainage holes.

HALF WHISKEY BARREL

HALF WHISKEY BARREL

DESCRIPTION: A wooden barrel, cut in half, that actually was used to make whiskey (or wine), though some are made just for planter use. All are made of hardwood staves or strips held together with metal bands, about 2½ feet in diameter at the top, and slightly narrow at the bottom; about 2 feet deep. The inside of the barrel often has been charred as part of the whiskey aging process. Sizes vary, but a typical big one holds about 3 cubic feet of soil.

USE: As large planters. Can also be used to create a miniature water garden if the residual whiskey or wine is thoroughly washed out first to avoid intoxicating the fish.

USE TIPS: Whiskey barrels used for aging whiskey and wine must be cleaned well with warm water and a stiff brush before they can be used as planters or for miniature water gardens, but it is not necessary to remove the charred section from the inside of the barrel. The charred sides actually "sweeten" the soil or water in the barrel—they absorb many unwelcome chemicals that tend to build up in soil. The staves in the barrel swell when wet, allowing the barrel to hold water for water gardening (lily pads and goldfish—why not?), though it may take several days for this to happen. If you are planning to use a whiskey barrel as a planter, drill several ½-inch holes in the bottom for drainage first. Because the metal bands that hold the staves in place are not treated to prevent rust, it may be a good idea to paint them.

BUYING TIP: Look for half whiskey barrels that have not been allowed to dry out and whose bottoms are not warped. When a whiskey barrel is overdry the staves are not tight and the metal bands become loose. Compare prices at different places, as the markup can vary greatly. You should have to pay no more than $25 for a half whiskey barrel—remember, they are discards from whiskey manufacturers.

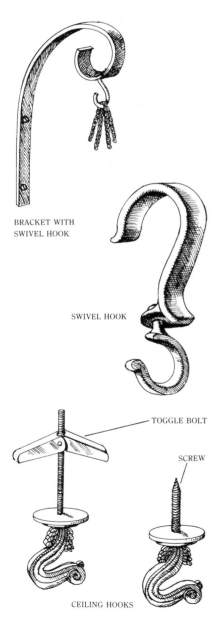

BRACKET WITH
SWIVEL HOOK

SWIVEL HOOK

TOGGLE BOLT

SCREW

CEILING HOOKS

HOOKS, HANGERS, AND BRACKETS

DESCRIPTION: Many ingenious designs are available, and most fall into the categories that follow. However, there are too many odd ones to list, such as those that stick on windows or hold hanging plants. Be sure to browse through several displays and ask for suggestions from the garden center if you aren't satisfied with what you see.

TYPES: *Brackets:* Decorative L-shaped or scroll hook of various sizes that is mounted on a wall and may be hinged, from which a hanging basket is suspended. Some models have a small scroll at the outward end in which you insert an S-hook, while others have a swiveling hook built in. Some of the best looking are made from wrought iron, though brackets made from all kinds of metal or wood can be found in a wide range of prices. They are adjustable to fit. Place pulleys at the base and tip, and with a cord and a cleat you can raise and lower a hanging basket to your level, especially handy if you're in a wheelchair, or to a high ceiling.

Ceiling hooks: Simple hook with a flanged base, like a big cup hook, usually made of cast aluminum in a decorative style (this may also be known as a *swag hook).* Sold with either a screw (for solid ceilings) or a toggle bolt (a winged device for hollow ceilings). Both kinds are generally used with a lightweight decorative chain and often sold in plastic bubble packs. A special design of ceiling hook is made for use on suspended ceilings. It slips over the thin metal runners that hold the ceiling panels. All are used with hanging baskets.

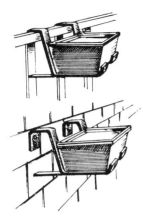

PLANTER BOX BRACKETS

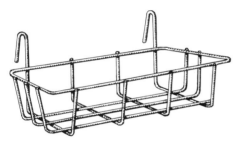

HANGOVER

POT CLIP

Macramé: Multiple strands of decorative woven rope or yarn, ranging from 2 to 6 feet in length; the strands come together at one or several points to hold potted plants. A metal eye at the top provides for hanging from a nail or hook.

Planter box brackets (also known as *hangovers, window box brackets,* or *flower box brackets):* Sturdy metal arms that hook over a deck, stair, fence railing, or windowsill, or attach to a wall to support a planter or window box. Most are adjustable, with a sliding assembly to accommodate the width of the railing as well as the width of the planter. Smaller versions for holding round pots are also available, called *hang-a-rounds.* Models for direct attachment to a wall are available, too, called *pot clips,* or *flowerpot holders.*

Pulleys: Grooved wheel assembly that can be attached to a ceiling.

S-hooks: Wrought iron, plastic, or steel strand, usually about ¼ inch thick, in the form of an S. Ranges in size from about an inch to half a foot.

Shelving: Lightweight metal shelving, usually 3 or 4 shelves to a unit, about 36 inches long and high.

Swivel hooks: These rotate so the plant can get sun on all sides.

Track: Long metal channel, about 1 inch deep, in which special hooks or eyes can slide; S-hooks or chains are hooked into each one, and the plant suspended by the chains.

USE: Hanging or supporting plants in containers near windows or on exterior walls.

USE TIPS: Hangers with swivel devices make it easier to rotate plants so that different sides are toward the light. Hooks and

TRACK

hangers with pulley devices make it easier to lower heavy pots and planters for watering and care. Measure your rails and planters before purchasing support brackets.

BUYING TIP: Hardware stores and gift shops also carry ingenious plant hanging items. Shop around.

JARDINIERE

DESCRIPTION: Decorative ceramic or stoneware jar that comes in a wide variety of shapes, sizes, and colors.

USE: Dresses up houseplant containers. Not often used for outdoor plants.

USE TIPS: Few jardinieres have drainage holes, so plants should not be planted directly in them but rather in containers, such as plain pots, that fit easily inside the jardiniere. A layer of gravel should be placed in the bottom to act as a reservoir for excess water underneath the plain pot. The container holding the plant should never sit in water unless the plant is a bog marginal (bog marginals are referred to as "plants that love wet feet").

BUYING TIP: A purchase determined by budget or aesthetic considerations only.

PLANT TRAY

DESCRIPTION: Shallow, clear or colored plastic tray with ribs and no drainage holes. *Window* or *windowsill trays* are designed to fit on windowsills, and are therefore long and narrow. Typically 20 or 22 inches long by 3½ to 10 inches wide. Usually sold with small aluminum brackets to hold them in place.

USE: Supporting flowerpots or other containers in a moist environment when filled with gravel, sand, perlite, or vermiculite. The gravel or other material holds a supply of water away from the roots to prevent rot and to maintain high humidity.

USE TIPS: Even in a greenhouse these are helpful, especially a window greenhouse. Collect sand or rocks from a favorite vacation spot and you'll have even more to enjoy.

BUYING TIP: Clear plastic for some reason is often more expensive. Search out the thicker, stronger trays.

PLASTIC PLANTER

DESCRIPTION: Commonly made of polyurethane and available in almost any size and shape. Color range is wide, but a popular color resembles terra-cotta. Many models, called *self-watering* or *reservoir planters* or *pots,* are available with a built-in reservoir for water in the bottom. This may be internal and airtight, or else a saucerlike attachment, with a capillary or wick system that draws up the water as needed. The better models have aeration ducts that maintain the proper humidity level in the soil, and sensors that shut the water on and off. *Hanging pots* are deep containers with attached saucers and three wires and a hook for hanging.

USE: Any type of planting. Those that look like terra-cotta are ideal for designs that call for this appearance but where weight is an issue, such as on roofs and balconies. Self-watering planters are good for people who find it hard to water regularly, with some models capable of going a month between waterings.

USE TIPS: Plastic is not porous and soils and media in these containers do not dry out as quickly as soil in a more porous clay pot, an important consideration in hot, dry places. But watch out for overwatering, the primary cause of houseplant failure, if you don't have a self-watering model. Soil should always be separated from water reservoirs by stones or else the roots will rot. Add a layer of charcoal to the bottom to absorb toxic chemicals and salts.

BUYING TIPS: Plastic pots are often less expensive than fiberglass ones. The choice of plastic pots is pretty much up to your needs and taste, though color is an important consideration. A good thick layer of gravel in the bottom may give a similar but less efficient effect as a more expensive built-in reservoir.

RED CLAY FLOWERPOT

DESCRIPTION: The quintessential flowerpot, available in the standard tapered shape, with a ridge that extends about one-fifth of the way down from the top, since time immemorial. The ridge indicates the level to which it should be filled with soil. Size ranges from tiny 2-inch-deep pots to those more than 3 feet deep. Standard-model clay pots are unglazed and unpainted, though glazed and painted clay pots are available.

RED CLAY FLOWERPOT

USE: Containers for houseplants or terrace or roof garden plants. Often houseplants in clay pots are summered outside in the garden or on the patio.

USE TIPS: Because clay pots are porous, the soil they contain dries out more quickly than soil in less porous pots. Clay pots are the only ones that "breathe." Experienced gardeners know when to water plants that are growing in clay pots by being observant of the color of the pot. As the soil dries out, the pots become lighter in color. The salts found in fertilizers and some water sources may build up on clay pots, appearing as a white chalky residue on the surface of the pot. If the pot is to be reused, this salt should be scraped off and the pot washed in a solution of warm water and chlorine bleach to remove other bacteria and fungi that may be on or in the clay. Pots that are kept wet develop algae, which appear as a green film. Algae are usually not harmful and can easily be washed off if the pot is reused for another plant. Note that pots do absorb heat quickly in hot weather, which may bake plant roots.

BUYING TIPS: Clay pots may not necessarily be any better than ones made from plastic or other materials, but they do seem to be the choice of serious gardeners, primarily because they absorb excess water and thus help resist damage from overwatering. They are less expensive than ceramic or stoneware pots and are generally considered more earthy and attractive.

STRAWBERRY JAR

STRAWBERRY JAR

ALSO KNOWN AS: Strawberry pot

DESCRIPTION: Urn or jar with an open top and holes in the sides. Most commonly made from unglazed fired red clay, but also made from glazed stoneware or other materials such as plastic or fiberglass. Size ranges from only 8 inches in height to as tall as 3 feet. Another version is a redwood *patio tower* with slats instead of holes, in either a slight pyramid or bookcase style.

USE: Traditionally used for growing strawberries, but also used to grow a miniature herb garden or a collection of succulents or other small houseplants, including African violets and miniature English ivy.

USE TIPS: Strawberry jars should be planted in layers. Soil should first be placed in the pot up to the first holes, plants then put in the holes, and soil added until the next level of holes is reached. A cardboard collar or tube made from paper towel rollers taped together should be placed in the center of the pot from top to bottom and filled with the small gravel such as is sold in pet stores for lining bird cages or aquariums, before the pot is filled with soil. The tube is removed when the pot is completely filled and planted, leaving a gravel core through which the pot can be uniformly watered. You may want to use soilless mixes because they are lighter, and put this planter on rollers so you can rotate it to give all sides some sun.

BUYING TIPS: The material you choose is strictly a matter of personal preference. Glazed stoneware pots are usually more expensive. Hand-thrown, unglazed, Italian clay strawberry pots are common and often not expensive.

WINDOW BOX

WINDOW BOX

ALSO KNOWN AS: Estate planter box

DESCRIPTION: Rectangular planter made of metal, plastic, wood, fiberglass, cast cement, terra-cotta, or ceramic. A standard window box fits on or hangs from a windowsill, and is as long as 3 feet and as wide and deep as 8 to 10 inches. Plastic and metal window boxes come in an assortment of colors, though green is the most common. Though not all boxes do, they should have two or more 1-inch drainage holes in the bottom, and feet to create a gap under the holes. Redwood and cedar are the most common woods used.

USE: Growing decorative plants outside windows and along balcony or porch railings.

USE TIPS: Many wooden or plastic window boxes are sold without drainage holes, but they should be drilled in the bottom before being used. Also, put the box on something to create a gap under it if it has no feet. Soil in window boxes dries out quickly, so frequent watering is essential for most plants. Be sure to place them where they are convenient for watering. A soil mix high in humus (see page 6) holds moisture longer. Metal boxes on sunny sills tend to heat up to dangerous levels, harming plant roots. Treat any wood other than cedar or redwood with a preservative that does not contain pentachlorophenol (also known as "penta"), such as Cuprinol. Special brackets (see page 269) are available for attaching window boxes to railings or fences as well as windows.

BUYING TIPS: Buy the deepest window boxes you can find (a minimum depth of 10 inches is preferred) and that your space can hold. The deeper the box, the longer it takes for the soil to dry out. Even though you can drill holes in window boxes that do not have them, it is better to buy boxes that already do. Color is an important consideration—many shades of green clash with the natural green of plant foliage. Window boxes in earth tones, if they go with the color of your house or apartment, are often good choices. Also, the more lightweight the box, the easier it is to mount outside your window—no small consideration. The only woods that hold up well to weathering are redwood and cedar.

WOODEN TUB

WOODEN TUB OR CONTAINER

ALSO KNOWN AS: Redwood planter, cedar planter

DESCRIPTION: Rectangular or octagonal container, usually held together by metal bands and sometimes lined with plastic or galvanized tin. Available in a variety of sizes from flowerpot size to large tubs that can hold a tree or shrub. Made of rot-resistant redwood, cedar, teak, or treated pine or other softwoods.

USE: Attractive, natural-looking containers for plants and shrubs. A carefully chosen collection of wooden containers on a terrace can give continuity to the overall design.

USE TIPS: If a wooden planter is not lined, a heavy plastic garbage bag can be placed on the inside in order to slow down the decay of the wood (be sure to put drainage holes in the plastic liner). If the planter does not have drainage holes, drill some before planting. Even a rot-resistant redwood planter can have its useful life doubled by using a plastic liner. The soil in unlined wooden planters tends to dry out more quickly than in lined or solid containers. Do not use treated wood planters for growing any edible plants—the treatment is usually toxic.

BUYING TIPS: Wooden containers have an insulating value that keeps soil from drying out as fast as it does in other types of containers. Look for lined planters with drainage holes. Avoid those treated with toxic preservatives, such as those used on decks (CCA is the most common), but if you must, get one that is treated for contact with the ground. Never even bother with creosoted wood—it is toxic to plants. The best planters are made of disease- and rot-resistant redwood or cedar. While teak is an excellent material for the construction of wooden planters, much of it comes from the commercial harvest of naturally grown teak that has been destroying tropical rain forests. Gardeners in particular should be concerned about this and avoid purchasing teak products that are produced from wild teak; look for teak labeled as "grown in managed forests."

Stakes, Supports, and Fencing

ABOUT STAKES, SUPPORTS, AND FENCING

Stakes and supports are used with all kinds of plants and to solve many different problems, so there is a wide array of types available.

There is no such thing as just plain "fencing"—each type has its specific function. Some are used to keep pest animals at bay, and are noted in chapter 4. Others are used for defining areas or for creating shade, and are noted here.

ANCHOR

DESCRIPTION: Short stakes made of wood, metal, or plastic, designed to be driven into the ground with a mallet or hammer.

USE: Holding down plastic sheeting, whether it be landscape fabric used as mulch (see pages 27–28), row covers (see pages 286–87), or protective netting (see page 112).

USE TIPS: Drive in deeply for extra holding strength and shield exposed end with rocks or potted plants to limit the chance of someone tripping over the stake.

BORDER FENCING

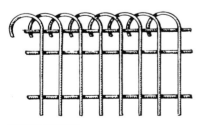

BORDER FENCING

ALSO KNOWN AS: Trim fence, bed guard, folding fence, flower border

DESCRIPTION: Small decorative fence of welded, plastic-coated or enameled wire, or of wooden pickets. Vinyl coated in green or white. Commonly sold in 8-, 10-, and 12-foot lengths, folded into sections, or in 20- and 25-foot rolls, 8 to 32 inches high, and in a variety of styles, such as round tops, angular tops, or Gothic tops. Picket patterns usually have model names like Colonial or Cape Cod. Wooden lattice panels also available. Also available is a 36- or 48-inch high version, called a *lawn guard*.

USE: Marking off flower beds and protecting them from people, pets, and lawn mowers.

USE TIP: If low fencing is to be placed near a popular shortcut, try to notice if people are tripping on the fence rather than going around it. If so, replace with a higher fence.

BUYING TIP: Avoid untreated pine fencing, as it will rot after just one year in the soil.

PLASTIC EDGING

EDGING

ALSO KNOWN AS: Plastic border, landscape border, grass stop, grass edging, lawn edging, border edging, bed divider, lawn border

POPULAR BRAND NAMES: Easy-Edge®, Sureedge

DESCRIPTION: Several different types available. Semirigid polyethylene, galvanized steel, or aluminum sheet, 4 to 6 inches high, meant to be driven into the ground vertically. The plastic version has a tubular edge that, when pushed into the ground, should just touch the surface (a small L on the bottom edge keeps the plastic from coming back up). Plastic models available in black, white, green, or redwood color, sold in rolls of 20 and 100 feet. Steel and aluminum come in the same lengths, silver or green in color, and usually in 40-foot lengths. Also available in 6-inch and 12-inch-high scalloped cedar slabs in 10- and 20-foot sections or in 3-inch diameter *pegs* or *logs* 4½ to 10 inches high, joined by a wire or rubber sheet in 3-foot sections. Still other types are made of pressure-treated pine (in a green-gray color) with decorative picket tops, or fake plastic "pegs." Better brands have a T or flared bottom to keep it from coming out.

USE: Making borders for flower beds and lawns. A particularly good way to keep creeping grass out of perennial beds and off walks.

USE TIP: Push metal or plastic in slowly so it does not buckle. The edging should be pushed into the soil deep enough to block any invasive roots and for a lawn mower to pass over it.

BUYING TIPS: Black plastic edging with the tubular top has largely replaced green metal and other forms of plastic edging and is considerably more durable. Some brands are guaranteed for twenty years. Avoid promotionally priced lightweight metal edging, as it is likely to bend when it is being installed.

PLANT STAKE

DESCRIPTION: Long thin piece of bamboo, hardwood, or steel tubing covered with PVC, ranging in size from small pencil diameters to 1 inch thick and from 2 to 8 feet long. Wooden and bamboo stakes may be either painted or unpainted. Usually sold in packages or bundles of 10 to 25, sometimes including an assortment of mixed sizes. *Tree stakes* are either of two kinds: 6-foot-long and 2- to 3-inch-thick pieces of rot-resistant cedar, or else sturdy 1-foot stakes that look much like tent stakes. Both are used with *guy wires* (lengths of galvanized steel wire) that are wrapped around the trunk with a rubber sleeve for protection and attached to the stakes. Rough-textured natural *fernwood poles,* made from the roots of large ferns, are also available. These are a few inches in diameter and 18 to 36 inches long.

USE: Holding up tall or heavy plants, like hollyhocks or tomatoes, and shrubs. Tree stakes keep newly planted trees from blowing over in high winds before their roots are established. Fernwood poles are used for houseplants.

USE TIPS: When tying plants to a stake, secure the tie or twist or string to the stake before tying it to the plant. This prevents the tie from slipping down the stake. Especially with vegetable crops like tomatoes, it is important that the tie be loose around the plant's stem. If it is too tight, the plant will strangle as it grows or the tie will cut into the stem. Use natural fiber string or twine to tie the plants. String or twine made from synthetic material will not decompose if left in the garden, and is harder to work with. Look for natural fiber materials such as jute or cotton; paper-covered wire is better than plastic ties.

BUYING TIPS: Determine how you are going to use the stakes and whether you will be using them for many years or not. If you need the stakes for a temporary job, buy the cheaper bamboo stakes. If you are planning to use the stakes for several years, the more expensive PVC-covered steel tubing is worth the extra money.

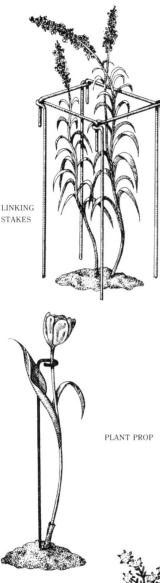

LINKING
STAKES

PLANT PROP

PEONY SUPPORT

PLANT SUPPORT

ALSO KNOWN AS: Cage, hoop, perennial support, flower support, flower support ring, border support

DESCRIPTION: Rust-resistant or plastic-coated stakes or wire hoops, loops, or grids with vertical wire legs, of various designs. *Peony supports* are single or double wire hoops attached to heavy vertical wires 24 or 35 inches long, making a cylinder. *Grow-through flower supports* have a large round grid, or frame, over the top of which plants grow. Another version has just a single stake with a small loop at the top, called a *blossom* or *bulb support, plant prop,* or *loop-stake.* And some, *link* or *linking stakes,* are just straight wire pieces available in three lengths, from about 1 to 3 feet, that are linked together as the gardener wishes, custom-designed for each plant or garden. *Tuteurs* (French for "tutors") are 6-foot-high supports for vines and climbing plants. All are usually dark green and available in a small range of sizes. Some designs fold flat for winter storage.

USE: Holding up top-heavy plants that have a tendency to flop over, whether due to their own weight or heavy winds and rain. Blossom or bulb supports are for single top-heavy flowers. The grow-through flower support, or grid, is more suitable for taller perennials. Linking stakes are most helpful in borders and beds.

USE TIPS: Place the supports over the plants just as they start to grow. Push the vertical wire in the ground around the plant so that the plant is centered in the hoop or hoops. Note that it is darn hard to push a full-grown plant with large blooms through a small opening, so put supports out when the plant is beginning to grow, not afterward, though linking stakes can be installed after plants have grown.

BUYING TIPS: Peony supports are not very expensive at under $2 for a single hoop and under $3 for a double hoop, although a homemade version using chicken wire is a good alternative, and it doesn't show that much. The chicken wire (about 1 foot square) is placed over the plant just as it starts to grow and is raised up by the lower leaves as it grows. The blooms appear above the wire. Linking stakes are the most versatile. Look for strong wire and smooth coatings. Though more expensive than tying plants to stakes, supports are easier.

PLANT TIE

POPULAR BRAND NAME: Twist-em®

DESCRIPTION: Thin wire sandwiched inside a ¼-inch-wide paper, usually green. Sold in reels ranging from a few feet to 250 feet long as well as in packages of precut pieces about 6 or 8 inches long. Alternatives include soft, natural *jute twine* (green or natural beige color), *vinyl ribbon, nylon loops,* and *foam-coated, cushioned wire,* some of which stretch as the plant grows. Most can be found in the color green.

USE: Temporary and gentle holding of plants against supports and stakes.

USE TIPS: Avoid sturdy plastic ties because they are more likely to restrict the growth of woody plants. Wire ties are easiest to use and can be tied with one hand.

BUYING TIP: Natural jute or sisal twine is generally cheapest and also biodegradable.

FAN TRELLIS

RIGID PLANT TRELLIS

DESCRIPTION: Sold in a variety of shapes, including the old-fashioned *fan trellis,* a wider-bottomed *flair trellis,* a rectangular *ladder* design, and the *diamond grid trellis,* also called *lattice.* Made of aluminum, plastic, fiberglass, or wood. An *arbor* (or *trellised arch)* is sort of a three-dimensional trellis that spans a walk like a freestanding doorway or arch, and a *tunnel* is a longer version. A *bean and pea tower* is merely 6-foot-long stakes bunched together at the top like a skinless tepee. An *A-frame trellis* consists of two 5-by-8-foot metal frames covered with a large mesh nylon net, and a similar rigid trellis is made of large panels that unfold like a Japanese screen.

USE: Supporting climbing or vining plants that cannot adhere to a wall. In some cases, you may not want vines on the wall (to avoid damage by invasive roots) or, in other cases, the trellis may create a natural wall of its own. Trellises also allow you to harvest vining vegetables without bending over.

USE TIP: Be sure that the trellis is well secured, particularly when growing woody or heavy vines. Excellent for those who have trouble reaching ground level, such as wheelchair-bound or elderly gardeners.

SHADE FENCING

SHADE FENCING

ALSO KNOWN AS: Snow fencing, shading fence

DESCRIPTION: Small, ⅜-inch-thick wooden boards, called *laths,* 3 to 6 feet long by about 1 inch wide, bound together with several rows of wire, twisted on both sides of each lath. Often stained or painted red or maroon. Sold in rolls of 50 feet. A similar type of protective fencing is woven from thin, chemically treated freshwater reeds, called *reed fencing.* It comes in 6-foot-high rolls 15 and 25 feet long.

USE: Breaks wind enough to control the drifting of snow and sand. Also functions as a simple windbreak for small shrubs and trees—an application particularly useful in areas where the winter winds can be damaging. Can also be used to shade newly planted seedlings or hardwood cuttings.

SPIRAL ALUMINUM TOMATO STAKE

SPIRAL ALUMINUM TOMATO STAKE

DESCRIPTION: Thick wire spiral with straight pointed end, 5½ feet tall and ½ inch in diameter, which can be stuck in the ground near a tomato plant.

USE: Holding tomato plants upright without tying: They grow through the tunnel that is created by the spiral.

USE TIP: Make sure the main stem is placed inside the spiral before branching occurs. Keeping sucker growth (buds and stems that appear between the main stem and a branch) pruned is more important with this kind of stake. Sucker growth not only saps the strength of the plant, but can create a bushier plant than this type of stake is designed to accommodate.

BUYING TIP: These are more expensive than other types of stakes. Try one out before deciding whether you want to use it for all your tomato plants.

TOMATO CAGE

ALSO KNOWN AS: Tomato stake cage

DESCRIPTION: Rust-resistant metal or plastic frame, 48 or 54 inches high, shaped like a cone, with the larger end of the cone on the top, or like a straight cylinder or rectangle. Several concentric wire rings are held together by vertical metal wires.

TOMATO CAGE

Some are made from pieces of large wire mesh formed into 18-inch cylinders.

USE: Supports tomatoes and other fruiting plants, eliminating the task of staking and tying.

USE TIP: Cages should be placed over the plants shortly after they have been transplanted into the garden, before they become too big to be easily caged.

BUYING TIP: Unless you grow hundreds of tomatoes, cages are not an expensive purchase. They can be used for many years and are much easier to use than stakes and ties.

TRELLIS NET

DESCRIPTION: Plastic netting designed to be strung between poles or posts.

USE: Temporary trellis for climbing vegetable crops, such as cucumbers, beans, and peas. Reduces the amount of space needed in the garden. They also make harvesting from vines easier.

USE TIP: Place poles and posts that are used to support nets close enough together to support the weight of the crops. Test and experiment to determine the best distance, and install so that they hold well.

BUYING TIP: Gardeners in the past made their own net vegetable trellises by stringing twine between upright poles. Plastic net trellises simplify this task, and they can be used for many more years than twine. Make sure the net you are buying can support the weight of the crop that you wish to grow on it.

WALL ANCHOR

ALSO KNOWN AS: Vine hanger, vine support, vine nail, wall nail, garden wall tie

DESCRIPTION: Extra-sturdy 1¼-inch nail (a masonry nail) with a soft lead arm, or clip, about an inch or two long. Another version is a small fiber disk with a 2-inch-long wire tongue, sold with a tube of weatherproof adhesive. The simplest version is a long steel wedge with a hole in the wide end, called a *vine eye.* Another type is the *pole pin,* a sturdy, long U-shaped pin that is pushed into soft wood.

USE: Holding up vines or other climbing plants on masonry or wooden walls.

USE TIPS: Bend the holding arm before attaching to a wall. Make sure you follow adhesive directions, leaving a thick pad of it between the wall and the anchor.

WIRE FENCING

DESCRIPTION: Welded wire fences are available with large mesh and fence posts in 36- and 48-inch-high models, sold in 50-foot rolls. *Hex netting,* also known as *poultry netting* or *chicken wire,* is available in 50- and 150-foot rolls, 24, 36, and 48 inches wide, of lightweight galvanized, woven wire. *Diamond mesh* is available galvanized or vinyl coated, usually with a 2½-inch woven mesh made of medium-weight wire, in 50-foot rolls, 36 or 48 inches high—it looks like the much stronger and heavier *chain link fences.* Welded mesh has square openings in various sizes, including ½ by 1 inch, 1 inch square, 2 by 1 inch, and 4 by 2 inches, and is available in 36- and 48-inch heights, sold in rolls 50 and 100 feet long. Some fencing labels refer to the "gauge" of the wire used, meaning the weight or thickness. A higher number is lighter weight: Below approximately 14 to 16 is heavy, and above 20 is lightweight.

USE: Containing animals and people on your property, or excluding them.

BUYING TIP: Welded fencing is stronger than woven fencing, and wire fence material that is galvanized after welding is better protected against the elements.

Protective Materials and Season Extenders

BURLAP

ALSO KNOWN AS: Wind shield, windbreak, plant protector

DESCRIPTION: Loosely woven, light brown cloth traditionally made from natural jute fiber, available in 7-ounce and lightweight 5-ounce versions. Sold in sheets from 20 inches square to 120 inches square or in rolls up to 125 yards long and in widths of 36, 40, 48, or 60 inches, called *bulk,* or *continuous, burlap.* May be treated (to prevent rot) or untreated. Very loosely woven (½-inch) untreated burlap is sold in 3-foot by 10-, 25-, 50-, and 100-foot rolls for use over newly seeded lawns. It decomposes after the grass grows through it. Longer rolls, 45 inches by 250 yards, are sold as *lawn netting* and may be made of twisted paper cord. Plastic version is also available. *Erosion cloth* is a term sometimes used to refer to the 5-ounce, lightweight, wide (or "open") mesh version. Available also in 8- to 12-foot squares, with grommets in each corner and reinforced edges for use as a leaf carrier; may be called *totes.*

USE: Seven-ounce rolled burlap is used to construct wind shields to protect sensitive plants from cold, damaging winter winds and snow. Sheets are used to wrap root and soil balls when transplanting or moving woody shrubs and trees. Smaller sheets, about 8 feet square, can be used for carrying large loads of raked leaves or other garden debris. Five-ounce erosion cloth and lawn netting are staked or pinned down on newly seeded or bare lawns, especially on gentle slopes and embankments.

USE TIPS: When wrapping root balls, wet the soil around the plant well to keep the soil in a compact ball. Be sure to use natural twine to bind a natural burlapped root ball, so that it decomposes after planting. Most burlap products, especially the lightweight version, are biodegradable and disintegrate naturally after one season—considered an advantage by most users. Remove lawn netting after grass sprouts if you don't want to wait. Do not use as a duster: The dust will go all over, not as directed, and is likely to pose a hazard to you.

BUYING TIP: Natural burlap is easier to use as it is more pliable than plastic, which does not allow plant roots to breathe and does not decompose in the ground.

CLOCHE

ALSO KNOWN AS: Season extender, plant protector, tepee, plant cover

DESCRIPTION: Plastic, glass, or fabric cone that is placed over a single plant, several plants, or an entire row of plants in a garden. Similar in theory to a cold frame (see next entry), but portable. Light passes through the material so that the green leaves can still photosynthesize. Many ingenious designs are available, from galvanized wire mesh covered with plastic to paper on wire hoops, as well as the familiar molded or formed

CLOCHE

plastic. A newer kind is a set of interconnected clear plastic tubes that are filled with about 3 gallons of water, forming a ribbed cone (sold under the brand name Wall-O-Water). The water retains heat from the day and releases it at night, acting as a temperature moderator and insulator.

USE: Protects young, tender crops during the early (and late) season from late (or early) frosts and cold winds. It is also used to extend the season into the cooler weather in the fall and to protect seedlings from birds, insects, and hard rains. Crops such as tomatoes, peppers, and other transplants can get a head start when a cloche is placed over them.

USE TIP: Be sure to remove the cloche when the day temperatures are particularly warm (75° F or over), as the plants may heat up too much. Replace the cloche when the temperatures begin to drop.

BUYING TIP: If you plan on using cloches for several years, buy the higher-priced fabric or solid plastic ones that will last, and store carefully between seasons. It will be worth the investment.

COLD FRAME

DESCRIPTION: Essentially a miniature greenhouse, consisting of an open pit dug in the ground up to 2 feet deep by about 3 or 4 feet long and wide, with a wooden (rot-resistant redwood most often), plastic (polycarbonate), or aluminum frame around the sides and a hinged glass or clear plastic top. Some models come with thermostatically controled tops that automatically open when the temperature reaches a certain point, or other automatic venting systems, or it can be a simple homemade job.

USE: Allows you to winter over tender plants as well as to start and protect seedlings in the spring. Can double during the summer as a small compost bin when it is not being used for plants.

USE TIPS: Cold frames should be opened when the day temperatures begin to climb, otherwise you risk a premature cooking of the plants within. Watch out that you don't drop the top and break the glass; plastic glazing is advantageous in this respect.

BUYING TIPS: Cold frames are so easy to make that most people (even those who are not handy) can put one together in an afternoon, using scrap lumber and old windows. However, the polycarbonate ones sold commercially are excellent—they even insulate a bit—and won't break if you drop the tops or accidentally step on them when chasing an errant shuttlecock or baseball. Look for ones with wind-protected vents.

ROSEBUSH PROTECTOR

ALSO KNOWN AS: Winterizer, plant protector, season extender, rose collar, rose cone

DESCRIPTION: Two basic types: one solid and one open. The solid one is a Styrofoam plastic cone about 1½ or 2 feet high that resembles a large wastebasket with a flange. Stakes, which are supplied, are driven through holes in the flange to hold the cone down. The open one is fiberglass screening or corrugated plastic in the form of a cylinder a foot high and from 1 to 1½ feet in diameter. It is filled with a light, insulating mulch, such as peat moss, peanut shells, or the like.

USE: Protecting rosebushes from winter weather extremes.

USE TIPS: Carefully prune your roses first. Clean and store properly to get long life out of your protectors.

ROW COVER

ALSO KNOWN AS: Fabric row cover, floating row cover

POPULAR BRAND NAME: Reemay®

DESCRIPTION: Essentially a sort of cold frame (see pages 285–86) brought to the plants instead of the other way around. Made of lightweight, translucent, spun-bonded polyester material in rolls between 5 and 6 feet wide and 250 to 2,550 feet long. Sunlight (75 percent) and water (almost 100 percent) penetrate easily. Some are slitted to prevent overheating during periods of temperature fluctuation.

USE: Protects seedlings from animals, flying pests, and seasonal temperature extremes (early spring and late fall) to a certain extent, while still allowing light and water to enter. Also helps retain moisture and heat in a seedbed.

USE TIPS: Support with some kind of light framework or stakes. Though the manufacturer claims that the material is so light it can be placed loosely over new plants or seedbeds, letting the plants push it up as they grow, tender seedlings might not be

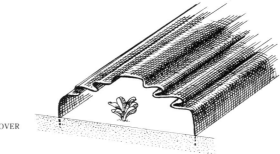

ROW COVER

strong enough to do this and could get damaged. Remove the fabric once the seedlings are established to avoid heating up the bed too much.

SHADE FABRIC

DESCRIPTION: Loosely woven black polypropylene fibers sold in 6-foot rolls in lengths up to 300 feet. It is graded according to the density of shade it provides, ranging from 30 to 92 percent (commonly 53, 63, and 73 percent). Price varies accordingly, with the densest costing roughly twice as much per square foot as the most open. The fabric is rot-proof, mildew-proof, UV ray resistant, and chemical resistant. *Shading compound* is a concentrated paint that is used on glass greenhouses to temper the sunlight. A different kind of compound is used on plastic. *Greenhouse film* is UV resistant plastic sheeting, 14 to 40 feet wide, sold in 100-foot rolls, used for the same purpose; it is secured with staples and *greenhouse tape,* an adhesive tape specially formulated for this purpose.

USE: Primarily for shading tender new seedlings and transplants but also for covering a planting bed where cuttings are rooting.

USE TIP: It is easier to install above a planting bed if it is attached to a wooden frame.

BUYING TIPS: As with many products sold by the roll, larger ones are cheaper to buy by the foot. Look for shade fabric that is UV tested, as this indicates it does not break down under sunlight.

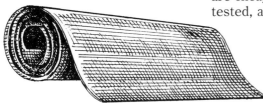

SHADE FABRIC

STEEL MESH TREE PROTECTOR

POPULAR BRAND NAME: Tree Tender®

DESCRIPTION: Soft, flexible, stainless steel mesh that is sold in small pieces 2⅜ inches by 7½ feet. Secured with clips supplied by the manufacturer. Can be cut to fit. Another version is made of sturdy foam rubber.

USE: One layer protects against rodent damage; multilayered wrap protects bark from string trimmer and mower damage. The open weave permits natural ventilation but discourages insect larvae development.

TREE SUPPORT KIT

DESCRIPTION: Collection of three 18-inch hardwood stakes, three 12-inch rubber sleeves (probably sections of old hose), and 30 feet of heavy galvanized wire. Others may include 6-foot cedar stakes instead, usually in urban areas.

USE: Holding a newly planted tree upright without damaging it.

USE TIPS: Wrap the wire around the stakes securely so that it really holds the tree if tension is placed on it. Position the hose around the tree's trunk, then wrap securely with the other ends of the wire. The hose will prevent the wire from cutting into the tree's bark. Place colorful ribbons on the stakes to prevent people from tripping over them. Remove after one year.

BUYING TIP: This is another item that is easily made at home, but is packaged merely as a convenience.

TREE TUBE

ALSO KNOWN AS: Tree guard

POPULAR BRAND NAMES: Ross Tree Gard®, Clark's Weed Whacker Guards

DESCRIPTION: A plastic tube slit along the side, sold in 36-inch lengths.

USE: Snaps onto trunks of young trees to protect them from insect and animal damage, as well as from excessive sun, like tree wrap (see next entry), but, because it is stiff plastic, it also protects street trees from minor bike or dog abuse, and provides particularly good winter protection. A new specialty model only 6 inches high has been developed for protecting against nylon string trimmers.

USE TIP: Remember to remove the tubing as the tree grows too big for it, although one advantage to slit tube or spirals is that they expand easily with the growth of the tree.

TREE WRAP

ALSO KNOWN AS: Tree paper, tree collar

DESCRIPTION: Waterproof paper, plastic fiber, vinyl, foam rubber, or burlap in widths from 3 to 6 inches. The woven wraps are sold in rolls of 100 or 150 feet, while the plastic wraps may be in 2- and 3-foot-long spirals. The paper type is dark brown kraft paper sandwiching a layer of weatherproof asphalt and given a "crepe" finish.

USE: Wound in a spiral around the bottom 6 feet or so of the trunks of small trees. Protects trees, especially young, newly planted ones, from damage by insects, pets, deer, rabbits, and weather (sunscald, windburn, or early frost), as well as from loss of moisture.

USE TIPS: Paper and natural fiber burlap are easier to work with and better for the tree than synthetic material, which when used as a tight fabric wrap does not expand as the tree grows, and if not removed, will constrict the tree. Tie with jute twine, which will rot off over time and not harm the tree as it grows. Solid plastic spirals should be avoided as they neither breathe nor decompose. Trees with lenticles (breathing pores) should not be covered with plastic tree wrap.

Personal and Miscellaneous Gear and Equipment

Protective Clothing and Gear

ABOUT PROTECTIVE GEAR AND SAFETY ITEMS

As tame a pastime as it may appear to be, gardening is not without its dangers—power tools, tools with sharp edges or blades, and toxic chemicals are some of the things that can be hazardous to the gardener who does not consider safety when using them. Many of the items listed here as personal gear are in fact safety items, designed to protect the gardener from harm. On the other hand, some are designed to make the gardener's job easier, or to help infirm or elderly gardeners get around an uncomfortable job. Both kinds are important.

When shopping for safety items, do not sacrifice quality for price. Be sure the items you are buying meet your own rigid standards for fit and function, and look for labels of government approval as well, such as OSHA (Occupational Safety and Health Administration) or ANSI (American National Standards Institute).

EAR PROTECTORS

ALSO KNOWN AS: Earmuffs, hearing protectors

DESCRIPTION: Similar to large audio headphones: two semi-

EAR PROTECTORS

spherical cups that are sound-insulated and foam-lined for easy fit. They fit over the ears and are held in place by a plastic or metal band that is worn over the top of the head.

USE: Prevent damage to the ears from the noise of power tools.

USE TIPS: Gasoline-powered tools such as lawn mowers, gas-powered string trimmers, chipper/shredders, generators for hedge trimmers, rotary tillers, and chain saws are particularly noisy and can cause damage to the ears. Ear protectors should be worn when using these tools and machines. Keep your eyes open for possible warnings from other people, because you won't be able to hear them when operating these types of equipment.

BUYING TIP: Try on ear protectors to test for comfortable fit and to test the level of noise they absorb.

HARD HAT

ALSO KNOWN AS: Safety hard cap

DESCRIPTION: Metal or reinforced plastic cap with a short bib visor in the front and a web lining. Available with transparent face shields (made of either plastic sheet or metal mesh) or ear protectors, in which case may be called a *safety helmet.*

USE: Protecting your head during overhead tree pruning or major clearing projects.

USE TIP: Adjust headband for snug fit.

BUYING TIP: Though not a standard item for all gardeners, it is recommended if you do a lot of heavy pruning. If you find that your are wearing a hard hat with your goggles and ear protectors, you may wish to look for hats that have these features built in. Consider the temperature when buying a hat with a face visor—a wire mesh face shield is cooler than a solid plastic one. Many different makes are available. Look for one that meets ANSI standards, the government test.

PROTECTIVE GOGGLES

ALSO KNOWN AS: Safety goggles, eye protectors

DESCRIPTION: Oversized plastic glasses with covered sides,

PROTECTIVE GOGGLES

large enough to fit over regular glasses, with rubber or elastic headbands that hold them in place. The side pieces also have vent holes to prevent the goggles from fogging up, though some goggles are now made of nonfogging plastic.

USE: Protect eyes from dust or flying particles of wood, grit, stone, or any other object that could damage the eyes. They are to be worn when using most power tools, such as chipper/shredders and string- or blade-type weed cutters, as well as large cutting tools such as axes and hatchets.

USE TIP: Goggles should be kept clean for better visibility. Certain power tools kick up so much debris that the goggles can become dangerously clogged, actually blinding you and possibly leading to an accident.

BUYING TIPS: Safety goggles are an essential gardening item if you use axes or power tools. Try them on before purchase to ensure a comfortable fit. Wear them for a few minutes to see if they fog up, and don't buy them if they do. Goggles should protect from dust and dirt as well as impact, and are marked as such. If you wear glasses, get a pair of goggles that are large enough to fit over them. There is no question that protection of your eyes is worth spending money on. Don't worry about finding great bargains here.

RESPIRATOR AND DUST MASK

ALSO KNOWN AS: *Respirator*—Breathing mask, gas mask; *Dust mask*—Pinch mask, face mask, painter's mask (this term is incorrect and misleading)

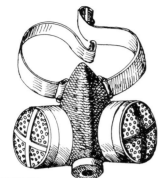

RESPIRATOR

DUST MASK

DESCRIPTION: Respirators are heavy-duty rubberized plastic devices that are strapped to the head and fit over the mouth and nose. A round filter cartridge is on each side. Some models, called "full-face" models, have a face shield that covers the entire face. Government specifications for whatever it can filter out are clearly indicated on the filter package.

Dust masks are only a few inches wide, fit loosely over the mouth and nose, and are held by a thin rubber band around the head. They are made of compressed paper fibers, are usually white, and a thin metal strip above the nose section of the mask is pinched tight for a more secure fit around the nose. The term *painter's mask* is incorrect as it generally does not protect against inhaling spray paint. Also available are slightly heavier plastic or rubber masks, roughly triangular in form, into which you insert small replacement filters; they provide a slightly snugger fit around the mouth and nose. Only a few designs are government approved.

USE: Respirators are used to filter out fine dust, mists, or toxic vapors, depending on the filter type. This kind of respirator is essential if you are using toxic chemicals; be certain to check the specifications of the filter cartridges. Dust masks are used to block out larger dusts and powders, but they do not filter out toxic vapors or mists.

USE TIPS: All masks must fit properly in order to do any good. Every gardener should keep good-quality paper dust masks on hand to wear when mixing soils, working with milled peat, and particularly for mixing soilless mixes that throw off a lot of dust, which can cause respiratory problems. *Paper dust masks are disposable and must be discarded after each use.* Clean a respirator and change its filter per directions.

BUYING TIPS: Depending upon the type of gardening you do and your exposure to toxic fumes, a respirator may not be necessary, but it is easily available these days and not too expensive. It seems a worthwhile investment in your health, even if used rarely. Dust masks, however, are inexpensive essentials. You must match the type of respirator to the job at hand. Filter cartridges are marked by their capacity for masking out dusts, mists, vapors, or fumes. Look for government approval, from either NIOSH (National Institute of Safety and Health) or MSHA (Mine Safety and Health Administration) or both. If your local garden center or hardware store cannot provide these items, check the Yellow Pages under "Safety Equipment" or "Industrial Supplies."

Comfort and Convenience Items

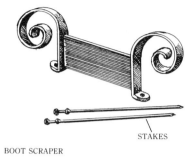

STAKES

BOOT SCRAPER

BOOT SCRAPER

DESCRIPTION: Many varieties, most of which fall into two categories: mat and brush type or H bar type. The former is like a metal doormat, with several rows of metal teeth instead of fiber or rubber, and the latter is a simple, flat, 6-inch-long piece of metal suspended between two uprights not more than a foot long. Stakes are driven into the ground through the uprights to hold it securely. Sometimes the mat kind has brushes fixed on either side, and instead of metal teeth, a wire brush that is replaceable. Certain models have waist-high handles, helping those of us who have trouble balancing on one leg, whether from lack of strength or mere exuberance.

USE: Forcibly removing mud from the bottoms and sides of boots.

GARDEN BOOTS

DESCRIPTION: High-top rubber boots with sturdy soles reinforced in the instep for digging (pushing a shovel by stepping on it) and a patch over the anklebone. Easily removable and waterproof.

USE: Allow unworrisome accumulation of mud on the feet, while keeping them dry.

BUYING TIPS: Typically black; most of the best models are English. Be sure to look for reinforcement where you push the shovel with your instep, and a sole pattern that does not hang onto mud.

GARDEN CLOGS

DESCRIPTION: Colorful clogs that look like wooden Dutch shoes, but are made of a rubberlike plastic. They have cushioned insoles that can be removed so that the clog can be cleaned with a hose.

USE: Gardening shoes that hold up to moisture and repeated cleanings.

USE TIP: The clog will outlast the insole, which is replaceable.

GARDEN SPEAKER

GARDEN SPEAKER

DESCRIPTION: Electronic hi-fi speaker in a decorative, weather-proof housing, often cylindrical and intended to be partially buried.

USE: Providing music in your garden from a remote source, usually your interior radio, tape deck, or record player.

USE TIPS: It is unclear which kind of music plants prefer. Watch your volume. Be careful not to disturb the neighbors.

GARDENING APRON AND TOTE

ALSO KNOWN AS: Gardener's apron

DESCRIPTION: Heavy canvas or cloth with pockets for small hand tools, plant labels, seed packets, notepad, pencils, and the like, designed to be worn like a kitchen apron or, in the case of the tote, like a holster on a belt.

USE: Keeping small and often-used gardening tools and accessories handy when not in use. Particularly useful during spring planting days.

USE TIPS: Aprons can be used for storage of these small necessities whether being worn or not. Hang the apron in an "open" position; this has the advantage of keeping the apron loaded and ready whenever you actually put it on. You may want to dedicate a belt to the gardening tote, so you can put it on over your gardening outfit, rather than having to take your own belt off each time you want to use the tote.

BUYING TIPS: Heavy-duty canvas aprons with many pockets and double seams are the best. Shorter aprons allow free movement, especially if you need to kneel, so the length should not go beyond the knees.

GARDENING GLOVES

ALSO KNOWN AS: Work gloves, protective gloves, garden gloves

DESCRIPTION: Constructed from cloth, canvas, leather, rubber, or some form of pliable plastic, lined or unlined. Gloves designed for pruning thorny brush or roses or picking fruit have long gauntlet-type cuffs to protect the arms and are coated with a plasticlike material that thorns cannot penetrate. They may be called *fruit picker gloves*. Lightweight, disposable plastic gloves are also available. So-called *ladies' gloves* are available in gingham, floral, and polka-dot patterns as well as plain, and tend to run in smaller sizes.

USE: Protect hands from blisters, dryness, cuts, and other damage that might occur during gardening, and provide a better grip in cold weather. Heavy plastic gloves made of *neoprene* are required for handling toxic materials, and lightweight, disposable ones for merely irritating chemicals. *Real* gardeners do *not* wear gloves to keep their hands clean!

USE TIPS: Wear the appropriate glove for the job you are doing. If you are transplanting delicate seedlings, don't wear heavy gloves that dampen your sense of touch. Unlined cloth gloves are good for light work and leather gloves that provide a good grip are for heavier or dangerous work. Check the directions for cleaning, because only some leather gloves can be washed. Most leather gloves that are soiled and damp become stiff and difficult to use when they dry, and should be treated with saddle soap or Murphy's Oil. Some pigskin resists this stiffness. Cotton gloves can be rinsed out in a rain barrel or sink. Gloves with holes in them will no longer prevent blisters and should be replaced. Models with lots of little rubber dots are excellent for gripping muddy tools and may wear longer.

BUYING TIPS: Gardeners should have several pairs of gloves. Check the gloves for a comfortable fit that is neither too tight nor too loose. Design varies greatly from brand to brand, and some makes offer a range of sizes, including those designed for women and men. The better designs take the natural curve of your grip into account. Look for material that resists cuts, snags, and punctures; goatskin is used in top-of-the-line products. Sheepskin, with its natural lanolin, is a real comfort if you can find it, and such gloves tend not to impede your dexterity (other skins, like goatskin, may offer the same quality, depending on the make). Look also for reinforced palms and seams. Work gloves are not an expensive investment, but generally the better gloves cost a little more (around $10 for good leather work gloves) and are worth it. When you find a pair that fits just right, you may want to buy several pairs right then.

GARDENING HAT

GARDENING HAT AND SUN VISOR

DESCRIPTION: Wide-brimmed, lightweight hat made of cloth, palm, plastic, straw, leather, or even paper and cardboard, in a wide variety of styles. A Panama hat is woven out of light straw.

USE: Personal, extremely portable sunshade. Wide brims keep gnats away.

USE TIPS: A hat or visor is essential protection against the harmful ultraviolet rays of the sun. Wear one as much as possible. And never underestimate the role of fashion in your choice of hats: A snappy-looking gardener is a better gardener, they say. Also, you might scare away some pest birds with some of the more adventurous or unsuccessful designs.

BUYING TIPS: Should be flexible, and a good-quality hat should "breathe" to keep you cool during hot days. There are no substitutes for genuine palm in terms of strength.

KNEELING BENCH

KNEE PROTECTORS

DESCRIPTION: Several products are sold that protect the knees from damage while gardening.

TYPES: *Kneepads:* Shallow rubber cups that fit directly over the knee and are held in place by straps that go around the leg. Sold in different weights and densities.

Kneeling pads: Rectangular foam rubber pads about 9 by 18 inches. Most have an elliptical hole that serves as a handle for carrying.

Kneeling bench (also known as *kneeler stool, bench/ kneeler,* or *garden stool):* A combination bench and kneeling pad design, this has become quite popular in recent years. Consists of a tubular metal frame about 20 inches high that supports a padded seat about 20 inches wide. When the bench is positioned with the cushion up, it is a comfortable, portable seat. When it is turned upside down, it becomes a kneeling pad with high handles for assisting the gardener in getting up and down. A bench or seat design is available with wheels, for scooting along as you garden, called a *garden scoot.*

USE: Reducing the pain of kneeling. The kneeling bench is particularly helpful to elderly gardeners and all those who have difficulty kneeling and bending.

USE TIP: It is probably a good idea to protect your knees even if you have no knee problem. Whether using a pad or not, stand up and stretch often while gardening.

BUYING TIPS: Rubber kneepads are convenient because they are attached to you and don't have to be carried around, but many gardeners complain about the slight discomfort caused by the strap that holds them on. The more expensive designs, with their heavier, denser material, tend to be worth it. Cheaper ones that don't work well make you pay with real discomfort. (One alternative is a homemade solution: Make large pockets for sponges on the knees of your gardening pants. Ready-made pants like this are available via mail-order.) Foam kneeling pads are light, inexpensive, and easy to use, but they have to be moved each time you move. The kneeling bench is more expensive but its combination design makes it versatile. It is particularly attractive to elderly or arthritic gardeners who find kneeling and bending difficult.

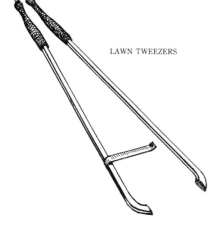

LAWN TWEEZERS

LAWN TWEEZERS

ALSO KNOWN AS: Cleanup caddy

DESCRIPTION: Lightweight aluminum tongs about a yard long with a hinge near the end. Plastic hand grips.

USE: Picking up litter without bending over or leaving a wheelchair, or reaching through thorny bushes

POISON OAK AND IVY CLEANSER

DESCRIPTION: Bottled salve.

USE: Applied within two to eight hours after exposure to these menaces, it removes the poison oil from your skin, actually preventing the dreaded rash. Relieves itching, slows spreading, and helps heal if applied to a rash directly.

TOOL HANGER

ALSO KNOWN AS: Tool hook

DESCRIPTION: Small steel tubing and brackets of various de-

HANDLE HANGER

signs. Longer brackets may have small balls welded on to keep tools apart. Some are designed to fit into the holes of Pegboard® while others are cliplike devices that slide over the top of a board which is in turn anchored to a wall. Another type, best for smaller tools, is a metal grid with specially made hooks. A popular design is a loop of tubular steel with both ends pointing out and up; it is attached to the wall at the center (a smaller version is merely a piece of stamped metal with two hooks). For larger tools there are *handle hangers* that look like large hooks placed sideways with hinges at the top—a long, straight tool handle is inserted in the hook by lifting it away from the wall and is held in place by friction.

USE: Holding tools on a wall.

USE TIPS: Draw an outline for each tool, or put a label above each hanger, so you can always fit the tools back where they came from. Make sure any supporting boards are securely anchored—a half dozen garden tools can be very heavy and quite dangerous should they fall. Hang pronged tools with their sharp tips facing the wall.

BUYING TIPS: Hangers are useful because they help avoid a dangerous clutter of tools on the floor, and keep the tools away from moisture as well. However, in many cases, large nails driven partway into a thick board, such as a two-by-four, that is in turn anchored securely to a wall, can do just as well. Look for systems that do not require two hands to use.

TOOL HOLSTER

TOOL HOLSTER

TYPES: *Sheath, Scabbard, Utility belt*

ALSO KNOWN AS: *Utility belt*—Tool belt

DESCRIPTION: Leather or canvas pouch that attaches to a belt, or in the case of a utility belt, a wide leather belt with hooks and compartments that goes over a regular belt.

USE: Keeping frequently used tools close at hand, especially knives, hatchets, pruning shears, and tree saws. Particularly useful for tools that are used throughout the garden, such as pruning shears, or those used when you are on a ladder.

USE TIP: Small items like pruning shears and pruning knives are less likely to be lost if they are placed in a sheath worn on the belt. Can be considered a safety item if you are working from a ladder.

BUYING TIP: Though most gardeners have no need for a heavy utility belt, any gardener with pruning shears and pruning knives will find the purchase of a quality holster a good investment. Look for well-sewn seams that are also riveted, and expect to pay between $5 and $10 for a good one.

TRUG

TRUG

ALSO KNOWN AS: Sussex trug, garden basket

DESCRIPTION: Shallow basket made of wide wooden strips, with short wooden feet and a large handle. Typically about 1 foot to just under 2 feet in length; size may be measured in capacity (e.g., 2 pints, 1.5 gallons, and 3 gallons). Made also of polyethylene.

USE: Handy way to bring small garden tools or your vegetable and flower harvest along with you as you work in the garden.

BUYING TIPS: Top-quality models are often English, made from chestnut and willow. Other common good materials are northern ash weavings and oak handles.

Birdhouses, Feeders, and Food

ABOUT BIRD EQUIPMENT

Almost all garden centers have a section devoted to birds, with birdhouses, bird feeders, birdseed, and other items designed to attract birds to the garden. Most gardeners get a particular thrill when birds find the garden pleasing enough to inhabit it. Furthermore, the presence of birds (and their singing) in a garden reminds gardeners that they are participating in a natural world that is larger than the dimensions of the garden itself. Though some birds become pests, and products are sold to rid the garden of them (see chapter 4), most birds are quite beneficial to gardens, consuming mosquitoes and other insect pests. In even the smallest garden (on apartment balconies, too) there is room for a bird feeder or a small birdhouse.

BIRDBATH

DESCRIPTION: Shallow basin that holds water, of almost infinite variety in design and detail. Some are classic and simple bowllike designs, others whimsical animal motifs (including one that recently appeared, ironically, in the form of a cat). Most birdbaths are set on a pedestal to keep them out of the reach of cats. Birdbaths can be made of stone, glazed clay, terra-cotta, cement, plastic, cast aluminum, brass, and still other materials.

USE: Attracting birds to your garden. Water is essential to attract birds, and a birdbath provides this water and is at the same time an attractive garden accessory.

USE TIPS: Place birdbaths in somewhat open areas so that birds can see any approaching cats while they are bathing. This is particularly important for basins that do not sit on pedestals or stands. Keep filled with fresh water and wash the bath out if algae begin to grow. In areas of the country where winters are harsh, basins should be heated with an *electric birdbath heater* or emptied of water. If not stored inside, they should be wrapped in plastic. Freezing water will expand and crack even a stone birdbath.

BUYING TIP: Cheap plastic birdbaths are not a good buy. Besides looking cheap (this should be considered a permanent decorative item), they are light, and the water-filled basin makes them top-heavy. There are almost unlimited alternatives. Shop for one that will complement your garden and be a focal point.

BIRD FEEDER

DESCRIPTION: A tremendous array of designs exist, from the whimsical and rustic to the extremely high tech, but all bird feeders consist of some type of chamber that holds birdseed and some place for birds to perch while feeding. Bird feeders can be round cylinders, rectangular boxes, or covered top shelters in which the seed is placed in a feeding tray. They are made of plastic, wood, glass, metal, and combinations of all these materials. Some are even designed to be mounted on a window. Most have some device for preventing squirrels from feeding, a *squirrel baffle,* a large plastic disk that fits on the support pole or hangs above a wire-held feeder. A *seed catcher,* a large saucer that attaches to the pole under the feeder, catches any stray

BIRD FEEDER

SQUIRREL BAFFLE

BIRD FEEDER

seeds that might fall. Baffles also are used for excluding heavier "nuisance" birds, such as blackbirds or pigeons.

USE: Bird feeders are most often used to attract birds to the garden during off-seasons, such as winter, when other food is scarce. Some feeders, however, are designed to attract a particular type of bird during seasons when they migrate through your area. Other feeders are used to attract particular types of birds in the spring in the hope that they will nest in or near your garden. Always keep your feeder full during its season(s) of use.

USE TIPS: Squirrels are the enemies of bird feeders, as they will enter and devour all the seed if at all possible. Place bird feeders in locations that make it difficult for squirrels (and cats, of course) to get to them, such as on metal poles and away from branches and climbable parts of buildings. Or add a squirrel baffle. Be mindful that sunflower seeds act as an herbicide and will kill your grass.

BUYING TIPS: Other than buying a sturdy, well-made feeder, particular consideration should be paid to whether the feeder is squirrel- or cat-proof. Squirrel baffles are sold separately, too. Look for models hung from wires or poles with circular squirrel guards. Bird feeders that have wide platform areas give squirrels a place to perch while raiding a feeder, and should be avoided. Window-mounted models may work better with one-way mirrors so you don't scare the birds away. The feeder should be able to adequately dispense the size of birdseed you wish to put in it. For example, finches, wrens, and many small birds feed on thistle seed and small grains. If the dispensing part of a feeder is too large, these smaller seeds will not be held well. Sunflower seed cannot be dispensed if the openings are too small. Buy feeders that will attract the specific birds you want. This information should be included in the packaging but can also be found in reference books.

BIRDHOUSE

DESCRIPTION: Made of wood, clay, plastic, or metal, birdhouses are constructed in certain sizes, shapes, and even colors to attract the specific type of bird they were built to accommodate. For example, the very social purple martins prefer to live and nest in groups and are attracted to white, well-ventilated, multicompartment houses that will house six to twenty-four nesting couples, usually perched on top of a tall pole (which has to be

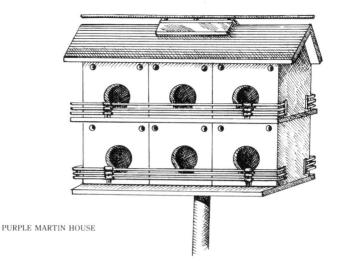

PURPLE MARTIN HOUSE

taken down, or the house lowered, each winter for cleaning). The wren, on the other hand, prefers to nest in a solitary small house that is protected by lush plant growth. The size(s) of the hole(s) in birdhouses determine(s) what birds will live in them, too. For example, house wrens and pygmy and brown-headed titmice use a house with a 1-inch hole; chickadees, Carolina wrens, tufted and plain titmice, and small woodpeckers need a small hole 1¼ inches in diameter; while bluebirds and swallows want a hole that is 1½ inches in diameter. As for materials, a popular type is a sawdust/clay/concrete mixture that looks and feels like wood or dried mud, the normal stuff birds make nests of. Also popular are those with genuine thatched roofs. Of all the woods, cedar lasts longest. Many have openings for cleaning out the houses.

USE: Attracting birds by providing a place for them to nest in your garden. Since many birds nest in the same place year after year, once you have housed nesting birds they should be with you for many years. Attracting nesting birds that are known to eat bugs is a great natural way of controlling many garden pests.

USE TIPS: Birdhouses should be placed in areas where cats cannot reach them. If this is not possible, then you must find ways to cat-proof the house, such as wrapping a wooden pole in a sheet of galvanized tin about 3 feet high to prevent cats from climbing up. How high a birdhouse is placed and what direction it faces are important considerations for getting the tenant you want to occupy it. This information can be easily found in your library, in most popular field guides and books and articles on attracting wildlife. You might also try checking your local Cooperative Extension bulletins.

BUYING TIPS: Look for sturdy birdhouses. Know specifically what birds you want to nest in your house, and buy one that is stated to have been made for that particular bird. Shop around, as prices do vary considerably. Martin houses, being bigger, are generally more expensive than others. Check your reference books to find out what size hole you need for the birds you want to attract, and measure the holes before buying—often they are not marked. As for "manufactured" wood versus natural, it seems to be a matter of personal preference. The birds are not choosy. What's important is that the house endures, and the clay/concrete mixture seems to be the sturdiest; furthermore, squirrels and predator birds are unable to enlarge the hole.

BIRDSEED

DESCRIPTION: Grains and seeds, usually mixed, including sunflower, safflower, peanut hearts, millet, sunflower chips, thistle, and cracked corn. Mixtures of different types of grain and seed are blended to match the diets of certain types of birds. Some garden centers sell the seed unmixed so that you can buy and mix your own, depending on the type of birds you have or want to attract.

USE: Placed in bird feeders primarily to supplement birds' diets during times when other food is scarce, such as in winter.

USE TIPS: Select the type of seed to attract the birds you want most. Avoid unshelled sunflower seeds if you have a squirrel problem, as this is their favorite. Mixes that contain unshelled sunflower seed are for larger birds. The shells of sunflower seeds contain a natural herbicide and kill vegetation if they collect on the ground under a feeder.

BUYING TIP: Birdseed is not expensive, so experiment to find those mixes that attract the birds you want. With a little research, you can easily learn what types of seed certain birds prefer.

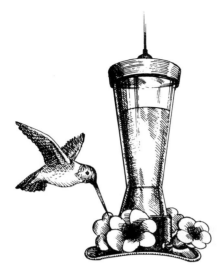

HUMMINGBIRD FEEDER

HUMMINGBIRD FEEDER

DESCRIPTION: There are several types of hummingbird feeders on the market but all have several things in common. Each has a reservoir for holding a liquid sugar mixture (often sold as *hummingbird nectar*). All or part of the feeders are red, as this color attracts hummingbirds. Feeding tubes that resemble the trumpet-shape flower that hummingbirds naturally take nectar from are attached to the sides. Feeders may have a single or several feeding tubes or fountains (small holes that the hummingbird sticks its beak into).

USE: Attracting this fascinating bird to the garden.

USE TIPS: If the liquid reservoir on your feeder is clear, a little red food coloring can be added to the nectar to help attract hummingbirds. Learning something about the hummingbirds in your area will help you attract them to your garden. For example, hummingbirds migrate through the northeastern United States in late summer, so this is the best time for putting out feeders there. Remember that hummingbirds feed from flowers, so the feeder should not be placed higher than where the birds will naturally look for it.

BUYING TIP: Hummingbird feeders are not expensive. Most will attract hummingbirds if they are in the area at all, but ones designed to be bee-proof are better.

SUET BALLS AND CONES

DESCRIPTION: Suet balls are made of animal fats or lard compressed into a small ball and embedded with birdseed. The ball has a string or a wire attached so that it can be hung from a tree. Suet cones are large pinecones that have been dipped in animal fats and sprinkled with birdseed.

USE: Supplement to birds' winter diet, when food is scarce. The suet itself is supposed to be helpful to the birds during cold weather.

USE TIPS: Note that suet balls and cones are primarily for winter feeding—they become a dripping mess in warm weather. A metal collar is necessary to act as a squirrel guard.

BUYING TIP: Suet balls are an inexpensive and easy way to feed birds in winter. As inexpensive as they are, some people find them a nice home project to make themselves.

Bonsai and Flower Arranging Tools and Equipment

ABOUT BONSAI

The enduring Japanese art of growing miniature trees, bonsai, is very popular in all parts of this country. The tree's leaves, branches, and roots are clipped regularly and trained with copper wire, forcing the plant to mature without getting large. Specialized tools have been developed to make this work easier.

Bonsai plants need gentle care. If you are not a serious bonsai hobbiest and receive a plant as a gift, take a course at a nearby botanic garden or search for some good books on the subject, of which there are many.

BONSAI PLANTER

DESCRIPTION: Shallow round, oval, or rectangular dish, usually of glazed ceramic material but also of plastic, with drainage holes. Commonly sold with matching saucer.

USE: Growing bonsai plants.

BUYING TIP: Although any container with drainage will do, these are more likely to fit the art form.

BONSAI SNIPS

DESCRIPTION: Specially adapted snips for more control and precision in the detail work required by bonsai gardening. More specialized tools may be found—these are the basics.

TYPES: *Scissors* (also known as *beginner's shears* or *bud shears*—these have small finger loops): Black wrought iron or carbon-steel scissors with short blades (about 1 inch—known as *Koryu* style) and long handles, either with small finger holes on the end or with large butterfly loops for the entire hand. Overall length about 6 inches.

Shears (also known as *trimming, Ikebana,* or *flower arranging shears):* Like scissors, but with slightly longer blades (about 2 inches) and butterfly handles—called *Ashinaga,* or more correctly, *naga ashi bonsai hasami*—*hasami* means "shears" in Japanese.

Branch nippers (also known as *concave cutter):* Black

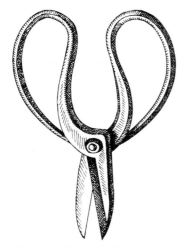

KORYU STYLE BONSAI SCISSORS

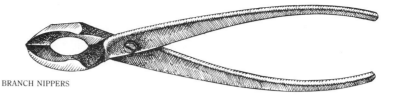

BRANCH NIPPERS

wrought iron pincers, with wide, beveled, curved jaws, about 1 inch long and ¾ inch wide. Resemble wide pliers. Long handles; tool is about 8 inches long overall. Variations include a *spherical cutter,* a *knuckle cutter,* and a *root cutter.*

Wire cutters: Resembles above-mentioned scissors, but 1-inch blades are thicker. Handles have finger loops at end.

USE: Maintaining bonsai plants with precision. The *scissors* are for leaf trimming; *shears* for cutting small branches and leaves; *branch nippers* for making concave cuts when removing branches; and *wire cutters* cut wire close to the branch. Choice of model is largely one of individual discretion.

BONSAI TROWELS

DESCRIPTION: Miniature versions of trowels (see pages 153–55) and scoops, usually made of one piece of metal.

USE: Careful moving of soil in bonsai planters (see page 306).

CEMETERY CONE

ALSO KNOWN AS: Funeral cone, cemetery vase

DESCRIPTION: Small plastic, galvanized steel, tin, or cast-iron cone, about the size of a jumbo soft-drink cup or ice-cream cone, often filled with a small bouquet of plastic flowers. Usually dark green. May have a spike on the bottom or a bracket on the side.

USE: Displays flowers on or near a gravestone. Attaches permanently to gravestones or is stuck into the ground nearby. Holds plastic or real flowers.

USE TIP: One of the best ways to leave flowers at a gravesite.

BUYING TIP: Usually carried only by those garden centers located near a cemetery.

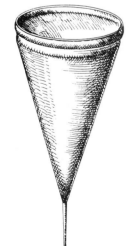

CEMETERY CONE

CUT FLOWER PRESERVATIVE

ALSO KNOWN AS: Cut flower food

DESCRIPTION: A type of fertilizer and conditioner for cut flowers in granular form.

USE: When mixed with water in a vase, can preserve cut flowers an extra week or so by cutting down on bacterial growth, which also keeps the water clear.

FLORAL FOAM

ALSO KNOWN AS: Foam brick, floral base, floral foam brick

POPULAR BRAND NAME: Oasis

DESCRIPTION: Stiff green Styrofoam block, sold in 6-inch cubes, that can be cut to size. Is treated with a floral preservative and may come with adhesive on one side for anchoring in a vase. *Dry floral foam* is similar, but is intended for use with dried and silk flowers (and plastic flowers, too, if you must). A similar product that is less common is *floral clay,* which works in much the same way as foam.

USE: Holding the stems of cut flowers in the bottom of a floral arrangement. Stems are merely stuck into the foam at any angle. The foam is first floated on water until it is saturated, then held down with waterproof adhesive floral tape (see next entry) made for this purpose.

USE TIP: Helps retain water and extend flower life.

FLOWER ARRANGING ACCESSORIES

DESCRIPTION: A variety of items that are convenient ingredients in floral arrangements, both fresh and dried.

TYPES AND THEIR USES:
Floral wire (also known as *florist's wire)* comes in green, straight, and coiled forms and is used to hold flowers in place in arrangements and corsages.

Floral tape (also known as *stemming tape* or *stemming wire)* is used to conceal the wires, especially on corsages.

Floral picks hold flower stems in the foam.

Floral adhesive, usually sold in 1-inch-wide tape form, holds the foam securely to the bottom of the vase.

FLOWER HOLDER

FLOWER HOLDER

ALSO KNOWN AS: Flower pin, needlepoint flower holder, *kenzan* (Japanese), floral holder, frog, flower frog

DESCRIPTION: Small, heavy, flat or domed disk or rectangle with many 1-inch spikes, usually green enamel or brass. Round ones are as small as 1 inch in diameter, with 4 inches a common size. May have a lead-weighted base surrounded by rubber. Some models on adjustable pedestals are made for putting short-stemmed flowers in with longer ones. An older version with notched copper hooks that look like hairpins instead of spikes is called a *hairpin frog.* Circular, interlocking models are called *sun-and-moon* flower holders.

USE: Holding the stems of cut flowers in the bottom of vases for floral arrangements such as *Ikebana.* Domed models are for splays of flowers.

BUYING TIP: Permanent and reusable, as opposed to floral foam (see page 308). Brass spikes are the most desirable, though galvanized steel does fine.

Garden Ornaments

ABOUT GARDEN ORNAMENTS

Garden centers that years ago limited their selections of garden art to designer urns, fancy teak chairs, benches, or a few pieces of sculpture are now selling all manner of lawn and garden ornaments, including gnomes, flamingos, and whirligigs.

The use of lawn and garden decorations has long been more popular in the South. Ironically, however, many of the major manufacturers are in the North, including Quebec, which is quite seriously north. The ornaments themselves have been sold in New England since the late 1700s.

These garden variety "objets d'art" give gardeners an opportunity to display their taste in public, leading one to ask, At what point does kitsch become art? This is a difficult question to answer, especially for a buying guide such as this. Excess and flamboyance may actually help develop our collective sense of taste. However, instead of the usual garden experts, it is more likely that archeologists, art critics, art historians, social commentators, and psychologists could provide answers—perhaps not definitive ones, but certainly more profound ones. Even some of the religious objects may be chosen for the same unspoken reason many of the animal or fantasy symbols are: some sort of basic, intimate desire for protection and a wish for continued fertility of the garden. It could be the sort of thing that taps into our collective unconscious and identification with archetypal symbols: We've moved on from totems, rocks, and petroglyphs, but not far—this is simply the modern version. As for the whimsey involved, this seems to be a way to keep the child within us alive, tying in with the theme of endless rejuvenation that is so appropriate to a garden. Anyway, it's probably something like that, but maybe not.

A final note: Once caught up in a collecting frenzy, some gardeners have difficulty curbing the impulse. In answer to the often-asked question, How much is too much? it appears that the answer is, according to one distinguished Southern gardener, "When it looks like you're selling the stuff!"

BARNYARD ANIMALS

HEN WITH CHICKS

DESCRIPTION: Cast either in plastic or cement in the shapes of familiar farm animals such as roosters, hens, chicks, ducks, ducklings, lambs, and sheep. Also available as wooden cutouts, painted, or covered with polyester imitation wool (in the case of sheep), or a sort of furry material that expands when wet to resemble the three-dimensional real thing. Sheep come in two styles: with heads down at grass level (grazing position) or up (looking position), and in small (1 foot), medium, and large (2½ feet) sizes. Some large sheep may also have a bell at their necks.

USE: To create a bucolic or "cute" effect.

USE TIP: Move your animals around the garden or lawn every day to create the illusion that they are alive. Excellent gift item, especially the fur-covered ones of the cuddly type.

BUYING TIPS: If you are buying a family of chickens, be sure to get the hen with the chicks, and not the rooster, even though he may be more colorful, in order to be biologically correct. Those animals that are curled up and looking out at the viewer are much more cuddly appearing than those that are in the standing position. Sheep with their heads in the "up" position generally cost $2 more, for no apparent reason. Large polyester-on-plywood pigs and sheep can cost as much as $70. Some sheep come in a set with Little Bo-Peep.

CARTOON CHARACTERS

DESCRIPTION: Disney characters and other familiar cartoon friends. Recent introductions to lawn and garden decor, they are almost always made of colorful plastic. Snow White and the Seven Dwarfs are sold as a unit of approximately eight pieces.

USE: Personal expression in public. These objects reflect your interest and personality more than most of the other ornaments.

USE TIP: Bambi may not go with more serious garden or landscape concepts.

BUYING TIP: Cartoon characters are among the most affordable of the lawn objects on the market. If you are on a limited budget but wish to collect, this would be a good place to start.

CLASSIC FOUNTAIN

CLASSIC SCULPTURE AND FOUNTAINS

DESCRIPTION: Figures and shapes of a variety so diverse as to be impossible to list here. Though derived primarily from Western European stock classic art styles, it ranges in style from the Greek to the Colonial to the representational to the abstract. The most popular include small svelte figures of nymphs and cherubs as well as a series of sea horses or scallop shells plumbed internally for cascading water. Pumps may or may not be included; some models are wired for lighting. Often edged in turquoise.

USE: Adds a touch of class to a garden.

USE TIPS: The higher the waterfall, the louder the noise. Do not place near popular nap locations.

BUYING TIPS: Some regional preferences may be reflected in the stock your garden center carries, such as a fountain in the shape of an oil well for the oil-producing areas of our country.

FAT FANNY

ALSO KNOWN AS: Gardening girl

DESCRIPTION: Wooden cutout of a rear view of a woman in a polka-dot dress bent over so that all you see is the polka dot–clad rump and two short legs, although now there is a thinner, bikini-clad version. Male version also available, sometimes called *Fat Freddy.* Sizes range from 16 to 24 inches high.

USE: To show the general public that you have a sense of humor.

USE TIP: Most effective when seen from a distance at high speed—excellent for those people who live near a major highway.

FAT FANNY

BUYING TIP: Look for well-painted wood that will stand up to the weather.

FLAMINGO

FLAMINGOS

DESCRIPTION: Invariably pink, large plastic or cement birds that usually stand a yard tall and are usually sold in pairs. The body is often cast or molded while the legs are extremely thin metal, plastic, or wood stakes made to be stuck into the ground. Some models are made with only one leg to imitate the flamingo's natural resting position, while others have two, to imitate a natural feeding position. *Herons* are a similar-looking but all white bird available in some garden centers.

USE: Adds a touch of drama to a yard. The farther away from the natural range of the subtropical flamingos you live, the more drama they add to your garden. Tropical colors give a sense of Miami Beach.

USE TIP: Flamingos should be taken in during the winter, as they appear particularly out of place in the snow. Furthermore, flamingos allowed to weather outside during the winter may lose their pink color, leaving the bird looking drab, which then quite defeats their purpose, as drab is not dramatic. Herons should be placed near a body of water to appear more natural-looking, as they do not add as much drama as flamingos.

BUYING TIP: It is a matter of personal taste as to whether the one-leg or two-leg model is preferable, but some gardeners find that the one-leg models make them nervous.

GAZING GLOBE

GAZING GLOBE

ALSO KNOWN AS: Reflective ball, witch's ball, lawn ball, buzzard ball, mirror ball

DESCRIPTION: Mirrorlike glass ball, 8 to 14 inches in diameter, usually placed upon a pedestal. Available in several colors, usually including sky blue, red, green, silver, and gold. Pedestals, which are also sold for birdbaths, may need an *extension* to hold the globe, and come in white or various shades of brown. They are made of concrete or clay.

USE: To attract attention. Rumored to kill weeds by reflection, but this is unproven at this time.

USE TIPS: Do not place near an active play area, as globes are made of glass. Bring inside during hailstorms.

BUYING TIPS: Look for the slightly irregular, hand-blown globes. Molded globes have seams and are of lesser quality.

GNOMES

GNOME

ALSO KNOWN AS: Dwarfs, dwarves, elfs, elves, trolls, leprechauns

DESCRIPTION: Elfish statues of "little people" in odd clothes and with old faces, ranging in size from less than a foot to around 20 inches high, though one model is 39 inches high; made of cast cement, bonded marble, plastic, or painted plaster. They may be the natural color of the material from which they are made or they can be painted to look more or less lifelike, depending on your taste. Some are wired with lights. Gnomes come with a variety of props, such as garden tools, pails, lanterns, golf clubs, watering cans, a large snail, a book, flutes, and an accordion. Props and poses can either reflect the owner's interests, personality, or some imagined and longed-for identity. Folklore has long linked these "little people" with the earth, trees, and water. Gnomes are European in origin and one of the better quality lines, Heissner Gnomes, has been manufactured in Germany since 1872. This may be the "Old World" that people so often link with "charm."

USE: Adding charm to your garden, and for good luck. A British scholar considers these phallic symbols.

USE TIPS: Gnomes tend to do well when partially hidden behind foliage or low branches, appearing to peek from behind plants. Remember that dwarfs and gnomes are social creatures and a single one does not look natural—place them in natural groupings of three or more.

BUYING TIPS: Though nothing lasts longer than concrete, the colors may fade. Only the very expensive makes are painted very accurately. Materials are largely a matter of personal taste. Gnomes should be bought to scale: Small gardens should have smaller gnomes than large gardens. If you want a lot of dwarfs, your best deal is to get a set of the Disney characters, such as Snow White and the Seven Dwarfs (see pages 311–12).

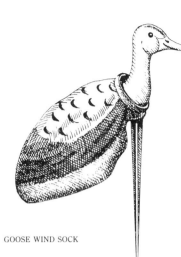

GOOSE WIND SOCK

GOOSE AND DUCK WIND SOCKS

DESCRIPTION: Large fabric socks printed to look like ducks or geese, attached to stakes that are stuck into the lawn. When the wind fills the fabric body of the birds they undulate and appear to be moving like the real thing; they hang limply when there is no wind. These work on the same principle as the fabric carps that are used in Japan to celebrate the birth of a boy child. Popularity began on the East Coast seashore.

USE: Adds movement to ornamentation in order to draw attention to your yard. Also tells you if the wind is blowing or not, and from which direction.

USE TIP: Use in groups of half a dozen or more, just as geese tend to land and feed in flocks.

JOCKEY HITCHING POST

JOCKEY AND SERVANT HITCHING POSTS

DESCRIPTION: Cast-iron, plaster, plastic, or cement statue of a 3- to 4-foot-tall jockey or servant in formal (red topcoat and tophat) or riding attire. His right arm is raised and often contains a small lamp or a ring for tethering a horse or mule. Until recently the jockey was black, but generally they are now white, reflecting a positive, though very minor, step in evolution of our society's race consciousness. Other hitching post lawn ornaments include the head of a horse with a ring through its nose, or a simple pole with a ring attached to the top.

USE: Originally to provide, perhaps, the mystique of the Old South, now nothing more than pure ornamentation, used primarily at the end of a walk or driveway.

USE TIP: Existing black jockeys may easily be painted white.

BUYING TIP: Not considered trendy.

JUST PLAIN BIZARRE ANIMALS AND FIGURES

DESCRIPTION: Large marine creatures (such as fish, clams, or sea horses) in chomping action, little dogs with their back legs raised (to be posed in an appropriate place, such as near the wheel of a car when it is parked in the driveway), other dogs (usually basset hounds) with "Welcome" or "Beware of Dog" painted on their ears, guttersnipes (urchins) in a variety of

BIZARRE MARINE FIGURE WITH NYMPH

poses, little sports players in action, seamen, drunkards, and servants. A new appearance has been made by dinosaurs, appropriately labeled "Tyrannosaurus," "Stegosaurus," and the like.

USE: To have something unusual on your lawn that your neighbor doesn't have yet, or to get otherwise taciturn visitors to ask you questions about your garden. Considered by some gardeners as necessary for providing a finishing touch to their landscaping. There is no logical explanation for the popularity of the little sports players as garden ornaments.

USE TIP: Manufacturers are coming up with new items all the time, and though the first time you see one of these it will seem extremely strange, as more and more people buy this new strange item it will become a familiar sight in our suburban landscape.

BUYING TIP: Expect a short life for your new and strange item because its uniqueness is bound to wear thin or completely off after a while. Frequent visits to garden centers will ensure that you will be one of the first people on your block to have the newest and the weirdest.

MUSHROOMS AND TOADSTOOLS

DESCRIPTION: Cast cement sculpture in a variety of sizes from 6 inches to as much as a yard high, available in single, double, and triple versions. May be painted in a variety of bright or even garish colors, including polka dots, or may be left unpainted, such as is often the case with cast cement. *Toadstool* refers to relatively flat-topped mushrooms.

USE: Making a complementary setting for gnomes, deer, and other decorative lawn and garden creatures.

USE TIP: If the top and the stem of the toadstool are two separate pieces, be sure that they fit together well. This could be a safety concern in the matter of larger, heavier models, not only for the nearby gnomes, but also for children or other visitors to your garden who might bump it.

BUYING TIP: If your other statuary is unpainted, choose toadstools that are also unpainted. Otherwise, the effect is an inconsistency similar to that of being lost between Kansas and the Land of Oz.

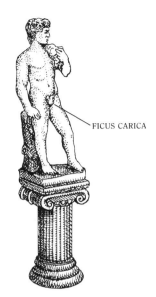

FICUS CARICA

DAVID ON PEDESTAL

NUDES

DESCRIPTION: Statues in plastic, cement, and stone without clothing, fig leaves, or loincloths. Many items also sold in covered versions—even Michelangelo's *David* is available with or without a fig leaf. Many consumers today are turning over a new leaf on what is acceptable in garden statuary, and are boldly displaying copies of classic nude sculptures, wood nymphs, Pans, and gods and goddesses. Only the Virgin Mother and Snow White seem to have escaped this revealing trend. May be sold as fountains. Available on both Ionic and Doric pedestals.

USE: To demonstrate your taste and standards of expression on a level wholly different from the other lawn ornaments noted here.

USE TIP: If you are shy about venturing into the exciting world of nude statues, you may wish to start out by positioning one modestly behind a small bush.

BUYING TIP: Expect to pay more for nudes: Art comes at a price.

JAPANESE LANTERN

ORIENTAL OBJECTS

DESCRIPTION: Japanese lanterns, fat Buddhas, meditating Buddhas, dragons, Japanese scholars, miniature pagodas, temple guard dogs, samurai warriers, Tiki gods, Tiki torches, and arched footbridges. Made of cast cement or bonded marble, natural cement color or artificially bronzed. Derived from traditional Japanese garden decor.

USE: To add a touch of the exotic to your landscape.

USE TIP: Do not mix samurai warriors with Buddhas.

BUYING TIP: Although "Tiki" generally implies a South Pacific style, some of the designs resemble Easter Island god-sculptures.

RELIGIOUS FIGURES

ALSO KNOWN AS: Saints and shrines

RELIGIOUS FIGURES AVAILABLE: Jesus, Mary, St. Joseph, St. Anthony, St. Fiacre, St. Francis, St. Jude, St. Patrick, St. Theresa (or St. Theresa of Avila)

MARY

ALSO KNOWN AS: *Mary*—Madonna, Blessed Mother, the Blessed Virgin, the Virgin Mary; *St. Anthony*—St. Anthony the Abbot; *St. Theresa*—the Little Flower, Little Flower of Jesus, St. Therese, St. Therese of the Child Jesus (St. Theresa of Avila is a different saint). Also spelled St. Teresa.

DESCRIPTION: Any one of a number of Catholic saints or important biblical religious figures in traditional religious poses, made of painted (often with several layers of acrylic lacquer) or plain cast cement, stone, marble, plastic, or lead, and ranging in height from 18 to 54 inches, most commonly including the ones listed above.

Most saints are left unpainted, but are also available in full color: *Jesus* and *Mary* are more often available painted in multiple colors, and in *Bleeding Heart* or *Sacred Heart* versions; both are shown in the forms of various apparitions, such as the Infant of Prague or Lady of Lourdes. Jesus, Mary, and Joseph may often be sold as a set, usually with Jesus shown as a child, in a year-round version different from the *nativity scene,* another common item. *St. Francis* is usually shown with a few birds. *Grottos*—small parabolic shell backdrop/shelters—are sold separately, and may have a provision for electric lighting, though some gardeners still prefer to use rare clawfoot bathtubs as backdrops. Grottos are usually painted royal or sky blue on the inside and fade to white on the outside; the inside top may be plain, with a gold star, scalloped with a radiant gold star or a gold sun, or with a radiant golden cross. *Praying children* and *cherubim* are also available, with similarly small grottos or the means to be attached to them. Some religious figures appear on the market in response to a momentary fad, such as a three-foot figure of the Pope during a tour here. One such model had nozzles in the fingertips from which water flowed.

USE: Adding inspiration to a garden, to demonstrate an affinity to whatever the religious personage stands for, or to fulfill a vow, ranging from promises to build a shrine for deliverance from disease to personal accomplishment. Some religious articles are seasonal and help to celebrate a particular holiday (e.g., a fully lighted, plastic nativity set complete with three wise men and a baby Jesus, for Christmas). Choice of most displays is influenced greatly by ethnic background and geographic location. An ancient tradition.

Jesus: All aspects of faith.

Mary: Most popular figure, perhaps because of relation of women to earth, as far as gardening is concerned, as

ST. FRANCIS

one of the most popular figures to pray to, or because reputedly appears in many visions.

St. Joseph: Patron saint of workers and families. Also, sometimes buried in the front lawn of a house that is proving difficult to sell in order to find a buyer.

St. Anthony: Patron saint of lost articles—particularly helpful for those gardeners who continually lose their tools.

St. Fiacre: Patron saint of gardeners, most appropriately. Usually depicted with a spade and a small plant.

St. Francis: Universal symbol for the love of animals and wildlife. Protestant Christians as well as Catholics put a St. Francis statue in a conspicious place in their garden to show their affinity with nature. Often accompanied by tiny animals.

St. Jude: Associated with lost and impossible causes, usually those more serious than a failed garden.

St. Patrick: If you have a snake problem, this one is for you (especially if you're Irish).

St. Theresa: "Little Flower" is often shown with a small bouquet of flowers or surrounded by roses (in relation to her experience of a miraculous shower of roses). Symbolic of a simple life. *St. Theresa of Avila* was a Spanish mystic with a good sense of humor who is associated with common sense. (It is not always clearly indicated to the consumer by the manufacturer which St. Theresa is being sold, but it is more likely to be the former.)

USE TIPS: Do not mix the sacred and the profane: Disney characters do not look natural beside a nativity crèche. If you bury a statue of St. Joseph, be sure to note where it is buried so that you can retrieve it after the house is sold.

BUYING TIPS: There are so many statues and shrines on the market today that you should be able to pick and choose the one that is suited for you at a price you can afford. Mary outsells all the saints ten to one at some garden centers (indeed, some stock only Mary). Because of the lack of difference between the two St. Theresas, accepting the one you bought as the one you want requires an act of faith. Some people relate the price of the shrine to the difficulty of the task involved in the vow it fulfills: Deliverance from death would seem to deserve, for example, more than a plastic Mary.

SPECIAL PLANTERS

DESCRIPTION: Plastic or cast cement planters in the shape of wheelbarrows, swans, geese, turtles, hippos, bears, frogs, lambs, burros (with or without sombrero-clad napping figure), or other creatures. Some burros, also known as mules, are accompanied by a walking figure, commonly referred to as "Pedro." These are similar to the same objects sold as lawn ornaments, but they contain an additional receptacle for holding plants.

DONKEY PLANTER

USE: As a decorative or attention-getting planter for terraces, roof gardens, or the lawn, especially in areas where there is little soil.

USE TIP: Once you have determined where the planter is most effective from a design point of view, select plants that can grow well in the light of that particular place. For example, put impatiens or caladiums in a shady or partially shady spot.

BUYING TIP: Unless they are being used for aquatic gardening, be sure that there are drainage holes in the bottoms of the planters. If it is impossible to add holes, place plenty of gravel and charcoal in the bottom before adding soil.

SPINNING DAISY

ALSO KNOWN AS: Lawn daisy pinwheel

DESCRIPTION: Brightly colored plastic flowers about 12 inches in diameter with thick wire "stems" for staking in the ground. The petals spin on their own stems, like pinwheels, when the wind blows through them. Some are available without propellers but with reflectors for lining driveways, or as an aid to snowplows.

USE: As a pure lawn decoration and also used to mark the entrance to your driveway for gardeners who entertain many out-of-town friends.

USE TIP: For the best motion, turn daisies to face the direction that the wind blows from most frequently.

BUYING TIP: Considered a safe fallback to add color to your garden if you do not have a green thumb.

ARMILLARY SUNDIAL

SUNDIAL

DESCRIPTION: Round, flat, cast bronze or stone clock face, almost always with Roman numerals. Designed to be mounted on a pedestal or rock, or as a wall plaque. A pointer, called a *gnomon,* is attached in the center and angles up over the XII. (The 4 on clock faces is written IIII instead of IV, for some reason.) A few are manufactured with Arabic numerals for those who resist the traditional (this kind of clock has been around for twenty-two centuries—that's a lot of tradition). Usually inscribed with phrases such as "Time takes all but memories" or *"Tempus fugit"* and/or decorated with American eagles, frogs, turtles, small boys fishing, or sailboats, any of which may double as gnomons. Another version is the *sun clock,* which has a half-circle band with Arabic numerals cut out, held at an angle over a flat piece (usually a star) and with a line down its middle. The reverse shadow of the appropriate numeral falls on the line to tell the time. Still another model is the *equatorial sundial,* in which the numerals are on a curved, angled band with a line, usually an arrow, at its axis; a full-sphere model is called an *armillary sundial.*

USE: Tells time on sunny days by the fall of the shadow from the gnomon.

USE TIPS: Follow installation directions carefully for accurate readings. Mount on a large rock or pedestal, and *make sure it is perfectly level.* Align the gnomon with the North Star (not magnetic north). The word *gnomon* is especially useful for those gardeners who play Scrabble.

BUYING TIP: Get good bronze (about 88 percent copper).

TORCHES AND CANDLES

DESCRIPTION: Wicks surrounded by citronella-scented wax, either in glass jars *(low boy candles),* small galvanized buckets, or on 3-foot-long wooden stakes. *Tonga torches* hold a quart of petroleum fuel (can be citronella-scented) and come in either bronze or black metallic finishes.

USE: Dramatic source of light which also repels mosquitoes.

USE TIPS: Large wax torches drip on the ground, so do not place them near a patio that must remain pristine. Do not use torches indoors.

PUMPING GIRL WHIRLIGIG

FLYING DUCK WHIRLIGIG

WHIRLIGIG

DESCRIPTION: Wooden or plastic decoration with propellers that are either linked to wires which move a figure or else are simply placed alongside in the shape or place of legs or wings. Designs of the former include women washing clothes, churning butter, or watering plants; men sawing wood, pumping water, starting a car, or being kicked in the derrière by a donkey; also excitable scarecrows and feeding chickens. Designs of the latter type include ducks, geese, flamingos, roadrunners, airplanes, Dutch windmills, American farm-type windmills, California raisins, Maine potatoes, cartoon characters (with the blades functioning as feet, not wings), and political figures. Usually painted bright colors. Mounted on long stakes that are stuck in the ground.

USE: Adds eye-catching action to a garden. A combination wind vane and novelty item. Often sold as folk art, particularly in the Smoky Mountains and parts of Appalachia. May also scare birds away and keep you from napping in the garden, depending on the amount of noise it makes. Originally used to repel moles: The vibrations set up by a moving whirligig scare them away.

USE TIP: When these are mounted on a pole, be sure that they are level and that the moving parts are well oiled. With the models of a person working, the greatest pleasure is commonly found in watching them work at top speed in the winds that occur just before a summer thunderstorm.

BUYING TIP: If you wish to have one of these moving weather vanes as a "folk art" item, buy only those that are handcrafted in wood. They will cost a little more than the less authentic, mass-produced plastic or wooden ones. Some people find the depiction of chores linked to the traditional gender sexist.

WILD AND DOMESTIC ANIMALS

DESCRIPTION: A wide variety of animals, including skunks (with or without a flower in paw), bunnies (with or without carrots), frogs, raccoons, cats, dogs, kittens, little lambs (with Mary), alligators, armadillos (also in boot scraper version), turtles, pelicans, deer, lions, giant flapping butterflies, birds, bees, ladybugs, donkeys, dogs, pheasants, and a few imaginary creatures. Frogs are available with lipstick and bow ties, depending on the sex, and playing various musical instruments. Butterflies and some birds may come with a clothespin-type clip or other clamp for

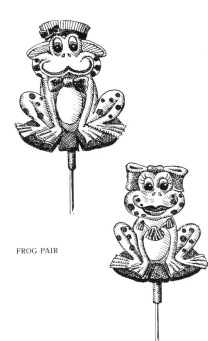

FROG PAIR

attaching to branches or parts of your house. *Flocked* models have lifelike, weatherproof fur. All are available in a range of materials, including plastic, aluminum, ½-inch-thick wooden cutouts with spikes for securing in the ground, or full-sized cast cement sculpture painted an unrealistic bronze color. Rabbits, ducks, and chipmunks are commonly available in sets as well. Certain manufacturers offer a number of wooden cutout animals with signs attached, such as "Skunk Crossing" or "Snail Trail." Others make cast brass signs with the animal and appropriate "_____ Crossing" underneath, including quail (both single and family group), flamingo, duck, bunny, frog, hummingbird, kitty, boy, and girl figures. Many dog and cat models are recognizable by breed.

USE: Often collected by people who are into collecting one type of animal—for example, there are people who collect only skunks or turtles or owls. But these animals could also be mixed and matched.

USE TIPS: Plastic and cement (painted and unpainted) in the same garden looks particularly unnatural. Stick with the same material, such as all unpainted cement. Some people like to treat their fur-covered animals with Scotchgard.

BUYING TIP: Animals with exceptionally expressive eyes tend to cost more.

WISHING WELL

DESCRIPTION: Plastic, plaster, cement, or wooden structure that resembles an old covered wellhouse above a well shaft. These replicas are often complete with bucket, chain or rope, and crank.

USE: To add a certain rustic charm to your garden, a charm that is particularly lacking in the suburbs.

USE TIP: People can't resist the urge to toss money into a wishing well, so locate yours near a heavily traveled thoroughfare and collect what you can.

BUYING TIP: Go for the larger sizes. Small ones especially tend to look more ridiculous than larger ones, almost like a child's beach toy, and should be avoided.

General Buying Guide for Bulbs, Seeds, Plants, Shrubs, and Trees

In keeping with the mandate of the title of this book—*The Complete Illustrated Guide to Everything Sold in Garden Centers (Except the Plants)*—the following is a simplified buying guide to the basic groups of live items—the "greengoods"—sold at garden centers, as opposed to the "hard lines" and "packaged goods" that are covered in the main body of this book. This appendix is not meant to be a detailed list of the items themselves (grass seed rates the detailed treatment it gets in the book because it is treated like a basic commodity and is such a common purchase). However, we couldn't resist giving just a few basic pointers on the most common groups of plants to help orient you as you walk back into the greenhouses and nurseries from the front part of the garden center.

A knowledgeable salesperson should ask you questions about your growing conditions—light, soil, and moisture—prior to selling you a plant. Seek out this kind of help.

A final note about names: You will be confronted by rows of plants labeled with Latin botanical names. While this may seem daunting, this type of labeling is much more accurate than relying exclusively on common names and gen-erally ensures that you get the plant you want, as the same common name can refer to two totally different plants. These botanical names are always made up of two components, and sometimes three. The first component is the *genus* name; the genus is the basic group that a particular plant comes from. The second component is the *species designate,* which when used with the genus denotes the species (the species is a distinct subgroup of the genus that possesses specific characteristics). In the case of *Geranium dalmaticum,* for example, *Geranium* is the genus name, while *Geranium dalmaticum* indicates the species. When a plant's name is repeated in a text such as this several times in a row, you will often find the genus name abbreviated by just its first initial after the first mention. In our example, *Geranium dalmaticum* would be shortened to *G. dalmaticum.*

Finally, our plant may be a *variety,* a variation within the species. If it is a naturally occurring variety, its name will appear in italics after the species name. If it is an artificially created variety, or *cultivar* (short for *cultivated variety),* or a *hybrid* (a cross between two different plants), its name will appear within single quotation marks in roman type, such as *Geranium dalmaticum* 'A.T. Johnson.' Keep in mind that cultivars usually can be propagated only by cuttings; they will not grow true to seed, meaning that if you harvest their seeds and plant them, the resulting plant will not possess the important characteristics (usually flower and leaf color, though it depends on what qualities it was bred for) of its parent.

BULBS

A seasonal item, most garden centers offer bulbs for sale twice a year in colorful displays. The banner announcing "The Dutch Bulbs Are Here," which goes up on garden centers in the early fall, heralds the arrival of the most popular ones, the spring-blooming bulbs whose appearance signals the end of winter. Bulbs are also well loved because they are colorful and require little care to make them bloom. Because most bulbs are not expensive, and a wide variety are stocked by most garden centers, this is a good kind of plant with which to experiment. Most bulbs are guaranteed to bloom at least once and often become "established" in the garden, rewarding the gardener with blooms for years to come. Others are easily grown indoors, even in the smallest apartment, and can be "forced," or made to bloom off-season (the most familiar of these are the popular amaryllis, commonly offered as a Christmas present in the northern parts of this country, or the paperwhite narcissus).

The basic definition of a bulb, many of which look like nothing more than an onion, is a plant that has a large storage root or stem or even an entire compressed plant which remains in the ground during a dormant season and from which the plant blooms again during its growing season.

As for quality, avoid "bargain mixes," which may be just a mix of bad or undersized leftovers. Always look for the largest bulbs of each type, too, and solid, not squishy ones. Don't buy bulbs with mold on their top crowns or basal plate (bottom). Solid plastic bags without holes are generally not good for bulbs, as they create conditions ripe for these problems—try those sold in net bags or loose.

The process by which bulbs establish themselves and multiply in a garden is called *naturalizing.* Most gardeners prefer bulbs that naturalize well—check your gardening books to find which kinds tend to naturalize. Beyond a few modest requirements, bulbs are carefree—they generally require only sunlight and good drainage to grow well. Some bulbs even grow and bloom in part shade. Although the spring-blooming bulbs are the best known, different types of bulbs bloom at all different times during the growing season. Always check the bloom time on the package and aim for a mixture of dates that suits your garden plan. Be sure to note the planting depth and the sun and water requirements. Store bulbs in a cool, dry place until you plant them. When you do plant bulbs, note that they need well-drained and aerated soil, as they may rot in overly moist soils. And do your best to wait until the right season to plant—too soon or too late will not do.

Some, such as the popular paperwhites, can be forced to bloom indoors. A little research and experimentation will show you which ones are easily grown on a dining room table in January, and stand up to various moves, including a stint in your refrigerator for rejuvenation. (If you do put them in your refrigerator to make them go dormant before forcing, make sure they are clearly marked and not confused with your shallots, or your next sauce may taste a little strange.)

A true bulb is one in which not only a plant part comprises the storage unit, but an entire plant that is compressed into an underground storage chamber. If you cut a true bulb in half, you will find a compressed basal plate or stem, roots, and even leaves. Daffodils, onions, narcissus, and lilies are true bulbs. However, not everything marketed as a bulb is a true bulb. The term *bulb* is used to describe underground storage units formed from modified roots, branches, buds, stems, or tubers.

The following are sold as bulbs:

• *Corms* are underground stems without the storage leaves that true bulbs have. If cut in half, the corm will not show the rings or layers (actually leaves and storage leaves) that you find in an onion, which is a true bulb. In corms, buds form at the top of these squat stems and produce the plant. Popular corms include gladiolus and crocus.

• *Rhizomes* are lateral underground stems. Roots develop from the underside of the rhizome and buds, called *pips,* along the top. Lilies of the valley, many iris, Chinese lotus, and ginger grow from rhizomes.

• *Tubers* are underground buds or underground stems, like the corm, that swell with stored nutrients. Tubers do not have a basal plate. Jerusalem artichoke, the white potato, and some begonias are tubers.

• *Tuberous roots* are swollen roots that store starches. A new plant will grow from the *eye,* or *bud,* found on a tuberous root. The sweet potato and the dahlia are well-known plants that grow from tuberous roots.

About Spring Bulbs

These bulbs are sold and planted in the fall to bloom in the spring. The smaller spring bulbs usually bloom first and are the jewels of the spring garden. These are followed by the daffodils and tulips. It is wise to buy a variety of bulbs to ensure bloom throughout the spring season. Hardy spring bulbs often need to go through a winter season where the temperature is near or below freezing before they will bloom in the spring. This is known as *stratification.* Hardy spring bulbs can be purchased at any time during the fall and planted as long as the ground has not frozen. It is often best, however, to get bulbs into the ground in the early fall so that roots will begin to grow before the winter freeze sets in. The exceptions to this rule are hybrid tulips, which, if planted too early, may actually start to sprout, only to be killed in the colder weather.

Superphosphate (see pages 73–74), bulb food (pages 67–68), or bone meal (pages 59–60) can be placed with soil in the hole with the bulb as it is planted. This will help with root development and produce better bloom in the spring.

About Summer and Fall Bulbs

In much of the country where winters are harsh, summer- and fall-blooming bulbs are offered for sale in garden centers in the spring. These are planted in the spring and, depending on the local climate, removed from the garden in the fall before the first hard freeze and stored over winter in a dark, dry place, such as a paper bag or dry peat moss, to be replanted the following spring after the ground has warmed up. In milder areas of the country, many summer- and fall-flowering bulbs can be planted in the fall and left in the ground to bloom year after year.

SEEDS

Flower and vegetable seeds are easy to buy. There is plenty of reference material in magazines and books to guide you at the beginning, and there is more information on each package, including a picture of the plant. For some of us, it's like being a kid in a candy store—the stuff is right there, it looks good, and doesn't cost much. But, hard as it may be to accept, you have to grow up and accept the fact that not all seeds are for you, at least for now.

To determine what's right for you, first look

at the back of the package to find the basic information as to what kind of light is needed, when to plant, and germination time (the time it takes the seed to sprout), and to get a feel for the general ease of cultivation of the item. There is plenty of choice, so pick one that fits your depth of experience and desire for involvement.

Seeds with germinating times over twenty-one days are usually very difficult for the home gardener to grow, because of the need to maintain uniform soil conditions, temperature, and moisture levels during that entire period. Gardeners need to rely on heating sources and controls; this is generally the case when starting seeds indoors for long germination periods. Seven to ten days' germination time is the most desirable for beginning gardeners.

Many flowers and vegetables do better in the garden if they are started indoors and then transplanted as seedlings. Check the packet to see if it is labeled as such, usually with the phrase "best if started indoors." Recommendations for container gardening are usually given as well.

In addition to sowing instructions, the seed packets also have a *test date.* This usually indicates the month and year in which the seed was last tested for *percentage of germination,* or the percent of seeds that will eventually grow into plants. This date should be *in the current growing year* for best germination of the seed purchased and the germination rate should be around 90 percent. In any case, when comparing two brands of the same seed, the one with the higher germination rate is the better buy. And don't squeeze the package to see how many seeds are inside—you'll break the seed coats and ruin the embryos.

About Vegetable Seeds

The first things you should look for on the packet are the *planting* and *maturing times.* The seed packets offer information on when to plant, saying, for example, "Plant indoors in February or March, and transplant in late April or May or when the temperature has reached a constant 70° F." However, if you are not familiar with starting seed indoors or do not have the required equipment, the same plants can be purchased as seedlings in April and May. Garden centers will offer these transplants for sale at reasonable prices when it is appropriate to plant them. Some of the vegetable plants that may be better purchased as seedlings include tomatoes, eggplants, and peppers. It is often fun, however, to try to grow these plants from seed indoors (see "Seed Starting Products," chapter 9).

If the seed packet says, "Plant directly in the garden when the soil has warmed up in late spring," it is considerably cheaper to buy the seed rather than seedlings. Some of the plants that can easily be grown from seed in late spring include cucumbers, squash, sunflowers, pole and bush beans, and corn.

Still other seed is offered that can be planted as soon as the soil can be worked in early spring. Crops that do best in the cooler temperatures of spring and fall are often referred to as *cold crops* (or *cold* or *cool weather crops).* Many plants in the cabbage family (cabbage, kohlrabi, boc choy, kale, collard greens) are cold crops. Other cold crops include lettuce, peas, radishes, and many other leafy green vegetables.

During the warmer summer season, heat-tolerant plants such as tomatoes and peppers can be planted in the same place that the cold crops grew. Cold crop seed can be sown again in early fall to extend the garden season up until hard frost time.

If you know the length of your growing season (for example, in the Northeast, the growing season is from April until October—about 210 days), you should choose seed that will produce fruit or crops well within that time span. This information is stated with a phrase such as, "Matures from 90 to 100 days." You should also know if you've had problems with certain pests or diseases in your soil, and look for seeds that have been treated or developed to be resistant to these problems. Some varieties of tomato seeds, for example, are available which are resistant to nematodes (labeled *N)* or the diseases verticillium wilt *(V)* and fusarium wilt (labeled *F,* or *F 1 & 2* if resistant to two types), or all three (labeled *VFN)*. Seeds may also be treated with a fungicide to control damping-off disease and noted as such on the packet.

About Flower Seeds

Growing flowering plants from seed is not costly. Seed packets are usually sold for under two dollars, so even if the seed does not germinate, it is not a great loss. Growing flowers and other plants from seed is highly recommended, if only for the fun of it. It is also an easy way to experiment in your garden.

There are three types of flowers: *annuals, biennials,* and *perennials.* Annuals are plants that grow, bloom, and set seed in one growing season—they bloom continuously during the season and then die. Popular annuals include marigolds, zinnias, cosmos, sweet alyssum, ageratum, celosia, salvia, and petunias. These plants do not survive, or *overwinter,* in areas where the winter temperatures dip below freezing. However, annuals are the easiest flowers to grow from seed.

Biennials are plants that grow in the wild for one season without blooming and then bloom during the second season, after which they die. Once established in a garden, however, biennials often *self-seed* (seed themselves) and then grow and produce a succession of blooming plants for many years to come. For this reason they are often confused with perennials. Popular biennials include hollyhocks, sweet william, Canterbury bells, and wallflowers. The latter is a much-neglected flower that is a fine addition to almost any border.

Perennials are plants that are *winter hardy,* meaning they will survive cold winters (that is, their roots survive, while their tops die off) and grow and bloom in the garden for many years; different plants blooming at different times of the season. Perennials can be purchased as grown plants, too. Among the popular perennials are hosta, peonies, lamb's ears, daisies, and periwinkle.

PLANTS

Most garden centers don't sell just "plants"—they sell *annuals, perennials, tropicals, woody plants,* and so on. Do a little shopping research in reference books first to save yourself some time at the garden center. Definitions for some of these terms are found in the preceding section on seeds. *Bare-root stock* refers to plants sold without any soil.

You should have in mind where you plan to put these plants, and be able to describe the kind of sun—northern or southern, direct or shade—and the temperature conditions: Near a drafty door? In a greenhouse? In a house where you lower the temperature at night? The personnel at the nursery should ask you these questions. Avoid sales clerks who are more interested in pushing a particular plant than in your growing conditions. Plants can't be plunked down anywhere willy-nilly, so don't buy something just because it's on sale, no matter how tempting it is. Conditions have to be right for a plant to grow. Don't buy until you know exactly where you want to put it.

Questions you should ask the clerks include: Does it bloom? How long will it bloom? Will it rebloom within the year? Will it drop leaves? Is it fragile or durable? Is it the kind that likes to "dry out" every now and then, or not? How sensitive would it be to my own schedule of watering, dictated by my life-style? How damp should I keep the soil? Is it basically an indoor or outdoor plant?

A few rules of thumb can be applied to buying most plants, whether bought as seedlings or full grown. Look for symmetry. Consult a good illustrated gardening book to figure if the leaves should be even in height or staggered, and how thick the leaves should be. Especially with those sold in small six-pack containers, look for flowers that are *not* blooming, but are about to do so. Blooms mean that the plant has been growing in that confined space for a long time and it may be stressed out, though of course a few blooms are necessary to judge color. Don't hesitate to squeeze the pot and pull roots apart a bit to stimulate them before planting. Avoid woody, thick stems on small plants. Look for signs of disease: Yellow leaves or leaves with brown edges are typical (brown tips are natural), though one or two bad leaves may be acceptable. Avoid plants with wilted leaves, or ones that are tall and spindly—look for compact and sturdy plants. Roots should not be poking out of the holes in the bottom of the pot, and there should be no weeds growing in it. Square pots are preferable—they keep the roots from growing in circles. And don't forget, when purchasing big plants for indoors, to check your door and ceiling heights first, as well as door widths. Figure out an appropriate route for such a heavy, big, and probably dirty object. Double-check the plant's sun and shade requirements, and notice if the garden center has met them. Make sure that your garden or home can meet them as well.

When purchasing spreading plants, get yourself a "deal" by finding a larger one with several stems. You'll be getting more plant for your money. The better plant buys at local garden centers are bedding annuals and vegetable seedlings.

It is hard to beat the quality you can expect from a plant sold by its grower. Look for garden centers with their own nurseries, and you will usually get better material. Of course, if the plants have been grown under special conditions, you may have trouble keeping the plant growing just as well. Ask. Natural conditions similar to your own are a better bet. Plants purchased from a mail-order source across the country may not be suited to your growing conditions, by this reasoning. Be sure you check your reference books thoroughly before making a purchase via catalog that might not grow in your area.

Bargains are not worth the money you save if the plant dies soon after you get it home. They are only bargains if you really know what you are doing and have the resources to handle plant problems.

SHRUBS AND TREES

Much of what goes for shrubs applies to trees as well. Check to see that no weeds or grass is growing on the burlap root ball or container. Remember to remove any plastic string that is binding the ball when you plant it—only natural jute should be left on to disintegrate in the ground. Remove it from the neck of the plant.

One of the first things to look for is a shrub or tree that appears balanced. If a specimen has symmetry, you're on the right track. As for details, check for wounds and any splitting where the branches join the trunk. Research before you buy: Some trees or shrubs need lots of care or drop potentially annoying seedpods. Most shrubs want well-drained soil with some full sun. If you are interested in a tree or shrub with ornamental berries or flowers, you should check to learn whether the male and female flowers occur on the same plant or on separate plants. An example of this is the hollies, where the fruit is found only on the female plant, or the pussy willow, where the attractive bloom is only on the male plant.

Be sure to arrange for delivery at a convenient time so you can get your trees and shrubs in properly placed and sized holes without having to rearrange your whole life. Then be ready for the delivery to be late and have to be rearranged anyway. Plan the placement very carefully by determining the plant's mature size, both in height and width. You'll probably have to plant them a bit farther apart than you originally thought so they can fill in naturally and not hit the house or each other. Don't expect to be able to move them if you place them poorly. Take your time and plan very, very carefully.

Don't forget to have a good water source, the right fertilizer, and plenty of peat moss and humus on hand for the planting. Make sure that trees have no roots broken off, are delivered with proper containers or burlapped balls, and are staked sturdily once they are planted.

Of course some trees are purchased dead: Christmas trees. When buying any kind of *cut greens,* as these are called, check the branches: They should be soft and supple, not brittle. If they are brittle and many needles fall when you shake them, it is dried out, and should be avoided.

One last note: The actual distinction between trees and shrubs is not perfectly clear. Probably the most common definition is that shrubs are less than 10 or 12 feet tall and do not have real trunks.

Items of Special Interest to Gardeners with Physical Limits

Many tools are found in garden centers which are particularly comfortable to use or helpful to gardeners who have difficulty gripping, bending, kneeling, reaching, or are confined to wheelchairs. The most useful ones are noted as such throughout this book and are listed here as well.

Unfortunately, some of the specially designed tools are quite expensive. For those gardeners desiring these tools but who are on a limited budget, or just habitually frugal, passing them by should be no hardship: There are many ways to adapt regular tools for comfort and convenience. Use your creativity and lots of tape and foam rubber—and bicycle handlebar grips, Velcro, insulating pipe tape, and so on. Additional grips (many available from mail-order catalogs) can be attached partway up a long wooden handle. Lightweight interchangeable systems of heads and handles, "ladies'," "floral," and children's tools can be handled more easily from a wheelchair than regular tools. Your local botanic garden or Cooperative Extension office should be able to advise you if you cannot find suggestions in magazines and books.

Furthermore, there is such a wide range of design among the common tools that seeking out one that is particularly good for you should not be hard. For example, cultivating can be done standing up with long-handled tools instead of hand-held ones used from a kneeling position. With the right tool, weeding can be done with push-pull movement or just a pulling movement, instead of a lifting and digging movement. Read the descriptions of all these items in this book to note the differences between them.

Finally, garden design and planning have as much to do with the handicapped gardener's ability to enjoy work as anything—indeed, some consider it the most important thing. There are many theories on low-maintenance gardening and landscaping found in numerous articles and books, including specific barrier-free design elements such as wheelchair-high raised beds and built-in irrigation systems. Just putting houseplants at a convenient level or hanging them on pulleys can solve the problem in the simplest cases. Using slow-release or natural organic fertilizers generally reduces the number of times you have to apply fertilizer (see chapter 3), and proper mulching (chapter 2) helps reduce weeds. Ultimately, gadgets are only part of the solution to the challenge of making gardening something everyone can enjoy.

Items of special interest include:

Chapter 5: Digging Tools and Wheel Goods
Bulb planter (long handle)
Cultifork (scoop-headed garden fork)
Dibble (long-handled)
Garden cart
Trowel (long handle, offset, and trigger grip)

Chapter 6: Cultivating, Weeding, and Raking Tools
Back-saver rake
Dandelion digger
Garden rake (made of tubular aluminum)
Hand fork (long-handled and trigger grip models)
Heart hoe
High wheel cultivator
Spiked wheel cultivator
The original weeder
Weed slicer
Weeding hoes
Yard arm, or handy weeder (or spring-operated puller)

Chapter 7: Pruning, Cutting, and Trimming Tools
All power tools, especially cordless models
Flower gatherer
Flower shears with butterfly handles
Grass shears with trigger grip
Long-handled grass shears
Long-reach fruit and flower picker
Long-reach pole saw and lopper (pump-style pole pruner)
Pruning shears (with long reach extension and lever, and with ratchet)
String trimmer
Swing blade and grass whip
Weed hook (pull-action pruner)

Chapter 8: Maintenance Tools and Equipment
Aerator sandals
Bags and accessories (hoop to hold bags open)
Blower
Compost aerator tool
Compression sprayer (pressurized hand sprayer)
Drip irrigation system
Hanging plant waterer (pump-action)
Herbicide applicator
Hose guides
Hose reel (and hose reel cart)
House hose
Quick-connect hose system
Shutoff valve
Soaker hose
Traveling sprinkler
Trombone sprayer
Water controller
Water wand
Water wick
Watering can (long-reach style)

Chapter 9: Starting Products and Gardening Aids
Capillary waterer
Hooks, hangers, and brackets (with pulleys and swivels, pot clips)
Plant ties (from reels, made of wire)
Plastic planter (with self-watering feature)
Rigid plant trellis
Seed-planting template
Seeder (long handle as well as hand-sized devices)
Trellis net

Chapter 10: Personal and Miscellaneous Gear and Equipment
Graden scoop
Knee protectors (pads and bench)
Lawn tweezers

Information Sources

Choosing products to use in your garden involves biology and philosophy as much as it does good common sense. While garden center personnel (and this book) can help you learn to differentiate among the various products available, to determine what your basic needs and desires are and what type of solution you feel comfortable with, you may want to consult with other experts. Three areas (besides the thousands of books and magazines available) are good places to start: your local Cooperative Extension, organizations and companies devoted to consumer awareness regarding fertilizers and pesticides, and your local botanic garden.

The *Cooperative Extension* is an agency of the Department of Agriculture and functions from the land-grant university in each state. A Cooperative Extension office is located in each county in the country, and is listed in your phone book under any of a variety of titles, though it should be the college name followed by "Cooperative Extension." Keep looking if you don't find it right away—it may be listed under the county name or with the county or state government offices. Call a botanic garden

for help if need be. Each office has many helpful publications and programs.

The activities and publications of each office are tailored to its constituency: In urban areas, they may help start community vegetable gardens in abandoned lots or teach classes in home economics; in rural areas, they may specialize in that region's crop, such as fruit trees or cotton, and so are oriented to help professional growers; all are active with the 4-H clubs. Suburban ones usually have information about chemicals and insects as well as houseplants and vegetables. A few have clinics or diagnostic labs available on a fee basis. Research at the state's land-grant college is often focused on a policy on particular products or weather conditions, such as droughts. Most offices have a list of publications available that indicates which are free and those for which there is a charge. Not all are oriented to the amateur gardener—many are geared to farmers, nursery owners, or landscape architects. Because of their relationship with the land-grant colleges and the FDA experiment stations, they are your best source of current research-based information.

Nothing is more fundamental to gardening than knowing the makeup of your soil, both in terms of structure and acidity (chapter 1) and in terms of nutrients (chapter 3). Though reference books can be a big help in analyzing your soil structure, and there are plenty of test kits available for analyzing the acidity and nutrient level of your soil, it makes sense to call on experts, especially for a first time, at Cooperative Extension offices. Most offices—and some of the larger garden centers—can do an extremely thorough and accurate soil test for you. Although there is a nominal fee for a soil test, usually under $10, the results are much more accurate than those you get from a simplistic, inexpensive, off-the-shelf kit. And it's a government service.

There are a good number of places to turn to for help in learning about fertilizers and pesticides. The synthetic chemical approach is pretty thoroughly covered by the bulk of advertising and existing literature, and the EPA (see address below) has many good publications. The catalogs that specialize in natural organic products, listed in appendix D, are an easy place to start for alternatives to synthetic chemical products. Check your library for numerous books and magazines on this subject which are not normally sold in bookstores and at newsstands. Many magazine editors will handle basic questions with ease or send you back issues on the subject you ask about. You can also write:

United States Environmental Protection Agency
Office of Pesticides and Toxic Substances
401 M Street, SW
Washington, DC 20460
Attention: Chief, Document Management Section (H7502C)
Information Services Branch
703-557-4474

Many publications are free, and detailed reports on individual chemicals are available for a standard fee. Ask for a list.

NCAMP (National Coalition Against the Misuse of Pesticides)
530 7th Street, SE
Washington, DC 20003
202-543-5450

Ask for brochures or newsletters on a variety of subjects.

Bio-Integral Resource Center
P.O. Box 7414
Berkeley, CA 94707
415-524-2567

Ask for their publications catalog. Newsletter is available.

Many botanic gardens or horticultural societies are terrific sources of all kinds of information, from the purely practical to the purely theoretical. Whether or not they have an educational program, most are staffed by gardeners who may informally share information you don't readily find in traditional sources, especially during the less busy seasons. Look them up in your phone book, or try the book *American Gardens: A Traveler's Guide* (Plants and Gardens Handbook Series #111, Brooklyn Botanic Garden Record, vol. 42, no. 3, 1000 Washington Avenue, Brooklyn, NY 11225). It lists some 250 public gardens around the country.

Mail-Order Catalog Guide

While there is no doubt that garden centers generally supply whatever the gardener really needs, as well as personal service and expertise, there is an element of dream and fantasy that mail-order catalogs provide what garden centers just do not, especially off-season. Think of them as a particularly convenient browsers' heaven. In any case, it is a firmly established tradition to shop by mail for many garden items.

In keeping within the parameters of this book, all noteworthy catalogs reviewed here feature tools and supplies—the hard lines and packaged goods. There are plenty of seed and nursery catalogs, but they are not listed, though many offer both types of items.

All mail-order sources back up their products with a guarantee, though some are explicitly more flexible and reassuring than others. Be sure to note the conditions before ordering. (If you are ordering seeds, bulbs, or plants, note that most catalogs have a Plant Hardiness Zone map, which you should refer to, or else call your local Cooperative Extension office to determine your zone or to see if a particular plant is borderline for your area. Many catalogs list the acceptable zones alongside each plant.) And don't let the term *mail order* limit you to the written word: Many catalogs have real folks at an 800 number who are more than willing to chat and, of course, take orders. Some have a fax number for electronic mail convenience and efficiency—a nice new twist. Many of the catalogs have a special number for customer service or technical questions in addition to the order number shown, but those numbers are not listed here.

One general note of interest: Virtually all of the catalogs contain a personal note from the owner, usually on the inside cover. This seems to be some sort of tradition, but in any case, it highlights the warm, personal feeling most of us have about gardening—and the high competition among the catalogs in regard to service and quality.

This listing is not meant to be all-inclusive but rather a sampling of the better-known catalogs that offer a variety of merchandise. Catalogs that feature only one manufacturer's items are not included. Omission or inclusion of a catalog does not reflect or imply approval or disapproval.

The Alsto Company—"Handy Helpers"

"Practical Products for Your Home, Yard, &
   Garden"
P.O. Box 1267
Galesburg, IL 61401
800-447-0048

Though at first glance this looks like many of
the other glossy color catalogs, the pictures are
not too clear and the copy is often quite long.
Consecutive editions feature mostly the same
items, but with a different layout and new
photos and copy.

The choice of items includes many common
and some uncommon high-quality garden supplies, tools, and gift items, such as an electronic
rain gauge that measures up to 100 inches of
rain and never needs emptying, garden furniture, products for cutting, splitting, and stack-
ing firewood, gloves, tools, rubber boots, and
many nongarden gadgets. Less than half the
pages are devoted to garden items—the rest is
general home maintenance, leisure, or furniture
products.

Bird'n Hand—"Pure seed bird feed"

40 Pearl Street
Framingham, MA 01701
508-879-1552

With a formal design and conservative range
of items well-suited to its gentle subject, this
catalog specializes in gourmet food for birds,
but also carries feeders of many designs. Feeds
listed contain no fillers of any kind and are a bit
more expensive per pound, but it goes farther
(so they claim) than normal seed. Twelve types
of seed are offered so you can tailor your feedings to attract your favorite birds. The birdseed
is backed with a full money-back guarantee. (A
larger but slicker, more commercial catalog is
put out by Duncraft®, Penacook, New Hampshire 03303-9020, Tel. 603-224-0200.)

A handy feature of this catalog is an Automatic Supply Shipment which can be paid up
yearly so you don't have to continually reorder.
All prices include freight.

Brookstone—Hard-to-Find Tools

127 Vose Farm Road
Peterborough, NH 03458
603-924-9541 (24 hours a day)

Brookstone wrote the book on browser-ori-
ented catalogs, so to speak, and has done very
well since the mid-1970s. Their bright and colorful layout, with crystal-clear color photos, is
cheerful and well written, though it is quite
busy and crammed with exclamatory headlines.

Not just a garden catalog, Brookstone's section of tools and equipment for the garden and
greenhouse fills under one-third of their summer catalog. Included are such items as sundials, hose guides, spigot extenders, edgers,
weeding tools, ultrasonic bird chasers, solid
brass hose fittings, tool hangers, hose repair
kits, a faucet rethreader, earth auger bits, folding wheelbarrows, a flat hose and reel, a back-
saving wheeled rake, a lightweight scythe, and
so on—a strong emphasis on the unusual.

Clapper's Garden Catalog

1125 Washington Street
West Newton, MA 02165
617-244-7909
Fax: 617-244-5260

An interesting hybrid of an organization,
Clapper's has an institutional and professional
background that dates from 1922. The catalog's
orientation is definitely toward those with, as
they say in their introductory note, "suburban
and country properties." Thus it is no surprise
to find that the first part of the catalog is devoted to furniture and accessories that include

a $4,000 circular tree seat made of teak and a $300 faux terra-cotta planter. The color photography is regular catalog photography, but because all the tools are grouped into one photo per spread, they are more clearly visible than in most catalogs.

Items featured include carts, wooden wheelbarrows, and a full selection of reasonably priced, well-made garden tools. There is a good assortment of hand tools, plus burlap, canvas totes, Wellington boots, gloves, plant supports, watering cans, sprayers, hoses, flower arranging accessories, wind chimes, and botanical prints, as well as a small selection of gift books. Their retail store is located in one of the fanciest suburbs of Boston, but their professional equipment is well chosen and well priced.

Gardener's Eden—A Garden Catalog from Williams-Sonoma

P.O. Box 7307
San Francisco, CA 94120-7307
415-421-4242

Published three times a year, this is a catalog with a refined feel, definitely for the up-scale, leisure- and convenience-minded gardener. Each catalog focuses on products appropriate for each season. Prices on selected items are often marked down 15 to 20 percent, at least in the late summer catalog.

There is a consistent style, quality, and tone to the gift-type products listed, which include French wire baskets, florist's buckets, odd ornaments like a bee skep (a woven grass beehive), English watering cans, many vases and beautiful containers, potpourri saucers, wreaths, shoe/boot brushes, wooden doormats, and garden furniture. Serious tools and practical equipment are listed in black and white on the order blank, under a category called "Simple Solutions," as though it was an afterthought.

Gardener's Supply—Innovative Gardening Solutions

128 Intervale Road
Burlington, VT 05401
802-863-1700 (24 hours, 7 days a week for credit card orders)

A pleasant, unpretentious catalog with reasonable prices and a large variety of items, with an emphasis on well-chosen selections of practical and serious equipment. Published twice a year, the spring catalog features seed starting products, while the fall catalog features chippers and shredders as well as equipment for canning fruit and vegetables. Some of the items are products that they developed themselves or helped develop in their own test gardens with the help of friends, test gardeners around the country, and the university as well as the State of Vermont. They also are active in a number of nonprofit gardening activities there and abroad, including the management of a compost pile that produces 700 tons annually. Each product description is quite informative, and the color photos feature many older people as "models," lending genuine, down-to-earth feeling to the whole production. Definitely for the serious gardener. A retail store and greenhouse/garden area are located in Burlington.

Gardener's Supply includes only organic fertilizers and safe, natural pest controls, as well as biodegradable trash bags. Standard listings are quite wide-ranging and include portable and permanent greenhouses, row covers, minimum/maximum thermometers, kneepads, boot brushes, trellises, bean poles, tomato ties, soil test kits, rotary tillers, sprayers, flower supports, garden carts, hand tools, edging, books, gloves, birdhouses and feeders, sundials, and a few pieces of modestly priced furniture. Surprisingly few everyday tools are listed—only special ones. One interesting item is Rodent Rocks, porous lava stones that have been soaked in an herbal formula containing garlic and onion. When buried, the rocks give off an odor that repels most rodents.

Gardens Alive!—Natural Gardening Research Center

> Highway 48 P.O. Box 149
> Sunman, IN 47041
> 812-623-3800

Of all the catalogs listed here, this is perhaps the least inviting to read, let alone look at. It has the smallest print and the smallest pictures of any of the catalogs reviewed, condensed into a dense layout. Furthermore, numerous "editions" are almost alike.

However, some of the copy is educational, including a nine-page section on pests complete with color photos. They have a comprehensive collection of organic, nontoxic, and biological controls for many pests, including a good selection of live insect predators like ladybugs and spined soldier bugs, as well as beneficial nematodes. Gardens Alive! also lists bird supplies (including one of the more exotic items, a bird-bath heater), seed starting equipment, watering equipment, row covers, dusters and syringes for biological controls, and their own organic fertilizers or soil conditioners, all with the Alive! name. There is plenty of information found among the product listings, if you can stand looking for it.

The Growing Naturally Catalog

> P.O. Box 54
> 149 Pine Lane
> Pineville, PA 18946
> 215-598-7025

An attractive annual catalog, with its green print on buff-colored paper, Growing Naturally is intended for gardeners and small-scale farmers who are dedicated to organic and "low input" farming and gardening. The copy is both friendly and informative, and gives the impression that each item has been carefully chosen at the exclusion of many others—unlike some more commercial catalogs that are equally effusive about similar items. Prices are very good.

Includes mostly natural organic fertilizers, conditioners, and pest control products, with a notably large section of beneficial insects and biological controls, some natural pet-care products, and a very tight selection of basic but high-quality tools, equipment, and watering devices.

Harmony Farm Supply

> P.O. Box 451
> Graton, CA 95444
> 707-823-9125
> Fax: 707-823-1734

A straightforward catalog that is dedicated to organic farming, it caters to small farmers as well as home gardeners. Almost half of the pages are dedicated to irrigation equipment, including some inexpensive drip irrigation material. Laid out clearly and simply in black and white on newsprint, most copy is extremely informative and thorough. Comes out two to three times a year. Started in 1980 by an entomologist and her irrigation engineer husband to help organic farmers—except for some noted exceptions, no materials are sold that do not meet the California Organic Foods Act, and nothing is synthetically compounded. The warehouse is open for visitors six days a week (4050 Ross Road, Sebastopol, CA).

Items include an incredible range of irrigation equipment, tools and equipment that run the gamut from kitchen utensils to power sprayers, and ten pages of books. Also lists their workshops—half a dozen during a typical summer—on ecological pest controls, pruning, and drip irrigation, for example.

Kinsman Company—Gardener's Catalog
"Special gardening items we use ourselves"

River Road
Point Pleasant, PA 18950
215-297-5613

Kinsman has an amusing range of items that are both fun and practical. Along with the top-quality English hand tools, they feature such everyday but hard-to-find items as barbecue covers and tool hooks, as well as a number of simple decorative items like weather vanes and leaded glass roundels, Victorian plant holders, and wall baskets. There is a fine assortment of watering cans, cold frames (including a portable one), pot hangers, specialized bags and aprons, a good selection of plant supports, arbors, leaf-exclusive gutters, and tool sharpeners. Prices are average and include the cost of freight. Kinsman has a warehouse store in Point Pleasant.

Langenbach—A Collection of the World's Finest Garden Tools

P.O. Box 453
38 Millbrook-Stillwater Road
Blairstown, NJ 07825
201-362-5886

Perhaps the least cluttered, easiest to read, and most focused of all the catalogs, Langenbach limits itself to a small number of imported, high-quality tools, equipment, and accessories, with an emphasis on hand tools. Very serious writing, though personal, with little comments in a number of captions. In fact, the whole enterprise is small and personal—Paul Langenbach himself might answer the phone if you call. But this is no fly-by-night family circus. The Langenbachs have a vineyard and winery in New Jersey and were on a quest for these tools for use on their property, then spent about four years putting the catalog together, getting the first one out in 1989. Superior reproduction of color photos on heavy stock.

Characteristically, they feature mirror-polished stainless steel Burgon & Ball English spades and forks on the cover and first four pages. Other high-quality items include Gardena tools and system, Felco pruners, and the Solo power system, and a stand-out selection of unusual wooden-handled English machetes and unique hoes, and a very cleverly designed British garden cart. Also includes a small collection of gift books.

Mellinger's—Garden Catalog for Year-Round Country Living

2310 West South Range Road
North Lima, OH 44452-9731
800-321-7444

Mellinger's once-yearly catalog opens up not only with the usual personal letter, but with a snapshot of at least three generations of Mellingers and in-laws who run the place, including founder Port B. Mellinger, in his eighties, who, according to the caption, "remains active at his desk every day." A traditional-looking catalog packed full of listings in columns, it is as useful to the professional grower (for whom there is a special section) as it is accessible to the home gardener. Brief copy lacks hyperbole, making it easy to read, and the range is all-inclusive (a complete index is found near the rear). Despite its "Ma and Pa" appearance, it is a very large operation with real business rules. Plants are guaranteed one year. Merchandise is "sold according to manufacturer's warranty," except sale items, and any product returned for general dissatisfaction is subject to a 10 percent handling charge.

Just under half of this catalog is devoted to hundreds of plants, while the rest lists one of the most complete selections of garden supplies, soil conditioners, tools, books, birdseed, beneficial insects, bonsai tools, and pesticides (including a special organic section) found in any consumer-oriented catalog. It has the most extensive book listing of all the catalogs, with over one hundred titles included, grouped by subject. Books may be returned and exchanged within seven days. Also includes a few pages of cooking utensils and processing accessories. Retail store at headquarters, which, a map says, is not near Lima, Ohio—*North* Lima is near Youngstown. Prices are competitive and there are many small items that can be had for just a few dollars.

The Necessary Catalogue—"From the Earth for the Earth"

Necessary Trading Company
New Castle, VA 24127
800-447-5354 (Answering machine. Open Saturdays in the spring)
Fax: 703-864-5186

Published annually since 1978, the Necessary is oriented to the serious organic gardener or small farmer, but also to the knowledgeable home gardener—it even includes pet and houseplant products. Specializing in the latest in biotechnological problem solvers that are natural, biologically safe, and nonpolluting, they claim to list only products that "fit into the natural cycle," which underlies the attitude that permeates the whole catalog. The copy is educational and interesting as well as straightforward, including details on how the products are derived, some IPM orientation, and a how-to box in most sections.

This is probably the most complete listing of natural pest control products among the catalogs. Items include slug and beetle kits, a fruit fly trap that looks like an apple, fly swatters, sticky yellow pest paper, an entire line of Bt products, dormant oil, animal traps, deer repellents, sulfur fungicides, sprayers and dusters, and a wetting agent for powders. There are

plenty of organic fertilizers and soil conditioners. Equipment includes advanced soil testing and analyzing equipment (including a $200 optical refractometer), compost turners, spreaders, and a soil thermometer. They also have green manures (cover crops planted in fall and turned under in the spring) and a good listing of books and pamphlets on subjects of interest to organic gardeners. Very orderly—there is a table of contents as well as an index. Prices are very competitive.

The Nitron Formula—Natural Products for Organic Gardening

Nitron Industries, Inc.
4605 Johnson Road
P.O. Box 1447
Fayetteville, AR 72702-0400
800-835-0123
Fax: 501-750-3008

One of the most educational catalogs to read, Nitron features few items but spends as much as a page on each. Nitron is a unique catalog for two reasons. The first pages are devoted exclusively to touting and explaining their basic product, a natural, nontoxic enzyme soil conditioner called Formula A-35, and much of their catalog is given over to explaining organic gardening. They sponsor an annual organic growers' seminar and even have a list of organic growers and suppliers as one of their products. Long testimonial letters fill one page and are scattered throughout the rest of the catalog, giving a feeling that Nitron is on some kind of mission. They put out five or six issues a year, and have been selling enzymes since 1977. Though they have a basic unconditional guarantee, it is expressed vaguely, albeit warmly: They just say to call them and talk to them about your problem.

Items made with their natural enzymes include compost starter, septic tank cleaners, jewelry cleaners, and pet deodorizers. Also listed are a few tools and gifts, a few books, water filters, soaker hoses and a good selection of organic fertilizers (including bat guano), soil builders, and conditioners such as earthworm castings and greensand. Although there is a page that explains "Enzymes and Trace Elements," it does not really define them satisfactorily. Prices are average.

Park Seed Co.—Flowers and Vegetables and Bulbs
"Park Helps You Grow"

Cokesbury Road
Greenwood, SC 29647-0001
803-223-7333
800-845-3369

Since 1868, Park Seed Co. has been family owned, and the catalog maintains an appropriate all-American, traditional tone. You actually have to hunt for the phone number—they are that traditional about "mail order." And there are pictures of cute kids chomping on corn on the cob or hovering around giant jack-o'-lanterns. But this is the largest company of its kind. The basic catalog is full of bright color photos of flowers, fruit, and vegetables for 123 pages, followed by 8 pages of seed starting and garden maintenance products. No tools are listed.

Catalogs are issued twice a year (one is just for bulbs), and products concentrate on seed propagation, of course, including seed trays, Jiffy-7 pots, seedbed mulches, pH measurers, soil heating cables, thermometers, plant supports, solar window openers, plant-light units, and growing media. A number of the products are their own inventions. It is convenient to order seed and supplies at the same time from this sensible selection.

Peaceful Valley Farm Supply

P.O. Box 2209
Grass Valley, CA 95945
916-272-GROW

This simply illustrated, straightforward catalog, printed on newsprint, has one of the most serious tones of all the catalogs. Featuring products for state-of-the-art sustainable agriculture, they include only ecologically sound growing supplies and services. They are so sincere that they offer comments on gardening techniques which would actually eliminate the need for the product being described, and offer on-site consultation by one of their staff members, classes, seminars, pest and irrigation management, comprehensive soil audits, animal feed analysis, and plant tissue analysis—all a great help for those new to organic farming. They also offer radionics testing "only to growers who are progressive, open minded and able to follow directions" *(sic)*. Very obviously oriented toward the small farmer, but large enough to have items for the home gardener as well. Open Monday through Saturday, 9:00 A.M. to 5:30 P.M.

Peaceful Valley carries animal health and pet products, books, chipper/shredders, cold frames, composting aids and equipment, seed mixes, hand tools, gourmet vegetable seeds, microbial inoculants, an extensive selection of natural pest control items, tools for monitoring pests, ladders, watering equipment, and heavy-duty farm equipment.

The Plow & Hearth—Products for Country Living

560 Main Street
Madison, VA 22727
800-527-5247

Well-printed color photos on good paper make this one of the nicer catalogs that arrive two or more times during the year, and they not only guarantee everything unconditionally, but offer a guarantee on lowest prices as well. However, the copy headlines tend to the declaratory, which wears thin after a while.

Only eight or so pages out of forty list garden tools and equipment. The rest is furniture, pet, and household gadgets and gift items. Garden items include planters, a small sundial, croquet sets, bird supplies, a bat box, several pages of Adirondack furniture (assembled and in kits), and novelty items like weather vanes and wind chimes. There is even a propane torch for burning weeds.

Ringer Lawn & Garden Products Catalog—100% Natural

"Ringer's natural products work to achieve and maintain a biologically active and balanced soil. The result is stronger, healthier plants."

> 9959 Valley View Road
> Eden Prairie, MN 55344-3585
> 800-654-1047 plus answering machine; 7 days during spring
> Fax 612-941-5036

Just to underscore the fact that organic gardening is nothing new, Ringer points out that they have been around since 1962, and they have a slick commercial image that makes their products, especially for lawns, compare directly with those from the big petrochemical companies. Their own line of fertilizing and soil-building products is substantial, and they are expanding into natural pest control items. A bright, all color, easily read catalog that comes out in spring and fall editions. Prices are average but include shipping, though a $1 handling fee is added to any order.

The catalog is filled chiefly with Ringer's own line of natural lawn and garden products. Their biologically safe, organic lawn fertilizers and conditioners differ from others in that they contain the microorganisms needed to break

the material down and make it accessible to the plants; they build the soil structure and increase the biological activity. Their long-range benefits to the soil and root development make them well worth any extra cost, although they are hard to compare directly to traditional products. A small variety of supplies and products from other manufacturers include grass seed, a soil testing service (unique among the catalogs, but more expensive than the Cooperative Extension), an inexpensive hand lawn mower, biodegradable garbage bags, a soil core sampler, stump remover, pruning tools, compost bins and supplies (and compost itself, in case you can't make your own), chipper/shredders, sprayers, watering accessories, and small plastic greenhouses.

Smith & Hawken—Catalog for Gardeners, Bulb Book, Garden Furniture, Rose & Gerard Catalog

> 25 Corte Madera
> Mill Valley, CA 94941
> 415-383-2000 or 800-777-4556
> Rose & Gerard: 415-383-4050
> Fax: 415-383-7030

The Smith & Hawken Catalog sets the standard for good design, effective copy, and general polite and respectful attitude toward the consumer. They even send a confirmation letter for orders that are going out the same day. Probably the most readable catalog of all.

Smith & Hawken has become one of the more popular garden supply catalogs, making a reputation among gardeners largely because of the quality of their merchandise, the variety of the selection, and the caring and often personal service one gets when ordering from them. They also demonstrate a corporate concern for the environment, doing things like buying teak from commercial tree plantations and otherwise showing an intelligent choice of suppliers.

Their choice of items is incomplete in the tool area but does cover the basics with a tinge of the whimsical. It includes genuine Panama hats, Sussex trugs (low baskets), some special vegetable seed collections, a few helpful books, pigskin garden gloves, sprayers, praying mantis egg cases, ladybugs, and other organic pest control items (these only in the spring), garden clogs, soil blockers, nursery flats, watering devices, Reemay floating row covers, Felco pruners, children's tools (good ones—not flimsy ones), plant supports, wildflower field mixes, sheep shears and other hand tools, top-quality English shovels and spades, as well as extensive and beautiful selections of accessories and furniture very obviously oriented to the gift market. Surprisingly for an outfit that stresses quality so much, their prices are average or only a few dollars more than in other catalogs. Service is excellent.

They started another forty-page catalog just for beautiful decorative and accessory items, "the garden as idiom" in their words, called *Rose & Gerard*. Some of the furniture is found in the regular catalog, but this catalog contains no tools. It does contain incredibly lush, romantic, flower-filled photos of fine garden furniture and accessories that range so far afield that they include terra-cotta candelabras and hand-loomed place mats, as well as French olive oil soap.

Walt Nicke's Garden Talk

36 McLead Lane
P.O. Box 433
Topsfield, MA 01983
508-887-3388

Published three times a year, this simple black-and-white catalog is particularly inviting, perhaps because of its personal feel. Enthusiastic but detailed descriptions satisfy your curiosity, and common and uncommon garden supplies and equipment are listed side by side. Illustrations are mostly simple line drawings though there are a good number of very, very gray photos on the plain paper. The layout is simple and clear, and there is an easy-to-read table of contents. Intended for the serious gardener as well as the gadget hound, prices are among the lowest of all the catalogs.

Tools, almost all of which are imported from Europe, include modified designs of planters, weeders, and hoes, including items like the West German hoelike tool that "cultivates ground without destroying the natural soil layers, thus preserving the subsurface microenvironment for soil bacteria. In addition, the Bio-Aerator is made of a copper alloy, and therefore, does not leave traces of iron in the soil to deplete oxygen." They also carry tools crafted specifically for gardeners with disabilities, such as a curved-handle, solid-cast trowel for people with carpal tunnel syndrome and arthritis. Other items include how-to books, a cold frame, small greenhouse equipment, and various propagation products, as well as lots of watering accessories. Despite all the practical items, it is not surprising somehow to see a listing for "gay blade" windmills, listed with the admonition, "Order a windmill and give yourself and the kids a giggle." At only $3.95, it is a nice complement to the $89.95 stainless steel spades.

Wind & Weather Catalogue

The Albion Street Watertower
P.O. Box 2320
Mendocino, CA 95460
800-922-9463

One of the few catalogs that specializes in a particular area, this one is entirely devoted to weather devices and sundials. Despite its narrow range, it is quite interesting and pleasantly readable, although it has a cluttered design with annoyingly small print. Items range from high-tech barographs to folk-art wind vanes, including humidity and rain gauges, all kinds of sundials (even a pocket model), wind chimes, books, cloud charts, calendars, and logs.

Catalogs for the Professional

Three catalogs stand out for range of choice, price, and service. However, before you call them up, please note that they cater to repeat business from professional horticulturalists, whether they be groundskeepers of institutions, growers, florists, growers, foresters, landscapers, or arborists. They do not relish handling small orders (though they all will, for a fee of a few dollars).

These three companies differ in two primary ways from the consumer-oriented catalogs listed here. First, their selection is much more extensive, with many more items than even a fully stocked garden center, in many cases without narrowing the choice for you (they may carry several lines of the same tool). Second, in place of the nice personal letter in the front, they usually have a "statement of terms of conditions of sale" in contract language, noting restrictions for returns and guarantees—quite opposed to those of the consumer catalogs. It is really quite a different ball of wax.

Good-Prod Sales, Inc.
825 Fairfield Avenue
Kenilworth, NJ 07033
201-245-5055
Fax: 201-245-6906
Tools, supplies, and ornaments (many items for resale).

A. H. Hummert Seed Co.
2746 Chouteau Avenue
St. Louis, MO 63103
800-325-3055
Fax: 314-771-5203
(Catalog costs $35)
Tools, supplies, nursery equipment, greenhouses, and greenhouse equipment Established 1934.

A. M. Leonard, Inc.
6665 Spiker Road
Piqua, OH 45356
800-543-8955
Fax: 513-773-8640
Quality tools and equipment only—no supplies. More amenable to consumer orders than the others. Two editions per year: Spring/Summer and Summer/Fall. Established 1885.

Index

Note: *Italics* indicate main item entries.